böhlau

Archiv für Diplomatik

Schriftgeschichte
Siegel- und Wappenkunde

Begründet durch
EDMUND E. STENGEL

Herausgegeben von

IRMGARD FEES und ANDREA STIELDORF

Beiheft 22

From Digital to Distant Diplomatics

Digital Diplomatics 2022

DANIEL LUGER, GEORG VOGELER (ed.)

BÖHLAU

Publikation mit finanzieller Unterstützung durch das Referat Wissenschaft und Forschung des Landes Steiermark, die Universität Graz sowie den Europäischen Forschungsrat (ERC): Projektnummer 101019327

Das Land Steiermark
Wirtschaft, Tourismus, Wissenschaft und Forschung

UNI GRAZ

erc European Research Council

Bibliographic information published by the Deutsche Nationalbibliothek:
The Deutsche Nationalbibliothek lists this publication in the Deutsche Nationalbibliografie; detailed bibliographic data available online: https://dnb.de.

Cover design: Michael Haderer, Wien
Cover image: Automatisch erkannte visuelle Merkmale einer spätmittelalterlichen Urkunde auf monasterium.net im Rahmen des internationalen Forschungsprojekts „Between Composition and Reception: the Authority of Medieval Charters (BeCoRe)“ (ANR-19-CE27-0021 bzw. I 4502 Internationale Projekte).
Typesetting: Bettina Waringer, Wien
Printed and bound: Hubert & Co, Ergolding
Printed in the EU

Vandenhoeck & Ruprecht Verlage | www.vandenhoeck-ruprecht-verlage.com
E-Mail: info@boehlau-verlag.com

ISBN print: 978-3-412-53090-7
ISBN openaccess: 978-3-412-53092-1

Inhalt

III. Charters and their Digital Editions

Preface

The "Digital Diplomatics 2022: From Digital to Distant Diplomatics" conference convened from September 28th to 30th, 2022, at the University of Graz, marking the fourth iteration of an international conference series originating from a workshop in Munich in 2004, with subsequent gatherings in Munich (2007), Naples (2011), and Paris (2013). In the long gap preceding this recent conference, considerable strides have been made in the digitization of mediaeval charters, instruments, and deeds, notwithstanding persistent challenges in the domain of digital diplomatics.

The impetus for this conference stemmed from the approval of the "From Digital to Distant Diplomatics" (DiDip) project by the European Research Council, which aims to revolutionise diplomatics by integrating data science and artificial intelligence, fostering a Virtual Research Environment facilitating harmonious collaboration between human researchers and machines. DiDip focuses on analysing European trends and regional disparities, particularly within 14th and 15th-century charters, probing the influence of institutions such as the Roman Church and the dissemination of Roman law, while also scrutinising authentication practices. Moreover, the project contextualises its findings within significant historical events such as the Western Schism and the Great Plague. Through these endeavours, we aspire to pose and address novel and stimulating research inquiries within our traditional discipline.

The realisation of our conference was enabled by the generous financial backing of the European Research Council, the Department of Science and Research of the Province of Styria, and the Rector's Office of the University of Graz, for which we extend our profound appreciation. We also wish to convey our sincere gratitude to the dedicated individuals and staff members of the Zentrum für Informationsmodellierung at the University of Graz for their enthusiasm and meticulous efforts in orchestrating this event. Special acknowledgement is due to Sandy Aoun, Florian Atzenhofer-Baumgartner, Gisela Decker, Franziska Decker, Tamás Kovács, Florian Lamminger, Angelos Nicolaou, Nicolas Renet, Elisabeth Steiner, and Walter Scholger for their invaluable contributions.

Each contribution to this volume underwent a stringent anonymous peer review process, and we are indebted to the reviewers for their discerning critiques and guidance, as well as to all the authors for their constructive engagement with our volume. All links contained in these conference proceedings were checked for validity by us in August and September 2024 and archived at http://web.archive.org/.

Finally, we express our gratitude to Irmgard Fees and Andrea Stieldorf for accepting our conference proceedings as a supplement to the Archiv für Diplomatik, and to the team at Böhlau Verlag, particularly Dorothee Wunsch and Jonas Hiese, for their seamless collaboration during the publication process.

Graz, summer 2024
The editors[1]

1 The larger part of the editorial work has been done by Daniel Luger. He could not attend the conference due the birth of his son Christian, so he decided to engage with its content through editing the printed contributions. I want to express my special gratitude to him for this effort, as infants are well known to take a lot of your time as well! (Georg Vogeler)

What makes the difference between Digital and Distant Diplomatics?

Georg Vogeler, Daniel Luger

The term "Digital Diplomatics" was introduced more than 15 years ago at an event organised by the University of Munich: the first "Digital Diplomatics" conference, taking place in Munich in 2007. This event was preceded by a workshop in 2004[1], in which international diplomatics scholars discussed the possibility of creating a data exchange format for digital charter editions with the help of XML[2]. Obviously, structural annotations of texts have a use case in the field of diplomatics as single sheet legal texts are highly structured and their structure is relevant for their legal validation[3]. However, scholars had been active in the application of digital tools to charters already in the 1970s. While archival sciences followed Luciana Duranti's proposal using the tradition diplomatics as a reference for establishing methods of authentication to electronic records[4], the community engaging with historical documents focussed on the creation of digital resources. The series of conference between 2007 and 2013[5] framed the concept of digital diplomatics in this way: The contributions dealt with methods to create digital representations of mediaeval and early modern charters: what should be included, what excluded from digitization and annotation? Which corpora are available? Which tools are available to create and present the data? Large scale digitizations like those pro-

1 https://www.cei.lmu.de/digdipl04/

2 Georg Vogeler, Ein Standard für die Digitalisierung mittelalterlicher Urkunden. Bericht zum Workshop (München, 5./6. April 2004), in: AfD 50 (2004) p. 23–24; Georg Vogeler, Towards a standard of encoding medieval charters with XML, in: Literary and linguistic computing 20 (2005) p. 269–280.

3 Michele Ansani, Diplomatica e nuove tecnologie. La tradizione disciplinare tra innovazione e nemesi digitale, in: Scrineum Rivista 1 (2003), p. 175-196, DOI: 10.13128/SCRINEUM-12097; Michele Ansani/Antonella Ghignoli, Testi digitali: nuovi media e documenti medievali, in: Les historiens et l'informatique. Un métier à réinventer, ed. Jean-Philippe Genet/Andrea Zorzi (Collection de l'École Française de Rome 444), Napoli 2011, p. 73–86.

4 Luciana Duranti, Diplomatics. New Uses for an Old Science, Lanham 1998.

5 https://didip.hypotheses.org/conference-2022/digital-diplomatics-conference-series

vided by Monasterium.net, the French charters portal in Telma, the Diplomata Belgica project, or the CEMA corpus provided by Nicolas Perreaux are milestones in this development. This included the conversion of diplomatic resources like the Vocabulaire Internationale de la Diplomatique as a semantic web resource[6] and other research on the modelling of charter data like Martin Roland's taxonomy of illuminated charters[7]. Based on the latter, a number of studies in the dialogue between diplomatics, art history and digital humanities were published, for example, in 2018[8]. Close to the core research in diplomatics are the creation of seals databases like the Portuguese Sigillvm[9], and the large scale projects John McEwan's Digisig[10], and Laurent Hablot's Sigilla[11]. A major change in the creation of digital representation of physical charters and their texts is defined by the rise of handwritten text recognition (HTR) technology. While Nicolas Perreaux's Cartae Europae Medii Aevi (CEMA) corpus relies mostly on material published in print[12], HTR gives access to the texts of yet untranscribed charters. The HIMANIS project turned, for instance, the full set of the French royal registers into a digital resource of images searchable by keywords[13].

The number of publications using digital charter material for statistical uses have increased in the meantime: Gelila Tilahun, Andrey Feuerverger and Michael Gervers have demonstrated how statistical distribution of phrases can help to date undated charters[14], Nicolas Perreaux has told many stories about terminology developing over time and space[15], Sergio Torres Aguilar, Pierre Chastang and Xavier Tannier have experimented with automatic information extraction[16]. This marks

6 https://www.cei.lmu.de/VID/ See also Georg Vogeler, Von der Terminologie zur Ontologie. Das "Vocabulaire international de la diplomatique" als Ressource des Semantic Web, in: Francia 40 (2013) p. 281–297.

7 Martin Roland, Illuminierte Urkunden im digitalen Zeitalter. Maßregeln und Chancen, in: Digital diplomatics. The computer as a tool for the diplomatist?, ed. Antonella Ambrosio/Sébastien Barret/Georg Vogeler (AfD Beiheft 14), Köln–Weimar–Wien 2014, p. 245–269.

8 Illuminierte Urkunden: Beiträge aus Diplomatik, Kunstgeschichte und Digital Humanities, ed. Gabriele Bartz/Markus Gneiss (AfD Beiheft 16), Köln–Weimar–Wien 2018.

9 http://portugal-sigillvm.net/EN/index.html

10 https://www.digisig.org/

11 http://www.sigilla.org/

12 https://cema.lamop.fr/aims/

13 http://himanis.huma-num.fr/app/

14 Gelila Tilahun/Andrey Feuerverger/Michael Gervers, Dating medieval English charters, in: Annals of applied statistics 6 (2012) p. 1615–1640.

15 See for example recently Nicolas Perreaux, Langue des capitulaires et langue des chartes: richesses, circulations, specificités, in: Die Sprache des Rechts. Historische Semantik und karolingische Kapitularien, ed. Bernhard Jussen/Karl Ubl (Historische Semantik 33), Göttingen 2022, p. 167–210.

16 Sergio Torres Aguilar, La reconnaissance des entités nommées dans les bases numériques de chartes médiévales en latin: le cas du Corpus Burgundiae Medii Aevi (xe-xiiie siècle), in: Mé-

the move of digital diplomatics into the radius of the "Distant reading" field, introduced into the Digital Humanities by Franco Moretti in 2001 and continuously used as a reference point in the discussion about the relationship between literary studies and digital methodology[17].

To map the current state of the relationship between diplomatics and digital methodologies as presented by the 20 papers collected in this volume, we take four different perspectives: Two of them can be considered representative to the "digital" approach to diplomatics: the challenges of digital editions of charters and the solutions of the archives preserving the charters. Others take the "distant" approach by computational methods, applying it to internal and external features. In the following we will discuss the contributions of the conference to these four fields, trying to highlight, why "digital diplomatics" still makes sense and how "distant diplomatics" is opening new paths for future research.

The first five contributions delve into the intricate challenges of editing charters within a digital context and explore the rich analytical potential therein. The GallRom project demonstrates the requirements of digital representations of charters for linguistics research: Martin Glessgen and Marguerite Dallas make a significant step forward in the study of mediaeval Gallo-Romance languages. By combining bibliographical data and editions with lexical data from reference dictionaries and philological data, GallRom creates a rich philological research tool. The database facilitates differentiated lexicological and grapho-phonetic analyses, shedding light on the linguistic evolution from Latin to Romance, geochronological changes in vocabulary in mediaeval documentary texts, and the development and diffusion of writing in the Gallo-Romance territory.

Delving into the intricate structures inherent in notarial documents within the Portuguese and Spanish kingdoms, Miguel Calleja-Puerta's paper on the NotFor project offers valuable insights into the major progress of diplomatic analysis utilising TEI-annotated charters, domain-specific XML markup and XQuery-based selections. Furthermore, Calleja-Puerta shows how a specific set of tags has

---

diévales. Langues, Textes, Histoire 73 (15 December 2017) p. 47–65. https://doi.org/10.4000/medievales.8182; Pierre Chastang/Sergio Torres Aguilar/Xavier Tannier, A Named Entity Recognition Model for Medieval Latin Charters, in: Digital Humanities Quarterly 15,4 (2021). http://www.digitalhumanities.org/dhq/vol/15/4/000574/000574.html; Sergio Torres Aguilar/Pierre Chastang/Xavier Tannier, Automatic medieval charters structure detection: A Bi-LSTM linear segmentation approach, in: Journal of Data Mining & Digital Humanities, 30 octobre 2022, https://doi.org/10.46298/jdmdh.8646.

17 On this topic, see for example Stefan Jänicke/Greta Franzini/Muhammad Faisal Cheema/Gerik Scheuermann, On Close and Distant Reading in Digital Humanities: A Survey and Future Challenges, in: Eurographics Conference on Visualization (EuroVis) (2015) https://doi.org/10.2312/eurovisstar.20151113

been developed to describe and analyse the specific diplomatic structure of notarial documents.

The Diplomatarium Serbicum Digitale (DSD) project, a pioneering initiative presented by Žarko Vujošević, displays a significant effort to edit Serbian mediaeval charters. One of the primary challenges of the project is the conversion of a local SQL database into an XML format using modified and extended TEI. The importance of this project cannot be overstated, as it addresses a serious desideratum in local research, which has so far lacked charter editions or records even in printed form.

Christian Domenig revisits his 2007 presentation, detailing his personal experience with developing a digital edition of the charters of the counts of Cilli. Initially based on a homemade Microsoft Access database, the project faced setbacks due to technical challenges. However, reconstruction using SemanticMediaWiki showcases the efficacy of such tools in zero-budget projects, particularly for educational purposes.

Balázs Csiba's paper on mediaeval diplomatic sources in Slovakia sheds light on the historical context of individual and institutionalised editing of charters and ongoing efforts to enhance accessibility through digital platforms. Currently, the editorial work is mostly handled by employees of Comenius University and the University of Trnava. In recent years, after overcoming initial challenges, the digitization process has also commenced and is partly displayed also on monasterium.net. Nevertheless, the majority of Slovak archival materials still remain unavailable in electronic databases.

While these editions are driven by scholarly selection criteria (linguistics, chancery, region), digital publication of charters can be driven by the current preservation in the archives. The Digitale Charterbank Nederland (DCN), presented by Jan Burgers and Rik Hoekstra, transforms archival descriptions and digitisations into a regional representation of diplomatic sources. It integrates a vast collection of mediaeval and early modern charters from various Dutch archives through a partnership with the software company De Ree, which serves many Dutch archives. For archives not using this software, data was exported automatically and added manually. This method has specific possibilities but also certain limitations, and Burgers and Hoekstra stress the necessity of thorough source criticism when using such databases.

While the DCN has to accept high variance in description of the charters in the archives, Stefan Bröhl report on a consistent collaborative effort among Southern German archives to publish about 7.000 descriptions of charters issued by the counts palatine of the Rhine: The counts palatine were one of the highest-ranking secular princes of the mediaeval Holy Roman Empire, but their archives are spread among various modern archives. The abstracts created in the project follow a common scheme to become consistent. They will be enriched with digital charter images, authority data and keywords using controlled vocabularies, allowing several types of presentation, access and research. In doing so, this pioneering project addresses a significant gap in late mediaeval research.

Offering insights into the digital processing of papal charters and letters for late mediaeval Poland, ADAM ZAPAŁA underscores the potential for advancing research in papal diplomatics by digital methodologies. The project digitally processes existing printed editions, automatically extracting and normalising their metadata, creating an XML database with persistent identifiers stored and managed in Wikibase. Zapała also outlines procedures for transcribing and preparing text for full-text publications, and moreover he rightly emphasises the importance of an international collaboration to comprehensively process 15th-century papal sources.

ÁDÁM NOVÁK and SÁNDOR ÓNADI introduce *Memoria Hungariae*, a digital online database encompassing mediaeval charters, manuscripts, seals, letters, and other material sources. It can apply new technologies to capture the materiality of the recorded objects. As part of a pilot project, they were able to use photo-geometric measurements and spatial imaging with optical object scanners for seals.. This enhances their presentation and preserves these fragile artefacts from inevitable deterioration. Moreover, this technique holds significant potential for academic research, education, and museum curation.

The creation of a systematic database of documents issued from 1526 to 1570 by the National Archives of Hungary is shown by the contribution of KRISZTINA ARANY and GYÖRGY LACZLAVIK. The project, they present, started in spring of 2016 aiming at identification, digitization, and processing of this corpus. The documents were processed in an online database dedicated to this data and in the generic database of the National Archives of Hungary. These databases offer a wealth of resources on the the history of the Kingdom of Hungary, county legislation and administration, and the opportunity to uncover previously unknown genealogical data.

Much distant diplomatics research is based on results from digital diplomatics work: The linguistic interest in digital charter data in TIMO KORKIAKANGAS' contribution can only be achieved by existing charter corpora. By highlighting the importance of annotations in general for Latin and structural annotations in the case of charters and the opportunities arising from the metadata on charters, he makes a case for a future of better digital linguistics with charters by increasing research material for the Latin-Romance transition, metadata automatically assigned by text or image classification, and machine created structural annotation of charters.

Already digitised texts are also at the core of EVELINE LECLERCQ's reflection on the style of charters from the Cambrai area in the 12th century. She studies stylometric methods on the example of the Cambrai bishop's chancery and can extend her earlier results in identifying one single dictator in finding methods identifying other dictators corroborated by close reading diplomatics. Her work documents parameters in which these methods are successful, in particular considering visualisation as the main method through which the distant analysis is conveyed. In a too distant view with larger corpora, it is hard to see the spots of diplomatics interest for close reading.

The distant view on internal features can go beyond the very text. The research on delegated jurisdiction in the Iberian peninsula of the 12th century presented by MARLENE ERNST, ALINA OSTROWSKI and MALTE REHBEIN discusses the concepts of automatic research on formulaic language in charters and can re-use the work of Iberia Pontificia for extracting from the charter metadata networks highlighting central actors and patterns in phrasing of the charter text.

As remarked above, HTR technology is one of the major steps towards distant diplomatics, as they allow creating large scale textual data sets from not yet edited charters. SERENA AMMIRATI, LORENZO LASTILLA, PAOLO MERIALDO and MARCO MAIORINO give an example of how this can be combined with digital diplomatics, when they tell their story of combining palaeographical teaching with the development of machine learning based automatic transcription and hand identification of the registers of pope Honorius III. Another example for the links between digital and distant diplomatics is the continuous need of data creation for the application of machine learning methods on large scale data sets. This is demonstrated by NICOLE BERGK-PINTO, JACQUELINE SCHINDLER and NIKLAS TSCHERNE who report on the paths from the "traditional" diplomatics concept of "charter landscapes" towards a machine learning based analysis of internal and external features relaying authority in mediaeval charters

A major change in the combination of digital methodologies with charters is the application of software to address the external features of charters. The NOTAE team (ZAHRA ZIRAN, FRANCESCO LEOTTA, MASSIMO MECELLA and ANTONELLA GHIGNOLI) still focus on the creation of a digital resource for early mediaeval graphical signs, but their work opens it up to distant diplomatics by two approaches: providing the data as semantic web data to ease facilitate combination with other data sets and deep learning based methods to detect and classify graphical symbols.

While most of the machine learning approaches used in distant diplomatics rely on statistical representations created from training data, MARK BELL, EIRINI GOUDAROULI, JOHN STELL and JANE WINTERS suggest assigning qualitative values from the relative topology in the document layout. This includes detection of temporal layers and opens a different path to distant diplomatics which can help the diplomatists understand the layout elements of large scale data sets.

TOBIAS HODEL and JONAS WIDMER show another way, how distant diplomatics can intersect machine learning based computer vision methods with close reading palaeography and diplomatics. They suggest using HTR technology beyond the pure computation of large data sets as a tool that can highlight palaeographical features resulting in HTR uncertainties which are expressed in the confidence matrices. They propose using these observations as contributions to hand identification.

The combination of distant diplomatics with machine learning technologies is also emphasised by John A. McEwan's approach to dating mediaeval seal matrices from Britain. He makes use of the verbal descriptions in seal catalogues to suggest dates in more precise date ranges as many catalogues provide.

Comparing the research from the origins of "digital diplomatics" 15 years ago with the current state of research collected in this volume, one cannot declare an opposition between a research program defined by digital diplomatics and a distant diplomatics one. However, if we define as distant diplomatics research looking at digital charter corpora through the statistical and computational lens, only these methods can provide us with the necessary tools to answer traditional classical questions of diplomatics for the mass of late mediaeval documentary material, such as the analysis of script, form and dictation[18]. In addition, we see tendencies to leave the realm of reconstructing the conditions of charter production as a major goal of diplomatics towards the study of charter use or general practices with charters. This corresponds with tendencies towards a cultural history of charters in the late 20th and early 21st century. We don't want to start a chicken-and-egg discussion, which of the approaches caused the other[19]. This volume shows that the digital and distant diplomatics discourse is much more driven by the epistemological consequences of digital and computational technology for knowledge representation and knowledge creation than by the diplomatics research trend. The impact of these technologies on our interpretation of charters as cultural artefacts and on their creation, preservation, and use – to reference Michael T. Clanchy's seminal study[20] – has still to be seen. It might be called "diplomatics in a cyborg world" to highlight that thinking about mediaeval and early modern charters in an environment in which human thinking capacity is intertwined with information processing machines. Or it might be called "computational diplomatics" focussing on the numerical representations and processes that give us new insights. Or it might simply blend into a larger "digital diplomatics" research program. In any way, it will still be diplomatics.

18 See for instance the possibilities collecting and analysing a corpus of charters related to the practice of arbitration described by Daniel Luger/Florian Atzenhofer-Bruck, De alto et basso: Ein Experiment aus dem Bereich der „Distant Diplomatics" zum Formular von Urkunden aus dem Schiedsgerichtswesen, in: Studia historica Brunensia 71 (2024) 239–247.

19 See, for example: Irmgard Fees, Diplomatik und Paläographie als Schlüssel zur Kulturgeschichte: Papstgeschichtliche Wende und Urkundengestaltung, in: Papstgeschichte im digitalen Zeitalter, ed. Klaus Herbers/Viktoria Trenkle (AfD Beiheft 46), Köln 2018, p. 95–108.

20 Michael T. Clanchy, From Memory to Written Record, Oxford 1993.

I. Diplomatics and Computational Methods: Internal Features

Patterns of Change

The DEEDS Database, Topic Modeling and Network Analysis in English Medieval Charters, and the Future of Digital Diplomatics

Michael Gervers, Gelila Tilahun

The following is in part an autobiographical sketch describing the path that led one author into an early stage of humanities computing in the 1970s, and how developments in the field brought about a long-term academic partnership with the other that focused on the applications of emerging machine learning methods for textual analysis. After first developing algorithms to calculate dates for the invariably undated medieval English charter, topic modeling and network analysis are now being successfully applied to the study of their diplomatic.

* * *

In the summer of 1956, my great aunt and uncle[1] took me on a tour of some medieval sites in Essex, the county that borders the northern banks of the River Thames from London to the English Channel. We picnicked in the churchyard of a small village called Little Maplestead (*the place of the maple tree*). [Fig. 1] This church was of some interest because it was one of England's rare round churches; its shape was inspired by the rotunda of the Church of the Holy Sepulchre in Jerusalem, itself representing the dome of Heaven, the Heavenly Jerusalem[2]. The rotunda was the

1 The late Oliver and Ruby Probert of Bevills, Bures, Suffolk, UK.

2 Michael GERVERS, Rotundae Anglicanae, in: Actes du 22e Congrès international d'histoire de l'art, Budapest, 1969, vol. 1, Budapest 1972, p. 359–376; Id., The Use and Meaning of the Twelfth-and-Thirteenth-Century Round Churches of England, in: Tomb and Temple Re-Imagining the Sacred Buildings of Jerusalem, ed. Robin GRIFFITH-JONES/Eric FERNIE, Woodbridge 2018, p. 376–386; Catherine E. HUNDLEY, The English Round Church Movement, in: Ibid. p. 352–375.

Fig. 1: Little Maplestead Church, Essex. Frontispiece by William WALLEN, The History and Antiquities of the Round Church at Little Maplestead, Essex, formerly belonging to the Knights Hospitallers of Saint John of Jerusalem (afterwards known as the Knights of Rhodes, and now of Malta). Preceded by An Historical Sketch of the Crusades, London 1836.

hallmark of the military crusading order of the Hospital of St. John of Jerusalem, to whom the village and the church had been donated in 1186[3].

Eleven years after that picnic on the lawn, I married a Hungarian archaeologist, Veronika Molnár, who quite coincidentally had recently written her PhD dissertation on the round churches of medieval Hungary. She identified 80 such monuments constructed between the late 10th through 13th centuries, the great majority having been inspired indirectly by Charlemagne's renowned palace chapel at Aachen, dating from the late 8th century. The Central European rotundas of the 12th and 13th centuries saw another wave of inspiration from that holy city via the crusades, and again from the military orders of the Hospitallers and the Templars[4].

The Hungarian rotundas reminded me of the church at Little Maplestead and I followed up by consulting one of the Essex volumes of the Victoria Country History (a detailed history and topography of England in 175 volumes, and still grow-

3 British Library, Cotton MS Nero E VI, fol. 305.

4 Vera GERVERS-MOLNÁR, A Középkori Magyarország Rotundái, Művészettörténeti Füzetek 4, Cahiers d'histoire de l'art, Budapest 1972.

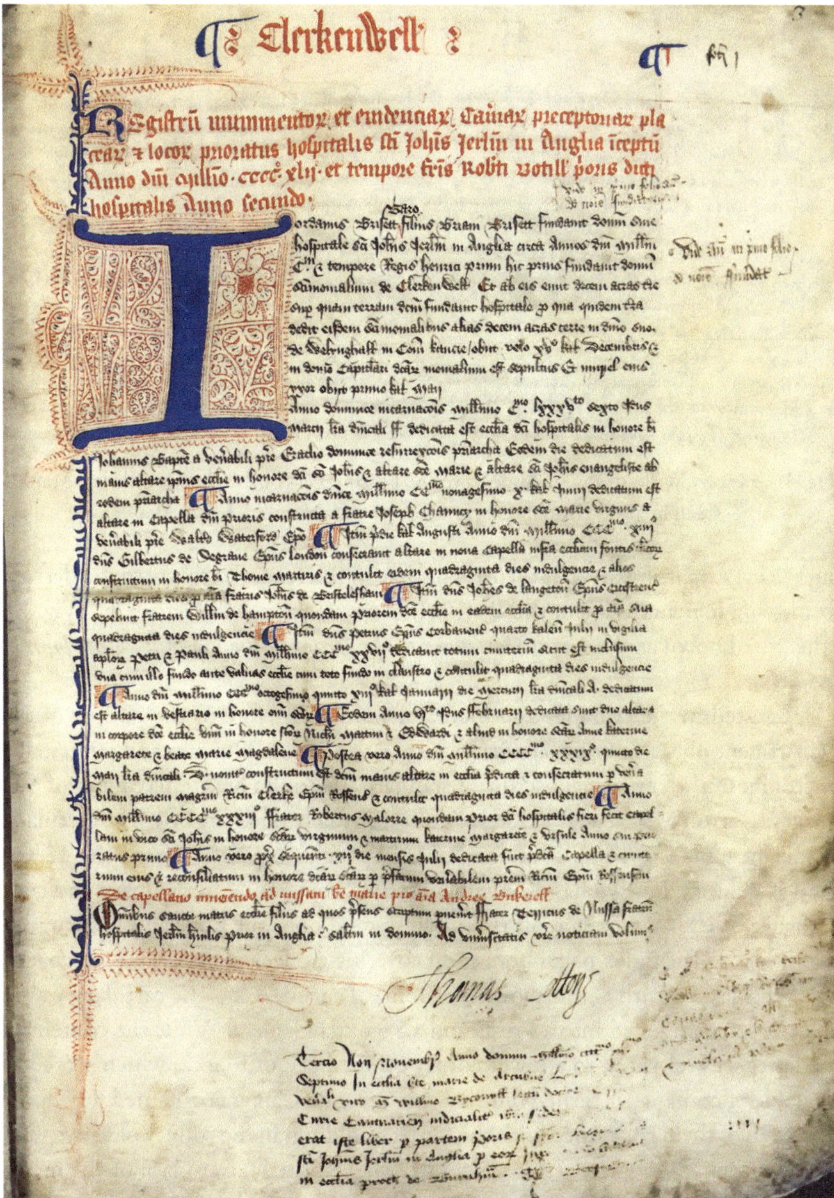

Fig. 2: Initial folio of the Great Cartulary of the Order of the Hospital of St. John of Jerusalem (British Library, Cotton MS Nero E VI), fol. 3r.

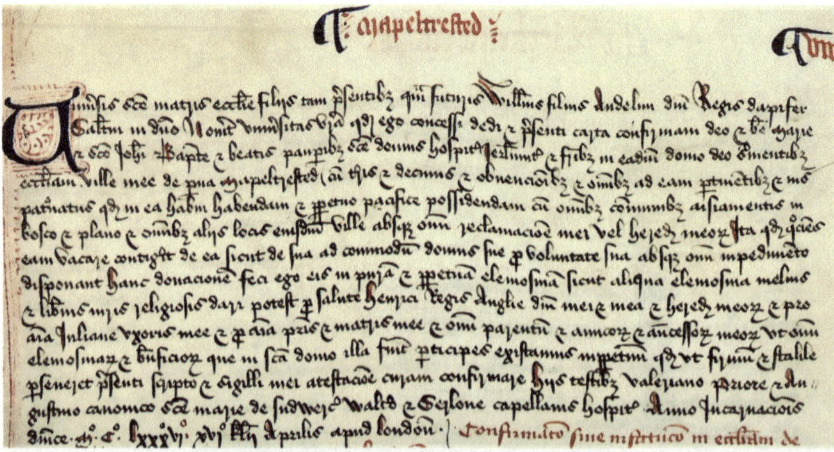

Fig. 3: Grant by William son of Audelin to the Hospitallers of the church of Little Maplestead in 1186 (British Library, Cotton MS Nero E VI, fol. 305r).

ing) to look up its history[5]. It turned out that all references to this rotunda derived from a single manuscript in the British Library: Cotton MS Nero E VI [Fig. 2], otherwise known as the *Great Cartulary of the Order of the Hospital of St. John of Jerusalem in England.*

Interested in the crusades and medieval warfare, I wrote to the Keeper of the Department of Manuscripts at what was then the British Museum and requested a microfilm of the entire manuscript. A standard microfilm held a maximum of 500 images; Cotton MS Nero E VI, at 467 folios, virtually filled the box. The cartulary, originally copied in 1442, contained over 3,000 charters dating from the 12th to the 15th century. It was a handsome manuscript (now bound in two parts as a consequence of its having fallen off the reading stand onto the floor and broken into two pieces[6]). The index pages bore tituli covering twelve counties, and the coat of arms of a seventeenth-century owner, Thomas Penruddock[7]. The cartulary was at an early stage arranged into a Prima and a Secunda Camera. While the content of the latter was relegated to a lower corner on the back of folio 2, which served as the table of contents, it turned out that this Secunda Camera contained 957 documents, all of them concerned with the Order's holdings in the county of Essex, with many of them falling under the titulus of 'Mapletrestede', our place of the maple

5 The Victoria History of the County of Essex, vol. 2, ed. William PAGE/J. Horace ROUND (1907) p. 178.

6 As reported to the author by the late C.N.L. Brook, who was using the manuscript at the time.

7 Philip MORANT, The History and Antiquities of the County of Essex, new ed., vol. 2, London 1816, p. 603. According to a note on fol. 2 of BL Cotton MS Nero E VI, Penruddock gave the MS to Sir Robert Cotton on 5 May 1628.

tree. The gift that transferred the village to the Order was made in a rarely dated charter of 1186 by William son of Audelin [Fig. 3], the steward of King Henry II (r. 1154–1189)[8].

To make a long story short, I subsequently undertook to make a transcription and critical analysis of the Secunda Camera the subject of my doctoral dissertation at the University of Toronto and devoted five years to the enterprise. The analysis was published in 1981[9] and the critical edition in two volumes in 1982 and 1996[10].

While working on the Hospitaller cartulary as a graduate student, I was deeply impressed by an article in the *Annales* by Lucie Fossier of the Institut de recherche et d'histoire des textes (IRHT) in Paris, and Marion Créhange, entitled *Un essai de traitement sur ordinateur des documents diplomatiques du Moyen Age*[11]. At the end of the decade she, together with Caroline Bourlet, Jean-Philippe Genêt, Christiane Klapisch-Zuber and others, produced the first issue of *Le médiéviste et l'ordinateur*[12]. This publication continued, I believe largely due to the enthusiasm and hard work of Caroline Bourlet, until 2003. At more or less the same time, that is from 1966 to 1976, David Herlihy and Christiane Klapisch-Zuber were involved in coding the content of the Florentine Catasto of 1427, "one of the first statistical surveys to use computers to analyze large amounts of data"[13]. The results were published in a highly praised book in 1978 entitled *Les Toscans et leurs familles: Une étude du Catasto florentin de 1427*. Herlihy and Klapisch-Zuber, like Madame Fossier, were well ahead of a younger generation of historians who were deeply motivated by the possibility of organizing and analyzing their data electronically. Among them were Peter Denley and Deian Hopkin who, in 1986, organized a conference in London on "History and Computing" that, surprisingly for all concerned, led to a meeting of 500 historians[14]. At that event, I met Manfred Thaller (a graduate of the University of Graz), an inspiring mind and a highly influential proponent of Digital

8 See n. 3 above.

9 Michael GERVERS, The Hospitaller Cartulary in the British Library (Cotton MS Nero E VI). A Study of the Manuscript and its Composition with a Critical Edition of Two Fragments of Earlier Cartularies for Essex (Studies and Texts 50), Toronto 1981.

10 The Cartulary of the Knights of St. John of Jerusalem in England. Essex, 2 vols., ed. Michael GERVERS, Records of Social and Economic History NS 6 and 23 (1982–1996).

11 Lucie FOSSIER/Marion CRÉHANGE, Un essai de traitement sur ordinateur des documents diplomatiques du Moyen Age, in: Annales. Histoire, Sciences Sociales 25/1 (1970) p. 249–284.

12 Le médiéviste et l'ordinateur, 1979–2003.

13 David HERLIHY/Christiane KLAPISCH-ZUBER, Les Toscans et leurs familles: Une étude du Catasto florentin de 1427 (Editions de l'Ecole des Hautes Etudes en Sciences Sociales), Paris 1978; translated into English as Tuscans and their families: a study of the Florentine catasto of 1427, New Haven 1985.

14 For a selection of the proceedings, see History and Computing, ed. Peter DENLEY/Deian HOPKIN, Manchester 1987.

Fig. 4: History and Computing, vol. 1, no. 1, 1989. Cover page.

Humanities[15]. Needless to say, he has long been a supportive colleague. The second London meeting led to the foundation of the journal *History and Computing*, published between 1989 and 2002 on which we and many other late twentieth-century digital historians served as Editorial Advisors for the duration [Fig. 4][16]. The frontiers were clearly expanding in the early years of this century, when *Le médiéviste et l'ordinateur* and *History and Computing* came to a simultaneous end, to be replaced by the *International Journal of Humanities and Arts Computing* which, since 2007, has born the subtitle *A Journal of Digital Humanities*[17].

It would be no exaggeration to say that in the first decade of the twentieth century, the torch for the digitization of charters and their diplomatic analysis was handed to Georg Vogeler, whose leadership in the field of Digital Diplomatics has been instrumental ever since. That leadership has brought us to where we are today,

15 https://dblp.org/pid/31/4693.html.

16 For background on the foundation of the journal "History and Computing" see the statement by its principal editor, R.J. MORRIS, History and Computing. A New Magazine, in: Historical Social Research/Historische Sozialforschung 15/1 (53) (1990) p. 118–120.

17 https://www.euppublishing.com/loi/ijhac

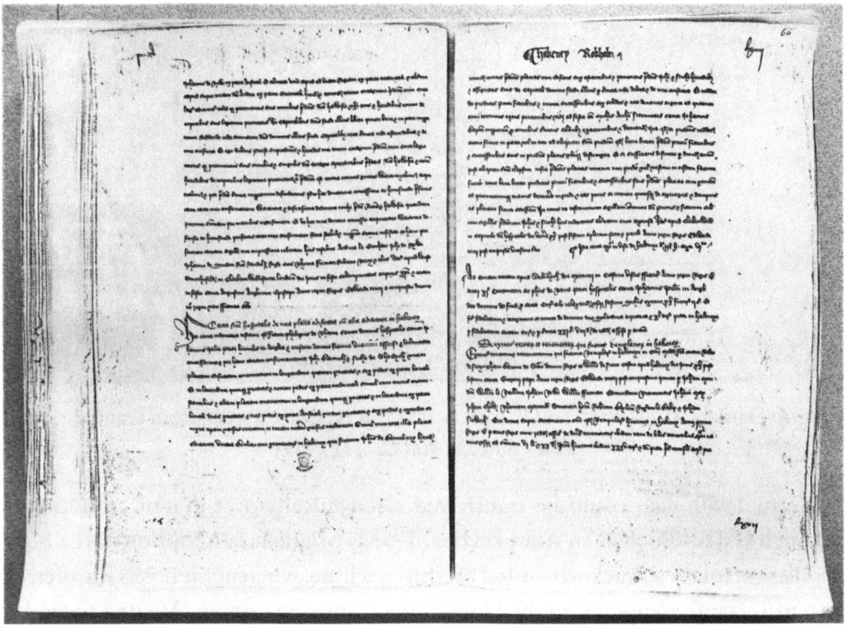

Fig. 5: CopyFlo print on large format paper from microfilm of British Library, Cotton MS Nero E VI, fol. 65v-66r.

a long way from when we were only slowly stepping away from totally manual approaches to charter scholarship forty to fifty years ago[18].

Then, we all used microfilm or microfiche readers[19], but making a full transcription using such a contraption was problematic and there were inventive options such as CopyFlo, by which an entire manuscript could be transferred from microfilm to print on large format paper[20] [Fig. 5]. The microfilm version of the Secunda Camera was transcribed directly from these CopyFlo sheets using an Olivetti Lettera 32 portable typewriter and three carbons[21]. When graduating to a standard desk-top typewriter some years later, one felt like a school boy getting his first bicycle, but carrying it was another matter. You may remember Daniel Couturier and Patrick Auffay lugging one around Paris in François Truffaut's classic film from 1959, *Les 400 Coups*[22] [Fig. 6].

18 https://didip.hypotheses.org/author/vogeler

19 Terence CROWLEY, Comparing Fiche and Film: A Test of Speed, in: Journal of Library Automation 14/4 (1981) p. 292–295.

20 George Robert GUFFEY, Standardization of Photographic Reproductions for Mechanical Collation, in: The Papers of the Bibliographical Society of America 62/2 (1968) p. 237–240.

21 https://www.macfilos.com/2012/12/25/2012-12-24-ancient-laptop-olivetti-lettera-32-typewriter/

22 https://www.youtube.com/watch?v=H9NtTRpLa78

Fig. 6: Daniel COUTURIER and Patrick AUFFAY in typewriter scene from François Truffaut's film *Les 400 Coups* (1959).

Circa 1980, data could be transferred electronically over dial-up phone lines through systems such as an Atari keyboard[23]. My original transcription of the Hospitaller cartulary was rekeyboarded on this machine, whereupon it was transferred to a mainframe computer on the University of Toronto campus. Making the index was still an entirely manual process, taking a year to prepare using 35,000 index cards with each entry manually typed on a separate piece of 3 x 5 inch note paper. Such was the normal, manual manner of preparing an extensive number of diplomatic documents for publication.

Other challenges followed, unfortunately not so quickly in the field of Natural Language Processing. The University boasted regularly of its acquisition of ever larger mainframe computers[24]. Those who wished, could request access to these number crunchers from the dean, who would hand out user time in the form of "computer dollars". A Department of Computer Services was established to support novice users, where one was directed for guidance in setting up the structure, for example, of a database [Fig. 7]. Computer Services spent the better part of an academic year sketching out such a structure in the only form then available, a hierarchical database[25]. We struggled with this arrangement using the hierarchical database software Mark IV for a decade, eventually getting nowhere and subsequently

23 Charles CANGIALOSI, The Electronic Underground: Computer Piracy and Electronic Bulletin Boards, 15 Rutgers Computer & Tech. L.J. 265 (1989). (https://heinonline.org/HOL/LandingPage?handle=hein.journals/rutcomt15&div=13&id=&page=; https://commons.wikimedia.org/wiki/File:Atari_800XL_with_Modem.jpg.

24 https://web.cs.toronto.edu/timeline (site visited 22 December 2022)

25 Dennis TSICHRITZIS/Frederick Horst LOCHOVSKY, Hierarchical Data-Base Management: A Survey, in: Computing Surveys 8/1 (1976) p. 105–123 (https://dl.acm.org/doi/pdf/10.1145/356662.356667.

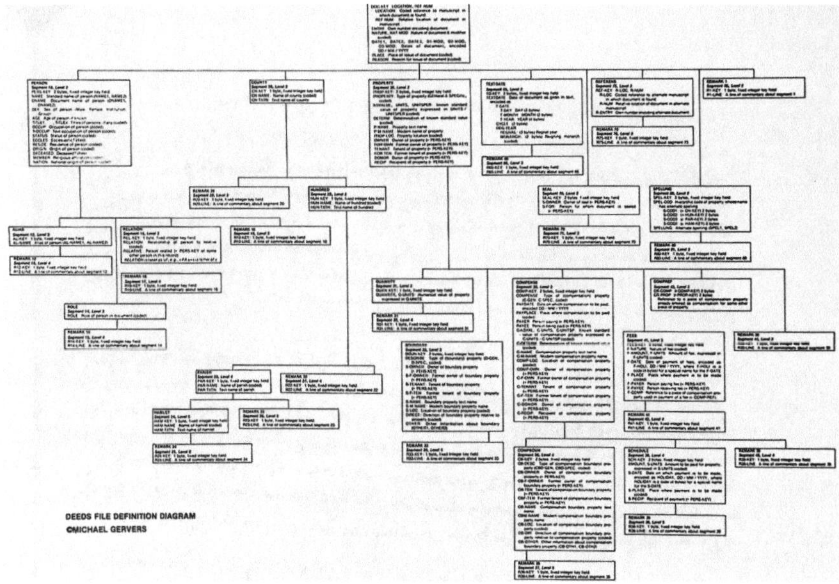

Fig. 7: Hierarchical file definition diagram for the DEEDS Project, ca. 1979.

abandoning it entirely[26]. One day, in about 1987, a student trainee walked into the DEEDS Project with a box under his arm containing a new product by a then virtually unknown Microsoft competitor called ORACLE[27]. The company was giving it away to universities and major administrative centres to encourage its use in building relational databases. Needless to say, the initiative was successful and we used the software for the next twenty years not only for the purpose of analyzing the content of medieval English charters, but also for training students and those from the mainframe world who desperately sought to retrain in the use of individual stand-alone machines and relational software[28]. Eventually, ORACLE's annual license became too expensive, so we transferred to MySQL.

* * *

Following the conquest of England by Duke William of Normandy in 1066, Norman diplomatic became the norm for English charters. Perhaps because the

26 Michael GERVERS, Medieval Charters and the Computer: An Analysis Using Mark IV, in: Computers and the Humanities 12/1 (1978) p. 127–136.

27 https://www.oracle.com/ca-en/research/. On the history of the company, see: https://www.britannica.com/topic/Oracle-Corporation

28 Michael GERVERS/Gillian LONG/Michael MCCULLOCH, The DEEDS Database of Mediaeval Charters: design and coding for the RDBMS ORACLE 5, in: History and Computing 1/3 (1990) p. 1–12.

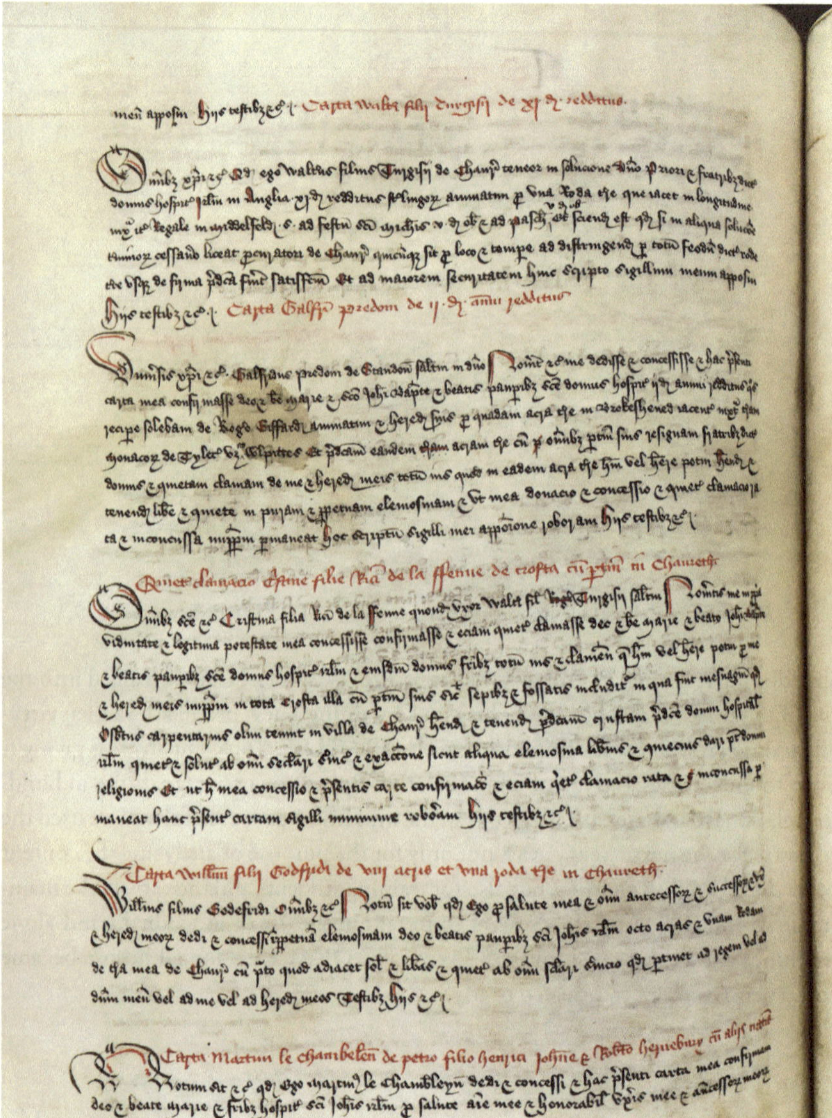

Fig. 8: Charters copied without witness lists, from British Library, Cotton MS Nero E VI, fol. 208v.

Normans were new to Christianity, literacy and the administrative system of the Roman Church and its extension to the chanceries of the monarchies of medieval Europe, they adopted an abbreviated form of the conveyance which, for two and a half centuries, saw approximately 97% of English charters issued without dates. Richard I, the crusader king who ruled largely in absentia from 1189–1199, was the first to introduce regular dating to the royal chancery, but such was not the case for private charters until the reign of Edward II, which began in 1307. No one has ever found a satisfactory explanation for this lack of chronological markers, nor how the English administrators of the time dealt with their absence, but they did. They obviously attributed more legal value to the names on the witness list, which from a chronological viewpoint can be confusing in cases where similar assemblages of names may recur in villages where grandsons bear the same names as their grandfathers. When editing the entries in the Hospitaller cartulary, the only recourse was to find names with counterparts appearing elsewhere in dated sources. In place of dates, therefore, names became the key to determining the chronological placement of the document, although the results could not be counted on to be accurate. If, furthermore, we step away from the original single sheet charters to cartularies, we find that with scribes being paid by the number of lines they copied, for economic reasons it was not uncustomary for the usually monastic patron to have documents copied without their witness lists [Fig. 8]. In such cases, the obvious alternative in the absence of paleographical analysis was, for modern researchers at least, to depend on the diplomatic of the charter. This approach led to attributing to English charters such vague dates as *Late twelfth century*, *First half of the thirteenth century*, *Mid-thirteenth century*, and so on.

At DEEDS, where we seek to identify social change across twelfth- and thirteenth-century English society, such solutions were far too vague to be of much historical use. The second half of the twentieth century being the heyday of the machine-generated concordance, we followed suit with the production of a concordance of the Hospitaller cartulary on microfiche, a medium which allowed for over 200 images on a single sheet [Fig. 9][29]. It was a considerable advance over microfilm, but then a special microfiche reader had to be available to read them. The result, however, was a breakthrough for us. We could now see words and phrases in context in documents without witness lists and link them to the circa dates previously attributed to each document. By choosing a dozen or so of these phrases, or word patterns, for each document, adding up their low dates and high dates, and averaging the two, it was possible to get an approximate date for the undated document that had lost its witness list. Calling it *dating by formulae*, this method was used for those hapless Essex documents devoid of their witness lists in the *Prima Camera* of Cotton MS Nero E VI that were eventually published in 1996[30]. As primitive and time consuming as this approach may have been, the results turned out to be a step on the way to what was produced by the far more advanced algorithms leading to the current dating system used at DEEDS and discussed below.

29 Michael GERVERS, A Microfiche Concordance of the Cartulary of the Order of St. John of Jerusalem, secunda camera (British Library, Cotton MS. Nero E VI, fols. 289–467), Toronto 1983.

30 See above n. 9, vol. 2 (1996) p. xxviii.

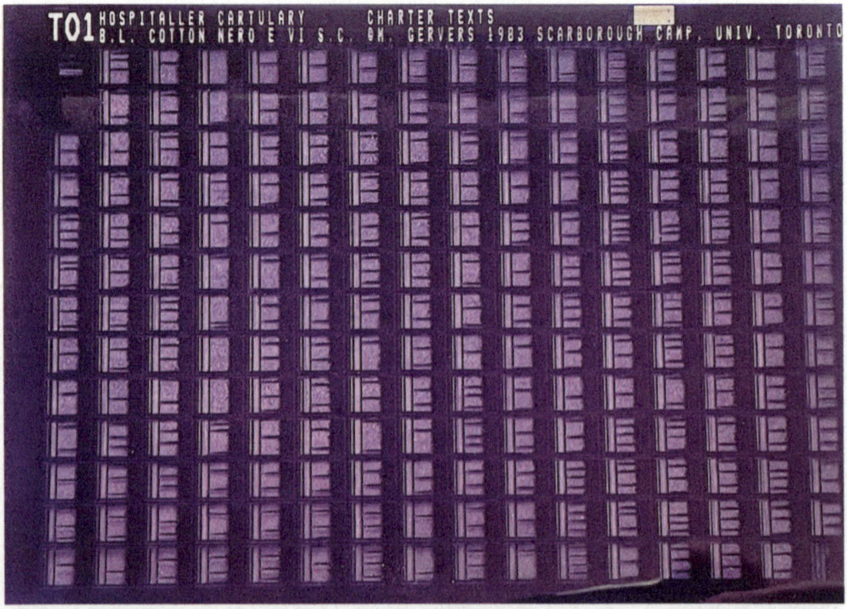

Fig. 9: Microfiche concordance of the first page with words starting with letter *T* from the secunda camera of British Library, Cotton MS Nero E VI.

In 1999, a conference was organized at the Collegium Budapest on the question of the undated charter, contributions to which were published a year later as *Dating Undated Medieval Charters*[31]. Among the participants were many familiar names: Véronique Gazeau, Benoît-Michel Tock, Nicholas Vincent, Georges Declercq, Zsolt Hunyadi, P.D.A. Harvey, and others. The following decade saw the publication of a number of articles as attempts to attribute dates to diplomatic documents by statistical means progressed. The period coincided with the beginning of what has been a long-term collaboration with statistician Dr. Gelila Tilahun, who received her PhD in 2011 based on the algorithms she developed to determine dates for the undated charters in the DEEDS database[32]. In the same academic year, DEEDS received a three-year grant from the Social Sciences and Humanities Research Council of Canada that provided funding for the creation of the current DEEDS database by the University's Information Technology Services [Fig. 10][33].

31 Dating Undated Medieval Charters, ed. Michael GERVERS, Budapest and Rochester 2000.

32 Gelila TILAHUN, Statistical Methods for Dating Collections of Historical Documents, Phil. Diss. Toronto 2011.

33 https://deeds.library.utoronto.ca

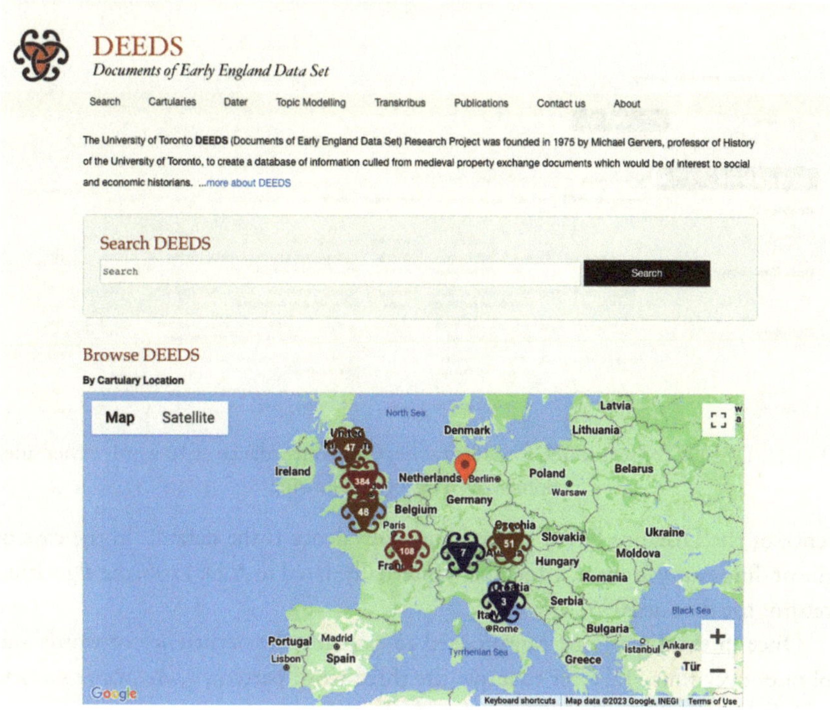

Fig. 10: Home page of the DEEDS Project (https://deeds.utsc.utoronto.ca).

This database provides users with a number of functions enabling them to analyze its content, first and foremost the essential SEARCH mechanism. This was, until very recently, unique in the field of charter studies. One can search on words, such as *anglis* (*to the English*), phrases such as *francis et anglis* (*to French and English*), with up to ten contextual words on either side [Fig. 11], and letters within a word (**gli**). A click on the header word will return hits in ascending numeric or alphabetic order. Any search can be refined or filtered at sixteen levels. Thirty years after producing a far less versatile concordance on microfiche, we now had an automated digital version of our own.

The next move was to implement Dr. Tilahun's dating algorithms, which after testing on dated documents, proved capable of returning dates accurate to within ±7 years about 80% of the time[34]. The algorithms are based on English charter diplomatic, but have been shown to respond relatively accurately to Continental charters of the 12th and 13th centuries. Turning, therefore, to the *Dater* on the home page, the user can date a document by one of two methods: the Maximum Preva-

34 Gelila TILAHUN/Andrey FEUERVERGER/Michael GERVERS, Dating Medieval English Charters, in: Annals of Applied Statistics 6/4 (2012) p. 1615–1640.

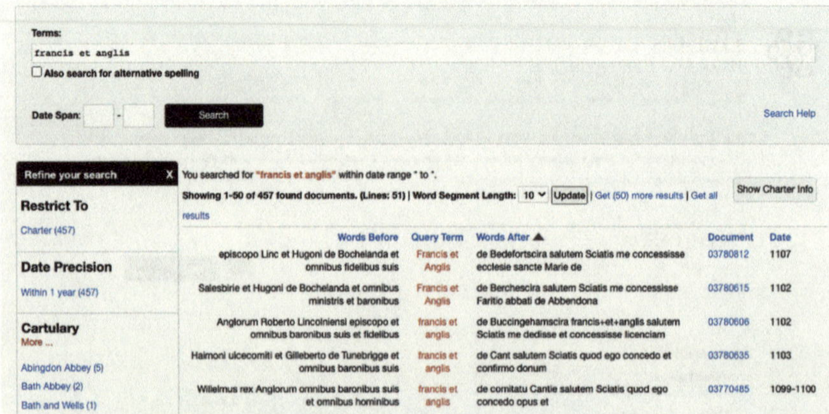

Fig. 11: DEEDS context search for *francis et anglis* as concordance of 10 words either side, alphabetized by word following.

lence or the Distance Based[35]. Maximum Prevalence is the default. In the case of the on-line *example* given, a document internally dated to A.D. 1100, the algorithm returns the date of 1096.

Once in the *Dater*, one can proceed to examine the occurrence of words and phrases over time. Take for example the three-word pattern, *beate Marie missam* and drop it into the *Text Pattern Search*. Two documents are returned from the entire database that contain this exact phrase: entries 00010098 and 00160091, both dated internally to 1237. This in itself is coincidental as one comes from the *Early Charters of St. Paul's Cathedral London*[36] and the other from the *Cartulary of the Monastery of St. John the Baptist in Colchester* (an ancient Roman town on the Essex border with Suffolk)[37]. A quick review shows that they are, in fact, one and the same document, each preserved in the registers of the monastic houses in ques-

35 On the Maximum Prevalence Method, see: Ibid.; on the Distance Based Method, see: Andrey Feuerverger/Peter Hall/Gelila Tilahun/Michael Gervers, Distance measures and smoothing methodology for imputing features of documents, in: Journal of Computational and Graphical Statistics 14/2 (2005) p. 255–262; and Andrey Feuerverger, Peter Hall, Gelila Tilahun/Michael Gervers, Using statistical smoothing to date medieval manuscripts, in: Beyond Parametrics in Interdisciplinary Research: Festschrift in Honor of Professor Pranab K. Sen 1, ed. Narayanaswamy Balakrishnan et al. (Institute of Mathematical Statistics Collections 1), Beachwood 2008, p. 321–332. For analysis on a larger dataset for Maximum Prevalence and Distance Based methods, see: Michael Gervers/Gelila Tilahun/Shima Khoshraftar/Roderick A. Mitchell, The dating of undated medieval charters, in: Archives [Journal of the British Records Association] LIII/137 (2018) p. 1–33.

36 Early Charters of St. Paul's Cathedral London, ed. Marion Gibbs (Camden Third Series 58), London 1939, p. 71–73.

37 Cartularium Monasterii sancti Johannis Baptiste de Colecestria, ed. Stuart A[rchibald] Moore (Roxburghe Club Publications 131), London 1897, p. 91–93.

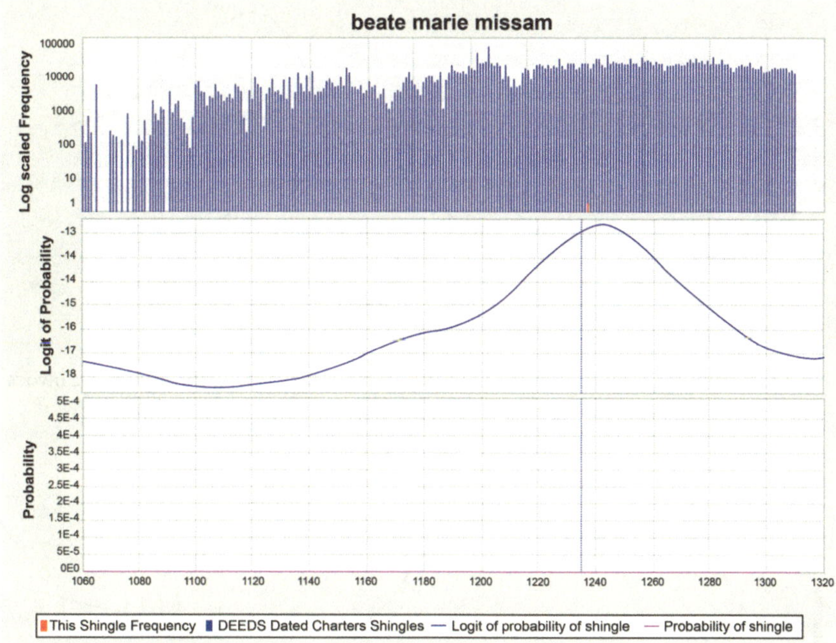

Fig. 12: Chronological plot showing the occurrence of the trigram *beate Marie missam* in the DEEDS database.

tion. The search phrase, *beate Marie missam* in these documents shows that in the first case it is preceded by *in altare*, while in the second by *in altari*. Whether this and numerous other small differences in the two transcripts are scribal or editorial errors cannot be determined from the DEEDS database as we have rarely had the opportunity to include links to the original sources to check the paleography, but in time that option will become available as the repositories make their holdings available online. When we plot *beate Marie missam* on the time scale we find that it sits neatly at 1247, with no competition from other points on the scale [Fig. 12]. A more familiar expression, *omnibus Christi fidelibus*, shows considerably more activity, especially from the latter part of the twelfth century, while *omnibus sancte matris ecclesie* flourishes earlier and diminishes over time [Fig. 13][38].

The *Text Pattern Comparison* function in the Dater allows one to compare word use over time. If, for example, we take our previously chosen *beate Marie* and compare it to *sancte Marie* we find that over a period of approximately 155 years, there is a growing preference in English charter diplomatic for the use of *beate Marie*

38 Michael Gervers, The Dating of Medieval English Private Charters of the Twelfth and Thirteenth Centuries, in: A Distinct Voice: Medieval Studies in Honor of Leonard E. Boyle, O.P., ed. Jacqueline Brown/William P. Stoneman, Notre Dame (Indiana) 1997, p. 455–504 (here p. 462–463).

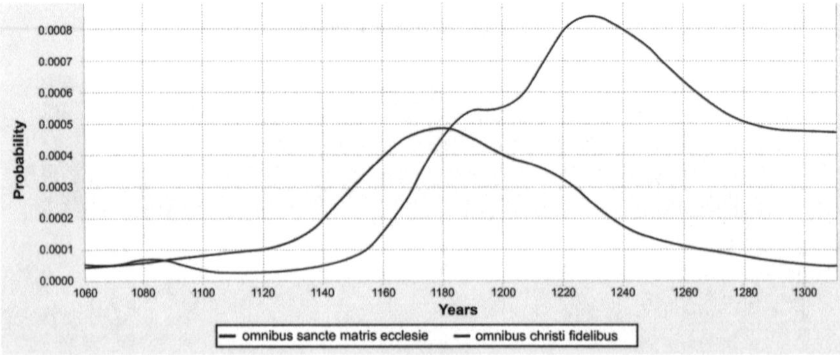

Fig. 13: Chronological plot showing the comparative occurrence of the diplomatic invocations *Omnibus sancte matris ecclesie* and *Omnibus Christi fidelibus.*

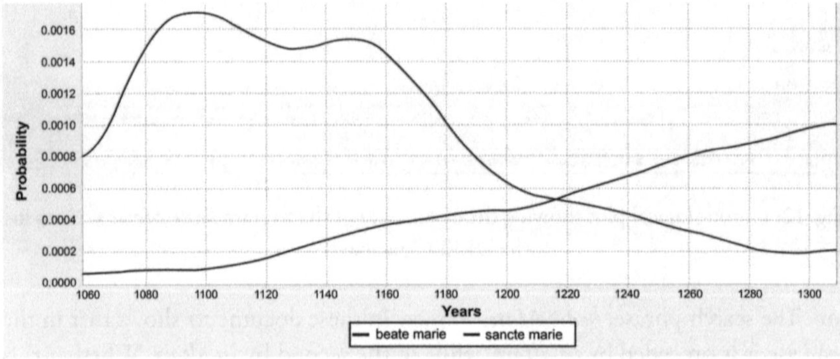

Fig. 14: Chronological plot showing the changing preference for the use of *beate Marie* over *sancte Marie.*

over *sancte Marie*, with the crossing point around 1217 [Fig. 14], a year after the tumultuous reign of King John (1199–1216) and the beginning of that of the then minor, King Henry III (1216–1272). The reason for this slow change of preference is yet to be determined. Such changes in diplomatic usage are by no means unusual. In fact, it is because of the frequency and extent of these changes that the functions behind the dating algorithms are able to work. They measure pattern change over time and, when calculated as a whole, provide a date for a document.

Having entered the realm of Digital Humanities by rendering portions of the Hospitaller cartulary into machine readable form, and then providing the means to attribute dates to undated charters through the development of a database of those rare dated charters issued from the eleventh through early fourteenth centuries, we next turned to analyzing the content of the tens of thousands of charters in the DEEDS database to determine what they could tell us beyond the confirmation of property transfer for which they were created. We are now experimenting with the degree to which changes in words and word patterns reflect economic and especially social change. We are doing so by the application of topic modeling[39].

Topic modelling is a statistical learning approach in the field of natural language processing that discovers latent or hidden *themes* (referred to here as *topics*) from a large textual collection or corpus. It is a popular technique for text categorization and approaches to textual analysis. A particular algorithm used for topic modelling which we have applied is called Latent Dirichlet Allocation or LDA[40]. This model assumes there to be a fixed number of recurring patterns of co-occurrences of words, or terms, in documents, called topics, and that each of the documents within the corpus exhibits the topics to a greater or lesser degree. The inputs for LDA are the textual corpus and the number of topics which the user wishes to be determined. For each one of these topics, the output returns the probability, or the likelihood, of occurrence of all the words from the corpus within the topic. The words (or terms) with relatively high values of probability are the basis from which the *theme* of the topic is determined. Another important output that is returned is the probability distribution of documents over the various topics, which means that every document is a composition of a weighted percentage of each of the topics[41]. This probability distribution measures the degree to which a document is composed of the different topics – the higher the composition of a document from a certain topic, the higher is the associated document-topic probability.

In the current analysis, we have used 16,976 documents dated to within a year of issue and comprised of over 3.5 million words. A histogram visualizes the distribution of the dates [Fig. 15]. As shown, most of the collection is from the thirteenth century. While the collection itself is an ad hoc assimilation, extracted from published sources, it may be considered representative of the overall repertory of legal acts used in the conveyance of property during the period. In addition to date, for each of the documents in the collection, metadata has also been collected, such as: place of issue, document type and the patronage of the sources, most of which are religious houses.

Prior to applying the LDA model, it was necessary to determine a priori the number of topics on which to implement it. Determining the optimal numbers through computational approaches is not always satisfactory[42] and even the most

39 David M. Blei, Topic modeling and digital humanities, in: Journal of Digital Humanities 2/1 (2012) p. 8–11.

40 David M. Blei, Andrew Y. NG and Michael I. Jordan, Latent Dirichlet Allocation, in: Journal of Machine Learning Research 3/1 (2003) p. 993–1022.

41 See notes 39 and 40.

42 Jingxian Gan/Yong Qi, Selection of the optimal number of topics for LDA topic model—taking patent policy analysis as an example, in: Entropy 23/10 (2021) p. 1301.

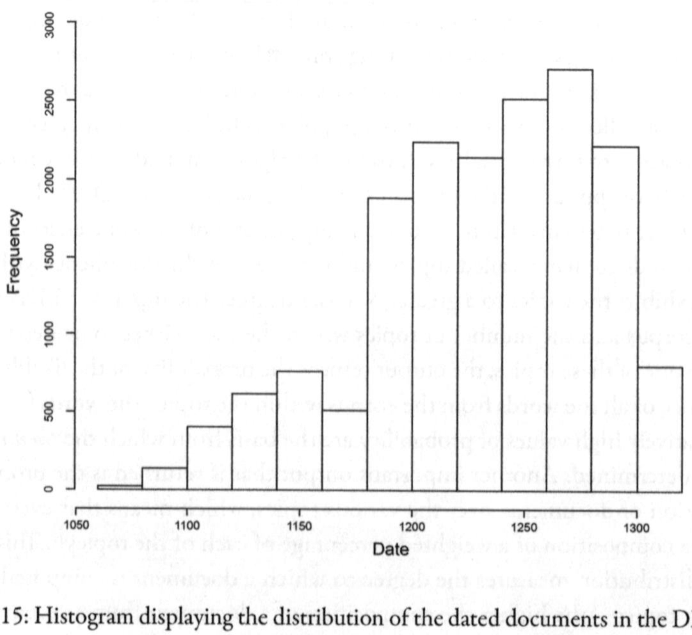

Fig. 15: Histogram displaying the distribution of the dated documents in the DEEDS collection. The majority are from the 13th century.

commonly used method, the perplexity metric[43] has pitfalls[44]. If the chosen number for topic modelling is too small, significant topics would not be identified, and if too large, the topics would risk becoming incoherent. Since relying purely on a computational approach to determine the optimal number of topics does not yield an interpretable result of satisfactory quality, we found it useful to employ domain experts (medieval historians) and/or other auxiliary data (in our case, metadata information on document types) in corroborating that the number of topics on which we ultimately settled, eight, was sensible. The choice of eight turned out to be appropriate for coherently interpreting the main themes arising from the corpus [Fig. 18]. With eight topics, the highest ranking words/phrases from each of the eight topics were more interpretable by the historian experts. Moreover, since we can quantify the extent to which a document belongs to any of the topics, when overlaying the metadata, we found documents which belonged to the same document type overwhelmingly clustered to the same topic [see Fig. 16]. When we ran the LDA with a smaller number of topics, the themes/topics could not be as

43 David M. BLEI/Andrew Y. NG/Michael I. JORDAN, Latent Dirichlet Allocation, in: Journal of machine Learning research 3/1 (2003) p. 993–1022.

44 See Stefano SBALCHIERO/Maciej EDER, Topic modeling, long texts and the best number of topics. Some Problems and solutions, in: Quality & Quantity 54 (2020) p. 1095–1108.

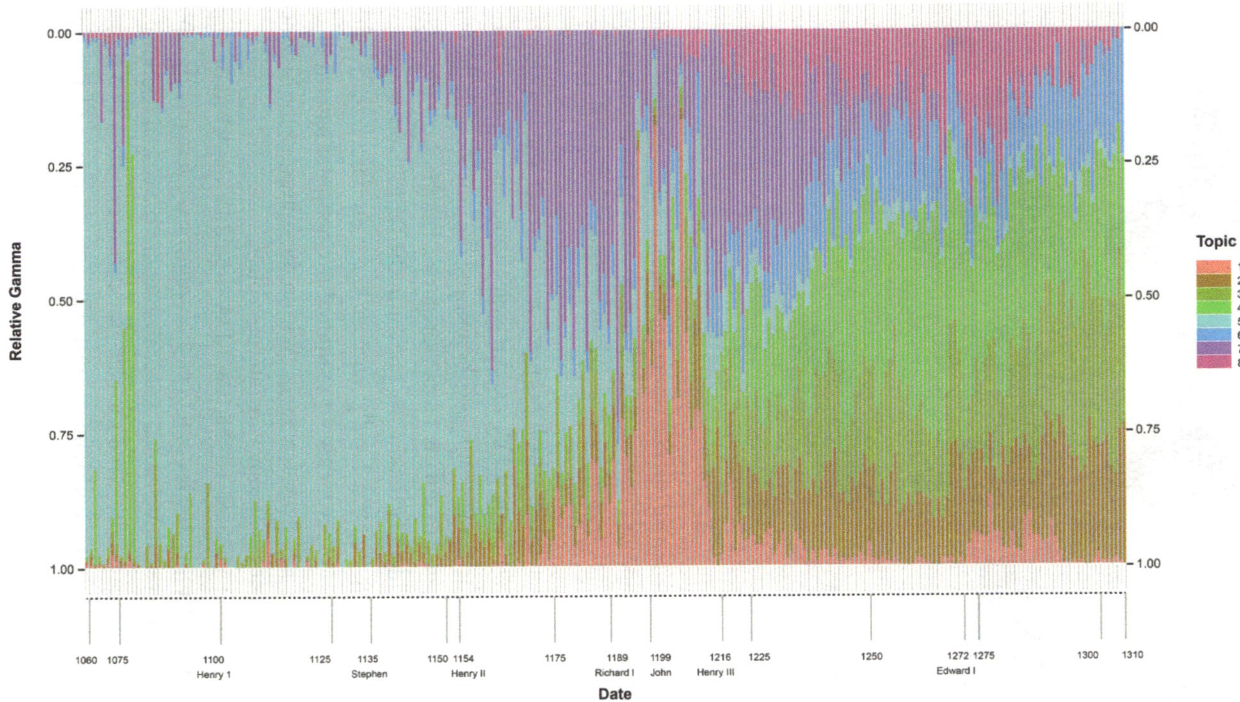

Fig. 16: Document-topic proportions displayed as bar graphs. The horizontal axis displays the date (1060 - 1310) and the vertical axis the value of the topic proportions. The colours correspond to the eight different topics selected.

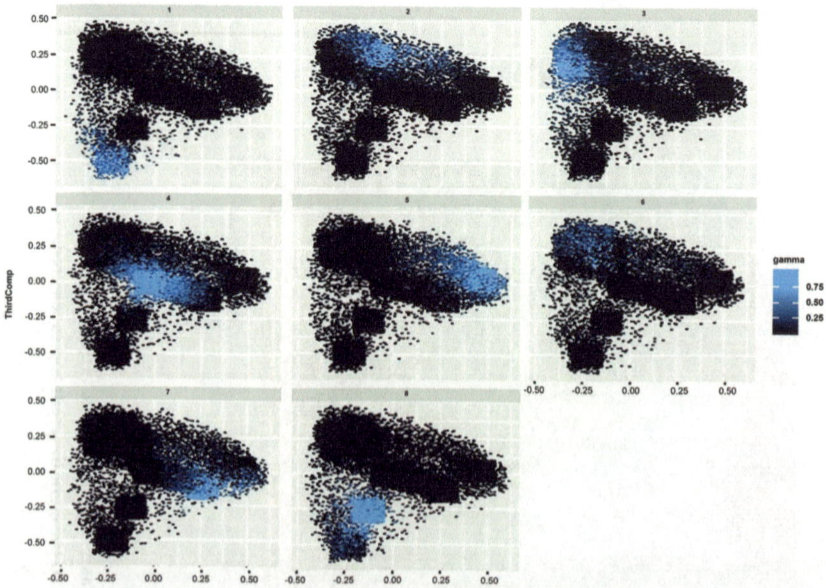

Fig. 17: A 2-D projection of 16,976 dated DEEDS documents using multidimensional scaling. Each point corresponds to a document and all panels are replicas of one another. Documents that have high in-topic proportion are lighter blue in colour.

easily discerned, and documents which belonged to different metadata clustered within the same topic. When the LDA was run with a topic number much larger than eight, the topics/themes were not as cohesive, and documents with the same metadata tended to disperse to different topic categories. For the form and nature of the words serving to identify the themes present in the DEEDS documents, we chose strings of three, or trigrams. Finally, since we know the dates of each of the documents, in all of our experiments we examined the temporal pattern of the prevalence of the topics across the date range. Within the context of the historical events of the time, the prevalent topics are interpretable[45].

In addition, since we determined that the LDA should be modelled on eight topics, the probability topic distribution of each document is consequently represented as a point in a seven-dimensional space. To visualize the spatial relationship between the documents, we projected the pair-wise distances onto a two-dimensional document space using multidimensional scaling[46]. Each one of the eight

45 Michael Gervers/Gelila Tilahun, Topic Modelling English Charters, 1066–1307, in: International Centre for Archival Research (ICARUS) (2020).

46 John C. Gower, Principal coordinates analysis, in: Wiley StatsRef: Statistics Reference Online (2014) [https://onlinelibrary.wiley.com/doi/book/10.1002/9781118445112]. The R Statistical Programming function used here for implementation of multidimensional scaling is *cmdscale*.

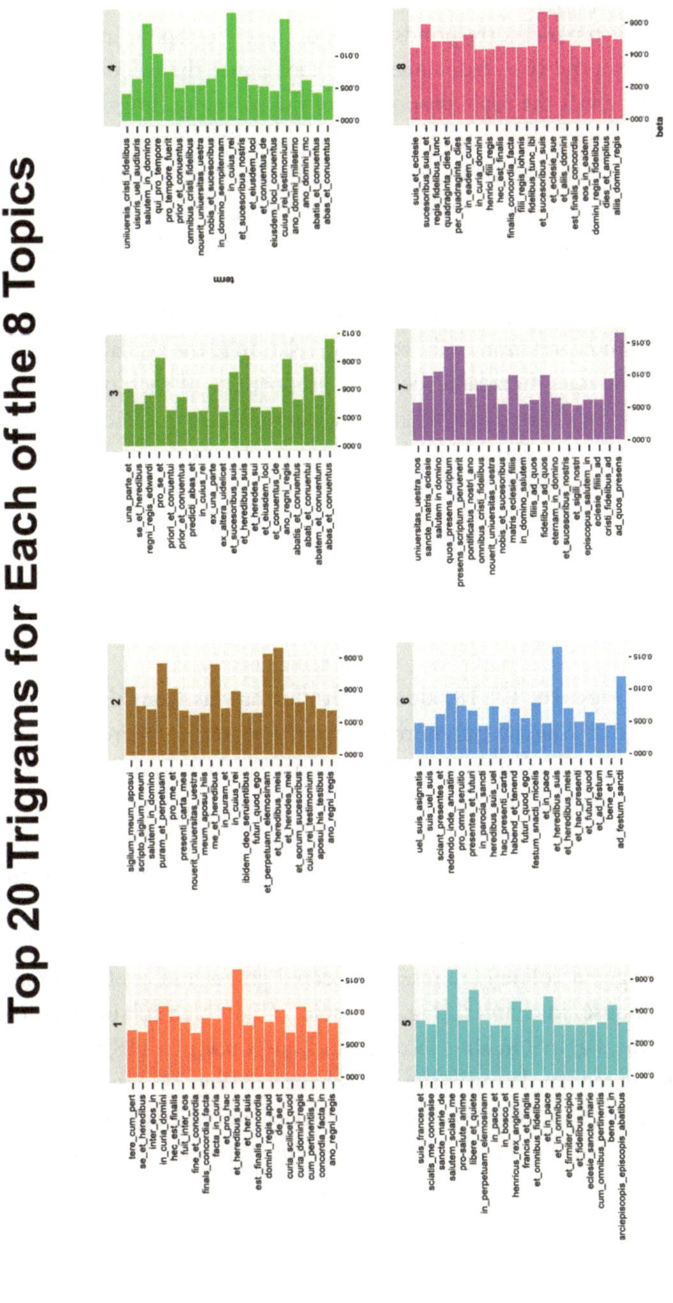

Fig. 18: Eight bar charts corresponding to each of the eight topics. For each term (rows) within a topic, the bar chart measurements show the probability (*beta*) of the term within the topic. The trigrams are the twenty top-ranked terms within each topic. Note that double consonants have been removed to facilitate search compatibility.

panels in Fig. 17 is a projection of the 16,976 documents onto a two-dimensional document space. Each panel corresponds to one of the eight topics, and each point corresponds to one of the 16,976 documents. In each panel, the colour gradients of each of the points reflect the topic proportion of the corresponding document for the topics associated with the respective panels, and the lighter the blue colour of a point, the higher the topic proportion. Documents that have a high degree of in-topic proportions lie near one another, as seen in the light blue areas. The twenty most significant tri-grams, as determined by topic modeling for the eight topics, enable us to establish marked differences within our corpus of documents [Fig. 18][47].

An interesting aspect of topic modelling appearing in the DEEDS collection is found through the interpretation of the results in relation to the available metadata. In Fig. 16, using the *date* metadata, the topic proportions of each of the 16,976 DEEDS documents are charted as a bar graph where the values are stacked and normalized in accordance with the date of the documents. The horizontal axis displays the date range of the documents, and the vertical axis (*relative gamma*) displays the normalized document-topic proportions. In reading the graph, the contribution of a topic is determined by the height of the bar corresponding to the colour of the topic. For example, many of the documents from the eleventh to the mid-twelfth century appear to have a high proportion from topic-5.

Information from Figs. 16, 17, 18, along with illustrations from the remaining metadata, are parts of a jigsaw puzzle that help in forming a coherent theme of the eight topics. In brief, what we found by evaluating the tri-grams for each of the eight topics was that: [Fig. 19] topic 1 (orange colour) was built around *Concordances* held in the royal archive known as the *Feet of Fines*[48]; [Fig. 20] topic 2 (brown colour) is composed of *Grants* in free alms to religious houses largely from the period following the reign of King John (r. 1199–1216); [Fig. 21] topic 3 (olive green colour) represents *Agreements* issued to, or by, religious houses after c. 1216; [Fig. 22] topic 4 (green colour) are internally dated grants and confirmations issued by religious houses in chapter; [Fig. 23] topic 5 (light blue colour) are largely externally dated royal grants in alms to religious houses prior to 1189 when King Richard introduced regular dating to the royal chancery; [Fig. 24] topic 6 (sky blue colour) are conveyances made in exchange for service and compensation starting in the second decade of the thirteenth century; [Fig. 25] topic 7 (purple colour) indicates internally dated episcopal documents running from c. 1170, with a dip

47 Note that in order to achieve conformity of spelling and thus the greater number of returns of any word, double consonants were reduced to single consonants in the search data.

48 Chris Phillips, *A Short Introduction to Feet of Fines, in: Foundations: The Journal of the Foundation for Mediaeval Genealogy 4 (2012)* p. 45–55; https://www.nationalarchives.gov.uk/help-with-your-research/research-guides/land-conveyance-feet-of-fines-1182-1833/

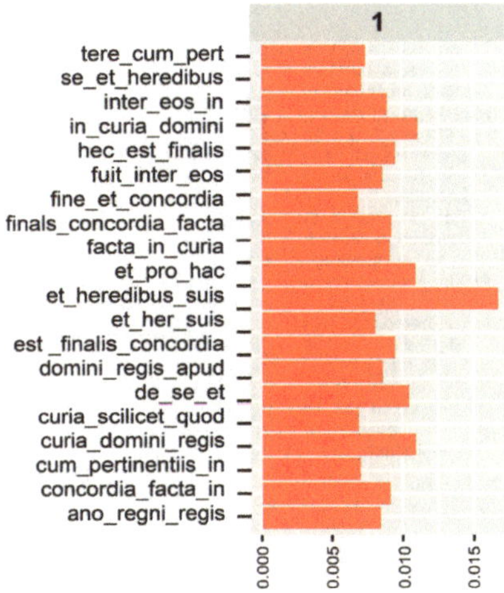

Fig. 19: Topic 1 (orange) represents *Concordances* found in the royal archives known as the Feet of Fines.

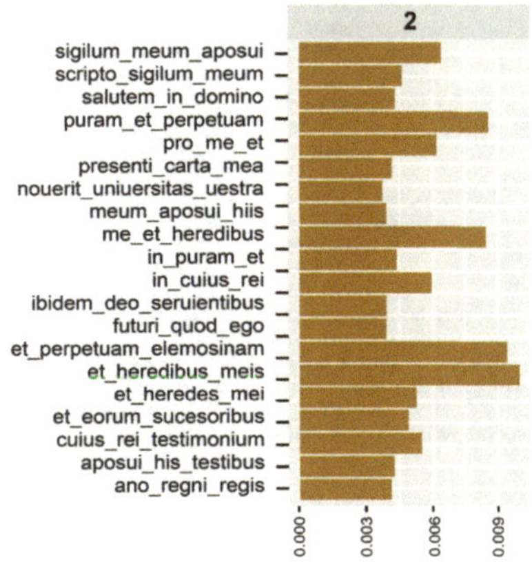

Fig. 20: Topic 2 (brown) represents *Grants* in free alms to religious houses predominantly from the period post 1216.

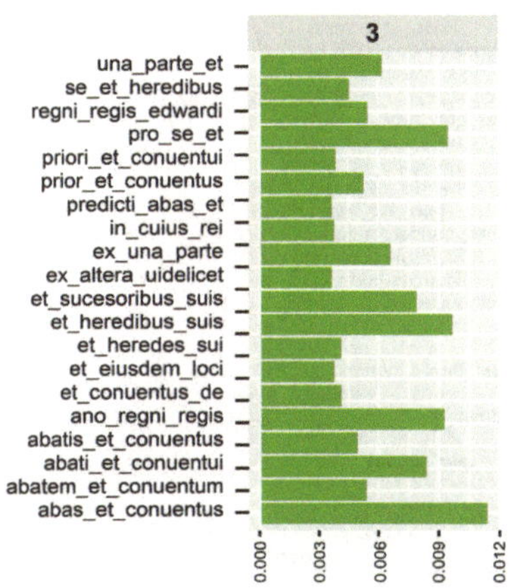

Fig. 21: Topic 3 (olive green) represents *Agreements* issued to, or by, religious houses after ca. 1216.

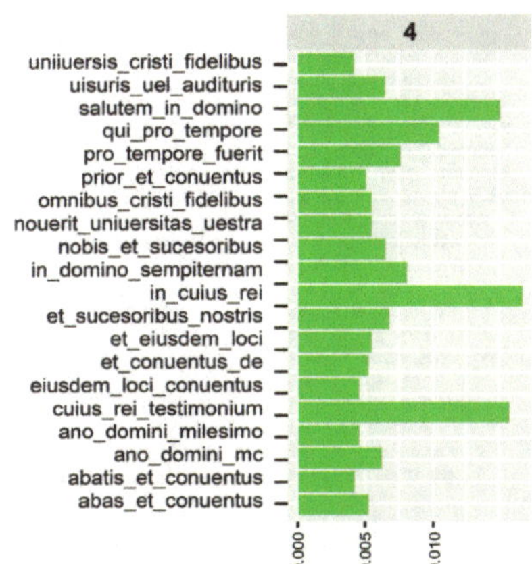

Fig. 22: Topic 4 (green) represents internally dated *Grants* and *Confirmations* issued by religious houses in chapter.

during the papal Interdict applied during the reign of King John, and continuing until c. 1250; [Fig. 26] topic 8 (reddish colour) reflects letters written by bishops to the king from the time of the Fourth Lateran Council in 1215 largely concerning matters of excommunication.

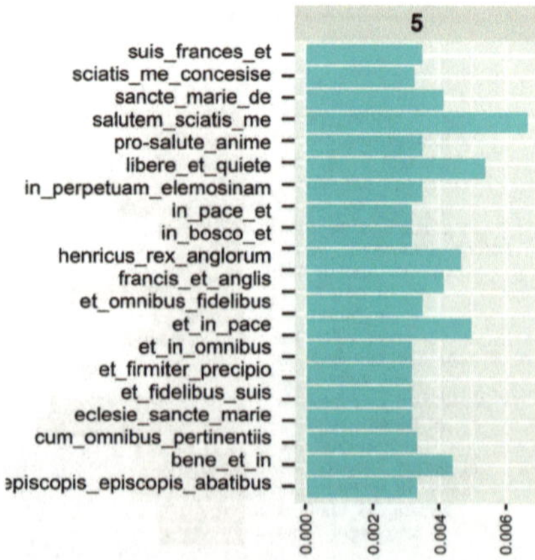

Fig. 23: Topic 5 (light blue) represents largely externally dated royal grants in alms to religious houses prior to 1189.

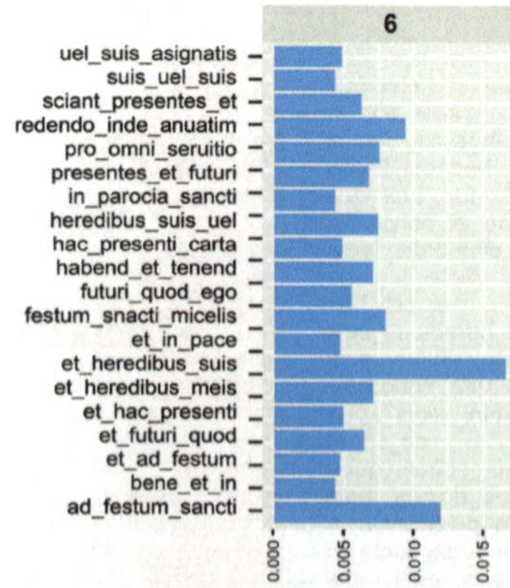

Fig. 24: Topic 6 (sky blue) represents *Conveyances* made in exchange for service and compensation from the second decade of the 13th century.

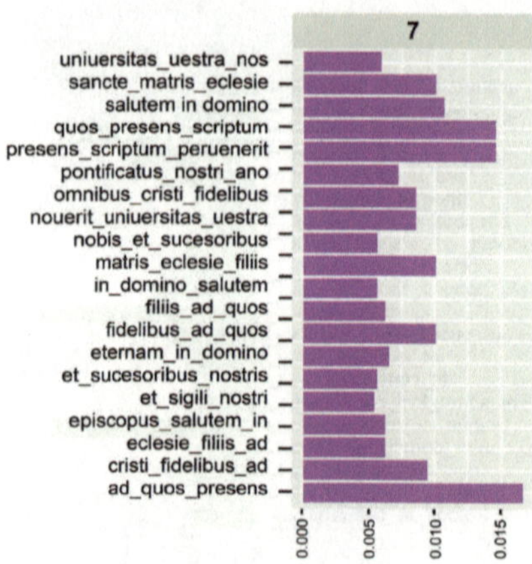

Fig. 25: Topic 7 (purple) represents internally dated episcopal documents from ca. 1170 to ca. 1250.

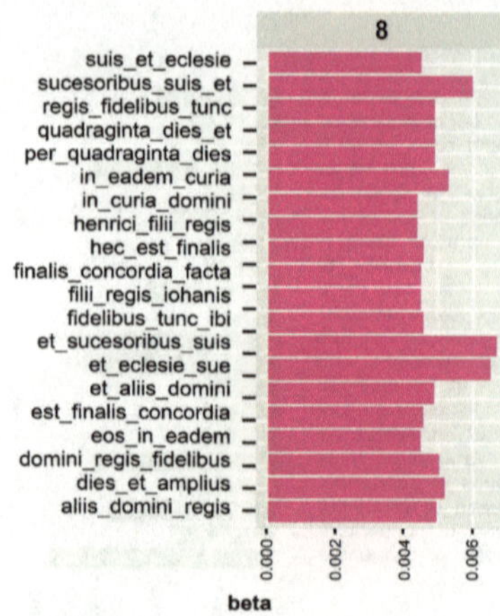

Fig. 26: Topic 8 (red) represents letters from bishops to the king following the Fourth Lateran Council (1215) largely concerning matters of excommunication.

Considering the significance of the assignment of documents to a topic, we investigated the degree to which each of the documents, in terms of percentage weight, were attributed to each one of the topics. Recognizing that the percentage weight of a document's association across all topics adds up to 100%, and considering 85%

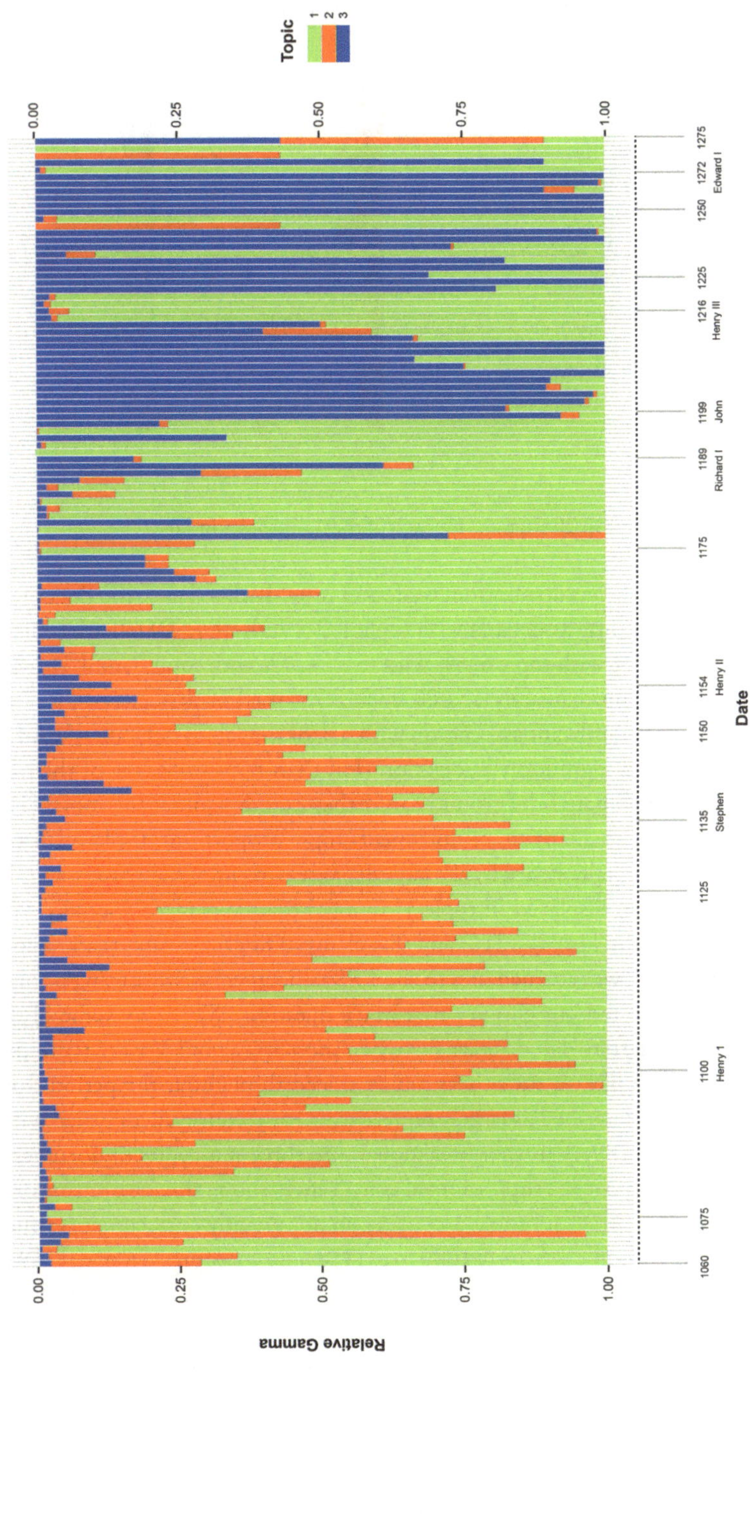

Fig. 27: Subtopic-1 (green): predominantly documents issued before c. 1200; subtopic-2 (orange) from c. 1080 to c. 1158; and subtopic-3 (blue) from c. 1189 to c. 1272.

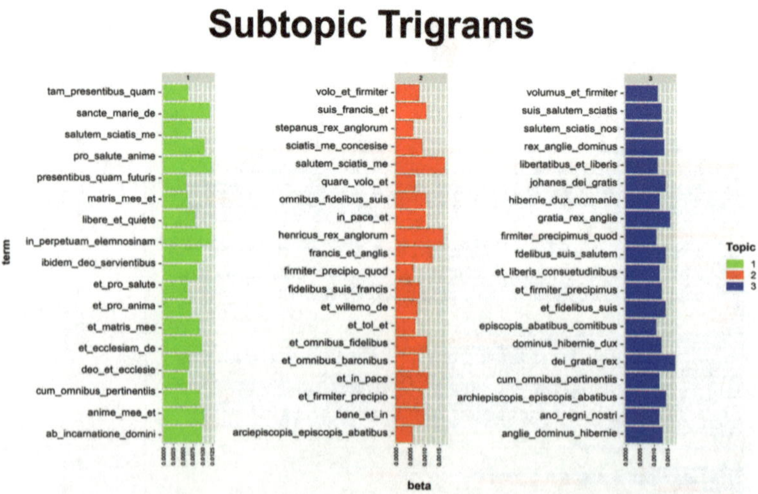

Fig. 28: Top 20 trigrams for each of the 3 subtopics in Fig. 27.

weight to be a significant attribution, we found roughly that 5% of the document collection is significantly associated with topic 1, 7% with topic 2, 8% with topic 3, 9% with topic 4, 11% with topic 5, 5% with topic 6, 7% with topic 7, and 5% with topic 8. From the approximately 17,000 documents used in this analysis, around half of them have a significant association with one of the topics only, and the other half do not have any significant association (less than 85%) with any of the topics. The foregoing prepared the ground for further examination of the topics [Fig. 16]. Looking again at the figure of document–topic proportions displayed as bar graphs, we were especially struck by the large expanse of topic 5 (light blue), and the very clear disruption displayed in topic 1 (orange) that coincided especially with the reign of King John (1199–1216) and that changed England's diplomatic record forever. To that end, we returned first to the 1,884 documents constituting primarily topic 5 and directed our enquiry to a single question: Why were some of the twelfth-century charters dated internally when most were not? We are reminded that topic-5, which like all the others can be traced throughout the period from 1060 to 1320, was described as largely representing royal conveyances issued without dates prior to 1189. A further breakdown into three sub-topics of documents which ranked highly for the topic of royal conveyances shows that by plotting only *Date* and *Religious Order*, subtopic-1 consists predominantly of documents issued prior to c. 1200; subtopic-2 from c. 1080 to c. 1158; and subtopic-3 from c. 1189 to c. 1272 [Fig. 27]. The twenty most common trigrams for each topic help to clarify their differences [Fig. 28].

Subtopic-1 is especially interesting because it provides a sizable number of internally dated documents from the early part of the time scale (11th and 12th centuries) where all the documents fall under the same topic. We discovered that some of the tri-grams that occurred in higher proportions in the internally dated documents than in the externally dated documents were of particular significance for our search [Fig. 29]. These included *et_ecclesiam_sancti*, *in_eadem_ecclesia*, and *super_altare_sancti*. When reviewed in context, these trigrams from internally dated documents turned out to represent grants made *of churches*, *in churches*, and consummated *on the altar* thereof.

amore dei et
anno ab incarnatione
anno domini incarnationis
anno incarnationis domini
de warena et
dedi et concessi
domini millesimo centesimo
ecclesiam sancti petri
ecclesie sancte trinitatis
et ecclesiam sancti
et rogero de
et sancto petro
henricus rex anglorum
huius rei testes
in eadem ecclesia
in eadem uilla
incarnat. dom. millesimo
ita tamen quod
omni seculari seruitio
patris et filii
pro remedio anime
pro salute animarum
que ad eam
rei testes sunt
super altare sancti

Fig. 29: Trigram words in Subtopic 1 (Figs. 27 and 28) that occur with statistical significance in higher proportions in the internally dated documents than in the externally dated ones.

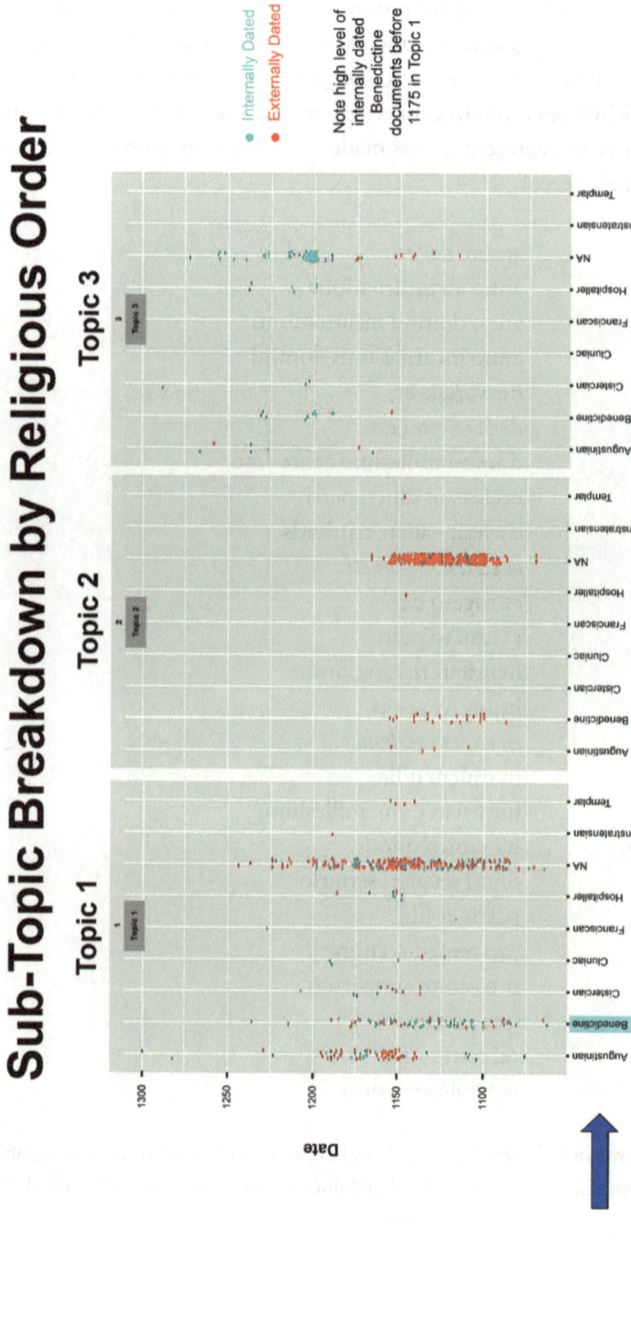

Fig. 30: Subtopics by religious order, showing the high level of internally dated Benedictine documents issued before 1175 in topic 1.

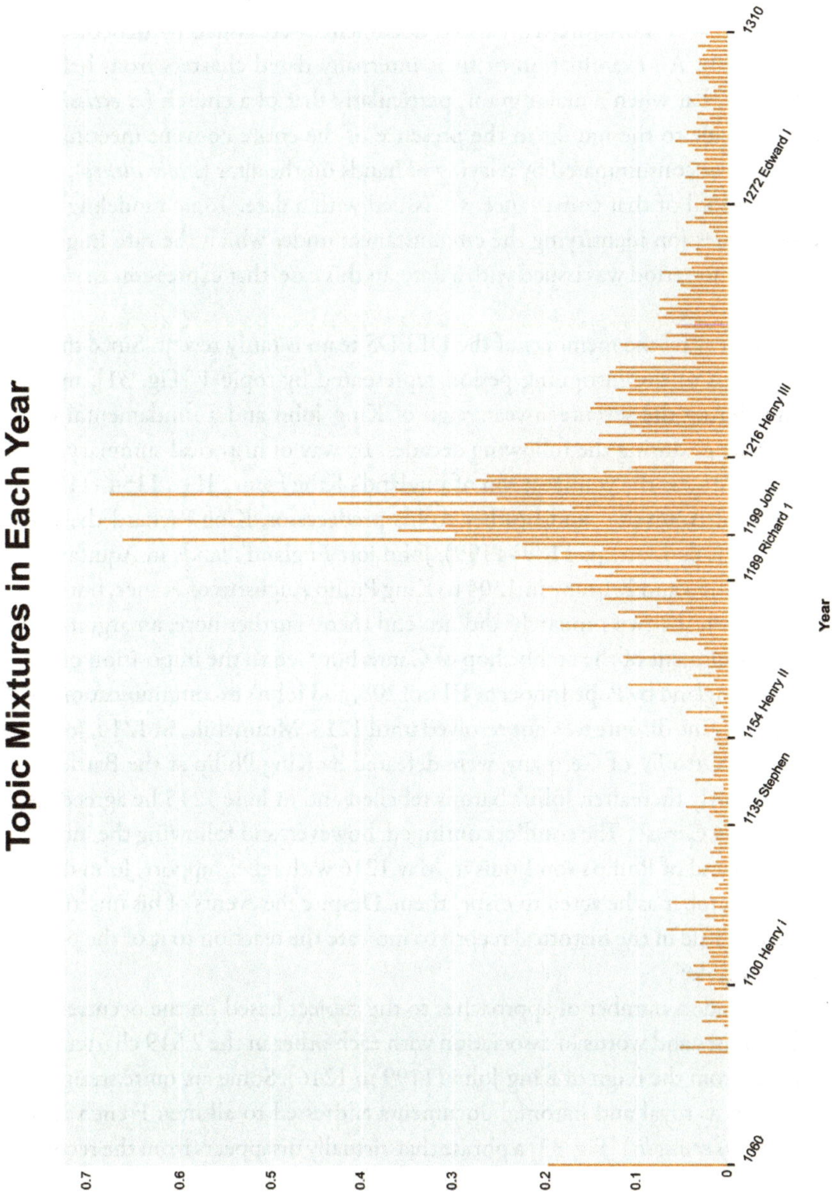

Fig. 31: Bar chart representing charters reflecting a high level of topic 1.

When the metadata heading of *Religious House* was called into play, it emerged that the majority of those internally dated documents were issued by Benedictine houses [Fig. 30]. An examination of their internally dated charters from before c. 1200 shows that when a major grant, particularly that of a church (*et ecclesiam sancti*), was made to the monks in the presence of the entire convent meeting in chapter, and was consummated by a laying of hands on the altar (*super altare*), the parchment record of that conveyance was issued with a date. Topic modeling led to the key expression identifying the circumstances under which the rare English document of the period was issued with a date; in this case, that expression is: *super altare*[49].

This discovery by the members of the DEEDS team is fairly recent. Since then, we have turned to the intriguing period represented by topic 1 [Fig. 31], most prominent during the seventeen-year reign of King John and a fundamental indicator of change during the following decades. By way of historical summary for the period, John was the youngest son of England's King Henry II (r. 1154–1189) and Eleanor of Aquitaine, and brother to his predecessor, King Richard the Lionheart (Coeur de Lion) (r. 1189–1199). John lost England's lands in Aquitaine, Normandy, Anjou and Brittany in 1204 to King Philip Augustus of France, but the conflict between the two monarchs did not end there. Furthermore, an argument over the appointment of the archbishop of Canterbury led to the imposition of an Interdict on England by Pope Innocent III in 1208, and John's excommunication in 1209 [Fig. 32]. The dispute was not resolved until 1213. Meanwhile, in 1214, John, together with Otto IV of Germany, were defeated by King Philip at the Battle of Bouvines. Shortly thereafter, John's barons rebelled and in June 1215 he agreed to sign the *Magna Carta*[50]. The conflict continued, however, and following the incursion into England of Philip's son Louis in May 1216 with rebel support, John died of illness in October as he acted to dispel them. Despite the events of his unsettled reign, there is little in the historical record to indicate the reaction to it of the population as a whole[51].

We have made a number of approaches to the subject based on the occurrence of words, phrases and words in association with each other in the 2,519 charters in the database from the reign of King John (1199 to 1216). Some are quite straightforward, such as royal and baronial documents addressed to all men French and English (*francis et anglis*) [Fig. 33] a phrase that virtually disappears from the record

49 Michael Gervers/Gelila Tilahun, Topic Modeling and the Resolution of a Medieval English Diplomatic Enigma, in: Archives and Archival Research in the Digital Environment, ed. Žarko Vujošević/Nebojša Porčić, Belgrade 2022, p. 149–168.

50 Danny Danziger/John Gillingham, 1215. The Year of Magna Carta, London 2003.

51 Christopher R. Cheney, King John and the Papal Interdict, in: Bulletin of the John Rylands Library 31 (1948) p. 295–317.

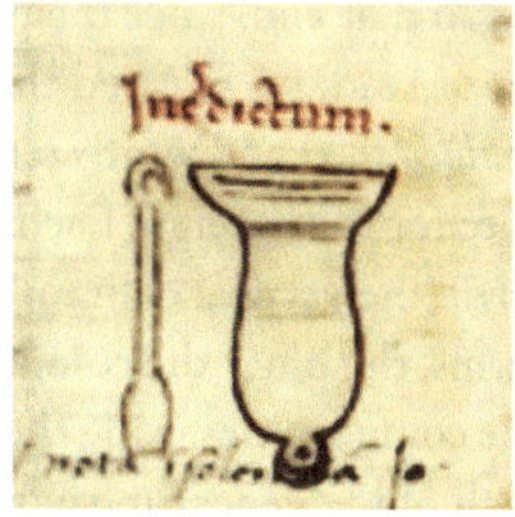

Fig. 32: Marginal drawing of a bell and clapper referring to the papal interdict (Royal MS 14 C VII, fol. 90r), England, S. (St Albans), 1250–1259.

immediately following England's loss of its French possessions in 1204[52]. Others are more subtle and here we are assisted by plots on a graph. During the Interdict and John's excommunication, grants in alms to religious houses rise markedly [Fig. 34]. Was that because people felt that by making grants to the Church when they were deprived of ecclesiastical services, they would stand a better chance of avoiding the everlasting terrors of Hell? One can take any number of words and find dramatic annual changes in their occurrence during John's reign, particularly from the period leading up to the Interdict of 1208 and his death in 1216. It is the visualization of these individual changes that encouraged us to penetrate more deeply into the vocabulary and diplomatic of the corpus as a whole.

52 Michael GERVERS/Nicole HAMONIC, *Pro Amore Dei:* Diplomatic Evidence of Social Conflict During the Reign of King John, in: Law as Profession and Practice in Medieval Europe. Essays in Honor of James A. Brundage, ed. Kenneth PENNINGTON/Melodie Harris EICHBAUER, Farnham, 2011, p. 231–259 (here p. 242–243).

To that end, since the primary purpose of the charters is to document the transfer of land, we selected the correlation between the word *terre* (*of* or *pertaining to arable land*) and words referring to administrative and ecclesiastical terms for each date for John's reign. Each small square in Fig. 35 measures the correlation between *terre* (the vertical column) and each of these other terms. The more correlated the terms, the bluer the colour of the squares. Using Network Analysis[53], we identified the communities using the Spineglass community detection algorithm[54] formed by each of the generating words. We then measured the similarities (distances) by using the Jaccard similarity measure[55] between each of the communities induced by the generating words within and across all the dates to produce this chart. Sketchy as it may seem, this visualization shows that there is a general similarity among the words surrounding *terre* from the beginning of John's reign until 1206, when there is a clear interruption. One may propose that this interruption reflects the reaction to the land market once people fully realized, over the next 18 months, the consequences of John's definitive loss of Normandy in June 1204. The situation falls off markedly with the inception of the Interdict and John's excommunication, becoming especially murky between 1214 and 1218. Thereafter, equilibrium is slowly re-established. We remember that John died in October 1216 when England was being invaded by Prince Louis of France. Louis was eventually defeated in August 1217 by English supporters of John's son, the then nine-year-old King Henry III (r. 1216–1272). The charters show that with peace restored, land-holders began to regain the confidence they appear to have lost in or about 1206, when John's forfeiture of his territories in France was still of recent memory.

The foregoing has demonstrated the extent to which words and word patterns in medieval diplomatic sources can, like the rings of an onion, be peeled off to reveal extensive evidence of change over time that is not rendered explicit in the sources themselves. The opportunities behind such approaches are endless, but we need to take advantage of the digital potential that is continuously being laid at our doorsteps to resolve the ever-increasing problems of our day and to facilitate and improve the gathering of data. Nothing happens on this planet that cannot be transmitted across the globe instantly. The transfer and linking of data is commonplace, as a consequence of which the stand-alone database is quickly becoming a thing of the past; and it should be because its reach is limited to its content, beyond which is a dark chasm, *une frontière impassable*, *eine wahre Grenze*. Current research is

53 David EASLEY/Jon KLEINBERG, Networks, crowds, and markets: Reasoning about a highly connected world, Cambridge 2010.

54 Gábor CSÁRDI/Tamás NEPUSZ/Vincent TRAAG/Szabolcs HORVÁT/ Fabio ZANINI/ Daniel NOOM/Kirill MÜLLER, igraph: Network Analysis and Visualization in R. (2023) doi:10.5281/zenodo.7682609, R package version 1.5.1, https://CRAN.R-project.org/package=igraph.

55 Paul JACCARD, The distribution of the flora in the alpine zone 1, in: New phytologist 11/2 (1912) p. 37–50. The Jaccard distance is found by simply subtracting the similarity value from 1.

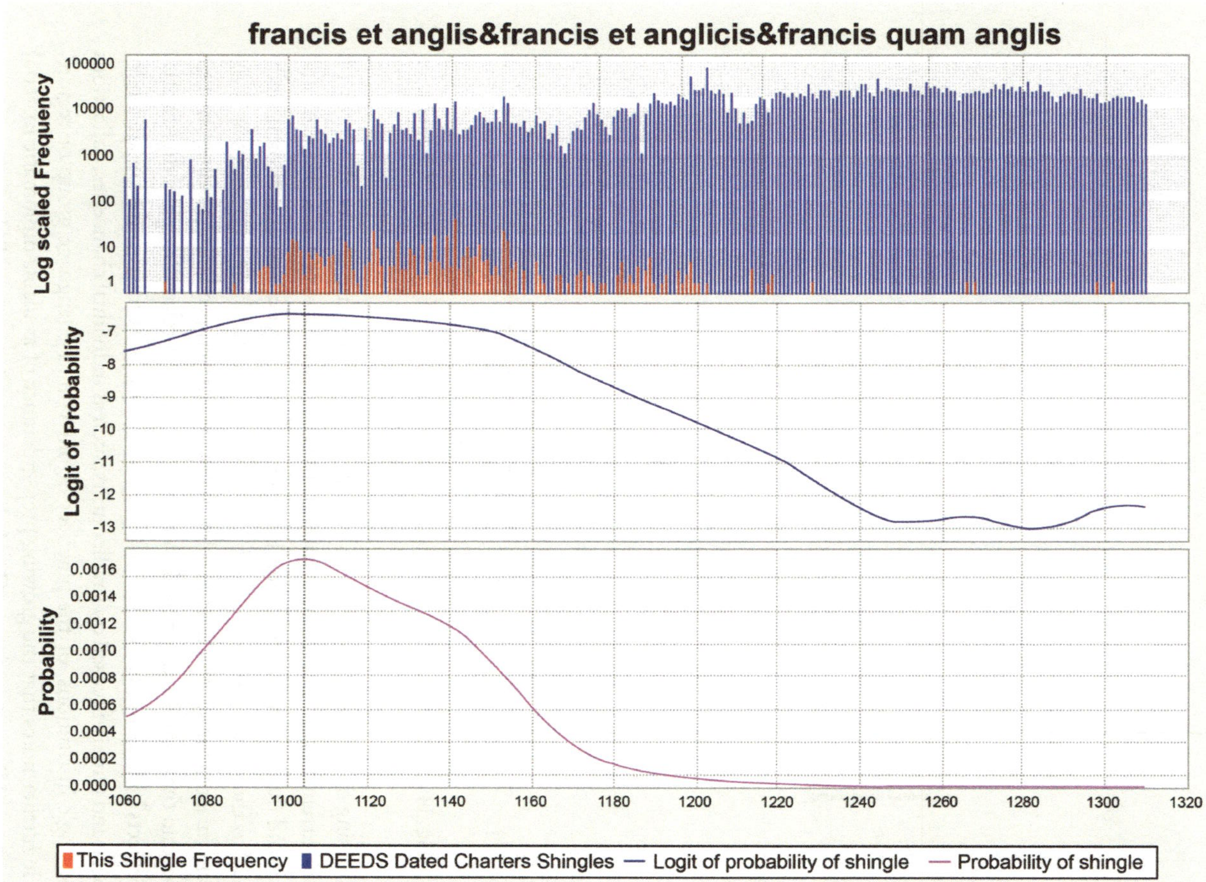

Fig. 33: Occurrence of charters addressed to *French and English* in the DEEDS database. Note the sudden drop in usage of the phrase after 1204.

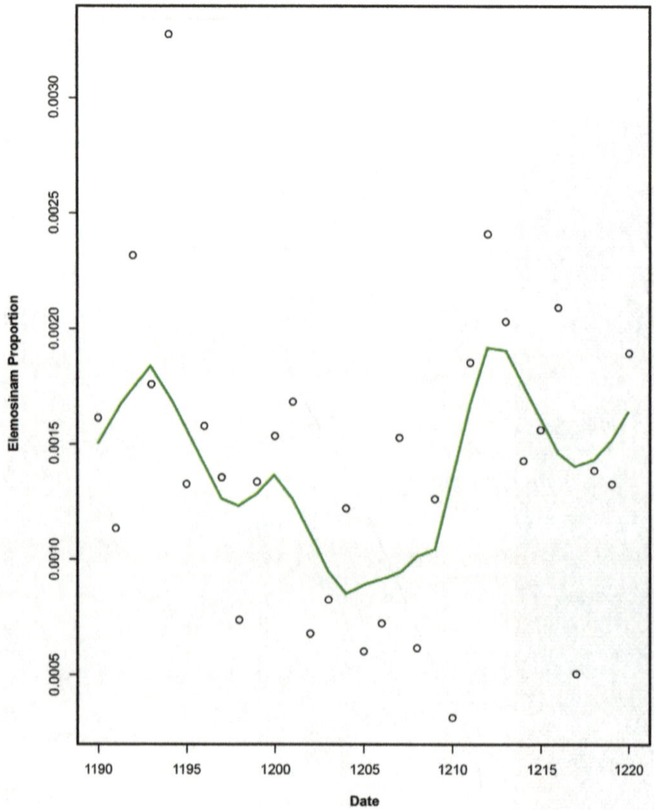

Fig. 34: Occurrence of the term *elemosinam* in charters from the reign of King John (1199–1216).

focusing on the means to cross that border. Georg Vogeler is leading the way with his current Digital Diplomatics project, DiDip, designed to organize, improve and expand the Monasterium corpus, not only bringing "modern computational methods to the transregional study of late medieval charters", but also applying "'distant' macroanalysis practices to a Europe-wide dataset, producing findings that go beyond the traditional regional and single-institution related scope of diplomatics projects". He reminds us that "the preponderance of studies in diplomatics have been and remain focused on smaller units, such as individual chanceries, collections of single institutions, or the practices of one country, language group or region". He further notes that the growing preponderance of available diplomatic material as the middle ages progresses "has led to a resignation among diplomatics scholars in the face of the large amount of documentation in the 14th and 15th century"[56].

56 Quotations are from the abstract of Georg Vogeler's Research Proposal [Part B] for an ERC Advanced Grant 2020 under the title "From *Digital* to *Distant* Diplomatics. DiDip".

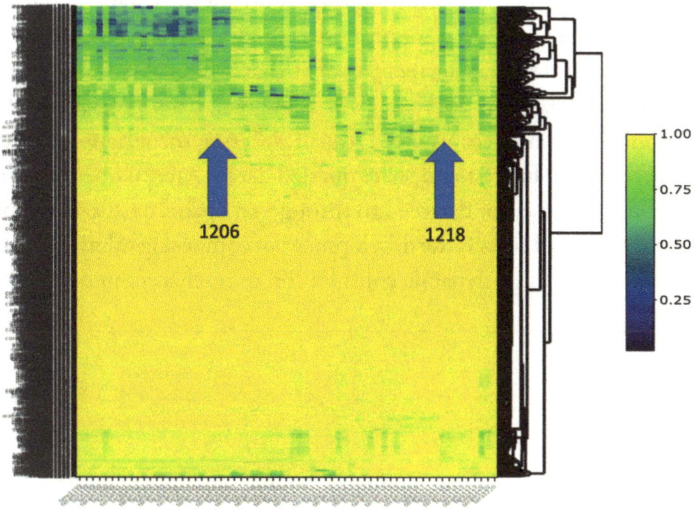

Fig. 35: Network analysis chart showing the result of measuring the distances between the communities of generating words related to "TERRE" in the charters within and across all dates from 1199 to 1220. A clear pattern break is visible between 1206 and 1207, which does not begin to 'normalize' again until 1218.

And the quantity does not stop there, as archivists across Europe have under their aegis, and attempt to make available on-line with whatever information they can, diplomatic documents reaching well into the Early Modern period and beyond.

The means are available to put the growing corpus of digital information at the disposal of the distant user. How to do so in an efficient and effective manner can be summed up in a single bigram: *collaborative cooperation*. For the most part, and with few exceptions, we have been approaching the question of digitization and database building on a one-to-one basis, with the result that we are all spending enormous amounts of money doing virtually the same thing, often using off-the-shelf components and functions. We contracted with the Information Technology Service of the University of Toronto to build the DEEDS database more than a decade ago for CAN $50,000.00. They never finished the job, claiming the funds were not enough. All of us are working with charters, conveyances, acts, legal records of one kind or another, in multiple languages, although for the medieval period mostly in Latin. We have only one sensible option which, from now on is, like building the International Space Station, to collaborate and to cooperate.

An objective of current research is to develop the means to link databases, to integrate the modules so that the questions raised can be analyzed first in a pan-European fashion, and ultimately to encompass the Mediterranean world and beyond. The challenge will be first to standardize our data and then to link it. The question is, how best to ensure continuing access to the growing number of documents available while at the same time allowing each contributing database to retain its individuality and purpose. What we propose is to join participating digital collections into a federated data management system that will enable the searching of connected repositories. This approach will allow data from geographically dispersed collections to remain decentralized, thus respecting the autonomy of the sources. The objective is to harvest and share queried data via access operations that are advantageous to all users and agreed to through an open, consultative process. What we must avoid at all costs is the development of competing solutions when far more is to be gained through dynamic consultation to reach a common objective.

Delegated Jurisdiction in the Iberian Peninsula of the 12th Century

Considerations on a Computational Approach to Personal Networks and Formulaic Language

Marlene Ernst, Alina Ostrowski, Malte Rehbein

The 'long' 12th century is a pioneering period of juridification and unification of legal culture in Latin Church history[1]. Delegated jurisdiction, whereby the investigation of disputes brought before the pope was entrusted to local officials who were endowed with papal authority for this purpose, played an important part in enforcing papal jurisdictional primacy[2]. The proceedings to be conducted by the delegates according to Roman canonical procedural law contributed significantly to the spread of uniform legal norms in Latin Europe. They linked ecclesiastical prelates with the papal curia and promoted the "communicative networking of the centre with the periphery", as MÜLLER describes it[3]. The Iberian Peninsula, with the empires of Navarre, Aragón, Castile, León, and Portugal as well as their close mutual relations and cultural links with the southern French region represents a particularly interesting field of research in this respect and is the centre of attention for the investigations within the DFG funded project "Delegierte Gerichtsbarkeit auf der Iberischen Halbinsel im 12. Jahrhundert. Struktur und computergestützte

1 Cf. Peter LANDAU, Der Einfluß des kanonischen Rechts auf die europäische Rechtskultur, in: Europäische Rechts- und Verfassungsgeschichte. Ergebnisse und Perspektiven der Forschung, ed. Reiner SCHULZE, Berlin 1991, p. 39–57; Orazio CONDORELLI/Franck ROUMY/Mathias SCHMOECKEL, ed., Der Einfluss der Kanonistik auf die europäische Rechtskultur 3, Köln et al. 2009.

2 Cf. Harald MÜLLER, The Omnipresent Pope. Legates and Judges Delegate, in: A Companion to the Medieval Papacy. Growth of an Ideology and Institution, ed. Atria LARSON/Keith SISSON, Leiden 2016, p. 197–219, DOI: 10.1163/9789004315280_011.

3 Translated from: Harald MÜLLER, Entscheidung auf Nachfrage. Die delegierten Richter als Verbindungsglieder zwischen Kurie und Region sowie als Gradmesser päpstlicher Autorität, in: Römisches Zentrum und kirchliche Peripherie. Das universale Papsttum als Bezugspunkt der Kirchen von den Reformpäpsten bis zu Innozenz III., ed. Jochen JOHRENDT/Harald MÜLLER, Berlin/New York 2008, p. 109–134, DOI: 10.1515/9783110210569.1.109, here p. 109.

Analyse eines urkundlichen Massenkorpus"[4]. Similar research has been conducted for Normandy[5], Canterbury[6], and Reims[7], thus offering a good overview on delegated jurisdiction for the northern French and Anglo-Norman area on both sides of the English Channel. In this project, however, digital approaches shall be applied in order to factor in a broad source base and gain new insights.

On the level of actors (persons as well as institutions) and their interconnections, methods of historical network research are applied for analysis[8]. Considering papal letters of justice, in which close connections to delegated court proceedings can often be seen, a special interest also lies in formulaic language. In order to grasp the dissemination of legal formulas and clauses, automated text analyses, especially in the form of text reuse detection, shall be used. The following pages offer theoretical concepts and first practical insights into a digital processing of documents related to 12th century delegated jurisdiction on the Iberian Peninsula.

Corpus Composition

For a wide-ranging examination of delegated judicial practice, a great number of documented (papal) charters is needed, especially when applying digital methodologies. For the core of the Iberia Pontificia corpus (IbePon corpus) we will draw upon approximately 1000 full-text editions, which are already available for further digital

4 The project is a collaboration between the Chair of Computational Humanities at the University of Passau and the Göttingen Academy of Sciences and Humanities (DFG project no. 495959196).

5 Harald Müller, Päpstliche Delegationsgerichtsbarkeit in der Normandie (12. und frühes 13. Jahrhundert): Teil 1: Untersuchung, Bonn 1997.

6 Jane E. Sayers, Papal Judges Delegate in the Province of Canterbury, 1198–1254. A Study in Ecclesiastical Jurisdiction and Administration, Oxford 1971.

7 John S. Ott, Men on the Move: Papal Judges-Delegate in the Province of Reims in the Early Twelfth Century, in: The Use of Canon Law in Ecclesiastical Administration, 1000–1234, ed. Melodie H. Eichbauer/Danica Summerlin, Leiden/Boston 2019, p. 23–50, DOI: 10.1163/9789004387249_003.

8 Recent years and studies have shown their applicability for medieval history, although none have used it for research on delegated jurisdiction so far. Cf. e.g. Eva Jullien, Netzwerkanalyse in der Mediävistik. Probleme und Perspektiven im Umgang mit mittelalterlichen Quellen, in: VSWG: Vierteljahrschrift für Sozial- und Wirtschaftsgeschichte 100/2 (2013) p. 135–153; Robert Gramsch, Zerstörte oder verblasste Muster? Anwendungsfelder mediävistischer Netzwerkforschung und das Quellenproblem, in: Handbuch Historische Netzwerkforschung, ed. Marten Düring/Ulrich Eumann, Berlin 2016, p. 85–99; Robert Gramsch-Stehfest, Von der Metapher zur Methode. Netzwerkanalyse als Instrument zur Erforschung vormoderner Gesellschaften, in: ZHF 47/1 (2020) p. 1–40, DOI: 10.3790/zhf.47.1.1.

Fig. 1: Places of issue of the registers in Iberia Pontificia I–V: total (1001 registers) in grey and filtered by entries marked as cases concerning delegated jurisdiction (258 registers) in red. Graphic created with Palladio.

processing, containing charters of Catalonia[9], Navarra and Aragón[10], Castile[11] as well as Portugal[12] and from the Vatican registers[13]. The older editions have been retro-digitised and are being prepared for further digital "upcycling"[14] in the form of transferring them into our data model. Another 200 charters are currently being edited by the partners of the Göttingen Academy of Sciences and Humanities. Additionally, eight volumes from the series 'Iberia Pontificia' covering registers for the bishoprics of Astorga, Ávila, Burgos, Calahorra, Ciudad Rodrigo, Coria, Huesca, León, Oviedo, Palencia, Pamplona, Plasencia, Salamanca, Segovia, Sigüenza, and Zamora[15] offer valuable information. These volumes cover not only all known doc-

9 Papsturkunden in Spanien. Vorarbeiten zur Hispania Pontificia I. Katalanien, ed. Paul Fridolin Kehr, Berlin 1926.

10 Papsturkunden in Spanien. Vorarbeiten zur Hispania Pontificia II. Navarra und Aragon, ed. Paul Fridolin Kehr, Berlin 1928.

11 Papsturkunden in Spanien: Vorarbeiten zur Hispania (Iberia) Pontificia. III. Kastilien, ed. Daniel Berger/Klaus Herbers/Thorsten Schlauwitz, Berlin/Boston 2020.

12 Papsturkunden in Portugal, ed. Carl Erdmann, Berlin 1927.

13 La Documentación Pontificia hasta Inocencio III. (965–1216), ed. Demetrio Mansilla (Monumenta Hispaniae Vaticana: Registros 1), Rome 1955.

14 Cf. Simon Donig/Malte Rehbein, Für eine „gemeinsame digitale Zukunft". Eine kritische Verortung der Digital History, in: Geschichte in Wissenschaft und Unterricht 9/10 (2022) p. 527–545.

15 Iberia Pontificia Vol. I. Dioeceses exemptae. Dioecesis Burgensis, ed. Daniel Berger, Göttingen

uments and acts of the popes and their legates up to the year 1198, but also deeds of judges delegate. Data provided by Daniel BERGER from volumes I–V[16] give us some indication of their geographical distribution and for which regions significant contributions for the posed topic of delegated jurisdiction can be expected (see Fig. 1).

In addition, for the end of the 12th century, reference can also be made to the more recent volumes of the 'Regesta Imperii', which record the papal charters of the years 1181–1195 for the whole of Europe[17]. Overall, the editing and recording of the Iberian papal charters has progressed to such an extent that the practice of delegated jurisdiction for this large region can be examined in the context of the general orientation towards the papacy and over the entire 12th century. The comprehensive source basis enables an overarching and comparative perspective. For this purpose, the main interests for the digital humanities components lie in two areas: actors in the form of historic network analysis as well as formulaic language and text reuse detection.

2012; Santiago, Iberia Pontificia Vol. II. Dioeceses Exemptae. Dioecesis Legionensis, ed. DOMÍNGUEZ SÁNCHEZ, Göttingen 2013; Iberia Pontificia Vol. III. Provincia Toletana. Dioecesis Palentina, ed. Daniel BERGER, Göttingen ²2021; Iberia Pontificia Vol. IV. Provincia Compostellana. Dioeceses Abulensis, Salmanticensis, Cauriensis, Civitatensis, Placentina, ed. Frank ENGEL/José Luis MARTÍN MARTÍN, Göttingen 2016;. Iberia Pontificia Vol. V. Dioeceses Ovetensis et Asturicensis, ed. Santiago DOMÍNGUEZ SÁNCHEZ/Daniel BERGER, Göttingen 2019; Iberia Pontificia Vol. VI. Dioeceses Pampilonensis, Calagurritana et Tirasonensis, ed. Frank ENGEL/Thomas CZERNER/Daniel BERGER, Göttingen 2022; Iberia Pontificia Vol. VIII. Dioeceses Secobiensis et Seguntina, ed. Daniel BERGER, Göttingen 2024; Dioecesis Zamorensis, ed. Santiago DOMÍNGUEZ SÁNCHEZ/José Luis MARTÍN MARTÍN/Frank ENGEL, Göttingen 2024.

16 An Access database with flags on delegated jurisdiction and several other additional information for (parts) of the volumes is the basis for this partial analysis.

17 Johann Friedrich BÖHMER/Katrin BAAKEN/Ulrich SCHMIDT, Regesta Imperii IV. Lothar III. und ältere Staufer 1125–1197. 4. Abt.: Papstregesten 1124–1198, Tl. 4, Lfg. 1: 1181–1184, Bd. 4, Köln/Weimar/Wien 2003; Johann Friedrich BÖHMER/Katrin BAAKEN/Ulrich SCHMIDT, Regesta Imperii IV. Lothar III. und ältere Staufer 1125–1197. 4. Abt.: Papstregesten 1124-1198, Tl. 4, Lfg. 2: 1184–1185, Bd. 4, Köln/Weimar/Wien 2006; Johann Friedrich BÖHMER/Ulrich SCHMIDT, Regesta Imperii IV. Lothar III. und ältere Staufer 1125–1197. 4. Abt.: Papstregesten 1124–1198, Tl. 4, Lfg. 3: 1185–1187: Urban III. und Gregor VIII., Bd. 4, Köln/Weimar/Wien 2012; Johann Friedrich BÖHMER/Ulrich SCHMIDT, Regesta Imperii IV. Lothar III. und ältere Staufer 1125–1197. 4. Abt.: Papstregesten 1124–1198, Tl. 4, Lfg. 4: 1187-1191: Clemens III., Bd. 4, Köln Köln/Weimar/Wien 2014; Johann Friedrich BÖHMER/Ulrich SCHMIDT, Regesta Imperii IV. Lothar III. und ältere Staufer 1125–1197. 4. Abt.: Papstregesten 1124–1198, Tl. 4, Lfg. 5: 1191–1195: Cölestin III., Bd. 4, Köln Köln/Weimar/Wien 2018.

Network Analysis

In analysing the content, we put special emphasis on the actors (bishops, abbots, and in the late 12th century also dignitaries of the cathedral chapters), their relations with each other and with the papacy. In order to determine the role of the actors in the spread of delegated jurisdiction on a personal as well as institutional level, the litigants and judges involved in the proceedings are systematically recorded and considered in the context of their other curial activities (e.g., acquisition of privileges). Through historical network analysis we aim at identifying spatio-temporal clusters of actors, places, institutions, and their relations with each other. Research questions to be answered are whether certain individuals or groups have a pioneering role and whether common characteristics (like origin, religious affiliation, career path, legal knowledge) are at the forefront and thereby represent a certain clerical group or milieu regarding delegated jurisdiction.

The interweaving of persons and places across documents in time can be modelled as a multimodal network or multipartite graph, a form of representation that has so far been little used by historical researchers due to its relative complexity[18]. This makes it possible to show the interrelationships of the persons involved in the procedures, whereby conspicuous clusters can be identified within the complex relationship structure of the Iberian episcopate, whose function and significance are to be determined in the historical context.

Since the transfer of all the diverse data sets into a uniform format and, more importantly, data model has yet to be completed, (partial) evaluations of the entire corpus are not yet feasible. However, first attempts and preliminary studies using the partial corpus of Iberia Pontificia I–V serve as feasibility studies and provide first insights into some aspects. In Fig. 2 which visualises a subset[19] of registers with reference to delegated jurisdiction, for example, we can see a focus on certain offices. Especially the Bishops of Burgos, an office which is connected to eight pontificates through over fifty mentions in the 12th century, play a significant role. But also, other bishops (e.g., Palencia, Sigüenza, Osma, and Segovia) as well as the Archbishop of Toledo are important in the context of judicial letters and mandates.

---

18 Cf. recent overview Alexander RAUSCH, Bimodale Netzwerke, in: Handbuch Netzwerkforschung, ed. Christian STEGBAUER/Roger HÄUSSLING, Wiesbaden 2010, p. 421–432, DOI: 10.1007/978-3-531-92575-2_37; on dimensional reduction recently Roberto INTERDONATO et al., Multilayer Network Simplification: Approaches, Models and Methods, in: Computer Science Review 36 (2020), 100246, DOI: 10.1016/j.cosrev.2020.100246; on visualisations Katy BÖRNER et al., Network Visualization in the Humanities (Dagstuhl Seminar 18482), in: Dagstuhl Reports 8/11 (2019) p. 139–153, DOI: 10.4230/DagRep.8.11.139.

19 Information on additional persons (and their offices) mentioned in the registers is offered for 65 of the 258 entries concerning delegated jurisdiction.

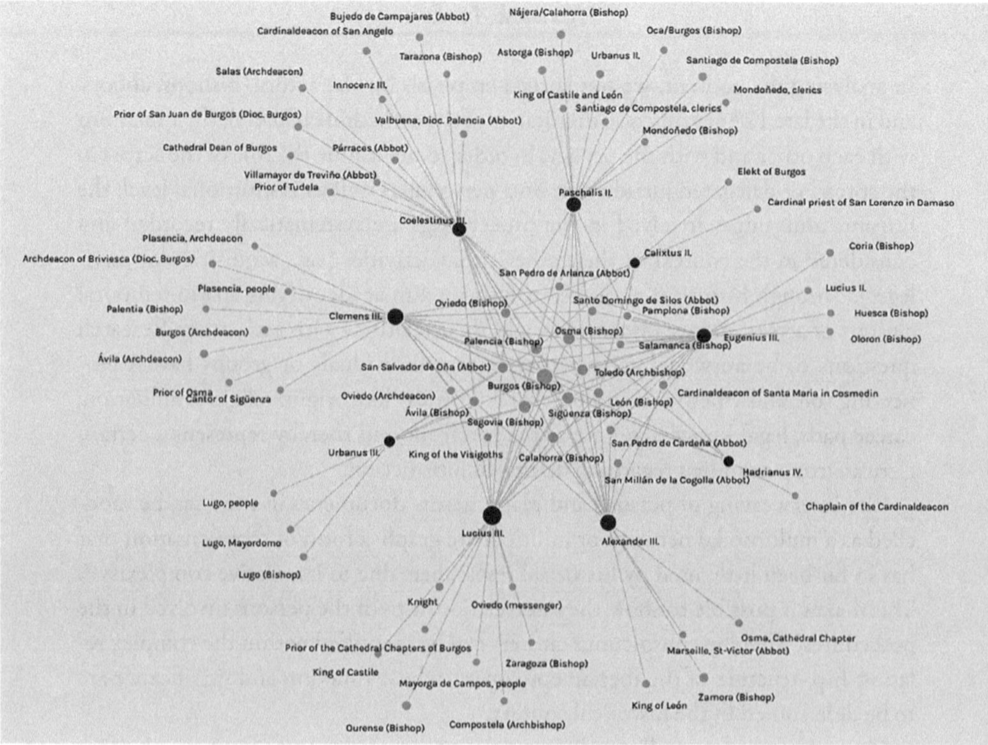

Fig. 2: Pontificates and connections to offices of further mentioned persons from a subset of the registers from Iberia Pontificia I–V. Graphic created with Palladio.

Another promising variation of the network analysis aspect is offered by not only focusing on the personal networks but exploring a connection between personal networks with content-related or linguistic features and recurring, formulaic language elements. This stage is still highly theoretical at the moment, but we created a first trial through linking issuers with three significant keywords. In many cases *mandare*, *praecipere* as well as *quatinus*, often in the form of the fixed sequence *mandamus et praecipimus, quatinus*, serve as introduction for the dispositive part of a charter. Our interest lies, e.g., in whether one or the other verb (or their combination) is more prominently used in cases where delegated jurisdiction is concerned and also which issuing context (i.e., issuers) they have. For such charters we can see (Fig. 3) a predominancy of the usage of *mandare* compared to *praecipere*. In most instances where *praecipere* or the adverb *quatinus* are used, the charters are issued by the popes themselves, as opposed to judges delegate or legates, and combined with forms of *mandare*.

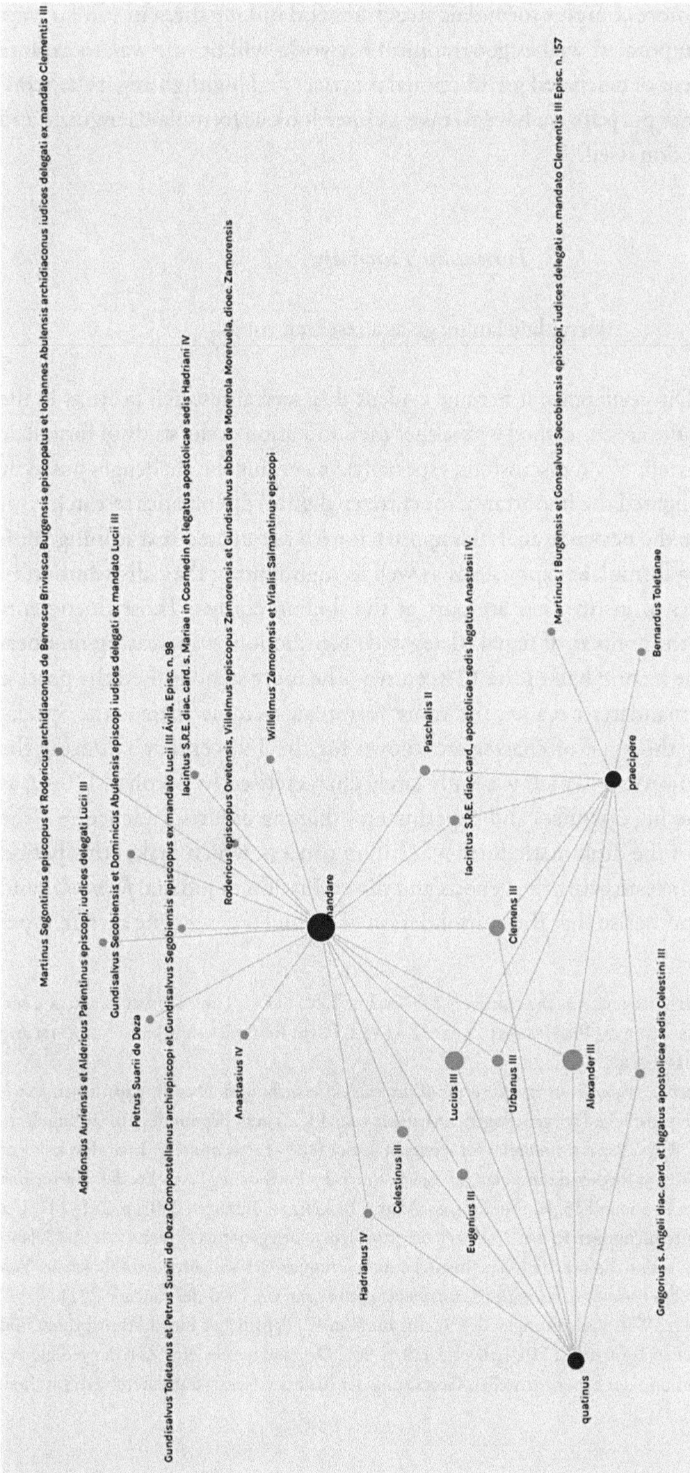

Fig. 3: Relation between keywords and issuers of registers concerning delegated jurisdiction from Iberia Pontificia I–V. Graphic created with Palladio.

Identifying more complex formulaic structures and linking them in similar ways to personal, temporal as well as geographical networks will be one way to explore the establishment of delegated jurisdictional practices and highlighting its key contributors. To that purpose we have to take a closer look at formulaic language and text reuse detection itself.

Formulaic Language

Formulaic language as a research topic

During the DiDip conference it became evident that several research projects in the field of diplomatics are concerned with either the annotation or the study of formulaic language in charters. Vivid discussions, especially concerning the challenges posed by this topic, highlighted the importance for current (digital) diplomatics research[20].

We combine the network analytics approach with automated text mining, aiming at detecting formulaic expressions as well as highlighting their distribution in the papal letters of justice that are part of the IbePon corpus. Those documents were issued in the context of papal (delegated) jurisdiction in increasing numbers mainly since the second half of the 12th century. The more standardised the process of issuing the mandates became, the more formulaic became their texts. Special formularies for this type of charter are known for the 13th century[21]. During the 12th century however – which was only lately characterised by Stephan Dusil as "a time of redacting openness and experimental shaping of jurisprudence"[22] – the consolidation of the diplomatic form was still in process, which makes this period well suited for investigating the genesis and dissemination of judicial *formulae* and clauses. We hypothesise that the consolidation of formulas describing certain types

20 Cf. the research presented at the conference by Eveline Leclercq, Timo Korkiakangas, Miguel Calleja-Puerta, Pia Geissel, Adam Zapała, Filipa Roldão with Joana Serafim and João Paulo Silvestre.

21 Cf. Peter Herde, *Audientia litterarum contradictarum*. Untersuchungen über die päpstlichen Justizbriefe und die päpstliche Delegationsgerichtsbarkeit vom 13. bis zum Beginn des 16. Jahrhunderts, Tübingen 1970; Id., Papal formularies for letters of justice (13th–16th centuries): Their development and significance for medieval canon law, in: Stagnation oder Fortbildung? Aspekte des allgemeinen Kirchenrechts im 14. und 15. Jahrhundert, ed. Martin Bertram, Tübingen 2005, p. 221–247; Ute Pfeiffer, Untersuchungen zu den Anfängen der päpstlichen Delegationsgerichtsbarkeit im 13. Jahrhundert. Edition und diplomatisch-kanonistische Auswertung zweier Vorläufersammlungen der Vulgataredaktion des *Formularium audientie litterarum contradictarum*, Città del Vaticano 2011.

22 Stephan Dusil, Wissensordnungen des Rechts im Wandel. Päpstlicher Jurisdiktionsprimat und Zölibat zwischen 1000 und 1215, Leuven 2018, p. 507. Original quote: 'eine Zeit der redigierenden Offenheit und der experimentellen Gestaltung des Rechtswissens' (translated by the authors of this paper).

of jurisdictional cases both indicates as well as accompanies a consolidation of the corresponding treatment of those cases. This is why the investigation of the development of formulaic language can give us new insights into the historical development of papal legislative culture. Usually, analyses of historical formulaic language are conducted in time- and resource-consuming research projects, meticulously close reading and comparing large quantities of text[23]. We are therefore assessing natural language processing (NLP) tools and whether they are suited to pre-process a charter corpus in a less time-consuming and more intersubjective way to answer questions posed by the historical sciences regarding the content of the source. Two different approaches to detect and analyse formulaic language in the IbePon corpus are being used. First, it comprehends the retrieval and tracing of known formulas. As already mentioned, contemporary papal formularies exist for the 13th century onwards[24]. Since the 12th century presents a gap of such sources, it is promising to trace back the formulas contained in these formularies to their first appearance. Their early stages, which may have slight variations to the later fully standardised formula, can furthermore point to the historical circumstances under which they were introduced into papal jurisdictional language.

Second, we search for yet unknown formulas. We presume different reasons for those formulas being unknown so far: They might not have been recognised by researchers due to the lack of an adequate quantity of source material, or due to the relative flexibility of a just newly developing formula. Maybe some formulas were also used exclusively in the 12th century and can therefore not be seen in later charters. Text reuse detection is employed to find recurring expressions that are used in a conventionalised form in the IbePon corpus and that convey a fixed meaning or concept. The last condition may, of course, vary according to their stage of conventionalisation.

Defining formulaic language

A major challenge in applying NLP methods is how to accurately define formulaic language and retrieve textual expressions corresponding to this definition. Even though the term *formulae* or 'formulaic' is widespread amongst publications on medieval diplomatics and a common understanding about the term seems to be presumed[25], a shared definition does not exist. Looking closely at what diplomatists

23 Cf. Natalia FILATKINA, Historische formelhafte Sprache. Theoretische Grundlagen und methodische Herausforderungen (Formelhafte Sprache – Formulaic Language 1), Berlin/Boston 2018.

24 Up until the 11th century the so-called *Liber Diurnus* was used as formulary, but it seems to haven't been as influential as later formularies: Hans-Henning KORTÜM, 'Liber Diurnus', in: LexMA 5 (1991), cols. 1942–1943.

25 Most introductory works use the word formula ('Formel' in German) without previous explanation of the word's exact meaning in this context, e.g.: Thomas VOGTHERR, Einführung in die Urkundenlehre, Stuttgart ²2017, p. 77–78; Christian ROHR, Historische Hilfswissenschaften.

(or historians in general) write about, when they use the word 'formulaic', the term gets fuzzy and covers a set of related but not necessarily identical phenomena[26].

The term *forma* was contemporarily used to denote the wording of a charter text, that was meant to serve as a boilerplate for constructing the legally binding charter by inserting specific names, locations, and dates (cf. Lexikon des Mittelalters)[27]. Those *formulae* were often recorded in formularies. In this definition, the whole charter text itself is formulaic. In scholarly discourse however, the terms 'formula' and 'formulaic' are often used to denote only specific parts of a charter. Often, it is the standardised formal structure of charters and its segments, e.g., the *intitulatio* or *sanctio*, that are considered formulaic. Accordingly on the textual level, phrases that indicate those segments are called formulas[28]. Those kinds of formulaic elements are still relatively easy to define and retrieve.

By contrast, formulaic elements that we are interested in are not those *formulae* found in most of the papal charters as part of the diplomatic segments. We are rather investigating elements that are specific to letters of justice and that can be used especially in the *narratio* and *dispositio* of a charter, depending on how the judges are ordered to treat the specific case. In other words, we are interested in a kind of formula that does not belong to the overall diplomatic structure itself, but to a semantic context of the charters, in our case to jurisdiction[29]. Sometimes, these formulas have been called 'sub-formulas'[30].

Examples for judicial formulas in papal charters are shown in table 1. Example no. 1 introduces a description of the circumstances of the case as brought before the pope; no. 2 is an instruction for the judge delegate to hear both parties (instead of favouring one party over the other); no. 3 is another instruction for the judge about how to handle the case; and no. 4 prohibits the litigants to appeal against the ver-

Eine Einführung, Wien/Köln/Weimar 2015, p. 37–123. Harry BRESSLAU didn't include a definition in his first chapter on 'Grundbegriffe und Definitionen' of his definitive work on charters (Handbuch der Urkundenlehre für Deutschland und Italien, 2 vols., ed. Hans-Walter KLEWITZ, Berlin 1958; c.1 in vol. 1, p. 1–11).

26 As Reinhard HÄRTEL (Notarielle und kirchliche Urkunden im frühen und hohen Mittelalter [Historische Hilfswissenschaften 4], Wien/München 2011, p. 274) puts it: 'Was die Wissenschaft Formeln nennt, ist letztlich eine Fülle von Abstraktionen, und aus diesen ergibt sich kein ganzheitliches System.' Similar: Heinrich FICHTENAU, Forschungen über Urkundenformeln, in: MIÖG 94 (1986) p. 285–339, here p. 286.

27 Peter HERDE, 'Formel, Formelsammlungen, Formelbücher. A. Lateinisches Mittelalter. I. Definition', in: LexMA 4, Lachen am Zürichsee 1999, p. 646–647.

28 This use of the word 'formula' can be seen in current as well as older introductive works: BRESSLAU, Urkundenlehre (as n. 25) p. 46–49; ROHR, Hilfswissenschaften (as n. 25) p. 43–51, 63–73.

29 Harry BRESSLAU used the word formula in this sense too, but without defining it explicitly. For example, he differentiates *formulae* for different types of legal acts, such as donations and certain grants of privileges, cf. BRESSLAU, Urkundenlehre (as n. 25) p. 55–57.

30 Cf. HÄRTEL, Notarielle Urkunden (as n. 26) p. 276; FICHTENAU, Forschungen (as n. 26) p. 286.

dict of the judge. Since those formulas and their corresponding instruction to the judges can be combined relatively freely according to how the pope wishes the case to be handled, they do not constitute a formulary, or in other words they cannot be used as set wording or pattern for the entire charter. The examples demonstrate a kind of formula, that is specific to the legal act represented by the written charter, in this case the delegation of a court case[31]. They are therefore more versatile than other formulas in their linguistic implementation in the charter text and may often be absent, e.g., when a case does not require their use.

Table 1: Examples of judicial formulas[32]

No.	Identifying title	Meaning	Examples
1	*ad audientiam nostrum pervenit*	Introduction to the report of the initial complaint: 'We have learned that...'	*veniens siquidem ad apostolice sedis clementiam in audientia nostra exposuit* (88) *ad apostolice sedis audientiam tua noverit fraternitas pervenisse* (91) *Pervenit ad audientiam nostram* (101) *ad audientiam apostolatus nostri pervenit* (195)
2	*rationes hinc inde audire*	Instruction to hear the arguments of both parties of the dispute.	*auditis tuis quam adverse partis racionibus* (41) *allegationibus ac rationibus hinc inde diligenter auditis* (64) *racionibus utriusque partis plenarie auditis et cognitis* (71) *rationibus hinc inde plenius intellectis* (176, 178, 180)
3	*veritatem rei diligenter inquirere*	Instruction to investigate the true facts of the case.	*veritatem rei diligenter inquiras* (88) *rem ipsam diligentissime inquiratis* (114) *veritatem super hoc diligenter inquiras* (177) *inquiratis diligentius veritatem* (195)
4	*appellatione remota*	Exclusion of the possibility for the litigants to lodge an appeal after the verdict.	*ut nullus appellationis locus parti alterutri relinquatur* (64) *sine appellationis obstaculo* (91, 112) *omni appellatione cessante* (105, 112) *omni appellatione remota* (125) *contradictione et appellatione remota* (178) *remoto apellationis obstaculo* (186) *nullius appellatione obstante* (186) *appelatione postposita* (195) *appelatione remota* (195)

For a better definition of this type of formulaic diplomatic language, it is helpful to consider what the term 'formulaic' means outside the context of charters:

31 Other charters may use formulas for other legal acts and contexts, like donations or privileging.

32 References in brackets refer to the number(s) of the charter(s) in PUU 3 (as n. 11) using the given expression.

Historical linguist Filatkina defines formulaic language as essentially all expressions whose meaning is revealed only when the expression is understood holistically, which have a conventionalised usage, and a special communicational function in spoken language or a structuring function in written language[33]. Formulaic language may thus include a wide range of linguistic phenomena, like sayings, set phrases, figurative language or even some one-word expressions. Although, this linguistic definition is too broad for specific historical research conducted here, it contains many elements that help construct a working definition of formulas. For example, judicial formulas often refer to a specific procedural stage or a certain legal act as part of the entire legal process, and their meaning, when understood in a holistic way, therefore exceeds those of the words that are actually used.

An important aspect that isn't necessary for the overall linguistic definition but needs to be specified in a definition of formulaic language in charters is the judicial context. Formulas are judicial in two ways: First, a certain formula is usually connected to certain circumstances of a legal case. This means that a trained judge or advocate can understand legal details based on the correct wording of fixed legal expressions, even if those legal details are not explicitly described in the expression[34]. As already mentioned, this can be seen as a special subtype of the holistically understood meaning that Filatkina sees as criterion for formulaic language. Second, the use and exact wording of a formula may impact the way in which the corresponding legal act of a trial is carried out. This corresponds to Filatkina's criterion of a formulaic expression having a special (here: instructing) function. While Schmitz stresses the binding wording of legal formulas, whose modification could render the formula invalid (cf. Handwörterbuch zur deutschen Rechtsgeschichte)[35], this is often not true for medieval charters in general and for the emerging and evolving formulas that we are investigating in specific, since both allow for some variety of expression. Especially the latter may have a formulaic character while still being rather fluid in their exact wording or sequence, which may not yet or never have existed. In the same way, the exact legal implications of a formula may change as the process of papal delegated jurisdiction evolves. Nevertheless, linguistic and procedural standardisation – for which formulas and which legal acts it occurs and on what level – might be worth exploring.

Based on the definitions and considerations presented above we can construct a first working definition for narrowing down the linguistic phenomena that we will

---

33 Filatkina, Historische formelhafte Sprache (as n. 23) p. 158–164, especially p. 164.

34 Härtel, Notarielle Urkunden (as n. 26) p. 34–35, 272.

35 Gerhard Schmitz, ‚Formel, Formular, Formelsammlung', in: HRG 1, Berlin ²2008, cols. 1616–1626, here col. 1616: „Unter Formel versteht man eine feststehende Abfolge von Wörtern. […] In allen Fällen gilt, dass die Formel ihre Gültigkeit verliert, wenn Wortlaut u. Abfolge nicht wie vorgeschrieben eingehalten werden."

focus on: We want to investigate judicial formulas in papal letters of justice. A judicial formula in this case denotes a linguistic expression that can be found in several charters[36] and has a relatively stable meaning concerning the legal circumstances of the case or delegation as well as a distinguishable linguistic form. Since we are investigating formulas in their early stage of conventionalisation this linguistic form may vary, but it must be relatively stable, meaning that two or more identical words or synonyms of those words are co-occurring to form the stable meaning of the expression. A stable syntax of a formula as well as a stable sequence of its lexemes may indicate and support its formulaic character but are not required conditions. It seems helpful not to draw a strict line between formulas and non-formulas, but to rather try to locate recurring expressions on a spectrum according to their grade of formulaicity. Expressions with a very fixed set of lexical components (e.g., table 1 no. 3) or with a fixed syntax (no. 4) would be considered more formulaic than expressions with more variation among their specific manifestations in charters.

As a next step, we face the challenge of refining and formalising this definition as well as developing a practical model for annotating formulas in the digital edition of the papal charters[37]. As seen in the working definition, all three language levels of syntax, lexemes, and semantics are relevant to the detection, classification, and evaluation of diplomatic formulas. The model therefore should include all those levels while being flexible enough to allow for the variation between different occurrences of the still developing formulas. It also must be pragmatic enough to enable an efficient editorial workflow.

Automatic detection of diplomatic *formulae* – current state of research

In addition to the annotation of formulas in the newly digitally edited charters, we try to detect formulas in already edited ones with the help of digital tools in order to investigate their evolution. Even though the detection and identification of diplomatic structures and formulas seems to be a perfect use case for digital methods due to the good formalisability of those structures, it is yet scarcely researched. In

36 The recurrence of expressions as condition for their formulaicity was reasonably challenged by Filatkina, Historische formelhafte Sprache (as n. 23) p. 159–160. Since in the case of charters the frequent recurrence of expressions has always been a crucial indicator of their formulaic character, we include this condition in this very basic working definition. Nonetheless, if singular, non-recurring formulaic elements turn out to be frequent, they may be of relevance in a later phase of the project.

37 The detailed annotation of formulaic language has to this day only been attempted in the field of (historical) corpus linguistics. In computer linguistics, formulaic language is often dealt with under the term of 'Multiword Expressions' (MWE) (cf. proceedings of the annual Workshop on MWEs: https://aclanthology.org/venues/mwe). Yet, other terms may be applied and can denote different (and often wider) concepts than that presented here.

2018 GALUŠCÁKOVÁ and NEUŽILOVÁ presented first experiments aiming at automatically detecting formal sections in charters issued by the King of Bohemia in the 14th century[38]. They used, among others, information retrieval methods, namely the calculation of string similarities between predefined known diplomatic formulas and text segments from their corpus to match those segments to the diplomatic section to which the matching formula belongs to. This worked well when dealing with short sections that can be clearly defined by a few characteristic formulas, like the *intitulatio*[39]. This example already shows that retracing known set phrases or formulaic elements of a few words in unknown texts is achievable with resource-saving methods.

Those results are underlined by a prototypic program for automatic detection of sections within charters (OSTROWSKI 2019)[40]. The program was designed to automatically annotate an unsegmented royal charter with its diplomatic sections according to the CEI standard. The basis for the classification is a Naïve Bayes algorithm, but sentences that cannot be matched to a section by calculating the probability using their lexical features are assigned by consulting other features like the assignment of their neighbouring sentences. This approach requires a skeleton of classified sentences, that help assign the sentences in between. Again, to achieve this, string-matching methods were applied to calculate a string similarity between the sentences to be classified, on the one hand, and the known formulas given as a resource, on the other. The string similarity calculation was extended by the possibility to provide certain levels of similarity, e.g., matching exact substrings, matching subsets, or just matching a certain similarity indicated by a Jaccard-coefficient, as well as providing certain positional characteristics as further condition for a match. Like the experiments of GALUŠCÁKOVÁ and NEUŽILOVÁ, the evaluation of the program showed: The more fixed a formulaic expression is, the more reliable is its detection via simple string-matching methods. Accordingly, the detection of the sections belonging to the *protocol* and *eschatocol* had very high precision and recall scores of 95 % to 98 %.[41]

In our context, these two approaches can be adapted to look for occurrences of already known formulaic expressions of the 9th and 13th century onwards. Nevertheless, applying simple string-matching methods is limited to instances of formu-

38 Petra GALUŠCÁKOVÁ/Lucie NEUŽILOVÁ, Low Resource Methods for Medieval Document Sections Analysis, in: Proceedings of the Eleventh International Conference on Language Resources and Evaluation (LREC 2018), Miyazaki, Japan, ed. Nicoletta CALZOLARI et al., 2018, p. 2344–2348, URL: https://aclanthology.org/L18-1371.

39 Ibid. p. 2347.

40 Alina OSTROWSKI, Automatische Erkennung und Klassifikation von Formularbestandteilen in Königsurkunden. Zur Aufbereitung digitaler Urkundenkorpora in der Mediävistik, in: Die Historischen Grundwissenschaften heute. Tradition – methodische Vielfalt – Neuorientierung, ed. Étienne DOUBLIER/Daniela SCHULZ/Dominik TRUMP, Wien/Köln/Weimar 2021, p. 139–166.

41 Ibid. p. 161.

las that have only slight lexical or syntactical variations, as stronger variations might not be detected.

We are therefore testing text mining methods such as text reuse detection (TRD) on the IbePon corpus. TRD is well researched and used, for example, in the context of plagiarism detection. The goal of a text reuse analysis is to establish links between texts where one or more documents serve as a source for another textual document that reused parts of their text. During the last decade, TRD has also been used for some historical analyses aiming at identifying references to earlier works in historical sources. Büchler (2013) presented a first comprehensive approach to the specifics of historical text reuse and the adoption of TRD methods for the analysis of historical data[42]. Since then, for example the analysis of allusions in Latin poetry[43] or the detection of biblical quotes and allusions in accounts of the first crusade[44] have applied these methods.

In the context of medieval charters, TRD was recently applied by Leclercq and Kestemont to support the interpretation of a stylometric analysis conducted over a corpus of charters of the bishops of Cambrai[45]. They report that their analysis yielded useful results and that many of them contained formulaic elements. The approach of Leclercq/Kestemont is similar to ours in that they did not try to find actual sources of documents, but rather tried to identify linguistically similar text fragments and thereby attempted to explain why two documents might be considered stylometrically similar to each other. Usually, the differentiation between a 'real' intended reuse of a source text and unintended intuitive reuse of language, such as idiomatic or multi word expressions, presents a big challenge to the detection of text reuse since they have similar characteristics and the detection methods find both phenomena alike[46]. In our case, however, this unwanted effect allows us to adapt TRD to our research question. Like Leclercq/Kestemont, we do not aim at establishing links between target and source charters but rather at finding common linguistic phenom-

42 Marco Büchler, Informationstechnische Aspekte des *Historical Text Re-use,* Leipzig 2013, URN: https://nbn-resolving.org/urn:nbn:de:bsz:15-qucosa-108515.

43 Neil Bernstein/Kyle Gervais/Wei Lin, Comparative rates of text reuse in classical Latin hexameter poetry, in: Digital Humanities Quaterly 9 (2015), URL: http://www.digitalhumanities.org/dhq/vol/9/3/000237/000237.html.

44 Torsten Hiltmann/Jan Keupp/Melanie Althage/Philipp Schneider, Digital Methods in Practice. The Epistemological Implications of Applying Text Re-Use Analysis to the Bloody Accounts of the Conquest of Jerusalem (1099), in: Geschichte und Gesellschaft 47/1 (2021), p. 122–156, DOI: 10.13109/gege.2021.47.1.122. In the paper they also extensively discuss epistemological challenges for historical TRD.

45 Eveline Leclercq/Mike Kestemont, Advances in Distant Diplomatics. A Stylometric Approach to Medieval Charters, in: Interfaces 8 (2021) p. 214–244, DOI: 10.54103/interfaces-08-10, here p. 223–224.

46 Cf. Büchler, Historical Text Re-use (as n. 42) p. 43–44 and p. 51 n. 37, who calls the two types 'Text Re-Use' (intended) and 'Language Re-Use' (unintended).

ena – regardless of whether they originate from a scribe using an older charter as template or whether they only represent a reuse of language commonly used in the chancery. The idea is to cross-reference the charters of the IbePon corpus, algorithmically considering each charter as both a possible source as well as target document, and then find 'reused' passages common to one or more charters, which in turn may indicate that a formulaic expression was used. We hope that TRD will prove especially helpful in finding formulaic expressions that have not been recorded by modern historical research due to a weak level of standardisation.

While the differentiation between intended and unintended text reuse can be neglected in the context of the detection of *formulae*, another differentiation is, in contrast, very relevant: Text reuse may occur in two main types. The most obvious of those types is a literal or near literal reuse that stays close to the original and uses nearly the same words and syntax as the source. Examples are quotes or idiomatic expressions. BÜCHLER calls them 'Syntactic Text Re-Use'. BÜCHLER'S second type, 'Semantical Text Re-Use', is a reuse of ideas expressed in one text, but used in the target text without staying true to the original lexical and syntactical features. Examples for this are paraphrases, allusions, or summaries[47]. TRD must be conducted with different parameters and needs different input data depending on which type of reuse it should be able to look for. For the case of papal charters this tackles a question already raised regarding the definition and the modelling of formulaic expressions in charters: Should the search for reoccurring *formulae* only consider expressions with a similar form (i.e., identical syntax or lexemes), or should it also take into account expressions with a different form but similar meaning? In general, formulaic language with its conventionalised linguistic form belongs to the first of these types, which is why we are mostly interested in the methods for detecting syntactic reuse.

However, as discussed in the modelling section, semantic reuse without syntactic reuse can occur when *formulae* are not yet standardised and appear in an early form that differs completely from the later, fully developed form yet represents the same function and meaning. The detection of such fluid expressions is one major challenge in investigating formulaic language with digital approaches, since semantic textual similarity is difficult to detect with common TRD approaches[48], especially if the formulaic expressions that we look for are short (cf. Tab. 1, No. 4), and language models based on the meaning of words might be needed to identify them[49].

47 Cf. ibid., p. 77, fig. 2.3.

48 Maria MORITZ/Andreas WIEDERHOLD/Barbara PAVLEK/Yuri BIZZONI/Marco BÜCHLER, Non-Literal Text Reuse in Historical Texts. An Approach to Identify Reuse Transformations and its Application to Bible Reuse, in: Proceedings of the 2016 Conference on Empirical Methods in Natural Language Processing, ed. Jian SU/Kevin DUH/Xavier CARRERAS, Stroudsburg 2016, p. 1849–1859.

49 E.g., Bernhard LIEBL/Manuel BURGHARDT, The Vectorian API. A Research Framework for Se-

Another challenge is the regional or temporal variance of formulaic expressions, since they might occur less frequently and can therefore not be detected using approaches that rely on textual repetition to identify formulas. To model the diachronic aspect of formulaic evolution, we experiment with dividing our corpus into different regional or time-specific subsets and using alternative detection methods that are based on features such as the use of uncommon vocabulary (which might be indicative of a specific legal term) or their use in contexts similar to those of already known, standardised expressions. Finally, during an experimental annotation of formulaic expressions in the IbePon corpus, variable elements (such as names, descriptions of circumstances etc.) and modifiers (such as adverbial additions) have proven to be a non-neglectable part of formulaic expressions, which should not be ignored during the digital text analysis[50].

All methods that we apply to investigate judicial formulaic expressions must themselves be evaluated with respect to their performance, since their results are bound to differ from those of traditional text analysis by close reading[51] and, furthermore, some kinds of formulas might simply not be detectable with these approaches. To be able to adequately interpret our findings, we – like any humanities researchers using computer-based methods – must be aware of such technical limitations and account for them in the final historical analysis.

Outlook

These first considerations concerning digital analyses of papal delegated jurisdiction on the Iberian Peninsula of the 12th century show how far reaching the topic as a whole is. Next steps include the finalisation of the uniform data model as well as the transfer of all relevant charters and registers into it in order to execute the presented ideas and considerations on a larger scale. We expect to gain significant insight into the development of formulaic elements and key institutions as well as key figures (and their interconnections) concerning papal jurisdictional practices through the presented digital methods which will be combined with the content-related expertise of the project partners from Göttingen who are currently working on closing the editorial gap of papal charters of the Kingdom of León and the Spanish knightly orders in order to enable a comprehensive analysis.

---

mantic Textual Similarity (STS) Searches, in: Digital Humanities 2022. Conference Abstracts, ed. Yifan Wang, Tokio 2022, p. 654–656.

50 Cf. the notion of 'VAR'-elements and common extensions by Marijn Koolen/Rik Hoekstra: Detecting Formulaic Language Use in Historical Administrative Corpora, in: Proceedings of the Computational Humanities Research Conference 2022, ed. Folgert Karsdorp/Alie Lassche/Kristoffer Nielbo, Antwerpen 2022, p. 127–151

51 Cf. Hiltmann et al., Digital Methods (as n. 44) p. 154.

Linguistic research on medieval Latin charters

What to expect of digital diplomatics?

Timo Korkiakangas

1. Objectives and background

The present paper has a twofold goal: first, it reviews how medieval Latin charters have been used as a source of historical linguistic research; after that, it discusses what kind of prospects digital diplomatic advances open up for such research.[1]

Traditional linguistic studies of medieval Latin charters have progressively taken diplomatic knowledge into account since the last half of the 20th century. Currently, Latin linguistics tends towards increasingly complex research settings based on large text corpora. Since charters continue to provide crucial evidence for the diachrony of Latin, there is an urgent need to find ways to put diplomatic information meaningfully into the service of historical Latin corpus linguistics. The solutions are bound to be digital diplomatic. The importance of digital diplomatics for linguistics lies in that it can allow for the peculiar text type of charters even in large-scale research designs. Diplomatically informed approaches are likely to help in ruling out extra-linguistic artefacts and epiphenomenal features and, thus, lead to an increased precision and reliability in linguistic argumentation. Corpus-linguistic

1 A comprehensive and still largely valid overview on the diverse aspects and research strands of digital diplomatics is found in the conference proceedings of the *Digital Diplomatics 2011* conference: Digital diplomatics: the computer as a tool for the diplomatist? (AfD Beiheft 14), ed. Antonella Ambrosio/Sébastien Barret/Georg Vogeler, Köln 2014. For a more recent panorama of digital diplomatic advances, see, e.g., Digitizing Medieval Sources – L'édition en ligne de documents d'archives médiévaux: Challenges and Methodologies – Enjeux, méthodologie et défis (Atelier de recherche sur les textes médiévaux 27), ed. Christelle Balouzat-Loubet, Turnhout 2020; Eveline Leclercq/Mike Kestemont, Advances in Distant Diplomatics: A Stylometric Approach to Medieval Charters, in: Interfaces: A Journal of Medieval European Literatures 8 (2021) p. 214–244; and the many diplomatically-inspired contributions to Natural Sciences, Technology, and Informatics in Manuscript Analysis (Manuscript cultures 15), ed. Oliver Hahn/Volker Märgner/Ira Rabin/H. Siegfried Stiehl, Hamburg 2020.

argumentation is based, by default, on quantitative and statistical inferences and, consequently, is well in accordance with the digital diplomatic research paradigm.

Medieval charters are a privileged source for historical linguistics because, when they survive as originals, their spelling and grammar derive with certainty from the date they indicate. The great majority of Italian, Frankish, and Iberian charters do indicate dates, and many even the name of the scribe. This permits modern-day scholars to make diachronic, sociolinguistic, and diatopic comparisons. On the contrary, practically all other written sources of early medieval Latin are transmitted through a multigenerational process of copying that in principle strove for a close reproduction of the model. While each round of copying unavoidably added new errors to the text, the anonymous copyists may also have emended errors – or forms they considered errors – that belonged to the original. In addition, manuscripts are often undatable. Consequently, one cannot know how much a text has changed from one manuscript generation to another, let alone how many generations there have been before the first surviving manuscript. Although ample parts of the most solemn typologies of medieval documents, such as royal diplomas and papal decrees, were undoubtedly copied from formularies or other exemplars, all documents also necessarily contain non-formulaic matter that records the case-specific details of the legal transaction at hand. Moreover, there is evidence that humbler private charters were largely reproduced from memory at least in the early Middle Ages. Charters can, thus, provide invaluable insights into medieval Latin usage if they are scrutinized carefully.

In medieval Europe, charters were written in various local linguistic varieties, and the researchers of modern European national languages have successfully drawn on medieval charter data to reconstruct historical stages of their own languages. This has been fruitful, for example, with Germanic languages, from which much material survives[2], but the import of charters for many other languages with less historical evidence is also central[3]. In some Romance-speaking areas, Latin was used until very late in the modern period. Since medieval Latin is not a direct pre-

2 Kurt GÄRTNER/Günter HOLTUS/Andrea RAPP/Harald VÖLKER, Urkunden des 13. Jahrhunderts als Quellen sprachlicher Untersuchungen zum Westmitteldeutschen und Ostfranzösischen: Korpus und Auswertungsbeispiele, in: Urkundensprachen im germanisch-romanischen Grenzgebiet: Beiträge zum Kolloquium am 5./6. Oktober 1995 in Trier, ed. Kurt GÄRTNER/Günter HOLTUS, Mainz 1997, p. 21–138; Carsten BECKER/Oliver SCHALLERT, Areal variation in Middle High German: A perspective from charters, in: NOWELE North-Western European Language Evolution 74 (2021) p. 199–241; The Languages of Early Medieval Charters: Latin, Germanic Vernaculars, and the Written Word (Brill's Series on the Early Middle Ages 27), ed. Robert GALLAGHER/Edward ROBERTS/Francesca TINTI, Leiden 2020.

3 For example, Finnish toponyms and anthroponyms in the medieval charters of Finland written in Latin or Swedish: Oliver BLOMQVIST, Bilingual personal designations in medieval Finnish sources, in: Onoma 55 (2021) p. 111–131.

decessor of any national language, it has not aroused nationalistic interests and has been largely ignored from a linguistic point of view.

2. Language, linguistics, and language-related historical studies

This section defines the typological classes into which linguistic and other language-related research is categorized in this article for ease of exposition. The ways in which language is approached in research designs concerning historical documents are manifold. A fundamental dividing line lies between self-contained and instrumental uses of language and linguistics. Such a division is vital to the understanding of the radically differing premises, aims, and data requirements of different research paradigms.

"[Linguistics is] the scientific study of the structure and development of language in general or of particular languages[4]." In other words, linguistics focuses on the building blocks of a/the language and how they vary. In the Saussurean tradition, linguistics is primarily the study of the system of the language (*langue*) in distinction to how language is used by individual speakers (*parole*)[5]. Since the latter part of the 20th century, however, linguists have been paying more and more attention to the actual use of language[6].

Thus, if a study of historical documents accumulates new information on the very system of a given language, it can be properly termed linguistic (or historical linguistic). If it utilizes linguistic knowledge instrumentally to attain a language-external goal, it may still be called, broadly speaking, linguistic, although it does depart from linguistics proper in that it compares the data under examination to what is aprioristically known of the (system of the) language and exploits this comparison to promote argumentation about something factually unrelated to that system. Such an instrumental study may exploit the linguistic properties of texts to explain, say, the mechanisms of historical second-language acquisition or, if understood very inclusively, even the circulation of new concepts and ideas in a given geographical space[7]. However, this last type of research often has very little in common with

---

4 Cambridge Dictionary, s. v. Linguistics. https://dictionary.cambridge.org.

5 Ferdinand SAUSSURE, Cours de linguistique générale, Paris 1916, reprint Paris 1971, p. 27–32 (c. III/2).

6 For example, Joan BYBEE, Language, cognition, and usage, Cambridge 2010.

7 Of notable importance concerning the latter are the studies of Nicolas PERREAUX: for example, Nicolas PERREAUX, L'écriture du monde (II). L'écriture comme facteur de régionalisation et de spiritualisation du *mundus*: études lexicales et sémantiques, in: Bulletin du centre d'études médiévales d'Auxerre (BUCEMA) 20 (2016). See also Shigeto KIKUCHI, Representations of Monarchical 'Highness' in Carolingian Royal Charters, in: Problems and Possibilities of Early Medieval Charters, ed. Jonathan JARRETT/Allan Scott MCKINLEY, Turnhout 2013.

linguistics proper, and, indeed, authors of such studies tend to ascribe their activity not to linguistics but rather to historiography or to some of its subdisciplines, such as the history of ideas or concepts or even diplomatics.

This article only deals with the proper linguistic research that focuses on the system of the Latin language. The instrumental use of linguistic knowledge for language-external purposes, which is called here language-related, is only touched upon in passing.

3. Overview of linguistic studies on medieval Latin charters

This section presents the outlines of linguistic research on medieval Latin charters up to the present day. Subsection 3.1. discusses studies based on traditional, non-digital, approaches, while subsection 3.2. is about digital, essentially corpus-linguistic, research.

The proper linguistic research of medieval Latin charters is a chronologically and geographically sharply divided field. Early medieval Latin charters of the Romance areas of Europe up to the 10/11th centuries have been and are actively being used as a source for linguistic studies of various descriptions, while the later medieval Latin charters of any region have virtually not been studied at all from the point of view of their linguistic system. This is because the early medieval Latin of the Romance areas can still be considered the writers' native tongue, whereas later medieval Latin is undeniably a second language. Second-language Latin does not arouse nationalistic interests similar to the early varieties of modern European national languages also attested in medieval charters.

In the early medieval centuries, a metalinguistic turn took place, at a different pace in different, originally Latin-speaking regions. This was when (initially only a few well-educated) language users came to consider their spoken vernacular a language distinct from Latin, which, in its late ancient stage of spelling and grammar, was continuously held as the sole standard for the written language. A corollary of this recognition of two distinct languages was that Latin was gradually canalized into the language of learned communication. Nowadays known simply as medieval Latin, it was a lingua franca which had to be learnt as a second language, relying on grammar books and, preferably, through the imitation of a set of (late) ancient and medieval (school) authors[8]. The Carolingian Latin reforms are thought to have

8 The conceptualization of two different languages is traditionally considered to be visible for the first time in the acts of the council of the bishopric of Tours in 813, which distinguish between Latin and the *rustica Romana lingua*, the "rustic Roman language", spoken and understood by the local population. See Marc van Uytfanghe, The consciousness of a linguistic dichotomy (Latin-Romance) in Carolingian Gaul: The contradictions of the sources and of their interpretation,

contributed to the rise of this awareness of the gap between the spoken and written language, although the specific way how this happened is still discussed[9]. Importantly, with this awareness, the window gradually closes that allows linguists to see glimpses of the spoken language in non-literary texts, chiefly charters, predating that metalinguistic change[10].

Although the vernacular of the writer is often recognizable in later medieval Latin texts as well, in terms of revelatory mistakes, it can be argued that, by and large, the link between the written Latin and the spoken language was broken in most places of the Romance-speaking world during the last centuries of the first millennium. Such a development is accompanied by concomitant attempts to put vernaculars into written form, which, however, only took place on a large scale in the later Middle Ages. Official charters in particular continued to be produced in Latin in the Romance-speaking areas up until the Modern period.

Because charters are practically the only source of non-literary Latin from the early Middle Ages, it is understandable that they have attracted the attention of Latin linguists who wish to detect linguistic developments of this very late variety of Latin that was not yet unequivocally a second language but was still a native tongue. Charters are expected to shed light on phenomena that bridge the gap between ancient Latin and early Romance grammars. In other words, linguistic attention has almost exclusively concentrated on charters dating from the early Middle Ages.

The other side of the coin is that Latin linguists, who typically gain their education focusing on ancient Latin sources, tend to consider medieval Latin acquired as a second language uninteresting and irrelevant for the history of Latin. However, it can be argued that medieval Latin is an organic part of the history of the Latin language, albeit essentially different in nature. In fact, various meaningful big-data-style research settings would be possible were scholars interested in meeting the challenge. For example, learner language studies on modern languages have shown that second-language learners' linguistic output forms systems peculiar to individual language learners' first language, social background, level of education, and idiosyncratic preferences[11]. Moreover, many more Latin texts survive from the later Middle Ages than from Antiquity and the early Middle Ages. All this considered, it is surprising how little truly linguistic research there is on (later) medieval Latinity.

---

in: Latin and the Romance Languages in the early Middle Ages, ed. Roger WRIGHT, University Park, Pennsylvania 1991, p. 114–129.

9 See the contributions in WRIGHT, Latin (as n. 8).

10 The *Placiti cassinesi*, written in Latin in the 960s, record the oral testimonies of witnesses in what was undoubtedly the local vernacular, showing that Central-Italian speakers had come to distinguish between two different languages by that time. See Arrigo CASTELLANI, I più antichi testi italiani: edizione e commento, seconda edizione, Bologna 1976, reprint Bologna 1980, p. 59–76.

11 Rod ELLIS/Gary BARKHUIZEN, Analysing Learner Language, Oxford 2005, p. 24.

This disparity is probably enhanced by the fact that many medieval Latin studies are carried out by literature scholars with no specific linguistic background, hence the nearly exclusive focus on literature in all popular manuals[12]. This is also symptomatic of the main scientific venues of Latin studies: two biannual conference series of Latin linguistics are regularly held, the *International Colloquium on Latin Linguistics* and the *International Colloquium on Late and Vulgar Latin* (*Latin vulgaire, latin tardif*), and pertinent linguistic research is constantly published in a plethora of journals, whereas no regular conferences are devoted to medieval Latin, with the congresses of the *International Association for Neo-Latin Studies* and *The Journal of Medieval Latin* being almost exclusively concerned with literature. The *Archivum Latinitatis Medii Aevi* does contain linguistic research, which is, however, focused on the early Middle Ages.

3.1. Traditional linguistic studies

Scholarly interest in early medieval Latin charters arose in the wake of the 19th-century history boom, which was originally tightly bound with documentary evidence. Massive source editions began to bring charter texts within the reach of scholars. The most influential series was the rigorous *Diplomata* section of MGH[13], although many important collections of both Italian and Frankish charters had already been published in local projects of varying quality[14]. The publication of Iberian charters and chartularies started somewhat later[15].

---

12 For example, Medieval Latin: An Introduction and Bibliographical Guide, ed. Frank Mantello/George Rigg, Washington 1996; Pascale Bourgain/Marie-Clotilde Hubert, Le latin médiéval, Turnhout 2005; Keith Sidwell, Reading Medieval Latin, Cambridge 1995. Only Handbuch zur lateinischen Sprache des Mittelalters 1–5, ed. Peter Stotz, Munich 1996–2004, comes close to a linguistic synopsis, whereas manuals such as Karl Strecker, Einführung in das Mittellatein, Berlin 1929, and Dag Norberg, Manuel pratique de latin médiéval, Paris 1968, are narrow and largely outdated.

13 The diplomas of Merovingian kings and majordomos in: Diplomata imperii 1, ed. Karl Pertz, Hannover 1872, and those of German emperors in: Diplomata regum et imperatorum Germaniae, beginning from 1879.

14 The Ravenna papyri in: I papiri diplomatici, ed. Gaetano Marini, Roma 1805; charters kept in the archives of Lucca in: Memorie e documenti per servire alla storia di Lucca (various volumes beginning from 1813); Italian charters of the Lombard period until 774 in: Codice diplomatico longobardo 4/III–V, ed. Carlo Troya, Napoli 1853–1855; the charters written in Lombardy up to 1000 in: Codex diplomaticus Langobardiae, ed. Giulio Porro Lambertenghi, Torino 1873; the 9th- to 10th-century charters conserved in the archive of the abbey of Cava dei Tirreni in: Codex diplomaticus Cavensis (beginning from 1873); the Merovingian diplomas of Francia in: Diplomata, chartae, epistolae, leges aliaque instrumenta ad res Gallo-Francicas spectantia 1–2, ed. Jean-Marie Pardessus, Paris 1843–1849, and Jules Tardif, Monuments historiques: cartons des rois, Paris 1866.

15 For example, Louis Barrau-Dihigo, Notes et documents sur l'histoire du royaume de León 1:

Although linguistics, itself an emerging field in the 19th century, heavily concentrated on the historical stages of European national languages, it initially made little use of medieval Latin charters. This was partly because of the general problems charters pose to their interpreters (as explained in subsection 3.2.), partly because, contrary to the high-quality MGH, many early editions were not accurate enough to be used for linguistic study, given that they normalized spellings and omitted recurrent formulaic phrases. Whereas the Merovingian charters of Francia were available in a reliable form thanks to the MGH and other early editions[16], the oldest Italian charters could not be subjected to linguistic study before Schiaparelli's new edition of the *Codice diplomatico longobardo* in the early 1930s[17].

Among the earliest linguistic studies that exploited charters alongside literary and inscriptional evidence, figure Schuchardt's groundbreaking work on Vulgar Latin phonology and Meyer-Lübke's equally monumental comparative grammar of the Romance languages[18]. The first studies that concentrated on charters, excluding some brief dissertations, include treatises which attempt to reconstruct the phonology, morphology, and syntax of Merovingian Latin[19].

It is to be noted that the language of Frankish formularies, that is, model document collections, was also studied rather early on[20]. This was probably not only because of the 19th-century preference for official legal documentation, but also because formularies, contained in single manuscripts, presented a more accessible and stable research data than individual charters, especially after the publication of the first reliable formulary editions[21]. Moreover, early scholars seem to have nurtured a Platonic disdain for reproduction as opposed to model, inasmuch as formularies were considered more authoritative and representative of the will of the authorities

chartes royales léonaises (912–1037), in: Revue hispanique 10 (1903) p. 349–454, and Documentos lingüísticos de España 1: Reino de Castilla, ed. Ramón Menéndez Pidal, Madrid 1919.

16 Pardessus (ed.), Diplomata (as n. 14); Tardif (ed.), Monuments (as n. 14).

17 Codice diplomatico longobardo 1–2, ed. Luigi Schiaparelli, Roma 1929–1932.

18 Hugo Schuchardt, Der Vokalismus des Vulgärlateins 1, Leipzig 1866–1867 (see p. 12); Wilhelm Meyer-Lübke, Grammatik der romanischen Sprachen 1–4, Leipzig 1890–1902 (see p. 16–18).

19 Henry d'Arbois de Jubainville, La déclinaison latine en Gaule à l'époque mérovingienne, Paris 1872; Jeanne Vielliard, Le latin des diplômes royaux et chartes privées de l'époque mérovingienne, Paris 1927.

20 Ezechiel Slijper, De formularum Andecavensium latinitate disputatio, Amsterdam 1906; Jules Pirson, Le latin des formules mérovingiennes et carolingiennes, in: Romanische Forschungen 24 (1909) p. 837–944.

21 Recueil général des formules usitées dans l'empire des Francs du Ve au Xe siècle 1–3, ed. Eugène de Rozière, Paris 1859–1871; Formulae Merowingici et Karolini Aevi (MGH Leges 5), ed. Karl Zeumer, Hannover 1886.

than individual charters copied from them. Later, the relationship between formularies and charters has been duly problematized[22].

In Italy, linguistic study of the early medieval Lombard charters only became possible after Schiaparelli, although it took time even then, works entirely devoted to Italian charters only beginning to appear from the late 1930s onwards[23]. Mainly focused on Italian charters, the Politzers' work represents what might be called an American school of vulgar Latin studies. It saw its rise in the 1930s with the works of Pei and Sas about Merovingian Latin and was backed by the theoretical considerations of Muller[24]. These scholars exposed charters to pioneering quantitative linguistic research, which they called "statistical"[25], but which limited itself to counting percentages and presenting simple bar charts.

More problematically, these American scholars more or less shared a view of the charters' Latin as the actual spoken language of the scribes[26]. Such an attitude arose from a defective understanding of the textual function and production context of charters. Previous scholars, such as Vielliard, though seemingly not having explicit diplomatic training, had had a philological understanding of charters as a specific type of historical source that has its possibilities and limitations[27]. The American school, on the other hand, considered charters pretty much ahistorical data, the original sin of corpus linguistics. This approach led to plainly erroneous conclusions concerning non-standard forms or constructions and, consequently, the general character of early medieval Latinity. Robert Politzer, for example, wishfully mapped together the syntactic function and surface morphology of the first declension genitive plural: "Examples of the use of the genitive are not numerous but enough to indicate that *-as* was imposing itself in the genitive function: *diae octabo kalendis magias* (No. 12), *tertio ... kalendas febroaria* (No. 3) [--][28]". It is, however, evident that the scribe had not understood the syntax of the traditional dating

22 Alice Rio, Legal Practice and the Written Word in the Early Middle Ages: Frankish Formulae, c.500–1000, Cambridge 2009, which also summarizes the subsequent research on Frankish formularies.

23 A rather succinct doctoral dissertation: Wilhelm Funcke, Sprachliche Untersuchungen zum Codice Diplomatico Longobardo, Phil. Diss. Münster 1938; Robert Politzer's dissertation: Robert Politzer, A Study of the Language of Eighth Century Lombardic Documents, Phil. Diss. Columbia, New York 1949; the Part 1 of Frieda and Robert Politzers' study: Frieda Politzer/Robert Politzer, Romance Trends in 7th and 8th Century Latin Documents, Chapel Hill 1953.

24 Mario Pei, The language of the eighth-century texts in northern France, New York 1932; Louis Furman Sas, The Noun Declension System in Merovingian Latin, Paris 1937; Henri François Muller/Pauline Taylor, A chrestomathy of vulgar Latin, Boston 1932.

25 Politzer, Study (as n. 23) Introduction.

26 Ibid. p. 1.

27 Vielliard, Latin (as n. 19) p. ix–xi.

28 Politzer, Study (as n. 23) p. 70.

phrase, while he still reproduced the originally pertinent accusative plural forms in *-as* because adherence to formulae was his job. Thus, reporting the mentioned forms in *-as* as genitive plurals is nonsensical. Similarly, the Politzers' conclusion about the increased openness of the phoneme /e/ in 8th-century northern Italian charters appears to be an artefact caused by their misguided approach, as suggested by Larson in his unfortunately unpublished Master's thesis[29].

It was Sabatini in his article on the Latin origin of Italian plurals who drew the research community's attention to the fact that linguistic study cannot treat what he called the "formulaic parts" of charters on a par with the "free parts", that is, the case-specific contents (mainly the *dispositio*) with which the scribe had to rely on his own language skills instead of prefabricated phrases[30]. Therefore, the formulaic parts of charters contain different errors than the non-formulaic parts. According to Sabatini, the errors in the formulaic parts, which reproduce age-old legal terminology alien to the scribe's everyday language, are typically based on misunderstandings or hypercorrections of the ancient vocabulary and syntactic constructions absent from early medieval spoken Latin[31]. A consequence of this observation was that linguists working with charters became increasingly aware of the diplomatic articulation of their sources. They had to draw on diplomatic literature in order to detect what is formulaic and what not, which also called for an understanding of what purposes the various phrases and entire sections were expected to satisfy. Although these ideas did not penetrate the field immediately, linguistic research is today sensitive to the presence of both formulaic and less formulaic textual matter in charters. No longer would scholars commit Funcke's error of treating original, copied, and even falsified charters alike in the same study.

Notable from the theoretical point of view are also Korkiakangas' findings[32], which specify Sabatini's conclusions by showing empirically on a corpus of 8th and 9th-century Italian Latin charters that different linguistic domains behave differently with regard to the formulaic/free distinction. Early medieval scribes seem to have memorized morphological and spelling-related features of ancient Latin better than its syntax because morphology and spelling are perceptually more salient phenomena than syntax. Morphology and spelling have audible and visible representations, that is, a certain amount of phonetic matter in oral utterances and a certain number of letters in writing, while syntax is abstract and its relation to audible/visible morphemes is not necessarily transparent. This difference in the per-

29 POLITZER/POLITZER, Romance Trends (as n. 23) p. 7; Pär LARSON, Gli elementi volgari nelle carte del *Codice diplomatico longobardo*, Phil. Diss. Firenze 1988.

30 Francesco SABATINI, Esigenze di realismo e dislocazione morfologica in testi preromanzi, in: Rivista di Cultura Classica e Medievale 7 (1965) p. 972–998.

31 Ibid. p. 975–977.

32 Timo KORKIAKANGAS, Spoken Latin Behind Written Texts: Formulaicity and Salience in Medieval Documentary Texts, in: Diachronica 35 (2018) p. 429–449.

ceptual salience that conditioned the ancient Latin acquisition of the scribes seems to have contributed to more classical morphology and spelling in the formulaic parts, whereas syntax tends to be equally classical or non-classical both in formulaic and free parts.

The Neapolitan school of Latin linguists, which specializes in the charters of Cava dei Tirreni, also emphasizes the modern context-aware approach[33]. In her ample linguistic oeuvre, Sornicola makes a strong point about the necessity of understanding the historical and textual context in which early medieval charter texts came about, as well as the legal, social, and cultural functions they fulfilled. Far from being a direct reflection of the spoken language of the scribes or of any other historical stage of the spoken idiom, the Latin of charters is to be seen as a set of highly artificial and historically stratified varieties. These varieties draw on different chronological stages of legal Latin, from the imperial legislation up to the local laws of the successor regimes, conditioned by tendencies oscillating between prestigious conservative wordings and blatant innovations, some of which originating from the spoken idiom. Given the work of the Neapolitan school, the charters of Cava currently form the best-known individual corpus of charters, and their minute examination has helped in specifying the complex relationship between the oral legal tradition and the vernacular, as well as in recognizing the free/formulaic distinction as non-dichotomous[34]. The linguistic study of other medieval corpora would benefit from a similar meticulous analysis of the circumstances and conditions under which the charters were produced.

A related novel linguistic approach is that of Galdi, who examines the language of a group of Luccan scribes well-defined in terms of diplomatics and scriptural history, the so-called circle of Gaudentius[35]. Through a careful comparison of these

---

33 Epitomized in the chapters of: Sistemi, norme, scritture: la lingua delle più antiche carte cavensi, ed. Rosanna SORNICOLA/Elisa D'ARGENIO/Paolo GRECO, Napoli 2017; see also Rosanna SORNICOLA, Bilinguismo e diglossia dei territori bizantini e longobardi del Mezzogiorno: le testimonianze dei documenti del IX e X secolo, in: Quaderni dell'Accademia Pontaniana 59 (2012) p. 1–102.

34 Rosanna SORNICOLA, "Transizione" e "transizioni" dal latino al romanzo: il progetto di analisi linguistica dei documenti cavensi del IX secolo, in: SORNICOLA/D'ARGENIO/GRECO (eds.), Sistemi (as n. 33) p. 13–26 (see p. 17). For previous research on the Cava charters: Giuliana FIORENTINO, Aspetti della morfosintassi nominale nelle carte cavensi del IX secolo, in: Archivio Glottologico Italiano 79 (1994) p. 23–50; Mariafrancesca GIULIANI, Il policentrismo campano alla luce della documentazione medievale, in: La lingua dei documenti notarili alto-medievali dell'Italia meridionale, ed. Rosanna SORNICOLA/Paolo GRECO, Napoli 2013, p. 191–213.

35 Giovanbattista GALDI, Osservazioni sulla lingua e sul formulario dei rogatari lucchesi (VIII–IX secolo), in: Lingue, scritture e società nell'Italia longobarda: un percorso di sociolinguistica storica, ed. Elisa D'ARGENIO/Roberto DELLE DONNE/Rosanna SORNICOLA, Napoli [in press]; Armando PETRUCCI, Scrittura e libro nella Tuscia altomedievale (secoli VIII–IX), in: Atti del V Congresso internazionale di studi sull'alto medioevo, Spoleto 1973, p. 627–643.

scribes' Latin, Galdi draws conclusions on their linguistic competences, on which basis he contributes to paleographical and diplomatic study, proposing, for example, that the scribes Ostripertus and Austripertus, considered different scribes by the editors of ChLA, are most likely to be one and the same person, an excellent example of how linguistic study can profit the field in general.

Thus, charters continue to be steadily used alongside other sources for diverse historical linguistic studies on Latin. Italian charters have been recently utilized to scrutinize the protohistory of Italian plurals and possessive constructions[36], while the members of the *Passages du latin au français* (PaLaFra) project have conducted numerous studies on the morphology and syntax of Merovingian Latin charters[37]. Though perhaps with a slightly lower intensity, similar initiatives have been ongoing with Iberian charters[38]. The fundamental works on the Latin of early medieval charters of the Spanish and Portuguese territory appeared in the 1940s to 1950s[39], while a notable part of later scholarship on the theme seems to be focused on the phonology/spelling interface, probably as a reaction to the seminal thoughts proposed by Wright about the "invention" of the Romance languages following an alleged pronunciation reform[40].

3.2. Digital linguistic studies

This subsection first discusses the potential of digital methods for the linguistic research of Latin charters and then presents the achievements of such approaches to date.

Latin is a highly inflectional language with a notably free word order. The grammatical functions and other relations between words are primarily expressed through inflectional endings rather than the linear sequence of words. Moreover,

36 Vincenzo Faraoni, L'origine dei plurali italiani in -e e -i, Alessandria 2018; Cecilia Valentini, L'evoluzione della codifica del genitivo dal tipo sintetico al tipo analitico nelle carte del *Codice diplomatico longobardo*, Firenze 2018.

37 The PaLaFra project: https://palafra.github.io/en/description.html; for more details, see subsection 3.2.

38 See García Leal's numerous linguistic studies especially on Asturian charters, beginning from Alfonso García Leal, El latín de la diplomática asturleonesa (775–1032), Oviedo 1988.

39 Augustus Campbell Jennings, A Linguistic Study of the Cartulario of San Vicente de Oviedo, Phil. Diss. Columbia, New York 1940 (cf. what was said above about the American school of linguists); Juan Bastardas Parera, Particularidades sintácticas del latín medieval: cartularios españoles de los siglos VIII al XI, Barcelona 1953; Norman Paul Sacks, The Latinity of dated documents in the Portuguese territory, Philadelphia 1941.

40 Carmen Pensado, How was Leonese Vulgar Latin read?, in: Wright, Latin (as n. 8) p. 190–204; Thomas Walsh, Spelling lapses in early medieval Latin documents and the reconstruction of primitive Romance phonology, in: Wright, Latin (as n. 8) p. 205–218; Roger Wright, Late Latin and Early Romance in Spain and Carolingian France, Liverpool 1982.

Latin nominals display a high rate of homomorphism, which means that the same ending is used to encode more than one grammatical function (for example, the ending *-is* can be nominative singular, accusative plural, or genitive singular in the third declension and dative or ablative plural in the first and second declensions). Consequently, Latin raw text only lends itself to linguistic analysis to a limited extent, contrary to many scantily inflectional languages with strict word order, like English, which permits advanced syntactic analyses based on merely tokenized text. This is also the reason why pioneering Natural Language Processing (NLP) was so successful with English. With languages with free word order and occasionally homograph subject and object forms, NLP tools must be more robust.

Thus, most linguistic research on Latin requires the text to be parsed. This means understanding the lemma, the morphological analysis of each relevant word, and the word's relation to other words in the sentence. In traditional research, scholars carry out this parsing in their mind more or less explicitly, applying it to sentences they find representative of the phenomenon under examination. Such studies usually rest on a few to tens of relevant occurrences or, at any rate, some kind of slicing of all the available data[41]. For linguistic conclusions to be more broadly generalizable, they should be based on a substantial number of occurrences from extensive text collections. This approach is called corpus linguistics, and it is essentially computer-driven. The grammatical rules that govern the language in question are then derived from the corpus using appropriate queries to return all the occurrences that satisfy desired conditions. In the case of inflectional languages, a corpus also typically contains some kind of linguistic parsing in the form of annotations attached to each word or to a set of words; if the syntactic relations between words have been annotated, the corpus is known as a treebank[42].

Any digital linguistic approach to the Latin of medieval charters is bound to be corpus-linguistic in that it targets a large number of electronic charter texts at a time, and in the case of Latin, the annotation of at least some linguistic features is in practice necessary to tackle grammatical relations. While balanced corpora of diverse genres and registers can be compiled for modern languages to imitate real-life use, historical languages must most often do with what survives. Historical corpora can, thus, hardly be considered representative of the whole system of that language, but they can, nevertheless, reveal what is typical of a specific text type or genre at a certain point in time, and, with due caution, the results can sometimes be generalized to other contexts.

While Medieval Latin charters might seem ideal for corpus linguistics, their inherent formulaicity sets them apart from most other corpora. First, the formulae

41 For example, FIORENTINO, Aspetti (as n. 34) p. 33, which only examines the most frequent 38 nouns.

42 Anatol STEFANOWITSCH, Corpus linguistics: A guide to the methodology, Berlin 2020.

that occur in each or almost every charter are repeated hundreds or thousands of times depending on the number of charters in the corpus and, thus, cause a severe overrepresentation of certain grammatical features. Second, other grammatical features are completely or almost completely lacking if they are not present in the formulae. It is obvious that the heavy repetition can skew linguistic analyses if it is not properly accounted for. This means that charter corpora cannot be used for direct comparative studies with other corpora or to sketch a panorama of the linguistic categories of early medieval Latin, but they can shed light on specific grammatical constructions that happen to be frequent enough in them. In practice, formulaicity also precludes the normal use of conventional metrics of lexical or grammatical richness and productivity, such as Type/token ratio or Baayen's *P*, because they measure the variation of a specific linguistic feature as a function of time. The diachronic change of the formulae tends to hide the real diachronic linguistic change in charter corpora.

Moreover, charters contain abbreviations and, as they are original documents, even mistakes (haplographies, dittographies), which are rectified in edited texts. All these textual features are typically indicated in diplomatic editions, but how they should be dealt with in corpus linguistics is still a rather open question (however, see below for LLCT).

Currently, there are three major Latin charter corpora, all consisting of early medieval charters. The above-mentioned Neapolitan school's recent work is largely based on a corpus of the charters of Cava dei Tirreni, which was being lemmatized and lightly annotated morphologically in 2017 (for example, lemma: *venditio*, morph: feminine singular)[43]. Thus, the corpus has been used to extract words or their co-occurrences (separated by *n* words) that satisfy query criteria concerning their morphological analysis, lemma, and/or form (strings of characters matched by regular expressions), while the query results can be further restricted to specific date ranges, regions, and/or document types encoded as metadata in each charter. Thanks to an additional semantic annotation layer of juridical terms, the corpus also enables studies on the grammatical properties of legal lexicon[44], alongside of synthetic investigations into morphology and some syntactic features[45].

---

43 Elisa D'Argenio/Mariafrancesca Giuliani, Dalla raccolta documentaria al corpus elettronico, in: Sornicola/D'Argenio/Greco (ed.), Sistemi (as n. 33) p. 57–66.

44 Elisa D'Argenio, Note sul lessico giuridico della Cartula, in: Sornicola/D'Argenio/Greco (ed.), Sistemi (as n. 33) p. 335–364.

45 For example, verbal morphology in: Simona Valente, La morfologia verbale: un quadro d'insieme, in: Sornicola/D'Argenio/Greco (ed.), Sistemi (as n. 33) p. 135–174; phrasal complementation in: Paolo Greco, La complementazione frasale, in: Sornicola/D'Argenio/Greco (ed.), Sistemi (as n. 33) p. 267–310.

A Latin corpus with a more extensive morphological annotation is the PaLaFraLat[46], compiled at the universities of Regensburg and Tübingen within the PaLaFra project, mentioned in subsection 3.1. The PaLaFraLat corpus mostly consists of literary texts, but it also has a section of forty Merovingian and Arnulfing charters (13,798 words) prior to ca. 750, as well as eight formularies (66,670 words). The corpus has been used to study the transition from Late Latin to Old French in a diachronic perspective, and it is currently the only Latin corpus deliberately built of different genres and with the texts distributed over the time span as evenly as possible. The texts have been lemmatized, POS-tagged, and comprehensively annotated morphologically (with universal dependency morph tags) using automated lemmatizers and parsers, and subsequently corrected manually. Owing to its rich morphological annotation, the corpus has enabled detailed enquiries into the morphology and morphosyntax of Merovingian Latin, although scholars who primarily analysed syntactic features have resorted to additional manual annotation. Studies that exploit the charters and formularies of the PaLaFraLat corpus examine, among other issues, the passive periphrases and the morphosyntactic alignment in Merovingian Latin[47].

For the present, the only real treebank of early medieval charters is the Late Latin Charter Treebank (LLCT),[48] in which syntactic relations have been annotated according to dependency grammar. LLCT also features comprehensive morphological annotation, lemmatization, as well as a light semantic annotation of verb types, in addition to the metadata indicating date, scribe, place of writing, and document type for each of the 1,040 charters (483,752 tokens). Importantly, LLCT even contains a coarse diplomatic annotation that distinguishes between sentences belonging, in Sabatini's terms, to the formulaic and free parts. This has made studies that scrutinize the spoken-language origin of specific morphological and syntactic features possible[49]. The first part of the corpus, LLCT1, was mostly annotated manually, while the second part, LLCT2, was parsed using algorithms trained on

46 Lars Döhling/Rembert Eufe/Sebastian Ortner/Elisabeth Reichle/Maria Selig/Christian Wolff, PaLaFraLat (Version 2.0), Regensburg (https://txm-bfm.huma-num.fr/txm/).

47 Lieven Danckaert/Achim Stein, Passive periphrases from Latin to Romance, in: Bridging the gap between Late Latin and Early Old French: Empirical investigations to (morpho)syntactic changes, ed. Anne Carlier/Céline Guillot-Barbance/Lieven Danckaert/Jasper Vangaever/Maria Selig [in press]; Timo Korkiakangas, Morphosyntactic alignment in Merovingian Latin, in: Carlier/Guillot-Barbance/Danckaert/Vangaever/Selig (eds.), Bridging (as above).

48 Timo Korkiakangas, Late Latin Charter Treebank: Contents and annotation, in: Corpora 16 (2021) p. 191–203. The treebank is accessible online: LLCT1 at https://zenodo.org/record/1197357#.XucVkdrVJPY and LLCT2 at https://zenodo.org/record/3633614#.XucVv9r-VJPY.

49 For example, Korkiakangas, Spoken Latin (as n. 32).

LLCT1, except for the diplomatic annotation, which is fully manual[50]. LLCT also seriously addresses the problem of how to annotate a non-standard language variety that has no adequate language description or reference grammar. A solution was developed that reduces the evolved grammatical forms attested in charters to those ancient Latin categories they derive from following two principles: the evolutionary principle and the parsimony principle[51]. To enable contextualized linguistic analysis, LLCT integrates diplomatic information about abbreviations, haplographies, and dittographies, as well as the restorations of missing letters or lacunae of modest size into the annotation[52]. In this way, abbreviated and damaged inflectional endings can be excluded from statistical analyses, although the expanded and restored words appear in full in the dependency tree structures where they are necessarily needed. As a result, LLCT is currently the most diplomatically informed corpus of charter Latin.

4. Digital diplomatic import to linguistic studies on medieval Latin charters

The above history of the studies on the Latin of medieval charters shows that scholars aspire to empirically more and more robust research designs, which, consequently, are increasingly complex and based on larger datasets (corpora) than ever. At the same time, scholars have grown aware that such corpus-linguistic analyses must take the diplomatic and scriptural-historical context of charters into account. In this quest, digital diplomatics is likely to play an important role. In what follows, three fields of application will be discussed where the current and future advances of digital diplomatics are expected to most benefit Latin linguistics: accumulation of new charter data in high-quality electronic text, automated detection of metadata, and automated detection of diplomatic units of charters, including individual formulae.

As suggested in previous sections, the requirement of reliable corpus linguistics on charters is a digital diplomatic edition with all the abbreviations, restorations, and other relevant editorial mark-ups indicated in a machine-readable format. While the majority of early medieval Latin charters are already published in good

50 For the process, see Korkiakangas, Late Latin (as n. 48) p. 197–199.

51 Timo Korkiakangas, Theoretical and pragmatic considerations on the lemmatization of non-standard Early Medieval Latin charters, in: Studi e saggi linguistici 58 (2020) p. 67–94; Timo Korkiakangas/Marco Passarotti, Challenges in annotating Medieval Latin charters, in: Journal of Language Technology and Computational Linguistics 26 (2011) p. 103–114.

52 Timo Korkiakangas/Matti Lassila, Abbreviations, fragmentary words, formulaic language: Treebanking medieval charter material, in: Proceedings of The Third Workshop on Annotation of Corpora for Research in the Humanities (ACRH-3), ed. Francesco Mambrini/Marco Passarotti/Caroline Sporleder, Sofia 2013, p. 61–72.

editions and much has even been converted into electronic format, the need for digital editions for later medieval charters that reflect Latin as a second language is all the more urgent.

Various digital paleographical and diplomatic initiatives notably contribute to making previously inaccessible charters available as electronic text, either drawing on existing printed editions (often with almost error-free results) or directly on the digital images of previously unedited charters. In this way, more and more linguistic research scenarios reach the critical mass, so to speak, that makes them realizable. Indeed, the immense number of late medieval charters will hardly ever be transcribed and published in electronic text without Handwritten Text Recognition based on artificial intelligence. The results achieved using models trained in platforms like Transkribus look promising[53], although the huge diversity of scripts used in medieval charters diminishes the scalability of any single model. However, geographically and chronologically limited models, such as the Bentham and the Documents of Early England Data Set (DEEDS) projects' joint model for 13th to 15th-century Latin[54], yield low character error rates on validation data (1.7%). Moreover, a model called Medieval Scripts 2.4 does strive to establish a generic model for the Latin scripts of the Middle Ages based on an expanding set of charter and book hands transcribed within a variety of projects[55]. It can be expected with good reason that nearly zero-error recognition of regular chancery scripts or scripts of single prolific scribes will be possible in the future.

On the other hand, digital linguists emphasize the importance of small error rates because mistaken characters lead to cumulative errors in subsequent NLP tasks. While language-inspired historical studies can well accept Key Word Spotting or Named Entity Recognition within imperfectly recognized texts, corpus linguistics that aims at representativity is seriously degraded by approximate transcriptions. A seemingly excellent error rate of 1% means that a text of 10,000 characters contains 100 wrong characters; if each of them happens to be in an individual word, the linguistic parser may stumble 100 extra times compared to an error-free input, and each stumble is likely to provoke additional errors in parsing the dependents of that word, thus multiplying parsing errors[56]. For example, the performance of a specific Named Entity Recognition application drops from 90% to 60% when the word error rate of the text rises from 1% to 7%[57].

---

53 Transkribus: https://readcoop.eu

54 Transkribus model "UCL–University of Toronto #7", https://readcoop.eu/model/medieval-latin/

55 Tobias Hodel, Transkribus model "Medieval_Scripts_M2.4", https://readcoop.eu/model/charter-scripts-german-latin-french/

56 Thi Tuyet Hai Nguyen/Adam Jatowt/Mickael Coustaty/Antoine Doucet, Survey of Post-OCR Processing Approaches, in: ACM Computating Surveys 54 (2021), article 124.

57 Ahmed Hamdi/Axel Jean-Caurant/Nicolas Sidere/Mickaël Coustaty/Antoine Doucet,

Nevertheless, accurate machine transcriptions form a solid foundation for post-correction. Many OCR pipelines exploit large lexica of word forms attested in the target language as well as information about their relative frequencies arising from real corpora to improve token recognition or to post-correct the final output[58]. However, like any list-matching procedure, this kind of lexicon comparison task does not only correct errors, it also tends to normalize the real variation of the sources, such as non-standard spellings and human mistakes. Therefore, digital diplomatics, which is aware of the variation in documentary language, is bound to have a central role in compiling such lexica from well-checked existing editions and transcriptions. This lexical component of the OCR pipeline should also be built robust enough to cope with abbreviations and lacunae, as well as the editorial symbols indicating them and the restorations of the lacunae in the case of printed editions.

Another field of application regards the quantity and quality of the metadata assigned to each charter. Not only are newly transcribed charters useless without appropriate metadata, but the descriptive practices observed by many existing editions are also insufficient and poorly consistent with each other. While one can easily adopt the metadata structure used, for example, in the Monasterium.net archive[59], it is hard to extract all that information from huge masses of charters in a coherent way. Thus, there is a strong need for (re)generating, systematizing, and improving metadata for large charter corpora.

For linguistic studies, the most crucial pieces of contextual information in charters are the time and place of writing and the juridical type of the document. The identity of the scribe is also important in case it can be located in a socio-historical environment known from elsewhere. Often, the date and place can be close-read directly from the text, but, in certain areas and periods, charters were left undated. Moreover, localization is even more often challenging in default of reliable knowledge of medieval topography[60]. An already classic example of metadata detection concerning dates is the work done within the DEEDS project on undated English

An analysis of the performance of named entity recognition over OCRed documents, in: Proceedings of the 2019 ACM/IEEE Joint Conference on Digital Libraries, 2019, p. 333–334.

58 Hai Nguyen/Jatowt/Coustaty/Doucet, Survey (as n. 56) c. 3/II; Satria Priambada/Dwi Hendratmo Widyantoro, Levensthein distance as a post-process to improve the performance of OCR in written road signs, in: Second International Conference on Informatics and Computing (ICIC), 2017, p. 1–6. Lexicon-matching approaches are currently being increasingly enhanced with machine learning solutions: e.g., Chantal Amrhein/Simon Clematide, Supervised OCR Error Detection and Correction Using Statistical and Neural Machine Translation Methods, in: Journal for Language Technology and Computational Linguistics 33 (2018) p. 49–76; Aishik Rakshit/Samyak Mehta/Anirban Dasgupta, A Novel Pipeline for Improving Optical Character Recognition through Post-processing Using Natural Language Processing, in: IEEE GCON 2023 Conference Proceedings (arXiv:2307.04245).

59 The Monasterium.net collaborative archive: https://www.monasterium.net/mom/home

60 Rachel Stone, Building a charter database 3: places and their relationships, in: The Making

charters of the 10th to 14th centuries[61]. Due to the formulaicity of charters, statistical comparisons based on word bigrams with the few dated charters enabled the scholars to attribute a date to any charter from the period with an accuracy of seven years[62]. Similar text-based approaches can be used to estimate the place of writing or even the scribe.

Multi-genre corpora typically assign genres, also known as registers or text types, to each document included because the genre is one of the most important predictors associated with linguistic variation[63]. The automated genre classification of big datasets is currently a hot topic because of its applicability to various NLP tasks[64]. In charters, the contents and juridical-communicative function and, consequently, the language and its register vary from one document type to another. A casual memorandum, for example, differs strikingly from a land dispute, let alone from a royal diploma, as far as their vocabulary, style, and grammar are concerned. Likewise, the early medieval writers of humble rural exchange contracts usually had a lower educational level than the professional scribes active in key chanceries, a social distinction that can be perceived as sociolinguistic differences in various levels of language[65]. In the later Middle Ages, the associations between document type, educational background, and language change as a result of increasing professionalization, the rise of legal university education, and the growth of the notaryship.

Like date and place, the document type can usually be inferred from the tenor of the charter text by close reading, but, with thousands of charters, the task proves to be time-consuming. Another challenge is the fluidity of document types and their variation over time and place, which make it difficult to maintain consistency in classification. Here, digital tools can help considerably. Supervised and unsupervised document classification techniques abound, and the results of both closed-class and open-class categorization constantly improve. Traditional corpus linguistics prefers closed classes of genres, although such an approach does not do due justice to the variability of the data. A document-type classification helps in detecting grammatical differences in charters written for different purposes and po-

---

of Charlemagne's Europe blog (25 Oct 2014) https://charlemagneseurope.ac.uk/blog/building-a-charter-database-3-places-and-their-relationships/

61 The DEEDS project: https://deeds.library.utoronto.ca

62 Gelila Tilahun/Andrey Feuerverger/Michael Gervers, Dating medieval English charters, in: The Annals of Applied Statistics 6 (2012) p. 1615–1640.

63 Douglas Biber, Register as a predictor of linguistic variation, in: Corpus linguistics and linguistic theory 8 (2012) p. 9–37.

64 For example, Veronika Laippala/Samuel Rönnqvist/Miika Oinonen/Aki-Juhani Kyröläinen/Anna Salmela/Douglas Biber/Jesse Egbert/Sampo Pyysalo, Register identification from the unrestricted open Web using the Corpus of Online Registers of English, in: Language Resources and Evaluation (2022).

65 Cf. Timo Korkiakangas, Spelling correctness as a witness of changing documentary culture in Tuscia (VIII–IX centuries), in: Early Medieval Europe 31 (2023) p. 220–251.

tentially by different scribes and, alternatively, in targeting linguistic queries to text types considered optimal for the research task at hand.

The chronological and geographical location of a charter can also be approached multimodally: it is not only reflected by the wording of its formulae, but also by its visual elements, including the general layout, the script, and graphical symbols, such as the papal rota or various personal signs of scribes. Therefore, the groupings of documents achieved by computer vision techniques may be indicative of their common provenance. Document image classification comes close to some digital paleographic and computer vision approaches. As of yet, they have been applied to medieval charters to detect illuminated items, layout types[66], as well as graphic symbols and signs[67].

Thirdly, a specific desideratum of linguistic research is the automated detection of diplomatic parts within a charter. As was emphasized above, the distinction between formulaic and non-formulaic text is important for the interpretation of the results of linguistic analyses. In LLCT, which is the only corpus with this distinction encoded so far, the formulaic and non-formulaic parts were annotated manually. A rough dichotomous annotation of limited new datasets is straightforward using standard parsers trained on manually annotated training sets of the same data type, and this is what is being currently done for the extension of the LLCT treebank, LLCT3[68].

On a big-data level, a dichotomous formulaicity annotation might be simply achieved by dividing the n-grams created from the charter corpus into those that surpass a certain threshold frequency and to those that fall below it. The n-grams or continuous sequences thereof that surpass the threshold would then be taken as "formulaic" and the rest as "non-formulaic" passages. Of course, a continuous, stepless formulaicity value might also be useful in statistical linguistic analyses. This kind of approach is, however, complicated by spelling variation, so the analysis should be based on lemmatization at least with word n-grams. More critically, simple thresholds run the risk of oversimplification because some evidently formulaic phrases are infrequent; they may have been borrowed from foreign documentary traditions

66 Vincent Christlein, Automatic Detection of Illuminated Charters, in: Illuminierte Urkunden: Beiträge aus Diplomatik, Kunstgeschichte und Digital Humanities (AfD Beiheft 16), ed. Gabriele Bartz/Markus Gneiss, Köln 2018, p. 45–52; Vincent Christlein/Martin Gropp/Andreas Maier, Technical Tools for the Analysis of High Medieval Papal Charters, in: Papstgeschichte im Digitalen Zeitalter: Neue Zugangsweisen zu einer Kulturgeschichte Europas, ed. Klaus Herbers/Viktoria Trenkle, Köln 2018, p. 45–53.

67 Zahra Ziran/Eleonora Bernasconi/Antonella Ghignoli/Francesco Leotta/Massimo Mecella, Accurate Graphic Symbol Detection in Ancient Document Digital Reproductions, in: Document Analysis and Recognition – ICDAR 2021 Workshops, ed. Elisa H. Barney Smith/Umapada Pal, Cham 2021, p. 147–162.

68 Korkiakangas, Late Latin (as n. 48) p. 199.

and occur, therefore, only once or twice in a given corpus. On the other hand, all repetitive sequences are not formulaic. A certain authority may have issued several charters concerning, say, farmhouses within the same geographical area. Although the name and the title of the authority, the farmhouse, and the toponyms may occur thousands of times within a corpus, they are not formulaic, but represent blanks in the formula. Thus, the results of n-gram-based identification of formulaicity should ideally be disambiguated by scholarly judgement[69]. A further issue is the linguistic variation between the instances of one and the same formula (see below).

The automated detection of more granular diplomatic parts or even individual formulae might also be potentially useful for linguists. Grammatical differences between diplomatic units may reveal differences in their origin and intended function. On the other hand, the variation in formulae always reflects political, administrative, cultural, intellectual, and even personal connections between chanceries or groups of scribes. Such information on the descendancy of specific formulae might help in managing the highly disparate linguistic matter in charter corpora that derives from different textual registers, geographical contexts, and language-evolutionary stages.

A few digital diplomatic projects have successfully detected diplomatic sections within relatively homogeneous datasets, such as royal diplomas[70], while the extraction of individual formulae in large and varied corpora still seems to pose major theoretical and methodological problems. The extraction of formulae from diverse datasets is bound to be inaccurate in the absence of cost-effective ways to tackle the above-mentioned inequation between repetitiveness and formulaicity as well as the linguistic variation of individual realizations of the same formulae. Medieval documentary formulae are difficult to define in linguistic terms because the formulae which are used interchangeably and appear to be factually identical permit notable variation in their vocabulary, word order, and other grammatical structure[71]. A significant part of this variation is likely to result from the formulae being reproduced

69 An attempt to quantify medieval Latin charter formulae as human-readable text reuse templates, which can be used to disambiguate instances identified by n-gram methods, is described in: Timo Korkiakangas, Documentary formulae as text reuse templates: *constat* and *manifestus* clauses in early medieval Latin charters, in: Digital Medievalist 16 (2023) p. 1–44.

70 Alina Ostrowski, Automatische Erkennung und Klassifikation von Formularbestandteilen in Königsurkunden: Zur Aufbereitung digitaler Urkundenkorpora in der Mediävistik, in: Die Historischen Grundwissenschaften heute, ed. Étienne Doublier/Daniela Schulz/Dominik Trump, Wien 2021, p. 139–166; Petra Galuščáková/Lucie Neužilová, Low Resource Methods for Medieval Document Sections Analysis, in: Proceedings of the Eleventh International Conference on Language Resources and Evaluation (LREC 2018), 2018, p. 2344–2348.

71 Cf. Michael Gervers, The Dating of Medieval English Private Charters of the Twelfth and Thirteenth Centuries, in: A Distinct Voice: Medieval Studies in Honor of Leonard E. Boyle, ed. Jacqueline Brown/William Stoneman, Notre Dame 1997, p. 455–480; Korkiakangas, Documentary formulae (as n. 69).

partly from memory, partly from physical models[72]. The problems resulting from the varying word order of formula instances can be alleviated by applying skip-grams instead of linear n-grams, although this will concomitantly decrease precision. Novel insights into formula detection that are even likely to deal with lexical and other grammatical variation can be expected from recent initiatives, such as a project of the Deutsche Forschungsgemeinschaft that is going to exploit both supervised string-matching techniques and Text Reuse Detection applications, such as Tracer, to extract repertoires of formulae and their variants used in 12th-century papal charters[73].

5. Conclusions

This paper first sketched a review on how medieval Latin charters have been used as a source of historical linguistic research. After that, it discussed what kind of prospects digital diplomatic advances have opened and will possibly open up for such research.

It became clear that charters have been amply utilized especially by linguistic studies that focus on the transition from Latin to the Romance languages. Charters are, indeed, a privileged source since they survive as originals from a period from which relatively little linguistic evidence remains. Moreover, their language is non-literary unlike most other Latin texts. Therefore, literary devices are largely absent, which leaves room for the influence of the spoken language. On the other hand, the very formulaicity of charters limits the possibilities how they can be used for linguistic analyses: the language of the most formulaic parts must be approached differently from that of the less formulaic parts.

Over the last decades, the average number of charters considered in single studies appears to have augmented, and accordingly the research designs have become increasingly complex. As a consequence of such a development, more and more research questions are operationalized within a corpus-linguistic framework. At the same time, scholars have grown to recognize the importance of the diplomatic and scriptural-historical context of charters.

The present paper argues that digital diplomatics plays a key role in reconciling such contextual diplomatic information about charters with corpus-based Latin

72 Timo Korkiakangas, From memory or formulary: How were medieval documentary formulae reproduced? in: Mirator 22 (2022) p. 4–24.

73 The Delegierte Gerichtsbarkeit auf der Iberischen Halbinsel im 12. Jahrhundert: Struktur und computergestützte Analyse eines urkundlichen Massenkorpus project: https://gepris.dfg.de/gepris/projekt/495959196?context=projekt&task=showDetail&id=495959196&. Tracer is a set of 700 algorithms that enables Text Reuse Detection sensitive to lexical variation in terms of user-customized and wordnet-based synonym lists: https://www.etrap.eu/research/tracer/.

linguistics. The first steps have been taken when various types of diplomatic and scriptural-historical information have been integrated into charter corpora, as is the case of the charters of Cava dei Tirreni and LLCT. It would be desirable to extend similar or more advanced practices to other corpora of medieval documents. The most urgent task is perhaps to enrich the linguistic annotation with an unequivocal encoding of those editorial interventions that affect the reading of the text, such as the expansion of abbreviations and the restoration of characters missing for various reasons.

Although most potential of digital diplomatics for Latin corpus linguistics still lies ahead, it is possible to anticipate some major lines. First of all, digital diplomatic methods, alongside digital paleography, can contribute to accumulating new charter data for linguistic study. In practice, this means mass digitization of previously inaccessible charters into machine-readable texts. Though the simple enhancement of the number of available charters may sound banal, it is important because coherent and large enough bodies of charters of the same document type, period, and geographical area are needed for reliable statistical research designs to be possible.

Digital diplomatic applications can also be used to extract metadata within large charter corpora. Methods for approximating date and place for undated and unlocated charters have already been applied with particularly good results for dates, but for corpus-linguistic studies of charters, the document type would be equally important. General document classification approaches could be adjusted to group charters of a similar juridical content into predefined categories or machine-generated clusters. Also, the similar visual layouts of the charters written in the same place during the same period and/or representing the same document type might be detected by computer vision techniques.

Finally, linguistic research would benefit from the automated detection of the diplomatic parts of charters. While a dichotomous distinction between, in Sabatini's terms, clearly formulaic and free matter is also likely to be sufficient for most linguistic studies in the future, a better understanding of the grammatical differences between individual formulae would help in estimating how charters' different textual registers affect corpus-linguistic research.

Reflections on charter redaction

An assessment of a stylometric approach in studying the Cambrai bishop's diplomatic landscape (12th c.)

Eveline Leclercq

In recent years, a tendency to digitisation and digitalisation has raised questions about how the 'traditional' methodological approaches of palaeography and the comparison of formulas may be translated into a digital approach[1]. Hence, a plethora of digital source corpora and tools has seen the light[2]. So far, the diplomatics field seems to get past the first steps to full digitisation, addressing first and foremost the problems of how, where and in what capacity the sources can be disclosed and published, and then studied. The use of computational tools and statistics seems to slowly find its way into diplomatics research, even though the traditional methods remain valuable in their expertise and are still widely used to analyse the medieval written production of various redactional milieus[3]. Currently, we are in

---

1 Rik HOEKSTRA/Marijn KOOLEN/Sebastiaan DERKS, et al., Methodologische vernieuwing en bronnenkritiek in het digitale tijdperk – 2018–2023, URL: https://www.academia.edu/36933241/Methodologische_vernieuwing_en_bronnenkritiek_in_het_digitale_tijdperk?email_work_card=title.

2 It is not possible to provide an exhaustive list of all the tools and possibilities available today for the diplomatist in a footnote. A few examples concern *Diplomata Belgica*, *monasterium.net*, *DEEDS* and *Chartae Galliae* for the online databases and *Transkribus* and *DigiPal* for the Palaeography. The recent conference "Actes à l'infini, des bases de données infinies ? Exploitation des données – Interopérabilité – Convergences", Luxemburg University, 17–18 February 2022, offered an overview of limits and possibilities for the diplomatist.

3 Bernhard BISCHOFF, Latin Palaeography: Antiquity and Middle Ages, Cambridge 1990; Olivier GUYOTJEANNIN/Jacques PYCKE/Benoît-Michel TOCK, Diplomatique médiévale (L'atelier du médiéviste 2), Turnhout/Paris 1993; James DRISCOLL/Elena PIERAZZO, Digital Scholarly Editing. Theories and Practices (Digital Humanities Series), Cambridge 2016; Nicolas PERREAUX, L'écriture du monde (I), Les chartes et les édifices comme vecteurs de la dynamique sociale dans l'Europe médiévale (VIIe–milieu du XIVe siècle), in: Bulletin du centre d'études médiévales Auxerre 19/2 (2015) ; ID., L'écriture du monde (II). L'écriture comme facteur de régionalisation

a pioneer yet chaotic phase, encountering various questions and problems while seeking solutions; to what extent are computational methods of use to the diplomatist? What challenges do diplomatists face in making these methods their own? How should the existing computational approaches be adapted to be used in the study of charters?

This article wishes to offer a reflection on (part of) these questions, by way of analysing the case of the Cambrai chancery, which is the subject of an ongoing study using stylometric methods on a charter corpus. 'Stylometric methods' as such is a very broad term, underlining the wide array available to the researcher. These various computer methods are aimed at the comparison of generally literary texts to determine their intellectual author, or to compare contested authorship in literary production. In recent years, these methods have started to find their way into medieval studies, in particular those pertaining to medieval literature and Latin philology[4]. Within the context of a Ph.D. study it was interesting to see if some of these methods could be of help to analyse a radically different type of text: administration[5].

The case of the Cambrai chancery was promising, as this is a particularly well organised chancery in an important diocese. The diocese of Cambrai formed a unity with the Arras diocese until 1192/93[6], both situated within the ecclesiastical province of Reims, and was flanked by the dioceses of Reims, Laon, Noyon, Amiens, Tournai and Thérouanne, with the Liège diocese at its right side. Cambrai was con-

---

et despiritualisation du mundus : études lexicales et sémantiques, in: Bulletin du centre d'études médiévales Auxerre 20/1 (2016).

4 Mike Kestemont in particular has adapted these methods to mediaeval literary texts: Mike KESTEMONT/Karina VAN DALEN-OSKAM, Predicting the Past: Memory-Based Copyist and Author Discrimination in Medieval Epics, in: Proceedings of the twenty-first Benelux conference on artificial intelligence (BNAIC 2009); Mike KESTEMONT, Stylometry for Medieval Authorship Studies. An Application to Rhyme Words, in: Digital Philology: A Journal of Medieval Cultures, 1/1 (2012) p. 42–72. ID., What Can Stylometry Learn From Its Application to Middle Dutch Literature?, in: Journal of Dutch Literature, 2/2 (2011). Mike KESTEMONT/Sara MOENS/Jeroen DEPLOIGE, Stylometry and the Complex Authorship on Hildegard of Bingen's Œuvre, in: Digital Humanities 2013. Conference Abstracts p. 255–258.

5 Eveline LECLERCQ, L'élaboration des chartes médiévales. L'exemple des évêchés d'Arras, Cambrai et Liège (XIe–XIIe siècles), 2 vols., unpublished Ph.D. dissertation, Université de Strasbourg 2019, 438+304 p.

6 Eveline LECLERCQ, L'élaboration p. 40 ; Nicolas RUFFINI, Église et aristocratie en Cambrésis (fin IXe-milieu XIIe siècle). Le pouvoir entre France et Empire au Moyen Âge central, unpublished Ph.D. dissertation, Université de Namur 2014, p. 296–333. Bernard DELMAIRE, Le diocèse d'Arras de 1093 au milieu du XIVe siècle. Recherches sur la *vie religieuse dans le nord de la France au Moyen Âge (Mémoires de la Commission départementale d'histoire et d'archéologie du Pas-de-Calais,* tome XXXI), 2 vols., Arras 1994, p. 39–60.

sidered the most western pillar of the *Reichskirche*[7]. Politically speaking, Cambrai spreads out over the territories of the Holy Roman Empire, the Cateau-Cambrésis region as well as parts of the County of Hainaut, the Duchy of Brabant and the Duchy of Basse-Lotharingie, bordering of the County of Flanders and the Crown lands of France. As such, the Cambrai bishop held a key position, in particular during the Investiture Controversy[8].

Its chancery is considered to be established in 1057 under the auspices of bishop Liébert, when he introduced the first episcopal seal and the first mention of a chancellor can be found[9]. By the twelfth century, this writing office flourished under the guidance of chancellor Werinbold III (1101–1155?)[10]. This chancellor dominated the chancery with his writing style, bringing the writing office together in a coherent and rather strict *dictamen* model. Literal references to the *Ecclesiasticus* in particular are introduced during his regime. Throughout the second half of the twelfth century, one can distinguish a strong continuation of many formulas introduced by Werinbold III even until the end of the 12th c., while allowing for the emergence of new phrases[11].

In fact, when it comes to the conservation of its sources, the Cambrai chancery offers a corpus of a decent size. Erik van Mingroot, in his study of the chancery, analysed 254 episcopal charters[12]. Nathalie Barré, in her comparison of the bishop's charters and the cathedral chapter charters, counted close to 800 episcopal charters for the whole of the 12th c.[13] During my own Ph.D., aimed at completing the lacunas in the research, I closely studied 347 charters of which the text was availa-

---

7 Eveline Leclercq, L'élaboration, p. 38. Michel Parisse/Jacqueline Leuridan, Atlas de la France de l'an mil. État de nos connaissances, Paris 1994, p. 17.

8 Eveline Leclercq, L'élaboration, p. 40. Nicolas Ruffini, Église et aristocratie en Cambrésis (fin IXe-milieu XIIe siècle) p. 296–333.

9 Erik Van Mingroot, Les chartes de Gérard Ier, Liébert et Gérard II, évêques de Cambrai et d'Arras, comtes du Cambrésis (1012-1092/93), Louvain 2005, p. 14–15.

10 Eveline Leclercq, Werinbold III : une influence partagée entre le chapitre cathédral et la chancellerie épiscopale à Cambrai (première moitié du XIIe s.) in : Écrire à l'ombre des cathédrales. Pratiques de l'écrit en milieu cathédral (espace anglo-normand et france de l'ouest, XIe-XIIIe siècle). Actes de colloque, ed. Grégory Combalbert/Chantal Senseby, Rennes [forthcoming].

11 Eveline Leclercq, L'élaboration p. 243–270.

12 Erik Van Mingroot, Acten der bisschoppen van Kamerijk (642-1103). Inventaris en diplomatische studie, unpublished Master's dissertation, Katholieke Universiteit Leuven 1959; Erik Van Mingroot, *De Bisschoppelijke Kanselarij te Kamerijk 1057–1130*, unpublished Ph.D. dissertation, Katholieke Universiteit Leuven 1969; Erik Van Mingroot, Les chartes de Gérard Ier, Liébert et Gérard II, évêques de Cambrai et d'Arras, comtes du Cambrésis (1012-1092/93), introduction, édition, annotation (Mediaevalia Lovaniensia 1: Studia), Leuven 2005.

13 Nathalie Barré, Chancellerie épiscopale, chancellerie canoniale : unicité ou pluralité des institutions à Cambrai au XIIe siècle?, in: Bulletin de la Commission royale d'Histoire 176/2 (2010) p. 129–146.

ble[14]. 245 of these were originals. For 149 of those originals, I have distinguished 21 hands[15]. No other type of 12th c. administrative document of the Cambrai chancery has survived to this day: no accounts or personnel lists are available to us.

The method used here, which was presented last year in a joint chapter with Mike Kestemont, remains unchanged through all of the current tests[16]. For the purpose of clarity and in order to value the method and its implications, it will be explained in five steps. For those who then wish to test it themselves, the code is freely available in a Zenodo link[17]. It is important to note that this method has currently been exclusively adapted to and applied to charter texts. The limited length of these texts provided a first challenge to general stylometric practices[18]. As such, the code has been specifically developed for the use with charters, since earlier stylometric studies have successfully analysed short texts[19].

The first step embodies building the corpus, first and foremost containing the episcopal chancery charters. As for stylometric research it is interesting to have contrasting charters to differentiate between these seemingly similar texts, due to their formulaic nature, the network around the bishop is taken into account. This includes charters coming from the cathedral chapter, as well as the beneficiaries of the episcopal charters. These are adjacent authorities such as other bishops, the pope, local institutions, lords, ladies and cities implied in the beneficiaries' charters. For each test, the corpus size varied, due to the period considered and these additional 'network' charters, all of which had to be collected in a short time. The *Diplomata*

14 Eveline LECLERCQ, L'élaboration p. 205–316.

15 Ibid. p. 89–156.

16 Eveline LECLERCQ/Mike KESTEMONT, Advances in Distant Diplomatics: A Stylometric Approach to Medieval Charter, in: Interfaces. A Journal of Medieval European Literatures 8 (2021) p. 214–244. URL: https://riviste.unimi.it/interfaces/article/view/14201.

17 DOI 10.5281/zenodo.5548217 and URL: https://doi.org/10.5281/zeno-do.5548217. This code was developed by Prof. Dr. Mike Kestemont of the University of Antwerp, who developed a very user-friendly code, useable by diplomatists who are not computer specialists.

18 Kim LUYCKX/Walter DAELEMANS, The Effect of Author Set Size and Data Size in Authorship Attribution, in: Literary & Linguistic Computing 25 (2010) p. 35–55; Moshe KOPPEL/Jonathan SCHLER/Argamon SHLOMO, Authorship Attribution in the Wild, in: Language Resources and Evaluation 45/1 (2011) p. 83–94.

19 Graeme HIRST/Olga FEIGUINA, Bigrams of Syntactic Labels for Authorship Discrimination of Short Texts, in: Literary and Linguistic Computing 22/4 (2007) p. 405–417; Joachim DIEDERICH/Jörg KINDERMANN/Edda LEOPOLD/Gerhard PAASS, Authorship Attribution with Support Vector Machines, in: Applied Intelligence 19/1 (2003) p. 109–123; Conrad SANDERSON/Simon GUENTER, Short Text Authorship via Sequence Kernels, Markov Chains and Author Unmasking: An Investigation, in: Conference on Empirival Methods in Natural Language Processing (Caussier 2006), University of Technology, Sydney, Australia, 22–23 July 2006, ed. Dan JURAFSKY/Eric CAUSSIER, Sydney 2006, p. 482–491.

Belgica[20] and the *Chartae Galliae*[21] databases proved to be crucial in doing this. These databases also offered the metadata to apply the code.

After composing the corpus by collecting the charter texts out of paper and digital editions or databases, the second step concerns the pre-processing of the corpus. Charter texts are not without variation, which posed the second challenge for this case. The easiest solution at this point was to separately encode and pre-process each text. In one large 'corpus' file, each text is encoded in UTF-8-format as a separate .txt document and given a unique identifier. In each charter text, the presence of text sections such as the *protocol*, the *dispositio* and the *eschatocol* is then marked using an *ad hoc* tagging scheme. In practice this step demands the most time as it is still done manually, since the charter texts can show a lot of variation. The tag "*dispositio*", containing the preamble, *narratio*, *dispositio*, *corroboratio*, *sanctio* and the announcement of the witnesses (*testes*), receives the most attention during analysis. These sections would in theory – as developed by Walter Prevenier[22] – be less formulaic and thus reveal more personal stylistic traits. In that same vein, named entities have been masked with the method of Stamatatos[23]. This counterbalances the weight these names, which are not specific to a chancery *dictamen*, would represent in the analysis. Finally, the entire *dispositio* has been lowercased and punctuation has been removed.

While collecting and pre-processing the individual texts, a separate spreadsheet containing charter specific metadata is prepared. Every charter receives the same unique identifier as its corresponding .txt-file so they can be matched. This step is still rather manual as well in the current testcase, as we build on the metadata recorded in existing editions and ideally, in online databases. Each piece of information, such as the date, issuer, beneficiary, subject, etc. was manually copied per charter into the spreadsheet. Extracting this information directly from the databases would automate the process further, which would ideally exclude human error and increase accuracy and efficiency. The metadata allows for reading and interpreting the visualized text map – otherwise we'd be left with a random looking collection of dots. It is possible to assign a number to a group of charters by choice, which will then show up in a different colour in the visualisation, allowing to highlight a group of charters in the whole.

---

20 Diplomata Belgica. The Diplomatic Sources from the Medieval Southern Low Countries, ed. Thérèse De Hemptinne/Jeroen Deploige/Jean-Louis Kupper/Walter Prevenier, Brussels: Royal Historical Commission, since 2015. URL: www.diplomata-belgica.be.

21 *Chartae Galliae.* URL: telma-chartes.irht.cnrs.fr.

22 Walter Prevenier, Oorkonden der graven van Vlaanderen (1191– aanvang 1206), Bruxelles 1964, p. 1–31.

23 Efstathios Stamatatos, Masking Topic-related Information to Enhance Authorship Attribution, in: Journal of the Association for Information Science and Technology 69/3 (2018) p. 461–473.

Thirdly, the analysis by the computer is conducted. For this, the code relies on a bag-of-words model, in which the frequencies of each word in each charter are measured within the encoded corpus. In this way, the method allows for a more objective view in which *all* words of the *dispositio* can be studied rather than certain formulas, chosen word groups or 'significant phrases' as is done in more manual dictamen analyses. Each charter is thus represented as a list of frequency values called 'a document vector'. These numbers are then scaled with TF-IDF normalization (term frequency-inverse document frequency). A relatively higher weight is given to terms that are relatively less frequent in the corpus, and thus more document-specific. The use of a bag-of-words model is limited to the 1,000 words of all kinds that have the highest frequency across the entire corpus. This model remains a useful tool however until more advanced techniques, such as sentence embedders, become sufficiently developed for medieval languages.

Using the Euclidean distance, the distance between each combination of two charters is then calculated and put in a square distance matrix. Hence, two more similar texts will show a smaller geometrical distance than two more differing texts. Here we encounter a limitation of the method of stylometry for charters. As we most often have no 'ground truth', that is, knowing with certainty what charter has been written by which clerk, this system is not optimal. Mike Kestemont has applied well-established parameters within the field. Therefore, the future testing of this method, with well-researched charters and more 'ground truths', is an important next step in assessing the method.

Finally, these distances are visualized in the fourth step with t-SNE (t-distributed Stochastic Neighbor Embedding)[24]. A scatterplot – here also named 'charter map' - is produced in which each charter is represented by a coloured dot[25]. The metadata of every dot becomes visible when hovering over it with the cursor. Charters with a similar stylistic profile can be expected to end up in the same region in the plot.

These four steps produced an automatic reading of the entire charter text by the computer code, presented in a visualised charter map. Step five of our method entails a close reading of the *dictamen* based on this charter map. For this test case, said close reading could be completed by the information gathered up front in a more 'classic' approach of comparing the charter text formulas in a *dictamen* study based on Els De Paermentiers' method, which takes the use of online databases into

24 Laurens Van der Maaten/Geoffrey Hinton, Visualizing Data using t-SNE, in: Journal of Machine Learning Research 9 (2008) p. 2579–2605.

25 In this example the blue dots represent the episcopal charters of Cambrai. The turquoise dots pertain to episcopal charters of other dioceses present in the corpus. Green dots refer to charters issued by the counts of Flanders. Finally, the pink dots point to papal charters.

Fig. 1: The visualisation of the Cambrai charters 1131–1200.

account[26]. These additional data facilitated determining the reasons for any clustering – in most cases however still no easy task. This step underlines once more the importance of gathering metadata: they allowed for an easier overview of the clusters, in particular for the charters not studied in detail during the *dictamen* study.

Even in this more traditional approach of the charter *dictamen*, automatization was an option by the use of a text reuse detection algorithm, based on the Python text-matcher package developed by Jonathan Reeve[27]. As the package has been developed for modern English-language text, adapting this for Medieval Latin is high on the priority list of fine-tuning the method. Enrique Manjavacas and Lauren Fonteyn currently focus on studying historical languages with digital tools[28]. The results of the text reuse detection are saved as separate documents which show the shared formulas between pairs of charters in a tabular format. In this example, the blue squares and the green squares show the two texts being compared, while the red squares highlight the matches.

One could easily search these files by typing in words and partial phrases in the search bar of the file where the results are saved. This led to a semi-automated approach in studying the texts up close, which in turn saves time when checking if a formula is significant within a set corpus or not.

26 For a more detailed explanation of this particular method, see: Els De Paermentier, Schrift in dienst van de macht. De grafelijke kanselarij in Vlaanderen en Henegouwen (1191–1244), Hilversum 2021, p. 66–87.

27 Jonathan Reeve, Text-Matcher: A simple text reuse detection CLI tool; https://github.com/JonathanReeve/text-matcherGitHub

28 Enrique Manjavacas/Lauren Fonteyn, Adapting vs. Pre-training Language Models for Historical Languages, in: Journal Of Data Mining & Digital Humanities (2022) p. 1–19.

left context	match	right context
udo nos ammonet ut eos propensius confouere et promouere studeamus qui religiose conuersationis propositum sectari satagunt et amplecti inde est quod	dilectis in christo filiis xxxxxx et sociis eius religionis habitum	in ecclesia sanctÄ™ xxxxx in pratis per dei inspirationem et institutionem consilii nostri suscipientibus eorum que sucessoribus altare sancti saluato
am eos precipue plenius confouere cohortari et adiuuare tenemur qui sanctÄ™ conuersationis iter artum et arduum amplecti et tenere ordiuntur propterea	dilectis in christo filiis xxxxxx et sociis eius religionis habitum	secundum ordinem et institutiones Ä™cclesiÄ™ sancti xxxxxxx xxxxxxxxx assumere proponentibus terram illam quÄ™ est inter ecclesiam sancti saluatoris

Fig. 2: Tabular result of Text Reuse Detection.

As of today, two major cases have been subjected to the code. The first one was firmly based within my Ph.D. research and is the subject of the joint article with Mike Kestemont[29]. We worked with a corpus of 545 charters consisting of firstly the episcopal texts and secondly, the texts produced for and by the 23 institutions or persons who appeared as beneficiaries in the episcopal charters. The goal was to discover if stylometric methods could use the texts by the scribe and dictator we named "RogF/JeanE" as ground truth. During the initial *dictamen* analysis the products of this scribe had already been determined using the specific phrase *commitimus...memoriali*[30]. Indeed, the software regrouped the charters by this scribe in a satisfying way, and we even managed to add charters to the list of texts he supposedly conceived of – even without *commitimus memoriali* in the text. As such, the method offered additional arguments to the search for the person responsible of a charter's production.

Following up on this first successful test case, a larger test of the Cambrai charters was envisioned for the occasion of the 'Formule au Moyen Âge V' conference held in 2020/2021[31].

Two questions were brought into focus: could the method serve even without the ground truth of RogF/JeanE, and what is the ideal corpus size for such research? This test case was less of a study of one particular dictator/scribe and more a large corpus in which the use of various methods and multiple revisions were possible. As such, an initial corpus of 4036 charters was encoded, corresponding to the twenty-one currently determined scribal hands which were active in the service of the bishops of Cambrai from 1131 to 1200. The initial results were less than stellar.

29 Eveline Leclercq/Mike Kestemont, Advances in Distant Diplomatics p. 214–244.

30 Eveline Leclercq, L'élaboration p. 311–315.

31 The detailed analysis of this test is described in the forthcoming article: Eveline Leclercq, L'usage personnel de formules dans une chancellerie: une tentative de dévoiler les rédacteurs individuels par l'analyse stylométrique des chartes épiscopales de Cambrai (1131–1200), in: La Formule au Moyen Âge V (in print).

Not only was the visualisation enormous and was any overview lost, the RogF/JeanE charters were dispersed over most of the scatterplot. The details of the first test case were lost in a too wide array of formulas spread over a research period of sixty-nine years.

A new starting point was needed. As the case of RogF/JeanA studied an example of a dictator and scribe being the same person, this idea could be expanded upon for the new test case. After all, dictator and scribe being the same person is certainly a possibility, a result found in multiple researchers' diplomatic research[32]. As such, the scribe dubbed "NicF/AlaA" (1142–1175) was a good candidate, as some indications of his work as a charter dictator were available from the preliminary research[33]. The initial corpus was scaled down from 4036 charters to 2153 texts, by leaving out the charters issued by higher authorities than the bishop, for example the pope, kings and emperors. This lead to a corpus spread over a period of forty-one years, in which eleven chancery hands were active under the three bishops Nicolas the 1st (1137–1167), Pierre the 1st of Alsace (1167–1173) and Alard (1175–1178). Alas, in this case the close reading *dictamen* study with the support of *text reuse detection* did not clearly reveal NicF/AlaA as the dictator of the charters of his hand. In analysing the charters by other identified chancery hands in that same corpus, the ones known as "NicI" (1155–1159) and "NicH" (1154–1162) lead to a few arguments considering the *dictamen* of certain groups of charters but nothing conclusive was found on their activity as the dictators of these pieces. It is currently unclear to what degree the results for these three scribes are due to them not being the dictators of the charters of their hand, or due to a limit of the method.

Fortunately, there was another option to investigate the possibilities of stylometry for the diplomatist during this second large test. The preliminary *dictamen* research had already revealed a palaeographic and stylistic link between a group of twelve episcopal charters and those issued by the lords of Oisy, a local aristocratic family[34]. Benoît-Michel Tock firstly remarked upon this connection in his edition of the charters connected to the abbey of Vaucelles, which is a foundation by the

32 The idea of dictator and scribe as the same person is thusly included in the definition by Cárcel Ortí: "(lat.: scriba, scriptor) est celui qui écrit matériellement une pièce. Il peut en être aussi le rédacteur. On dit aussi écrivain. Il peut aussi en être le notaire." Maria Milagros Cárcel Ortí, n° 274 : « le scribe », [en ligne] *Vocabulaire international de la diplomatique*. URL : http://www.cei.lmu.de/VID/?282. For Cambrai in particular Erik Van Mingroot considers most of the scribes as the dictators of the pieces they put in writing. Van Mingroot, *De Bisschoppelijke Kanselarij* p. 714–736.

33 Eveline Leclercq, L'élaboration p. 97 and 112–114. Nicolas Huyghebaert, Quelques chartes épiscopales fausses pour Saint-Pierre au Mont Blandin à Gand forgées aux XIIe et XIIIe siècles, in: Bulletin de la Commission royale d'Histoire 148 (1982) p. 31–37.

34 Eveline Leclercq, L'élaboration p. 291–295.

lords of Oisy[35]. The corpus of the second test was scaled down a second time, to a group of 513 charters dated from 1131 to 1200. These texts were issued by the bishops of Cambrai, by the Cambrai chapters of Notre-Dame, Saint-Aubert, Saint-Géry, Saint-Lazare and Saint-Sépulcre, by the local lords Adam 1st of Walincourt, Simon of Oisy and Hugues III of Oisy, as well as the Vaucelles charters. Higher authorities were omitted once again, to bring the focus to the local playing field. The goal of this case was to learn more about a possible service rendered to local elite by the episcopal chancery. This study lead to other examples in which chancery hands or stylistic links could be found in the charters issued by the Oisy family, the Walincourt family, Gautier le Tonnerre and the lords of Saint-Aubert. In doing so, the network around the bishop was brought to the fore. A more extensive analysis of these stylistic links with the charters issued by the local aristocracy in the Cambrésis region is underway. This last test case is an example of opening up stylometric methods to wider questions than author attribution.

The current results of the preceding test cases have underlined a few limits and questions of the method. Whereas the first major test opened up the stylometrics field to a benchmark test, the second test was more focused on feeling out the limitations of the current code. From these tests, multiple questions about corpus size and corpus bias have arisen. Firstly, it was important to determine the sweet spot for a clear overview, while allowing for a significantly large basis of comparison. Currently, the best results seem to lie around 500 charters: both the RogF/JeanE case and the Oisy case produced the most interesting results. With this corpus size, the visualisation is sufficiently clear for the researcher; determining clusters and identifying individual texts in the charter map is still feasible.

This is connected to a limit of the current visualisation method concerning the labelling of each dot. One can find all provided metadata by hovering with the cursor over one coloured dot, but one cannot automatically search for an individual text within the charter map. Searching for certain texts in a charter map is very time intensive. The alternative is running the visualisation again and again, which changes the overall shape of the visualisation – though the calculated distances between the charter texts remains the same. In that same vein, the researcher must keep in mind that when adapting the corpus by adding or omitting charter texts, the distances are recalculated and the charter map will change. Similar texts will still be clustered in largely the same manner, but the search for individual texts starts anew. The visualisation is also limited to eight colours, before it starts to repeat itself. The researcher must carefully choose which cluster to highlight and compare.

---

35 Benoît-Michel Tock, Les chartes de l'abbaye cistercienne de Vaucelles au XIIe siècle, Turnhout 2010, p. 33.

When it comes to providing a sufficiently large basis of comparison, the researcher must keep tabs on which sub corpus dominates the visualisation: is it the one being tested (here, the episcopal charters) or do other authorities, such as dukes, counts, the pope or monastic institutions, come into play strongly? During the benchmark tests, a distortion of the charter map became noticeable when all papal charters were included. These texts were clustered on the sides of the charter map – showing a distinctly separate *dictamen* group. At the same time, the inclusion of charters by the Count of Flanders and the Duke of Brabant provided additional information on certain clusters within the charter map. These charters were most often somewhat spread out over a section of the visualisation and showed examples of a mixed *dictamen* or of influence from these authorities' chanceries.

In 'reading' the charter map, this 'additional information' is certainly of importance: a large part of the research consists of figuring out why the charters are clustered the way they are, which becomes easier the better the researcher knows his corpus up front. This method does currently not allow for a blind reading of the map. The use of ground truths as a starting point remains a necessity for a good functioning of the code.

This ties in to the counter argument to not automatically discount large corpora, as in theory these provide more information for the comparison. The corpus of 4036 charters was too large to find individual dictators: the overview was lost and higher authorities dominated the scatterplot. But could the general chancery practices of Cambrai emerge better in a larger corpus? The possibility of comparing multiple episcopal chanceries at once would be an interesting test case, which could be explored based on large ongoing edition projects such as ACTÉPI, which is set to collect the episcopal charters of twenty-five dioceses[36]. Such a larger investigation would allow the analysis of the additional question of corpus bias. To what degree is the type of charter an influence? These types would largely be determined by the formulas used, as evidenced by Walter Prevenier in the case of the Flemish Count's writs[37], but it seems this hasn't been properly researched yet with stylometric methods. In his study of the Burgundian episcopal charters, Nicolas Perreaux underlines one should not confuse corpus bias and the structural repartition of the studied texts – that what might seem biased could indeed provide important information[38]. If corpus bias constitutes a true problem for the code is an element which will be considered in future tests[39].

36 *Actépi. Les actes épiscopaux français du Moyen Âge – édition multimodale et exploitation.* This is an ongoing project by the Agence Nationale de la Recherche, scheduled from 2019 until 2023. URL: https://actepi.hypotheses.org/a-propos.

37 Walter Prevenier, De Oorkonden der graven van Vlaanderen p. 7–31.

38 Nicolas Perreaux, L'écriture du monde (I).

39 I thank Sébastien Barret for his remarks concerning corpus bias and how this doesn't necessary discount the results of stylometric research.

Preferably, this digital approach in its current form is viewed as an enhancement of the existing traditional methods. Based in the method of studying charter dictamen as developed by Els de Paermentier and her predecessor Walter Prevenier, the code keeps in line with tradition while opening up to larger questions. The greatest value of the existing code lies exactly in its ability to compare large text corpora within a short amount of time. Paired with a close reading of the corpus we arrive at a hybrid approach, which allows a 'distant' overview while not losing contact with the sources.

The need for easy access to these sources becomes once more apparent in applying this method. Whereas the pre-processing of the corpus can be very time-intensive, this is offset by an easy access to the texts. Especially quick access to the metadata proves to be essential. It's still a manual labour to enter these data into the spreadsheet prepared alongside the coding of the charters themselves, but this could be aided by automatic extraction out of databases, if the permission is granted.

The charters in question largely determine the digital approach used: 'stylometrics' remains a field with various methods and cannot be seen as a static given. Each new test demands to check up on the existing code. Currently, the existing code used in the tests described above all concern the same type of source as well as the same type of question. The code has been adapted to analyse charter texts; the ad hoc tagging scheme in particular, where diplomatic sections are designated, adheres to this genre. The question of 'authorship' in the literary sense and thus the study of signal words is equally embedded in the current code. In case one would wish to compare literary texts (hagiographical, historiographical, poetical, etc.) with the charter corpus, a review of the method is very much necessary. Such research would be much in the same vein as Jeroen De Gussem's approach of comparing a Saint-Denis charter ascribed to Suger of Saint-Denis with this dictator's literary work, presented in 2018[40]. Another practical adaptation – to which we alluded above - would be finetuning the text-matcher package to medieval Latin.

Hence, technical knowledge is most certainly needed, especially to keep the code up to date, as computer code and programs tend to 'age' rapidly. It can be a challenge to optimise technical skills and keep abreast of new developments in the field. In the case of the Cambrai episcopal charters, the collaboration between a medievalist and a specialist of stylometric methods proved most fruitful. The expertise of a diplomatist and palaeographer served well in formulating the correct questions needed to analyse this type of text – for example the comparison of formulas - which was then translated by Mike Kestemont into the right stylometric method

40 Jeroen De Gussem, Forgery in Saint-Denis: A Stylometric Study in the Donation of Charlemagne, presentation during the conference 'Digital humanities: New tools for the medievalist', Namur May 7th 2018.

that could be of use to us – for example text reuse detection - and developing and adapting the appropriate tools withheld in the current code. The importance of collaborations and cross-pollinating between the fields is once more underlined. Here, the field of 'digital humanities' is already responding to these needs with the emergence of various coding, data analysis and data mining classes in universities and research programmes.

In this vein, these methods are clearly still under development. It remains of great importance to communicate with other researchers about these methods and share as freely as possible the codes, methods and results of each test case. This should be a given in academic research, as we often are not aware of what other researchers are doing in the field. This seems to stem from the rather slow spread of stylometric methods in diplomatic research circles.

Additional testing of these limitations and possibilities in a more tangible manner are envisioned in a collaboration with Prof. dr. Els De Paermentier at the University of Gent in Belgium and with Prof. dr. Mike Kestemont, of the University of Antwerp. The corpus of 608 charters by the Counts of Flanders during the first half of the 13th century, as studied by prof. Els De Paermentier[41], permits us to examine a case with sufficient preliminary knowledge on the chancery *dictamen* as well as a group of identified clerks (*dictatores*) and chancery hands (*scriptores*).

The first of these additional tests will focus on taking some distance and determine to what degree stylometric methods can review, confirm, contradict or expand upon the results booked by Els De Paermentier. This will consist of a test in which the 608 count's charters are tested against a diverse corpus of 608 'other' charters, in which we focus on the chancery *dictamen*. Next, a more detailed view of these charters pertaining to the cases of the clerks is envisioned. After having assessed these results, we will proceed with testing the method on an even larger corpus of charters issued during the government of Margaret II of Flanders during the second half of the 13th century. This case would offer more challenges to test the code against as we currently only have partial results for the *dictamen* study. Another challenge is posed by the increasing importance of vernacular languages in charters, which leads to a separate French and Latin corpus to work with[42]. The code will be revised for these test cases.

41 Els De Paermentier, Schrift in dienst van de macht. De grafelijke kanselarij in Vlaanderen en Henegouwen (1191–1244), Hilversum 2021.

42 In the *Diplomata Belgica* database, only two charters in Dutch are present for the Counts of Flandres, both from countess Joan of Constantinople. Joan of Constantinople for Halle, 1225, DiBe ID 17622 in Diplomata Belgica. The Diplomatic Sources from the Medieval Southern Low Countries, ed. by Thérèse de Hemptinne/Jeroen Deploige/Jean-Louis Kupper/Walter Prevenier (Brussels: Royal Historical Commission, since 2015). URL: www.diplomata-belgica.be/charter_details_en.php?dibe_id=17622. Joan of Constantinople for Razo VII of Gavere, 1231,

On a separate research track, the Cambrai case still offers much to discover on the network around the bishop, in particular the local peers and the cathedral chapter. For this project, the existing corpus is enlarged with the charters of the local aristocracy. If possible, the bishop's letters and notices as well as the literary production of this region (more specifically of the chapter and the bishop) will be included, which too would demand a review of the code. The first half of this project – testing the bishop's charters against the aristocracy's charters – has been presented during the "Les évêques en leur monde: reseaux, communautés, influences (Xe-XIIIe siècle)" conference in May 2023 in Nancy.

Through this collection of tests, we hope to provide a contribution to the cross-pollination of stylometry within the field of diplomatics, be it significant or humble. The preliminary results are promising in any case and offer a lot of potential for broadening and optimising their application to diplomatic source material.

DiBe ID 27017 in *Diplomata Belgica. The Diplomatic Sources from the Medieval Southern Low Countries*. URL: www.diplomata-belgica.be/charter_details_en.php?dibe_id=27017.

II. Diplomatics and Computational Methods: External Features

Image processing and semantic technologies in digital humanities

The NOTAE experience[1]

Zahra Ziran, Francesco Leotta, Massimo Mecella, Antonella Ghignoli

Introduction

Digital humanities (DH) is a field that combines humanities studies with digital technologies. It involves digital approaches uses and methods to analyze, interpret, and represent cultural artifacts such as texts, images, and other media. Digital humanities are an important area of study because it enables us to better understand and appreciate our cultural heritage, and it also offers new ways to analyze and interpret that heritage. One of the most significant benefits of digital humanities is the preservation and accessibility of cultural heritage. By digitizing historical documents, art, and other cultural artifacts, they can be made available to people worldwide, allowing for their study and preservation. This is particularly important for artifacts that are fragile, rare, or located in remote areas. By digitizing these materials, scholars and researchers can access them more easily and study them in greater detail. Digital humanities also offer new opportunities for interdisciplinary collaboration. By bringing together scholars from different fields, including computer science, linguistics, history, and art, digital humanities can generate new insights and perspectives. This collaboration can lead to the development of new tools and methods that allow us to better understand and interpret cultural artifacts. Digital humanities can also be used to promote public engagement and education. By creating digital exhibits and other interactive tools, cultural institutions can engage the public and provide new ways for people to learn about history and culture. This can lead to a greater appreciation for cultural heritage and can help people better understand the significance of cultural artifacts. Furthermore, digital humanities can

1 This research is part of the NOTAE project: "NOT A writtEnword but graphic symbols", which has received funding from the European Research Council (ERC) under the European Union's Horizon 2020 research and innovation program (Advanced Grant 2017, GA n. 786572, PI Antonella Ghignoli). (For details see: https://notae-project.digilab.uniroma1.it)

also lead to research and scholarship advancement. By leveraging digital approaches and methods, researchers can process large amounts of data and analyze it in ways that would not be possible through traditional methods. For example, text mining and natural language processing can be used to identify patterns and trends in large collections of texts. This can help researchers identify new research questions and areas of study. Computational Humanities (CH) is a subfield of digital humanities that involves the use of computational and statistical methods to study cultural artifacts such as texts, images, and other media. With this, CH is helping digital humanities in several ways. Firstly, these methods can help researchers process large amounts of data quickly and efficiently. For example, text mining, image processing and natural language processing can be used to analyze large collections of texts and images to identify patterns and themes. Secondly, computational methods can help researchers to visualize data in new and interesting ways. For example, data visualization techniques can be used to create interactive maps, timelines, and other visual representations of data. This can help researchers to identify patterns and relationships that might not be apparent through traditional methods of analysis. Thirdly, computational methods can help researchers to test and refine theories. For example, simulation and modeling techniques can help to test hypotheses and predictions about how cultural artifacts evolve over time. This can help researchers to refine their theories and better understand the dynamics of cultural change. Finally, computational methods can help researchers to collaborate across disciplines. Because computational methods are used in many different fields, including computer science, statistics, and mathematics, providing a common language for researchers from different disciplines to work together. This can lead to new insights and discoveries that might not be possible through traditional methods of collaboration. In general, computational humanities is helping digital humanities to become more robust and sophisticated. By integrating computational methods with the study of cultural artifacts, researchers can develop new insights and perspectives that can help us to better understand and appreciate our cultural heritage. Computational humanities are sometimes met with skepticism from humanists who perceive these methods as imprecise and approximate, not meeting the rigorous standards of their research. The system can be continuously updated and refined with feedback from human experts to enhance its precision and accuracy, ensuring that computational humanities remain useful and relevant in humanities research. However, computational humanities are defined by a strong human-in-the-loop component, meaning that the methods used become more intelligent and precise over time with feedback from human experts. These methods are not meant to replace humanists, but rather to aid them in their research, providing analytical capabilities and new insights into their topics of interest. The human-in-the-loop component ensures that the results generated by these methods align with the goals and expectations of humanists. Incorporating computational methods in humanities research enhances research capabilities and provides new perspectives. With the active involvement of human experts, the precision and accuracy of computational humanities can be improved over time, enhancing the overall quality of humanities research. In this paper, we introduce the NOTAE project, which combines digital and computational humanities to study graphic symbols in historical documents. It provides a unique platform for experts to store information about the language, writer, social and economic status, purpose, and position of graphic symbols in a document. The project captures all possible historical implications associated with the use of graphic symbols and enables scholars to gain new insights and perspectives. Additionally, the project includes geographical analytics and a knowledge graph that plays a critical role in the NOTAE system. The subsequent section of this paper will delve into NOTAE's knowledge graph, highlight the significance of expertise in the project, and describe the methods and techniques used to assess the quality of symbol detection in ancient documents. Furthermore, we will explain how humans in the loop can improve the results of the proposed method.

The paper is structured as follows: first, the *related works* are discussed, followed by a section on *the experience of the NOTAE project*, where the project's contributions to digital and computational humanities are highlighted. Then, the NOTAE Knowledge Graph is introduced in a *NOTAE Knowledge Graph* section. The section *Graphic Symbol Detection in NOTAE* presents a new approach to graphic symbol detection that combines deep learning and set transformation. The crucial role of humanists in the loop is also discussed, as they provide expert knowledge and context to guide the analysis and interpretation of the detected symbols. The results of the method are presented in the *Classification Results* section. Finally, the paper concludes with some suggestions for future work.

Related Works

Having explained the essential functions of digital humanities and computational humanities in the study of cultural artifacts, this study will proceed to review significant research in these fields. For instance, as described by Jockers[2], digital humanities has expanded its capabilities through the creation of extensive and all-inclusive databases, the digitization of literary works, and the ongoing advancement of search engines. These resources enable scholars to pose significant research questions and conduct macroanalysis, which allows them to examine and interpret large-scale literary trends, patterns, and linguistic connections across thousands of texts in digital libraries. With the ability to retrieve keywords, phrases, and other linguistic patterns through computational analysis, researchers can use quantifiable evidence to

2 Matthew L. Jockers, Macroanalysis: Digital methods and literary history, Urbana 2013.

make determinations about the use of literary trends over time, across periods, within regions or demographic groups, and to assess how cultural, historical, and societal factors bind individual authors, texts, and genres into a larger literary culture. Jockers[3] introduces the concept of large-scale literary computing and the possibilities of macroanalysis as a new approach to literary interpretation. By focusing on large collections of digital material, researchers can better understand and contextualize individual works within the context of these collections, surpassing the limitations of close reading methods. Liu discusses the potential of library data collections to support a range of data workflows in humanities and social sciences, with the aim of promoting open, shareable, and reproducible data research[4]. Drawing on the example of in silico science, Liu suggests that humanities and social sciences can benefit from methods and standards developed by science for tracking data provenance, annotating and visualizing data analysis workflows, and comparing data workflows across different fields. This would involve identifying common data-analysis "moves" and vulnerable points in the data trajectory that require library support. Liu also proposed a reverse direction of influence, whereby humanities and social sciences can offer new perspectives on the narrative motifs and moves that are essential to analyze data workflows in any field. Ultimately, Liu argues that to analyze data workflows require a narrative approach that can match narrative motifs and moves with data workflow moves. The preservation, analysis, and representation of digital information in archives and other media pose complex challenges for historical researchers, archivists, and librarians. Theimer et al. introduced a framework called digital historiography that provides a critical, interdisciplinary approach to understand the interaction between digital technology and historical practice[5]. The American Historical Association (AHA)[6] panel aimed to explore key theoretical and methodological questions surrounding the intersection of digital archives and historical practice, including the selection and preservation of materials, the contextual information provided by archives, and the political, social, economic, and cultural power structures that shape archives. Participants emphasized the need for collaboration between historians and information professionals, including archivists, to create critical contextual information and new scholarly works that harness the power of digital archives. These efforts require further exploration of research areas and methodologies, as well as the development of practical

3 Ibid.

4 Aan Liu, Digital Humanities and Academic Change, Sept. 2009 [Online] https://liu.english.ucsb.edu/digital-humanities-and-academic-change/.

5 Katharina Hering/Michael J. Kramer/Joshua Sternfeld/Kate Theimer, Digital Historiography and the Archives, in: Journal of Digital Humanities 3/2 (2014); https://journalofdigitalhumanities.org/3-2/digital-historiography-and-the-archives/

6 https://www.historians.org/research-and-publications/perspectives-on-history/january-2014/digital-historiography-and-the-archives

models for diverse user communities. DH and its development over the past 70 years in applying computing to cultural heritage is introduced by Nyhan and Flinn[7]. It discusses the difficulties in writing history of DH and outlines the approach taken in the book. DH is defined as the intersection of computing and cultural heritage aimed at transforming how humanities study artifacts and phenomena. It differentiates itself from routine uses of computing in research and teaching. Histories of DH are necessary to understand its evolution and continued impact on humanities. In recent years, DH, also known as humanities computing, has rapidly emerged as a field of research. DH involves the use of computational tools to support the study of the humanities, social sciences, and cultural heritage. DH has emerged as a response to the growing demand for semantic text or image-analysis methods, as well as for intelligent data discovery, linking, querying, and visualization. At the intersection of computing sciences and humanities, current DH research aims to create digital embeddings of texts, images, musical compositions, and other semiotic artifacts that are accessible, searchable, and analyzable. This facilitates quantitative and automated analysis of large data sets, including sets of data that have not yet been examined in the relevant field of study. Computational tools such as textual search, visual analytics, data mining, statistics, and natural language processing are widely employed to support humanities researchers. There are many massive digitization projects and platforms dedicated to creating, curating and utilizing data in humanities and social sciences. The shift from traditional digital humanities to computational humanities has brought a greater emphasis on online accessibility, facilitating the widespread use of these tools by people worldwide. The transition from traditional digital humanities to computational humanities has resulted in a greater focus on online accessibility for widespread use by people around the world. For instance, B. Peterfi and K. Arany proposed[8] a method to provide an overview of new initiatives of the National Archives of Hungary (NAH) in the areas of digitization projects and developing online databases, public interfaces, and improved research opportunities. S. Bröhl investigates the challenges of standardization, archival description authority data in projects with multiple archival, and the common goal of presentation of the charts in one archiving portal to make accessible and publish online about 7000 late medieval charters and copies from cartularies. Although creating comprehensive archives of documents is essential, as J. Burgers and R. Hoekstra proposed, the Netherlands have preserved tens of thousands of original charters from the Medieval and Early Modern eras in hundreds of archival funds across numerous archival institutions, and yet this important resource is rarely used in historical research. To address this issue, the Digitale Char-

7 Juliane Nyhan/Andrew Flinn, Computation and the humanities: towards an oral history of digital humanities (Springer Series on Cultural Computing), Cham 2016.

8 For the following, see the corresponding papers in these conference proceedings.

terbank Nederland (DCN) was suggested to create an integrated database that would make this corpus available. Still, the user's search options are restricted by the method of data collection to content descriptions and a time stamp. DH also involves obtaining knowledge from historical documents, in addition to having online access to historical documents, digitization, and search engines. Computational Humanities is specifically interested in using computing to solve humanities research questions effectively. The right software can process large data sets, providing new and useful ways to approach questions in the traditional humanities. Nevertheless, before applying these techniques, it is crucial to identify the demands and difficulties facing the humanities. These issues fall under four categories: the interaction between researchers in the humanities and computer science; measuring the effectiveness of a computer system for processing humanities data; identifying research issues best suited for computational approaches; and examining the factors that affect the interpretability of the output produced by these algorithms from the perspective of humanities researchers[9]. In Piotrowski, the term "digital" in the context of "digital humanities" has various interpretations[10]. These interpretations identifies as (1) the use of digital tools and data, (2) the use of digital methodologies or methods, and (3) research related to cultural phenomena and digital artifacts[11]. These three aspects are closely related to data, tools, methodologies, and research, and involve both the humanities and computer technology. In addition to having online access to historical documents, the digitization of materials, and search engine capabilities, obtaining knowledge from historical documents is a significant component of CH, as noted by Biemann et al.[12]. CH is particularly interested in solving humanities research questions effectively through computing. The right software can process large datasets, enabling new and useful ways to approach traditional humanities questions. The transition from DH to CH has led to massive digitization projects, that curate and use humanities and social science data by relying on text analysis techniques and novel hybrid approaches formed from the relevant research communities[13]. One area of research within CH is Artificial Intelligence (AI) for the digital humanities, which focuses on studying the role of artificial intelligence methodologies, techniques, and tools in supporting digital human-

9 Chris Biemann/Gregory R. Crane/Christiane D. Fellbaum/Alexander Mehler, Computational humanities – bridging the gap between computer science and digital humanities (Dagstuhl Seminar 14301), in: Dagstuhl reports, Schloss Dagstuhl-Leibniz-Zentrum für Informatik, 2014.

10 Michael Piotrowski, Ain't no way around it: why we need to be clear about what we mean by 'Digital Humanities', in: SocArXiv Papers (2020); https://doi.org/10.31235/osf.io/d2kb6

11 Rute Costa/Bruno Almeida/Margarida Ramos/Maria I. B. Campos, The Role of Linguistics in the Age of Digital Humanities, in: Linha D'Água, 34/2 (2021) p. 1–8.

12 Biemann, Computational humanities.

13 Ibid.

ities research[14]. The research areas in this field mainly concentrate on effective information and document retrieval, natural language processing, extracting high-quality knowledge from textual resources, automated reasoning, and developing resources and applications according to Semantic Web and Linked Data best practices. While the transition to CH has introduced many new computational tools and methodologies, it is crucial to identify the demands and difficulties facing the humanities[15]. Therefore, it is necessary to evaluate the advantages and disadvantages of each method and achieve a balance between digital technologies and human involvement[16]. Agent-Based Modeling (ABM) is a proposed method of computational analysis that has been discussed in the context of the transition to CH[17]. ABM creates a simulated environment and measures the interactions of individual agents within that environment. One of the weaknesses of this model is, ABM does not depend on human interaction and just can be run many times by changing variables. VAST (Values Across Space and Time) is another project that discusses the vision of the transition from digital to computational humanities, focusing on the fundamental European values that are widely acknowledged as the foundational elements of society[18]. VAST studied how moral values change over time and space by digitizing historical content with document annotation modules and tools to support historians and humanities scholars in the extraction of value-related knowledge from sources[19]. They adopted semi-automatic solutions for the progressive enrichment of the reference vocabulary based on machine learning techniques[20] and offered interactive dashboards with content value organization[21]. VAST also outlined a human-in-the-loop participatory storytelling approach, where users can add their perspectives and express their likes or dislikes for other users' proposals, helping to define a value interpretation[22]. The role of artificial intelligence, data sci-

14 Michael Gavin, Agent-Based Modeling and Historical Simulation, in: Digital Humanities quaterly 8/4 (2014); http://www.digitalhumanities.org/dhq/vol/8/4/000195/000195.htm

15 Biemann, Computational humanities.

16 Gavin, Agent-Based Modeling.

17 Ibid.

18 Silvana Castano/Alfio Ferrara/Stefano Montanelli/Francesco Periti, From digital to computational humanities: The VAST project vision, in: SEBD 2021: Italian Symposium on Advanced Database Systems (CEUR Workshop Proceedings 2994), Pizzo Calabro 2021, p. 24–35.

19 Ibid.

20 Silvano Castano/Mattia Falduti/Alfio Ferrara/Stefano Montanelli, The LATO knowledge model for automated knowledge extraction and enrichment from court decisions corpora," in: COUrT 2020: CAiSE for Legal Documents (CEUR Workshop Proceedings 2690), Grenoble 2020, p. 15–26.

21 Silvana Castano/Alfio Ferrara/Stefano Montanelli, Topic summary views for exploration of large scholarly datasets, in: Journal on Data Semantics 7 (2018) p. 155–170.

22 Silvana Castano/Alfio Ferrara/Stefano Montanelli, Crowdsourcing task assignment with online profile learning, in: On the Move to Meaningful Internet Systems. OTM 2018 Con-

ence, and cutting-edge digital technologies is fundamental in this transition[23]. However, it is crucial to keep people "in-the-loop" to support massive-scale human processes, such as annotating, commenting, rating, and reviewing, and the methodical, task-based creation and uploading of content[24]. By addressing the challenges and demands of the humanities and evaluating the advantages and disadvantages of different computational tools and methodologies, it is possible to achieve a balance between the use of digital technologies and human's involvement in the research process. In the field of digital humanities and computational humanities, the concept of human-centered AI was proposed in Novak et al.[25], which aims to relate to human emotions and motivations, challenge assumptions, and provide alternative ways of looking at problems while still allowing room for human creativity and intuition. The objective of this approach is to enhance human decision-making and support human goals at both individual and societal levels, while also considering potential negative scenarios, such as AI developing decision-making processes that are difficult for humans to comprehend or that aim to replace humans. To achieve the best results, methods that include humans in the loop should be used to obtain feedback from AI. Furthermore, it was suggested in Hyvönen[26], that research on CH semantic portals should shift towards tools that support DH research, as well as automatic knowledge discovery and artificial intelligence. The proposed Sampo model, which leverages Semantic Web (SW) technologies and Linked Open Data (LOD) publishing, aims to address issues with information silos and data publishing. While computational techniques such as text categorization, information extraction, text mining, and automatic semantic markup have been successfully used in natural language processing, their scope of application could be broadened to include a wider range of texts, leading to new types of text hermeneutics and more powerful insights into literary text content. In El-Hajj et al., the potential for machine learning to scale up the analysis of historical content to larger corpora was discussed, and a method was proposed for digit recognition in numerical tables using a small number of annotated digits to train a neural OCR model[27]. In Cornia

---

ferences: Confederated International Conferences: CoopIS, C&TC, and ODBASE 2018, Valletta, Malta, October 22-26, 2018, Proceedings, Part I, Cham 2018, p. 226–242.

23 Gavin, Agent-Based Modeling.

24 Ibid.

25 Andrzej Nowak/Paul Lukowicz/Pawel Horodecki, Assessing artificial intelligence for humanity: Will AI be the our biggest ever advance? Or the biggest threat [Opinion], in: IEEE Technology and Society Magazine 37/4 (2018) p. 26–34.

26 Eero Hyvönen, Digital humanities on the Semantic Web: Sampo model and portal series, in: Semantic Web 14/4 (2023) p. 729–744.

27 Hassan El-Hajj et al., An ever-expanding humanities knowledge graph: The sphaera corpus at the intersection of humanities, data management, and machine learning, in: Datenbank-Spektrum 22/2 (2022) p. 153–162.

et al., algorithms for visual-semantic retrieval in the context of cultural heritage were developed using a semi-supervised approach that does not rely on labelled data in the artistic domain, which could lead to more powerful insights and analyses in the field of digital humanities[28]. Interactive storytelling was also described as an interdisciplinary field where the humanities and AI intersect, and the examination of narrative models in the humanities could provide better access to models and new adaptation strategies for AI researchers[29]. According to Gödel, human experts provide meaning to causal chains and logical propositions[30], which highlights the limitations of AI as a tool within a formal system. Humanities researchers are credited for their unique knowledge and perception, while AI is credited for following through on repetitive and specifiable tasks. Therefore, in the evolution of computational humanities into digital humanities, sound AI applications require expert knowledge, such as: verifying authenticity, identifying anomalies, and documenting intellectual works based on database evidence. By examining important studies in digital humanities and computational humanities, we have gained a more thorough understanding of the benefits that these fields bring to the humanities. We will now explore the NOTAE project and its use of digital humanities and computational humanities, which can provide us with a more comprehensive understanding and performance of the project.

The Experience of the NOTAE Project

The NOTAE project is a unique combination of digital humanities and computational humanities. As illustrated in Fig 4, it offers scholars the opportunity to investigate the use and significance of graphic symbols in written documents from Late Antiquity to early medieval Europe. A graphic symbol in historical documents refers to a visual element that encompasses alphabetical and other graphic signs, to convey meanings beyond the text. The message conveyed by a graphic is determined not only by its intrinsic properties but also influenced by the historical background in which it originated. Various types of documents with diverse functions in a range of social and cultural contexts employed a wide range of graphic symbols, ranging from unique to recurring and originating from individuals with varying levels of

---

28 Marcella Cornia/Matteo Stefanini/Lorenzo Baraldi/Massimiliano Corsini/Rita Cucchiara, Explaining digital humanities by aligning images and textual descriptions," Pattern Recognition Letters 129 (2020) p. 166–172.

29 Hartmut Koenitz, Interactive Storytelling Paradigms and Representations: a Humanities-Based Perspective, in: Handbook of Digital Games and Entertainment Technologies 1, ed. Ryohei Nakatsu/Matthias Rauterberg/Paolo Ciancarini, Singapore 2017, p. 361–376.

30 Kurt Gödel, Über formal unentscheidbare Sätze der „Principia Mathematica" und verwandter Systeme 1, in: Monatshefte für Mathematik und Physik 38 (1931) p. 173–198.

literacy. This project provides a comprehensive understanding of the historical implications of graphic symbols and capturing all the possible historical implications associated with their use as shown in Fig 5. The core of the NOTAE project is the NOTAE System, which consists of two parts. First, a back-office web application for experts, where all the information gathered on graphic symbols is stored in the NOTAE database. Second, a public web application for people to explore this information. The NOTAE system provides a unique platform for experts to store information about the language, writer, social and economic status, purpose, and position of graphic symbols in a document. The public web application enables the public to learn about the rich cultural heritage of graphic symbols. The database serves as a public repository of graphic symbols collected from original documentary sources, making it easily accessible to scholars and researchers. Scientists outside of the project can access and analyze this information through the NOTAE system's web interface, which provides a valuable resource for scholars to study and understand the use and significance of graphic symbols in written documents from Late Antiquity to early medieval Europe.

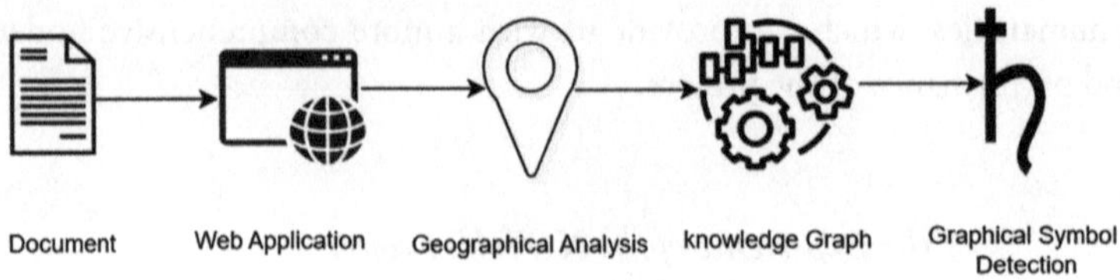

Fig 1: The NOTAE Project.

The NOTAE project also includes geographical analytics and a knowledge graph, which plays a critical role in the NOTAE system. The project employs methods and techniques to assess the quality of symbol detection in ancient documents. By combining digital humanities and computational humanities, the NOTAE project provides a more comprehensive understanding and performance of the project. It attempts to capture potential historical implications linked with the utilization of graphic symbols, potentially offering scholars new insights and perspectives into the significance and usage of these symbols within written documents of that era. The NOTAE project is an excellent example of how the combination of digital humanities and computational humanities can contribute to a deeper understanding of the humanities. In the following section of the paper, we will delve into NOTAE's geographical analytics, describing the correspondent knowledge graph, which plays a critical role in the NOTAE system. The section will also highlight the significance of expertise in the functioning of the NOTAE system. Subsequently, we will examine the methods and techniques used to assess the quality of symbol detection in ancient documents.

Fig 2: Surface Specific Multilayer (SSM).

NOTAE Knowledge Graph

The benefits of a knowledge graph in humanities research are numerous and can greatly enhance the value and usefulness of a database. Firstly, interconnectivity is a key advantage of knowledge graphs. The ability to connect and link together various pieces of information and data in a structured and meaningful way provides a better understanding of relationships between different elements such as people, events, and places in the medieval period. This interconnectedness can help researchers uncover new relationships, patterns, and insights that would otherwise be difficult to discern through traditional search methods. Another advantage of knowledge graphs is their reusability. By making data more accessible and reusable for future research, knowledge graphs enable other researchers to build upon previous work and find new uses for the data. This can help to advance the field and contribute to a more comprehensive understanding of the data. Semantic search is another key benefit of knowledge graphs as researchers can perform more complex and sophisticated search queries and easily search for entities related to a specific time or event. This enhances the value of a database in humanities research, providing a more comprehensive and interconnected view of the data and making it easier for researchers to uncover new insights and connections. Finally, knowledge graphs can provide a visual representation of the relationships between different pieces of information, making it easier for researchers to understand and interpret the data. This visual representation can greatly enhance the value and usefulness of a database, providing a more comprehensive and interconnected view of the data and making it easier for researchers to uncover new insights and connections. In Bernasconi et al. and various relevant online repositories and services, the aim is to create a semantic ecosystem that enhances information accessibility and supports knowledge discovery[31]. Currently, while some services offer data as Linked Open Data, none offer an integrated view of the field or allow for straightforward exploration of data and historical analysis. The proposed tool has the potential to promote collaboration among researchers and engage casual users by making niche topics, such as ancient documentary texts studied by the NOTAE project, more accessible. The NOTAE knowledge graph (KG) aims to address the lack of a shared vocabulary and integration among various digital cultural efforts, which is regarded as a significant drawback in the field. Many websites, such as Pleiades[32], Papyri.info[33], MANTIS[34], Open Context[35], and Trismegistos[36], provide valuable resources and information, they operate independently and without a common framework for integrating their data. In contrast, our model shares similarities with a study conducted by Broux and Depauw which utilized the Trismegistos data to produce a prosopography of individuals living in Ptolemaic Egypt[37]. The NOTAE knowledge graph also has the potential to complement the international Pelagios consortium's efforts[38], which uses the Linked Open Data (LOD) approach and the Pleiades gazetteer to connect online resources related to places in the ancient world. Our model

31 Eleonora BERNASCONI et al., Exploring the Historical Context of Graphic Symbols: the NOTAE Knowledge Graph and its Visual Interface, in: IRCDL 2021. Italian Research Conference on Digital Libraries. Proceedings of the 17th Italian Research Conference on Digital Libraries, Padova 2021, pp. 147–154.

32 https://pleiades.stoa.org/; see M. Alain GLEYZES/Lionel PERRET/Philippe KUBIK, Pleiades system architecture and main performances, in: The International Archives of Photogrammetry, Remote Sensing and Spatial Information Sciences 39 (2012) p. 537–542.

33 https://papyri.info/

34 http://numismatics.org/search/

35 https://opencontext.org/

36 https://www.trismegistos.org/; see Mark DEPAUW/Tom GHELDOF, Trismegistos: An interdisciplinary platform for ancient world texts and related information, in: Theory and Practice of Digital Libraries – TPDL 2013 Selected Workshops: LCPD 2013, SUEDL 2013, DataCur 2013, Held in Valletta, Malta, September 22–26, 2013. Revised Selected Papers 3, Cham 2014, p. 40–52.

37 Yanne BROUX/Mark DEPAUW, Developing onomastic gazetteers and prosopographies for the ancient world through named entity recognition and graph visualization: Some examples from trismegistos people," in: Social Informatics. SocInfo 2014 International Workshops, GMC and Histinformatics (Barcelona, Spain, November 10, 2014), Cham 2015, p. 304–313.

38 Leif ISAKSEN/Rainer SIMON/Elton T. E. BARKER/Pau DE SOTO CAÑAMARES, Pelagios and

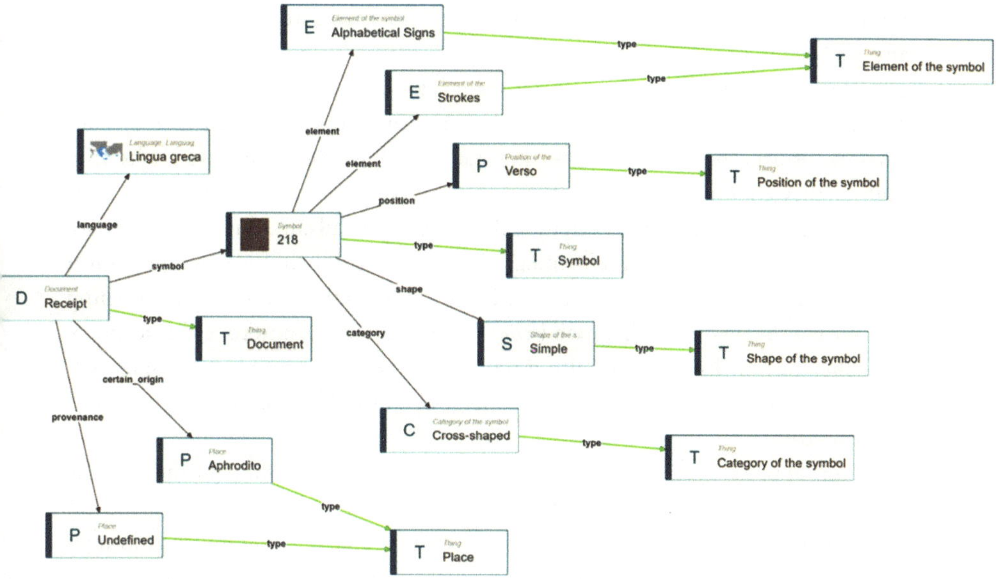

Fig. 3: NOTAE KG exploration example: Figure3 describes an example of how to derive historical implications from a knowledge graph.

can offer valuable contributions to the Pelagios consortium and help advance their goals. The knowledge graph is built on top of the NOTAE Database, which is updated daily through an ETL (Extract, Transform, Load) process. The NOTAE KG uses multiple vocabularies and RDFS (Resource Description Framework Schema) and OWL (Web Ontology Language) standards for data integration. The data is stored in a Blazegraph triplestore and is accessible through a SPARQL endpoint. The visualization and exploration of the NOTAE KG is based on the ARCA project tool. Classes and properties in the KG are defined using schema.org, DBpedia, FOAF, geo, and other namespaces. The KG can be used to find all entities that connect two terms of interest, such as a symbol and its associated document. An example of NOTAE KG exploration can be seen in Fig. 3.

Graphic Symbol Detection in NOTAE

The use of artificial intelligence and data science in the humanities is on the rise, as researchers seek to leverage computational methods to gain new insights into cultural heritage and historical documents. One promising application of AI in the

the emerging graph of ancient world data, in: Proceedings of the 2014 ACM conference on Web science, 2014, p. 197–201; https://doi.org/10.1145/2615569.2615693

humanities is graphic symbol detection, which involves automatically identifying and classifying specific symbols or patterns in images, such as those found in historical manuscripts or artwork. By detecting and analyzing these symbols at scale, researchers can potentially uncover hidden patterns and knowledge that may have been overlooked or undiscovered using traditional methods. However, achieving high-quality graphic symbol detection remains a challenge, as the task requires not only sophisticated algorithms and models, but also careful curation of training data and ongoing evaluation and refinement of results. In this paper, we present a novel approach to graphic symbol detection based on a combination of deep learning and set transformation, which we believe can significantly improve the accuracy and efficiency of this task. We also discuss the potential benefits of our approach for the humanities, particularly in the context of cultural heritage preservation and interpretation.

In our approach, we consider humanists to be essential experts in the loop, as they provide expert knowledge and context to guide the analysis and interpretation of the detected symbols. Their involvement ensures analysis's results are grounded in a deep understanding of the cultural and historical context where the documents were produced, and that any detected symbols are accurately interpreted and classified. The methodology used in this paper for graphic symbol detection involves a three-step approach[39]. First, the digital reproduction of a document undergoes image enhancement to improve image quality. Second, image segmentation is applied to find "boxes" that potentially contain graphic symbols. This step helps to isolate image areas where symbols may be present. Third, box classification is used to determine whether the box contains a graphic symbol or not. The classification model used in this step is trained using symbols previously identified by experts. They receive suggestions about potential symbols from the system and confirm or discard them while adding symbols not identified by the system. This process enables the system to improve through active learning, as the human expert's feedback is used to improve the system's accuracy in identifying graphic symbols. Overall, this methodology provides an effective way to detect graphic symbols in historical documents, enabling researchers in the humanities to extract valuable information and deepen their understanding of cultural heritage. The lack of dataset for training a machine learning model can occur due to various reasons such as limited availability of data, high cost of data collection and annotation, or the complexity of the task. This can be a major bottleneck for the performance of the model, as the lack of data can lead to overfitting, where the model fails to generalize well to new unseen data. To address this problem, data augmentation is a technique that is used

39 Zahra Ziran/Francesco Leotta/Massimo Mecella, Enhancing Object Detection in Ancient Documents with Synthetic Data Generation and Transformer-Based Models, in: CoRR, vol. abs/2307.16005, 2023, doi: 10.48550/ARXIV.2307.16005

to increase the size and diversity of the dataset by generating new examples that are like the original ones. This can help improve the model's performance by applying different transformations to the original data, such as flipping, rotating, scaling, or adding noise, to generate new examples that retain the same underlying structure and meaning. In the case of symbol recognition in documents, the basic dataset is composed of symbols manually identified by experts on analyzed documents. However, this dataset may not be sufficiently large or diverse enough to cover all the variations and styles of handwriting that can occur in different contexts. To overcome this limitation, data augmentation techniques can be used to generate new symbols that resemble the ones in the dataset, but with different variations and perturbations. One approach to data augmentation is to use generative models, such as the Set Transformer neural network architecture[40], to produce geometrical representations of symbols. These models can learn to generate new symbols that are similar to the ones in the dataset, but with variations that can improve the robustness and generalization of the model. For example, the model can generate symbols with different line thickness, curvature, or orientation, to simulate different handwriting styles and variations. These generated symbols can be added to the original dataset to increase its size and diversity and improve the performance of the model.

One common issue with datasets is that they may only contain positive examples, while the lack of negative examples can hinder machine learning models' performance. To tackle this problem, we employ a Generative Adversarial Network (GAN)[41] to generate negative examples and train a discriminator as a classifier. The intuition is that the generator produces fake samples that resemble the real ones, while the discriminator learns to distinguish between the fake and real samples. In this approach, the generator and discriminator play a game, with the generator trying to fool the discriminator, and the discriminator trying to correctly classify the samples. In our model for binary image classification, the discriminator acts as a classifier that assigns true or false labels to the input images. In this case, a true label means that the image contains a graphic symbol, whereas a false label indicates that it is identified as a non-symbol. The generator provides input images, and the created images should be labeled as false, while the original images found by database curators should be classified as true. We used 125 examples from the NOTAE database of graphic symbols and created a dataset for learning. After training, the dataset for the experiment of binary classification contains 800 instances, half of

40 Juho LEE/Yoonho LEE/Jungtaek KIM/Adam R. KOSIOREK/Seungjin CHOI/Yee Whye TEH, Set transformer: A framework for attention-based permutation-invariant neural networks, in International conference on machine learning, PMLR, 2019, p. 3744–3753; https://arxiv.org/abs/1810.00825

41 Alankrita AGGARWAL/Mamta MITTAL/Gopi BATTINENI, Generative adversarial network: An overview of theory and applications, in: International Journal of Information Management Data Insights 1/1 (2021); https://doi.org/10.1016/j.jjimei.2020.100004

Fig 4: The NOTAE Project.

which are labeled as false, and the other half are labeled as true. This means that the GAN-based data augmentation approach allowed us to increase the dataset's size by 540%, providing more diverse examples for training and potentially improving the classifier's performance. This way, the GAN-based data augmentation approach can help to overcome the problem of limited datasets and improve the performance of the classifier.

Classification Results

In our method, we have a classifier that predicts whether an image belongs to a certain label or not. We use a metric called the precision-recall curve to evaluate the accuracy of our classifier. AUC stands for Area Under Curve[42], and it's a way to measure a classifier's performance. The precision-recall curve shows us how well the classifier is performing, and the AUC value gives us an overall measure of this performance. The higher the AUC, the more accurate the classifier is as can be seen in 5. To make sure our classifier is really accurate, we tested it using a method called cross-validation. We split our test data into two halves and evaluated our classifier on both halves. The results were slightly different, but we took the average of the two AUC values to get a more accurate estimation of how well our classifier is performing.

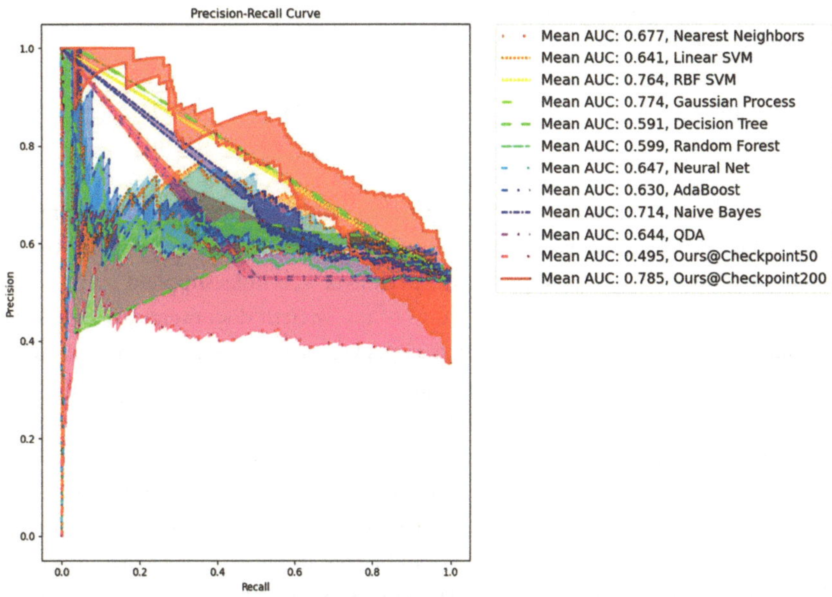

Fig. 5. Evaluation results for image classification. Checkpoints 50 and 200 refer to training epochs in our adversarial training.

An accurate classifier that minimizes incorrect predictions is desired. A recall of less than 0.4 and a precision greater than 0.8 were set as the criteria for the classifier to perform well and avoid harming the user with incorrect predictions. Evaluation

42 David J. Hand, Measuring classifier performance: a coherent alternative to the area under the ROC curve, in: Machine Learning 77/1 (2009) p. 103–123.

results showed in Table 1: Area Under Curve (AUC) of the Precision-Recall curve for 11 different classifiers including oursthat our developed model passed this test by achieving roughly 80% accuracy. Therefore, the developed method is effective in predicting image labels, which is crucial for applications such as digital assistants.

Table 1: Area Under Curve (AUC) of the Precision-Recall curve for 11 different classifiers including ours.

Classifier	Test 1 AUC	Test 2 AUC	Mean AUC
Ours	0.834	0.735	0.785
Gaussian Process	0.766	0.746	0.756
Radial Basis Function SVM	0.761	0.738	0.750
Naive Bayes	0.721	0.656	0.689
Neural Net	0.654	0.624	0.639
Quadratic Discriminant Analysis	0.628	0.638	0.633
Nearest Neighbors	0.644	0.605	0.625
AdaBoost	0.637	0.585	0.612
Decision Tree	0.553	0.628	0.592
Random Forest	0.580	0.540	0.561

Object detection involves identical processes of image augmentation, template matching, and object classification[43]. Initially, we deployed a web scraper bot to fetch document images from public databases via web links supplied by NOTAE database curators. The document pictures of the ancient documents are digital reproductions of historical artifacts such as papyrus and wooden parchments. Due to the age of these documents, their digital reproductions require image enhancement as a pre-processing step. Next, human experts actively binarize the pictures by selecting a binarization threshold value for each picture separately. As a result of image enhancement, humans are actively involved[44] in our object detection system's learning process. Finally, the enhanced picture of documents is prepared for object localization and classification as can be seen in Fig. 6. Due to the number of document images available in public databases and the active role of human experts in the system, a hybrid approach to annotating images for object detection was per-

43 Zahra ZIRAN/Eleonora BERNASCONI/Antonella GHIGNOLI/Francesco LEOTTA/Massimo MECELLA, Accurate Graphic Symbol Detection in Ancient Document Digital Reproductions, in: Document Analysis and Recognition, ICDAR 2021 Workshops, Lausanne, Switzerland, September 5-10, 2021, Proceedings, Part I, ed. Elisa H. BARNEY SMITH/Umapada PAL (Lecture Notes in Computer Science 12916), Cham 2021, p. 147–162. doi: 10.1007/978-3-030-86198-8_12.

44 Shubhomoy DAS/Weng-Keen WONG/ Thomas DIETTERICH/Alan FERN/Andrew EMMOTT, Incorporating expert feedback into active anomaly discovery, in: 2016 IEEE 16th International Conference on Data Mining (ICDM), Barcelona 2016, p. 853–858.

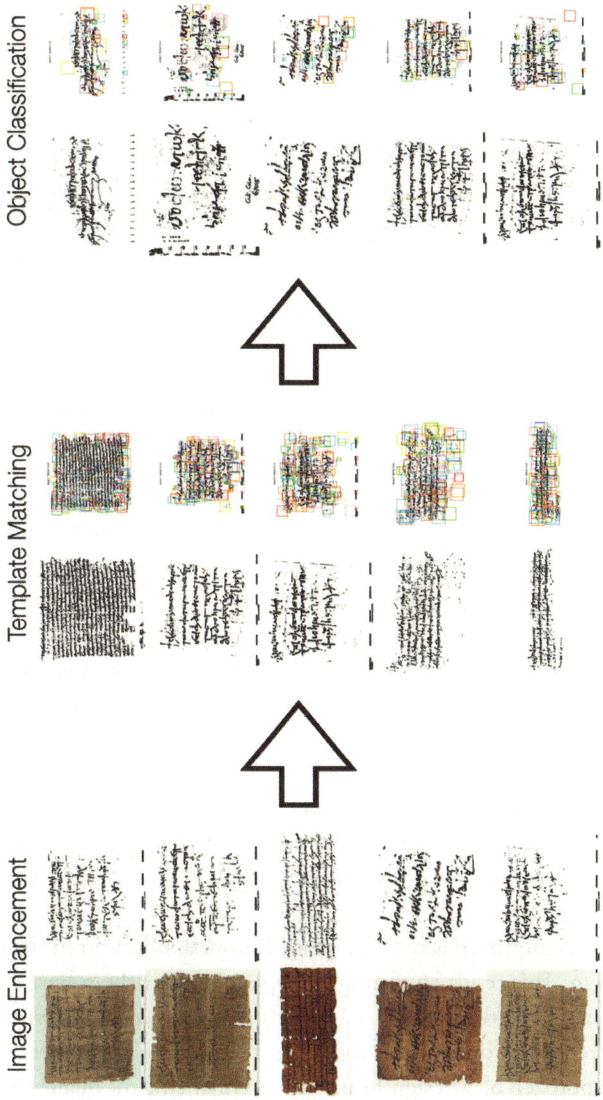

Fig. 6: Graphical Symbol Classification

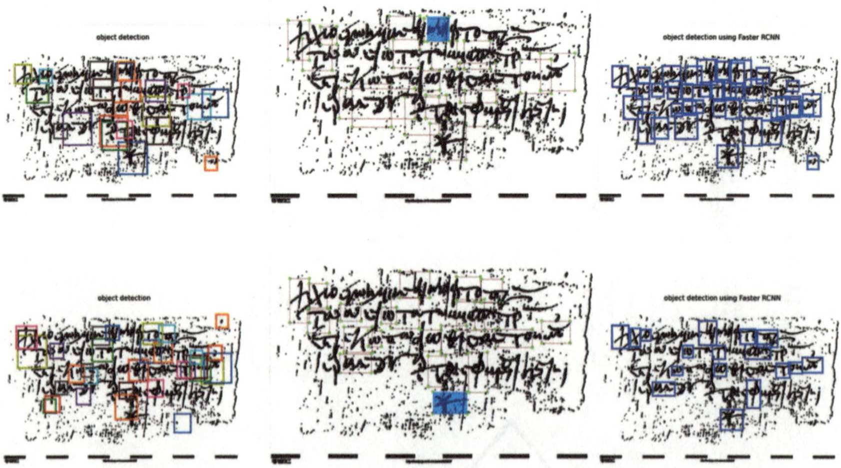

Fig. 7: The generation and evolution of ground truth data for the object detection task. The top row shows data version at checkpoint 50 whereas the bottom row is data version 200.

formed, utilizing both automatic and manual techniques. Ground truth data for training modern object detectors, such as Faster RCNN[45], consists of bounding box coordinates and their associated labels. To obtain this ground truth data, document images were first enhanced and annotated in two sequential steps: automatic annotation using our detector, followed by manual annotation using human experts. The resulting annotations were then divided into subsets in a ratio of two to one for training and evaluation.

Two sets of automatic annotation data were accessible in the image recognition experiment, utilizing two distinct variants of our classifier (checkpoints 50 and 200). To cross-validate the detector's performance, we manually labeled the pair of data sets separately, denoted by Checkpoint 50 and Checkpoint 200 and the result shown in Fig. 7.

The performance has improved across the board for our application in the case of the NOTAE system. This result confirms our hypothesis that the robust training of our classifier has a positive impact on object detection's accuracy, which is correlated with respect to the outcome of the image recognition experiment. The human-in-the-loop approach plays a significant role in enhancing the quality of the results by enabling the system to continuously improve its object detection capabil-

45 Shaoqing Ren/Kaiming He/Ross Girshick/ Jian Sun, Faster r-cnn: Towards real-time object detection with region proposal networks, in: Advances in neural information processing systems 28 (2015); https://arxiv.org/abs/1506.01497

ities. By incorporating such feedback, the system can better align with humanities community goals and more accurately identify their needs. Furthermore, the system's ability to improve itself based on expert feedback facilitates a more accurate recognition of the target society's structure. As a result of this process, the proposed method leverages the insights and knowledge of experts to enhance the learning process and improve the overall quality of the object detection system.

Conclusion & Future work

In conclusion, the NOTAE project demonstrates the potential of combining digital humanities and computational humanities to deepen our understanding of historical cultural artifacts. By employing advanced image processing techniques and developing a comprehensive meta-digital library of documents from Late Antiquity to early medieval Europe, the project aims to uncover the significance and use of graphic symbols within these historical records. The integration of a knowledge graph and an interactive symbol identification system provides valuable insights into the origin, meaning, and function of these symbols. Moreover, the project's interdisciplinary approach brings together experts from diverse fields to collaborate and generate new perspectives and discoveries. Ultimately, the NOTAE project's findings could revolutionize the study of digital and computational humanities, leading to novel advancements and a greater appreciation for our cultural heritage.

Future work could be done to further enhance the capabilities of our symbol recognition system's capabilities. One area of research would be the automatic suggestion of symbol categories, reducing the need for human intervention in the classification process. Another area of interest would be the automatic description of symbol categories in terms of their unique traits and geometric forms, allowing for better understanding and categorization of the symbols. Finally, detecting association rules between employment of specific symbols and historical context would enable a deeper analysis of the symbols and their significance in various cultural and historical contexts. These three areas of research have the potential to greatly expand our understanding of the meaning and usage of graphical symbols in the humanities and social sciences.

Roman medieval documents meet machine learning

An experience of research and teaching.

Serena Ammirati, Lorenzo Lastilla, Paolo Merialdo, Marco Maiorino[1]

Introduction

This contribution is dedicated to recounting our experience of researching the documents of medieval Rome, initiated in 2016 thanks to *In codice ratio*[2]. *In codice ratio* is a research project conceived by Paolo Merialdo that aims to develop innovative methodologies and tools for the analysis and study of manuscript sources. In its initial phase, the project involved the collaboration of the Department of Humanistic Studies of Roma Tre University and the Vatican Apostolic Archive in the application of machine learning techniques to create software capable of automatically recognizing and transcribing manuscript sources from the medieval period.

1. The papal registers

To initiate the project, it first became necessary to identify documents of undoubted historical interest written in a homogeneous medieval script. It soon became clear that the papal registers of the 13th century corresponded perfectly to these criteria. The choice fell in particular on the registers of Honorius III, which present a script, the diplomatic minuscule, characterized by a marked homogeneity in the realization of the alphabetical characters and in the abbreviative system, and at the same time constitute a source for medieval European history still largely unpublished,

---

1 The contribution is divided as follows: Serena Ammirati (Introduction, §§ 3-4 and Conclusions); Lorenzo Lastilla (§ 5) Paolo Merialdo (§ 2); Marco Maiorino (§ 1).

2 http://www.inf.uniroma3.it/db/icr/index.html, to which we also refer for an updated bibliography.

although widely explored especially thanks to the valuable collection of registers by Pietro Pressutti[3].

In little more than ten years of his pontificate Honorius III addressed many crucial issues: he confirmed and promoted the founding of new religious orders (Friars Minor and Preachers); he dealt with various ecclesiastical pastoral issues, as well as the organization of the crusade; and he worked to ensure a certain balance of power between the papacy and the Holy Roman Empire[4]. All this activity is reflected in the documents issued (and received) by the pope, transcribed in the *Registra Vaticana* 9–13[5]: in their entirety, they collect 5204 documents, to which a fair number of *litterae in eodem modo* is added; according to practice, in a *littera in eodem modo* only the *inscriptio* is generally indicated. This is undoubtedly a substantial documentary heritage, although it represents only a limited portion of the documents issued by Honorius III, many of which, as we know, were not copied into the registers.

It is known that registers of Honorius III were produced in the chancery[6], at which they had to be kept for some time. In December 1613, all papal registers were transferred to the first Pauline room of the *Novum Archivum*, soon to be called the Vatican Apostolic Archive or the Vatican Secret Archives, beginning in the mid-17th century[7].

Before presenting the results achieved by the *In codice ratio* project, we provide the essential data of Reg. Vat. 12, on which our attention was focused, currently preserved in the Vatican Archives.

3 Regesta Honorii Papae III, ex Vaticanis archetypis aliisque fontibus, ed. Petrus Pressutti, vol. 1, Romae 1888; vol. 2, Romae 1895.

4 Honorius III's vast activity is extensively described and discussed in the various contributions collected in: Nuovi studi su Onorio III, ed. Christian Grasso (Italia Sacra. Studi e documenti di storia ecclesiastica NS 3), Roma 2017.

5 Città del Vaticano, Archivio Apostolico Vaticano, Regg. Vatt. Latt. 9-13.

6 See Martino Giusti, I Registri Vaticani e le loro provenienze originarie, in: Studi sui registri di bolle papali, ed. Ibid. (Collectanea Archivi Vaticani 1), Città del Vaticano 1979, p. 3–79 and *Appendice II*, p. 129.

7 For the history of the preservation of the papal registers until the creation of the *Novum Vaticanum Archivum* at the initiative of Paul V see: Sergio Pagano/Marco Maiorino, Dalle camere segrete all'Archivio Apostolico: la separazione dell'Archivio papale dalla Biblioteca Vaticana, in: Storia della Biblioteca Vaticana, vol. 3: La Vaticana nel Seicento (1590-1700). Una biblioteca di biblioteche, ed. Claudia Montuschi, Città del Vaticano 2014, p. 243–278; Marco Maiorino, Gli antefatti: l'archivio papale fra Quattro e Cinquecento negli antichi inventari, in Religiosa archivorum custodia. IV Centenario della Fondazione dell'Archivio Segreto Vaticano (1612-2012). Atti del Convegno di Studi, Città del Vaticano, 17-18 aprile 2012, Città del Vaticano 2013, p. 23–64.

Reg. Vat. 12
years of pontificate: VII-VIII (1222–1224)
written sheets: 211 (422 sides)
number of documents: 230 (tome VII) + 534 (tome VIII) + 8 letters n.n. and a numerical jump = 771 (excluding *litterae in eodem modo*)
heading: no special annotations: on f. Iv : "Liber septimus domini Honorii tercii, quem scripsit dominus Radulphus Iaquetelli et debet poni cum libro VIII° eiusdem Honorii, quem scripsit Johannes Noleti Cathalaunensis diocesis"; f. cxiiv : "[Dominus Radulphus] Iaquetelli scripsit de isto libro (VIII) [LXXXI folia] quelibet [continentur] [...] [lineas] que [...] Thierricus Thome scripsit de isto libro [...] folia"; "folium continet LXXII lineas [...]". Both notes provide insight into the composition of the copy of the register commissioned by Urban V.

2. Machine transcription based on machine learning and crowdsourcing techniques

State-of-the-art approaches for automatic transcription of handwritten text are based on the adoption of machine learning techniques. These solutions require a considerable amount of training data, which, in the case of transcription, consists of fragments of manuscript images (e.g., words or lines) each associated with the corresponding textual transcription. While with modern scripts and in living languages it is fairly straightforward to produce these training data, in the case of medieval manuscripts, such as the papal registers of Honorius III, the production of the training data requires a thorough knowledge of medieval Latin language and script, and of the numerous abbreviations used by the scribes of the time. Therefore, in the case of setting up a system capable of learning from whole-line transcriptions, the production of training data would require onerous intervention by "transcription professionals" (paleographers, diplomatists, archivists...).

To avoid burdening experts with the production of these data, we tackled the problem by experimenting with an original solution, based on a crowd-sourced approach. Our idea was to involve people without paleographic experience and knowledge (specifically, high school students)[8] to whom we entrust a very simple task of visual recognition. Basically, through a web application, they are shown a small portion of the manuscript (typically a word) and are asked to mark the image fragments corresponding to one of the symbols (simple letters or abbreviations)

8 We would like to take this opportunity to thank hereby Prof. Marica Ascione of the Liceo Scientifico "Giovanni Keplero" in Rome, who was the first to enthusiastically accept the proposal to involve the students of her institute in this important phase of training data collection. She is credited, among other things, with the name given to the project *In codice ratio*.

used in the writings of the manuscripts under study. This is repeated several times, with different portions of the manuscript for all symbols. The image fragments thus identified and associated with the relevant symbols are then used to train the system to recognize them. An algorithm is then given the task of composing words and lines of text from the results produced by character recognition.

Fig. 1 (a and b) shows the Web application. The user (not necessarily an expert in paleography) is asked to mark the portion of the manuscript shown in the central part of the screen in order to highlight the fragment that is visually similar to the symbol, examples of which are shown above in the green box. Note that the user does not necessarily need to know the meaning of the symbol, but only needs to visually identify its shape most similar to the examples proposed in the image (word) below.

Fig. 1a: The user is asked to mark fragments of the word in the center of the screen that are visually similar to the symbol shown in the green bar.

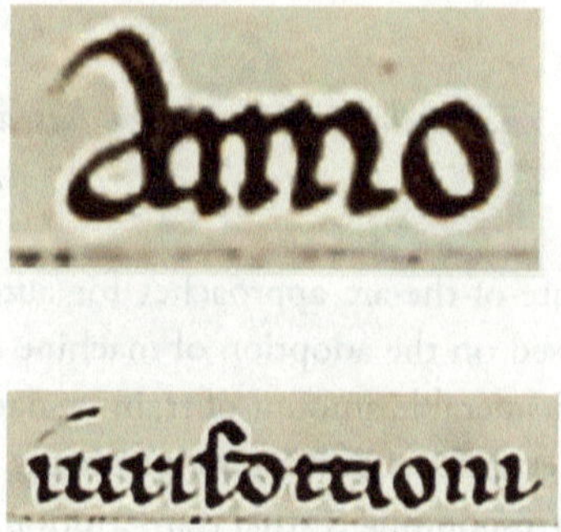

Fig. 2: Words than can lead to a wide range of trascription solution, if only based on pure segmentation

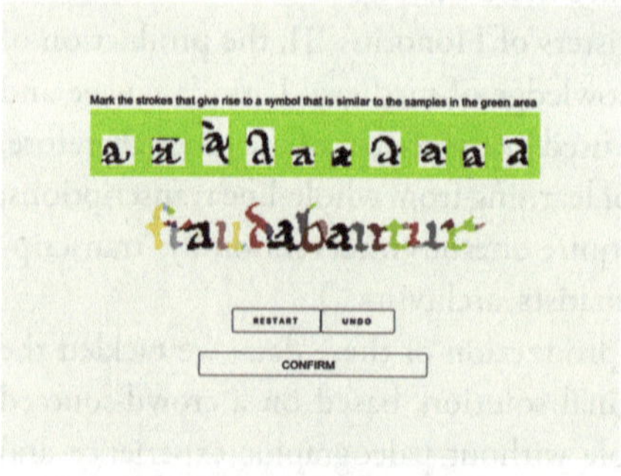

Fig. 1b: The user marked the fragments he recognized as visually similar to the symbol shown in the green bar.

The information gathered through the Web application allows a set of images to be associated with each symbol, each containing a representation of that symbol (simple letter or abbreviation). These images are then used to train a machine learning system capable of recognizing the different symbols in the script. Technically, such a system is implemented through a classifier based on a convolutional neural network (CNN).

The classifier can recognize individual letters with very high accuracy. However, producing a transcription for handwritten texts such as those in the papal regis-

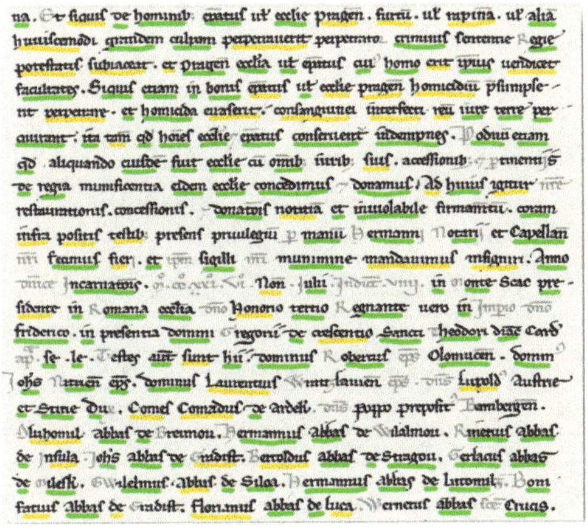

Fig. 3: Intuitive presentation of the results: On a page of 296 words: 62%: correct transcription (green); 20% at edit distance 1 (yellow); 18% not processable (gray). Failures are due to: segmentation errors (many); symbol recognition errors (a few).

ters of Honorius III on the basis of character recognition alone is an inherently ambiguous task: characters in words must be correctly separated to be correctly recognized; at the same time, correct recognition is often required for correct character separation. This ambiguity is known as "Sayre's paradox"[9].

As an example, consider the word image in Fig. 2: depending on how it is segmented, it can lead to a wide range of solutions other than "anno" (which is the correct transcription): "aimo" or "aniio" or even "aiiiio". Similarly, the word which corresponds to "iurisditioni", could be confused with "iurisdittiom", "uirisditioni" or other variants.

To overcome these problems, we use a strategy that relies on text over-segmentation with the goal of isolating elementary text segments (potential alphabet symbols) that are a superset of the actual ones in the word.

Most of these segments (or combinations of segments) contain real characters, but many of them are spurious: to this end, our CNN model is jointly trained both to distinguish correct segmentations from spurious ones and to classify characters, through two separate outputs.

A set of candidate transcripts is then produced for each word by assembling the results of the classifier. A search algorithm evaluates the candidate transcripts and chooses the most plausible one, based on both character recognition reliability and a language model.

In Fig. 3 you can see the results of this approach.

9 Kenneth M. SAYRE, Machine Recognition of Handwritten Words: A Project Report, in: Pattern Recognition 5 (1973) p. 213–228.

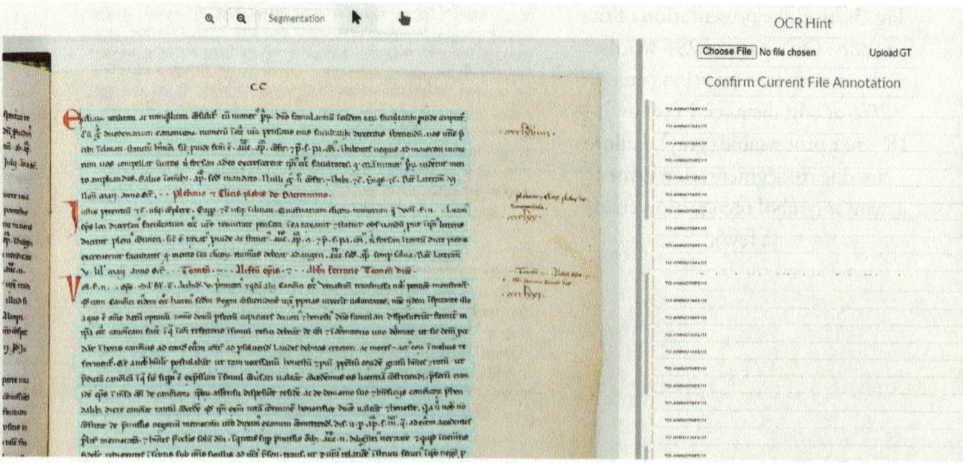

Fig. 4: Line-by-line transcript entry mask.

3. *Automatic transcription based on machine learning techniques and training set developed by experts. Future perspectives.*

Evaluation of the results obtained with crowdsourced training led us to try a new mode, an "advanced approach", in which the system is trained not with individual letters or abbreviations, but with entire lines of writing; in this way, visual and linguistic knowledge are not separated, but learned contextually. This mode of training is based on the use of "quality" data, that is, correct and accurate transcriptions made by individuals with high linguistic and paleographic expertise: by professionals, in short (paleographers, diplomatists, archivists). The production of these data is therefore an absolutely manual activity, which requires - as those who do it for a living know - time and concentration. To make the task less burdensome, we have therefore developed a working interface that is as user-friendly as possible. The image of the portion of text to be transcribed is uploaded to the software, which then segments the lines of text, creating a coherent mask into which the transcription can be entered line by line (Fig. 4).

The trained neural network operates with the same interface; by scrolling through the lines of text in the image these are highlighted in yellow, and so is the corresponding transcript. The expert can check the transcript produced and take action to correct it, thus contributing to the training of the system (Fig. 5).

In this way, a much more complex neural network is trained. We entrusted the creation of the training data, i.e., the transcription of about 20 folios of *Reg. Vat.* 12, to a research fellow in paleography, Francesca Galli, and used 5 folios of the same manuscript as a test set. The software then produced the transcription of all 211 folios of *Reg. Vat.* 12. The results obtained are encouraging, considering that 20 folios

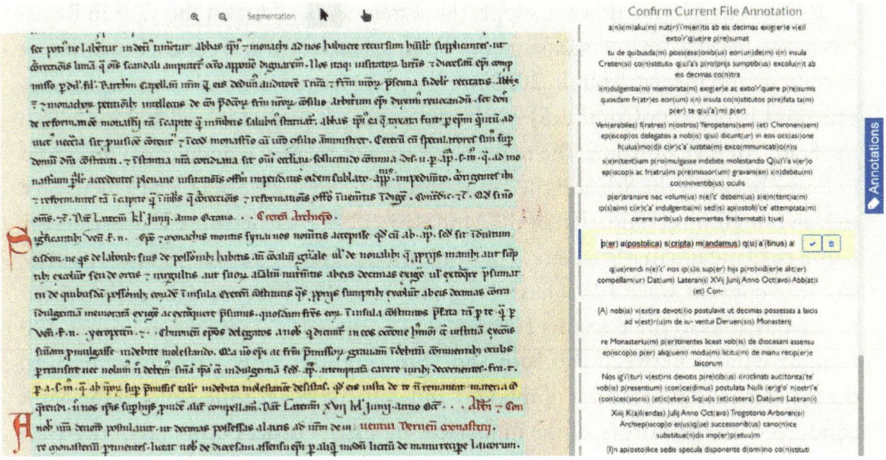

Fig. 5: The transcription of the line of text highlighted in yellow, made by the system, can be corrected by the expert.

as a training set is a rather small number, especially for texts so varied in content and so densely peppered with abbreviations: out of an average of 80 characters per line, the errors do not exceed 8, and are often concentrated on a few lines. When examined in detail, these errors, which mainly involve – as is to be expected – the dissolving of abbreviations, must be blamed either on the non-occurrence of that specific compendium in the training pages, or on an inconsistency in the transcription system: an abbreviated word dissolved in different ways (*Christo/xpisto*) by the trainer. It can happen, but the correctness and quality of the training data is inescapable[10].

4. Matrices: the present of In codice ratio

The technology we have developed so far has been a harbinger of other collaborations: with the Chamber of Deputies of the Italian Parliament, for the transcription of some nineteenth-century documents related to the Commission on Brigandage, and has proved equally effective for reading some printed tax documents[11].

10 "From big data to good data": this topic has been repeatedly drawn attention to in recent years by Andrew Ng, a pioneer in artificial intelligence (https://www.andrewng.org), who in 2022 launched a research topic called "data-centric AI", calling it "the discipline of systematically engineering the data used to build an AI system", an approach focused on finding ways to enhance the data for many practical applications. When dealing with data, it is important to be consistent if you want improvement in performance. Getting "Small Data" right will probably yield more immediate rewards. Small Data is crucial for various reasons, which is why it must be tackled separately from a larger Big Data endeavor (https://datacentricai.org).

11 The technology-cultural heritage combination has also had a good media echo: in 2019 Google

The next development was to apply the system worked out on the Vatican Registers to medieval Roman documents similar in textual form and epoch, but different in content and format. Thus in 2020 *Matrices* (seMAntic annotaTion over heteRogeneous hIstorical doCumEntS) was born: a research project in collaboration with the State Archive of Rome, the main repository of medieval documents produced in Rome between the 8th and the 14th centuries[12]. Again, we decided to focus on a rich and interesting fund, that of the Monastero delle Benedettine e Clarisse dei SS. Cosma e Damiano in Mica Aurea (in Rome, in the Trastevere area). The monastery, women's convent since 1235, has a long and complex history which can be reconstructed thanks to the documents preserved in original (parchment and paper, 470 in total, datable between the 10th and 18th centuries, only partially edited), to the registers and inventories of modern and contemporary times, and to the work conducted on the history of the monastery by sister Orsola Formicini in the 16th century. The oldest documents, edited in the late 19th century by Pietro Fedele, are irregular in shape and text alignment, but regular in repetitions of formulas and distribution of the content. One element of no small interest is the presence of identical hands in different documents (even from different funds), as is to be expected for medieval ecclesiastical institutions, which often used the same *notarii*, *scriniarii* and *iudices*[13].

selected our research as a showcase project for its AI platform (https://youtu.be/v-FgOACRgfs), and we have been able to tell about our research experience not only in peer-reviewed journals or high science journals, but also in newspapers in several countries (Italy, Germany, Spain, the United States). Two Roma Tre students founded a startup to take advantage of the technology developed in the project (MyBiros.com). Their goal is to offer a service to automate data entry processes.

12 As is well known, the State Archives of Rome is a so-called "archivio di concentrazione": established by Royal Decree No. 605 of December 30, 1871, following the Unification of Italy, today in the 'Pergamene' collection it preserves e.g. the documents extracted for the most part from the archives of suppressed religious corporations and hospitals, and, for the remainder, purchases made mainly between 1884 and the beginning of our century. Later, the parchment series of archival funds acquired over time were included.

13 The charters up to the year 1100 were published by Pietro FEDELE in: Archivio della Società Romana di Storia Patria (1898 and 1899), and lately reprinted, with indices by Paola PAVAN in: Carte del monastero dei SS. Cosma e Damiano in Mica Aurea. Testo latino a fronte, Vol. 1: Secoli X-XI, Roma 1981. On the Chronica of Orsola Formicini see G. GUERRINI FERRI, Il Liber monialium ed il Libro d'Antiquità di suor Orsola Formicini. Le Clarisse e la storia del venerabile monastero romani dei Santi Cosma e Damiano in Mica Aurea detto di San Cosimato in Trastevere (Biblioteca Nazionale Centrale, mss. Varia 5 e Varia 6), in: Scrineum Rivista 8 (2011) p. 81–111.

5. *Matrices: future of In codice ratio*

The subject of hand identity led us to develop collaterally some experiments: first, of scribal hand recognition, using some manuscripts preserved in the Vatican Library as a case study.

This problem has also been a particularly challenging case study to test the performance of self-supervised learning (a deep learning approach recently developed) in the paleographic field, and, as a result of the experiments conducted, to demonstrate the positive impact of the application of this methodology with respect to the scribal hand recognition task[14]. Among the strengths of self-supervised learning techniques, their capability to leverage large amounts of unlabeled data turned out to be particularly positive for the paleographic domain, characterized by a chronic problem of data scarcity (i.e., many digitized manuscripts are available, but just a few of them are labeled, so that most of the data is not useful when applying traditional deep learning techniques to this domain).

After these experiments, an explainability (also called xAI) analysis of the methodology was (and is currently being) carried out, to understand and highlight which parts of a page contribute the most to the scribal hand prediction of the deep neural network. Several explainability techniques have been considered and tested, with the aim of producing convincing visual explanations of the predictions, in particular: LIME[15], SHAP[16], and GradCAM[17]. The analysis is carried out at different levels of granularity, going from a pixel-level assessment to the evaluation of the importance of character-level, intra-line, and inter-line visual features, searching for possible connections with the features adopted by paleographers for the scribal hand recognition task. The outcome of this research could be the last stage of an effective system of training data set-up and evaluation of the results obtained, which may in time gain the confidence of even the most skeptical scholars in the application of machine learning techniques to traditionally humanistic study activities, such as hand recognition of different copyists.

14 Lorenzo Lastilla/Serena Ammirati/Donatella Firmani/Nikos Komodakis/Paolo Merialdo/Simone Scardapane, Self-supervised learning for medieval handwriting identification: A case study from the Vatican Apostolic Library, in: Information Processing & Management 59/3 (2022); https://doi.org/10.1016/j.ipm.2022.102875

15 Marco Tulio Ribeiro/Singh Sameer/Carlos Guestrin, "Why should I trust you?" Explaining the predictions of any classifier, in: Proceedings of the 22nd ACM SIGKDD international conference on knowledge discovery and data mining, 2016; https://doi.org/10.48550/arXiv.1602.04938

16 Scott M. Lundberg/ Su-In Lee, A unified approach to interpreting model predictions, in: Advances in neural information processing systems 30 (2017) p. 4768–4777.

17 Ramprasaath R. Selvaraju (et al.), Grad-cam: Visual explanations from deep networks via gradient-based localization, in: Proceedings of the IEEE international conference on computer vision (2017) p. 618–626; https://doi.org/10.1109/ICCV.2017.74.

Indeed, we believe that, with the appropriate involvement of traditional analysis methodology in the software development phase, it will not only lead to an optimization of the training data set-up (and, consequently, of the results obtained by the application), but also to the construction of a 'virtuous' workflow, in which the dialogue between humanities and computer science expertise, which is now necessary, is truly constructive and based on mutual trust.

Conclusions

To conclude: from the perspective of the paleographer and humanist, the experience of *In codice ratio* has given and continues to give many insights not only on the level of research, but also in traditional academic teaching, suggesting new learning tools. Being able to contribute to the creation of an informatics tool at the service of historical research has convinced us that, if developed and applied appropriately, artificial intelligence techniques can be a resource for paleographers and diplomatists, and that none of this is scientifically effective without constant dialogue and collaboration between different expertise.

BeCoRe – Between Composition and Reception

The Authority of Medieval Charters

Nicole Bergk-Pinto, Jacqueline Schindler, Niklas Tscherne

Medieval charters are complex objects, which combine linguistic (the text itself and its contents), visual (various graphical elements) and material signs (such as attached seals, which themselves also contain visual and textual features) within one process of communication[1]. While it may at first seem obvious to place emphasis on the textual aspects of these objects, the graphical features which they exhibit have historically taken on a wide range of roles, from the purely decorative, to making a document recognizable to an audience in a society of widely varying levels of literacy, to ones vital to their validity as legal documents. The former may be exemplified by the rich illustrations and flourishes that are found on illuminated charters, while the latter include well-known examples such as the "Bene Valete" or the "Rota" of papal bulls.

The possibility of the systematic analysis of graphical elements contained in large corpora of medieval charters is a recent development. New technologies as well as unprecedented access to research material through large-scale digitization efforts by numerous institutions today offer new opportunities for researchers to engage with the material, and even to potentially automatize some processes through the use of machine learning algorithms.

The BeCoRe project[2] aims at developing new ways of exploring and interpreting the graphical signs found on charters, by developing tools to automatize the search for and recognition of such signs, and integrating them into an online resource (the

---

1 Peter Rück, Beiträge zur diplomatischen Semiotik, in: Graphische Symbole in mittelalterlichen Urkunden: Beiträge zur diplomatischen Semiotik (Historische Hilfswissenschaften 3), ed. Peter Rück, Sigmaringen 1996, p. 3.

2 https://digital-humanities.at/en/dha/s-project/between-composition-and-reception-authority-medieval-charters-becore

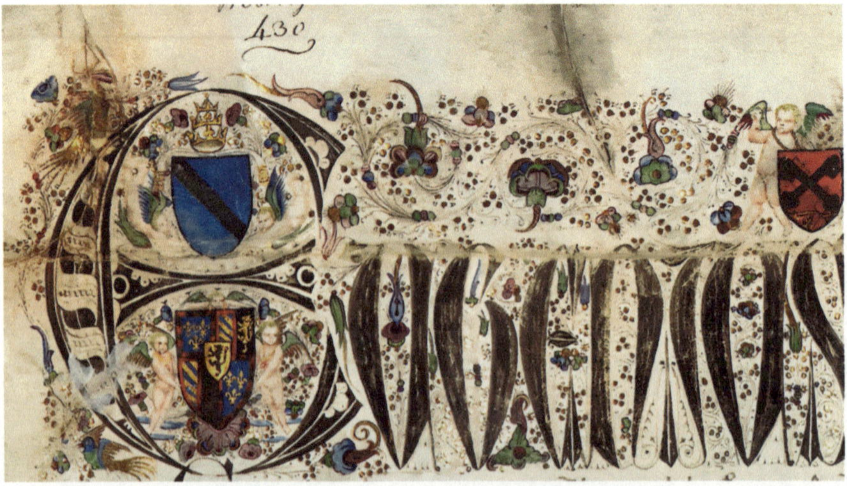

Fig. 1: Source: Illuminierte Urkunden 1439-07-06_Paris, in: Monasterium.net, URL /mom/IlluminierteUrkunden/1439-06-06_Paris/charter>

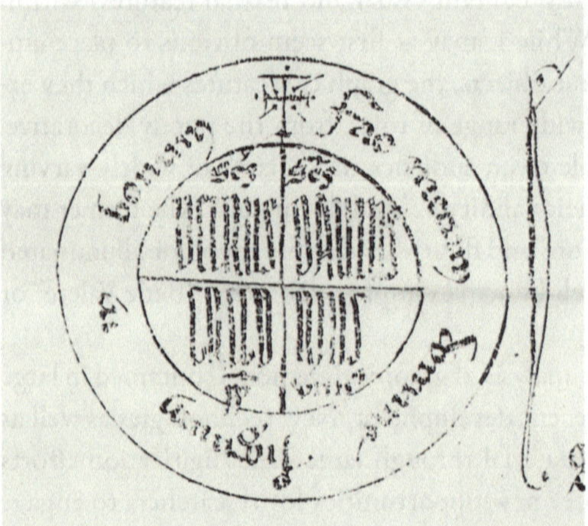

Fig. 2: Source: Illuminierte Urkunden - Papsturkunden 1236-03-18_Engelberg, in: Monasterium.net, URL /mom/IlluminierteUrkundenKurie/1236-03-18_Engelberg/charter>

Monasterium.net virtual archive) that hosts a large collection of charters. These tools will be making use of computer vision-based approaches to classifying images and detecting graphical signs. Our hope is that this will enable us to gain new insights from comparative analysis of charters of various origins, specifically regarding symbols of authority and validity, their use and reception. For this purpose, this project intends to extend the Monasterium.net database through new corpora, enhance the platform's data and metadata structures to allow work on newly developing research questions, and to create tools for the automatic analysis of visual features which can then be integrated into the website. This should then aid in further study of the visual features of charters in the broader context of their creation and reception.

The material that will be used in this project consists of five corpora of French and Austrian origin, namely the abbeys of Cluny and Fontenay as well as the Austrian abbeys of Lambach, Göttweig, and Lilienfeld, with a total of over 6000 charters. This selection allows us to study a lesser known period of Cluniac history as well as compare the developments of Benedictine and Cistercian monasticisms in Austria with those in France during the same period. Some of this material had already been published on Monasterium.net by the start of the project, while the rest was added subsequently, as will be described.

BeCoRe in context

BeCoRe is not alone in exploring its subject matter – there has been an increase in interest in the study of the visual features of charters and their symbolic significance in recent years (here we can give the example of the "Illuminierte Urkunden als Gesamtkunstwerk"[3] project, a cooperative effort by experts from art history, diplomatics, and digital humanities backgrounds, in the course of which Monasterium.net was enriched with a large number of illuminated charters). The following two brief examples of projects which are part of this development may give some additional context to the work of BeCoRe, and illustrate the kinds of questions that are of interest in the area of visual charter analysis.

The first is the NOTAE project[4] by Antonella Ghignoli, which focuses on the analysis of graphic symbols in documentary records as a historical phenomenon from Late Antiquity to the early medieval period[5]. It focuses primarily on data collection, seeking to give an inventory of symbols and their images from the available sources, analyze these symbols and place them in relation to their authors and historical/geographic context, create a database as a research tool for the project, and conduct comparative, diachronic studies based on the results of the work.

The Models of Authority project[6] has analyzed medieval Scottish charters and, combining diplomatic and paleographical approaches, aims to offer new perspectives on the origins of government in Western Europe[7]. Proceeding from the expec-

3 https://illuminierte-urkunden.uni-graz.at/de/

4 http://www.notae-project.eu/

5 Antonella Ghignoli, The NOTAE project: a Research between East and West, Late Antiquity and Early Middle Ages, in: Comparative Oriental Manuscript Studies Bulletin 5/1 (2019) p. 29–42. See also the paper by Francesco Leotta in this volume.

6 http://www.modelsofauthority.ac.uk/

7 Dauvit Broun, Introducing the 'Models of Authority' project: Scottish charters c. 1100–c. 1250 in: Models of Authority (2015); http://www.modelsofauthority.ac.uk/blog/intro/

tation that the changing nature of government also influences the production of charters, it has focused on the great visual similarities between English and Scottish charters, such as the use of quick, informal, cursive script. While this type of writing in English royal charters is likely a practical consequence of many documents needing to be processed in a short time, its appearance in charters from the comparatively less busy Scottish king's chapel seems to be an instance of visual mimicking for the purpose of increasing the document's authority. The project has made use of a digital database of charters, People of Medieval Scotland[8], which provides "essential information such as dating each text and identifying the people and places involved"[9].

Similarly, BeCoRe is particularly interested in graphical signs as symbols of authority and power, and what they tell us about how these symbols were used. The possibility of machine learning-supported analysis of larger groups of charters can hopefully enable us to make progress in studying these topics. One example in which progress could be made is the question of so-called "diplomatic landscapes".

Diplomatic landscapes

The notion of the diplomatic landscape (germ. "Urkundenlandschaft") is not entirely new (having been originally invented by the Austrian historian and diplomatist Fichtenau), but the strictness of the exact definition has varied through time and place, particularly when the originally German term is translated into other languages[10]. In the sense that it is used here and based on the definition given by Härtel[11], the term refers to an area within which charters have displayed a certain degree of similarity over a certain amount of time, and can therefore be understood to some extent as a distinct unity. This similarity can refer to both external features (physical aspects such as materials, format, and visual signs), as well as internal features (such as formulaicity and textual contents). In this sense, a comparison can be drawn between a diplomatic landscape and a linguistic dialect.

Such landscapes can develop for a variety of reasons: Political systems and forms of government can bring with them their own forms and traditions of creating char-

8 https://www.poms.ac.uk/

9 http://www.modelsofauthority.ac.uk/blog/intro/

10 Reinhard Härtel, Urkundenlandschaften zwischen Donau, Rhein und Adria, in: Urkunden – Schriften – Lebensordnungen, neue Beiträge zur Mediävistik; Vorträge der Jahrestagung des Instituts für Österreichische Geschichtsforschung aus Anlass des 100. Geburtstags von Heinrich Fichtenau (1912 - 2000), Wien, 13.–15. Dezember 2012 (Veröffentlichungen des Instituts für Österreichische Geschichtsforschung 63), ed. Andreas Schwarcz/Katharina Kaska, Wien, Graz und Köln 2015, p. 193–212, 193–195.

11 Ibid. p. 193.

ters, and both and cultural borders may create borders of diplomatic landscapes. Such borders are, however, often softened by legal and social circles that practice their own, separate traditions. More recent theories have taken a closer look at the relationship between diplomatic and physical landscapes, diplomatic and natural borders. Factors such as availability of safe roads, flows of traffic, relative remoteness and isolation of certain areas, mountains and rivers can all play as much into the spread of diplomatic practices as they do into the spread of any other cultural features. What also seems clear is that diplomatic landscapes are not set in stone, but subject to change over time and as a result of political, cultural and social shifts. Similarly, some types of charters may reflect different kinds of landscapes than others[12].

Concerning the analysis of charters preserved in the archives of monasteries (or at least until the institution's dissolution, in the cases of Fontenay and Cluny), one can pose the question of the correlation between the features of the charters whose production is linked to the monastic institution, and those from outside, which reflect the diplomatic features of the assumed diplomatic landscape into which the monastery is geographically embedded. Here, several aspects have to be taken into account. Monks have acted as carriers of cultural tradition, and may therefore have brought new diplomatic features to a monastery's environment, even if they did not necessarily innovate them, since this would have made them a kind of "diplomatic foreigners", potentially causing problems with the acceptability of their documents. Particularly until the 13th and 14th centuries, the influence of monasteries could be quite important, as those religious institutions were a kind of "literacy hub" in a society relying mostly on oral communication. In this context, the classic diplomatic question of whether a charter was produced by the issuing party or the recipients (or even by a third party) is of great interest, as this may provide evidence about the institution's role in the spread of diplomatic knowledge in particular and of written culture in general, in other words, whether the local population produced its own charters or had to refer to the monks' writing skills. Concerning this point, time, place, and degree of literacy have to be taken into account, since the evolution in the use of the written word brought about significant changes in society, and thus the situation in the 13th century cannot be compared with the situation at the end of the 15th century[13].

12 Ibid. p. 197–200

13 (Late) Medieval literacy is a highly discussed topic, cf. as a brief introduction: Mark Mersiowsky/Joachim J. Halbekann/Anja Thaller, Pragmatische Schriftlichkeit im Spätmittelalter und in Esslingen: Eine Einführung, in: Schreiben – Verwalten – Aufbewahren: neue Forschungen zur Schriftlichkeit im spätmittelalterlichen Esslingen (Esslinger Studien 49), ed. Mark Mersiowsky/Joachim J. Halbekann/Anja Thaller, Ostfildern 2018, p. 9–12.

Another significant aspect in this context is the influence of a monastery's affiliation with a monastic order (in our case the Benedictines and the Cistercians) on its diplomatic output. The latter especially are known for their advanced administration and handling of the written word[14], so one could assume that they acted as vectors of the development of new diplomatic elements. Could there even be, and this is a very bold assumption which, even if true, would be very difficult to prove, a link between the order's spirituality and the design of their charters, which was then (unconsciously) taken over by the monasteries' "neighborhood"? All these supposed diplomatic influences can possibly be analyzed at different levels, through the internal and external features of charters. By focusing on the latter and in particular on the graphic signs and the charters layout, we hope to bring new elements to the discussion about diplomatic landscapes and their evolution, in particular by using new methods adapted to the large quantities of charters preserved from the late medieval period.

The concept of the diplomatic landscape has been discussed for quite some time, be it as a means to an end (that is to say, to another research question), or, though less frequently, as a topic of research in its own right. The phenomenon has so far not been conclusively proven to be valid in the broader picture, and for areas beyond the vicinity of Austria, which has historically been the country most concerned with the question of diplomatic landscapes[15]. One reason for this may be the sheer quantity of material that would need to be examined in order to come to definitive conclusions – the overwhelming quantity of charters especially from the late medieval period being a common challenge in diplomatics. It is precisely problems of this kind which seem to lend themselves particularly well to machine learning-based, automated approaches, and we hope to be able to make progress in this regard in the course of this project. The search for diplomatic landscapes would thereby form part of the more general investigation of graphic signs of power and authority, which stands independently of whether such landscapes can be located. But if so, the insights thus gained could be of great value.

14 Elke Goez, Pragmatische Schriftlichkeit und Archivpflege der Zisterzienser. Ordenszentralismus und regionale Vielfalt, namentlich in Franken und Altbayern (1098–1525) (Vita regularis 17), Münster [usw.] 2003; Peter Rückert, Legitimation – Tradition – Repräsentation. Pragmatische Schriftkultur bei den Zisterziensern im deutschsprachigen Südwesten, in: Kulturtopographie des deutschsprachigen Südwestens im späteren Mittelalter. Studien und Texte (Kulturtopographie des alemannischen Raums 1), ed. Barbara Fleith/René Wetzel, Tübingen 2009, p. 99–120.

15 Ibid. p. 197 & 202.

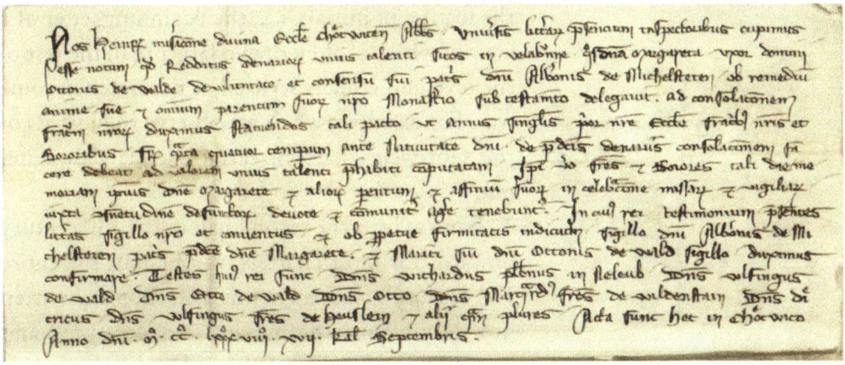

Fig. 3: Source: Göttweig, Stiftsarchiv Urkunden (1058-1899) 1288 VIII 16, in: Monasterium.net, URL </mom/AT-StiAG/GoettweigOSB/1288_VIII_16/charter>

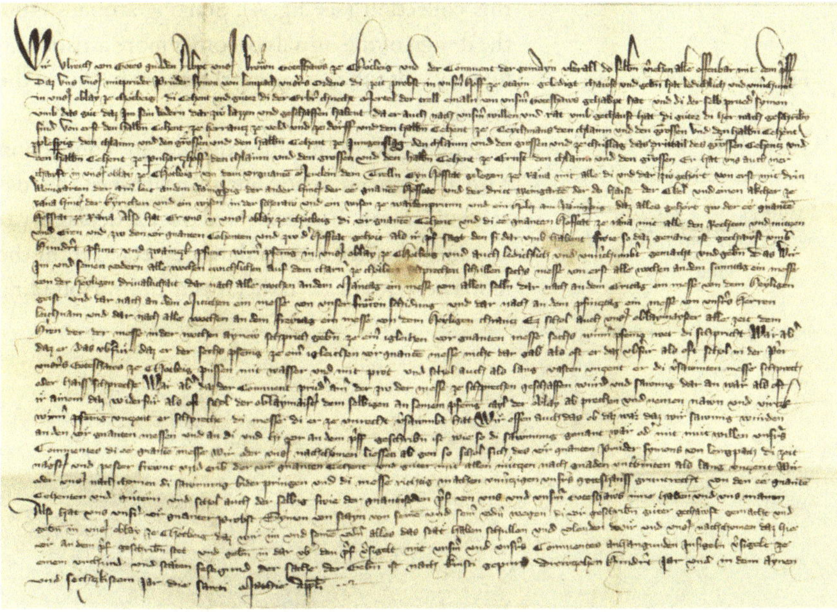

Fig. 4: Source: Göttweig, Stiftsarchiv Urkunden (1058-1899) 1361 II 24, in: Monasterium.net, URL </mom/AT-StiAG/GoettweigOSB/1361_II_24/charter>

Initials in Austrian charters

The Austrian charters that BeCoRe works with (from the Göttweig, Lambach and Lilienfeld monasteries) offer an opportunity to investigate the question of diplomatic landscapes and the visual development of charters over time by focusing on

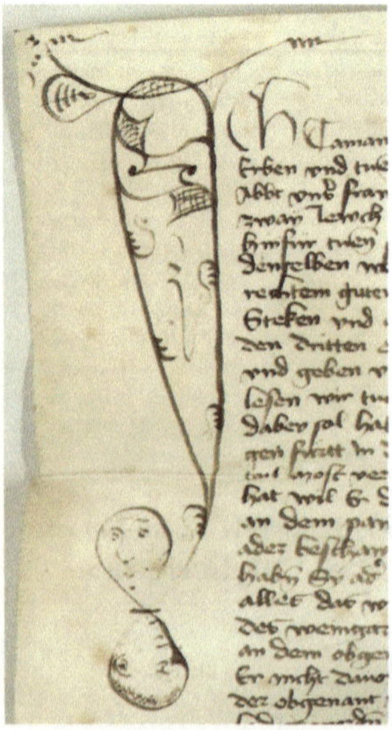

Fig. 5: Source: Göttweig, Stiftsarchiv Urkunden (1058–1899) 1444 XII 13, in: Monasterium.net, URL </mom/AT-StiAG/GoettweigOSB/1444_XII_13/charter>

the feature of initials, i.e., the beginning letter of a charter which is often drawn larger than the rest of the text, and visually stylized or decorated in some way. For example, when we observe the initials of the Göttweig charters, certain tendencies stand out.

From at least the second half of the 13th century onward (for most charters, throughout the entire 13th century), charters in this collection are written in a very plain fashion, with standard script and initials being largely unadorned and only slightly enlarged (see fig. 3). Towards the end of the 14th century, a significant increase in the size of the initials becomes noticeable on many charters from this collection (see fig. 4). Starting around 1400, the design of the initials becomes more artistic and flowery – at times covering the entire height of the charter.

Questions to be investigated in connection with this phenomenon include whether this development can be connected to particular writers, and whether this tendency emerged from the monastery itself, or rather from the surrounding

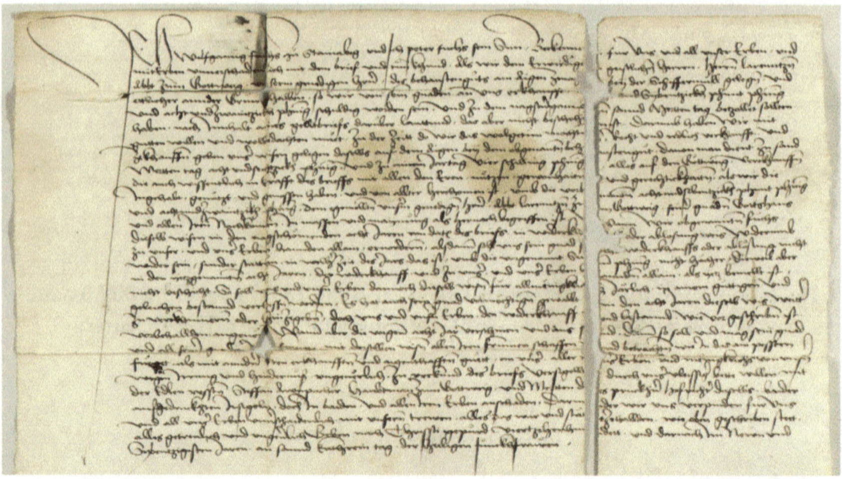

Fig. 6: Source: Göttweig, Stiftsarchiv Urkunden (1058-1899) 1479 XI 25, in: Monasterium.net, URL </mom/AT-StiAG/GoettweigOSB/1479_XI_25/charter>

areas. Fast, large-scale processing of images offers new possibilities for investigating whether the illustrations of given initials can be reliably matched to a writer, a scriptorium, or a "school" or tradition of charter composition. It will be interesting to see which styles of initials the machine learning algorithm even identifies as initials, and which would it potentially miss (notice the minimalist initial in fig. 6 as compared to the elaborate initial in fig. 5), and whether initials that were added at a later date are successfully distinguished from those that were added during the initial writing.

One practical approach that may lend itself for these kinds of questions is to use a clustering algorithm (for example, K-means clustering) to see which charters consistently cluster together. This process groups images that the algorithm determines as belonging to the same cluster, based on the similarity of certain features. The determination of these features, i.e. that which the machine actually "learns", is of central importance to this part of the work, and makes the difference between clusters that are actually meaningful and clusters that are merely incidental. For this, various means of feature extraction (such as convolutional neural networks and histogram of oriented gradients [HOG]) will be attempted. From the discovery of clusters, conclusions might then also be drawn about the context of the charter's creation. We also hope that such a process can be extended to signs of authority and power more generally, where the clustering approach may help discover differences in usage and meaning of such signs. However, this process can in practical application also be misleading, if we approach the material with the wrong expectations and assumptions – some of the potential dangers of this approach will be discussed later.

Monasterium.net

The primary resource the BeCoRe works with is Monasterium.net[16], the largest digital archive of medieval and early modern charters. The goal of the Monasterium.net project has been the creation of a digital platform that makes the vast collection of central European charters available to both the scholarly community as well as interested laypeople[17]. It has grown steadily since its beginning in 2002 (then with the goal of gathering a variety of ecclesiastical documents and materials, before later settling on digital representations of charter as its object of focus), and currently contains over 650 000 charters originating from over a dozen European countries in its database.

16 https://www.monasterium.net/mom/home

17 Karl Heinz, Monasterium. net: Auf dem Weg zu einem mitteleuropäischen Urkundenportal, in: Digitale Diplomatik. Neue Technologien in der historischen Arbeit mit Urkunden (Afd Beiheft 12), ed. Georg Vogeler, Köln/Weimar 2009, p. 70–77, 70.

The material that is available on Monasterium.net is very heterogeneous, and comes in widely varying stages of completion. The website supports the representation of both archival fonds and collections, and the state of the charters themselves can range from relatively crude OCR to items with richly detailed diplomatic descriptions, transcriptions, multiple photographs, and indices of persons and places. The continuing refinement and improvement of this material are a central concern of the Monasterium.net project[18]. To facilitate this process, the website encourages users themselves to participate in adding and improving contents via the Edit-MOM editor, which allows them to add abstracts, modify transcriptions, etc. Users may create personal copies of charters, even create their own collections, and then publish their work on the website.

Under the hood, Monasterium.net uses the eXist-db[19] XML database, which uses XQuery to query the database and XSLT for transforming data. Large parts of the HTML widgets that the user actually sees are created by querying the XML database with XQuery and displaying the results on page embedded into the regular HTML and CSS. Charters are stored in the CEI format, which was developed by the Charters Encoding Initiative[20] as an alternative to the TEI XML standard, and which is more specifically focused on the needs of diplomatists in representing charters digitally (for example, by providing tags for the various standardized formulas that appear throughout the text of a charter). More recently, the development of TEI-P5 has made many of these changes obsolete, and work has already been done to prepare a migration to the TEI-P5 standard[21] at some point in the future. Until that point, however, CEI remains in use on Monasterium.net.

Enhancing Monasterium.net

Part of the work that has been accomplished so far in the course of the project has been to both extend the Monasterium.net database with new collections of charters, as well as to enhance both the CEI schema and the user interface of the website. The corpus of Fontenay abbey[22] was originally available in the TEI format, and had to be converted to CEI before being imported into our database. This process involves consideration of numerous concerns, such as: Is there an analogous CEI annotation for a given TEI annotation? Can that annotation be conveyed without

18 Ibid. 71.

19 http://www.exist-db.org/exist/apps/homepage/index.html

20 https://www.cei.lmu.de/

21 Georg Vogeler, 'Monasterium.net'–eine Infrastruktur für diplomatische Forschung, in: Digitale Mediävistik und der deutschsprachige Raum (Das Mittelalter 24/1), ed. Roman Bleier et al., Berlin 2019, p. 247–252.

22 https://www.monasterium.net/mom/Fontenay/collection

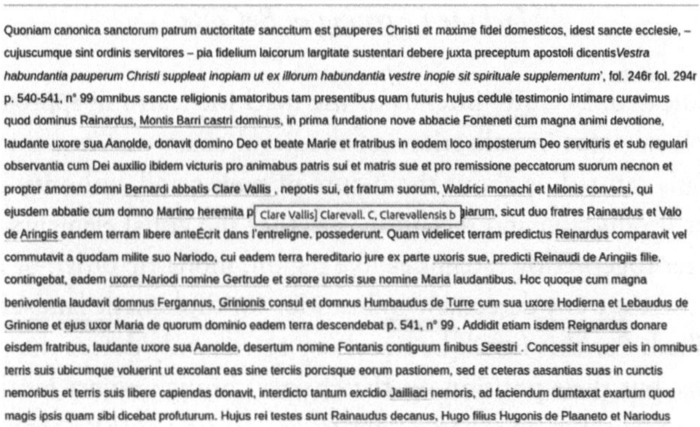

Quoniam canonica sanctorum patrum auctoritate sanccitum est pauperes Christi et maxime fidei domesticos, idest sancte ecclesie, – cujuscumque sint ordinis servitores – pia fidelium laicorum largitate sustentari debere juxta preceptum apostoli dicentis*Vestra habundantia pauperum Christi suppleat inopiam ut ex illorum habundantia vestre inopie sit spirituale supplementum*', fol. 246r fol. 294r p. 540-541, n° 99 omnibus sancte religionis amatoribus tam presentibus quam futuris hujus cedule testimonio intimare curavimus quod dominus Rainardus, Montis Barri castri dominus, in prima fundatione nove abbacie Fonteneti cum magna animi devotione, laudante uxore sua Aanolde, donavit domino Deo et beate Marie et fratribus in eodem loco imposterum Deo servituris et sub regulari observantia cum Dei auxilio ibidem victuris pro animabus patris sui et matris sue et pro remissione peccatorum suorum necnon et propter amorem domni Bernardi abbatis Clare Vallis , nepotis sui, et fratrum suorum, Waldrici monachi et Milonis conversi, qui ejusdem abbatie cum domno Martino heremita p[Clare Vallis] Clarevall. C, Clarevallensis b]giarum, sicut duo fratres Rainaudus et Valo de Aringiis eandem terram libere anteÉcrit dans l'entreligne. possederunt. Quam videlicet terram predictus Reinardus comparavit vel commutavit a quodam milite suo Nariodo, cui eadem terra hereditario jure ex parte uxoris sue, predicti Reinaudi de Aringiis filie, contingebat, eadem uxore Nariodi nomine Gertrude et sorore uxoris sue nomine Maria laudantibus. Hoc quoque cum magna benivolentia laudavit domnus Fergannus, Grinionis consul et domnus Humbaudus de Turre cum sua uxore Hodierna et Lebaudus de Grinione et ejus uxor Maria de quorum dominio eadem terra descendebat p. 541, n° 99 . Addidit etiam isdem Reignardus donare eisdem fratribus, laudante uxore sua Aanolde, desertum nomine Fontanis contiguum finibus Seestri . Concessit insuper eis in omnibus terris suis ubicumque voluerint ut excolant eas sine terciis porcisque eorum pastionem, sed et ceteras aasantias suas in cunctis nemoribus et terris suis libere capiendas donavit, interdicto tantum excidio Jailliaci nemoris, ad faciendum dumtaxat exartum quod magis ipsis quam sibi dicebat profuturum. Hujus rei testes sunt Rainaudus decanus, Hugo filius Hugonis de Plaaneto et Nariodus

Fig. 7: Source: Fontenay OCist Fontenay 1003015757, in: Monasterium.net, URL </mom/Fontenay/Fontenay_1003015757/charter>

loss of information in a given case? Will the CEI standard have to be extended to accommodate all the information that is given in the TEI version? Will the Monasterium.net charter HTML view have to be modified to adequately display these modifications to the schema? If so, in what ways? And so forth.

The corpus of the Cluny abbey (a part of which has been imported into Monasterium.net only as a private collection for internal work, since the material is already public) had been made available for the charters up to 1300 by the CBMA-Project[23] in various formats. This was first converted into an XML file via the tool OxGarage[24], and the resulting XML then once again converted into CEI. As part of the project, substantial effort is also going into the transcriptions of the charters of the late medieval period (i.e. after 1300) from this collection.

Particularly in the process of preparing the Fontenay corpus for import into Monasterium.net., the CEI schema was extended by numerous elements and attributes to avoid loss of information from the original TEI. Likewise, this preparatory process gave us the opportunity to make numerous enhancements to the site's user interface. Among others the display of indices of persons and places has been reworked, more detailed bibliographic information has been allowed, and the display of a critical apparatus in the single charter view has been added, which marks textual passages where variants exist, and displays lemmas and the list of variants as a tool tip (see fig. 7). These kinds of improvements are not only useful for our project, but make Monasterium.net a better platform for all users.

23 Corpus Burgundiae Medii Aevi: http://www.cbma-project.eu/

24 Now TEIGarage: https://teigarage.tei-c.org/

Machine Learning in BeCoRe

As already indicated, BeCoRe intends to use machine learning approaches to investigate graphical signs in collections of medieval charters. We want to explore what these signs can tell us about the nature of power and authority in the context of charter production and reception, whether the visual elements of charters naturally cluster together by categories like region, monastic order, or monastery, and whether there are any detectable indications for diplomatic landscapes as previously described. For this it will be necessary to not only detect the presence of graphical signs, but their position on the charter through object localization. In addition, we are working on a named-entity recognition (NER) approach to extracting the issuers of a charter, which could provide great assistance to these tasks. To develop this NER approach, one of the collections we are working with, the Göttweig corpus, was annotated to tag all the issuers of the charters, and a natural language processing library is used to test various ways of automatizing the detection of the issuer of a charter.

Several simple tests have already been conducted, and the project is currently in the process of moving into its machine learning-driven phase. At this stage it is crucial to be aware of the challenges and potential dangers of approaching our material with the tools of machine learning, one of the major ones being the temptation to "cherry-pick". The mathematical concept called the "no free lunch theorem", as used by David Wolpert and William Macready[25], tells us that there is no universally superior optimization algorithm. Any such algorithm, applied across all possible problems, will do as well or as badly as any other optimization algorithm. Of course, in practice we don't apply random algorithms to random problems, but this emphasizes the point that an algorithm has to be adapted to what we are looking for – everything depends on the data and the use case. The danger is that we then fall into a loop of continuously tweaking both our data and our algorithm, which will cause us to distort our results. When data is limited and classifiers are unlimited (as is the case through the almost infinite ways to tweak the parameters of the model), an algorithm can ultimately be pushed to find whatever it is we want to find, regardless of whether or not the result actually represents anything real and meaningful about the material itself.

A related, potential stumbling block is the tendency to be too rash with interpreting our results as confirmation of our theories. We will employ a clustering approach in looking for similarities between charters, and cluster diagrams can be something of a Rorschach test in which we see whatever we want to see, if we are not deeply aware of details of our chosen visualization, our (hyper-)parameters, and

25 David H. Wolpert/William G. Macready, No free lunch theorems for optimization, in: IEEE Transactions on Evolutionary Computation 1/1 (1997) p. 67–82.

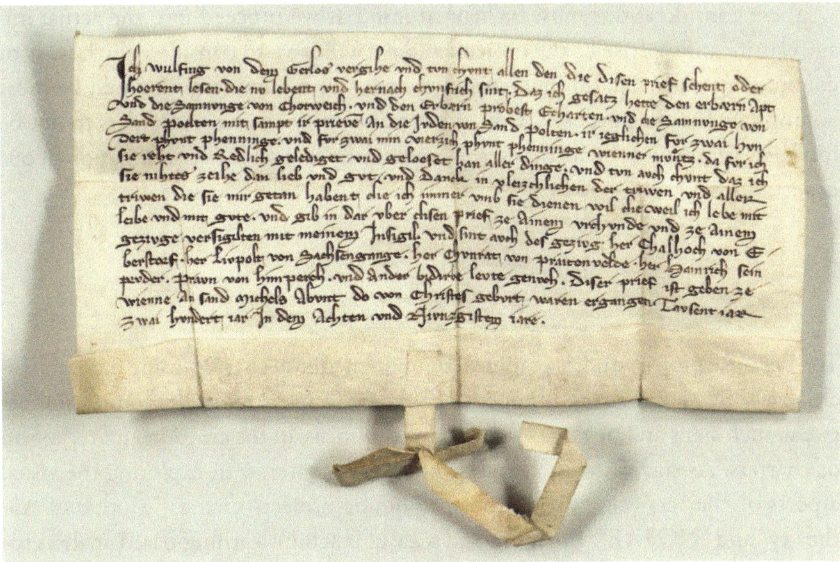

Fig. 8: Source: Göttweig, Stiftsarchiv Urkunden (1058-1899) 1298 IX 28, in: Monasterium.net, URL </mom/AT-StiAG/GoettweigOSB/1298_IX_28/charter>

so forth. If we neglect this, things like distances and cluster sizes on a diagram may not mean as much as we think they do, randomness may not look like randomness, and we are in danger of getting an altogether wrong idea of what we are looking at.

And if we are indeed looking for similarity between individual charters or groups of charters, we also have to consider what exactly we mean here by "similarity" – similar in what regard? Certain clusters exhibiting similarity must not be taken as an automatic confirmation of a hypothesis, since computer vision algorithms may respond to all kinds of features that we did not consider. To take a very obvious example from the BeCoRe research material: The Austrian photographs usually contain a color control patch placed next to the charter, while the French images do not, and this is obviously a significant visual feature that would cause Austrian charters and French charters to create separate clusters for reasons entirely unrelated to diplomatic aspects. As mentioned, this is a very obvious mistake that could only happen by accident if one were entirely unfamiliar with the research material, and failed to account for this difference. However, there are more subtle features that could distort the results without being noticed as easily: For example, in some images a charter's plica is unfolded manually, and the person's fingers will be captured in the photo, creating yet another visual feature that will be "noticed" by the algorithm. Even differences in camera angles when taking the photographs could distort results.

These considerations must be kept in mind as we proceed into the actual image classification phase of the project, and we will have to consider which ways of countering them (e.g., through cropping or image manipulation) would be most appropriate for our purposes. Most importantly, they serve as reminders to not be too hasty in treating results that seem superficially favorable as confirmation of our expectations.

Conclusion

The BeCoRe project studies graphical signs on medieval charters using modern machine learning approaches. It hopes to gain new insights about the connection between such signs and notions of power and authority in the creation and reception of charters. As such, it demonstrates the growing interest in exploring the visual aspects of charters using digital tools, alongside projects such as "Models of Authority" and "NOTAE". The speed and scale of machine learning-based analysis today allows us to gain new perspectives on questions in diplomatics that themselves are not necessarily new. One of these is the concept of the "diplomatic landscape", which describes the external and/or internal similarity of charters in a given region. Through automatized analysis of the charters' graphical features and understanding of their use, we hope to gain new insight into the usefulness of this idea.

During the "enrichment" phase of the project, in which much of the material was prepared for the machine learning analysis to follow, a lot of material was added to Monasterium.net, the main platform used by BeCoRe. As part of this process, we have also been able to make numerous improvements to the platform itself, be it through extensions to data and metadata structures or through improvements to the user interface, which benefit not only us, but all of its users. As we now proceed into the machine learning phase proper, and learn which techniques and approaches are the most useful to us, we must be very careful with our assumptions, and be aware of the ways in which results may become distorted and misinterpreted in our attempts to confirm our prior expectations.

From archives to archaeology via machine learning

An automated approach to dating medieval seal matrices from Britain

John A. McEwan

Introduction

The date is an essential part of any seal catalogue entry, because the date situates a seal in its historical context[1]. A seal is most often known in one of two forms: a seal matrix [Fig. 1] – the stamp used to make seal impressions – or a seal impression [Fig. 2], usually in wax. Cataloguers often date medieval seal matrices by comparing them with other seals that are already securely dated. The best source of securely dated seals are those known from seal impressions. Seal impressions normally survive attached to documents, which often include the date of the document's creation, or other information that allows the cataloguer to date the document [Fig. 3][2]. Unfortunately, manually and thoroughly gathering securely dated seals that are comparable to a particular seal matrix is time-consuming work.

This paper explores the feasibility of using existing archival seal catalogues and other similar sources to create an automated system that assists cataloguers in dating medieval seal matrices[3]. Many generations of archivists and scholars have re-

---

1 For the significance of seals, see: Brigitte Bedos-Rezak, Medieval Identity: A Sign and a Concept, in: American Historical Review 105/5 (2000) p. 1489–1533; see also: John A. McEwan, The Past, Present and Future of Sigillography: Towards a New Structural Standard for Seal Catalogues, in: Archives and Records 39/2 (2018) p. 3.

2 English documents from the reign of Edward I (1272–1307) typically include a date: Michael Gervers, The Deeds Project and the Development of a Computerised Methodology for Dating Undated English Private Charters of the Twelfth and Thirteenth Centuries, in: Dating Undated Medieval Charters, ed. Michael Gervers, Woodbridge 2000, p. 14.

3 For a list of published seal catalogues, see: Elizabeth Anne New, Seals and Sealing Practices, London 2010, p. 128–130; Paul D. A. Harvey/Andrew F. McGuinness, A Guide to British Medieval Seals, London 1996, p. 120–121.

corded information about the seals that are preserved in archives, with a view to enabling scholars to access to them [Fig. 4]. Could this information be repurposed and applied to the problem of dating the seal matrices that survive as archaeological artifacts, using machine learning? Machine learning is now widely used in many areas of research, including archaeology[4]. In medieval studies, there have been notable applications of machine learning to the transcription of documents, but these projects are in many respects different from the one described in this paper, which is based on text rather than images[5]. This project aims to employ the wealth of catalogue data that scholars and archivists have gathered on the seals that survive in archives.

For the purposes of this study training data for the machine learning process was drawn from the publicly accessible Digital Sigillography Resource (DIGISIG), which assembles sigillographic information from a wide variety of sources[6]. The system was then used to date a sample of the seal matrices listed in the Portable Antiquities Scheme (PAS) catalogue[7]. The PAS catalogue offers a good test case: it is one of the largest catalogues of seal matrices from England, but as an ongoing project that includes both polished and schematic records, the quality of its entries is uneven[8]. Moreover, because scholars have not yet definitively established when the

4 Simon H. Bickler, Machine Learning Arrives in Archaeology, in: Advances in Archaeological Practice 9 (2021) p. 186–191. On the history of computer technology in archaeology, see: Jeremy Huggett, Disciplinary Issues: Challenging the Research and Practice of Computer Applications in Archaeology, in: Archaeology in the Digital Era: Papers from the 40th Annual Conference of Computer Applications and Quantitative Methods in Archaeology (CAA), Southampton, 26–29 March 2012, ed. G. Earl et al., Amsterdam 2014, p. 13–24. Archaeologists have been using computers to sort and organize collections of artifacts since the 1960s: George L. Cowgill, Computer Applications in Archaeology, in: Computers and the Humanities 2/1 (1967) p. 20–21.

5 This is a very active area of research. A few notable contributions include: Guenter Muehlberger et al., Transforming Scholarship in the Archives through Handwritten Text Recognition, in: Journal of Documentation 75(5 (2019); see also: Joe Nockels et al., Understanding the Application of Handwritten Text Recognition Technology in Heritage Contexts: A Systematic Review of Transkribus in Published Research, in: Archival Science 22/3 (2022), p. 367–392. For another related application, see: Mike Kestemont/Vincent Christlein/Dominique Stutzmann, Artificial Paleography Computational Approaches to Identifying Script Types in Medieval Manuscripts, in: Speculum 92/1 (2017) p. 86–109.

6 The project is accessible at: https://www.digisig.org/. On the history of the project, see: John A. McEwan, New Approaches to Old Questions: Digital Technology, Sigillography and Digisig, in: Digital Medieval Studies: Practice and Preservation, ed. Laura K. Morreale/S. Gilsdorf, Leeds 2022, p. 33–49. See also: John A. McEwan, The Challenge of the Visual: Making Medieval Seals Accessible in the Digital Age, in: Journal of Documentation 71/5 (2015) p. 999–1028.

7 The catalogue is accessible at: https://finds.org.uk. On the history of the PAS, see: David W. J. Gill, The Portable Antiquities Scheme and the Treasure Act: Protecting the Archaeology of England and Wales?, in: Papers from the Institute of Archaeology 20 (2010) p. 1–11.

8 For how seals are recorded in PAS, see: https://finds.org.uk/counties/findsrecordingguides/seal-matrices/.

various types of seal were in circulation, all the dates for the seal matrices need to be periodically revised to take into account recent discoveries. The accuracy of the pioneering dating system presented and evaluated here does not rival a skilled and dedicated human cataloguer, but humans are comparatively slow and their labor is expensive. This system, even in its prototype state, can revise the dates assigned to the thousands of seal matrices in the PAS dataset quickly and at minimal cost. Thus, a computational approach to dating seal matrices can assist cataloguers of seal matrices, especially in situations where there are insufficient human resources available to date seals manually.

Training Data

Archaeologists are using machine learning, so the method itself is not novel. However, different types of artifacts require different approaches, and medieval seal matrices are challenging artifacts because they vary in size, shape and design. Consequently, training a computer to recognize the full range of types of seals and their periods of circulation requires a large training dataset. An initial challenge, therefore, involves gathering sufficient cases to serve as training data.

Fig. 1: Seal matrix. Handle (left): trefoil suspension loop on a double collared tapering hexagonal section handle. Face (right): full length figure of Saint Catherine, holding in her right hand a spiked wheel: round (21 mm). Discovered in South Gloucestershire, 14th Century. Recorded and dated by K. ADAMS (2004). Portable Antiquities Scheme, GLO-2AE0B3, available at: https://finds.org.uk/database/artefacts/record/id/76972. Photograph: Bristol City Council.

Fig. 2: Seal impression. Full length figure of Saint Catherine, holding in her right hand a spiked wheel, within an ornate border: round (21 mm). Saint Bartholomew's Hospital Archives, deed 1394, dated 2 Oct 1372. Available at: http://www.digisig.org/entity/10031891. Photograph: John A. MCEWAN (2023).

As already mentioned, seals are most often known in one of two forms: a seal matrix [Fig. 1] or a seal impression [Fig. 2]. As seal matrices are made from hard materials, such as metal, stone or bone, they can survive in the ground[9]. Many of the medieval seal matrices we have today were probably lost or discarded by their original owners[10]. If a seal is discovered during the course of a formal archaeological investigation of a site, evidence in the stratigraphy or in other accompanying artifacts may indicate when the seal was deposited. A few matrices were deliberately interred in tombs and thus can be dated based on the dates of the tombs[11]. However, most medieval seal matrices are recovered by members of the public from rural land. If the seal matrix is found in a field by someone using a metal detector, the context in which the seal matrix is discovered may offer little indication of when the seal matrix was deposited[12]. In such situations, the cataloguers of seal matrices must rely on the features of the seal matrices themselves to determine their dates. To do so, cataloguers often gather seals that are similar to the seal in question and already dated, and use those dated seals as an indication of when the seal in question was in circulation. For instance, Linenthal and Noel suggest that they made considerable use of Ellis' seal catalogues when dating their collection of seal matrices[13]. Similarly, the Portable Antiquities Scheme's cataloguers report that they use a variety of reference works. For example, the cataloguer of a "cast copper alloy seal matrix, oval

9 On the making of seals, see: Thomas Alexander Heslop, Seals as Evidence for Metalworking in England in the Later Twelfth Century, in: Art and Patronage in the English Romanesque, ed. F.H. THOMPSON/Sarah MACREADY (Occasional Papers of the Society of Antiquaries of London NS 8), London 1986, p. 50–60; John A. MCEWAN, Making a Mark in Medieval London: The Social and Economic Standing of Seal-Makers, in: Seals and Their Context in the Middle Ages, ed. Phillipp R. SCHOFIELD, Oxford 2015, p. 77–88.

10 Michael ANDERSON, Medieval Seal Matrices Found at Castle and Castle Mounds in Denmark – What Does Archaeology Tell Us About Their Use?, in: Good Impressions: Image and Authority in Medieval Seals, ed. Noël ADAMS/John CHERRY/James ROBINSON, London 2008, p. 71–72. Cherry notes that seal matrices could be defaced or broken to ensure that they could not be used in the future, but adds that the practice may have been most common in the twelfth and thirteenth centuries: Richard Rawlinson & His Seal Matrices: Collecting in the Early Eighteenth Century, Oxford 2016, p. 13–14. Another way to destroy a matrix may was to recycle its metal into a new object: MCEWAN, Making a Mark, p. 78, fn. 31.

11 For example, a silver seal matrix of Isabella, wife of Philip II of France, who died at age 21 in 1190, was buried with her: British Museum, 1970,0904.1, https://www.britishmuseum.org/collection/object/H_1970-0904-1.

12 About 90% of finds recorded in the Portable Antiquities dataset are discoveries of members of the public using metal-detectors: Katherine ROBBINS, Portable Antiquities Scheme: A Guide for Researchers, Portable Antiquities Scheme [website] 2014, p. 14, https://finds.org.uk/documents/guideforresearchers.pdf.

13 Richard A. LINENTHAL/William NOEL, Medieval Seal Matrices in the Schøyen Collection, Oslo 2004, p. xiv; Roger H. ELLIS, Catalogue of Seals in the Public Record Office: Monastic Seals, London 1986; Id., Catalogue of Seals in the Public Record Office: Personal Seals, 2 vols., London 1978–81.

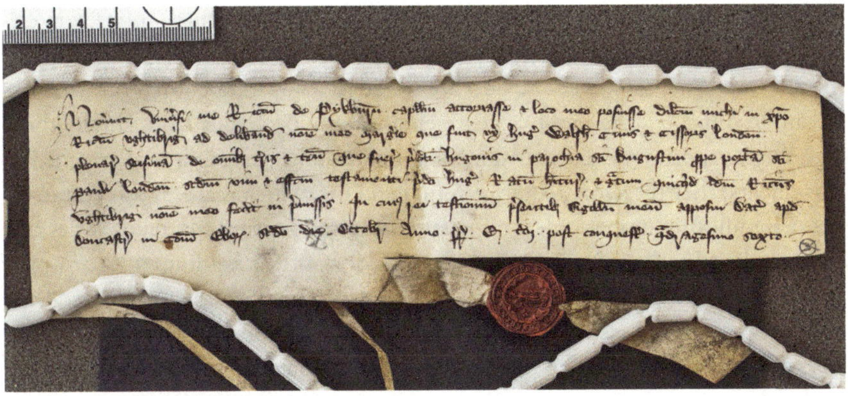

Fig. 3: Power of attorney given by Richard de Pykburn. Doncaster, Yorkshire, 2 Oct 1372. Saint Bartholomew's Hospital Archives, deed 1394. Photograph: John A. McEwan (2023).

in plan and inscribed with a sun motif with radiating linear rays" dates the object to between 1600 and 1700 [Fig. 5]. In support of this date, the cataloguer refers to a guide to British artefacts, which describes a seal matrix with a similar design, and comments that there are "similar examples recorded on the [PAS] database ... and [they] are all dated from the 17th century"[14]. This process produces dates that are generally broad and subject to revision, as Linenthal and Noel observe[15].

In contrast to seal matrices, which typically come out of the ground, seal impressions are found in archives. Typically made from wax, medieval seal impressions are fragile objects that normally survive attached to documents [Fig. 3][16]. A cataloguer can therefore determine the date of a seal impression by examining the document[17]. As someone might use a seal matrix multiple times over many years, multiple impressions of the same seal may survive attached to different documents. Thus, cataloguers of seal impressions assemble all known examples of a particular seal's impressions to determine, as far as possible, the range of dates when the seal was in use[18]. Whether cataloguers have one or multiple impressions of a seal, those

14 A. Tyacke, *CORN-9D9531: A Post Medieval Seal Matrix,* Portable Antiquities Scheme [website] *2012,* https://finds.org.uk/database/artefacts/record/id/505851.

15 Linenthal/Noel, Schøyen Collection, p. xiv.

16 Charles Hilary Jenkinson, A Guide to Seals in the Public Record Office, London 1968, p. 31.

17 On using seals to date difficult to date documents, see: Paul D. A. Harvey, Seals and the Dating of Documents, in: Dating Undated Medieval Charters, ed. Michael Gervers, Woodbridge 2000, p. 208–210.

18 On the difficulties of using dated seal impressions to infer when a seal matrix was fabricated: Jenkinson, Guide to Seals, p. 22. On the importance of including a fabrication date in catalogues of corporate seals used by religious houses, see: Brigitte Bedos-Rezak, Reviews of: Roger H.

impressions – provided they are attached to datable documents – offer firm evidence of when a seal was in circulation.

Seal impressions and seal matrices are stored in many different repositories, and it can be difficult to assemble a representative group of seals from the holdings of a single repository[19]. Furthermore, seal impressions are fragile and attached to documents; they therefore require careful handling, which makes it difficult to access a significant number of seal impressions at once. Fortunately, repositories that hold medieval seals typically provide descriptions of their holdings in the form of catalogue entries [Figs. 4, 6, 7]. Scholars have also surveyed seals and shared their descriptions in print, as websites, or as datasets[20]. Transforming these descriptions into data for a computer's use provides a practical alternative to working directly with original seals.

Two types of seal descriptions exist. A computer may be trained on one type or a combination of both; the quality of the data is more important than the type of the description. Seal cataloguing has historically largely proceeded collection by collection, with each institution recording its own holdings[21]. As museums typically take custody of seal matrices, while archives preserve documents with seal impressions, a given seal catalogue tends to deal with seals known either from seal matrices or from seal impressions. Cataloguers use the same basic metadata template in either

ELLIS, Catalogue of Seals in the Public Record Office: Monastic Seals, London 1986; and René Laurent, Sigillographie, Brussels 1985, in: Speculum 64/1 (1989) p. 158–162.

19 The National Archives probably has a representative set of seals for England as it holds "a vast quantity of seals" associated with records drawn from across the Kingdom, but the seals remain only partially catalogued and thus are difficult to access: JENKINSON, Guide to Seals p. ix. The seals in the British Library are also significant in number, but the existing catalogue covers a fraction of the seals in the collection and focusses on the seals of the privileged members of society: Walter de Gray BIRCH, Catalogue of Seals in the Department of Manuscripts in the British Museum, 6 vols., London 1887–1900; Andrew F. MCGUINNESS, Non-Armigerous Seals and Seal-Usage in Thirteenth-Century England, in: Thirteenth Century England. Vol. 5: Proceedings of the Newcastle on Tyne Conference 1993, ed. Peter R. COSS/S. D. LLOYD, Woodbridge 1995, p. 165; Paul D. A. HARVEY, Personal Seals in Thirteenth-Century England, in: Church and Chronicle in the Middle Ages: Essays Presented to John TAYLOR, ed. G. A. LOUD/Ian N. WOOD, London 1991, p. 117–118. Other archives also have significant numbers of seals, but they are often associated with a part of England: W. GREENWELL/Charles Henry Hunter BLAIR, Catalogue of Seals in the Treasury of the Dean and Chapter of Durham, Archaeologia Aeliana: or Miscellaneous Tracts Relating to Antiquity 8–9, 11–12, 14–17, third series (1911–1921). On the situation in France, see: Martine FABRE, Sceau Medieval: Analyse d'une Pratique Culturelle, Paris 2001, p. 219–224.

20 Phillipp R. SCHOFIELD et al., Seals and Society: Medieval Wales, the Welsh Marches and Their English Border Region, Cardiff 2016, p. 127–326; John A. MCEWAN, Seals in Medieval London, 1050–1300: A Catalogue, London 2016.

21 On the recording of seals in archives, see: JENKINSON, Guide to Seals, p. 31. He urges archivists to record seal impressions as part of the process of cataloguing documents.

GB Seal no.2047 1322
Raby, Thomas of
Charter granting a tenement to Sir John of Pollow, clerk. In 1315 Thomas was denounced as excommunicate (R.P.D., II, 740); see also S.D., IV, 39.
Size: 25 x 19 mm.
Seal design: Rounded oval, St Catherine standing, on dexter side RA, on sinister BI.
Inscription: S' THOME DE RABIE...

Seal attached to document reference: 3.16.Spec.2Digitised version

Fig 4.: Seal impression catalogue entry. Durham University Library Archives & Special Collections Catalogue: Medieval Seals, GB Seal no. 2047, https://n2t.durham.ac.uk/ark:/32150/s1vh53wv76d.xml#GB-2047. Photograph: C. H. BLAIR.

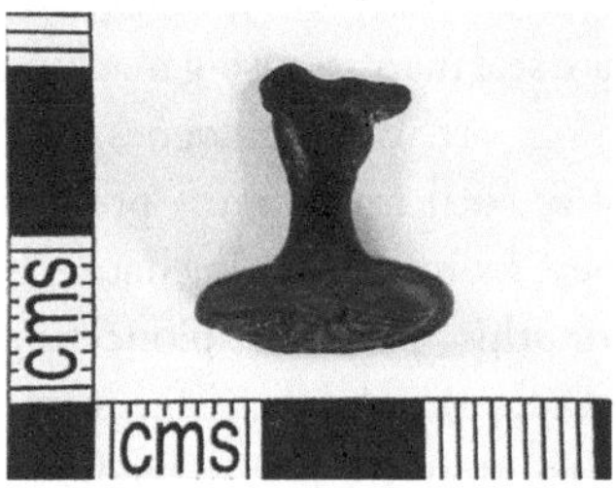

Fig. 5. Seal matrix. Handle: broken with only base remaining. Face: a sun motif with radiating linear rays: round (12.6 mm). Discovered in Cornwall, 17th Century. Recorded and dated by D. WILDING (2020). Portable Antiquities Scheme, WILT-2D77D7, available at: https://finds.org.uk/database/artefacts/record/id/1008327. Photograph: Royal Institution of Cornwall.

case, for they need to convey information about the size, shape, and content of the seals, in addition to setting them in their historical contexts[22]. But cataloguers dealing with seal matrices can also document the shape of the seal matrix and its material [Fig. 6][23]. Given that the aim of the machine-learning system is to date seal matrices, it might seem that the training dataset should rely on data from catalogues of seal matrices. However, although the additional data would be useful, the critical issue is the quality of the dates in the records[24]. As already discussed, date information is not derived directly from seal impressions and seal matrices, but rather from the contexts in which they are discovered. Thus, the key issue is the relative quality of the dates cataloguers attribute to seal impressions as compared to seal matrices.

Thus, both catalogues based on seal impressions and those based on seal matrices are potential sources of training data. They each provide information on the features of seals, and catalogues based on the seal matrices have the additional benefit of describing the matrices themselves as physical objects. However, the contexts in which seal impressions survive (in contrast to those of seal matrices) offer cataloguers significantly more precise information about the date of the seals. Therefore, for

22 For a seal recording metadata template, see: Robert-Henri BAUTIER, Vocabulaire International de la sigillographie, Rome 1990, p. 37.

23 LINENTHAL/ NOEL, Medieval Seal Matrices p. xiv-xvi.

24 When cataloguers speak of a seal's date, they may mean the period when the seal matrix was in use or the moment when it was made.

926. Bronze, oval, with hexagonal conical handle ending in a pierced trefoil. St. Catherine standing, facing, with her wheel in her l. hand, a palm-branch on either side of her. Legend, within pearled borders, * SAVNCA CATERINA *

Early 14th century.

Plate XXVII.

0·92 in. × 0·7 in. 2·3 cm. × 1·8 cm. 1865.

Rough work.

For a number of seals with the figure of St. Catherine connected with Hyde Abbey, Winchester, and found in the muniment-room of Winchester College, *see Proc. Soc. Antiq.* ix, pp. 368 ff.

926

Fig. 6.: Seal matrix catalogue entry. A. B. Tonnochy, "926", in: Catalogue of British Seal-Dies in the British Museum, London 1952, p. 199, plate XXVII.

1. Seal of: 2. Dates:

SEAL

3. Shape: 4. Dimensions:

5. Legend:

6. Description:

IMPRESSION

7. Material: 8. Colour:

9. Mode of attachment:
Nature of the attachments

10. State of conservation:

11. Counter-seal, see:

DOCUMENT

12. Date:

13. Nature and purpose:

14. Sealing clause:

15. Dimensions:

REFERENCES

16. Cast: 17. Photograph:

18. Publications:

Fig. 7.: Seal recording template for archival use, adapted from: Robert-Henri Bautier, Vocabulaire International de la Sigillographie, Rome 1990, p. 37.

the purposes of training a computer to date seal matrices using machine learning, archival catalogues that draw on seal impressions provide the best source of training data.

For this paper, a pioneering dataset for training machine learning algorithms for British medieval seals was constructed. The data was gathered, via DIGISIG, from repositories including The National Archives, the British Library, and the National Library of Wales, as well as the Huntington Library (California) and various cathedral archives, civic archives, university archives, and county archives in the United Kingdom. At the time of writing, DIGISIG holds records for more than 43.000 seals, but only a fraction of those seals and their records are suitable for this project. Seals known from seal matrices were excluded, to ensure that no seal matrix data was used in training dataset. Furthermore, incomplete seal records (those missing information about the size, shape or content of seals) were also excluded. In addition, for this pioneering effort, seals of corporate bodies, including the officials of monarchies, cathedrals, and religious houses, and towns, as well as kings, queens, bishops and members of the nobility were excluded. They often used exceptionally large seals, to evoke their standing, so their inclusion would complicate the task of training the computer[25]. Moreover, corporate seals have been extensively studied by scholars, so they are comparatively easy for cataloguers to recognize and date. In contrast, cataloguers struggle with seals used by people outside the aristocracy, yet those types of seals predominate in the Portable Antiquities Scheme dataset. Therefore, DIGISIG was queried for British seals, known exclusively from seal impressions, dated between 1100 and 1500 to a precision of five years or less, with complete information on their size, shape and content. Then seals known to be associated with corporate bodies or their officers, or members of the aristocracy, were excluded. The result was a dataset of about 6.000 cases.

Those 6.000 cases include many different types of seals, well-distributed both temporally and geographically. There are just over a hundred twelfth century cases, a small number that reflects the lack of evidence for this period. By contrast, there is strong representation for the period 1200–1500: just short of 2.000 thirteenth century cases, about 2.700 fourteenth century cases and 1.200 fifteenth century cases. Spatially, the cases are distributed across Britain. England is well-covered, with a mix of seals used in rural and urban areas. There is an important group of about 2.000 cases from the north of England and several hundred cases from the midlands and the south-west, but the bulk of the cases originate in the south and east of England, with a particularly large concentration of approximately 1.900 cases from London. In addition, there are about 450 seals from Wales and 60 from southern Scotland. The dataset includes seals displaying a wide range of different motifs. The most important group of motifs (36%) are seals that feature an object, such as a shield of arms. In about 18% of cases, the seal's central motif is a human figure, and in 26% of cases an animal. The remainder (21%) are various miscellaneous devices, such as stylized lilies. With a training dataset of this size and scope, how well can the computer date medieval English seal matrices?

System Design

The system created for this project is designed to assist a human cataloguer. When cataloguers date seal matrices, they typically employ a two-step process. A cataloguer will start by assessing the matrix's features and then consider the problem

25 John A. McEwan, Does Size Matter? Seals in England and Wales, ca. 1200–1500, in: A Companion to Seals in the Middle Ages, ed. Laura Whatley, Leiden 2019, p. 109–110.

of date[26]. As already discussed, a human cataloguer typically dates medieval seal matrices by identifying similar and securely dated seals that provide an indication of when the type of seal in question was in circulation[27]. In practice, cataloguers need to manually survey the published seal catalogues to discover these seals (perhaps with the assistance of tools such as DIGISIG). Ideally, cataloguers would not do this basic research work themselves, but instead would rely on reference works created by expert scholars[28]. Unfortunately, the considerable scholarship on the history of seals and sealing practices in Britain has tended to focus on certain types of seals. Seals used by kings, bishops, and institutions are well-studied, but seals used by people outside the aristocracy have been largely overlooked[29]. Thus, in the absence of complete taxonomic guides to British seals, cataloguers of seal matrices are often left to do their own research. Cataloguers can measure seals and describe their contents, but a computer can assist them in performing the laborious research and data analysis involved in dating seal matrices.

If a human cataloguer supplies a computer with information about the size, shape, and content of the seal that needs dating, then the computer can survey catalogues to find seals with similar features. However, if the computer treats each facet (size, shape and content) of the seal as an independent variable, then the search results may include irrelevant cases. Alternatively, if the computer only searched for exact matches, then it might overlook useful cases. A more sophisticated system would prioritize the features, or combination of features, that are most indicative of date. Thus, the computer needs to understand the relationship between the various features of the seal and their historical development. As already mentioned, scholars have yet to construct a definitive history of all the various types of seals people used in Britain. But the computer can create its own provisional history using machine learning. The machine learning process involves providing the computer with data on a large number of examples and then directing it to look for patterns in that data. In the case of medieval seal matrices, the computer can consider the relationship between the features of seals and their dates, using the corpus of existing catalogue entries. With that information, the computer can construct a model of how seals change overtime. Then, when presented with a seal matrix, the computer can use what it has learned from its training to suggest a date.

26 The Portable Antiquities offers cataloguers detailed guidance on how to describe the features of seal matrices, but little on how to date them: Helen Geake, Seal Matrices, Portable Antiquities Scheme [website] 2020, https://finds.org.uk/counties/findsrecordingguides/seal-matrices/.

27 Linenthal/Noel, Medieval Seal Matrices p. xiv.

28 For a general guide to artifacts: Michael Lewis/Kevin Leahy, Finds Identified, Witham 2018.

29 Harvey, Personal Seals p. 117–118; Elizabeth A. New, Reconsidering the Silent Majority: Non-Heraldic Personal Seals in Medieval Britain, in: A Companion to Seals in the Middle Ages, ed. Laura Whatley, Leiden 2019, p. 279–309.

Machine learning is a term that describes a set of algorithms with different features. This investigation employed the decision tree regressor algorithm. This algorithm aims to create a sequential chain of decisions, known as a decision tree, to sort cases into groups[30]. Applied to the seal data, it sorts seals into groups based on their features. Once the decision tree is constructed, the computer can then use the decision tree to date any seal matrix. The decision tree can be graphed and passed to a cataloguer or researcher to show exactly how the computer determines a seal's date. By contrast, seal cataloguers rarely set out explicitly their reasoning for assigning a date to a particular seal. Consequently, it can be difficult to assess any individual cataloguer's consistency and to compare different cataloguers' methods. A computer using the decision tree regressor algorithm is transparent about its decision-making process. For the purposes of a pioneering use of machine learning to date medieval seal matrices, transparency is an important feature of the system.

Seal catalogue records include information about shape, size, and content, all of which can be used in training the system[31]. DIGISIG classifies seals by shape using a set of 17 categories; as the algorithm can work with categorized data, the shape data can be fed directly into the algorithm[32]. By contrast, DIGISIG stores size data as separate horizontal and vertical measurements. To ease the machine learning process, these figures are combined into a single value by calculating an estimated area for each seal. Then, to provide the machine learning system with information about the graphical content of each seal, it is fed DIGISIG's seal motif classification information. DIGISIG uses a hierarchical system of about a hundred classes to sort seals according to their central motif. Although the motif classification system is a crude tool for describing the meaning of the graphical feature of a seal, it is currently the best available classification system for translating textual seal descriptions into data that a computer can analyze[33]. Consequently, the machine learning algorithm receives, in addition to the date of the seal, its shape classification, its size (area expressed in square millimeters), and its motif classification.

30 This study uses Scikit-learn's implementation of the CART algorithm: 1.10. Decision Trees, Scikit-learn [website], https://scikit-learn.org/stable/modules/tree.html.

31 The nature of the text on a seal can also be used for the purposes of dating, for letterforms changed over time: Jenkinson, Guide to Seals, p. 22–23. However, catalogues inconsistently report this information. As this project required as many cases as possible, it was not possible to take letterforms into account.

32 The shape categories are adapted from: Paul D. A. Harvey, Computer Catalogue of Seals in the Public Record Office, London, in: Janus 2 (1996) p. 29–36.

33 The system was originally designed to help cataloguers search for and identify cases where multiple damaged impressions of the same seal survived: McEwan, Challenge of the Visual p. 1008. In DIGISIG, the classification system has been re-purposed to provide a mechanism to facilitate searches across catalogues that use different vocabulary for describing seals.

The computer can create a decision tree of various sizes and shapes, but for the purposes of this study it was limited to a tree with seven levels. As the computer divides the seals into groups, the number of seals in each group diminishes; a minimum number of cases per group must be set to ensure that the groupings do not become so small that they lose significance[34]. Although the computer is constrained to create a decision tree with seven levels, it determines how to group seals. In this study, the computer found the most useful variable to be size. Consequently, the first decision in the decision tree divides seals according to whether they are greater than or equal to 191 squared millimeters in area[35]. Many subsequent decisions are also based on size, but there are decision points at which the computer considers the seal's shape or content. Take, for example, a seal matrix with a stylized lily motif, a pointed-oval shape, 33 x 21 mm, dated by the PAS to circa 1200 to 1300[36]. Following the decision tree, the dating algorithm passes through decisions on size, shape, content, and then on size again, to arrive at a predicted date of 1279.

A consequence of constraining the size of the tree is that the range of possible dates the model predicts is also constrained. This particular decision tree divides the seals in the training dataset into about 70 groups that include seals with similar features and date. When the algorithm is given a new seal, it uses its features to assign it to one of these groups, and then returns the date assigned to that group as the predicted date for that seal. (In this case, the dates of the groups range from 1184 to 1447.) The question is whether those predictions are sufficiently reliable that they have scholarly value.

Evaluating Results

The decision tree's purpose is to allow the computer to estimate a seal matrix's date, but measuring the decision tree's accuracy is challenging. One method involves applying the decision tree to cases in which the seals' dates are known. During the training process, a portion of the training data is set aside. When the decision tree is tested with this data, the predicted dates often diverge from the known dates. In a few cases, the predicted dates are centuries off the expected values. Occasional large errors are inevitable, because there are seals in the dataset whose features make them outliers. For example, some later seals were deliberately designed to imitate or

34 When the groupings become too small the decision tree is 'overfit', in machine learning terminology, and will not 'generalize' well to new cases.

35 For a discussion of the close relationship between size and date, see: McEwan, Does Size Matter p. 107–108.

36 M. Broomfield, SUR-97ADBB: A Medieval Seal Matrix, Portable Antiquities Scheme [website] 2015, https://finds.org.uk/database/artefacts/record/id/728768.

evoke the characteristics of earlier seals, and the algorithm has no capacity to detect such anachronisms. However, large errors in dating are exceptional; the median of the difference between the actual and predicted dates is 27 years. This suggests that the computer can date seals to within a few decades.

A few decades might seem like a considerable margin of error, but it is important to recognize that exact precision is impossible. With more training data, the computer might create a better decision tree that could date seals more accurately, but it will never be able to place seals exactly in the year when they were in circulation. The types of seals people used did not change so rapidly that certain types were restricted to specific years, or even decades. The totality of seals in circulation changed gradually, as each subsequent generation developed slightly different preferences. As already discussed, the decision tree algorithm groups together seals with similar dates and features. Consequently, although the decision tree algorithm suggests a precise date for each seal matrix, those suggested dates should be understood as representing a point roughly in the middle of a period of time when seals with those features were in circulation. Thus, the divergence between the predicted dates and the actual dates indicates a need for additional training data, but it also suggests the breadth of the span of time during which distinct types of seals circulated.

The decision tree's predictions may also be evaluated by comparing them to the dates assigned by human cataloguers to seal matrices listed in the Portable Antiquities Scheme (PAS). At the time of the preparation of this study, there are about 7.500 seal matrices listed in the PAS catalogue. Of those, about 6.200 are identified by the cataloguers as medieval. As already mentioned, the PAS catalogue is under continual revision, so records tend to improve over time. Nonetheless, at the time of writing, the dates predicted by the decision tree – even if they are treated as spans of a few decades – are significantly more precise than those assigned by PAS. PAS cataloguers typically date seals to periods of a century or more. Moreover, the tendency of PAS cataloguers to assign seals to centuries implies that the turn of the century witnessed dramatic change, when in practice change was constant and gradual. By placing seals in the vicinity of particular years, rather than in a particular century, the decision tree better positions seals in time.

Although the decision tree approach results in dates that are more precise and better distributed over time, its predicted dates do fall within the periods already assigned by the PAS cataloguers. For the purposes of this study, the decision tree was asked to predict dates for about 1500 seal matrices already dated by PAS cataloguers. In almost every case, the predicted dates fell within the spans of time assigned by the PAS cataloguers. Where the decision tree dates fell outside those bounds, the differences were often small. As already mentioned, the PAS cataloguers are fond of dating seals to particular centuries; seals that circulated in periods that straddled those centuries can be positioned by the decision tree just outside the periods predicted by PAS. Large discrepancies in the dates predicted by the decision tree and

PAS often seem to arise from cases where the PAS catalogers or the decision tree failed and made a serious error. In most cases, the decision tree predictions are consonant with the dates assigned by the PAS cataloguers, which further suggests that the machine learning method results in generally reliable dates. An outstanding question is to how the precise dates offered by the decision tree method should be broadened into span dates, to better express the period of time when the seals were in circulation.

Conclusion

An automated tool for dating medieval seal matrices is feasible. To train a computer to understand changes in seal usage over time, the computer needs thousands of cases. By bringing together information from many different repositories, the DIGISIG project makes it more convenient for human cataloguers to work with the existing data, but it also enables computational methods of analysis. With a training dataset of about 6.000 cases drawn from seals known through seal impressions preserved in archives, a computer can learn how seals changed over time. The dates that the computer then proposes for the surviving seal matrices may not be as reliable as those produced by a knowledgeable and dedicated human cataloguer. However, seal matrices survive in large numbers, and more are continually being discovered; it is difficult for human cataloguers to keep up. Thus, rather than give over the task of dating seal matrices entirely to a machine learning algorithm, human cataloguers might best treat the computer as an assistant who can quickly generate dates that the cataloguer can check or refine. A computational approach to dating seal matrices can assist cataloguers of seal matrices, especially in situations where there are insufficient human resources available to date seals manually.

A machine learning approach to dating seal matrices provides clear benefits to archaeologists, but it also offers benefits to documentary scholars. Simply applying machine learning to the problem of how seals changed over time may help sigillographers better understand how quickly sealing practices developed. Moreover, an important question for sigillographers who work on seals that survive in archives is the extent to which those seals are representative of the full range of seals in circulation. It is easy to suspect that archives disproportionately preserve the seals used by more privileged members of society, whose affairs were more likely to be recorded in documents preserved in archives. The seal matrices that archaeologists and members of the public find in the ground, which were discarded or lost by their original owners, probably include relatively more seals used by people from more humble backgrounds. By helping cataloguers to situate the seal matrices more precisely in time, the computer contributes to the creation of new information that scholars can use not only to discern not only how quickly seals changed over time, but also to improve our understanding of the full range of seals in circulation.

The machine learning method outlined in this paper is a pioneering effort. There are ways that the method could be improved. With additional training data, the computer could better model how seals change overtime and thus provide better predictions. Scholars could improve their methods of classifying the seals according to their motifs, so that the computer could gain a more refined understanding of what the seals depict. Cataloguers could compile information on the writing on seals, so that this could be used in training the computer. Other machine learning algorithms might be tested and prove superior. Nonetheless, this project shows the enormous potential of a digital diplomatics approach to sigillography. By assembling a large amount of information about medieval documents, seal impressions and seal matrices, and using a computer to aid in analysis, scholars can arrive at a deeper understanding of seals and sealing practices.

Qualitative Space in Digital Diplomatics

Mark Bell, Eirini Goudarouli, John Stell, Jane Winters

Introduction

The digitisation of collections held by cultural heritage institutions has transformed research in the late 20th and early 21st century. It has enabled the exploration and study of collections in new ways. However, the variety of formats, scale, complexity and heterogeneity of digital collections have raised a number of challenges in the existing modes of access to these collections.

Providing novel modes of access to digital collections has been a central strategic priority for cultural heritage institutions around the world as they reimagine the ways that digital collections can be used by the public[1]. At the same time, there has been a growing emphasis within the academic and research communities on the exploration, complex analysis and interpretation of large-scale digital heritage collections, using advanced computational techniques (e.g. text mining, machine learning, network analysis).

Existing access techniques are unable to deliver the views of digital collections that vast and complex new digital archives require. For example, catalogues and keyword search do not readily support analysis of the spatial and temporal aspects of primary source materials or the relationships present within and between collections. Additionally, keyword searching allows only the study of words in isolation (or with some limited context), making it difficult to view large-scale collections as connected wholes, rather than as multiplicities of separate fragments.

This paper argues that being able to go beyond keyword searching of digital collections will enable the exploration and identification of evidence based on their qualitative spatial and temporal relationships, offering exciting new avenues to researchers in the humanities and social sciences. Moving past keyword searching also

1 For example, https://www.nationalarchives.gov.uk/about/our-role/plans-policies-performance-and-projects/our-plans/our-digital-cataloguing-practices/project-omega/.

has the potential to open up new directions and generate new perspectives for researchers working in digital fields (such as computer scientists, interface designers, user experience researchers and digital archivists).

It also suggests new ways of exploring heritage collections as traces of dynamic processes and approaching documents as processual narratives, focusing on their spatial structure and interconnections. This approach allows researchers to reconstruct how documents came into being; to tell stories about when, how and by whom they were created; and to uncover the complex relationships both between the constitutive elements of an individual document and between documents within an archive. The spatial relationships in documents, such as where pieces of text are placed on a page, and the temporal relationships, such as knowing that one annotation was added after another, contribute significantly to meaning and interpretation. Relationships between multiple documents form complex networks, which shed light on how they have been created, used and reused. These networks include relationships such as the spatial (within a building or collection) and the temporal (between authors, versions or dates of accession to a collection).

The paper aims at using all these relationships as an aid to understanding and navigation. To do so, it will introduce Qualitative Spatial Representation (QSR) as a method to explore the spatial and temporal dimensions of digital document collections, focusing on the structure of the documents themselves and how they may have developed over time. The spatial arrangement of different parts of a document is often a key aspect of both original significance and the history of changes through time.

The layout of a document often conveys structure and meaning; consider how space is used to separate paragraphs, data is presented in regular columns, or the elements of an item of correspondence (address, salutation, signature) are positioned on the page. Werner analysed the relationship between visual aspects of papal documents and their intended recipients[2]. Spatial features examined included percentage of the page covered by text, relative distances of components of the documents, margin widths, and the size of capital letters. The interpretation of annotations depends on their placement in relation to both prior and subsequent writing. The positioning of individual signatures can denote relationships of importance. While experts can make judgements about the visual elements of an individual page, digital humanists are applying computational methods to large-scale collections to extract and analyse content. The field of document layout analysis has provided many methods for analysing document structure. Using computational techniques such

2 Judith Werner, Gestaltung der Urkunde, Gestaltung Europas – Urkundenlayout zwischen europäischem Empfängereinfluss und päpstlicher Vereinheitlichung, in: Papstgeschichte im digitalen Zeitalter. Neue Zugangsweisen zu einer Kulturgeschichte Europas, ed. Klaus Herbers/Viktoria Trenkle (Beihefte zum AKG 85), Cologne 2018, p. 109–134.

as machine learning and computer vision, vast amounts of data can be extracted from archival collections of documents, but these techniques can sometimes leave a large gap between essentially numerical data and the ways in which human experts describe documents in academic discourse. One way to bridge this gap is through the use of QSR which concerns relationships between entities in space. It is an important building block of Commonsense AI[3], combining mathematical logic and commonly understood concepts and language. This area, within Artificial Intelligence and Knowledge Representation, links digital representation with the kinds of spatial relationships that humans use in informal descriptions.

Children from the age of five in the UK are taught 'positional language' and 'repeating patterns'[4], both of which are used to understand spatial relations in documents. Examples include: *overlapping* (of some text and an annotation); *being to the left of* (of one block of text and another); *being underneath* (of the vertical arrangement of text and image, or a line beneath a word); *sequence of evenly spaced lines* (a possible definition of a block of text). Qualitative relationships have been used to represent humans' knowledge of space[5], and reasoning with spatial relationships is part of QSR (the R often signifying both representation and reasoning). Temporal relationships can be included; conceptualising time spatially as a line[6] or more complex branching structures with uncertain relationships between some events. A physical document is often both evidence of a process (accumulating annotations, additions, etc.) and a component in other processes (creating new versions, generating responses, political interactions, etc.). Exploring archival collections as traces of dynamic processes is limited without the ability to describe the spatial structure of successive changes. Machine learning can help to identify that a piece of text is an annotation, but it is QSR which can help us tie that annotation spatially to the text it addresses. These spatial connections can be essential for reading documents as narratives of processes.

While machine learning can achieve remarkable results, a well-known drawback is the lack of explanation associated with how those results are derived. This has led to the search for 'explainable AI' (XAI) as a way to allow decisions to be questioned and reduce the likelihood of bias due to unrepresentative training data. There is an increasing focus in archives on the importance of XAI for maintaining the trans-

3 Ernest DAVIS/Gary MARCUS, Commonsense reasoning and commonsense knowledge in artificial intelligence, in: Communications of the ACM 58/9 (2015) p. 92–103.

4 https://assets.publishing.service.gov.uk/government/uploads/system/uploads/attachment_data/file/335158/PRIMARY_national_curriculum_-_Mathematics_220714.pdf.

5 Anthony COHN/Jochen RENZ, Qualitative Spatial Representation and Reasoning, in: Handbook of knowledge representation, Elsevier, eds. Frank VAN HARMELEN, Vladimir LIFSCHITZ and Bruce PORTER, Amsterdam 2008, p. 551–596.

6 James F. ALLEN, Maintaining Knowledge about Temporal Intervals, in: Communications of the ACM 26 (1983) p. 832–843.

parency of process that underpins trust in the documentary record. In their consideration of AI in the archive, Rolan et al. 2019 distinguish between rule-based systems, statistical models and deep learning models, noting that the two former offer greater transparency and are more susceptible to inspection. Bunn[7] takes this framework as a starting point for considering the significance of XAI for recordkeeping and archival practice, highlighting 'the vital importance of transparency to the proper functioning of societies'. These considerations have influenced the choice of method explored in this chapter.

The research field of 'neuro-symbolic AI'[8] aims to combine the advantages of machine learning, the neural part, with logic and knowledge representation, the symbolic part. To adapt a simple example from an account of DARPA's XAI program[9] consider the task of classifying a portion of a document as either a later annotation or part of the original document. A purely machine learning approach might learn a classification function and be able to report 'later annotation, probability 0.87' based on the examples used in learning. An ideal XAI approach would still learn from examples but, instead of just learning a classification function, would learn a structured model of the process of classification. This model could be used to explain that 'later annotation' was chosen because (for example) the portion was overlapping a larger area of text on the page and was at an angle to it. This explanation uses the relationships: 'larger than', 'overlapping' and 'at an angle to'. To deliver explainable AI like this it is necessary to determine the appropriate relationships. In addition, the logical properties of these relationships are important to support deductive reasoning within explanations. Working with documents, spatial facts such as 'If two things are next to each other then they have nothing between them', can be used to build explanations.

So far, there is existing use of spatial relationships in document processing and document understanding. However, these are essentially restricted to identifying document genre and reading-order for text blocks[10]. The use of structure and layout can improve the quality of textual search results[11], but this does not treat the visual

7 Jenny BUNN, Working in contexts for which transparency is important: a recordkeeping view of explainable artificial intelligence (XAI), in: Records Management Journal 30 (2020) p. 143-153.

8 Pascal HITZLER et al., Neuro-symbolic approaches in artificial intelligence, in: National Science Review 9/6 (2022), https://doi.org/10.1093/nsr/nwac035; Vaishak BELLE, Logic meets Learning: From Aristotle to Neural Networks, in: Neuro-Symbolic Artificial Intelligence: The State of the Art, ed. Pascal HITZLER/Md Kamruzzaman SARKER, Amsterdam/Berlin Washington D.C. 2022, Chapter 3, p. 78–102.

9 David GUNNING/David W. AHA, Darpa's Explainable AI (XAI) Program, in: AI Magazine 40/2 (2019) p. 44–58, fig 3.

10 Floriana ESPOSITO et al., Machine learning for digital document processing, in: Machine Learning in Document Analysis and Recognition, ed. Simone MARINAI/Hiromichi FUJISAWA, Berlin/Heidelberg 2007, p. 105–138.

11 Marco AIELLO, Document understanding for a broad class of documents, in: International Journal of Document Analysis and Recognition 5 (2002) p. 1.

aspects of a document as features of interest which encode meaning. They do not provide a way to help users locate documents based on criteria such as 'the spatial structure of these elements should be similar to this example', where spatial structure is specified qualitatively (e.g., 'I want this to appear in between these other elements'). QSR can be used as an aid to understanding and navigation of document collections but it is almost entirely unexplored in this context.

This paper will introduce the ideas of QSR and demonstrate the relevance of these techniques to digital diplomatics through examples drawn from ongoing work at The National Archives UK in which we have been evaluating the role of spatial relationships in the analysis of documents. It will also explore how the spatial (e.g., relationships between blocks of text) and temporal (e.g., visible editorial and transmission histories) aspects of documents and collections may be used to enhance navigation through and interpretation of digital archival materials.

Document Layout Analysis

Document Layout Analysis (DLA) is among the first operations in Document Image Analysis[12]. DLA systems are primarily aimed at analysing digital documents, such as academic papers in PDF format, but a further sub-field of DLA focuses on the analysis of historical documents.

A survey of papers published at ICDAR, the bi-annual International Conference for Document Analysis and Recognition, held since 1991, identified three main tasks being addressed by researchers: pre-processing for image quality, identification of regions with homogeneous content, and textual content recognition[13].

The second of these is most relevant to QSR, and within this category several sub-tasks were identified: text line segmentation, baseline detection, text detection, symbol detection. The authors further summarised the application of deep learning technology as mapping inputs (e.g., a digitised page) to outputs (page, region, table, text-line, bounding box, transcribed text, image patch, image), with the algorithms generally classifying at the pixel level. Eskenazi et al. separate identification into physical (typed, text, images, decorations) and logical/functional (header, footer, main body), and define a typology of segmentation algorithms with three classes: (1) algorithm constrained, i.e., segmentation of specific layouts without needing

12 Galal M. BINMAKHASHEN/Sabri A. MAHMOUD, Document Layout Analysis: A Comprehensive Survey, in: ACM Computing Survey 52/6 (2020), Article 109.

13 Francesco LOMBARDI/Simone MARINAL, Deep Learning for Historical Document Analysis and Recognition – A Survey, in: Journal of Imaging 6/10 (2020) p. 110.

training; (2) parameter constrained (e.g., font size, connected components size); (3) potentially unconstrained (e.g. neural networks)[14].

Current state of the art approaches use deep learning to segment images. Mechi et al. used a U-Net, previously applied to medical image segmentation, for text line identification in historical documents[15]. Vogtlin et al. presented DIVA-VAF, a deep learning framework for separating text and side notes[16], while Pandey and Harit used top-down visual saliency models to identify four types of annotation: underlines, encirclements, inline text, marginal text[17]. Li et al. applied self-supervised learning to segmentation, using a cross-modal approach which incorporated textual content with semantic components (titles, text blocks)[18]. Wei et al. evaluated three machine learning classifiers for pixel level labelling of periphery, background, text, and decoration[19]. Machine learning models require datasets to train them, and Nikolaidou et al.[20] have surveyed 65 such datasets, classifying them by task. Of those related to document structure, 25 contain annotations for layout components, 27 for text-lines, 7 for tables, and 11 for graphics or images. Four include reading order. Examples of layout components include text regions, main body text, footnotes, page numbers, table of contents, marginalia, paragraphs. One dataset includes text features, such as italics or capitalisation, and separates handwritten from typed text. The dataset of the Oficio de Hipotecas de Girona includes a notarial typology, which can be identified by entries in the left margin aligned with the beginning of a

14 Sébastien ESKENAZI/Petra GOMEZ-KRAMER/Jean-Marc OGIER, A comprehensive survey of mostly textual document segmentation algorithms since 2008, in: Pattern Recognition 64 (2017) p. 1–14.

15 Olfa MECHI/Maroua MEHRI/Rolf INGOLD/Najoua ESSOUKRI BEN AMARA, Text Line Segmentation in Historical Document Images Using an Adaptive U-Net Architecture, in: International Conference on Document Analysis and Recognition (ICDAR), Sydney, NSW, Australia (2019) p. 369–374.

16 Lars VOGTLIN/Paul MAERGNER/Rolf INGOLD, DIVA-DAF: A Deep Learning Framework for Historical Document Image Analysis; State of the art results on separating text and side notes, 2022. (Accessed at https://arxiv.org/abs/2201.08295.

17 Shilpa PANDEY/Gaurav HARIT, Handwritten Annotation Spotting in Printed Documents Using Top-Down Visual Saliency Models, in: ACM Transactions on Asian and Low-Resource Language Information Processing 21/3 (2022) Article 58.

18 Peizhao LI/Jiuxiang GU/Jason KUEN/Vlad I. MORARIU/Handong ZHAO/Rajiv JAIN/Varun MANJUNATHA/Hongfu LIU, SelfDoc: Self-Supervised Document Representation Learning, in: IEEE/CVF Conference on Computer Vision and Pattern Recognition (CVPR), Nashville, TN, USA (2021) p. 5648–5656.

19 Hao WEI/Micheal BAECHLER/Fouad SLIMANE/Rolf INGOLD, Evaluation of SVM, MLP and GMM Classifiers for Layout Analysis of Historical Documents, in: International Conference on Document Analysis and Recognition, Washington D.C. 2013, p. 1220–1224.

20 Konstantina NIKOLAIDOU/Mathias SEURET/Hama MOKAYED, A survey of historical document image datasets, in: International Journal on Document Analysis Recognition 25 (2022) p. 305–338.

paragraph[21]. This is an example of semantic meaning of text being inferred from its spatial relationship with other text.

Earlier attempts at document layout analysis did use logic-based approaches. Esposito used spatial relations (top and left alignments, and touching), and qualitative size (small, medium, large), within a rule-based algorithm, combining with machine learning to optimally define the size categories. Aiello extended Allen Intervals to define Thick Boundary Rectangle Relations[22] (TBRR) in order to smooth the unevenness of text lines in historical documents. As an example, take two parallel text lines, A and B, where A is above B. Line A has x-coordinates of (100, 200) and B has x-coordinates (101, 201). Using Allen Intervals, the lines will be classified as overlapping, while to the human eye they will appear identical, since they differ by a single pixel at each end. TBRR provides a parameter, T, which defines how close two points can be to be considered equal (e.g. with T=2; 98–102 are all equal to 100).

Ishitani combined geometrical and logical layout analysis, using Gestalt principles of proximity, adjacency, and contextual similarity, to group objects on the page[23]. QSR has also been explored by Stell in relation to poetry where the layout can contribute key aspects of the meaning of the poem[24].

Controlled vocabularies of document features are available. Codicologia has a detailed vocabulary built from three databases (Vocabulaire codicologique, Le Lexicon[25], Arabic codicological glossary)[26]. Themes range from page layouts (long text, columns), and text regions (paragraphs, marginalia, lines) to signs such as brackets, underlines, and carets. SegmOnto aims to present a compromise between the detail of Codicologia and the limited range of features provided by PAGE XML (a standard schema for document layout), categorising layout features as zones and lines. Zone types include main text, margins, stamps, and tables, while line types include headings, drop capitals, and default text. Nikolaidou's[27] survey of datasets, and the

21 Lorenzo Quiros/Lluís Serrano/Vicente Bosch/Alejandro H. Toselli/Rosa Congost/Enric Saguer/Enrique Vidal, Oficio de Hipotecas de Girona. A dataset of Spanish notarial deeds (18th Century) for Handwritten Text Recognition and Layout Analysis of historical documents (1.0) [Data set] (2018); https://doi.org/10.5281/zenodo.1322666

22 Aiello, Document understanding p. 1.

23 Yasuto Ishitani, Logical structure analysis of document images based on emergent computation, in: Proceedings of the Fifth International Conference on Document Analysis and Recognition. ICDAR '99 (Cat. No.PR00318), Bangalore, India (1999) p. 189–192.

24 John G. Stell, Qualitative Spatial Representation for the Humanities, in: International Journal of Humanities and Arts Computing 13/1–2 (2019) p. 2–27.

25 Philippe Bobichon, Mise en page et mise en texte des manuscrits hébreux, grecs, latins, romans et arabes (Publications pédagogiques 5), Paris 2008.

26 http://codicologia.irht.cnrs.fr/theme/liste_theme/422.

27 Nikolaidou et al., A survey of historical document image datasets. https://doi.org/10.48550/arXiv.2203.08504.

literature on algorithmic approaches to DLA, suggests that the field has so far been focused on identification of major features of documents – paragraphs, lines, images – rather than the larger range of philological features included in Codicologia. Although some approaches identified have used spatial logic, they have used it as a means to an end–identifying region order, or classifying documents by type–not as a representation of the document itself.

Qualitative Spatial Representation (QSR)

QSR can be traced back to philosophical objections to a mathematical theory of space based on abstract points and uninformed by human experience. Whitehead notes that geometry as a deductive science is not grounded in the physical world, and asks 'How is space rooted in experience?'[28]. Whitehead was not the first to raise the mismatch between mathematical space and the space of experience. However, the theory of extensive connection[29] developed by Whitehead provided the basis for the development of the Region-Connection Calculus (RCC)[30]. The RCC consists of axioms for spatial regions, based on relationships between regions. It is generally applied to two-dimensional regions in the plane with relationships such as overlapping, touching at their boundaries, etc. Regions in this sense can be areas of text on a page, not necessarily rectangular nor of a single piece. The most commonly used form, RCC-8, includes eight relationships. Studies by Renz, Rauh and Knauff provide evidence that topological relations are important in human understanding of space, and 'the level of granularity given by the RCC-8 relations is particularly important'[31]. Each relationship consists of a precise mathematical definition, and a human interpretable, qualitative, description. For example, the relationship 'partially overlapping' is defined as 'there exists a part of a region X which is also a part of region Y and there is also some part of X which is not a part of Y'. The term 'part' also has a precise definition.

The relationship can also be more intuitively understood using circles to indicate two regions [Fig. 1]:

28 Alfred North WHITEHEAD, An Enquiry Concerning the Principles of Natural Knowledge, Cambridge ²1925, p V.

29 Alfred North WHITEHEAD, Process and Reality. An Essay in Cosmology, Cambridge 1929.

30 David A. RANDELL/Zhan CUI/Anthony G. COHN, A spatial logic based on regions and connection, in: Knowledge Representation 92 (1992) p. 165–176.

31 Jochen RENZ/Reinhold RAUH/ Markus KNAUFF, Towards Cognitive adequacy of topological spatial relations, in: ed. Christian FRESKA et al., Spatial Cognition II, Lecture notes in Artifical Intelligence 1849 (2000) p. 184–197, p 194.

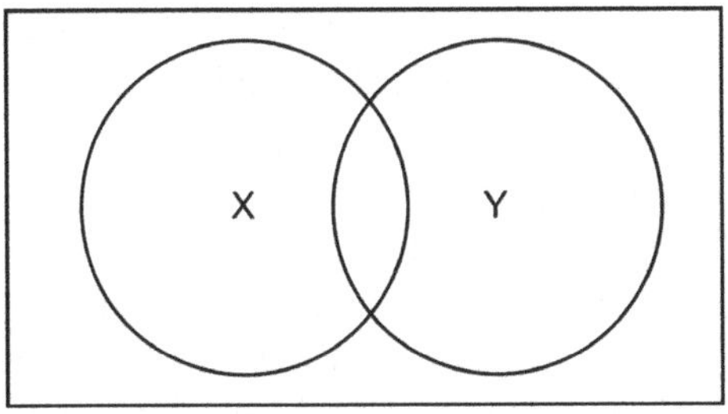

Fig. 1: Region X partially overlaps region Y.

For relationships between one-dimensional time intervals, the algebra of Allen[32] pre-dates the RCC and the development of computational QSR, but can now be understood as another system of relationships in the QSR mould. In this case the definition of two overlapping time intervals X and Y is that 'the beginning of Y occurs after interval X starts, but before it ends, and Y ends after X ends'. Again, a pictorial representation, this time using lines, is more intuitive [Fig. 2]:

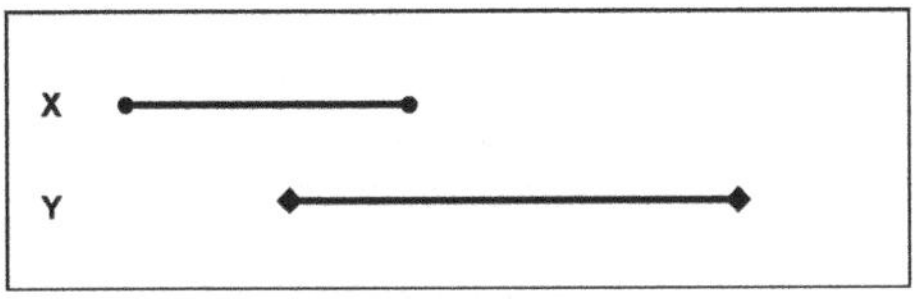

Fig. 2: Interval X overlaps interval Y.

The inverse of the 'overlaps' relationship is 'overlapped by'. In this case Y would begin before X and end during the interval X. The Allen algebra comprises 13 relationships: 6 (before, meets, starts, finishes, during, overlaps) plus their 6 inverses (after, met by, started by, finished by, contains, overlapped by), and the 'Equals' relationship.

Several extensions to Allen's original relations have been proposed, and we will make use of Thick Boundary Rectangle Relations[33] (TBRR) and Extended Allen Intervals[34] (EAI) in the experimentation section. TBRR recognises the imprecision of historical documents. While a paragraph may be left justified, the alignment of the beginnings of each line is generally approximate, especially at the pixel level, and may be further affected by skew from the digitisation process. To counter this imprecision the extremes of two intervals are considered equal if they are closer than a fixed distance T (setting T=0 is the equivalent of standard Allen intervals).

32 James F. Allen, Maintaining Knowledge about Temporal Intervals, in: Communications of the ACM 26 (1983) p. 832–843, p. 832.

33 Aiello, Document understanding p. 1

34 Renz, Towards Cognitive adequacy.

Returning to Fig. 2, if the beginning of Y was within distance T of the beginning of X, then the relationship under TBRR would be 'X starts Y'. The best value of T for an application may be identified through experimentation or derived using statistical or machine learning methods.

One criticism of Allen intervals is that they do not capture the degree of overlap; there is no distinction between two-one minute intervals overlapping by 59 seconds or by a single second. EAI addresses this issue by using the midpoint of each interval to make 27 relations. For example, the 'overlaps' relation becomes four relations which express the degree of overlap (o) by introducing the terms 'most part' (m) and 'least part' (l). These relations are: most part of X overlaps most part of Y (mom), least part of X overlaps least part of Y (lol), most part of X overlaps least part of Y (mol), least part of X overlaps most part of Y (lom). Fig. 3 shows the four overlapping relationships.

We also propose two simplified versions which will be referred to as Allen-2 ('overlap', 'no overlap') and Allen-3 ('before', 'overlap', 'after'). Following this naming convention, the standard Allen algebra will be referred to as Allen-13, the Extended version as Allen-27, and TBRR as Allen-13T.

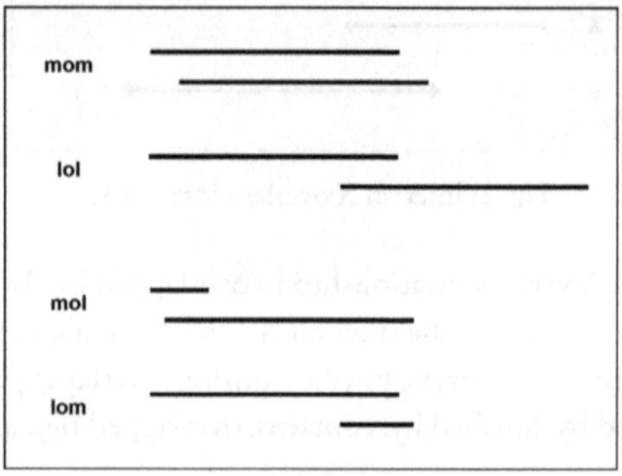

Fig. 3: Overlapping relations in EAI.

Allen intervals can also be applied to two-dimensional space. The Rectangle Algebra (RA) uses Allen-13 in both the x and y directions, which results in 169 possible relations between two rectangles. While this provides more nuance than RCC-8, it may make reasoning overly complex. For document features such as text lines, using Allen-2 (or 3) should be sufficient for one of the dimensions (vertical for text written across the page), reducing the algebra to 26 (or 39) relations. However, using Allen-27 for the other dimension increases would create up to 81 relations. The famous aphorism, 'All models are wrong, some are useful'[35], seems particularly appropriate when applying a qualitative representation. The algebra

35 George E. P. Box, Robustness in the strategy of scientific model building, in: Robustness in Sta-

used will always be a compromise between the nature of the problem being solved and the computational complexity of the solution.

Qualitative relationships have been analysed for directions such as 'left of', 'north of', etc, and also for relationships of distance such as 'near' and 'far'. These were not used in the experimentation reported here, but for a general overview of many spatial calculi see Cohn and Renz[36].

Applying QSR to Historical Documents

We have experimented with a number of documents to explore the value of QSR for identifying, categorising and perhaps even interpreting historical documents. Some are from the collections of the National Archives (TNA), and others come from the cBAD[37] document layout dataset. They have been selected to demonstrate the concepts of QSR but do not exhaustively represent the range of spatial features we may find in historical documents. The documents from TNA include medieval charters, which show how spatial relationships demarcate sections of a document, and incorporate visual features which group information together. Approaching charters in this way draws on the long tradition of diplomatics, a sub-discipline of archival science and legal theory that was developed to establish the authenticity of precisely such documents. Diplomatics plays an important role in the understanding of the form of individual documents, of what should and should not be present in a typical charter or contract from a particular time, region, or jurisdiction.

As Duranti notes, 'Any written document ... contains information transmitted or described by means of rules of representation, which are themselves evidence of the intent to convey information: formulas, bureaucratic or literary style, specialized language ... and so on'[38]. The present research is not concerned with authenticity, but it does seek to explore whether the same features that allow experts in diplomatics to assess whether a document is genuine can also shed light on document type at scale.

---

tistics, ed. Robert L. Launer/Graham N. Wilkinson, New York/San Francisco/London 1979, p. 201–236.

36 Anthony Cohn/Jochen Renz, Qualitative Spatial Representation and Reasoning, in: Handbook of knowledge representation, Elsevier, eds. Frank van Harmelen, Vladimir Lifschitz and Bruce Porter, Amsterdam 2008, p. 551–596.

37 Markus Diem/Florian Kleber/ Robert Sablatnig/Basillis Gatos, cBAD: ICDAR2019 Competition on Baseline Detection, in: International Conference on Document Analysis and Recognition (ICDAR), Sydney, NSW, Australia (2019) p. 1494–1498.

38 Luciana Duranti, Diplomatics. New Uses for an Old Science, Part I, in: Archivaria 28 (1989) p. 7–27, p. 15.

In addition to the medieval charters held at the National Archives, more modern documents have been examined, for example the drafts and final version of a speech made by Prime Minister Margaret Thatcher to President Ronald Reagan in 1982[39]. These pages are used to show how QSR can be deployed to establish and represent the evolution of a document over time. From the cBAD dataset we have chosen letters and documents with columnar layouts. This application of a common method over documents of widely differing types is again grounded in existing diplomatic practice. Writing in 1989, Duranti argued that 'notwithstanding the technical problems presented by some contemporary documents, the different structure of their text and the specific procedures governing their creation, maintenance, and use, the basic diplomatic principles and methodology formulated for the evaluation of medieval diplomas are still valid today'[40]. A charter might begin with an invocation and end with a dating clause and witness list, but an email is equally identifiable through the presence of a 'To' field containing at least one email address, CC/BCC fields, and a subject line (among other elements). Using form as a means of categorising, grouping, and connecting digitised and born-digital documents in heterogeneous collections would help historians to gain insights into the scope and shape of those collections and allow them to move between close, distant, and mid-scale reading.

QSR does not identify objects on a page it is solely a method for representing relations between them. Therefore we need other methods to identify the objects. The field of Document Layout Analysis has advanced significantly since the advent of deep learning and has produced many models for segmenting lines in digitised documents. We have applied one such model, ARU-Net[41], to identify baselines in our documents. Figs. 4(a)–(f) show the output of running ARU-Net on a selection of the documents we used. In many cases features of interest may be subtle, or beyond the capabilities of the current generation of machine learning models (or more likely, sufficiently large datasets of visual features to train them are unavailable). In preparing the examples for this paper we have also used the manual annotation tool VIA[42] to label lines and other features in documents. We found, for our purposes, that it was most pragmatic to draw baselines for text lines, and draw rectangles or polygons around symbols, underlinings, and other non-textual

39 https://discovery.nationalarchives.gov.uk/details/r/C13317582

40 Duranti, Diplomatics p. 23.

41 Olfa Mechi/Maroua Mehri/Rolf Ingold/Najoua Essoukri ben Amara, Text Line Segmentation in Historical Document Images Using an Adaptive U-Net Architecture, in: International Conference on Document Analysis and Recognition (ICDAR), Sydney, NSW, Australia (2019) p. 369–374.

42 Abhishek Dutta/Andrew Zisserman, The VIA Annotation Software for Images, Audio and Video, in: Proceedings of the 27th ACM International Conference on Multimedia (MM '19), October 21–25, Nice, France. ACM, New York, NY, USA, 4 pages, 2019.

annotations. We also used metadata labels to separate typed text, handwriting, and handwriting from different hands. From baselines we can generate rectangles, by naively filling the space vertically until encountering the next baseline, or by deciding on a standard height for each rectangle. A more sophisticated approach would use computer vision techniques to identify connected components above each baseline and derive a bounding box around them. Some segmentation models produce complex polygons, and jagged baselines, which closely follow the outline of the text. While these may benefit Handwritten Text Recognition (HTR) models, they introduce unnecessary computational complexity to deriving qualitative relationships. We therefore recommend simplifying the objects to rectangles and straight lines as much as possible.

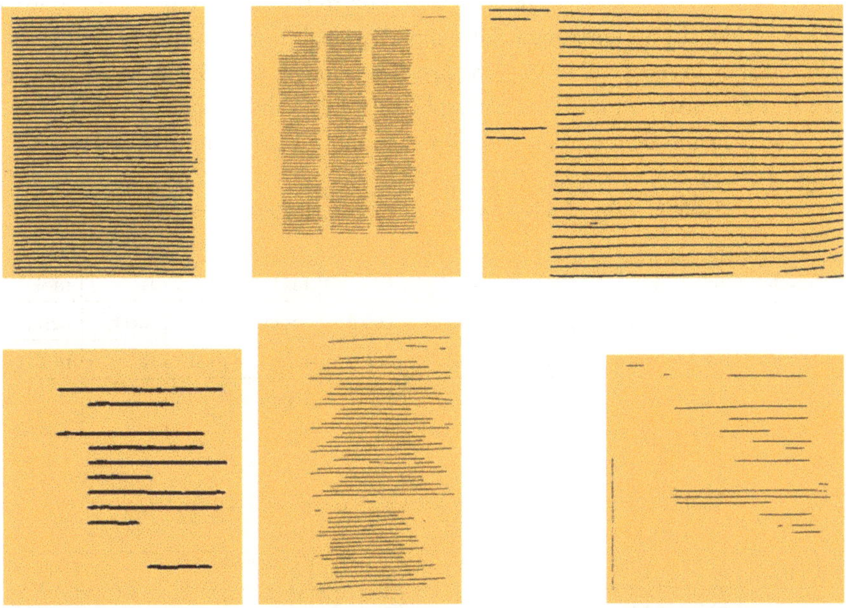

Fig. 4(a)-(f) clockwise from top left: (a) Page from a 19th century Will; (b) 3 column page from the cBAD dataset; (c) Paragraphs with headings in left margin; (d) Letter from cBAD dataset; (e) poem in the form of a tree; (f) first page of a speech.

QS Representation of Documents

Working with rectangles suggests the Region Connection Calculus as an appropriate starting point for documents. However, the majority of rectangles would be non-overlapping, or may overlap but not in a meaningful way. To create an interval-based representation of a document, we firstly derive baselines which as data consist of a y-axis position (y-pos), and x-axis start (x-start) and end (x-end) positions. Each interval is compared to its nearest neighbours, based on vertical distance, and a relation is calculated between the first overlapping neighbour below, and to the right. If there is no overlapping neighbour below, then the first non-overlapping neighbour is used instead. A configurable limit can be set on vertical distance, so an interval may have no close neighbours.

In Table 1, we have classified the 27 relations of Allen-27 according to their directional tendency ('before' implies a large shift to the right from one text line to the next; 'equals', no horizontal shift; 'momi', a small shift leftwards), and the implied change in size ('cdi' implies the first line is longer than the next; 'cd' implies the first is shorter; 'mom' does not explicitly imply a difference in length). Table 2 shows the equivalent table of Allen-13 relations (TBRR shares these relations).

Table 1: Allen-27 relations by size effect and directional tendency.

stretch	lom	lf	rd	mf	cd	ms	ld	ls	mol
	after	met by	loli	momi	equal	mom	lol	meets	before
shrink	lomi	lsi	ldi	msi	cdi	mfi	rdi	lfi	moli
	← **Left**					**Right** →			

Table 2: Allen-13 relations by size effect and directional tendency.

stretch				f	d	s			
	pi	mi		oi	e	o		m	p
shrink				si	di	fi			
	← **Left**					**Right** →			

Fig. 5: Hinton diagrams of relations for Fig. 4(a), (page of continuous, even length lines of text). From left to right, Allen-13, Allen-13T (T=8), Allen-27.

A Hinton diagram is used to visualise the relative values in a 2-D array. Fig. 5 shows three such diagrams. The positions in each 3x9 grid map to the relations in Tables 1 and 2, and the more times a relation occurs in a document the bigger the white square in the diagram. For example, the fourth square in row two of the left-hand Hinton diagram represents the number of 'overlapped by' (oi) Allen Intervals in a document. Each diagram in Fig. 5 depicts the central tendency of the document, with no blocks to the extreme left or right. However, both Allen-13 (left-hand diagram) and Allen-27 (on the right) have a lot of noise, with a high percentage of relations indicating horizontal shifts as the text descends down the page. The middle diagram shows the behaviour of Allen-13T in accounting for small differences in the beginnings and ends of lines (in this case up to 8 pixels). This is a much more accurate representation of the document.

Fig. 6: Hinton diagrams of relations for Fig. 4(e), (poem in form of tree). From left to right, Allen-13, Allen-13T (T=8), Allen-27.

All three diagrams in Fig. 6 capture the expansion and contraction of the lines as they go down the page. This is evidenced by the top and bottom boxes in the middle column of each diagram. Allen-13T also captures the left alignments of the lower lines which represent the trunk of the tree. Allen-27 also shows relations which are not captured by the other two representations. For example, there is a single 'ldi' relation which occurs when interval X is near the beginning and wholly during interval Y. This may not be an important distinction but it does capture some of the unevenness of the document.

Fig. 7: Hinton diagrams of relations for Fig. 4(d), (informal letter). From left to right, Allen-13, Allen-13T (T=8), Allen-27.

In Fig. 7, each diagram provides a very different picture of the document. There is not much difference between the Allen-13T diagram and the left-hand image in Fig. 5, even though the documents are very different in layout. Allen-13 produces a distribution which is similar to that of the poem in Fig. 6. Only Allen-27, with its broader range of relations, captures the very uneven nature of the document. The way in which a collection of qualitative relationships is able to detect different characteristics in a document is similar to the use of QSR in identification of events from video data[43]. In that case, different types of events are identified partly by making use of the patterns of change to spatial relationships between areas in each video frame occupied by certain objects. Conceptually, the pattern of relationships in a particular example is like a spectrum detected by a measuring instrument in analysing the example.

The most natural data structure for storing these relations is a network graph. The nodes are objects on the page (text lines, symbols, annotations), and the edges are relations. The graph is necessarily directed, meaning that an edge with relation 'before' from nodes A to B does not also imply that B is before A. To capture the inverse 'after' relation, an edge could be created from B to A. We may also create alternative graph representations of a page. A subgraph (a subset of nodes and edges from the graph) of closely related nodes could be combined into a single node. For example, the rows of each column of text in Fig. 4(b) could be represented by a single node, resulting in a graph with 3 nodes (say, L,M,R). Working from left to right we have the relations: 'L before M', 'M before R'. A distinction should be made between text in columns, and data in tabular form. The latter could be represented in two ways, equally valid. The first representation consists of a node for each row of data, the second consists of a node for each column. This is an important aspect of QSR; it is not a prescriptive set of rules but a language and framework for representing spatial relationships, and the representation chosen will vary by application.

The R of QSR can also stand for Reasoning. The mathematical definitions of each relation enable logical assertions to be made. For example, using the fact that each Allen relation has an inverse, if A is before B, it is implied that B is after A. If L is before R and R is before M, then we infer that L is also before M without explicitly identifying the relationship between L and M. The given relations thus provide a basis from which others can be deduced without having to store every possible relationship that might be useful. A query about whether a certain relationship holds can often then be answered by checking whether it follows from the given ones.

Fig. 4(c) shows a commonly seen document structure consisting of paragraphs of text, the start of each being vertically aligned to a shorter line or two in the left margin. One way of representing this structure is to merge the left margin text into the rows of text immediately to their right. Assuming Allen-13T has been used, each line of paragraph text has the same x-start and x-end values, other than the shorter lines at the end of the paragraphs. We will also assume the margin text lines have the same x-start values. With these assumptions, we can describe the documents as sequences of relations (the first being relative to the top edge of the page). Two such sequences are shown in Table 3:

43 Krishna S. Dubba et al., Learning relational event models from video, in: Journal of Artificial Intelligence Research 53 (2015) p. 41–90.

Table 3: Sequences of relations between text lines and their immediate vertical neighbour.

TBRR: Fig. 4(c)	TBRR: Fig. 4(e)
Finished by	Contains
Equals	During x 3
Finished by	Finishes
Equals x 9	Contains
Started by	During x 3
During	Finishes
Equals	Contains
Finished by	Finishes
Equals x 14	During
Started by	etc.

These are examples of repeating patterns. In column one, the pattern 'finished by', followed by multiple 'equals' relations, is the general pattern of a line of text followed by a block of indented text. The indentation is reversed by a 'started by' relation. In the right-hand column the distinctive tree pattern of the poem consists of repetitions of 'contains', 'during' (multiple times), and 'overlapped by'. The pattern breaks down at the third tier due to the inherent messiness of a handwritten document, but resumes further down the page. This representation lends itself well to searching for documents based on their layout. Possible approaches include regular expression pattern matching, vectorised representation (as used in large language models), or sketch based image retrieval.

The example documents presented so far all read from left to right, and down the page. Fig. 8 shows a document containing text written at three different orientations, with lines coloured by orientation. The vertical lines on the left of the page read from bottom to top, while on the right of the page the horizontal lines read from left to right, and the vertical lines from top to bottom. What this example highlights is that orientation is an important attribute of each object on the page. For comparisons between intervals it makes sense to make them relative to the expected reading order of the language.

For example, the vertical line furthest to the left of the page is left of the next line along, but from the perspective of the reader it is above. The entire block of text itself would still be considered to be 'before' the block of text on the right (in the horizontal direction).

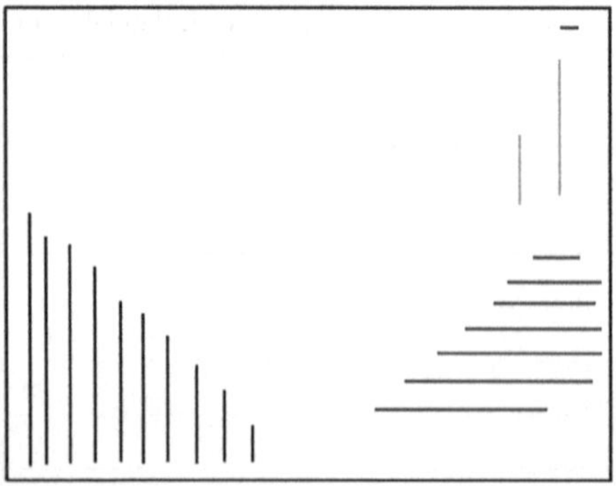

Fig. 8: Document with multiple text orientations.

Representing Change over Time

Fig. 9 shows a document with a Public Record Office (PRO) stamp. Without the contextual knowledge of when the document was written (c.1220), and when the PRO was formed (1838), a reasoning engine would not be able to decide whether the shape of the lines formed around the stamp, or whether it coincidentally formed a handy space to put a stamp. The spatial representation therefore requires a temporal dimension.

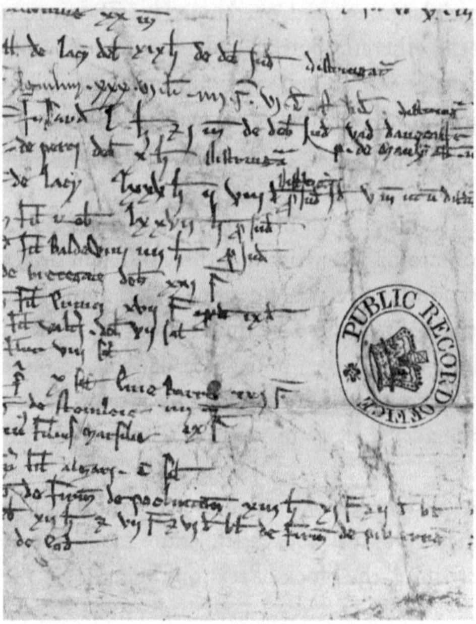

Fig. 9: Stamped document.

There are two draft versions of the speech made by Prime Minister Margaret Thatcher to welcome President Reagan on his visit to the United Kingdom in 1982, which will be used as an example of representing change over time. The layout of the first draft is that of a typed essay, several left justified paragraphs, with an indented first line. It is heavily annotated in black pen, including crossings out, encirclements, notes and replacement text between the lines and in the margins, and arrows. The sequence of events (typed speech, handwritten annotations) can be trivially represented on a timeline. Qualitative representation means we don't need to know the actual timeline. It is enough to state that the annotations came after the typed text. If there are multiple annotations, e.g. a blue pen, and a black pen, we will not necessarily know which came first but we know they are both 'after' the typed text. This can be modelled as a period of review 'after' the document was written, with each annotation occurring 'during' this period. No relation is derived between the annotations themselves. The temporal representation is enhanced when combined with the spatial arrangement of the annotations, and their relationship to the text.

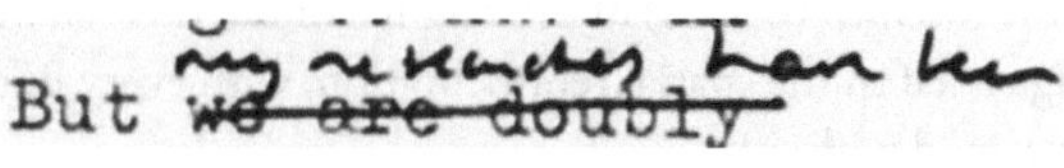
But ~~we are doubly~~

Fig. 10a: Crossed out text with replacement.

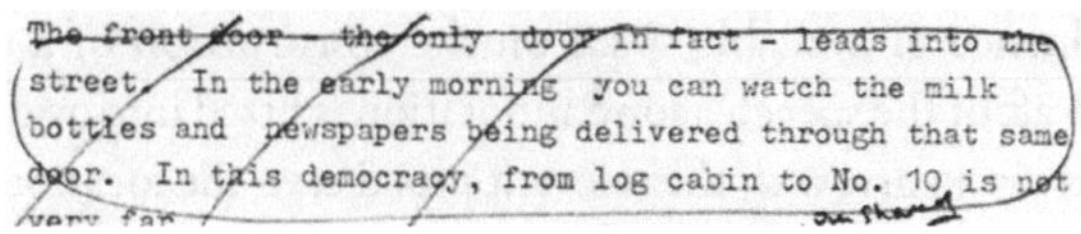
~~The front door – the only door in fact – leads into the~~
street. In the early morning you can watch the milk
bottles and newspapers being delivered through that same
door. In this democracy, from log cabin to No. 10 is not
very far

Fig. 10b: Crossed out and enclosed text

Fig. 10(a) shows three words of text crossed out, with a suggested replacement written above the line. Without reference to a specific spatial calculus, the handwritten text line is above the typed line, and is also between two typed lines. The hand-drawn line shares the same space as the text it is crossing out; it overlaps in both dimensions. In Fig. 10(b) the crossing out lines only overlap partially with a small subset of the text. The line circling the section of text encloses most of the words but only overlaps some of them. The handwritten-text line can be represented by Allen Intervals, with the temporal dimension separating it from the flow of the typed text. The hand-drawn annotations are better represented by a 2-d calculus, such as RCC-8. This is another case where approximation is most likely better than exactness. While we could represent line 2, say, as being contained within (or a non-tangential proper part of, in the language of RCC-8) the ellipse, and line 1 as partially overlapping it, that overcomplicates the representation and misses the intention of the annotation. Specifying that the entire text is a tangential proper part (contained and touching the edges) of the ellipse would be more pragmatic and better capture the purpose of what has been drawn.

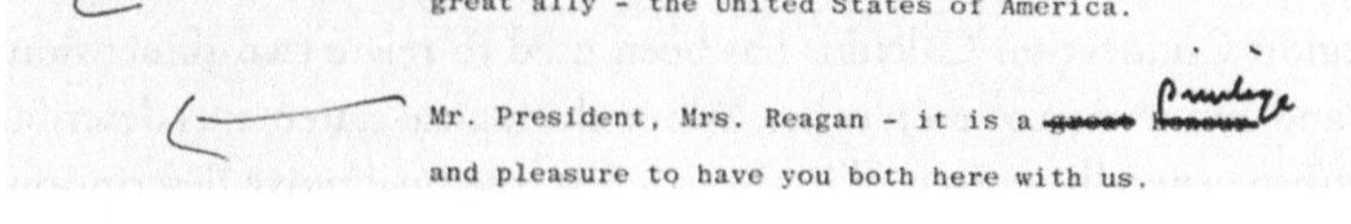
We are here today to welcome and ~~do~~ honour ~~to~~ our
great ally – the United States of America.

Mr. President, Mrs. Reagan – it is a ~~great honour~~
and pleasure to have you both here with us.

Fig. 11: Crossed out text with replacement

Moving to the second draft, there are fewer amendments to the text but the layout has subtly changed. The left margin is wider, which has the effect of stretching the text (the bottom line appears half way down the page in the first draft). Every line is left justified, and there is a large gap between the end of one sentence and the next - presumably to aid reading in public. Fig. 11 shows the drawing of two arrows which are requests to unindent the first lines of each paragraph. The effect of this instruction is seen in Fig. 4(f). Each new sentence starts on a new line, the font size is increased, as is the space between lines, and the length of the third paragraph means it gets a page to itself. The net effect is that the first page of the speech contains only the top fifth (6 lines) of the original draft. This can be modelled by including the page itself in the spatial representation, with every line and annotation being fully contained within it.

Further investigation is needed to understand how QSR could aid reasoning about the influence of available space on the construction of a document. Elsewhere in the draft of the speech a long annotation is fitted into available whitespace and connected via an arrow to the relevant typed text, the location of the stamp in Fig. 9 is unrelated to the adjacent text, and other documents which have informed our thinking include some lines that were tightly squeezed into a space set aside for one author amongst many.

Concluding Remarks

This paper approaches heritage collections as traces of dynamic processes and processual narratives. The key component of this work is to examine documents based on their spatial structure (such as where pieces of text are placed on a page), temporal relationships (such as knowing that one annotation was added after another) and spatiotemporal interconnections. Focusing on relationships between multiple documents that form complex networks revealing knowledge about how the documents have been created, used and reused, the paper puts these relationships at the forefront.

The examples presented have demonstrated how existing spatial relation algebras can be applied to historical documents and can be approached as an aid to understanding and navigation of large heritage collections. Allen Intervals, in various forms, have been used to evaluate the alignment of adjacent lines of text in the horizontal and vertical directions, and to track changes to a document over time. The Region Connection Calculus has been used to relate two-dimensional areas of text and annotation to each other. While the logical statements describing each relationship generally work well in this context, the qualitative descriptions of the relations are not always appropriate for describing documents. The term 'Non-tangential proper part' from RCC-8, meaning 'region X is wholly inside region Y', is unlikely to be understood by historians. The terminology of Allen Intervals is rooted in temporal language - saying line X occurs 'during' line Y makes little sense. This suggests that a spatial calculus using language which is meaningful to humanists is needed.

Each variety of Allen Intervals that we tested had advantages and disadvantages. The TBRR variety is certainly superior to Allen-13 when working with historical manuscripts as it smooths out the unevenness in handwritten documents. Setting the T parameter to 0 is also equivalent to Allen-13. The extended version of Allen provides more nuance in that it provides an indication of magnitude when intervals partially overlap, and direction when they fully overlap. A thick bordered variety of Allen-27 would improve its application to historical manuscripts. The downside of Allen-27 is that it consists of more than double the possible relations of Allen-13, which will have a computational cost when reasoning. The number of relationships can be reduced. In some applications, the inverse relations may not be applicable, particularly the 'most-most' relations such as 'mom' (most of X overlaps most of Y). In a paragraph of text the difference between 'mostly started' and 'mostly started by' could be down to whether line X is slightly shorter than Y, or vice versa. It may not be a meaningful difference. Equally, there may be applications where we wish to increase the number of relations. The 'during' relations ('ld','cd','rd') and their inverses offer no reference to relative length beyond that one interval is shorter than the other. One possibility is to incorporate the delta calculus in the QSR which would compare the lengths of two intervals. For example, a relation such as 'X centrally during and more than half length of Y' could be defined. In two dimensions, the eight relations of RCC may seem limited in applications to document understanding, but the Rectangle Algebra could range from 26 relations (Allen-13 x Allen-2) to 729 (Allen-27 x Allen-27), which probably makes too many distinctions for a useful qualitative relation. RCC-8 can be extended to incorporate degree of connection. For instance, 'partially overlapping' could be split into 'just' and 'well' overlapping; 'non-tangential proper-part' (NTPP) becomes 'just inside' and 'well inside'. RCC also lacks any notion of direction. Combining it with a direction calculus could give rise to relations such as 'overlapping from left' or 'overlapping from above'. An RCC with added direction and degree of overlap would consist of 23 relations: disconnected x {left, right, above, below}, externally connected x {4 directions}, partially overlapping x {4 directions} x {well, just}, NTPP (and its inverse) x {well, just}, TPP (and its inverse), and equal.

The examples presented in this paper are QSRepresentation. The derived relations only state that, say, two objects on the page happen to overlap. In order to attain QSReasoning human knowledge is needed. Take for example, a hand-drawn line. If it goes through a word it is an instruction to remove that word, below the word it may be interpreted as emphasis. If it connects an annotation to a line of typed text, it could be an instruction to insert or append the annotation text. The margin text in Fig. 4 is interpreted as the beginning of a section. The authors of that document also drew vertical lines down the left side of each paragraph to explicitly group those lines together. Other documents use symbols for the same purpose, while spacing between lines or sub-headings may also have the same meaning.

Figs. 12(a)–(c)[44] show three ways of drawing brackets. Visually they differ considerably but semantically they are the same. Indentation and spacing can be used to the same effect. In 12(a) the author of the document has used this bracketing only in the cases where the left margin text does not align with the top line of the section; they show an awareness of how spatial relationships are interpreted.

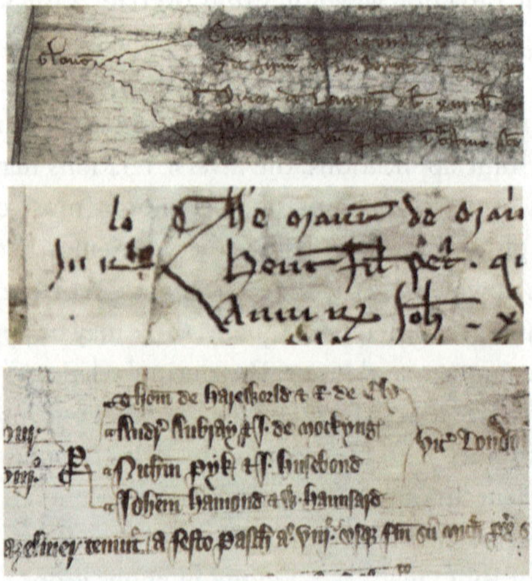

Fig. 12a–c: Brackets to group lines of text.

This paper has introduced Qualitative Spatial Representation (QSR) as a method to explore the spatial and temporal dimensions of digital document collections. It is a complementary technology to machine learning for technology-based document layout analysis and understanding, but it can be applied separately to automated techniques. We have identified several applications for the technology, including: representing spatial relationships between objects on a page, and how they evolve over time; enhanced search capabilities such as searching text 'near to' an annotation, or finding documents similar to a certain layout; human understandable explanations of the results of machine learning based layout analysis; and a language for communicating human knowledge of document layout to algorithms. In order to progress these applications, experts in history and diplomatics need to work with computer scientists to develop qualitative representations which comprise relationships that are applicable to the study of historical documents, and to curate datasets which will encourage further exploration of this technology.

44 The National Archives, UK: a) E 368/3 b) E 368/5 c) E 372/179

Combining Automatic Text Recognition with Digital Paleography

New Trajectories for Digital Diplomatics

Tobias Hodel, Jonas Widmer

What if we place trust in a machine-learning model? Can it answer questions that have not been part of its training process? This is the central inquiry explored in the following pages. By utilizing the output of a text recognition model, we seek to investigate if paleographically significant statements can be deduced. In other words, can the certainty and alternative readings provided by a text recognition model enable us to identify comparable scripts, potentially even the scribes[1]?

The process of digitization has opened numerous possibilities for analyzing charters. Image reproduction enables efficient visual comparisons[2], text recognition allows for easy searching and reading of documents, and computer vision can successfully identify visual entities such as heraldry and categorize and identify drawn objects[3]. These technologies are replicating "traditional" research questions and endeavoring to apply them to larger datasets with higher accuracy or more "objec-

1 This paper is the result of a small side-project, trying to use the output of models creatively. The authors are heavily indebted to Philip Kahle from the READ COOP for exporting confidence matrices from the Transkribus platform and to Gundram Leifert for explaining and discussing the concept of confidence matrices as well as the HTR+ workflow until they were understandable to the first author. Since these tests have been carried out, HTR+ has been removed from the Transkribus platform. Thus, it is unfortunately not possible anymore to access the mentioned confidence matrices. To provide a form of reproducibility the used confidence matrices (in the form of csv) have been published on Zenodo: 10.5281/zenodo.10148236.

2 As offered, for example, through www.e-codices.ch.

3 See e.g. for heraldry, Torsten Hiltmann/Sebastian Thiele/Benjamin Risse, Friends with Benefits: Wie Deep-Learning basierte Bildanalyse und kulturhistorische Heraldik voneinander profitieren, DHd 2020 Spielräume: Digital Humanities zwischen Modellierung und Interpretation. 7. Tagung des Verbands «Digital Humanities im deutschsprachigen Raum» (DHd 2020), Paderborn 20.02.2020. Online: https://doi.org/10.5281/zenodo.4621890.

tive" accounts. Machine learning, the predominant technology behind these developments, also offers other research paths when the output of machine learning algorithms is taken seriously.

Given that this issue of Archiv für Diplomatik concerns digital diplomatics, an introduction is almost unnecessary. The collected articles showcase what a digitized diplomatics world looks like: Machine learning tools are used regularly, ontologies are constructed, and data is provided in open formats and as linked data. Although technology and algorithms are constantly evolving, medievalists have always been at the forefront of the digital turn in digital humanities. The self-help group "Digital Medievalist" has existed for 20 years and has evolved into a learned society, complete with a journal and a dynamic group of contributing scholars and scientists.

The main focus of this article is exploring how machine learning, more specifically Handwritten Text Recognition, can be creatively used in paleography. By applying text recognition models, we can make large amounts of charters searchable and readable. Furthermore, machine learning algorithms offer a unique opportunity to make some of their decision-making process visible, potentially allowing us to identify scribes through the analysis of handwriting styles. Therefore, the question is relatively simple: Can we apply such machine-learning approaches for text recognition to make (machine-based) paleographical assumptions? On a methodological level, we take the machine's output seriously, as if the system could understand paleographical traits similar to a trained scholar. This approach is therefore an approach to help us understand the inner workings of Handwritten Text Recognition algorithms.

We thus use such models to compare writing styles by scoring similarities on identified characters and adjacent incorrect alternatives stored in confidence matrices. In theory – or at least we believe so – the information could be harvested to determine scribes. However, for our purpose, it is paleography on a scale, allowing us to analyze characters' similarities from a computational point of view. On a methodological level, this will help us explain how a deep learning algorithm "sees" a text line or, more precisely, parts of a single character. It is not the goal to develop a "better" approach to writer identification, specific and custom-made approaches are much more successful with this task[4].

In the article, we will, in ultimate brevity, discuss the development of digital paleography and explain in-depth the concept of confidence matrices, which are

4 As an introduction to writer identification see: Vincent CHRISTLEIN/Markus DIEM/Florian KLEBER et al., Automatic Writer Identification in Historical Documents: A Case Study, in: Zeitschrift für digitale Geisteswissenschaften, 2016. Online: https://doi.org/10.17175/2016_002. Mike KESTEMONT/Vincent CHRISTLEIN/Dominique STUTZMANN, Artificial Paleography: Computational Approaches to Identifying Script Types in Medieval Manuscripts, in: Speculum 92/1 (2017) p. 86–109. Online: https://doi.org/10.1086/694112.

the basis for our data analysis approach. We will then demonstrate the potential of this approach by applying it to a data set from Switzerland and highlighting the insights gained from the combination of confidence matrices. Finally, we will draw some lessons from this experiment for both paleography and deep learning in the humanities.

Digital Paleography, Text Recognition, and the State of the Art

Paleography and diplomatics developed in parallel in the digital turn. Both profited immensely from the vast masses of digitized material that became available in the past decades and honed their method based on scholarly-led inquiries. Briefly put, analog approaches have been translated into and adapted for the digital space.

In an exemplary manner, up to 2014, an annotation suit for visual features was developed within the DigiPal ERC project[5], formalizing the analysis of visual features and annotating manually. This ground-breaking project focused on using and segmenting the available digital imagery, allowing for an in-depth analysis of glyphs and letterforms on a scale. However, the work bore similarities to the approaches used by earlier generations who attempted to examine particular forms in order to distinguish scribes, understand their distinctions, and identify shared characteristics.

At the same time, the project was one of the first to implement a fully working framework (in the sense of a software solution) that acted as a virtual research environment running on web technologies for the humanities. Some projects still rely on this framework, and we can easily imagine other uses for the software in the future[6].

In the meantime, automatic text recognition received much attention, and new machine-learning-based platforms and engines emerged. To name a few, Transkribus resulted from an EU-funded infrastructure project that developed specific engines[7], eScriptorium was built based on Kraken and is currently being developed,

5 See, e.g., Peter A. Stokes, Modeling Medieval Handwriting: A New Approach to Digital Palaeography, in: Digital humanities 2012 – Conference abstracts, ed. Jan Christoph Meister, Hamburg 2012, p. 382–384.

6 *DigiPal: Digital Resource and Database of Manuscripts, Palaeography and Diplomatic*. London, 2011–14. Available at http://www.digipal.eu/

7 Günter Mühlberger/Louise Seaward/Melissa Terras et al.,Transforming scholarship in the archives through handwritten text recognition: Transkribus as a case study, in: Journal of Documentation 75/5 (2019) p. 954–976. Online: https://doi.org/10.1108/JD-07-2018-0114; [30. Oktober 2017]; Joan Puigcerver, PyLaia, 01.01.2022 [30. Oktober 2017]. Online: https://github.com/jpuigcerver/PyLaia.

taking a multitude of languages and writing systems into account[8]. At the same time, OCR4all is foremost being used for complex print types[9]. All these approaches and most other existing engines switched to an approach involving neural networks. From a computer science point of view, text recognition is based on this, understood as basically a solved problem[10].

At the same time and as a result, we can rely on a growing number of available documents, offering new possibilities. Since the quality can ever be improved and out-of-the-box models need large amounts of training material, the project "HTR united" started to collect ready-made transcriptions that can be re-used to train handwritten text recognition models. At the same time, they also acknowledge the work done by scholars and volunteers[11]. Still, various challenges remain since neural networks are usually trained from scratch and adapt to the used character sets. For example, the handling of abbreviations depends not only on the system's user's goals and interpretation, but also on the expected input to the system.

Thanks to the growing number of available image-aligned transcriptions, we do have access to many languages and a variety of writing styles; we are consequently currently on the brink of making so-called general models available that are capable of recognizing similar handwriting and entire writing styles, thus leading to a minimization of the necessary training material for specific handwriting styles[12]. Still, some questions remain open, as has been mentioned earlier, especially about topics of importance to medievalists, like character-sets and the treatment of abbreviations. For the moment, it is furthermore unclear what character error rates can be reached for completely unseen handwriting styles. One thing can be stated with confidence: for the time being, the automatically generated results will not be comparable to scholarly editions and require ways of dealing with uncertainty.

In the context of medieval charters, this approach continues to offer numerous opportunities for efficiently handling extensive document collections featuring comparable handwriting styles. It also paves the way for advancing the fields of diplomatics, history, and paleography on a broader scale. In essence, distant diplo-

8 Peter A. Stokes/Benjamin Kiessling/Daniel Stökl Ben Ezra et al., The eScriptorium VRE for Manuscript Cultures – Classics@ Journal, in: Classics@ 18 (2021). Online: https://classics-at.chs.harvard.edu/the-escriptorium-vre-for-manuscript-cultures/.

9 Christian Reul/Dennis Christ/Alexander Hartelt et al., OCR4all—An Open-Source Tool Providing a (Semi-)Automatic OCR Workflow for Historical Printings, in: Applied Sciences 9/22 (2019) p. 4853. Online: https://doi.org/10.3390/app9224853.

10 Tobias Hodel, Konsequenzen der Handschriftenerkennung und des maschinellen Lernens für die Geschichtswissenschaft. Anwendung, Einordnung und Methodenkritik, in: Historische Zeitschrift 316/1 (2023) p. 151–180. Online: https://doi.org/10.1515/hzhz-2023-0006.

11 See online: Alix Chaqué/Thibault Clérice, HTR-United/htr-united, 26.02.2021. Online: https://github.com/HTR-United/htr-united.

12 For medieval scripts see for example the large model made available on the Transkribus platform: https://readcoop.eu/transkribus/public-models/.

matics could serve as an initial and prominent illustration of how text recognition technology enables entirely new avenues of research. The recently started *DiDip: From Digital to Distant Diplomatics* project leads the way.

Confidence Matrices: Access to the Deliberations of an Algorithm

As a form of experimenting with machine learning output, this article takes the result of a text recognition algorithm seriously. It does not search for potentially wrong assumptions that need to be corrected by knowledgeable humans. When applying text recognition, some recognition engines, like HTR+ by Planet AI (usable within the Transkribus platform until the end of 2022), not only decide on the most likely character for a particular image slice but also the likelihood of all characters appearing in the training set for the said slice in a so-called confidence matrix. A confidence matrix is conceptually similar but not identical to a character confusion matrix. A confusion matrix assumes that there is a correct character to be recognized, an assumption that we ignore here completely. These confidence matrices are tables that can be used for advanced search approaches, which result in exceptionally high recalls (over 99,5%), even if the recognition model is only partially fitting to a specific script or handwriting[13]. This output is gained before in another step (mostly through beam-search) tries to improve the output based on language models.

The focal point of this article is not to improve search operations, but to extract paleographical information from documents. This paper assumes that a large recognition model would or should similarly identify similar letter forms. Using confidence matrices for this purpose assumes that forms of letters can be indirectly deducted by analyzing the second, third, or fifth (etc.) most likely character for a specific slice of a line[14].

---

13 For more in-depth information see, Gundram LEIFERT/Roger LABAHN/Joan Andreu SÁNCHEZ, Two Semi-Supervised Training Approaches for Automated Text Recognition, in: 2020 17th International Conference on Frontiers in Handwriting Recognition (ICFHR), Dortmund 2020, p. 145–150. Online: https://doi.org/10.1109/ICFHR2020.2020.00036 ; Tobias STRAUSS/Max WEIDEMANN/Johannes MICHAEL et al., System Description of CITlab's Recognition & Retrieval Engine for ICDAR2017 Competition on Information Extraction in Historical Handwritten Records, in: CoRR abs/1804.09943, 2018. Online: http://arxiv.org/abs/1804.09943; Tobias STRAUSS/Gundram LEIFERT/Tobias GRÜNING et al., Regular expressions for decoding of neural network outputs, in: CoRR abs/1509.04438, 2015. Online: http://arxiv.org/abs/1509.04438, Stand: 29.06.2018.

14 The notion that it is a slice, not an actual character, is significant. To reach decent results, splitting into characters didn't allow for a worthy recognition of textual entities. The slicing approach is highly adaptable and works for most tested writing systems.

In a sense, this combines the DigiPal approach of identifying and comparing letters, letterforms, and glyphs but only relies on a calculated output. This requires a brief introduction to confidence matrices since the "magic" (or, more specifically, the building of confidence, in the mathematical sense of the word) happens before the text is outputted as a transcription by an engine.

The main result of the text recognition process is, in most engines, not the transcribed lines but rather a table (a matrix) consisting of all possible readings at a specific slice of a line. Only from this table is the transcription inferred in the decoding process, and the recognized text appears on a screen. A recognition process is run for each line, creating an entire table. The table consists of columns of all letters or, more generally, characters occurring in the training set of the HTR model. For each character, it is calculated how likely it is to appear at a defined position. According to this calculation, the confidence of the HTR model at a specific slice of the line is written into the column. This also explains the name "confidence matrix".

If we look at some lines in an example table, we will encounter one "character" with a high frequency and high confidence: a so-called "feed-forward" ("Vorschub" in German). If the HTR model doesn't recognize a character with certainty, it proceeds while storing a "feed-forward" signal. After finishing up the recognition process, all "feed-forward" get deleted or, correctly put, ignored.

0.43	0.00	0.05	0.00	0.00	0.00	0.00	0.00	0.00	0.00	0.00	0.00	0.00	0.00	0.00	0.00	0.00
0.58	0.00	0.15	0.00	0.00	0.00	0.00	0.00	0.00	0.00	0.00	0.00	0.00	0.00	0.00	0.00	0.00
0.27	0.00	0.04	0.00	0.00	0.00	0.00	0.00	0.00	0.00	0.00	0.00	0.00	0.00	0.00	0.00	0.00
0.61	0.00	0.02	0.00	0.00	0.00	0.00	0.00	0.00	0.00	0.00	0.00	0.00	0.00	0.00	0.00	0.00
0.43	0.00	0.04	0.00	0.00	0.00	0.00	0.00	0.00	0.00	0.00	0.00	0.00	0.02	0.00	0.00	0.00
0.36	0.00	0.46	0.00	0.00	0.00	0.00	0.00	0.00	0.00	0.00	0.00	0.00	0.02	0.00	0.00	0.00
0.33	0.00	0.20	0.00	0.00	0.00	0.00	0.00	0.00	0.00	0.00	0.00	0.00	0.00	0.00	0.00	0.00
0.40	0.00	0.02	0.00	0.00	0.00	0.00	0.00	0.00	0.00	0.00	0.00	0.00	0.00	0.00	0.00	0.00
0.58	0.00	0.01	0.00	0.00	0.00	0.00	0.00	0.00	0.00	0.00	0.00	0.00	0.00	0.00	0.00	0.00
0.69	0.00	0.03	0.00	0.00	0.00	0.00	0.00	0.00	0.00	0.00	0.00	0.00	0.00	0.00	0.00	0.00
0.36	0.00	0.04	0.00	0.00	0.00	0.00	0.00	0.00	0.00	0.00	0.00	0.00	0.00	0.00	0.00	0.00
0.65	0.00	0.05	0.00	0.00	0.00	0.00	0.00	0.00	0.00	0.00	0.00	0.00	0.00	0.00	0.00	0.00
0.31	0.00	0.02	0.00	0.00	0.00	0.00	0.00	0.00	0.00	0.00	0.00	0.00	0.00	0.00	0.00	0.00
0.60	0.00	0.01	0.00	0.00	0.00	0.00	0.00	0.00	0.00	0.00	0.00	0.00	0.00	0.00	0.00	0.00
0.43	0.00	0.00	0.00	0.00	0.00	0.00	0.00	0.00	0.00	0.00	0.00	0.00	0.00	0.00	0.00	0.00
0.54	0.00	0.01	0.00	0.00	0.00	0.00	0.00	0.00	0.00	0.00	0.00	0.00	0.08	0.00	0.09	0.00
			!	"	#	$	&	'	(	)	*	+	,	-	.	/

Fig. 1: Red marked in the first column are activated feed-forward (with a numerical certainty). Image by Tobias Hodel, CC-BY.

In decoding, an independent algorithm processes the confidence matrix (the table) and chooses the character that is identified to be most likely at a particular position. You encounter the result then as a single character on the recognized line.

The process gets inverted for specific search algorithms in the sense that the decoding process is skipped. Using so-called Keyword spotting (KWS), the confidence matrices get searched, and the outputted text is ignored. By using KWS, a minimal confidence level is assumed as a threshold. As a standard, only characters

a	b	c	d	e	f	g	h	i	j	k	l	m	n
0.13	0.01	0.01	0.02	0.07	0.01	0.01	0.01	0.04	0.00	0.00	0.01	0.04	0.07
0.16	0.01	0.01	0.02	0.05	0.00	0.01	0.01	0.07	0.00	0.00	0.01	0.04	0.12
0.04	0.02	0.01	0.01	0.02	0.00	0.01	0.01	0.02	0.00	0.00	0.02	0.01	0.14
0.01	0.01	0.01	0.02	0.01	0.00	0.01	0.01	0.01	0.00	0.00	0.01	0.01	0.05
0.07	0.01	0.02	0.03	0.07	0.00	0.05	0.02	0.05	0.00	0.00	0.01	0.03	0.04
0.04	0.01	0.01	0.01	0.06	0.00	0.07	0.01	0.02	0.00	0.00	0.00	0.01	0.03
0.01	0.00	0.00	0.01	0.06	0.00	0.06	0.01	0.02	0.00	0.00	0.01	0.01	0.09
0.01	0.00	0.00	0.01	0.05	0.00	0.02	0.01	0.01	0.00	0.00	0.01	0.01	0.06
0.09	0.01	0.00	0.01	0.22	0.01	0.04	0.01	0.01	0.00	0.00	0.01	0.02	0.04
0.02	0.00	0.01	0.01	0.07	0.00	0.01	0.01	0.02	0.00	0.00	0.01	0.01	0.05
0.04	0.01	0.01	0.03	0.04	0.01	0.02	0.01	0.02	0.00	0.00	0.01	0.03	0.16

Fig. 2: Reading from top to bottom, the word "anen" can be identified. At the position of the "a" (second row of the image), the algorithm also identifies an "n" with a confidence of 12%. Image by Tobias Hodel, CC-BY.

appearing at a specific position with a likelihood of 5% or higher (marked red in the images) get looked up (this will eliminate most of the characters in the table and speed up the process). Of course, it is possible to alter this value and, e.g., only take characters with a confidence of 25% or higher into consideration, but this will result in fewer hits. We use the term Keyword Spotting here as a definition of a specific search approach relying on Confidence Matrices. Others refer to Keyword Spotting as an approach with a predefined list of keywords that an algorithm learns to identify[15].

i	j	k	l	m	n	o	p	q	r	s	t	u
0.28	0.00	0.00	0.01	0.00	0.02	0.02	0.00	0.00	0.01	0.01	0.01	0.26

Fig. 3: In the row, an "i" (28%) or a "u" (26%) are potential characters occurring at the slice. Image by Tobias Hodel, CC-BY.

For our experiment to work, we need a model trained on a large dataset that does not focus on the traits and particularities of a single hand but can recognize an entire writing style. The existence of such models has been proven, mainly based on documents from the 19th century in German Kurrent[16]. For these tests, we rely on a

15 See e.g. Sebastian Sudholt/Gernot A. Fink, PHOCNet: A Deep Convolutional Neural Network for Word Spotting in Handwritten Documents, 05.12.2017. Online: https://doi.org/10.48550/arXiv.1604.00187; Jon Almazan/Albert Gordo/Alicia Fornes et al., Word Spotting and Recognition with Embedded Attributes, in: IEEE Transactions on Pattern Analysis and Machine Intelligence 36 (12) p. 2552–2566. Online: https://doi.org/10.1109/TPAMI.2014.2339814. 01.12.2014.

16 Tobias Hodel/David Schoch/Christa Schneider et al., General Models for Handwritten Text Recognition: Feasibility and State-of-the Art. German Kurrent as an Example, in: Journal of Open Humanities Data 7 (2021). Online: https://doi.org/10.5334/johd.46. See also

model based on what is probably the largest amount of training data to this date for medieval scripts. The "Medieval Scripts 2.4" model has been trained on more than seven million words, which represents approximately one million lines of text[17]. All texts were written between the 13th and 15th centuries in Latin, German, Dutch/Flemish, and French. The model is quantitatively biased towards Dutch/Flemish and German since most of the material in the training set is from documents written in these two languages. Besides charters, it also includes book scripts; therefore, we avoided an overfitting or specialization towards textual structures, contents, and vocabularies primarily found in charters.

Since the past three years have seen a considerable improvement in text recognition and a diversification of text recognition engines, large amounts of transcribed text, alongside digitized materials and alignment of text and images, have become available. Therefore, the first large and general language models have become available[18]. And in the foreseeable future, we will even be able to produce further models that specialize not on a hand or a group of scribes but instead focus on a language and a time frame alongside even larger recognition models[19], resulting in high-quality first results for a variety of scripts.

But for this approach, the recognition quality is of lesser relevance. And going forward, we will not care about the quality of the recognition process. As a general impression, the recognition resulted in reliable text. Important for this experiment is the availability of a large model alongside the possibility of accessing the confidence matrices of several recognized documents that demonstrate the opportunities offered by the technology.

Ariane PINCHE, Generic HTR Models for Medieval Manuscripts The CREMMALab Project, 04.02.2023. Online: https://hal.science/hal-03837519.

17 For more information see https://readcoop.eu/model/charter-scripts-german-latin-french/. Links to published training and validation sets can be found there as well.

18 HODEL et al., General Models for Handwritten Text Recognition.

19 Phillip STRÖBEL/Simon CLEMATIDE/Martin VOLK et al., Evaluation of HTR models without Ground Truth Material, in: LREC 2022, Marseille, 21 Juni 2022 – 23 Juni 2022, European Language Resources Association, 2022. Online: https://doi.org/10.5167/uzh-219356.the usual data split into training, validation, and test data sets allows the evaluation of models in terms of accuracy or error rates. However, the evaluation process becomes tricky as soon as we switch from development to application. A compilation of a new (and forcibly smaller These approaches are based on the TrOCR framework provided by Microsoft; Minghao LI/Tengchao LV/Lei CUI et al., TrOCR: Transformer-based Optical Character Recognition with Pre-trained Models, in: ArXiv abs/2109.10282, 2021.

The Data Set and Approaches to Variants

As a first assumption, we take the output of the recognition process and, consequently, the confidence matrix seriously. This means we do not correct the output, and when comparing outputs of confidence matrices, we assume that the recognized character is correct and, in that sense, fixed. Also, we concentrate only on the lower-case alphabet. Even though the used model also outputs the likelihood of an abbreviation sign, of some Hebrew and Greek characters that have been occurring in the large model, or of the upper-case letters, all those characters are ignored. Furthermore, we only consider recto pages and neglect dorsal notes and other writing on the back of charters.

To make assumptions about paleographical traits, we take the most likely character at a specific slice as given (characters at the bottom). As a second step, we sum up all alternative readings of said character over the whole charter. For each lower-case character, we receive a value larger than 0. Applied to all lower-case characters, this results in a two-dimensional matrix that can be understood as a "fingerprint" of a charter. This «fingerprint» is highly influenced by the applied model, which means at the same time that we must automatically recognize all charters in question with the same model. Based on this fingerprint, charters can easily be compared.

For clarity, we produced heat maps, indicating higher values in darker green. This allows for a visualization by overlaying several matrices and running it as a sequence in a loop.

We built our corpus of 87 charters from the archives of the monastery of Einsiedeln (available on www.klosterarchiv.ch), written between the end of the 14th and the end of the 15th century[20]. To process a relatively uniform set of charters with the chance of finding documents written by the same hand, this approach seemed both feasible—due to the available images—and promising, thanks to a relatively dense charter production.

As a first, expected and apparent results are patterns of characters that have a certain visual similarity. These patterns appear over several charters frequently and form clusters: The characters "c" and "t" are good examples, which proofs the assumption that visual similarities do result generally over several charters in higher values. This means that they are often considered "similar" by the recognition engine. Similarly, the character "f" and "s" (the latter presumably as a long s) are also

20 As an introduction to Einsiedeln and its archives Joachim SALZGEBER, Das Kloster Einsiedeln, Einsiedeln 2006; Andreas KRÄNZLE, Das Klosterarchiv Einsiedeln, in: Traverse: Zeitschrift für Geschichte 19/2 (2012) p. 7–17. Online: https://doi.org/10.5169/seals-391037; Martin WERLEN/Andreas MEYERHANS/Peter NIEDERHÄUSER et al. (Ed.), Äbte, Amtsleute, Archivare: Zürich und das Kloster Einsiedeln (Mitteilungen der Antiquarischen Gesellschaft in Zürich 76), Zürich 2009.

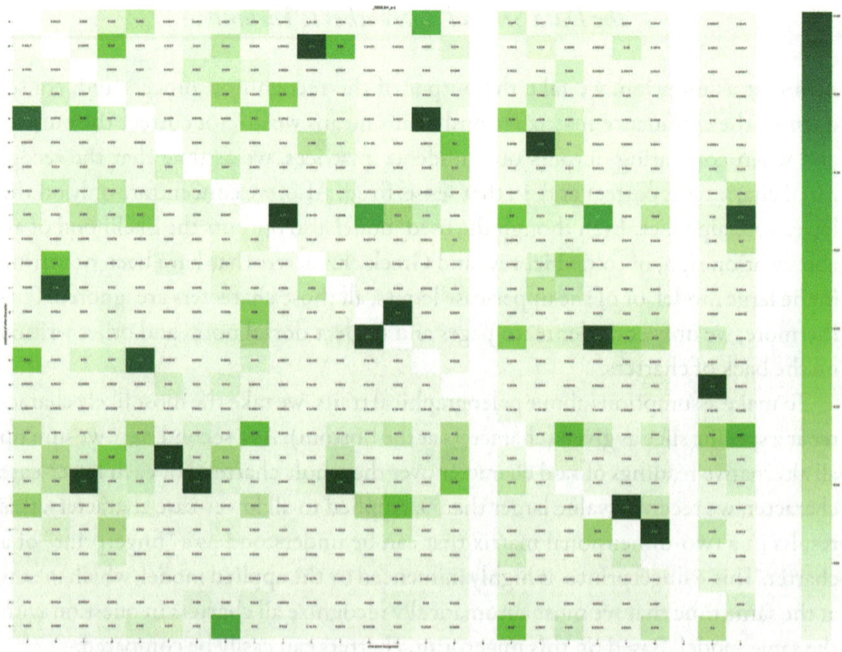

Fig. 4: Two-dimensional matrix, to be read from below, indicating the recognized character and the sum of all likelihood that another character could be appearing at all occurrences instead of the character (left). Blank columns indicate that a character has never been identified as the most likely character in the document.
How to read the table: Instead of the character "o" (see "o" at the bottom of the table), the character "e" could appear with a likelihood of 0.51 (see column "o", row "e").
Analyzed charter: Klosterarchiv Einsiedeln, KAE A SR 26 12. Image derived from www.klosterarchiv.ch.

often shown resulting in higher values. As expected, "u" and "v" also result in high similarities, while it remains unclear whether this results from the used model. In some of the data used to train the large model, "u" and "v" have been distinguished based on shape, while in other datasets that also were used for training, the distinction was based on their usage as consonants or vowels. Consequently, we must acknowledge that the text recognition model never learned to follow one approach to distinguish "u" and "v".

If we look at "m" and "n," we recognize that the latter ("n") is—as expected—confused with the first ("m"). An "n" can be considered part of an "m", which explains why in the "n" column the "m" value is high. "n" can also be identified as an "m" but with a far lower frequency. Finally, "m," "n," and "l" show a similarity to "i", but the "i" column doesn't result in higher values for "m", "n" and "l".

As an interim result, we conclude that visual similarities lead to spikes in the values of a confidence matrix. Those characters are often confused by paleography students as well, which hints at the fact that the visual analysis of the text recognition model is comparable to the interpretation by students in introductory courses.

Another frequently occurring pattern points to a different direction altogether. Vowels are associated with being similar to each other. For "e" and "o," this can easily be explained by the letter shape. But the similarity between "a" and "e", "e" and "i", or "a" and "i" is more surprising and not explainable due to visuality. The interpretation of this occurrence is based on the fact that in the training process, not single characters get segmented, but whole lines are the input that gets learned. The output of the trained model does not have access to a formal language model (such as a list of existing words/n-gram or similar), but the model learned representations based on visual inputs of entire lines and became thus aware of language patterns. In the trained languages (as in most Indo-Germanic languages), the position of vowels is rather strongly determined. Therefore, we identify a sort of "expectancy" (in the sense of overfitting in machine learning terms) by the model. The model learned that the next character is in certain cases most likely a vowel and rates all vowels as more likely in the output due to the learned patterns of occurrence of this class of characters. Therefore, we conclude that besides the shape, linguistic structures are also to be considered by the model and thus are reflected in the resulting confidence matrix.

Some charters exhibit more specific patterns. In one example (KAE A SR 26 5), the character "f" was identified as potential "g." This gothic cursive script has distinctively bold downward strokes, which probably explains the confusion. This observation suggests that both forms of patterns are occurring: 1) Very frequent patterns that indicate similarities due to the general writing style. 2) Individual patterns, which point towards singularities of specific hands.

Consequently, we can assume that a fine-grained divergence of documents can be detected through the similarity patterns between characters that are visually similar. Nonetheless, we ask for caution for two reasons: First, we assumed that the most likely identified character is the correctly identified character. This is, of course, not a given, and maybe thresholds should be used, and characters that have only been identified with lower confidences (e.g., below 50%) should be ignored. Second, we simply added up all the variant readings of a character. For each charter, we therefore sum up the likeliness that an "a" could be read as a "c" and so forth for all other lower-case characters, resulting in one value per identified character. The variant readings of characters that are identified more often will result in higher values. For future similar approaches, means or mean root squares could be more indicative measures.

We already showed that linguistic structures, especially the position of vowels, are represented in the matrix. Now, due to the adding up of all the variants as explained above, we take even more and unconsciously linguistical patterns into consideration. Therefore, we have to take into account that languages and language variants do use specific characters or syllables more or less frequently[21].

Clustering the individual charter fingerprints

In order to produce a visually comparable graph of all analyzed charters, we reduce the number of dimensions: For this we rely on a rather crude visual clustering of the charters through a Principal Component Analysis (PCA), that reduces the 676 dimensions (26^2 = all lower-cased characters of the latin alphabet) of a charter's confidence matrix (or fingerprint) to only two components[22].

Despite the loss of information inherent to the dimensionality reduction, the matrix fingerprints, still prove to be an ideal basis for experiments. Based on the derived clusters, we want to qualitatively check, whether narrowly clustered charters are visually similar. At the same time, we want to emphasize that PCA is but one step in the process and has to be checked by the qualitative analysis of the clusters to determine the appropriateness of the method. The results of such an analysis are to be carefully appraised to avoid jumping to conclusions.

The two outliers (in light orange in the top right corner) jump right into view, and on closer inspection, they are united by a problem with the layout analysis[23]. The lines of those two charters have been incorrectly identified (broken into very short parts of the actual line), and the recognized text is thus wholly gibberish. The patterns and mainly the frequency of occurring characters produce such an outlier. Again, we see that the clustering approach resulted in interpretable outcomes.

In the produced cluster, besides the outliers (top right corner), we see two larger clusters divided through differences in the y-axis. The violet and green cluster consist of Latin charters. Blue and red clusters are charters in German. We already mentioned the linguistic differences represented in the matrices. Thus, it's not surprising that we see such a divide. This also suggests that one of the two principal components indicates the language as a component.

However, when comparing very narrowly clustered documents, the approach demonstrates its shortcomings. Charter KAE AB 9 is identified as highly similar to charter KAE A SR 26 19. While the first one was produced in 1390, the second one was written in 1493 with no indication that either one has been pre- or post-dated.

---

21 See, e.g., figure 4: "q" has never been identified as the most likely character. We can thus assume that this is a charter in German. Medieval German uses "q" much less frequently than Medieval Latin, which is also present in the corpus.

22 Hervé Abdi/Lynne J. Williams, Principal component analysis, in: WIREs Computational Statistics 2/4 (2010) p. 433–459. Online: https://doi.org/10.1002/wics.101.

23 Such errors occur frequently with documents which have a darker coloration, maybe due to exposure to light and/or air.

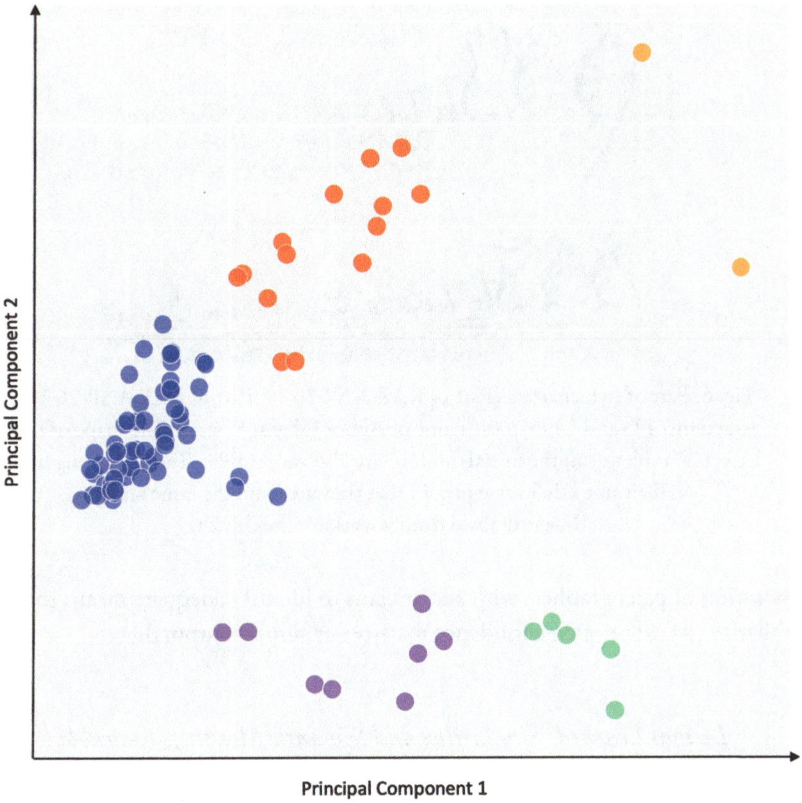

Fig. 5: Two-dimensional representation of the two most frequent principal component (PC1 & PC2). Clustered in five clusters. Based on the summed-up «fingerprints» of the charter. X (PC1) and Y (PC2) axis represent the two most likely calculated factors of the PCA process. Each point depicts one charter. Five clusters have been generated based on the PCA output. The X-axis represents feature 1, the Y-axis feature 2 of the PCA output. Fig. produced by Jonas Widmer. CC-BY.

Completely different is the assessment of the next closest charter KAE A SR 26 20: Like KAE A SR 26 19 the document has been issued in the name of the abbot of the Abbey of Rheinau, Johann Konrad, issued in 1495 only two years after the charter we compared it with. The two charters do probably have the same scribe, which demonstrates that the output of the Principal Component Analysis partially results in meaningful patterns.

At the end of this part, we want again to make aware of the limitations of the approach. The clustering is based on Principal Component Analysis, a form of analysis that has to be carefully checked for its results. Further research and the use of more elaborate clustering needs to be tested. We encourage further the close col-

Fig. 6: Part of two charters (Part of KAE A SR 26 19/Part of KAE A SR 26 20) issued in 1493 and 1495 in the name of Abbot Johann Konrad. The shape of the letters "s" is identical; the initials and "o" are also very similar. This is a strong hint (albeit not a definitive proof) that they are from the same scribe. Image derived from www.klosterarchiv.ch.

laboration of paleographers with statisticians to identify adequate means to define similarity (based on such confidence matrices or similar outputs).

Lessons Learned: Similarities and Semantic Meanings Embedded

Summarizing this first experiment, the analysis of confidence matrices is fruitful in identifying visual and, to a certain degree, linguistical similarities of charters (or other forms of handwriting). However, the method needs to be refined considerably to make it reliable. Compared to other processes requiring manual labor, the method could be applied on large scales. With more and more collections being made available based on automatic text recognition, this could be a useful method for detecting similarities in handwriting.

The method offered nonetheless valuable insights into the recognition process. We could demonstrate that beside visual forms being analyzed for the recognition – which is a fascinating insight and not a given *per-se* – linguistic patterns, for example the expectancy of a recognition model for a vowel at specific positions were showcased. This demonstrates how machine learning algorithms are relying heavily on the input data and learn to prefer to recognize specific patterns. This should be considered one way of bias, for which we have to be on the outlook.

For future work, we encourage to dive further into the analysis of confidence outputs while refining the statistics of the approach. Also, the method should be tested to distinguish different writing styles (e.g., running scripts versus book scripts) to get more insights about the method.

For a precise writer identification, the approaches presented here were too coarse, but the potential has been showcased. The output of machine learning approaches can be creatively used to address adjacent questions that are not the focus of a specific model. Using handwritten text recognition to determine similarities in handwriting is but one case to provide such an example.

III. Charters and their Digital Editions

The *Documents et analyses linguistiques de la Galloromania médiévale* (*GallRom*) – a new potential for interpretive research

Martin Glessgen, Marguerite Dallas

Introduction to GallRom

The new database *Documents et analyses de la Galloromania médiévale* (GallRom) is the result of the transformation and fusion of no less than six previously independent linguistic and philological projects relating to the textual witnesses of the four medieval Gallo-Romance languages: French, Francoprovençal, Occitan and Gascon. Of particular interest in the context of the discipline of digital diplomatics is the fact that it is home to the *Documents linguistiques galloromans* (henceforth DocLing). DocLing is the digital edition of a collection of original legal and administrative documents conserved in national and regional archives throughout the territory of modern-day France, Switzerland and Belgium, dating from the medieval period and written in the four Old Gallo-Romance vernaculars.

A first version of the DocLing corpus was accessible online at the University of Zurich from 2009 onwards. Two further editions were produced in 2013 and 2016, the number of subcorpora increasing with each one. A radically enlarged fourth edition, offering a significantly larger number of texts covering more regions, has recently been made available within GallRom. Crucially, both the content and the metadata are now linked to resources which enable researchers to exploit the corpus to its full potential. These consist of tools for scriptological analysis as well as complementary materials such as dictionaries and bibliographies.

This paper will consist of a short presentation of the periods and regions covered by the collection of documents (1). The description will be followed by a glimpse at how the textual editions are transcribed and encoded (2). We will then provide an overview of the architecture of the database, touching on some of the issues which arose during the fusion of the different modules (3). We will conclude with several examples of the types of investigation to which the database lends itself (4).

Over the last twenty-five years, the development of this highly complex and extensive system has absorbed the attention and energies not only of many junior and senior researchers in the fields of philology and linguistics, but also of a large number of computer scientists[1].

1. The documentary texts: significance for historical linguistics and geochronological scope

Documentary texts are particularly valuable for research in historical linguistics as they survive in original form and can generally be accurately dated and even localised. To a greater or lesser extent, collections are to be found for all regions, whereas literary or religious sources are linked to cultural centres and the nature of their chronological and regional distribution varies greatly. The immediate usefulness of original documents for diachronic investigation therefore surpasses that of texts belonging to other genres, as these are generally transmitted by later copies, display complex linguistic stratification and rely on a number of factors involving several different specialist fields for an approximate dating and localisation.

The DocLing corpus represents the continuation in electronic form of the series *Documents linguistiques de la France*, begun by Paul Meyer at the École des Chartes in Paris at the beginning of the last century and continued by his successors Clovis Brunel and Jacques Monfrin[2]. It was established in order to document the very beginnings of the written vernacular tradition of legal and administrative texts throughout the Gallo-Romance territory, with the aim of examining the nature of the evolution of the Gallo-Romance varieties from Latin and the constitution of written regional languages. The criteria governing the selection of the documents are thus necessarily chronological and geographical, the objective being to expand the collection to cover the whole of the territory. The earliest witnesses to vernacular writing for each region are included, and the latest texts generally date from the first decades of the fourteenth century, when the influence of the variety of French

---

1 Martin Glessgen exercises sole responsibility for the overall architecture of GallRom. The LiRI team at the University of Zürich is responsible for the technical management of the database. This task is currently performed by Jonathan Schaber, who took it over from Johannes Graen.

2 Cf. Martin Glessgen, L'écrit documentaire et le projet des Plus anciens documents linguistiques de la France, in: Manuel de la philologie de l'édition (Manuals of Romance Linguistics/MRL 4), ed. David Trotter, Berlin/Boston 2015, p. 267–295; and Id., Les 'Documents linguistiques' de la France. Histoire, présent et perspectives d'un projet centenaire, in: Comptes rendus des séances de l'Académie des Inscriptions et Belles-Lettres (CRAI) 161/3 [juill. à oct. 2017] (2018) p. 1261–1292 for a complete history of the evolution of the project; cf. also Jacques Monfrin, Introduction [= «Les études sur les anciens textes gallo-romans non littéraires»; «Le recueil des documents linguistiques de la France» etc.], in: Jean-Gabriel Gigot, Documents linguistiques de la France (série française), vol. 1: Chartes en langue française antérieures à 1271 conservées dans le département de la Haute-Marne, Paris 1974, XI–LXXX.

used by the Royal Chancellery began to be used in regional centres, resulting in the elimination of diatopically marked features.

As regards the sub-genres of the documentary discourse tradition, charters are preferred as they offer the widest variety of linguistic phenomena, particularly in the domains of morphology and syntax. The sheer number of participants involved in the various types of situation they reflect gives rise to a polyphonic constellation requiring a high degree of syntactic elaboration.

The corpus currently consists of 41 subcorpora. 15 of these represent the digitisation of the volumes published between 1909 (Meyer) and 1988 (Coq). The documents contained in each volume have been carefully re-edited and, in certain cases, newly collated by means of a comparison with the photographic reproduction of the original document wherever possible. Some corpora have been enlarged by the addition of previously unedited documents located in and collected from the respective regional archives. A further 7 are collections which had remained unpublished before their integration into the digital repertoire and are thus newly available to researchers. The remaining 19 subcorpora represent recent endeavours under the direction of Martin Glessgen and Françoise Vielliard, in collaboration with a number of their respective colleagues. DocLing thus offers a wealth of new diplomatic and linguistic material.

The extent of the coverage of the Gallo-Romance territory currently provided by the corpus is illustrated in the following tables. As can be seen from the dates of each subcorpus, documentary writing did not begin at the same time in all four Gallo-Romance languages, and, within each of these languages, marked differences may be observed at the regional level.

According to the evidence currently available, the first vernacular language to be used for documentary writing was Occitan[3].

Table 1: Sub-corpora for medieval Occitan.

Siglum	Department or region	Dates	Number of documents
ChOccAnc	Toulousain, Albigeois, Rouergue	1034–1200	541
DocAlpM	Alpes-Maritimes	1070–1630	62
DocHAlp	Hautes Alpes	1199–1568	20
DocArles	Arles	1318–1532	91
DocMars	Marseille	1319–1555	48
DocAlpHPr	Alpes de Haute Provence	1332–1570	70
DocAix	Aix	1387–1547	32

3 Cf. Clovis Brunel, Les plus anciennes chartes en langue provençale, Recueil des pièces originales antérieures au XIIIe siècle, Paris 1926.

It should, however, be noted that documents dated before ca. 1100 are written in a variety of Latin that displays the beginnings of vernacular word order and into which a large number of lexical vernacular forms have been incorporated.

Occitan was followed much later by the northern French variety of Picardy, where the first document dates from 1204. The Royal Chancery and the Prévôté de Paris only began to use the vernacular from the middle of the 13th century onwards (essentially from ca. 1260 to 1280), showing that the chronological variation is not only regional, but also institutional.

Table 2: Sub-corpora for medieval French (preliminary distribution).

Siglum	Department or region	Dates	Number of documents
ChDo	Douai	1204–1270	506
ChMo	Moselle	1214–1271	273
ChPoit	Charente-Maritime, Deux-Sèvres, Vendée, Vienne, Maine-et-Loire	1219–1300	340
ChSL	Saône-et-Loire	1221–1331	100
ChFland	Flandre orientale et occidentale	1224–1271	73
ChMe	Meuse	1225–1270	132
ChAub	Aube, Seine-et-Marne, Yonne	1230–1271	103
ChMM	Meurthe-et-Moselle	1232–1265	290
ChHM	Haute-Marne	1232–1275	276
ChMa	Marne	1234–1272	230
ChV	Vosges	1235–1275	146
docHain	Hainaut	1236–1270	129
COr	Côte-d'Or	1239–1306	231
ChOise	Oise	1241–1286	224
ChR	Chancellerie Royale	1241–1300	140
ChHS	Haute-Saône	1242–1300	132
Doc-Norm	Seine-Maritime, Calvados, Manche, Eure-et-Loir	1250–1332	290
ChN	Nièvre	1289–1330	34

Francoprovençal was spoken throughout a large area around Lyon, extending from Grenoble to Besançon and into present-day Switzerland. Mainly attested through documentary texts, its written tradition began in the 13th century and developed between 1340 and 1480. The language of the documents is often mixed; while the grapho-phonetic surface forms are French, the grammar and vocabulary are Francoprovençal[4]. The same phenomenon can be observed in texts from the regions of Charente and Poitou, where a French surface *scripta* conceals an underlying Occitan variety close to the spoken language of these regions, which, for this reason, are known in scientific circles as the '*Occitania submersa*'.

Table 3: Sub-corpora for medieval Francoprovençal (preliminary distribution).

Siglum	Department or region	Dates	Number of documents
DocLyon	Lyonnais	[1225]–1425	49
ChDoubs	Doubs	1233–1271	306
DocNCh	Neuchâtel	1238–1379	182
ChJu	Jura	1243–1296	95
ChJuBe	cantons Jura and Berne	1244–1374	299
DocVauGe	Genève/Vaud	1247–1406	72
DocForez	Forez	1260–1498	63
DocAin	Ain	1265–1466	18
DocFrib	Fribourg	1296–1496	74
DocGrenoble	Grenoble	1338/1339	*Comptes consulaires*
Codi	Dauphiné	ca. 1200 (?)	*Somme du code*

For Gascon in the south-west, clearly a language in its own right, documentary texts are a particularly valuable source, as they constitute the only evidence available for the medieval period. The Gascon corpus is currently in the process of being prepared for integration into the GallRom database and will consist of approximately 120 documents dated between 1220 and 1320.

2. Philological component: the digital editions

To produce the digital editions, the documents are first transcribed directly from photographs of the original documents into a Word file. The transcription is then prepared for insertion into the database by the addition of XML tags. Both the transcription and the encoding follow criteria which have been specially devised in order to faithfully reproduce the typographical and morphological features of a non-standardised, highly variable written language. The criteria also account for aspects pertaining to diplomatics. In the following examples, each element will be

4 Cf. Hélène Carles, Écrire en deux langues: la coexistence des systèmes français et francoprovençal dans les scriptae médiévales de la Suisse romande, in: Revue de Linguistique Romane 87 (2023) p. 375–426.

illustrated by two images of the same charter from the eastern French region of Meurthe-et-Moselle detailing the conditions of land tenure and dating from 1235. The first image will show the tags, while the second will show the view generated by the tags. Excerpts from the manuscript will be provided wherever helpful.

First of all, the elements contained in the descriptive table providing external historical and codicological information about the document are encoded. This includes the instances involved in its production, as well as the *scriptorium* in which it was produced. The identification of the latter is based on the observation of a combination of linguistic and codicological criteria.

tagging	<rd0><abbreviation>AbbSalival</abbreviation></rd0>
critical edition	SCRIPTORIUM (CHA AbbSalival

In the text itself, each element of diplomatic discourse is then tagged separately:

tagging	<pub><div num=“1“><maj>C</maj>onue chose soit à<punct>-</punct>toz</div></pub>
critical edition	1 Conue chose soit à-toz

Each line is numbered in accordance with the corresponding line in the manuscript:

tagging	<maj>C</maj>onue chose soit [...] at laissié à Wirion <zw num=“1“/>
critical edition	1 Conue chose soit à-toz *que* li abes *et* li chapitles de Salinvas · at laissié à Wirion

Each paragraph is then further divided into separately-numbered semantic units, referred to as ‘divisions’, in order to facilitate the comprehension of the content and to provide coherent subsections for use within the dictionary module of GallRom (see section 3 below):

tagging	<div num=“1“><maj>C</maj>onue chose soit à<punct>-</punct>toz</div>
critical edition	1 Conue chose soit à-toz

The medieval punctuation is also transcribed and tagged, separately from the modern punctuation inserted for the benefit of the modern reader:

manuscript	transcription with tagging	diplomatic edition
	anz<punct original=“.“>	anz ·

The individual occurrences of lexemes and grammatical words are then enriched with tags designed to highlight all linguistic and philological features of thirteenth-century written French. The restitution of contracted and abbreviated forms is rendered visible by the use of italics. This is essential in a corpus which is to be used for grapho-phonetic analysis, in order to avoid unreliable results:

manuscript	transcription with tagging	critical edition
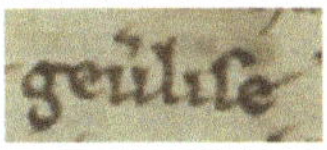	Gev<abr>er</abr>lise	Geverlise

Similarly, words which are illegible or missing due to damaged parchment and which are restituted by the editor are enclosed within square brackets, and are eliminated from any data selected for analysis. These forms are also excluded from the dictionaries.

Another common issue is the absence of capitalisation of the initial letter of a word at the beginning of a sentence or of proper names and place names, and, conversely, the use of a capital letter for common nouns. The letters are transcribed according to modern principles and all capital letters introduced by the scribe are indicated by the use of bolding:

manuscript	transcription with tagging	critical edition
	<maj>C</maj>i	**C**i

A more complex issue concerns the boundaries between lexemes, or between lexemes and morphemes. For example, definite articles are often fused with the nouns they determine. Again, the editor transcribes the forms according to modern principles, and the lack of separation in the manuscript is indicated by the insertion of an apostrophe between the two units:

manuscript	transcription with tagging	critical edition
	l<punct>'</punct>an	l'an

Finally, two types of footnote are added. The first is intended for problems relating to transcription, such as illegibility, while the second is for explanations or doubts concerning linguistic, geographical or socio-cultural aspects:

tagging	<ful><abr>Les</abr><abr>Vowes</abr> ou <abr>des</abr> <abr>Vowes</abr>?</ful>
critical edition	[3] *Les Vowes ou des Vowes?*

The tagging is designed to allow each text to be displayed according to three different methods of edition: 1) diplomatic, that is, exactly as it appears in the manuscript; 2) critical or semi-diplomatic, with every editorial intervention visible; and 3) interpretative, the aim of which is to render the content immediately accessible to the non-linguist.

A further, more unusual feature of the system which sets it apart from others is that the encoding is designed to allow modifications to be made to the editions even after they have been integrated into the database.

In the screenshot below, a single occurrence can be seen, displayed as an XML token for editing. Editing is carried out in three ways: a single token can be modified, two tokens can be united, and a single token can be split into two. The modifications are automatically applied throughout the entire system, providing an up-to-date view of the edited elements of the document wherever they appear.

This interface is essential as linguistic work on texts, particularly that of a lexicological nature, always results in the discovery of transcription and interpretation errors. The accuracy of the editions can thus be continually improved.

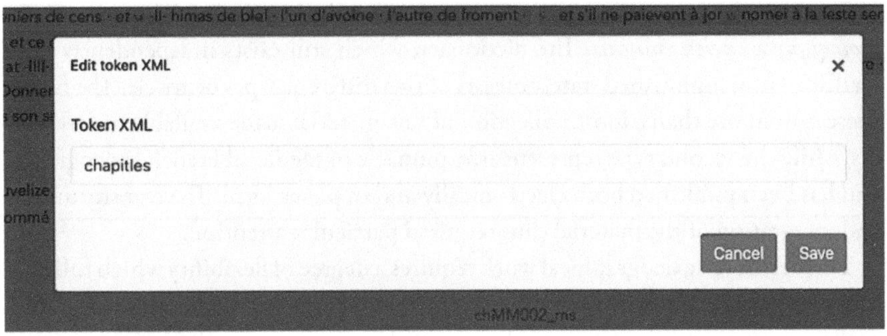

3. Further components of the GallRom database: overview of the architecture

Within the database GallRom, the editions of documentary texts are linked to three other modules – lexicographical, bibliographical and scriptological –, all of which are essential tools for the linguistic analysis of medieval Gallo-Romance. The project thus constitutes a network linking the textual production and the independent resources available for all four languages, rendering them accessible for linguistic and philological research.

In order to allow the reader to fully appreciate the nature of the enterprise, it should be mentioned that the previous version of the editorial system described above, which also included a lemmatisation module, was linked via a purpose-built interface to the *Dictionnaire étymologique d'ancien français* (DEAF), the most methodologically advanced dictionary of medieval French. This allowed the manual importation of lemmatised DocLing occurrences directly into the dictionary's database, where they could be integrated into the corresponding articles[5]. Parallel to this, the Dictionary Writing System (DWS) of the DEAF was duplicated and modified for the purposes of the digitisation of the material which had been collected during the course of the 20th century for a second dictionary, the *Dictionnaire d'ancien gascon* (DAG).

Between 2020 and 2021, every aspect of these disparate components (DEAF, DocLing and DAG) was analysed by an interdisciplinary team consisting of computer linguists and linguistic philologists, with a view to their transformation and integration into a single relational database.

5 Cf. Sabine Tittel, Historical Corpus and Historical Dictionary: Merging two Ongoing Projects of Old French by Integrating their Editing Systems in: Proceedings of the XVIIIth EURALEX International Congress: Lexicography in Global Contexts, 17–21 July, Ljubljana, ed. Jaka Čibej et al., Ljubljana 2018, p. 453–465 [DOI: 10.13140/RG.2.2.22835.12328] for a technical description of this process and Martin Glessgen/Marguerite Dallas, L'intégration du vocabulaire des Documents linguistiques galloromans dans le DEAF électronique, in: Lexicographica 35 (2019) p. 235–267 for linguistic and philological aspects.

The principal problems arose from the complexity of the *Dictionnaire étymologique d'ancien français*. The dictionary, which still exists independently from GallRom in an unfinished state, consists of two different types of article. The first of these is no more than a loose collection of raw material made available to researchers, while the second type represents the pinnacle of medieval French lexicography, and has been published both electronically and in paper form. The transformation and integration of the material thus required particular attention.

Furthermore, lexicographical work requires a degree of flexibility which fully-automated systems do not allow. This is all the more true of medieval lexicography, as the structure of different parts of each article can vary according to the nature of the data, and additional comment on the material is often necessary. Within the original DEAF DWS, this flexibility had been guaranteed by a mixture of manual and automated processes, resulting in the need for extensive manual corrections after the transformation, particularly as work carried out manually had produced a multitude of errors and inconsistencies in the use of mark-up and labelling. The parallel transformation of the bibliographies of the two dictionaries (DEAFBibl and DEAGBibl) was affected by the same issues, as fields contained different types of information requiring systematic separation[6].

As far as the documentary texts are concerned, the integration of the new textual module for DocLing necessitated the creation and implementation of new versions of each of the previously existing editorial tools and features. On the other hand, the transformation has eliminated serious technical issues arising from the instability which characterised previous versions of the technology. As mentioned above, the most important feature of the editorial system has always been the fact that it allows for the correction of the transcriptions of the documents even after their integration. In the previous system, the XML file for a document had to be exported, the corrections carried out and the document reimported. Each token had been assigned an identity number to ensure that it would be updated throughout the different parts of the system – the public consultation website, the editing system and the lemmatisation module (although this feature did not extend to the dictionary). These corrections frequently consisted in the addition of a token, necessitating the realignment of the numbering of the tokens within the document concerned upon reimportation. A momentary lapse in the internet connection during importation resulted in an error in the renumbering, which, in turn, affected any mark-up which had been added to the tokens, causing considerable loss of time.

---

6 Martin Glessgen/Marco Robecchi, Méthodologie et perspectives philologiques de la numérisation des bibliographies du DAO et du DAG, in: La littérature occitane médiévale dans sa tradition manuscrite. Témoins, traditions, corpora, ed. Caterina Menichetti/Federica Fusaroli/Aude Sartenar, Roma [in press].

The new relational system in conjunction with the dedicated and powerful infrastructure designed to support linguistic corpora has eliminated the possibility of such events.

The diagram below shows the general architecture of the immense database, consisting of bibliographical material, the document collections themselves, a dictionary and glossary section, and a module for scriptological analysis, all connected:

Documents		Analyses	
GallRomBibl Bibliographie des textes galloromans médiévaux	**DocLing** Documents linguistiques galloromans	**LEGaMe** Lexique étymologique de la Galloromania médiévale	Scripta Analyse scriptologique de la Galloromania médiévale
+ C. Menichetti, F. Möhren	+ H. Carles, Fr. Duval, P. Videsott	+ M. Dallas, H. Carles, Th. Städtler	+ P.Videsott, C. Dusio, J. Meierhofer, M. Robecchi, J. Schaber
DocLingBibl	Documents français, francoprovençaux, occitans et gascons	DocLingGloss Glossaire intégral des Documents linguistiques galloromans	Territoires français, francoprovençal, occitan [et gascon]
DEAFBibl (Frankwalt Möhren)		TEAF Trésor étymologique d'ancien français et d'ancien francoprovençal [= ex-DEAF + DocLingGloss (fr., frpr.)]	
DEAOBibl / RepCrit (Caterina Menichetti)		DEAG-DEAO Dictionnaire étymologique d'ancien gascon et d'ancien occitan [= ex-DAG + ex-DAO + DocLingGloss (gasc., occ.)]	
DEAGBibl			

The vast bibliography contains information on vernacular texts of all genres dating between the 9th and the 15th centuries, accompanied by philological and critical commentaries on the editions.

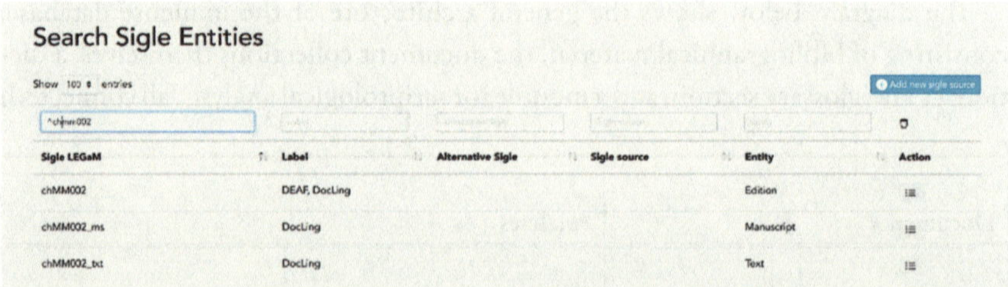

Three entities are distinguished for each entry. Returning to our example of the charter from 1235, these entities are: the edition, entitled ChMM002_GA [= Glessgen/Arnod, cf. the bibliography below] based on the names of the department and the editors; the manuscript itself, labelled AD_MM_H_1244, after the regional archives in which it is conserved and finally, the text, which bears the simple designation ChMM002. Each document is thus linked to its complete bibliographical description.

The lexicological database allows the analysis and interpretation of the vocabulary contained in the documentary texts, resulting in a diplomatic glossary for each of the four medieval Gallo-Romance languages, including a separate one for onomastics.

The transfer of data from one module to another is automatic. Each occurrence in the XML file for each document can be annotated for the purposes of lemmatisation:

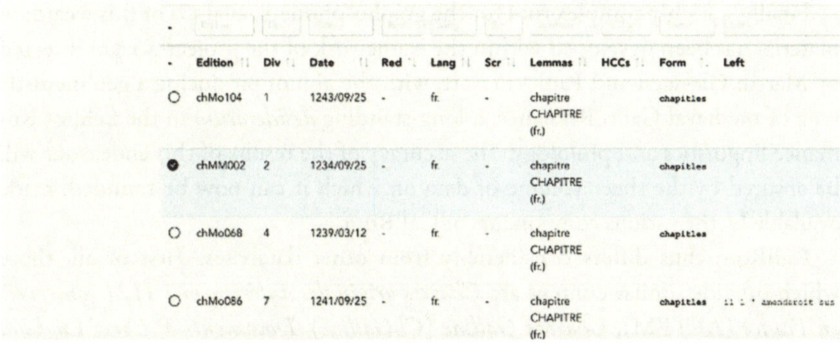

Each lemmatised wordform is then immediately visible in the article bearing the corresponding headword.

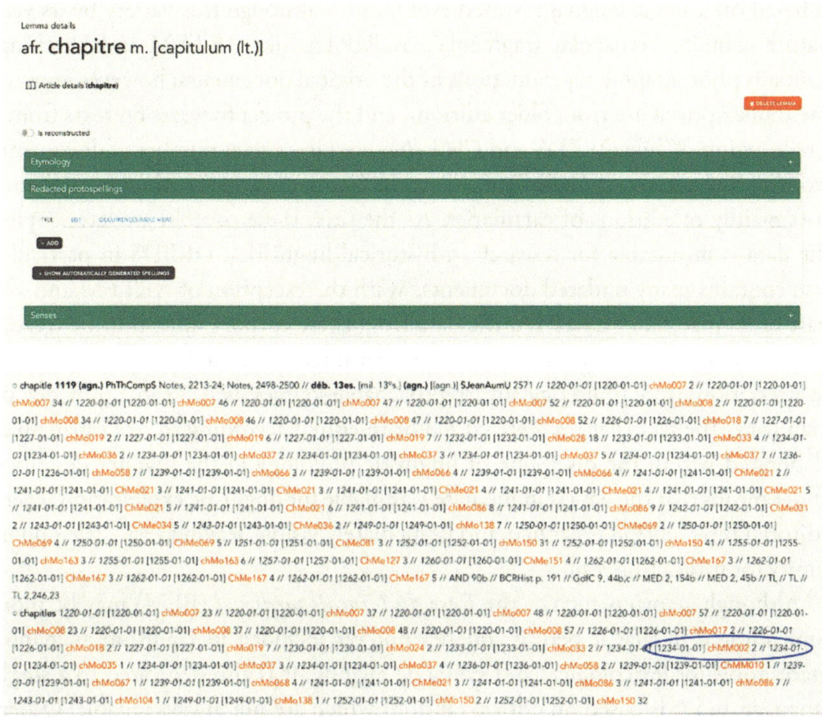

Here, the occurrence is grouped together with other occurrences of the same lexeme from all other textual genres, presenting an unparalleled opportunity for the establishment of differential definitions as well as for observations of an etymological and encyclopaedic nature.

Finally, a highly complex tool for the grapho-phonetic analysis of this wealth of material has been developed within the framework of the project *Scripta* directed by Martin Glessgen and Paul Videsott, with the aim of producing a geolinguistic map of medieval Gallo-Romance, a long-standing *desideratum* in the field of Romance linguistics and philology. The accuracy of the results of this endeavour will be ensured by the sheer volume of data on which it can now be founded, made available by the various components of GallRom.

GallRom thus differs considerably from other databases. First of all, those which provide similar content are *Chartes originales antérieures à 1121 conservées en France* (ARTEM), *Chartae Galliae* (*ChGalliae*), *Documents of Early England Data Set* (DEEDS) and *Site Caennais de Recherche Informatique et de Publication des Textes Anciens* (SCRIPTA).

Of these, only ARTEM is comparable in terms of philological standards, but it is based on a single language – medieval Latin – although this variety by its very nature contains vernacular fragments[7]. SCRIPTA, like ARTEM and DocLing, contains photographic reproductions of the original documents; however, most of the transcriptions are from older editions, and the project focusses on texts from a single region. While DEEDS and *ChGalliae* contain a great number of documents from a wide variety of Gallo-Romance and Germanic regions, the material consists mainly of editions of cartularies. As the texts these contain are later copies, the data is unsuitable for research in historical linguistics. DEEDS in particular also contains many undated documents. With the exception of ARTEM and, for part of its material, SCRIPTA, the data from these corpora must thus be treated with circumspection and can only be used for linguistic analysis as a complement to attestations from philologically irreproachable sources such as those provided by GallRom. The fact that texts are edited or re-edited according to strict principles elaborated within the discipline of linguistic philology in the manner described above means that the data is immediately available for linguistic exploitation. Every editorial intervention is explicit and immediately visible, leaving very little opportunity for misleading results.

Although a corpus such as the *Base du français médiéval* (BFM) may be more sophisticated in that it permits queries not yet included in GallRom as it integrates tools for lexicological and syntactic tagging, it is also dedicated to a single language and it is based on critical editions which are not always reliable. Others are restricted to the works of a single author or literary tradition. It must further be noted that although GallRom is currently specialised for grapho-phonetic and lexicological investigation, this does not preclude morphological and syntactic research in the future.

---

7 Hélène Carles, Trésor galloroman des origines. Les trajectoires étymologiques et géolinguistiques du lexique galloroman en contexte latin (*ca* 800–1120) (ÉLiPhi), Strasbourg 2017.

4. *Analyses*

The lexicological and grapho-phonetic work carried out on the basis of the material contained in GallRom allows not only a detailed investigation into the transformation between Latin and Romance but also an analysis of the precise nature of the medieval diasystem, as well as the identification of linguistic characteristics displayed by important writing centres.

A detailed investigation into the nature of the regionalised vocabulary contained in the documents from the eastern part of the Gallo-Romance area is underway. These are grapho-phonetically French; however, the pervasive presence of Francoprovençal lexemes and morphological markers bears witness to the fact that these regions, or parts of these regions, actually belonged to the Francoprovençal-speaking area during the early medieval period[8]. The documents displaying this phenomenon originate from the departments of Jura and Doubs, as well as – albeit to a lesser degree – the Haute-Saône, Côte-d'Or and Saône-et-Loire regions.

The long unanswered question of the genetic relationship between Occitan and Gascon has been clarified[9], and an investigation into the very conspicuous traces of Occitan which persist in 13th century documentary texts from the regions of Charente and Poitou has been conducted[10]. It has also been possible to observe the extent to which Latin documentary texts contributed to the elaboration ('Ausbau' as defined by Kloss[11]) of all four Gallo-Romance vernaculars through lexical, morphological and syntactic models, as well as through *Lehnprägung* (that is, the substitution of Latin lexemes via the semantic remotivation of etymologically unrelated existing vernacular lexemes), and direct translation[12]. This also suggests that vernacular customs may rely on earlier written legal and administrative traditions rather than on oral transmission. Finally, the database offers an unparalleled opportunity for the comparison of the etymological composition and the lexical evolution of the four Gallo-Romance languages from a typological perspective.

---

8 Cf. once again Carles, Écrire en deux langues.

9 Cf. Glessgen, Pour une histoire textuelle; and Id., L'identité linguistique; cf. Seraina Montigel, Le statut lexical du gascon médiéval. Étude étymologique et typologique des domaines gascon et occitan, University of Zurich/Université de Paris-Sorbonne 2023, version élaborée à paraître en 2024 (ÉLiPhi) Strasbourg.

10 Cf. Marco Robecchi, Entre oc et oïl: le changement linguistique en Poitou médiéval. [in prep.].

11 Heinz Kloss, Abstandsprachen und Ausbausprachen, in: Zur Theorie des Dialekts. Aufsätze aus 100 Jahren Forschung mit biographischen Anmerkungen zu den Autoren, ed. Joachim Göschel/Norbert Nail/Gaston van der Elst (Zeitschrift für Dialektologie und Linguistik 16), Wiesbaden 1976, p. 301–322.

12 Cf. Marguerite Dallas, Le lexique des Documents linguistiques galloromans - une analyse dans une clé diasystématique, ms. de thèse de doctorat en cotutelle, University of Zurich/Université de Paris-Sorbonne 2023, version élaborée à paraître en 2024 (ÉLiPhi) Strasbourg.

The same research methods naturally also lead to new historical perspectives, such as an accurate description of practices pertaining to different aspects of daily life, the legal and administrative system regulating these practices and the nature of the socio-political relationships characterising 13th and 14th century society. The diffusion of technical vocabulary highlights the role of monastic orders in industry during the 12th century in particular, linking the British Isles and the Continent and extending into Germanic territory, while the diffusion of vocabulary belonging to the fields of agriculture and construction is suggestive of municipal networks[13].

Epilogue: evolution and updating of the database

For French, the regional coverage is evolving constantly and a corpus of Anglo-Norman documentary texts will be added. For Gascon, the editions which constitute the sources of the lexemes treated by the DEAG will be integrated.

Lexicological work on the glossaries of all four languages will continue. Maps showing the variational distribution of Gallo-Romance grapho-phonetic phenomena and lexemes will be generated.

Bibliography

The bibliography contains all works referred to above, as well as suggestions for further reading. Explanations and user guides for each module of GallRom can be found at <https ://gallrom.linguistik.uzh.ch>.

1. DocLing

The DocLing corpus has undergone several successive editions, the number of edited documents and functions increasing with each version:

1a. *Les plus anciens documents linguistiques de la France. Édition électronique*, Collection fondée par Jacques MONFRIN, poursuivie par Martin GLESSGEN, première édition en collaboration avec Françoise VIELLIARD/Olivier GUYOTJEANNIN (^{1}2009). [= annotated edition of ca. 1,133 original French documents, dating from 1224 to 1275 and accompanied by photographic reproductions, preserved in the archives of the following departments: Marne, Haute-Marne, Meurthe-et-Moselle, Meuse]

1b. *Les plus anciens documents linguistiques de la France (DocLing). Édition électronique*, dirigée par Martin GLESSGEN, en partenariat avec Frédéric DUVAL/Paul VIDESOTT.

---

13 Ibid.

Deuxième édition entièrement revue et élargie (^{2}2013), [<www.rose.uzh.ch/docling>]. [= annotated edition of ca. 2,185 original French documents, dating from 1204 to 1331 and accompanied by photographic reproductions, originating from northeastern France (Flanders, Champagne, Lorraine, Franche-Comté, Burgundy) and from the Royal Chancellery]

1c. *Documents linguistiques galloromans (DocLing). Édition électronique*, dirigée par Martin GLESSGEN, en partenariat avec Hélène CARLES/Frédéric DUVAL/Paul VIDESOTT. Troisième édition revue et fortement élargie (^{3}2016), [<www.rose.uzh.ch/docling>]. [= annotated edition of ca. 2,400 original French documents, dating from 1204 to 1331 and accompanied by photographic reproductions, originating from northeastern France (Flanders, Champagne, Lorraine, Franche-Comté, Burgundy) and from the Royal Chancellery; edition of ca. 1,000 documents, dating from ca. 1250 to ca. 1450 from the *Oïl* region of Switzerland as well as from the Francoprovençal regions of France and Switzerland.]

1d. *Documents linguistiques galloromans (DocLing). Édition électronique*, dirigée par Martin GLESSGEN, en partenariat avec Hélène CARLES/Frédéric DUVAL/Paul VIDESOTT. Quatrième édition revue et fortement élargie (^{4}2024), *in*: GallRom.

2. Primary sources

DocMM_GA = *Documents linguistiques galloromans: Meurthe-et-Moselle (1232–1265)*. Édition électronique sur la base de l'édition dactylographiée de Michel ARNOD (1974), entièrement revue et élargie par Martin GLESSGEN. Version PDF (2015).

3. Electronic databases and dictionaries

ARTEM = Cédric GIRAUD/Jean-Baptiste RENAULT/Benoît-Michel TOCK, Chartes originales antérieures à 1121 conservées en France, Orléans, Institut de recherche et d'histoire des textes (2010), [<www.cn-telma.fr/originaux>].

BFM = Céline GUILLOT-BARBANCE/Serge HEIDE/Alexei LAVRENTIV, Base de français médiéval: une base de référence de sources médiévales ouverte et libre au service de la communauté scientifique, in: Diachroniques 7 (2017) p. 168–184; [<https://halshs.archives- ouvertes.fr/halshs-01809581>].

ChGalliae = AA.VV., *Chartae Galliae*, Orléans, Institut de recherche et d'histoire des textes (2014), [<www.cn-telma.fr/chartae-galliae>].

DAG = Kurt BALDINGER (dir.), Dictionnaire onomasiologique de l'ancien gascon, 23 fasc., Tübingen/Berlin 1975–2021.

DEAF = DEAF/DEAFél = Dictionnaire étymologique de l'ancien français, fondé par Kurt BALDINGER, continued by Frankwalt MÖHREN/Thomas STÄDTLER, Tübingen/Berlin/Boston 1974–, [<http://www.deaf-page.de>].

DEAG = Martin GLESSGEN, Dictionnaire Étymologique de l'ancien gascon (2024–), in: GallRom.

DEAFBibl = Frankwalt MÖHREN, Dictionnaire étymologique de l'ancien français. Complément bibliographique, Berlin/Boston ^{5}2021.

DEEDS = *Documents of Early England Data Set*, Michael Gervers (dir.), [<https://deeds.library.utoronto.ca>].

GallRom = Martin Glessgen (dir.), *Documents et analyses linguistiques de la Galloromania médiévale* (2024–), [<https ://gallrom.linguistik.uzh.ch>].

LEGaMe = Martin Glessgen (dir.), *Lexique étymologique de la Galloromania médiévale* (2024–), in: GallRom (as for the DEAG).

SCRIPTA = *SCRIPTA, Database of medieval norman documents*, Bauduin, Pierre (dir.), Caen, CRAHAM-MRSH (2010–2016), [<http://www.unicaen.fr/scripta/>].

4. Monographs, articles and essays

a. History of the project Documents linguistiques and evolution of GallRom

Clovis Brunel, Les plus anciennes chartes en langue provençale, Recueil des pièces originales antérieures au XIIIe siècle, Paris 1926.

Martin Glessgen, L'écrit documentaire et le projet des Plus anciens documents linguistiques de la France, in: Manuel de la philologie de l'édition (Manuals of Romance Linguistics/MRL 4), ed. David Trotter, Berlin/Boston 2015, p. 267–295.

Martin Glessgen, Les 'Documents linguistiques' de la France. Histoire, présent et perspectives d'un projet centenaire, in: Comptes rendus des séances de l'Académie des Inscriptions et Belles-Lettres (CRAI) 161/3 [juill. à oct. 2017] (2018) p. 1261–1292.

Martin Glessgen/Marguerite Dallas, L'intégration du vocabulaire des Documents linguistiques galloromans dans le DEAF électronique, in: Lexicographica 35 (2019) p. 235–267.

Martin Glessgen/Marco Robecchi, Méthodologie et perspectives philologiques de la numérisation des bibliographies du DAO et du DAG, in: La littérature occitane médiévale dans sa tradition manuscrite. Témoins, traditions, corpora, ed. Caterina Menichetti/Federica Fusaroli/Aude Sartenar, Roma [in press].

Caterina Menichetti, Le nouveau Répertoire critique des manuscrits littéraires en ancien occitan: objectifs et méthodes, in: Revue de Linguistique Romane 85 (2021) p. 133–158.

MeyerDoc = Paul Meyer, Documents linguistiques du Midi de la France, Ain, Basses-Alpes, Hautes-Alpes, Alpes-Maritimes, Paris 1909.

Jacques Monfrin, Introduction [= «Les études sur les anciens textes gallo-romans non littéraires»; «Le recueil des documents linguistiques de la France» etc.], in: Jean-Gabriel Gigot, Documents linguistiques de la France (série française), vol. 1: Chartes en langue française antérieures à 1271 conservées dans le département de la Haute-Marne, Paris 1974, XI–LXXX.

Sabine Tittel, Historical Corpus and Historical Dictionary: Merging two Ongoing Projects of Old French by Integrating their Editing Systems in: Proceedings of the XVIIIth EURALEX International Congress: Lexicography in Global Contexts, 17–21 July, Ljubljana, ed. Jaka Čibej et al., Ljubljana 2018, p. 453–465 [DOI: 10.13140/RG.2.2.22835.12328].

b. Analytical monographs produced on the basis of the material in GallRom

Alessandra Bossone, Le Dictionnaire des régionalismes du français médiéval (DRM). Principes méthodologiques, résultats et perspectives, [in prep.].

Marguerite DALLAS, Le lexique des Documents linguistiques galloromans - une analyse dans une clé diasystématique, ms. de thèse de doctorat en cotutelle, University of Zurich/Université de Paris-Sorbonne 2023, version élaborée à paraître en 2024 (ÉLiPhi) Strasbourg.

Seraina MONTIGEL, Le statut lexical du gascon médiéval. Étude étymologique et typologique des domaines gascon et occitan, University of Zurich/Université de Paris-Sorbonne 2023, version élaborée à paraître en 2024 (ÉLiPhi) Strasbourg.

Marco ROBECCHI, Entre oc et oïl: le changement linguistique en Poitou médiéval. [in prep.].

c. Suggestions for further reading on the history and the nature of the four medieval Gallo-Romance languages

Hélène CARLES, Trésor galloroman des origines. Les trajectoires étymologiques et géolinguistiques du lexique galloroman en contexte latin (ca 800–1120) (ÉLiPhi), Strasbourg 2017.

Hélène CARLES/Martin GLESSGEN, History of the Occitano-Gascon Lexicon in: The Oxford Encyclopedia of Romance Linguistics (ORE), dir. Michele LOPORCARO et al., Oxford (forthcoming).

Hélène CARLES, Écrire en deux langues: la coexistence des systèmes français et francoprovençal dans les scriptae médiévales de la Suisse romande, in: Revue de Linguistique Romane 87 (2023) p. 375–426.

Gerhard ERNST et al., Romanische Sprachgeschichte/Histoire linguistique de la Romania. Ein internationales Handbuch zur Geschichte der romanischen Sprachen und ihrer Erforschung/Manuel internationel d'histoire linguistique de la Romania (Handbücher zur Sprach- und Kommunikationswissenschaft 23/1–3), 3 vol., Berlin/New York 2003, 2006, 2008.

Martin GLESSGEN, Pour une histoire textuelle du gascon médiéval, in: Revue de Linguistique Romane 85 (2021) p. 325–384.

Martin GLESSGEN, L'identité linguistique du gascon médiéval: analyse scriptologique des genres textuels, in: Revue de Linguistique Romane 86 (2022) p. 35–94.

Martin GLESSGEN, A New Companion to the Romance Languages [accepted for publication, 2024].

Heinz KLOSS, Abstandsprachen und Ausbausprachen, in: Zur Theorie des Dialekts. Aufsätze aus 100 Jahren Forschung mit biographischen Anmerkungen zu den Autoren, ed. Joachim GÖSCHEL/Norbert NAIL/Gaston VAN DER ELST (Zeitschrift für Dialektologie und Linguistik 16), Wiesbaden 1976, p. 301–322.

Martin MAIDEN/Adam LEDGEWAY, The Oxford guide to the Romance languages, Oxford 2016.

El etiquetado de los documentos notariales para el análisis diplomático

Experiencias del proyecto NotFor[1]

Miguel Calleja-Puerta

El propósito de este artículo es hacer un balance de las aportaciones del proyecto NotFor al tratamiento electrónico de los documentos diplomáticos.

NotFor, o *Notariado y construcción social de la realidad (siglos XII–XVII)*, fue un proyecto de investigación financiado por la Agencia Estatal de Investigación del Gobierno de España, dentro de la convocatoria 2018 de proyectos de I+D del programa de Generación de Conocimiento, con una duración de 4 años, entre el 1 de enero de 2019 y el 31 de diciembre de 2022.

La propuesta científica de partida se proponía avanzar en el conocimiento del documento notarial en la Corona de Castilla y el reino de Portugal en los siglos del Antiguo Régimen, así como de la institución que lo sustentaba. Por un lado, se proponía profundizar en áreas de trabajo iniciadas con anterioridad; pero al mismo tiempo se proyectaba avanzar en el conocimiento de ámbitos, épocas o espacios poco estudiados hasta el momento, como el reflejo de los formularios en la praxis notarial, la extensión del notariado público al mundo rural, a los señoríos eclesiásticos, a las colonias americanas o a la Edad Moderna.

A su vez, la ampliación del ámbito de estudio hizo ver la posibilidad y la necesidad de avanzar a medio plazo a estudios comparativos que abarcasen porciones significativas del espacio de estudio, en especial en las fórmulas que componen los documentos. Si el lenguaje notarial articula el marco jurídico de la sociedad y la describe sobre categorías específicas, también varía de unos lugares a otros, contribuyendo a definir centros y periferias, áreas de influencia y flujos culturales.

1 Proyecto PGC2018-093495-B-I00 financiado por MCIN/ AEI/10.13039/501100011033/ y por FEDER Una manera de hacer Europa.

Avanzar hacia ese tipo de estudios, menos centrados en una oficina notarial concreta y más volcados a un análisis de tipo transversal, requería a su vez el perfeccionamiento de las herramientas de análisis, que permitiesen un análisis más sistemático de las evidencias documentales. Por ese motivo, una de las líneas de investigación del proyecto se centró en el desarrollo de un modelo de codificación específico, aplicable al documento notarial del Antiguo Régimen, y que permitiera un análisis sistemático de la formulación de tipos documentales concretos que pudieran filtrarse con cierta variedad de criterios: desde luego por la oficina productora, la tradición diplomática, la cronología o el área geográfica de referencia, pero también por la categoría social de los participantes en el negocio o por el tipo de bien que era objeto del documento.

Los antecedentes

El interés del grupo por la aplicación de técnicas digitales a la compilación, descripción y análisis de la documentación diplomática se remonta a hace más de diez años. Entre 2009 y 2010, la parte del equipo radicada en la Universidad de Oviedo ya se encargó de reunir y convertir a soporte digital en cadena de caracteres los documentos medievales relativos al territorio actual del Principado de Asturias que entonces estaban ya editados, cuyo número superaba las seis mil unidades documentales[2]. La valoración conjunta de ese material, sin embargo, en seguida permitió ver que reunía piezas de naturaleza muy variada, en primer lugar en lo referido a las oficinas productoras, y luego en lo relativo a las tipologías documentales; la situación se hacía aún más compleja a partir del siglo XIV, con la aparición de los libros administrativos. En consecuencia, para caracterizar materiales de archivo tan diversos mediante una ficha descriptiva común se hizo necesario identificar las categorías básicas que permitiesen armonizar sus elementos descriptivos, y que obviamente fueron seleccionándose dentro de los parámetros propios al análisis diplomático[3].

El segundo problema que entonces quedó planteado fue el del tratamiento con recursos digitales de los materiales que se iban acumulando, con vistas a su explotación para la investigación. La primera evidencia a tener en cuenta fue el hecho de que las bases de datos relacionales al uso implicaban encasillar la información de cada documento en una serie bastante limitada de categorías, que además se estan-

2 María Josefa Sanz Fuentes/Miguel Calleja Puerta, Edición digital del patrimonio documental de Asturias (I). Diseño de la aplicación y digitalización de los documentos medievales publicados, in: La escritura de la memoria: los registros, ed. Elena Cantarell Barella/Mireia Comas Via, Barcelona 2011, p. 379–385.

3 Sobre la tensión entre respeto al texto y navegabilidad por sus contenidos, véase el trabajo de Georg Vogeler, The 'assertive edition'. On the consequences of digital methods in scholarly editing for historians, in: International Journal of Digital Humanities (2019) p. 309–322.

darizaban con vistas a la recuperación de la información. La operación de describir cada pieza y reducir su forma y contenido a parámetros muy específicos facilitaba el análisis conjunto, pero también suponía un alejamiento de los textos que le servían de base y de las sugerencias que podía ofrecer el análisis fino, recortando así las posibilidades analíticas del estudio de una gran masa documental. Se entendía que, sin perjuicio de que pudieran homogeneizarse una serie determinada de metadatos, la riqueza de los textos diplomáticos requería que la herramienta descriptiva informática conservase la remisión inmediata al documento original, y que las distintas etiquetas descriptivas que se generasen pudiesen adaptarse a éste.

A partir de ahí, la búsqueda de soluciones tecnológicas adecuadas a las necesidades analíticas planteadas condujo a un análisis de los proyectos de edición digital que en 2009 tenían presencia en la red internet, un repertorio muy variado que iba desde pequeños fondos reproducidos en facsímil con intención divulgativa a colecciones de regestos o documentos digitalizados y disponibles en línea, con o sin instrumentos de búsqueda[4].

De ese análisis se concluyó que el lenguaje XML y el estándar TEI ofrecían en principio perspectivas favorables para satisfacer las necesidades del proyecto: por un lado distinguían datos y metadatos, preservando la transcripción fidedigna de los documentos y yuxtaponiéndole las descripciones analíticas que fuesen necesarias para su análisis. Con ello, la flexibilidad del metalenguaje XML solucionaba las constricciones de espacio o de soporte propios de los programas de software comercial que se habían utilizado con anterioridad como Microsoft Access. Su perdurabilidad en el tiempo lo convertía igualmente en elemento clave de la elección, por encima de la obsolescencia de las aplicaciones de visualización. Y sobre todo, el carácter extensible del lenguaje de codificación abría la puerta a enriquecer los estándares ya existentes como TEI –que en seguida nos parecieron prometedores– y adaptarlos a las necesidades del análisis diplomático, siguiendo la línea ya iniciada en la Charters Encoding Initiative[5].

Por aquellos años, las posibilidades teóricas de la aplicación de TEI ya estaban siendo reconocidas en algunas publicaciones científicas españolas, no solo desde la perspectiva más amplia de los textos medievales y su estudio filológico[6], sino

---

4 Santiago Rodríguez Pérez, Ediciones diplomáticas en formato digital: modelos y lenguajes, Tesina de licenciatura Universidad de Oviedo 2009.

5 La trascendencia del Vocabulaire international de Diplomatique como sistematización jerarquizada del conocimiento de la Diplomática y presupuesto esencial para los retos de la digitalización ya fue tempranamente advertida por Michele Ansani, Diplomatica (e diplomatisti) nell'arena digitale, in: Scrineum 1 (1999) p. 1–11. Véase Georg Vogeler, Towards a standard of encoding medieval charters with XML, in: Literary and linguistic computing 20 (2005) p. 269–280.

6 José Manuel Fradejas Rueda, La codificación XML/TEI de textos medievales, in: Memorabilia. Boletín de literatura sapiencial 12 (2009) p. 219–247.

también aplicadas de forma específica al análisis diplomático de los documentos de archivo[7].

Sin embargo, la aplicación práctica de aquellos presupuestos ha sido escasa en número y muy lenta en su desarrollo. La edición digital del *Becerro galicano* del monasterio de San Millán de la Cogolla fue concebida a principios de la década en una base de datos MySQL, si bien con posterioridad se enriqueció con una edición de cada uno de sus documentos según el estándar TEI[8]. A mediados de la década arrancó también el proyecto *Siete Partidas digital*, que reúne y edita los manuscritos del código legal de Alfonso X en TEI[9]. En el ámbito del análisis diplomático, sin embargo, los progresos con trascendencia pública fueron aún menores. La Red Charta, que había iniciado la aplicación de TEI al estudio filológico de los documentos de archivo, publicó en 2020 un manual de etiquetado relativo a este tipo de testimonios, pero las aportaciones para el análisis diplomático se reducían a un apéndice donde se proponían algunas etiquetas básicas para el etiquetado de la estructura documental, aun reconociendo que la propuesta "en ningún modo pretende ser exhaustiva", y abriendo la puerta al desarrollo ulterior de etiquetas específicas "para cada elemento diplomático"[10].

Por su parte, la edición digital académica se ha ido convirtiendo en una línea de investigación cada vez más relevante en el área de Ciencias y Técnicas Historiográficas de la Universidad de Oviedo, aunque a un ritmo igualmente muy lento que en buena medida dependía de las discontinuas oportunidades de financiación[11]. M. Calleja-Puerta adquirió formación en TEI en la Oxford Summer School de 2010, F.J. Álvarez Carbajal colaboró con el proyecto DiXiT en 2014–17, y ambos coordinaron el seminario *La edición diplomática del documento notarial y concejil en la era digital – The Diplomatic Edition of Notarial and Municipal Charters in the Digital Age* (Avilés, 10–11 de octubre de 2016), con apoyo del proyecto *Escritura, notariado y espacio urbano en la Corona de Castilla y Portugal (Siglos XII–XVII)*, finan-

7 Asier Romero Andonegi, Nuevas herramientas para el estudio de la diplomática: los lenguajes de marca TEI y EAD, in: Documenta & Instrumenta 6 (2009) p. 91–118.

8 https://www.ehu.eus/galicano/?l=es. Véase también el análisis de Francisco Javier Álvarez Carbajal, The Digital edition of the Becerro Galicano de San Millán de la Cogolla, in: RIDE 2 (2014); doi: 10.18716/ride.a.2.3.

9 https://7partidas.hypotheses.org/

10 Carmen Isasi Martínez/Leyre Martín Aizpuru/Santiago Pérez Isasi/Elena Pierazzo/Paul Spence, Edición digital de documentos antiguos: marcación XML-TEI basada en los criterios CHARTA, Sevilla 2020, p. 79–80.

11 En el mismo sentido, Eliana Magnani, Des chartae au Corpus. La plateforme des CBMA – Chartae/Corpus Burgundiae Medii Aevi, in: Digitizing Medieval Sources: challenges and methodologies – L'édition en ligne de documents d'archives médiévaux: enjeux, méthodologie et défis, ed. Christelle Balouzat-Loubet (Atelier de recherches sur les textes médiévaux 27), Turnhout 2019, p. 57–67.

ciado por la Agencia Estatal de Investigación y coordinado desde la Universidad de Sevilla por P. Ostos Salcedo.

De todo ello pronto se concluyó que era necesario un modelo de codificación que extendiera TEI y CEI para responder de forma más precisa a las necesidades analíticas de los estudios diplomáticos. Como bien ha advertido Vogeler, la aproximación de los historiadores a la documentación suele ir especialmente orientada al contenido y lleva aparejada comúnmente una serie de elementos de contextualización que son menos comunes en las ediciones filológicas[12]; esa es la razón de que pareciera adecuado mantener la estandarización de nombres de persona y lugar o de instituciones, pero también extender el repertorio de metadatos descriptivos de cada documento editado, añadiendo categorías propias de la caracterización diplomática de cada pieza. A esto debe añadirse que los estudios diplomáticos tienen como cuestión medular el análisis de la forma documental, lo cual hacía pensar en la necesidad de enriquecer la biblioteca de etiquetas que describen en el propio texto los elementos del discurso diplomático.

En cualquier caso, el esquema de necesidades esbozado en 2011[13] tardó varios años en empezar a plasmarse en realizaciones concretas y en ponerse a prueba mediante el etiquetado manual sobre colecciones documentales específicas. A lo largo de la década se fueron generando sucesivas versiones de un modelo de codificación de documentos diplomáticos adaptados a la producción documental de distintas oficinas. El objetivo básico era aprender a filtrar la información etiquetada mediante el uso de expresiones XPath que ofreciesen conjuntos de datos relevantes para el análisis diplomático; sin embargo, a falta de personal especializado que pudiese prestar apoyo técnico, no se llegó a desarrollar un documento ODD propiamente dicho y el proyecto avanzó de forma muy rudimentaria.

Álvarez Carbajal inició un análisis específico para la documentación señorial que no llegó a término[14], y Calleja-Puerta desarrolló un modelo de carácter más general que añadía a varios de los módulos de TEI un repertorio de etiquetas procedentes de CEI y otras de creación propia, que alcanzó su primera versión en la primavera de 2017 (en adelante, DocuLab)[15]. El principio básico que ha ido guiando su desa-

12 Vogeler, The 'assertive edition' (como n. 3) p. 310–312.

13 Sanz Fuentes/Calleja Puerta, Edición digital (como n. 2) p. 384. En ese momento se planteaba un trabajo progresivo, primero la codificación de "referencia archivística, tradición, data, oficina de producción, nombre de escribano, otorgantes y destinatarios; y para una segunda fase algunos elementos esenciales de la estructura documental: invocaciones, preámbulos, verbos dispositivos, sanción y sistemas de validación".

14 Francisco Javier Álvarez-Carbajal, La producción documental de los condes de Luna: hacia un modelo de digitalización de su estructura diplomática, in: Escritura y sociedad: la nobleza, ed. Ana Suárez González, Santiago de Compostela 2017, p. 421–430.

15 Se consideró más adecuado seguir trabajando sobre el modelo de TEI, en perjuicio de otras posibilidades que se han ido desarrollando en los últimos años, como la que proponen John Brad-

rrollo es el de su usabilidad. El objetivo principal de éste era añadir a los metadatos descriptivos de cada pieza una serie de elementos que se consideraban esenciales para el análisis diplomático: en primer lugar, la acción jurídica documentada y el objeto sobre el que recaía, identificados respectivamente como <actio> y <object>; en segundo término, los autores del documento a los que se identificaba como <persona>, distinguiendo con atributos su categoría socio-profesional y su papel como otorgantes o destinatarios de la acción documentada; a continuación se dedicaba un elementos específico a la identificación de la oficina productora y su implantación territorial, descrita como <oficina>; y en fin, se empleaban etiquetas adicionales para describir el tipo de redacción –objetiva o subjetiva–, y el lugar de cada testimonio descrito dentro de la tradición diplomática del documento. De forma subsidiaria, se desarrollaron etiquetas específicas para describir los elementos básicos del discurso diplomático, sin más propósito en aquel momento que el de conseguir un banco de pruebas para posteriores concreciones.

Sobre esa base, la contratación de una persona como técnico de apoyo y gestión en 2017–18 vinculada al proyecto *Escritura, notariado y espacio urbano en la Corona de Castilla y Portugal (Siglos XII–XVII)* permitió ampliar notablemente el corpus de documentos volcados manualmente a soporte electrónico a través de aquel modelo de codificación. Ahora el esfuerzo se centró en reunir aquellos producidos en oficinas notariales y concejiles y en adaptarlos a la versión del modelo DocuLab. De este modo, parte de los documentos asturianos ya disponibles en pdf y word fueron transferidos a xml y se les añadieron metadatos conforme a aquel esquema. Con ello, se siguió el mismo procedimiento de conversión a formato digital de otras muchas ediciones diplomáticas, ahora ya a escala de la península Ibérica, aunque centradas especialmente en los territorios de Asturias, Galicia y Andalucía Occidental. En el momento de cerrar este proyecto de investigación, a finales del año 2018, se habían reunido 3.674 documentos.

Naturalmente, la incógnita que subyace a todas estas laboriosas operaciones es determinar si el esfuerzo de compilación y descripción conduce a una herramienta de análisis eficiente que permita un avance sustancial en los estudios diplomáticos; y este problema tiene dos vertientes. Por un lado, parece conveniente comprobar si el tiempo invertido en aprender la lógica de la codificación y su aplicación práctica, que es largo[16], proporciona retornos aceptables en un tiempo razonable para cada investigador. Y con ello, es inevitable plantearse si es mejor desarrollar un modelo

---

LEY/Alice RIO/Matthew HAMMOND/Dauvit BROUN, Exploring a model for the semantics of medieval legal charters, in: International Journal of Humanities and Arts Computing xiii/1–2 (2019) p. 136–154.

16 En el mismo sentido, Antonella AMBROSIO, L'edizione critica digitale dei documenti medievali: le forme degli atti di Octavianus notarius, in: Ingenita curiositas. Studi sull'Italia medievale per Giovanni Vitolo, ed. Bruno FIGLIUOLO/Rosalba DI MEGLIO/Antonella AMBROSIO, Battipaglia 2018, p. 1153–1173 y p. 1160.

conforme a TEI, que requiere un conocimiento de sus métodos para las categorizaciones jerárquicas del que no disponíamos en el equipo; o bien se optaba por sacrificar la interoperabilidad con otros usuarios de la Text Encoding Initiative, obteniendo a cambio unos resultados más rápidos en el análisis propiamente diplomático mediante la simple creación de nuevos elementos que facilitaban el proceso de marcado y su procesamiento posterior.

Para tratar de dilucidar la viabilidad de esta segunda opción, en los últimos años se han hecho algunas pruebas en varios trabajos académicos defendidos en la Universidad de Oviedo. Una parte de ellos han intentado adaptar la documentación que editaban al estándar TEI, con resultados apreciables: fue lo que hizo F. Floriano Fernández, que trabajó sobre 46 documentos regios de variada tipología copiados en un cartulario de finales del siglo XIV[17], o E. Albarrán Fernández, que realizó la edición de 384 documentos notariales asturianos comprendidos entre fines del siglo XIII y mediados del siglo XIV[18]. La necesidad de reflejar determinadas cuestiones relevantes para el análisis diplomático se resolvió en ambos casos dentro del marco de TEI. En el primero de ellos, dedicado exclusivamente a documentos regios, la tipología documental se expresó simplemente como un atributo subtype dentro de cada elemento <div>, y los elementos del discurso diplomático se representaron como atributos dentro de elementos <seg>[19]. El segundo, por su parte, con el apoyo de una estancia en l'École nationales des chartes procuró adaptar a TEI las etiquetas creadas en el modelo DocuLab, de modo que incorporó al encabezamiento de cada edición digital elementos identificativos de la oficina productora, la acción jurídica, el objeto sobre la que esta recae, el estilo objetivo o subjetivo de redacción y la tradición documental. En cuanto a los elementos del discurso diplomático, se siguió la misma opción de emplear la etiqueta genérica <seg>, añadiendo a cada caso atributos de función, tipo y subtipo.

La explotación de los datos ofrecía resultados tan consistentes como esperanzadores, que llevaban a ambos autores a concluir enfatizando el poder analítico del nuevo marco de trabajo. Pero la planificación de búsquedas cada vez más complejas y facetadas nos permitía anticipar también una serie de dificultades. En primer lugar, la expresividad de las etiquetas en un esquema jerárquico resultaba bastante limitada, toda vez que, para cada elemento, estos dos trabajos solo aplicaron los

17 Fernando Floriano Fernández, Modelo de codificación con tecnología XML:TEI para una edición digital del Libro Becerro, ms 9 del Archivo de la Catedral de Oviedo, Trabajo fin de Grado, Universidad de Oviedo, Oviedo 2020.

18 Elena Albarrán Fernández, La implantación de los notarios públicos del rey en Asturias (1260–1350 ca), Tesis doctoral Universidad de Oviedo 2022.

19 También valora su uso Víctor Caballero Gómez, La codificación XML en el ámbito de las Ciencias y Técnicas Historiográficas. Algunas propuestas para su uso y desarrollo, in: Revista de Humanidades Digitales 4 (2019) p. 57–68. Sin embargo, ya había planteado algunos inconvenientes Álvarez-Carbajal, La producción documental de los condes (como n. 14) p. 426.

atributos @type y @subtype, sin llegar a utilizar taxonomías ni avanzar en el uso del módulo Feature Structures. Esto era preocupante en un contexto en el que la edición digital se contemplaba cada vez más como una herramienta de análisis que como un medio de publicación de resultados[20]. A partir de ahí, el aprovechamiento del material resultaba igualmente limitado, pues obligaba a expresiones XPath de gran complejidad para resultados relativamente sencillos.

De forma paralela, otros trabajos académicos han ido aplicando el modelo DocuLab, y permitiendo ver además la necesidad de seguir desarrollándolo a medida que se incorporaban al sistema nuevas realidades documentales que no se habían contemplado en el momento inicial. Fue el caso del trabajo de C. Miyar Azcano, que etiquetó 168 entradas del catálogo de manuscritos de la Biblioteca Universitaria de Oviedo que había confeccionado A.C. Floriano Cumbreño a mediados del siglo XX[21]. A diferencia de los casos anteriores, donde todos los documentos estaban confeccionados en oficinas homólogas –ya fuesen regias o notariales–, la colección de manuscritos de la Universidad de Oviedo, que es una colección facticia formada hace menos de un siglo, reúne materiales muy variados en su naturaleza y cronología, y con ello invitaba a la elaboración de un modelo donde la jerarquía de etiquetas fuera lo más amplia posible. Por su parte, I. Morago Olaya codificó según el modelo DocuLab la edición de 32 documentos del siglo XIV procedentes del archivo monástico de San Bartolomé de Nava[22], que permitieron ver las posibilidades analíticas de filtrar la documentación de un fondo de archivo por la oficina productora, y a partir de ahí proceder al estudio particularizado sobre la estructura y contenido de series documentales específicas[23].

La puesta en marcha del proyecto NotFor, con vigencia de 4 años a partir de 2019, perseguía profundizar en aquellos antecedentes tomando la documentación notarial como campo de aplicación específico de las experiencias previas y del modelo de codificación DocuLab.

La financiación concedida no fue suficiente para contratar personal con capacitación de ingeniería técnica informática que pudiera trabajar como programador desarrollando una aplicación de automatización de consultas, pero sí fue posible obtener un contrato predoctoral vinculado al proyecto al que se formó específi-

20 Coincidimos aquí con el planteamiento de Vincent Jolivet, Éditions ou données? API et (re) publications, in: Actes royaux et princiers à l'ère du numerique, ed. Olivier Canteaut/Olivier Guyotjeannin/Olivier Poncet (Cultures, arts et sociétés 10), Pau 2020, p. 59–68.

21 Cristina Miyar Azcano, Edición digital del catálogo de manuscritos de la Biblioteca Universitaria de Oviedo (cajas 259–264): transferencia a XML y valoración del método de codificación, Trabajo Fin de Grado Universidad de Oviedo 2019.

22 Ignacio Morago Olaya, Edición digital de los documentos medievales de San Bartolomé de Nava (1351–1400), Trabajo Fin de Grado Universidad de Oviedo 2020.

23 Véase en este sentido la experiencia que describe Ambrosio, L'edizione critica digitale (como en n. 16) p. 1167.

camente en el uso de lenguajes de marcado, y que los está utilizando para trazar el mapa de la extensión de los notarios públicos en el reino[24]. Por consiguiente, a lo largo de los últimos años la base de datos elaborada dentro del grupo ha seguido creciendo, sobre todo en lo referido a documentación notarial de la Baja Edad Media castellana. Y sobre esa documentación se ha ido progresando en los aspectos que se detallan a continuación.

La representación de los actores del documento en los metadatos

Los documentos de archivo, por su propia naturaleza, están repletos de referencias a individuos y organizaciones que pueden ser descritos con los detallados procedimientos que ofrece TEI al respecto. Sin embargo, las posibilidades de llevar a cabo esa caracterización son muy limitadas en lo que se refiere a las identidades personales: en la Baja Edad Media castellana, toda la sociedad acude de forma habitual ante el notario público, de modo que con frecuencia estos documentos notariales son las únicas noticias escritas sobre la mayoría de esas personas. Por consiguiente, no es posible hacer un registro de entidades que permita el reconocimiento y desambiguación de cada uno de los actores presentes en el corpus, de los que generalmente se desconoce su ocupación, fechas de nacimiento o muerte.

En la fase actual de la investigación se ha optado por etiquetar solo a aquellas que pudieran ser relevantes para el análisis diplomático en cuanto notarios, otorgantes o destinatarios, pero se ha renunciado a identificar uno a uno a los testigos de cada acción documental, de los que generalmente no se sabe nada más. Además de eso, se ha puesto su caracterización funcional por delante de su identidad, ya que esa es la manera en la que estamos habituados a conceptualizar el documento, y con la que hemos sido capaces de generar expresiones XPath sobre la masa de documentos etiquetados que proporcionasen resultados pertinentes al tipo de investigación que nos interesa.

La identificación de los actores del documento, ya sea como otorgantes o destinatarios de la acción documental, o bien como los responsables de su escrituración, es uno de los elementos básicos de cualquier estudio diplomático y suele actuar como eje vertebrador de muchas investigaciones: por un lado, la oficina productora impone una forma específica a los documentos que elabora; por otro, otorgantes y des-

24 Una primera aproximación en César Quijano Martínez, La implantación del notariado público en la Corona de Castilla: un conflicto entre poderes (1250–1350), in: Poder y poderes en la Edad Media, ed. Raquel Martínez Peñín/Gregoria Cavero Domínguez (Monografías de la Sociedad Española de Estudios Medievales 16), Murcia 2021, p. 361–373.

tinatarios pueden influir en ella, generando sesgos específicos[25]. Para ambos casos hemos creado etiquetas específicas.

En lo que hace a la oficina productora, una de las primeras cosas a tener en cuenta es su categorización como cancillería regia, oficina concejil, despacho notarial, etc.; y dentro de cada una de ellas, será posible definir subtipos que puedan servir como criterio para el análisis y el estudio comparado, particularmente la implantación territorial de la oficina o el tipo de jurisdicción a la que pertenece. Para satisfacer estas necesidades utilizamos la etiqueta <oficina> que, además de identificar a su responsable de forma particularizada, la categoriza con una taxonomía de atributos de tipo y de lugar. En una base de datos documental esto permitirá, por ejemplo, ceñir la búsqueda solo a los documentos producidos en oficinas notariales; dentro de ellos, será posible a continuación seleccionar los notariales de determinada localidad y, a su vez, elegir exclusivamente los de una notaría en concreto. En su interior, finalmente, sería fácil automatizar las búsquedas para dilucidar la huella que su personal puede imprimir a los documentos que confecciona.

Más allá de la oficina y de las personas responsables de la elaboración de los documentos, resulta igualmente necesario categorizar en los metadatos los distintos tipos de personas e instituciones que participan de la acción jurídica que aquellos contienen, ya que estas componen una de los primeros criterios de filtrado de la información en los documentos etiquetados. La propia naturaleza de la documentación que analizamos no permite dilucidar en el momento del etiquetado si el que intitula un documento actúa como particular o como institución. Más aún, en la inmensa mayoría de los casos su identificación se plantea como imposible. Sobre esa base, aplicar las etiquetas de TEI que distinguen con claridad personas y organizaciones planteaba problemas y obligaba a búsquedas demasiado complejas y a la postre ineficientes. Por ese motivo, y partiendo del hábito de distinguir personas físicas o jurídicas en las acciones documentales, hemos utilizado la etiqueta <persona>, que permite tipificar tanto a individuos como colectivos o instituciones, facilitando con ello la representación digital de las distintas modalidades de intitulación, ya sean individuales, conjuntas o colectivas. Un atributo de tipo caracteriza a cada uno de estos agentes con referencia a una taxonomía –papa, obispo, arcediano, arcipreste...–, y a este se suman un atributo de rol, que describe si la entidad que se está caracterizando actúa como otorgante o destinatario, y otro de género, que permite filtrar los resultados considerando este criterio. Todo ello facilita, en suma, seleccionar los resultados mediante la combinación de todos estos elementos, y así obtener listados de fenómenos muy específicos cuya obtención por procedimientos

25 El modo en que se codifican estos aspectos en el marco del proyecto NotFor ya fue presentado en un póster por Miguel Calleja Puerta, con el título The encoding of agency in Iberian notarial charters (XIIth–XVIIth centuries), al congreso Data for History 2021: Modelling Time, Places, Agents (Berlín – virtual conference), el 2 de junio de 2021.

convencionales sería tan ineficiente en sus resultados como costosa en el tiempo necesario para alcanzarlos.

Finalmente, en el campo de los metadatos la acción jurídica se representa dentro de la etiqueta <actio>, complementada por un elemento <object> que describe el objeto de la acción documentada. Ambos se completan con sendos atributos de tipo, de nuevo con vistas a comprobar el grado en que la acción jurídica y los objetos sobre los que recaen pueden modular el formulario documental.

Describir un documento de archivo con los parámetros anteriores consume poco tiempo. Sin embargo, navegar en la colección diplomática filtrando los resultados por varios de aquellos elementos conduce rápidamente a la obtención de listados muy específicos, muy costosos de obtener con recursos tradicionales. Esto es lo que permitió, por ejemplo, abordar el estudio de los escribanos del concejo de Ribadavia como fenómeno singular en los orígenes del notariado[26]. La búsqueda de escribanos que se calificasen como *públicos* en fechas anteriores a 1250 en seguida permitió identificar en aquella localidad una oficina que no había sido objeto de estudio, y que en su largo proceso de formación sumaba un centenar de documentos repartidos por media docena de archivos distintos. A partir de ahí, secuenciar sus testimonios por fecha permitió la identificación de sus titulares durante casi medio siglo. Luego, la búsqueda particularizada de cada uno de ellos condujo no solo al reconocimiento de su actividad previa al trabajo para el concejo, sino también a la demostración de una conciencia cada vez más clara de la naturaleza de su oficio, comprobada a través de sus suscripciones.

Obviamente, la fortaleza del sistema se incrementa a medida que el corpus documental crece, y se multiplica cuando estos filtros sirven para abordar el estudio de cláusulas singulares. Si la elaboración de listados de las suscripciones notariales sirvió para pulsar el ritmo y consistencia con que aparecen las referencias a su condición de *jurados* y *públicos*, el seguimiento de otros elementos del discurso diplomático permitió plantear problemas nuevos y ofreció conclusiones igualmente interesantes. En cuanto a la génesis documental, la serie de los actores del documento permitió ver la aparición de la figura de los procuradores o personeros, así como analizar la denominación con que se les caracteriza. El listado cronológico de las datas tópicas iluminó la actividad de los escribanos tanto en el burgo como en otras localidades del municipio y permitió observar cómo se enfatizaba su carácter público. Y el seguimiento de las suscripciones permitió describir tanto la estructura de la oficina como el peso de los testigos en la validación documental, cuya caracterización se completa con el análisis de la quirografía y sellos.

Por su parte, el análisis de la forma documental plantea incógnitas igualmente interesantes. La presencia o no de ciertas formalidades permite valorar la existencia

---

26 Miguel Calleja-Puerta, Antes del notariado alfonsí: los escribanos de Ribadavia en la primera mitad del siglo XIII, in: Journal of Medieval Iberian Studies XIV/3 (2022) p. 424–444.

de minutas previas a la expedición del documento definitivo. La variada formulación del contenido negocial hace que deba descartarse el empleo de formularios y abre la puerta a valorar la influencia de los clientes en la formulación. A su vez, la valoración de esta influencia es sencilla por cuanto el sistema permite filtrar los resultados según la categoría social de los actores del documento: la presencia consistente de invocaciones en las compraventas donde participan algunas comunidades monásticas resulta tan relevante como el uso esporádico de las cláusulas de saneamiento, obligación o reserva que denotan la influencia del Derecho nuevo, y todo ello ofrece matices inesperados en el análisis sistemático de fórmulas aparentemente poco expresivas.

Naturalmente, no hay nada de lo antedicho que no pudiera hacerse con fichas manuscritas o con bases de datos relacionales. La diferencia seguramente estriba en la velocidad con que es posible filtrar la información aplicando varios criterios a la vez, y así obtener esta cascada de informes parciales que extraen la literalidad de la formulación de los documentos filtrada por criterios muy variados.

El estudio de cláusulas singulares

En efecto, una de las mayores potencialidades del empleo de lenguajes de marcado sobre documentos diplomáticos reside en su capacidad para generar listados de cualquier elemento de la estructura documental, y a partir de ahí para analizarlos en función de un número variado de criterios que se hayan etiquetado previamente: en el tiempo y en el espacio, por oficinas y por escribanos dentro de ellas, según la clientela o según el tipo documental[27].

El interés en comprobar esas posibilidades fue el que condujo a ensayarlas en el ámbito de los preámbulos, que en su condición de composiciones que acentúan el componente ideológico y literario ofrecían a sus autores un excelente campo de experimentación retórica y a los investigadores una parcela de estudio igualmente brillante, que ha conducido a tipificaciones ya bien conocidas. Una de sus modalidades más características es la del preámbulo de memoria, y el modelo de codificación DocuLab fue el que sirvió para el estudio de un tipo de preámbulo de memoria singular, que enfatiza los valores de la equidad y el derecho y acentúa el valor de lo

27 Un análisis inspirador en este sentido es el de Els DE PAERMENTIER, Instruments of Administrative Identity and Princely Power. Repetitive Protocol and Dispositive Text Formulas in the Charters of the Count(esse)s of Flanders and Hainaut (1191–1244), in: La formule au Moyen Âge II, ed. Isabelle DRAELANTS/Christelle BALOUZAT-LOUBET (Atelier de Recherches sur les Textes Médiévaux 23), Turnhout 2015, p. 17–33.

escrito para su conservación; su uso era bien conocido en la documentación asturiana de los siglos XII y XIII, pero carecía de un análisis específico[28].

La revisión de la base de datos disponible en el momento de redactar aquel trabajo permitió localizar 420 muestras de su empleo a lo largo de más de un siglo a partir del primer caso localizado, del año 1165, y a partir de ahí la investigación pudo dirigirse en dos direcciones concretas.

En primer lugar, y en relación al origen de esta composición retórica, la identificación de las primeras oficinas que lo emplearon dirigió el interés hacia el cabildo de la catedral de Oviedo, y dentro de él llamó la atención sobre uno de sus miembros, el canónigo Adriano, que durante aquellos años redactaba solemnes documentos para los sectores más privilegiados de la sociedad local. Sin embargo, el análisis de la trayectoria notarial de este individuo permitió ampliar su radio de acción mucho más allá del espacio asturiano, ya que se le encuentra activo en la década anterior en la cancillería del rey Alfonso VII de León y Castilla. A su vez, la obtención del listado de preámbulos que estuvieron en uso en la cancillería regia durante su reinado –que forma parte de otro proyecto de investigación en marcha– desveló que los conceptos de equidad y justicia venían manejándose allí desde los años treinta del siglo XII, y que la idea de *ratio scripta* se había incorporado a los preámbulos del monarca precisamente en los años en que Adriano trabajaba a su servicio[29]. Lo interesante es que, de regreso a Oviedo, el escribano Adriano se mostraba capaz de transformar las fórmulas aprendidas en la cancillería del Emperador, y que varios escribanos del entorno ovetense de la época lucían elaboraciones propias sobre la memoria y la escritura. Pero desde el punto de vista de la metodología de la investigación interesa tener en cuenta que esta argumentación solo es posible combinando la búsqueda por escribanos y fórmulas concretas, y combinando corpus documentales que habitualmente han sido tratados por separado, en este caso uno de documentación regia y otro de documentación privada.

En segundo término, el análisis de la extensión de su uso permitió ver cómo se conforma una región diplomática en torno a algunas formalidades específicas compartidas por una comunidad gráfica. Tras la presumible canonización de su forma en el entorno catedralicio ovetense, en las décadas siguientes su uso aparece compartido por un grupo de escribanos que en buen número declaran su condición eclesiástica –monjes, curas parroquiales, presbíteros en general–, y que generalmente escrituran negocios relativos a la ciudad episcopal de Oviedo y a un anillo

28 Miguel Calleja-Puerta, Equum et rationabile est: extensión y usos de un preámbulo de memoria en la ciudad de Oviedo (siglos XII–XIII), in: Traditio 77 (2022) p. 107–127.

29 También se han estudiado las arengas de su cancillería en Miguel Calleja-Puerta, El valor de la escritura en los preámbulos de la cancillería de Alfonso VII, in: Poderes, espacios y escrituras. Los reinos de Castilla y León (siglos XI–XV), ed. Carlos M. Reglero de la Fuente, Madrid 2018, p. 179–202.

de unos cuarenta kilómetros a la redonda. Sin embargo, su extensión no alcanza la totalidad de una diócesis cuya superficie era mucho mayor, y en sus márgenes aparecen elaboraciones distintas, generadas en centros eclesiásticos cuyos escribanos muestran una personalidad diferenciada[30].

En tercer lugar, hay que contar también con el modo en que aquellos escribanos manejaban un preámbulo que, a principios del siglo XIII, parece haberse convertido en un lugar común. Filtrar los datos por el responsable de la escrituración permitió analizar su uso en oficinas o escribanos concretos. Y así destaca el caso del muy documentado presbítero Pedro Bono, que lo emplea con llamativa estabilidad a lo largo de su carrera, en la primera mitad de la centuria; pero que también es capaz de adaptarlo a distintos tipos documentales mediante pequeños cambios en su formulación. Del mismo modo, combinar la búsqueda con el tipo de clientes para los que trabajaba ayuda a explicar las modificaciones y mejoras de algunos casos. En su centenar largo de documentos destacaba una donación de 1235 otorgada por el chantre de la catedral: las modificaciones en una arenga que ahora habla de discreción, bondad y honestidad permiten suponer que en este caso Pedro Bono trabajaba al dictado de su culto cliente. Como contrapartida, en otros escribanos la evidencia de los errores cometidos se convierte en indicio de sus dificultades crecientes con el latín, y explica que a mediados del siglo XIII las oficinas mejor documentadas oscilen entre la eliminación de la fórmula o su traducción al romance asturiano.

En fin, la desaparición de este preámbulo en el último tercio del siglo XIII fue acompasada con la renovación radical de las oficinas que supuso la implantación del notariado público: escribanos laicos que abandonaron por completo el viejo preámbulo en beneficio de procedimientos de elaboración de escrituras cada vez mejor definidos, cuya formulación entraba también en un progresivo proceso de transformación[31]. Más aún, en aquellos casos en que se podía reconocer en estos primeros notarios públicos una carrera anterior como oficiales de la pluma, se observa que en aquella etapa previa sí conocían y usaban el preámbulo, que fue abandonado en el momento de acceder al oficio de la notaría.

---

30 Véase a este respecto el trabajo de José Antonio Álvarez Castrillón, Nuevas perspectivas sobre la colonización cisterciense en el noroeste peninsular: la renovadora gestión del abad Gómez Pérez (1230–1262) y su huella, in: Medievalismo. Boletín de la Sociedad Española de Estudios Medievales 32 (2022) p. 15–39.

31 Recientemente ha procedido a su edición y estudio Olaya Rodríguez Fueyo, Los inicios del notariado público de nombramiento real en Oviedo (1263–1350). Edición y estudio, Tesis doctoral Universidad de Oviedo 2023.

El estudio comparativo de la documentación notarial

Evidencias como las que se acaba de presentar convierten el estudio del formulario en un campo de notables posibilidades para comprender las implicaciones de la extensión del notariado público del rey en la Corona de Castilla. A lo largo de las últimas décadas, el estudio de la documentación notarial ha sido uno de los ámbitos de mayor desarrollo dentro de la investigación diplomática desarrollada en este espacio. Los territorios de Asturias, Galicia y Andalucía son los ámbitos geográficos que han conocido el mayor número de investigaciones, y el esquema típico de esta serie de trabajos pasa por la identificación de los escribanos, el estudio de su proceso de implantación, la reconstrucción de la génesis documental y el análisis de sus caracteres externos e internos, con particular atención a su tipología.

En este último aspecto, a medida que el conocimiento de la institución y sus documentos se amplía, la diversidad formularia se hace cada vez más evidente, en particular si se remite como posible referente a los formularios de la obra normativa del rey Alfonso X, que al fin y al cabo pasa por ser el principal promotor de la extensión del notariado público en el reino. Por consiguiente, una de las intenciones del proyecto NotFor era avanzar hacia estudios comparativos que permitiesen ver hasta qué punto la nueva institución notarial había articulado la sociedad castellana en categorías bien definidas, o bien había necesitado adaptarse a situaciones preexistentes. Para ello, se ha seguido madurando el modelo de codificación de la estructura diplomática de los documentos notariales[32], y también se han desarrollado algunos estudios particulares.

Una muestra de ese tipo de investigación ha venido facilitada por el caso excepcional del archivo de un artesano que vivió en Oviedo en las décadas centrales del siglo XIV, y del que se ha conservado un importante lote de 128 pergaminos en el archivo del monasterio de San Pelayo de Oviedo[33]. Su fortuna no parece haber sido excepcional, por cuanto no resulta un personaje destacado en la sociedad local de la época. Sin embargo, la profesión monástica de uno de sus hijos es seguramente la responsable de que se haya conservado parte de su archivo personal, que aquél debió transferir al monasterio. Debe subrayarse, entonces, que la recurrencia en los actores del documento, detectada con un simple listado de destinatarios de compraventas, fue el hilo conductor para individualizar en el fondo de pergaminos de San Pelayo de Oviedo un subcorpus inesperado, que es el de los documentos acumulados a lo

32 El 30 de octubre de 2021 se presentó en modalidad virtual un póster al congreso Next-Gen TEI. TEI Conference and Members' Meeting 2021, con el título Encoding the diplomatic structure of notarial charters at the NotFor Project.

33 Ha sido objeto de la investigación doctoral de Jorge Felpeto Cueva, El archivo de un artesano del siglo XIV: el orfebre Alfonso Fernández de Oviedo, Tesis doctoral Universidad de Oviedo 2023.

largo de su vida por el orfebre Alfonso Fernández. Esos documentos permiten, por una parte, recomponer una porción significativa de una parentela en la que, junto a este afortunado artesano, se identifica una serie de primos caracterizados como escuderos o caballeros, y también un tío abuelo que destacó como canónigo en la catedral de Oviedo, consolidando la posición del grupo familiar en la ciudad.

Pero más allá de la reconstrucción familiar y su interés para la historia social, el orfebre Alfonso Fernández de Oviedo destaca en su archivo patrimonial como comprador de bienes inmuebles en la aldea de Borondes (Grado), a unos veinte kilómetros de su residencia en Oviedo, y de donde procedía parte de su familia. Su archivo ha conservado 113 documentos de compraventa que, al tener en todos los casos al mismo comprador, limitan los posibles efectos del cliente en el formulario y permiten un acercamiento más sistemático al trabajo en la oficina notarial. Más aún, ese centenar largo de documentos de compraventa fue escriturado en una veintena de notarías públicas repartidas principalmente entre dos localidades distintas: en primer lugar la ciudad episcopal de Oviedo, que tenía una centenaria tradición como lugar de redacción de documentos en torno a sus centros eclesiásticos y a su poderoso concejo urbano; y en segundo término la villa de Grado, promovida por el rey Alfonso X a mediados del siglo XIII y donde los nuevos notarios públicos habían reemplazado a los escribanos rurales y a un episódico escribano del concejo[34].

Todo ello ofrecía una excelente oportunidad de cotejar los formularios en uso en ambas localidades, y los resultados de la pesquisa resultan francamente llamativos, al extraer listados comparativos de determinados elementos del discurso diplomático y comparar su uso entre las distintas localidades y notarías. En primer término, permiten ver a un notariado que en Oviedo resulta más conservador y apegado a las formulaciones tradicionales: allí perdura más tiempo el uso de las invocaciones, o de fórmulas obsoletas como los falsos testigos de la ley visigótica.

Pero resulta particularmente significativa la comparación de otros elementos aparentemente poco expresivos, como la fórmula de notificación[35]. En los años setenta del siglo XIII, los formularios del documento de compraventa incluidos en la obra legislativa de Alfonso X que se ha tomado como referencia para la regulación

---

34 Véase el trabajo de Guillermo Fernández Ortiz, Práctica notarial en el concejo de la puebla de Grado (Asturias) durante el siglo XIII. De los escribanos rurales al notariado público, in: Lugares de escritura: la ciudad. XII Jornadas de la Sociedad Española de Ciencias y Técnicas Historiográficas (Zaragoza, 16 y 17 de junio de 2014), ed. Pilar Pueyo Colomina, Zaragoza 2015, p. 171–188.

35 Se referían a la notificación como une formule sans grande importance Olivier Guyotjeannin/Jacques Pycke/Benoît-Michel Tock, Diplomatique médiévale (L'atelier du médiéviste 2), Turnhout 1993, p. 79. Abunda en el interés de estudiar estas poco expresivas fórmulas Olivier Guyotjeannin, Vie et mort des clauses, circulation des formules, in: Actes royaux et princiers à l'ère du numérique (Moyen Âge – Temps modernes), ed. Olivier Canteaut/Olivier Guyotjeannin/Olivier Poncet (Cultures, arts et sociétés 10), Pau 2020, p. 84–99.

del oficio y su praxis, tanto el *Espéculo* como las *Partidas*, privilegiaban la forma *Sepan quantos esta carta vieren*, que de hecho terminaría por convertirse en elemento de identidad del documento notarial castellano[36].

Sin embargo, en la muestra analizada su uso resulta tan escaso como tardío. En primer lugar, se contrae a tan solo 18 casos, que resultan un porcentaje muy bajo dentro de la muestra analizada. Además de eso, el primero en utilizar esta formulación fue Juan Pérez, notario público de Grado, del que solo se conserva un documento, en fecha tan tardía como 1340. Luego, sus sucesores en el oficio en la villa parecen hacer un empleo consistente de la fórmula en los años subsiguientes. Pero resulta mucho más llamativo lo que ocurre en Oviedo, donde la muestra documental es más amplia, pero resulta que solo unos pocos notarios emplean la expresión del formulario regio, y además lo hacen de forma prácticamente excepcional. Esto quizá refleja el funcionamiento de unas oficinas donde el notario se limitaba a validar la carta, toda vez que cumpliese los requisitos legales, y sin que importasen demasiado variantes expresivas que no afectaban a su legitimidad; en este contexto, destaca el arraigo de la expresión tradicional *Connosçida cosa sea a quantos esta carta vieren*, que se mantuvo en uso durante décadas. En suma, llama la atención que las notarías de localidades tan próximas entre sí hagan un empleo tan diferenciado de la fórmula de notificación, y esto abre la puerta a un estudio más extensivo –ya en curso– de la cronología de su extensión por todo el reino, que puede actuar como indicador del ritmo al que el formulario de la norma regia se fue extendiendo de forma efectiva. De nuevo, la posibilidad de filtrarla por zonas, oficinas y clientela se plantean llena de posibilidades.

En el mismo sentido, resultan de gran interés otros comportamientos locales que distinguen a las notarías de Oviedo con respecto a las de Grado. Se trata de la cláusula de donación de la demasía o plusvalía, que en Oviedo aparece hasta en 86 ocasiones frente a los 4 exiguos casos de las notarías de Grado. Esta había aparecido tempranamente en la ciudad de Oviedo, y con una formulación que la vincula a expresiones similares localizadas en el Midi francés. El análisis sistemático de estas concomitancias es de nuevo una hipótesis por demostrar, una vez que hayamos etiquetado de forma sistemática la documentación anterior a la implantación del notariado. Pero de momento puede plantearse la posibilidad de que el importante componente de población franco que se documenta en la ciudad episcopal de Oviedo desde el siglo XII haya actuado también como transmisor de usos y fórmulas documentales que se habrían perpetuado incluso después de la implantación del notariado, demostrando sin embargo una limitada capacidad de irradiación a unas

36 Véase en particular el trabajo de Pilar Ostos Salcedo, Derecho es que se fagan lealmente. El formulario de la compraventa de Sevilla en la segunda mitad del siglo XIII, in: La formule au Moyen Âge IV, ed. Élise Louviot/Charles Garcia/Stephen Morrison (Atelier de recherches sur les textes médiévaux 31), Turnhout 2021, p. 74.

villas del entorno cuyo proceso de creación y base poblacional habrían tenido un perfil más tardío y local. En el mismo sentido, el seguimiento de las expresiones formularias en los documentos de compraventa, que reflejan la idea de justo precio en las transacciones, puede venir a compensar la pérdida de las bibliotecas asturianas de entonces, revelando el conocimiento y extensión entre la sociedad urbana de la Asturias de los siglos XII y XIII de las preocupaciones de los canonistas, romanistas y teólogos que estaban considerando estas cuestiones.

A modo de conclusión

Mucho han cambiado las cosas desde que Robert-Henri Bautier reconociera en los ordenadores "la seule méthode rationelle pour l'exploitation des sources notariales"[37], aunque no fuera más que para la indexación de los documentos o la extracción de listados y tablas, más útiles para la historia económica y social que para los estudios diplomáticos propiamente dichos. En los tiempos de las fichas perforadas, los trabajos suponían una descomunal tarea de análisis y codificación de los datos para unos resultados que, por más que fuesen rigurosos en el recuento de las categorías descritas, imposibilitaban luego volver con rapidez sobre los textos originales, y con ello suponían una ruptura con los métodos tradicionales que resultaba difícil de asumir.

Desde entonces, sin embargo, las posibilidades tecnológicas han permitido pasar del análisis de valores numéricos extraídos de los textos originales a la categorización de los propios textos. Con ello, ha ido formándose una noción de edición digital académica donde el entorno virtual es el medio natural y ya no es necesaria la transferencia a otro formato con la consiguiente mutilación de sus posibilidades analíticas[38].

Las experiencias de los últimos años en el empleo de lenguajes de marcado para el análisis de documentos notariales del Antiguo Régimen nos animan a ofrecer una reflexión final. La primera premisa es que, una vez asumido que los documentos de aplicación de derecho son una representación de la realidad, el análisis diplomático de su estructura y formulación es una operación necesaria para cualquier investiga-

37 Robert-Henri BAUTIER, Les demandes des historiens à l'informatique. La forme diplomatique et le contenu juridique des actes, in: Informatique et histoire médiévale. Actes du colloque de Rome (20–22 mai 1975), ed. Lucie FOSSIER/André VAUCHEZ/Cinzio VIOLANTE (Collection de l'École Française de Rome 31), Rome 1977, p. 179–186 y p. 180. Puede verse un balance de las últimas décadas en el trabajo de Miguel CALLEJA-PUERTA/Guillermo FERNÁNDEZ ORTIZ, El ordenador como herramienta para la investigación diplomática: evolución y perspectivas, in: Documenta & Instrumenta 21 (2023) p. 13–35.

38 Patrick SAHLE, What is a Scholarly Digital Edition?, in: Digital Scholarly Editing. Theory and Practice, ed. Mathew DRISCOLL/Elena PIERAZZO, Cambridge 2016, p. 19–39.

ción histórica que se fundamente sobre su testimonio. A partir de ahi, distinguir en cada documento las expresiones más formularias de aquellas que suponen una descripción más espontánea de situaciones concretas se convierte en una operación esencial, que motivará un acercamiento diferenciado al análisis de unas y otras.

En relación con lo anterior, identificar los elementos del discurso diplomático es una práctica que se acomoda bien a los lenguajes de marcado, que permiten categorizarlos de forma precisa sin renunciar al análisis de sus variantes expresivas. Sobre esa operación previa, es sencillo obtener listados de fórmulas específicas, y también filtrar esos resultados por cualquiera de los criterios que se hayan considerado como metadatos, ya sea la naturaleza de otorgantes o destinatarios, su género o su identidad, el tipo de negocio y los bienes a los que se refiere el documento, las oficinas donde se crea o el lugar que ocupe en la tradición diplomática. Todo ello contribuye a una caracterización más precisa de los usos diplomáticos y su variación en el tiempo y en el espacio, así como de los distintos factores que influyen en su composición.

Sin embargo, y quizá lo más importante, la codificación no es solo una herramienta útil para la rápida obtención de estos listados, sino que también se convierte en un estímulo a definir mejor la estructura del documento y las funciones de cada uno de sus componentes. La necesidad de asignar una categoría concreta a cada elemento del discurso diplomático va de la mano con la posibilidad de testar la validez de la respuesta en un corpus más amplio con el que se puede establecer una comparación inmediata. De resultas de lo anterior, la combinación de velocidad y sistematicidad permite identificar fenómenos que, de otro modo, quizá pasarían inadvertidos. Al mismo tiempo, la experimentación sobre distintos lotes de fuentes plantea permanentemente la necesidad de ampliar y flexibilizar el modelo inicial de etiquetado[39]. Y así, se cumple doblemente la situación de provisionalidad como característica esencial de las ediciones digitales: no es solo que se pueda disponer de los textos transcritos desde el primer testimonio estudiado, antes de llegar a la edición crítica definitiva[40]; además de eso, la situación del corpus documental como conjunto abierto permite ir modulando el modelo de marcado a medida que la colección documental se amplía. Todo ello redunda en una definición cada vez más neta de la edición digital como laboratorio de experimentación para la investigación diplomática.

39 En el mismo sentido, Ambrosio, L'edizione critica digitale (como en n. 16) p. 1168.

40 Así lo plantea Benoît-Michel Tock, La diplomatique numérique. Une diplomatique magique?, in: Digital diplomatics. The computer as a tool for the diplomatist? ed. Antonella Ambrosio/Sébastien Barret/Georg Vogeler (AfD Beiheft 14), Köln–Weimar–Wien 2014, p. 15–22.

Diplomatarium Serbicum Digitale

Eine Wiederaufnahme zwischen Datenbank und digitaler Edition

Žarko Vujošević

Vor etwa zehn Jahren in Neapel wurde die Idee einer digitalen Datenbank aller Urkunden und Briefe serbischer mittelalterlichen Aussteller zum ersten Mal der wissenschaftlichen Öffentlichkeit präsentiert[1]. Diese hat sich in der Zwischenzeit zu einem Unternehmen entwickelt, das im Rahmen vom internationalen Projekt „Community as Opportunity: The creative archives' and users' network" (CO:OP, 2014–2018), angetrieben durch das International Centre for Archival Research (ICARUS), Ergebnisse erzielt hat – das Diplomatarium Serbicum Digitale (DSD)[2]. In den letzten Jahren haben jedoch finanzielle und institutionelle Umstände dazu geführt, dass das DSD für eine Weile ins Stocken geraten ist. Seit kurzem darf man sich aber auf eine Wiederaufnahme freuen, die einerseits das Aufleben der alten Datenbank in einer neuen Applikation, andererseits eine neue Perspektive in der Übertragung des gesamten Materials in das Format XML eröffnet. In diesem Beitrag wird zunächst der Bestand dargestellt, mit dem sich das Projekt befasst, und dann eine kurze Projektgeschichte skizziert, mit dem Schwerpunkt auf der aktuell laufenden Phase, in der die neue Applikation weiterentwickelt und ins Netz gestellt wird. Im Vordergrund steht dabei die Vorstellung der neueren Projektentwicklung mit einem Ausblick, in dem die Forschungsaspekte der Datenbank

1 Žarko Vujošević/Nebojša Porčić/Dragić M. Živojinović, Das serbische Kanzleiwesen. Die Herausforderung der digitalen Diplomatik, in: Digital diplomatics. The Computer as a Tool for the Diplomatist?, hg. von Antonella Ambrosio/Sébastien Barret/Georg Vogeler (AfD Beiheft 14), Köln u. a. 2014, S. 133–147.

2 Die im Rahmen des genannten Projektes entstandene Datenbank wurde präsentiert in Žarko Vujošević, Old Wine into New Skins. The Charters Database *Diplomatarium Serbicum Digitale*, in: Power in Landscape. Geographic and Digital Approaches on Historical Research, hg. von Mihailo St. Popović/Veronika Polloczek/Bernhard Koschicek/Stefan Eichert, Leipzig 2019, S. 215–225.

und deren Nutzung für diplomatische Fragestellungen aus persönlicher Sicht und ohne vergleichende Analyse mit ähnlichen Konzepten bzw. Methoden abgehandelt werden. Schließlich, stellen wir die erwähnte XML-Perspektive des Projektes mit ihren Möglichkeiten an konkreten Beispielen vor.

Das Projekt „Diplomatarium Serbicum Digitale“ ist insofern „Diplomatarium“, indem es sich mit mittelalterlichen Urkunden und Briefen beschäftigt, und insofern „Serbicum“, weil es Dokumente in Betracht zieht, die von „serbischen“ Ausstellern stammen[3]. Somit enthält die Sammlung also nicht Dokumente, die im heutigen Serbien aufbewahrt werden, auch nicht (nur) diejenigen, die in (alt)serbischer Sprache verfasst wurden, sondern all jene Urkunden und Briefe, die aus den „Kanzleien“ (hier als Verabredungsbegriff verwendet) serbischer Herrscher, Territorialfürsten und kirchlicher Würdenträger des Mittelalters hervorgegangen sind. Inwiefern es auch ein Diplomatarium „Digitale“ ist oder werden kann, ist eine Frage für sich, deren Antwort die hier im Folgenden dargestellten Ergebnisse und Möglichkeiten zu berücksichtigen hätte. Dementsprechend wäre das Unternehmen derzeit in Kürze wie folgt zu beschreiben: Das DSD Projekt gilt der editorischen und kritischen Bearbeitung von Urkunden und Briefen serbischer Aussteller des Mittelalters, sowie ihrer Darstellung in digitaler Form.

Es folgen einige grundlegende Angaben zum Bestand[4]. Es handelt sich dabei um ungefähr 600 Dokumente bzw. „diplomatische Einheiten“[5]. Zusammen mit der verschiedenartigen kopialen Überlieferung kann man mit mindestens 1.000 Stücken rechnen. Von den 600 diplomatischen Einheiten wurde etwas mehr als Hälfte

3 Der Begriff „Diplomatarium“ gilt hier einer Sammlung der edierten und kommentierten vollständigen Urkundentexte (wie z. B. bei Diplomatarium Suecanum – https://riksarkivet.se/diplomatariet – oder Diplomatarium Danicum – https://diplomatarium.dk) und nicht etwa einem Kopialbuch oder einem Regestenwerk. Dementsprechend wäre er mit „Urkundenbuch“ oder „Codex Diplomaticus“ bedeutungsgleich. Der Konzept und Inhalt des „serbischen“ Diplomatariums werden im Folgenden detailliert dargestellt.

4 Ausführlich bei Žarko Vujošević, Das Phänomen Herrscherkanzlei im mittelalterlichen Serbien, in: AfD 66 (2020) S. 239–276, hier S. 244–249.

5 Eine „diplomatische Einheit“ ist ein Dokument als Rechtsakt (bzw. in einem Dokument zusammengesetzte Verfügung/-en desselben Ausstellers), der in einem oder mehreren Exemplaren/Überlieferungen beliebigen Typs (Original, Abschrift, Nachzeichnung, Registereintrag, Transsumpt, Fälschung usw.) aufbewahrt werden kann. In diesem Zusammenhang schreibt Georg Vogeler, Versioning Charters: On the Multiple Identities of Historical Legal Documents and their Digital Representation, in: Versioning Cultural Objects. Digital Approaches, hg. von Roman Bleier/Sean M. Winslow (Schriften des Instituts für Dokumentologie und Editorik 13), Norderstedt 2019, S. 127–150 vom „legal act” und „written artefact” (vgl. auch Žarko Vujošević/Georg Vogeler, Encoding Charters in preparation for a Diplomatics Semantic Web. Combining the TEI with the Vocabulaire International de Diplomatique, 2025. Preprint auf Zenodo - https://doi.org/10.5281/zenodo.14696237. Bedeutungsgleich unterscheidet die interne DSD-Dokumentation auf Englisch zwischen „diplomatic unit“ (= legal act) und „diplomatic item“ (= written artefact).

(330) von den Herrschern ausgestellt, die als zentrale Träger der „Staatshoheit" während des Mittelalters angesehen werden können – nämlich die Herrscher aus den Dynastien Nemanjić (um 1166–1371: Großgespanen, Könige und Kaiser), Lazarević (um 1371–1427: Fürsten und Despoten) und Branković (1427–59: Despoten). Ein so definierter Bestand deckt den Zeitraum zwischen 1186 – als die erste bekannte Urkunde verfasst wurde – und 1457 – als zwei Jahre vor dem endgültigen Fall Serbiens unter die osmanische Herrschaft die letzte serbische Herrscherurkunde entstand[6]. Die restlichen Dokumente stammen von Territorialherren (insbesondere nach dem Zerfall des Nemanjidenkaiserreichs 1371), sowie den serbischen Titulardespoten in Südungarn bis zum Anfang des 16. Jahrhunderts, aber auch von lokalen Fürsten, kirchlichen Würdenträgern und anderen Ausstellern[7].

Was die Typologie der Dokumente betrifft, werden diese allgemein in Urkunden und Briefe unterteilt, und zwar nach dem jeweiligen Betreff bzw. Zweck, und nicht nach ihren formellen Merkmalen[8]. So werden unter Urkunden alle Stücke verstanden, mit denen ein dauerhaftes Recht, ein Privileg oder eine Besitzung erteilt oder bestätigt wird (einschließlich Verträge), während zu den Briefen Dokumente gezählt werden, die sich auf die laufende Korrespondenz (Nachrichten, Verordnungen, Verwaltung) beziehen. Im erhaltenen Bestand sind Urkunden klar in der Mehrheit, und zwar mit 70% gegenüber 30% an Briefen. Nach Empfängern ist das Material wie folgt strukturiert: etwa 45% entfallen auf kirchliche Destinatäre

6 Vujošević, Herrscherkanzlei (wie Anm. 4) S. 244 (die Editionen der beiden genannten „Rahmenurkunden" in der Anm. 11 ebenda). Das Mitte des 20. Jahrhunderts am Historischen Institut der Serbischen Akademie der Wissenschaften (heute Historisches Institut Belgrad) begonnene Projekt des „Serbischen Diplomatars" bezog auch die Dokumente aus Bosnien und Dubrovnik ein und rechnete dadurch mit etwa 1.000 diplomatischen Einheiten (zwar nur in Kyrillisch). Als Zwischenergebnis dieses Unternehmens ist 2011 der erste und bisher einzige Band mit 148 Urkunden und Briefen (einschließlich Deperdita) bis zum Jahr 1321 erschienen: Zbornik srednjovekovnih ćiriličkih povelja i pisama Srbije, Bosne i Dubrovnika I, hg. von Vladimir Mošin/Sima Ćirković/Dušan Sindik, Beograd 2011 (die Titel der in der Regel kyrillisch verfassten serbischen Veröffentlichungen werden hier in lateinischer Transliteration wiedergegeben, ggf. mit ihren Übersetzungen in fremdsprachlichen Abstracts oder Zusammenfassungen).

7 Zum allgemeinen historischen Kontext siehe u. a. die immer noch relevante deutschsprachige Darstellung bei Konstantin Jireček, Geschichte der Serben, 2 Bde., Gotha 1911–1918; weiterhin Sima Ćirković, La Serbie au Moyen Âge, Paris 1992; und John V. A. Fine, The Late Medieval Balkans. A Critical Survey from the Late Twelfth Century to the Ottoman Conquest, Ann Arbor 1994.

8 Vujošević, Herrscherkanzlei (wie Anm. 4) S. 244–245. Zur Typologie der serbischen mittelalterlichen Urkunden unter anderen Aspekten siehe Ljubomir Maksimović, Das Kanzleiwesen der serbischen Herrscher, in: Kanzleiwesen und Kanzleisprachen im östlichen Europa, hg. von Christian Hannick (AfD Beiheft 6), Köln u. a. 1999, S. 25–53, hier S. 34–35 (Dokumentenamen) und Nebojša Porčić, The Menologem in Serbian Medieval Document-Making, in: Perivolos I. Mélanges offerts à Mirjana Živojinović, hg. von Dejan Dželebdžić/Bojan Miljković, Belgrade 2015, S. 285–298, hier S. 288–289 (äußere und innere Merkmale).

(Klöster, Kirchen, Bistümer, Geistliche), 40% auf ausländische Städte (35% alleine auf Dubrovnik) und 15% auf Laien von unterschiedlichem Status[9]. Auf die weiteren Merkmale des Bestands gehen wir an dieser Stelle nicht näher ein, da eine ausführlichere Analyse bereits in den zitierten Veröffentlichungen erfolgte. Hier wollen wir lediglich die beiden wohl auffälligsten Charakteristika erwähnen: einerseits die Mehrsprachigkeit, weil Dokumente in drei Sprachen verfasst wurden (Altserbisch – 80%, Latein – 12%, Griechisch – 8%), sowie andererseits die weite geographische Streuung der erhaltenen Exemplare, wobei das Archiv der Stadt Dubrovnik in Kroatien und mehrere Klöster auf Athos ungefähr 65% der Dokumente aufbewahren, während in Serbien selbst nur etwa 5% zu finden sind[10].

Gerade der schwierige Zugang zu den Dokumenten – auch weil es noch keine vollständige gedruckte Edition oder ein Regestenwerk gibt, sondern lediglich mehrere unvollständige Sammlungen – war das Hauptmotiv, eine digitale Datenbank zu erstellen[11]. So startete im Jahr 2015 das „Diplomatarium Serbicum Digitale" im Rahmen des von der Europäischen Union geförderten „CO:OP" Projektes mit dem Ziel, das gesamte Quellenmaterial elektronisch zu bearbeiten und ggf. online zugänglich zu machen. Die gewählte Darstellungsform richtet sich nach Vorbildern der „klassischen" Druckeditionen und hat dementsprechend die folgenden Bestandteile: Kritische Textedition, diplomatische Beschreibung, diplomatische Analyse, Bibliographie, editorische Methoden, Abbildungen (falls vorhanden und zugänglich), Verzeichnis von Deperdita. Bis zum Auslaufen von „CO:OP" Ende 2018 wurde eine Datenbank mit eigener Software online gestellt, in der ungefähr 75% des Bestands (453 diplomatische Einheiten) in Form von neuen Editionen, Metadaten mit diplomatischem Kommentar und Abbildungen präsentiert wurden. Das an der Serbischen Akademie der Wissenschaften und Künste durchgeführte Projekt wurde dann nach zweieinhalb Jahren Stillstand vom Institut für Balkanstudien, dessen Webserver mit der Datenbank 2020 abgeschaltet wurde, im Juni 2021 an das Audiovisuelle Archiv und Zentrum für Digitalisierung (AVA-Zen-

---

9 Nebojša Porčić/Žarko Vujošević, Treaties between Serbia and Dubrovnik (Ragusa): Reflections of Political Relations in Diplomatic Forms (12th–15th Centuries), in: Quellen zur Geschichte der „internationalen" Beziehungen zwischen politischen Zentren in Europa und der Mittelmeerwelt (ca. 800–1600): Briefe – Urkunden – Verträge. Beiträge des 15. Kongresses der Commission Internationale de diplomatique (Leipzig 2018), hg. von Wolfgang Huschner/Sebastian Roebert (Italia Regia. Fonti e richerche per la storia medievale 7) – im Druck.

10 Vujošević/Porčić/Živojinović, Kanzleiwesen (wie Anm. 1) S. 134–136 (mit zwei Karten).

11 Zur Editionspraxis in Serbien (und Montenegro) bis etwa 2006 siehe Žarko Vujošević, Diplomatik in Serbien und Montenegro, in: AfD 52 (2006) S. 531–540, hier S. 534–536. Darüber hinaus ist neben dem in Anm. 6 oben erwähnten ersten Band des „Serbischen Diplomatars" noch eine umfangreichere kommentierte Edition zu erwähnen: Nebojša Porčić, Dokumenti srpskih srednjovekovnih vladara u dubrovačkim zbirkama. Doba Nemanjića [engl. Zusammenfassung: Documents of Serbian Medieval Rulers in Dubrovnik Collections: the Nemanjić Period], Beograd 2017.

trum) übergeben. Eine Finanzierung der weiteren Tätigkeit erfolgte erst im Jahr 2022 durch das serbische Kultusministerium. Die Aufgabe: Die bestehenden Dateien vollständig in ein neu zu schaffendes (und inzwischen auch fertiggestelltes) online-Portal des AVA-Zentrums zu übertragen sowie die editorische Bearbeitung des bislang noch nicht bearbeiteten Bestands vorzunehmen[12]. Somit wurde die alte Datenbank in einer neuen Form wiederbelebt.

Jedes Dokument in der Datenbank wird durch 35 Merkmale in Form von „Rubriken" bzw. Einträgen dargestellt. Deren Verzeichnis wird in der folgenden Tabelle mit kurzen Beschreibungen bzw. Erklärungen gegeben.

Dokumentidentifikator	Zusammengesetzt aus Datum, Aussteller und einer internen „Arbeitsnummer" (z. B. „13810808 Lazar 0336")
Aussteller	In formalisierter kürzester Form (z. B. „Stefan Dečanski" und nicht „König Stefan Uroš III. Dečanski")
Empfänger	Wie oben (etwa: „Hilandar" und nicht „das Kloster Hilandar")
Kurzregest	Was (Dokumenttyp), wer, wem, wovon, Ort, Datum (in Klammern, normale Form); Beispiel: „Urkunde des Stefan Dečanski dem Hilandar über die Muttergotteskirche in Prizren (8. Februar 1327)"
Ausstellungsdatum	Formalisierte Datumsangabe (wie oben im Dokumentidentifikator)
Ausstellungsort	Wiedergabe in heutiger Form
Vollregest	Ausführliche Beschreibung des Inhalts
Überlieferungstyp	„Original", „Glaubwürdige" oder „Verunechtete Abschrift" (darauf weitere Erklärung in freier Form: zweifelhaft, interpoliert, spurium nach echter Vorlage, Pseudooriginal...), „Fälschung"[13]
Selbstbezeichnung	Wie das Dokument sich selbst „nennt" (falls angegeben)
Aufbewahrungsort	Ort – Archiv-/Klostername – Signatur (ggf. „Verschollen" oder „Vernichtet")
Aufnahmen	Ort – Archiv-/Einrichtungsname – Signatur (falls vorhanden bzw. bekannt)
Geschichte des Dokuments	Falls relevant, in freier Form
Bisherige Editionen	Bibliographisches Verzeichnis
Sekundärliteratur	Wie oben

12 Die Applikation ist auf https://ava.sanu.ac.rs zugänglich. Das DSD findet sich unter den „work-in-progress Projekten" auf https://ava.sanu.ac.rs/o-avi/mustra2/3, zwar noch inaktiv (die „Beta-Version" ist hier auf den Abb. 2–5 dargestellt).

13 In einer weiteren Entwicklung der Datenbank wäre hier an die Verlinkung mit dem fachspezifischen „Vocabulaire international de la Diplomatique" (VID) zu denken (s. Anm. 23 unten). Auch andere Linked Open Data Funktionalitäten, etwa bei den Ausstellungs- oder Aufbewahrungsorten der Urkunden, könnten künftig bereitgestellt werden.

Beschreibstoff	„Pergament", „Papier" oder „Mauer" (ggf. mit Besonderheiten in freier Form, etwa „Kodex von 105 Blättern"). Die Bezeichnungen „Unzugänglich" (Dokument liegt nicht vor, auch nicht als Abbildung) und „Keine Angaben" (Dokument verschollen) erscheinen ggf. auch in allen weiteren Einträgen, die die Beschreibung der äußeren und inneren Merkmale des Dokuments betreffen
Beschreibung des Zustands	Beschreibung in freier Form
Dimensionen	Länge x Breite in mm
Wasserzeichen (falls vorhanden)	Kürzeste Form, Belegjahr(en), Literaturhinweis
Sprache	„Serbisch", „Griechisch", „Latein", „Italienisch", (ggf. mit Kommentar, etwa: „Italienisch – ursprünglich Serbisch")
Schrift	Schriftart, Stil (z.B: „Kyrillisch, Schnellschrift")
Andersfarbige Buchstaben	Farbe, Beschreibung (welche, was, wo, wie)
Graphische Symbole und Verzierungen	Kurze Beschreibung, wie oben
Siegel	Falls vorhanden: Kurze Beschreibung mit einem Link zur Siegeldatenbank mit detaillierten Angaben; Andere Möglichkeiten: „Reste", „Spuren", „Beschreibung" (bei Transsumpten oder Übersetzungen), „Erwähnung" (etwa in der Corroboratio), „Nicht vorhanden", „Unzugänglich", „Keine Angaben"
Unterfertigung	Übersetzt mit Zeilenangabe
Logos-Formel (falls vorhanden)	Wie oben
Zeugen	Wie oben
Spätere Notizen (dorsual und/oder marginal)	Beschreibung; Der Wortlaut wird unter dem Urkundentext wiedergegeben
Datumsangabe (wie im Dokument angeführt)	Übersetzt mit Zeilenangabe
Ortsangabe (wie im Dokument angeführt)	Wie oben
Schreibervermerk bzw. Beurkundungsbefehl	Wie oben
Vorurkunden und andere erwähnte Dokumente	Chronologisch angeführt, ggf. mit dem Hinweis auf die Liste von Deperdita
Kommentar	Nach Bedarf wichtige Bemerkungen und Schließungen zum Inhalt bzw. den diplomatischen Eigenschaften
Editionsvorlage	„Autopsie", „Aufnahmen" (mit Signaturen), (ältere) „Edition(en)"
Text	Kritische Edition in moderner Schrift, normiert und mit aufgelösten Abkürzungen
Abbildungen (falls vorhanden)	Links auf vorhandene Abbildungen aller Exemplare

Bei mehrfach überlieferten Texten eines Dokuments (bzw. einer diplomatischen Einheit) werden Originale vollständig (wie in der Tabelle oben) erfasst. Weitere Exemplare werden nur teilweise beschrieben (so etwa Registerabschriften ohne äußere Merkmale) und verweisen auf das jeweilige Original; dabei werden variante Fassungen in der Edition nicht zusammengeführt, sondern als einzelne Texte belassen.

Das vorherige Benutzerinterface wurde 2022 durch ein neues ersetzt. Dieses ist ein Teil der modularen Applikation des AVA-Zentrums, in der auch andere digitale Sammlungen (Dokumente verschiedener Herkunft, Bücher, Bilder usw.) vorhanden sind [Abb. 1]. Die Abbildungen 2–5 zeigen, wie eine Urkunde, die durch mehrere Auswahlmöglichkeiten („Filter" – nach Aussteller, Empfänger, Chronologie oder Aufbewahrungsort) gesucht werden kann, repräsentiert wird („Beta-Version")[14]. Es handelt sich um eine synoptische Darstellung mit paralleler Anzeige von Abbildung und Text – hier zunächst die Metadaten bzw. die oben genannten Einträge, danach der kritisch edierte Text des entsprechenden Dokuments.

Abb. 1: Startseite der modularen Applikation des Audiovisuellen Archivs und Zentrums für Digitalisierung der Serbischen Akademie der Wissenschaften und Künste (DSD erstes von rechts oben).

---

14 Hier die Urkunde von Stefan Uroš III. „Dečanski" an das Kloster Hilandar über die Muttergotteskirche in Prizren, ausgestellt am 8. Februar 1327; zur neuesten gedruckten Edition siehe Siniša Mišić, Povelja kralja Stefana Uroša III manastiru Hilandaru [frz. Abstract: Charte du roi Stefan Uroš III au monastère de Chilandar], in: Stari srpski arhiv 5 (2006) S. 65–81.

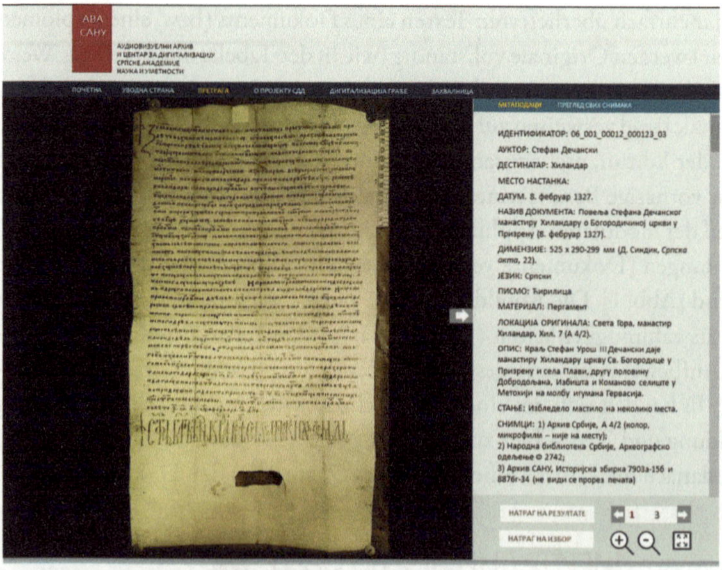

Abb. 2: Darstellung eines Dokuments (Teil 1) – Aufnahme links, (ein Teil von) Metadaten rechts.

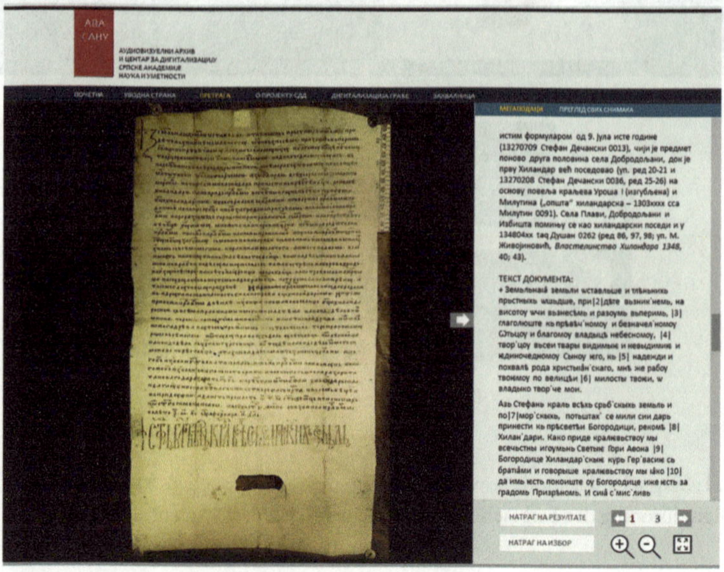

Abb. 3: Darstellung eines Dokuments (Teil 2) – Aufnahme links, kritische Edition (Anfang) rechts.

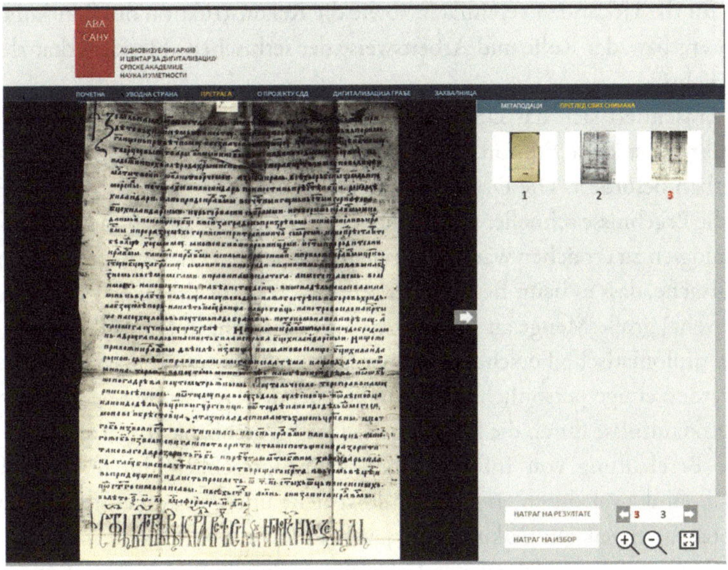

Abb. 4: Darstellung eines Dokuments (Teil 3) – Auswahl der vorhandenen Aufnahmen.

Die neue DSD-Applikation ist zwar elektronisch zugänglich bzw. durchsuchbar und wird (wieder) im Netz veröffentlicht, stellt aber als eine lokale SQL-Datenbank noch keine digitale Edition dar[15]. Doch wird sie als ein wichtiger Beitrag für die regionale Forschungsgemeinschaft betrachtet, die sonst, wie oben erwähnt, über keine vollständige Sammlung von Editionen oder Regesten verfügt. Das erneuerte DSD schafft also mit seinen einheitlichen Texteditionen sowie seiner erleichterten Zugänglichkeit, Übersichtlichkeit und Durchsuchbarkeit des Materials einen klaren „Mehrwert" für die serbische Diplomatik, der es noch an Analysen aus der Gesamtschau mangelt. So wird vor allem die Festlegung allgemeiner Echtheitskri-

15 Eine (kritische) digitale Edition verstehen wir im Sinne von Patrick Sahle als eine „erschließende Wiedergabe historischer Dokumente im digitalen Paradigma", die dementsprechend „ohne wesentliche Informations- und Funktionsverluste in eine typografische Form nicht gebracht werden kann": Patrick Sahle, Digitale Editionsformen. Zum Umgang mit der Überlieferung unter den Bedingungen des Medienwandels, Bd. 2, Norderstedt 2013, S. 138, 148–149 (zu der Abgrenzung von digitaler zu anderen Typen von Editionen, etwa „elektronischer" oder „digitalisierter" siehe ebd., S. 148–155). Für weitere Definitionen sowie die Entwicklung des Konzepts der „Digitalen Edition" siehe Digital Critical Editions, hg. von Daniel Apollon/Claire Bélisle/Philippe Régnier, Chicago 2014; Elena Pierazzo, Digital Scholarly Editing: Theories, Models and Methods, Farnham 2015; Patrick Sahle, What is a Scholarly Digital Edition?, in: Digital Scholarly Editing. Theories and Practices, hg. von Matthew James Driscoll/Elena Pierazzo, Cambridge 2016, S. 19–39.

terien für die Urkunden vereinfacht sowie die Rekonstruktion des Beurkundungsverfahrens bzw. der Rolle und Arbeitsweise der serbischen „Herrscherkanzlei(en)" ermöglicht[16].

So präsentiert sich das DSD mehr als Werkzeug und weniger als Methode – das heißt, es ist keine Edition, die die Forschung mithilfe von digitalen Methoden wesentlich befördert. Die Datenbank dient vor allem der Arbeitsökonomie: Man kann die Ergebnisse schneller und effektiver erreichen, die auch ohne Informationstechnologien zu erreichen wären. Im Falle von DSD liegt das erwartungsgemäß an der Tatsache, dass es beim Bestand der serbischen mittelalterlichen Urkunden um keine (sehr) große Menge an Daten bzw. Textsammlungen handelt. Das Potenzial für die diplomatische Forschung ist aber keinesfalls zu unterschätzen. Im Folgenden werden einige persönliche Erfahrungen bei der Gewinnung neuer diplomatischer Erkenntnisse durch die Nutzung der DSD-Datenbank vorgestellt.

Die Beschaffung von Informationen ist hauptsächlich durch Suchanfragen möglich, und zwar durch einfache Volltextsuche und Zusammenstellung von bestimmten Gruppen von Dokumenten [Abb. 5] sowie besonders wertvoll durch die kombinierte Suche verschiedener Urkundenmerkmale (bzw. „Rubriken" – Abb. 6: hier wird die alte Applikation gezeigt, weil bei der neuen diese Funktion noch zu programmieren ist). Dabei können verschiedene Einsichten entstehen, die sich sonst nur schwer oder vielleicht gar nicht durchsetzen würden. So war z. B. bei einer Fallstudie über die Beglaubigung von Urkunden des Kaisers Stefan Uroš (1355–71) schnell festzustellen, dass das verbindliche Beglaubigungsmittel seiner „Kanzlei" die Unterschrift und nicht das Siegel war[17]. Zudem wurde auf diesem Weg deutlich gemacht, dass die Verwendung von Siegeln anscheinend empfänger-

16 Vgl. Vujošević/Porčić/Živojinović, Kanzleiwesen (wie Anm. 1) S. 133–140 (Beispiele zur Untersuchung einzelner Fragen in Bezug auf die dilpomatische Produktion S. 140–147 ebenda). Zur Kanzleifrage und Kanzleiforschung in Serbien siehe Vujošević, Herrscherkanzlei (wie Anm. 4) S. 239–243. Als wegweisende Beispiele des computergestützten „quantitativen Approachs" in der Analyse des Beurkundungsverfahrens seien hier genannt Els De Paermentier, *Diplomata Belgica*. Analysing medieval charter texts (dictamen) through a quantitative approach. The case of Flanders and Hainaut (1191–1244), in: Digital diplomatics. The Computer as a Tool for the Diplomatist?, hg. von Antonella Ambrosio/Sébastien Barret/Georg Vogeler (AfD Beiheft 14), Köln u. a. 2014, S. 169–185; sowie die beiden Aufsätze Dies., L'apport des éditions èlectroniques à l'étude diplomatique: l'exemple d'une recherche sur l'influence des chancelleries royales sur la chancellerie comtale en Flandre (XIIe – début du XIIIe siècle) bzw. Olivier Canteaut, Quantifier l'activité des chancelleries à l'aune de la tradition des actes: l'exemple de la chancellerie des derniers Capétiens (1314–1328), in: Actes royaux et princiers à l'ère du numérique (Moyen Âge – Temps modernes), hg. von Olivier Canteaut/Olivier Guyotjeannin/Olivier Poncet, Pau 2020, S. 79–82 bzw. S. 101–111.

17 Žarko Vujošević, Über den Status einiger Urkunden des serbischen Kaisers Stefan Uroš (1355–1371): Ein Beitrag zur Kanzleiforschung, in: Initial. A Review of Medieval Studies 4 (2016) S. 109–124. Siehe auch die Abb. 6 hier.

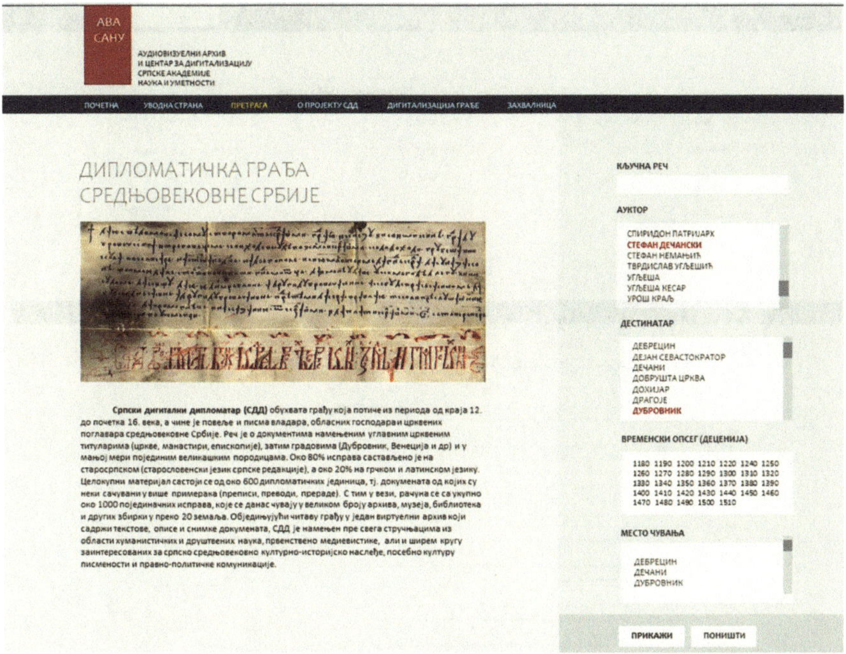

Abb. 5: DSD Suchanfragen (rechts von oben nach unten): Volltextsuche („Schlüsselwort" in der ganzen Datenbank) sowie Dokumentsuche nach Aussteller, nach Empfänger, Chronologisch und nach Aufbewahrungsort.

orientiert war, denn diese befinden sich an allen Urkunden für die Stadt Dubrovnik, während sie bei Klosterurkunden nur in wenigen Ausnahmen vorkommen. Ein weiteres Beispiel, das hier zu nennen ist, wäre die Erwähnung des geographischen Begriffs „Albanien" in den Intitulationes und/oder Unterschriften der serbischen Herrscherurkunden. Dieser kommt nämlich nur in den fremdsprachig (hauptsächlich Latein) verfassten glaubwürdigen Dokumenten vor, während die seltenen serbischsprachigen Urkunden mit diesem Element in der Forschung als unecht oder verunechtet gelten. Dadurch sind wir von dieser schnell und einfach gewonnenen Erkenntnis dazu angeregt, die Glaubwürdigkeit einer Abschrift einer neuerlichen Untersuchung zu unterziehen[18].

18 Es handelt sich um insgesamt 15 Urkunden und Briefe, ausgestellt zwischen 1333 und 1451, in denen „Albanien" meistens als Teil der Intitulation erwähnt wird. Die genannte Abschrift, die ggf. neu zu bewerten wäre, bezieht sich auf die Urkunde des Kaisers Stefan Dušan an das Kloster der Erzengel Michael und Gabriel in Jerusalem vom 8. März 1350. Dazu siehe Žarko Vujošević, Vranjina i Sv. arhanđeli u Jerusalimu – još jedan osvrt na tradiciju darovne povelje cara Stefana Dušana [engl. Zusammenfassung: Vranjina and the Holy Archangels Monastery in Jerusalem – another look at the tradition of Emperor Stefan Dušan's donation charter], in: The Historical

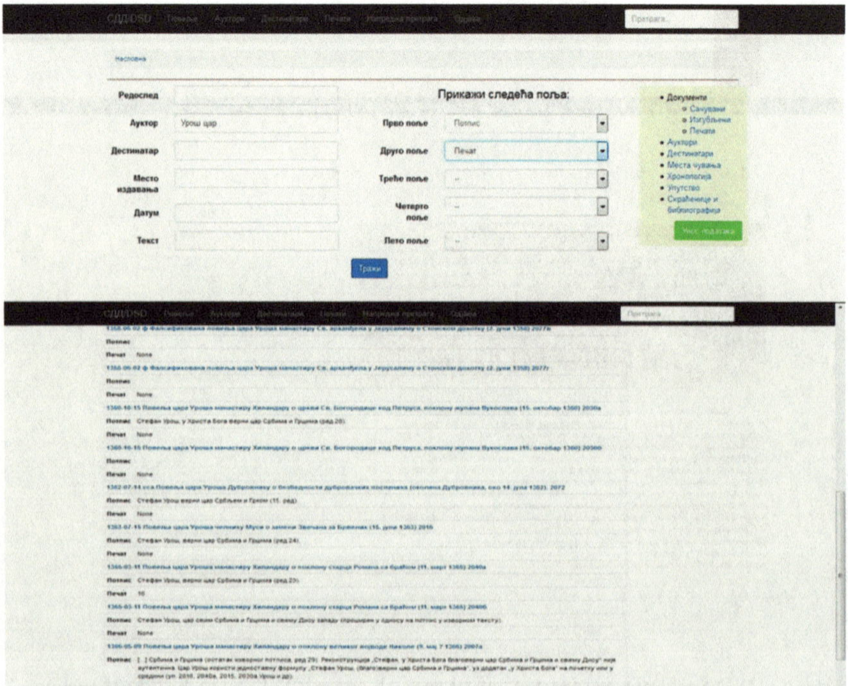

Abb. 6: DSD kombinierte Suche durch „Rubriken“: Hier wird nach allen Urkunden des Kaisers Stefan Uroš mit Unterschrift und Siegel gesucht (wobei im Falle eines fehlenden Inhalts leere Felder bzw. ausdrückliche negative Aussagen – „none“ – angezeigt werden).

Was wäre allerdings ohne die DSD-Datenbank nicht oder nur sehr schwer erreichbar? Zum Beispiel die Suche nach einem Begriff/Wort im Kontext – eine Funktion, die auch gerade programmiert wird. Dadurch werden Fragestellungen, aber auch in weiterer Folge neue methodische Überlegungen möglich, die ohne dieses Werkzeug nicht aufkommen könnten. Hier gibt es zwar noch keine eigene Erfahrung, doch einige Aussichten lassen sich dennoch vorstellen – etwa hinsichtlich der Untersuchung einzelner Bezeichnungen von Immunitäten und ihrer Zusammenhänge in der Dispositio, die bislang noch nicht systematisch erforscht wurden[19]. Auf diesem Weg nähert man sich digitalen Methoden an und kann über

Review 66 (2017) S. 237–255; und Porčić, Dokumenti (wie Anm. 11) S. 236–243 (mit der Edition aller drei erhaltenen Exemplare).

19 Zur „Institution“ der Immunitäten im mittelalterlichen Serbien auf der Grundlage der bis 1321 an kirchliche Empfänger ausgestellten Urkunden siehe Miloš Ivanović, Razvoj institucije imuniteta u srpskoj srednjovekovnoj državi do kraja vladavine kralja Milutina [engl. Zusammenfassung: Development of the institution of immunity in the Serbian medieval state until the end of reign of King Milutin], in: The Historical Review 66 (2017) S. 49–83. Erkannt werden Immu-

weitere Schritte nachdenken, etwa im Bereich der Diktatanalyse. Die Suche nach autorenspezifischen Wörtern oder Phrasen könnte etwa helfen, die Verfasser von den sowohl zahlreichen als auch bedeutungsreichen serbischen Arengen zu ermitteln. Was wir bisher in diesem Bereich versuchen konnten – und zwar ohne Nutzung von Informationstechnologie – war eine Untersuchung der verwendeten Bibelzitate, die unter Hinzuziehung entsprechender narrativer Quellen (insbesondere Herrscherbiographien) einige bekannte kirchliche Würdenträger als Akteure der Urkundenproduktion erahnen ließ[20].

Bei den letztgenannten Beispielen, bzw. Fragestellungen scheint die DSD-Datenbank eigentlich überfordert zu sein, und dies vor allem deshalb, weil sie bislang nicht mit anderen Urkunden- und Textcorpora vernetzt werden kann. Dies wäre umso mehr möglich, wenn ihre zugrundeliegenden Daten in einem standardisierten XML-Format bearbeitet wären. Gerade diese neue Perspektive eröffnete sich dem Projekt in der „Interimszeit" (2020–2021) dank der Zusammenarbeit mit dem Zentrum für Informationsmodellierung der Universität Graz. Somit kann die Wiederaufnahme des DSD-Projektes mit Recht als „zweigleisig" bezeichnet werden. Der erste Schritt, der auf „Gleis zwei" vorgenommen wurde, ist die Überführung des DSD-Inhalts in das XML-Format, was unter Verwendung des Standards der Text Encoding Initiative (TEI) durchgeführt wird[21].

---

nitätentypen mit Blick auf rechtliche und steuerliche Aspekte, die um 1300 „durch bestimmte Formeln klar definiert werden". Inwiefern die Art und Weise der verfügten Immunitäten für die in den Urkunden geschaffene Rechtsqualität sowie den Status der Privilegierten gegenüber den Aussteller bedeutend sein können, zeigt z. B. die Entwicklung eines neuen Privilegientyps in der diplomatischen Produktion Ludwigs des Frommen: Theo Kölzer, Kaiser Ludwig der Fromme (814–840) im Spiegel seiner Urkunden, Paderborn 2005, S. 27–29 (vgl. Die Urkunden Ludwigs des Frommen I, MGH Diplomata Karolinum II, hg. von Theo Kölzer u. a., Wiesbaden 2016, S. LXXV).

20 Zusammenfassend bei Žarko Vujošević, On the Role of the Clergy in the Composition of Serbian Medieval Royal Charters, in: Initial. A Review of Medieval Studies 7 (2019) S. 73–82, hier S. 79–81. und Ders., Herrscherkanzlei (wie Anm. 4) S. 262–263 mit der älteren Literatur.

21 Schon 2004 wurde von den Diplomatikern ein eigener Beschreibungsstandard vorgeschlagen – ein XML Schema für Urkunden, genannt Charters Encoding Initiative (CEI); dazu u. a. Georg Vogeler, Charters Encoding Initiative (CEI): Zu Möglichkeiten der Integration mit Hilfe eines Standards für Urkundendigitalisierung, in: Alte Archive – Neue Technologien, hg. von Thomas Aigner/Karin Winter, St. Pölten 2006, S. 181–198. Obwohl die CEI ihre Stellung in der Welt der digitalen Diplomatik behauptet hat (z. B. als grundlegendes Schema für das Urkundenportal www.monasterium.net), hat sich inzwischen das viel allgemeinere und umfangreichere TEI–Schema als Hauptreferenz für Geisteswissenschaften durchgesetzt (https://tei-c.org). Zur Verwendung von der TEI in der editorischen Arbeit mit Urkunden siehe Georg Vogeler, Die Text Encoding Initiative (TEI) als Werkzeug des Urkundeneditors – Erfahrungen und Desiderate, in: Papsturkundenforschung zwischen internationaler Vernetzung und Digitalisierung. Neue Zugangsweisen zur europäischen Schriftgeschichte, hg. von Irmgard Fees/Benedikt Hotz/Benjamin Schönfeld, Dokumentenserver res doctae, Göttingen 2015, [S. 1–11, https://doi.org/10.26015/adwdocs-441].

Das TEI-Schema kann allerdings die Ansprüche der Diplomatik nicht vollständig erfüllen. So fehlen etwa Elemente zur Beschreibung mehrerer diplomatischer Phänomene (wie etwa Unterfertigungen, Schreibervermerke, Logos-Formel u.a.m.), oder wenn diese vorhanden sind, so ist unter Umständen deren Verwendung in bestimmten Kontexten vom TEI-Schema nicht erlaubt[22]. Deshalb ist eine sinngemäße und auch kreative Anpassung dieses Standards nötig, was am besten durch das Integrieren bereits etablierter fachspezifischer Systeme gelingen kann. So ein System ist das schon in den 90er Jahren veröffentlichte und inzwischen auch digital zugängliche „Vocabulaire international de la Diplomatique" (VID), dessen Terminologie in die TEI-Elemente und Attribute mit gewissen Modifikationen aufgenommen wird[23]. Als Ergebnis der Zusammenarbeit mit Georg Vogeler wurde ein Schema verfasst, das schon bei der TEI-Konferenz 2021 dargestellt wurde und nun für die gerade laufende Überführung des DSD-Inhalts in das XML-Format genutzt wird[24]. Derzeit werden die Metadaten überführt; in einem nächsten Schritt ist die direkte Auszeichnung der Urkundentexte geplant. Somit kann eine „echte" digitale Edition aufgebaut werden, die das Potenzial der computerunterstützten Erschließung von Dokumenten erheblich erhöht. An folgenden Beispielen wird gezeigt, wie die Darstellung von Metadaten innerhalb des „TEI-Headers" aussehen sollte und welche Lösungen bei der XML-Markierung der Urkundentexte vorgeschlagen werden.

---

22 Hinsichtlich dieser Umstände sind Vorschläge für eine Erweiterung der TEI mit verschiedenen für die Diplomatik spezifischen Konzepten bereits zu verfolgen – siehe u. a. Sean M. Winslow, Authenticating Features in the TEI, in: Journal of the Text Encoding Initiative 13 (May 2020 – November 2022, Online seit 23. September 2021) [S. 1–21, http://journals.openedition.org/jtei/3608].

23 Vocabulaire International de la Diplomatique, hg. von Maria Milagros Carcél Ortí, Valéncia 1997 (1. Auflage 1994, online Version auf https://www.cei.lmu.de/VID). Zum VID als einem (werdenden) Teil des Semantic Web siehe Georg Vogeler, Von der Terminologie zur Ontologie. Das „Vocabulaire International de la Diplomatique" als Ressource des Semantic Web, in: Francia 40 (2013) S. 281–297.

24 Die (virtuelle) TEI Konferenz 2021 (Next Gen TEI) fand im Oktober 2021 statt. Der Beitrag Georg Vogeler/Žarko Vujošević, Using non-TEI vocabularies in TEI descriptions, wurde begleitet durch die Präsentation, abrufbar auf https://online.uni-graz.at/kfu_online/wbFPCompsCallBacks.cbExecuteDownload?pDocStoreNr=6886779. Wie die Terminologie der VID im TEI-Umfeld verwendet werden kann, wird im Detail und an mehreren Beispielen in Vujošević/Vogeler, Encoding Charters (wie Anm. 5) dargestellt.

Beispiel 1 – TEI-Header[25]

Das Beispiel kombiniert die bestehenden Elemente und Attribute der TEI mit den nummerierten VID-Einträgen[26]. Hier werden sie zu besserer Verständlichkeit und Übersichtlichkeit um ihren deutschen Bezeichner ergänzt sowie fett gedruckt – daher erscheint kein wohlgeformtes XML.

<teiHeader>
<fileDesc>
<titleStmt>
<title><idno>13471212 F Dusan (0104)</idno> <term ana="VID:385"> Urkunde</term> des Kaisers<persName ana="VID:16" **Aussteller**>Dusan</persName>an<orgName ana="VID:17" **Empfänger**>Hilandar</orgName>zur Schenkung von Livada und Paleokometica (<placeName ana="VID:563" **Ausstellungsort**>Landenge von Athos</placeName>, <date ana="VID:560" **Datum**>12. Dezember 1347</date>).</title>
</titleStmt>
<sourceDesc>
<listWit>
<witness xml:id="A">
<msDesc>
<msIdentifier>
<repository ana="VID:add_27" **verschollenes Objekt**>Unbekannt (verschollen)
</repository>
</msIdentifier>
<msContents>
<textLang>Serbisch</textLang>
<msItem>

25 Im Folgenden werden die Metadaten einer diplomatischen Einheit, die in drei Exemplaren aufbewahrt wird, in Auszügen dargestellt (Quelle für die Metadaten: DSD 13471212 F Dušan 0104 auf Deutsch übersetzt). Es handelt sich um eine Fälschung mit dem Datum 12. Dezember 1347, dem Kaiser Stefan Dušan zugeschrieben; zuletzt abgehandelt von Aleksandra Fostikov, Povelja cara Dušana o poklonu Livade i Paliokometice Hilandaru (Hil. 34) [engl. Zusammenfassung: The charter of Emperor Stefan Dušan about the gift of Livada and Paliokometica to the monastery of Hilandar], in: Stari srpski arhiv 16 (2017) S. 29–56 (mit der Edition eines der Exemplare).

26 Dabei werden auch einige in Vujošević/Vogeler, Encoding Charters (wie Anm. 5) vorgeschlagene VID-Erweiterungen verwendet und zwar: add_8 – Selbstbezeichnung; add_11 – Logos-Formel; add_12 – rote (oder andersfarbige) Buchstaben und Zeichen; add_14 – Dorsualnotizen; add_15 – Marginalnotizen; add_22 – Schrift; add_23 – Schriftart; add_27 – verschollenes Objekt (zu finden auf: https://github.com/GVogeler/VID/tree/FSGervers).

<filiation ana=“VID:24” **Überlieferung**><term ana=“VID:116”>
Fälschung
</term></filiation>
</msItem>
</msContents>
<physDesc>
<objectDesc>
<supportDesc>
<support><material>Pergament (nach Angaben in der Literatur)
</material></support>
<extent><dimensions>
<height>Unbekannt</height>
<width>Unbekannt</width>
</dimensions>
</extent>
<condition>Stellenweise Flecken und Blässe [...] (nach dem Lichtbild)
</condition>
</supportDesc>
</objectDesc>
<scriptDesc>
<scriptNote> <term ana=“VID:add_22” **Schrift**>Kyrillisch</term>
<term ana=“VID:add_23” **Schriftart**>Halbunzialschrift</term>
</scriptNote>
</scriptDesc>
<decoDesc>
<decoNote ana=“VID:add_12” **rote Buchstaben/Zeichen**>
Unterschrift<ref>Аврамовић (1847) 51; Леонид (1868) 62.
</ref></decoNote>
<decoNote ana=“VID:145” **grafische Symbole**>Entwickeltes NI-KA-Kreuz der Invocatio symbolica [...]</decoNote>
</decoDesc>
<sealDesc ana=“VID:540 VID:add_27” **Hängesiegel; verschollenes Objekt**><condition ana=“description”><p>Auf dem Lichtbild ist nur der Schnur sichtbar [...]. Beschreibung und Abzeichnung des verschollenen Siegels bei [...] </p></condition>
</sealDesc>
</physDesc>
<history>
<origin><origPlace>Hilandar</origPlace><origDate>Zweite Hälfte des 15. Jahrhunderts</origDate></origin>

```
      <provenance>Das Dokument befand sich im Kloster Hilandar, als
      es dort […] aufgenommen wurde […]</provenance>
    </history>
    <additional>
      <surrogates><list type="photographs">
        <item><placeName>Belgrad</placeName><orgName
        type="archives">Archiv der Serbischen Akademie […]
        </orgName><idno>8876-60</idno></item></list>
      </surrogates>
    </additional>
  </msDesc>
  <listBibl ana="VID:19" Edition>
    <bibl>J. Рајић, История разныхъ славенскихъ народовъ […]</bibl>[…]
    <bibl>F. Miklosich, Monumenta Serbica […]</bibl>[…]
  </listBibl>
  <listBibl type=»literature» >
    <bibl>Д. Аврамовић, Света Гора […]</bibl>[…]</listBibl>
</witness>
<witness xml:id="B">
  <msDesc>
    <msIdentifier>
      <settlement>Belgrad</settlement>
      <repository>Museum der Serbischen Orthodoxen Kirche</repository>
      <collection>Sammlung von Radoslav Grujić</collection>
    </msIdentifier>
    <msContents>
      <textLang>Serbisch</textLang>
      <msItem>
      <filiation ana="VID:24" Überlieferung><term
      ana="VID:53">Abschrift (aus A)</term></filiation>
      </msItem>
    </msContents>
    <physDesc>[…]</physDesc>
    <history>[…]</history>
    <additional>[…] </additional>
  </msDesc>
  <listBibl ana="VID:19" Edition>
    <bibl>P. J. Schaffarik, Serbische Lesekörner […]</bibl>
  </listBibl>
  <listBibl type="literature">
    <bibl>P. J. Schaffarik, Übersicht […]</bibl>[…]</listBibl>
```

```
        </witness>
        <witness xml:id="C">
          <msDesc>
            <msIdentifier>
              <geogName>Athos</geogName>
              <repository>Kloster Hilandar</repository>
              <idno>Хил. 34 (A 4/14)</idno>
            </msIdentifier>
            <msContents>[...]</msContents>
            <physDesc>
              <objectDesc>
                <supportDesc>
                  <support><material>Papier</material><watermark>Waage
                    im Kreis [...] </watermark></support>
                  <extent><dimensions unit="mm">
                    <height>580</height>
                    <width>310</width>
                  </dimensions>
                </extent>
                <condition>Stellenweise Nässe- und Tintenflecken [...]</condition>
              </supportDesc>
            </objectDesc>
            <scriptDesc>[...]</scriptDesc>
            <decoDesc>[...]</decoDesc>
            <sealDesc>[...]</sealDesc>
            </physDesc>
            <history>[...]</history>
            <additional>
              <surrogates><list type="photographs">
                <item>Belgrad, Archiv Serbiens A 4/14 (Mikrofilm)</item>[...]
              </list></surrogates>
            </additional>
          </msDesc>
          <listBibl ana="VID:19" Edition>
            <bibl>А. Фостиков, Повеља цара Стефана Душана [...]</bibl>
          </listBibl>
          <listBibl type="literature">
            <bibl>Л. Славева – В. Мошин, Српски грамоти [...]</bibl>[...]</listBibl>
      </witness>
    </listWit>
  </sourceDesc>
```

</fileDesc>
<profileDesc>
<textClass>
<keywords ana="VID:385"><term>Urkunde</term></keywords>
<keywords ana="VID:add_8" **Selbstbezeichnung**><term>Златопечатни хрисовуль/слово </term></keywords>
<keywords ana="VID:add_11" **Logos-Formel**><term>Словом, Словеси (A); Царство ми, Словеси (C)</term>
</keywords>
</textClass>
<abstract>
<p>Kaiser Stefan Dusan besucht Athos, beschenkt die dortigen Klöster [...]</p>
</abstract>
<handNotes ana="VID:347" **Dorsualnotizen, Marginalnotizen**>
<handNote sameAs="A"><locus ana="VID:add_15 **Marginalnotizen**>[...]</locus> <locus ana="VID:add_14 **Dorsualnotizen**>[...]</locus> </handNote>[...]</handNotes>
</profileDesc>
</teiHeader>

Beispiel 2 – Textmarkierung[27]

<text>
<body>
<div ana="VID:add_16" **Protokoll**>
<ab ana="VID:146" **symbolische Invokation**>+</ab>
<ab ana="VID:196" **Arenga**>Принесѣмь убѡ и мыи кь прѣдстателнѣи царици нашеи, владычици Богородици, трьжьство сь дарьї, юже пронарече богоѡтьць Давидь сїице: <cit type="Bible"><quote>"Прѣдста царица вь ризахь ѡзлаштенахь ѡдѣана и прѣоукрашенаа".</quote><ref>(Ps 45,9.13) </ref></cit> Приводима бываѥть вь светоую црьковь [...]</ab>

27 Hier wird der edierte Text einer Urkunde Kaiser Stefan Dušans an das Kloster Hilandar, ausgestellt in den ersten Monaten des Jahres 1348, in wesentlich gekürzter Fassung dargestellt (Quelle für den Text: DSD 134804xx taq Dušan 0262). In der Forschung wird dieses (einzig) erhaltene Exemplar als eine glaubwürdige Abschrift betrachtet; die letzte gedruckte Edition mit Kommentar: Siniša Mišić/Marija Koprivica, Opšta hrisovulja cara Stefana Dušana Hilandaru [engl. Zusammenfassung: General chrysobull of tsar Stefan Dušan to Hilandar monastery], in: Stari srpski arhiv 14 (2015) S. 65–106. In diesem Beitrag orientiert sich die Markierung hauptsächlich an den Elementen des Urkundenaufbaus, während die Auszeichnungen der Textzeilen, Namen, des kritischen Apparatus u. a. m. ausgelassen sind.

<ab ana="VID:197" **Narratio**>Тѣмже и<seg ana="VID:187" **Intitulatio**> азь, вь Христа Бога благовѣрныи и Богомь поставлѥнїи Стефань царь всѣмь Срьблѥмь и Грькомь и Западнои странѣ, рекоу же Алаванїи и Поморию и всемоу Дисоу.</seg> Божьствьною бо благодатию [...]</ab>
</div>

<div ana="VID:198" **Dispositio**>
<ab ana="VID:491" **Zahlungsauftrag**> [...] и приложисмо ѡть всега добитка живога што се находи оу царьства ми десетькь всако годиште. [...]</ab>
<ab ana="VID:395" **Immunitätsprivileg**> [...] освободи царьство ми ѡть всѣхь работь царьства ми [...]</ab>
<ab ana="VID:436" **Stiftung**>И оучини царьство ми вьноутрь у монастыри болницоу [...]</ab>
<ab ana="VID:438" **Ausstattungsschenkung**>И да се даѥ ѡть полате царьства ми [...] </ab>
<ab ana="VID:51" **Bestätigung**> [...] исписасмо имена метохиіамь всѣмь по Срьблѥхь и по Романїи. Села по земли Срьбьскои: село Кроушево [...] Оу Полозѣ црьковь Мати Божіа Хтѣтовска и [...] црьковь Светы Николае,<note ana="VID:97" **Vorurkunden**>што приложи царьство ми Богородици Хтѣтовскои</note> [...]</ab>
<ab ana="VID:395" **Immunitätsprivileg** >И сиіази села и метохиѥ освободии царьство ми ѡть всѣхь работь [...]</ab>
</div>

<div ana="VID:182a **Eschatokoll**">
<ab ana="VID:211" **Verpflichtung der Nachfolger**>И молю, ѥгоже Богь изволи по мнѣ царьствовати [...]</ab>
<ab ana="VID:237" **Sanctio**>Ктѡ ли се наге такѡвыи оухыштрениѥмь дїавѡлскыимь инако прѣложити [...]</ab>
<ab ana="561" **Datumsformel**>Сіи <seg ana="VID:add_8" **Selbstbezeichnung**> хрисѡвоуль</seg>написа се кьди приде царьство ми у <placeName ana="VID:563" **Ortsangabe**>Светоу Горю,</placeName><date ana="VID:562" **Zeitangabe** period="1347-09-01 to 1348-08-31">вь лѣто <choice><orig>҂s.w.н.s.</orig> <reg>6858</reg></choice></date></ab>
<ab ana="VID:259" **Unterschrift**>СТЕФАНЬ ВЬ ХРИСТА БОГА ВѢРНИ ЦАРЬ</ab>
</div>

<div ana="VID:347" **Dorsualnotizen, Marginalnotizen**><ab ana="VID:add_15" **Marginalnotizen**>Donation für das Kloster Hilendar, über die von dem servischen <sic>König</sic> Stevan, und<sic>Königinn</sic> Helena, geschenkte Dörfer, und davon beziehende Zehend de anno 1348.</ab>

```
    </div>
  </body>
</text>
```

Abschließend bleibt noch zu erwähnen, dass sich das „XML-Gleis“ des DSD besonders auf das neugegründete Fach „Digitale Diplomatik“ freuen darf, welches ab dem Studienjahr 2022/23 im Masterstudium der Abteilung für Geschichte der Philosophischen Fakultät Belgrad angeboten wird. Somit könnte das DSD-Projekt auch der praktischen Arbeit mit den Studierenden dienen und auf diesem Weg die treibende Kraft der Digitalen Diplomatik in Serbien werden.

Quellen zur Geschichte des Alpen-Adria-Raumes

Digitale Urkundenedition auf Basis von MediaWiki

Christian Domenig

1. Geschichtswissenschaft im Medienwandel

Die letzten drei Jahrzehnte waren geprägt von einem rasanten Medienwechsel sowie Medienwandel. Als Geschichtsforschende zwischen 2020 und 2022 aufgrund der Corona-Pandemie mehrfach vor verschlossenen Archiv- und Bibliothekstüren gestanden sind und plötzlich zu Hause arbeiten mussten, etablierte sich endgültig die Überzeugung, dass wissenschaftliches Arbeiten ohne digitale Komponenten nicht mehr möglich sei. Die Digitalisierung nicht nur des Forschens, sondern auch des Lehrens machte einen großen Schritt nach vorne.

Gemäß einer Theorie zum Medienwechsel dauert es eine gewisse Zeit, bis das spezifisch Neue eines Mediums erkannt wird und eigenständige Formen gefunden werden[1]. Entsprechend stellte Stephan Freisler für frühe digitale Projekte 1994 fest, „daß die derzeit produzierten Hypertexte allesamt ‚elektronische Inkunabeln' sind", die nur das Buchformat nachahmen[2]. Für das Internet wurden eigene Formen erst im Web 2.0 sichtbar, das sich ab der Jahrtausendwende etablierte. In dieser Zeit wurde mit unmittelbarer Interaktion und Kollaboration die spezifische Ausprägung dieses neuen Mediums deutlich. Der eigentliche Auslöser dieser Veränderung war aber, die Statik und Fadesse der frühen Internetseiten zu überwinden und – angesichts der beginnenden Kommerzialisierung des WordWideWeb – auf möglichst einfache Weise zu Content zu kommen. So entstand als ein Paradebeispiel für Web

1 Bernd Ulrich Biere/Werner Holly, Zur Einführung: Medien im Wandel. Neues in alten, Altes in neuen Medien, in: Medien im Wandel, ed. Werner Holly/Bernd Ulrich Biere, Opladen/Wiesbaden 1998, S. 7–11, hier S. 7.

2 Stefan Freisler, Hypertext – eine Begriffsbestimmung, in: Deutsche Sprache 22 (1994) S. 19–40, hier S. 20.

2.0 im Jänner 2001 die Online-Enzyklopädie *Wikipedia*, die innerhalb weniger Jahre die klassischen, gedruckten Nachschlagewerke vom Markt fegte.

Auf den digitalen Wandel muss auch die Geschichtswissenschaft eingehen, selbst wenn sie allgemeinen Entwicklungen gerne hinterherhinkt. Das gilt besonders für die Quellenbearbeitung und ihre Aufbereitung für eine Edition. Im Prinzip werden Quelleneditionen ähnlich verwendet wie Enzyklopädien. Das Werk wird nicht von vorne bis hinten gelesen, sondern es werden gezielt gesuchte einzelne Stücke für die Forschung benötigt. Zugleich erfolgt auch die Bearbeitung nicht in chronologischer Ordnung, sondern nach pragmatischen Gesichtspunkten wie bearbeiteten Archiven.

„Wider Erwarten ist mit der Digitalisierung kein neues Zeitalter der Quelleneditionen angebrochen", musste ich andernorts feststellen[3]. Die Gründe dafür sind vielfältig. Der Aufwand einer peniblen Bearbeitung von Quellen ist hoch, entsprechend lange – mehr als 100 Jahre[4] – sollte die Nutzungsdauer sein. Bis heute kann das eine elektronische Veröffentlichung weder von der Hard- noch von der Software her leisten. Jede digitale Lösung braucht ein regelmäßiges Service, denn Daten müssen stets auf neue Hardware überspielt und neuer Software angepasst werden. Für beides sind zudem laufend finanzielle Mittel aufzubringen. Schon früh wurde klar, dass die Langzeitarchivierung elektronischer Daten eine gewaltige Herausforderung werden wird[5]. Ein Buch über Jahrhunderte aufzubewahren ist demgegenüber relativ einfach.

In verschiedenen Wissenschaften ist das Arbeiten mit Datenbanken in der Frühen Neuzeit entstanden. Durch den starken Anstieg der Publikationen nach Erfindung des Buchdrucks war eine Neuorganisation des Wissens notwendig geworden[6]. Schon im 19. Jahrhundert verbreitet waren Kartotheken bzw. Zettelkataloge, mit denen z. B. Bibliotheken erschlossen wurden. Sie haben die älteren Bandkataloge abgelöst. Der Soziologe Niklas Luhmann verstand seinen Zettelkasten, dem er auch ein Eigenleben zusprach, als „eine Art Zweitgedächtnis, ein Alter ego, mit dem man laufend kommunizieren kann"[7]. Leo Santifaller beschreibt 1937 für die historische Quellenarbeit eine Grundstruktur, mit der noch heute gearbeitet

---

3 Christian DOMENIG, Geschichte in Bewegung. Das Mittelalter jenseits der Politik, Stuttgart 2022, S. 219.

4 Bruno MEYER, Zur Edition historischer Texte, in: Schweizerische Zeitschrift für Geschichte 1 (1951) S. 177–202, hier S. 199.

5 Uwe M. BORGHOFF/Peter RÖDING/Jan SCHEFFCZYK/Lothar SCHMITZ, Langzeitarchivierung. Methoden zur Erhaltung digitaler Dokumente, Heidelberg 2003.

6 Helmut ZEDELMAIER, Gelehrtes Wissensmanagement in der Frühen Neuzeit, in: Die Frühe Neuzeit als Epoche, ed. Helmut NEUHAUS (Historische Zeitschrift Beihefte 49), München 2009, S. 77–89.

7 Nikolas LUHMANN, Kommunikation mit Zettelkästen. Ein Erfahrungsbericht, in: Nikolas LUHMANN, Universität als Milieu. Kleine Schriften, Bielefeld 1992, S. 53–61, hier S. 57.

werden könnte: Neben einer chronologischen Hauptreihe der Urkunden sollen in eigenen Kartotheken Aussteller, Empfänger, Archive usw. aufgenommen werden[8]. Während aber der Weg hin zu Lochkarten von einigen noch eingeschlagen wurde, schien den meisten Forschenden der Umstieg auf eine Computerdatenbank als zu schwierig. Abgesehen von Programmierkenntnissen gab es vor allem ein Hindernis: Historische Daten sind selten konsistent, diese Fehlstellen verzeihen elektronische Datenbanken aber nicht.

Noch ein weiterer Aspekt erschwerte die Digitalisierung: Der Personal Computer wurde ab den 1980er Jahren eher als elektronische Schreibmaschine denn als Rechner verstanden. „Damit ließ sich der Computer in die kulturelle Traditionslinie des Buchdruckes einschreiben“[9]. So kam die Historische Fachinformatik nach euphorischen Anfängen in den späten 1960er und frühen 1970er Jahren rasch in eine Randlage. Der vielseitige technische Wandel im Computerbereich stand zudem Forschungsinteressen, die auf lange Nutzbarkeit aufbauen, entgegen.

Editionen mit Computereinsatz sind nach der Aufstellung von Patrick Sahle in den letzten Jahrzehnten unter vier Bedingungen erfolgt: Retrodigitalisierung (einscannen), Hyperedition (Bearbeitung am Computer, aber klassischer Druck), elektronische Edition (früher auf CD-ROM bzw. heute im Internet) und digitale Edition (mit Links)[10]. Erst letztere wird dem Medium Internet wirklich gerecht und diesen Ansatz möchte das in weiterer Folge vorgestellte Portal *Quellen zur Geschichte des Alpen-Adria-Raumes* verwirklichen. Mit einer digitalen Edition ergibt sich eine faszinierende Möglichkeit: Datensätze können – sofern sie weiter gepflegt werden – immer wieder neuen Gegebenheiten angepasst werden. Zwar gibt es damit keine abgeschlossene Edition mehr, dafür aber eine immer aktuelle Edition. Gerade das ist der größte Mehrwert.

2. Digitale Quellenedition

Der Kern einer modernen Computeredition liegt zuerst in der Trennung von Darstellung und Inhalt. Nur wenn diese verschiedenen Ebenen ausreichend gekennzeichnet sind, lassen sie sich computergestützt weiterverarbeiten. Die Ausgabeform – ob pdf zum Druck oder App am Smartphone – wird dabei nebensächlich. Möglich ist das durch die Verwendung einer Auszeichnungssprache. Die älteste Richtschnur dafür bietet die *Standard Generalized Markup Language* (SGML),

8 Leo SANTIFALLER, Urkundenforschung. Methoden, Ziele, Ergebnisse, Weimar 1937, S. 16f.

9 Peter HABER, Digital Past. Geschichtswissenschaft im digitalen Zeitalter, München 2011, S. 25.

10 Patrick SAHLE, Digitale Editionsformen. Zum Umgang mit der Überlieferung unter den Bedingungen des Medienwandels. Teil 2: Befunde, Theorie und Methodik (Schriften des Instituts für Dokumentologie und Editorik 8), Norderstedt 2013, S. 149.

die schon 1986 zur ISO-Norm wurde. Darauf baut die Internetsprache HTML genauso auf wie das Format XML zum Datenaustausch. Auf XML baut die *Text Encoding Initiative* (TEI) auf, die bereits 1987 entstand. Dabei steht die Textauszeichnung selbst im Mittelpunkt, weshalb sie sich in den Geisteswissenschaften besonders rasch durchgesetzt hat. 1994 wurden die ersten Richtlinien veröffentlicht, bei denen gleich mehrere Erfassungsebenen von Text und Sprache wie physische und logische Struktur oder Textauszeichnung berücksichtigt wurden[11]. Damit ist es einem Programm möglich, mit der Ambiguität von Wörtern umzugehen. Ein Computer kann einen Text erschließen, weiterverarbeiten und aufbereiten. Auch die Aufbewahrung elektronischer Daten lässt sich so leichter bewerkstelligen. TEI ist mittlerweile Standard in der professionellen geisteswissenschaftlichen Textarbeit, für den Spezialfall Urkunden hat sich 2004 die *Charters Encoding Initiative* gebildet.

Was bislang fehlt, ist eine einfach zugängliche und leicht einrichtbare Software zur Eingabe und Darstellung der Daten. Hier wurde und wird meist für jedes Projekt eine individuelle Lösung entwickelt. Dieser Weg verlangsamt die eigentliche Projektarbeit, erhöht die Kosten und verhindert allzu oft die Weiternutzung der geschaffenen Daten. Eine Open-Source-Software, die von vielen weiterentwickelt wird, ist hingegen geeigneter, die Daten dauerhaft benutzbar zu halten. Ein führendes Projekt in diesem Rahmen ist *MediaWiki* – die Software, mit der *Wikipedia* betrieben wird. Sie wird von zehntausenden Webseiten weltweit benutzt[12]. *MediaWiki* vereint zahlreiche Vorteile, die auch bei einer wissenschaftlichen Textedition zum Tragen kommen: kollaboratives Schreiben, Plattformunabhängigkeit und Langlebigkeit. Zudem ist die Software barrierefrei und unterstützt sämtliche Unicode-Zeichen sowie Permalinks. Das Wikipedia-Prinzip ist außerdem allgemein bekannt, Installation und Wartung erfordern nur geringe Informatikkenntnisse. Besonders hilfreich sind spezielle Erweiterungen der Software, die eine Erhöhung der Funktionalität gewährleisten. Eine – im Informatik-Jargon – mächtige Erweiterung ist *Semantic MediaWiki*. Sie baut auf dem Konzept des Semantic Web auf. Damit werden die sonst unstrukturierten und informellen Informationen auf Internetseiten zu strukturiertem und formalem Wissen, das elektronisch weiterverarbeitet werden kann[13]. Der nun in einer Wiki-Umgebung mögliche Einsatz von semantischen Annotationen kann nach den Richtlinien der TEI und CEI gestaltet werden.

---

11 Nancy M. IDE/C. Michael SPERBERG-MCQUEEN, The TEI: History, Goals, and Future, in: Computers and the Humanities 29 (1995) S. 5–15, hier S. 7.

12 https://www.mediawiki.org/wiki/MediaWiki/de.

13 Ansgar SCHERP/Gerd GRÖNER, Semantic Web, in: Handbuch der Künstlichen Intelligenz, ed. Günther GÖRZ/Ute SCHMID/Tanya BRAUN, Berlin/Boston [6]2021, S. 783–815, hier S. 783.

Die Aufbereitung von Quellen mittels Mediawiki und semantischen Tags bedeutet, den Inkunabelstatus von Online-Editionen zu überwinden und eine eigenständige Präsentationsform zu finden, die modernen Anforderungen eher gerecht wird als andere Veröffentlichungen.

3. Quellen zur Geschichte des Alpen-Adria-Raumes

Als praktisches Beispiel für die Umsetzung dieses Konzeptes dient nun die Internetseite *Quellen zur Geschichte des Alpen-Adria-Raumes*[14]. Diese Region umfasst die historischen Länder Kärnten, Steiermark, Krain, Friaul und Istrien. Trotz der heutigen politischen Aufteilung auf vier Staaten (Italien, Österreich, Slowenien, Kroatien), hat der Raum im Mittelalter eine stark verwobene Geschichte. Kirche und Adel waren über die heutigen Grenzen hinweg meist in allen Teilen vertreten und agierten als politische Akteure. Die Bevölkerung war durch verschiedene Ebenen weltlicher und kirchlicher Herrschaftsorganisation vielfältig miteinander verbunden. Der Name des Portals wurde bewusst offen gewählt und umfasst keine zeitliche Einschränkung. Vorerst sollte es um die mittelalterlichen Urkunden des Alpen-Adria-Raumes bis zum Tode Kaiser Maximilians I. im Jahr 1519 gehen. Ziel ist es, einerseits ältere, mittlerweile gemeinfreie Editionen und Regestenwerke einzuarbeiten, andererseits Originalurkunden neu zu edieren. In weiterer Folge sind narrative Quellen und Verwaltungsschriftgut angedacht. In diesem Portal werden ebenfalls die seit 1999 gesammelten Urkunden der Grafen von Cilli online in einem eigenen Bereich veröffentlicht[15]. Zudem könnte das Portal zu einem Geschichtslexikon der gesamten Region ausgebaut werden. Immerhin sind neben den Quellen auch weitere Daten wie Personen, Orte und Archive erfasst. Diese Seiten können beliebig ausgebaut und (z. B. mit verschiedenen Normdaten gefüllt) verknüpft werden.

Der technische Ausgangspunkt des Vorhabens liegt in einer Access-Datenbank, die 1999/2000 im Rahmen des FWF-Projektes *Die Quellen zur Geschichte der Grafen von Cilli (1341–1456)* entwickelt wurde[16]. Sie folgt im Aufbau den Richtlinien für die Regestierung von Urkunden des Arbeitskreises für Editionsgrundsätze von 1965[17]. Nach Projektende im Jahr 2005 wurde sie in die *Klagenfurter Urkunden-*

---

14 Quellen zur Geschichte des Alpen-Adria-Raumes, ed. Christian Domenig, www.quellen-alpen-adria.eu.

15 Christian Domenig, Cillier Urkunden, in: Quellen zur Geschichte des Alpen-Adria-Raumes, ed. Christian Domenig, http://www.quellen-alpen-adria.eu/quellen/index.php?title=Cillier_Urkunden.

16 Die Grafen von Cilli, wwwg.uni-klu.ac.at/cilli.

17 Arbeitskreis für Editionsgrundsätze, Richtlinien für die Regestierung von Urkunden, in: Blätter für deutsche Landesgeschichte 101 (1965) S. 1–7.

datenbank überführt[18]. Diese Internetseite erlebte ein typisches Schicksal: Die Programmierer konnten als Werkvertragsnehmer immer nur Teile ausgestalten und wechselten sich häufig ab, womit jeder viel Zeit für das Einarbeiten in die Vorleistungen aufwenden musste. Zudem standen strikte Vergaberichtlinien von Förderstellen einer stabilen Finanzierung entgegen. So konnte das Projekt nicht abgeschlossen werden. Der Umstieg auf eine selbst administrierbare Open-Source-Software war der logische nächste Schritt. Seit 2013 ist deshalb das Portal als Semantic-Wiki online.

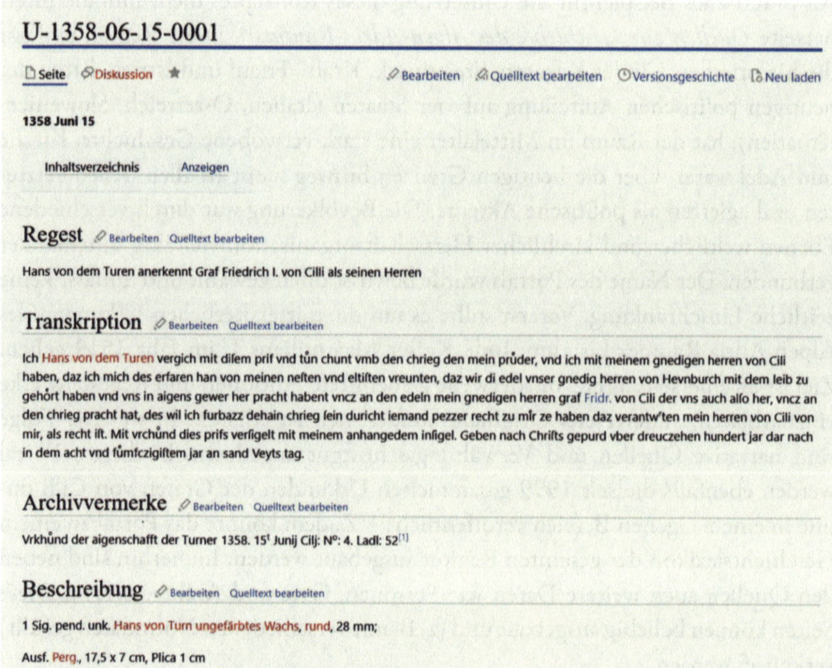

Abb. 1: Urkunde. © Christian Domenig 2023.

Das Äußere der Seite folgt einem Wikipedia-Layout [Abb. 1], der große Unterschied liegt im Quelltext. Schon in der Testphase stellte es sich heraus, dass der Einsatz von Tags der Textgestalt der Quellen wesentlich besser entgegenkommt als eine starre Datenbankstruktur. Gestaltung und Einsatz der Markierungen waren trotzdem eine Herausforderung, sie sind der Schlüssel zu jeder Informationsabfrage. Auch wenn mit TEI und CEI Tag-Bibliotheken vorliegen, eignen sie sich

18 Christian Domenig, Die Klagenfurter Urkundendatenbank, in: Digitale Diplomatik. Neue Technologien in der historischen Arbeit mit Urkunden, ed. Georg Vogeler (AfD Beiheft 12), Köln/Weimar/Wien 2009, S. 78–83 und S. 344f.

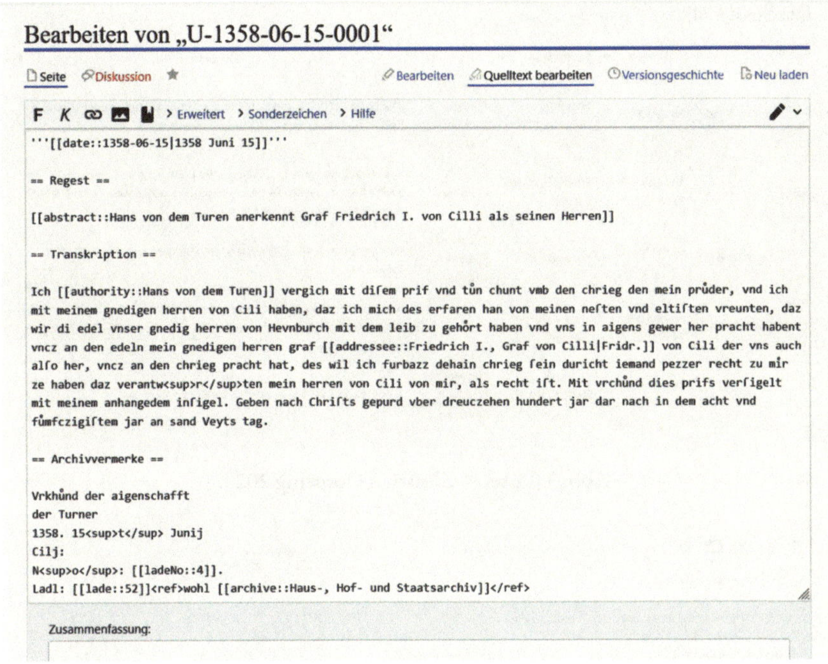

Abb. 2: Tags in der Urkunde. © Christian Domenig 2023.

nicht problemlos für jede Fragestellung. Sie sind formal-strukturell gehalten und passen für Standardangaben wie Datum, Ausstellungsort und Regest, aber sie erschließen den eigentlichen Inhalt eines Textes nur wenig [Abb. 2]. Gerade diese Informationen sind jedoch für ein geschichtswissenschaftliches Quellenportal von Relevanz. Ausgewertet werden sollte mit einer simplen, in die jeweilige Seite eingebauten Abfrage z. B. wer welche Titel und Funktionen in einem gewissen Zeitraum inne hat, welche Art von Gebäuden sich in einem Ort befinden, wo Mauten und Gerichte liegen oder welche Vorfahren und Nachkommen eine Person hat. Nur wenn die Tags richtig gesetzt sind, ist in weiterer Folge eine automatische Listener-stellung möglich. Die Abfrage könnte dann z. B. die Beschäftigten in einer Kanz-lei aufzählen oder welches liturgische Gerät in einer bestimmten Kirche zu einem Zeitpunkt vorhanden ist – also eine Amtsliste oder ein Inventar erstellen [Abb. 3]. Gerade diese Informationen sind ansonsten nur schwer zu generieren. Die Abfragesyntax ist dabei überraschend einfach anzuwenden [siehe Abb. 4].

Zu problematisieren ist die Tiefe der Erschließung. Eine große Anzahl von Tags zu setzen benötigt viel Zeit. Zudem hängt die Art der Tags von der jeweiligen Fragestellung ab. So benötigt eine regionalhistorische Auswertung andere Markierun-

Die Stadt Celje Bearbeiten Quelltext bearbeiten

	Datum	Person	Bauwerk	Regest
U-1364-06-24-0001	24 Juni 1364 JL	Weigand von Bleiburg Heinrich, Pfarrer von Cilli	Hospital Pfarrkirche Friedhof Spitalskapelle	Die Grafen Ulrich I. und Hermann I. von Cilli bestätigen dem Spital vor Cilli seinen Besitz und statten es mit Rechten aus.
U-1374-09-14-0001	14 September 1374 JL	Friedrich, Pfarrer von Cilli	Pfarrhaus	Graf Hermann von Cilli I. stiftet in der Pfarrkirche St. Daniel zu Cilli eine ewige Messe gemäß der letzten Verfügung seines Vaters Graf Friedrich I. und seines Bruders Graf Ulrich I.
U-1451-04-11-0001	11 April 1451 JL	Stadtrichter	Stadtmauer Zeughaus Rathaus	Graf Friedrich II. von Cilli gewährt den Bürgern und der Stadt Cilli Privilegien.
U-1458-02-27-0001	27 Februar 1458 JL	Gregor Dienstel, Vizedom		Kaiser Friedrich III. ordnet seinen Dienstleuten an, alle Einnahmen bei Friedrich Abprecher, Pfarrer von Tüffer, und Gregor Dienstel, Vizedom von Cilli, abzugeben.
U-1717-09-18-0001	18 September 1717	Stadtrichter	Stadtmauer Zeughaus Rathaus	Kaiser Karl VI. bestägigt der Stadt Cilli ihre Freiheiten

Abb. 3: Liste. © Christian Domenig 2023.

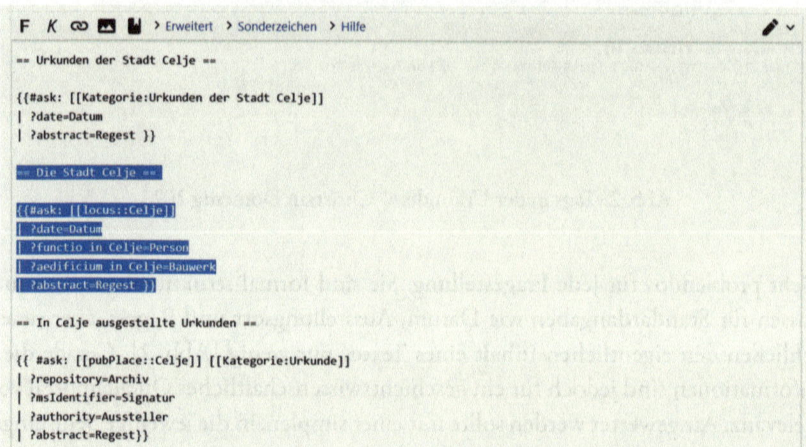


```
== Urkunden der Stadt Celje ==

{{#ask: [[Kategorie:Urkunden der Stadt Celje]]
| ?date=Datum
| ?abstract=Regest }}

== Die Stadt Celje ==

{{#ask: [[locus::Celje]]
| ?date=Datum
| ?functio in Celje=Person
| ?aedificium in Celje=Bauwerk
| ?abstract=Regest }}

== In Celje ausgestellte Urkunden ==

{{ #ask: [[pubPlace::Celje]] [[Kategorie:Urkunde]]
| ?repository=Archiv
| ?msIdentifier=Signatur
| ?authority=Aussteller
| ?abstract=Regest}}
```

Abb. 4: Abfrage. © Christian Domenig 2023.

gen als eine kunsthistorische. Für eine Ersterschließung müssen Personen und Orte genügen, eine Tiefenerschließung kann erst im zweiten Schritt erfolgen.

Noch umzusetzen ist eine Weiterverarbeitung der Daten. So sollen visuelle Informationen auf Karten zur Verfügung gestellt werden. Zur Georeferenzierung von Daten gibt es verschiedene Bestrebungen. Das Vorhaben wäre allerdings ein größeres Teilprojekt, das in Kooperation mit der historischen Geographie durchgeführt werden müsste. Ebenfalls noch nicht umgesetzt ist der Datenexport inklusive Ausgabe von Sammlungen als pdf. Allerdings gibt es hier gute Erweiterungen von MediaWiki, die z. B. die Erstellung von Büchern aus Wiki-Artikeln ermöglichen.

Nicht angedacht ist der Einbau von Abbildungen auf den Seiten. Abgesehen von Copyright-Fragen würde das die zur Verfügung stehende Festplattenkapazität des Servers schnell sprengen. Links zu entsprechenden Portalen sind ohnehin problemlos gesetzt, sie müssten allerdings dort stabil bleiben.

Ein großer Vorteil von Mediawiki ist, dass eine große Community am Gesamtprojekt und den Erweiterungen arbeitet. Die Installation der Software auf einem Server ist mit geringen Informatik-Kenntnissen möglich. Das spart Kosten, denn Aufgabe der Geschichtswissenschaft ist es, die Vergangenheit zu erforschen und nicht Informatik-Projekte zu finanzieren.

Der Einsatz von Open-Source-Software kommt außerdem den abnehmenden Finanzierungsmöglichkeiten von Quelleneditionen entgegen. Diese sind die eigentliche geschichtswissenschaftliche Grundlagenforschung und brauchen personelle und finanzielle Kontinuität über einen langen Zeitraum. Die Forschungsförderung ist hingegen risikoscheu geworden und unterstützt nur noch Projekte, deren Erfolg innerhalb eines kurzen Zeitrahmens garantiert ist. So geht trotz steigender Publikationszahlen die wissenschaftliche Innovation insgesamt zurück[19]. „Der inhärente Konservativismus mit Impact-Garantie dominiert gegenüber risikobehafteter, transformativer Forschung auf neuen Gebieten, auf denen zunächst nur eine kleine Community die Arbeiten zitieren kann“[20]. Quantität ist ausschlaggebender geworden als Qualität. Damit wird die Edition der so genannten „Privaturkunden“ zu einer Privatangelegenheit. Die Geschichtswissenschaft verliert angesichts moderner Fragestellungen zunehmend ihre Quellenbasis. Mittlerweile gibt es in der Forschung schon heftige Kritik daran, dass immer dieselben Quelleneditionen ausgewertet werden müssen. Innovative Fragestellungen, die aufgrund eines neuen Blickwinkels andere Quellen benötigen, haben es deshalb schwer. Keine Förderungen zu erhalten ist allerdings auch ein Vorteil. Die Forschenden sind weder von Vorgaben der Förderinstitutionen noch vom Wohlwollen der Gutachtenden abhängig. Gewisse Seilschaften sind ausgeschaltet. Forschende können autonom über das Projekt und dessen Ausgestaltung entscheiden und dieses Vorhaben auch problemlos in das nächste Dienstverhältnis mitnehmen.

Es bleibt zu hoffen, dass mit einem entsprechenden technischen Unterbau endlich ein neues, digitales Zeitalter der Quelleneditionen beginnt. Unentdecktes gibt es mehr als genug in Archiven und Bibliotheken.

---

19 Michael Park/Erin Leahey/Russell J. Funk, Papers and patents are becoming less disruptive over time, in: Nature 613 (2023) S. 138–144.

20 Wilhelm Krull, Die vermessene Universität. Ziel, Wunsch und Wirklichkeit (Wissenschaft – Transformation – Politik), Wien [2017], S. 27.

Editing Mediaeval Diplomatic Sources in Slovakia

Balázs Csiba

The focus of the DiDip 2022 conference was on the digital support in the analysis of historical documents, on digitisation projects and future trends of the digital diplomatics. This relatively new research field is still evolving and is in the process of exploring its potentials, therefore the printed editions cannot be ignored. This article attempts to provide a brief overview about the editions of mediaeval sources published by Slovak scholars and the digital databases of archival materials in Slovakia. It is important to keep in mind that the territory of today's Slovakia was part of the Kingdom of Hungary until 1918, hence sources about its history were and are still published by Hungarian researchers as well[1].

The beginnings (until 1918)

In comparison with the Hungarian or Czech historiography, the first editions by Slovak scholars were published somewhat belatedly, in the second half of the 19th century. These works were issued in various collective volumes, mainly in Letopis Matice slovenskej (1870–1874), Slovenský letopis (1876–1883) and Zborník Muzeálnej slovenskej spoločnosti. The editors of these editions were, above all, the most productive Slovak historian of the 19th century František Víťazoslav Sasinek, archivist in Kremnica Pavol Križko, and museologist (but primarily medical doctor) Ján Petrikovich. The aforementioned scholars did not have a profound method of editing and their works can be considered as rudimentary with national-apolo-

1 For a summary of the latest and ongoing Hungarian projects and source editions see Balázs Csiba, Publikovanie stredovekých listín v Maďarsku a súčasný stav maďarskej diplomatiky [Publishing Mediaeval Charters in Hungary and the Current State of the Diplomatics], in: Slovenská archivistika 51/1 (2021) p. 11–26.

getic character. The main priority was to draw the attention to the Slovak people and their historical role in the Kingdom of Hungary.

The first scholarly editions (1918–1945)

Only after the founding of the Comenius University in Bratislava (1921) were created the favourable conditions for the institutionalisation of editorial work. From the era of the First and Second Czechoslovak Republic (1918–1938, 1938–1939) and the Slovak State (1939–1945) must be mentioned mainly three scholars, who played a significant part on that matter. Mária Jeršová-Opočenská, to whom is often referred as the first erudite Slovak archivist, in 1927 edited charters related to the history of Slovak and Czech people from the Austrian Haus-, Hof- und Staatsarchiv[2]. A decade later, she published an inventory of sources from the archive of the Slovak National Museum in Martin[3]. Václav Chaloupecký is another important figure of Slovak historiography, who issued two source editions. In the first one, he edited an exceptionally rare and important source, the so-called Law Book of Žilina[4], and in his next book presented Czech/Slovak letters from the 15th century[5]. Alexander Húščava, who influenced the development of the Slovak diplomatics for more than 30 years, brought to light besides numerous articles in form of modern diplomatary the archive of the noble family from Okoličné, with which he set an example to be followed[6].

Real socialism (1949–1989)

The first scientific editions were products of uncoordinated efforts of individuals without any systematic planning or management. Nonetheless, after World War II the editorial work leant on the achievements of the previous era, but at the same time continued to develop. One of the most influential Slovak scholars and university teachers to date in the field of diplomatics, Darina Lehotská, wrote primarily text- and handbooks of diplomatics[7], but she also collaborated on the editing of

2 Slovenika uherských listin v domácím, dvorním a státním archivu ve Vídni v období let 1243-1490, ed. Mária Opočenská (1927).

3 Inventár archívu Slovenského národného muzea v Turčianskom sv. Martine, ed. Mária Opočenská-Jeršová (1938).

4 Kniha Žilinská, ed. Václav Chaloupecký (1934).

5 Středověké listy ze Slovenska. Sbírka listů a listin psaných jazykem národním, ed. Václav Chaloupecký (1937).

6 Archív zemianského rodu z Okoličného, ed. Alexander Húščava (1943).

7 In that matter, above all must be mentioned Darina Lehotská, Príručka diplomatiky, Bratisla-

the inventory of sources stored in the exceptionally rich archives of Bratislava[8]. Another important figure of the Slovak historiography and the Comenius University, Branislav Varsik published in 1956 letters written in Czech/Slovak language from the 15th and 16th centuries with detailed commentaries[9]. Three years later, Richard Marsina, the most significant and well-known Slovak mediaevalist, in collaboration with archivist Michal Kušík edited in two volumes the oldest urbaria from the territory of today's Slovakia[10].

In the 1970s and 1980s, the focus of the long-term publishing activities shifted to the Institute of History of the Slovak Academy of Sciences. After years of preparation and several partial studies, in these decades were issued two of the most important and known Slovak series to date, commonly referred to them as Slovak diplomatary[11] and Slovak regestary[12]. The idea of the former arose in the 1950s. The goal was to publish every historical document that has connection to the territory of Slovakia from the oldest to the extinction of the Árpád dynasty (1301). Marsina in the first two volumes edited full text sources to the year 1260. The editor of the Slovak regestary was Vincent Sedlák. The project aimed to publish documents at least to the beginning of the reign Sigismund's of Luxembourg (1387). From the era of the Angevin kings (1301–1387) have survived significantly more sources, therefore editing full texts did not seem a practical solution, so Sedlák had to choose a different approach – regests, however in the first volume he published the previously unedited charters in extenso. His abstracts are not actual regests in the strict sense of the word, but rather abbreviated texts of the documents. Although the said series are to date the most frequently cited source publications by Slovak scholars, unfortunately in the beginning of the 1990s, after two published volumes in each series was in the Institute of History determined, that editorial work is no longer the primary interest of the historical research. In the previous years, there were many rumors and plans among historians about the future of these projects, nevertheless the continuation is still uncertain.

va 1972; Id., Transkripčné pravidlá, odborná terminológia a ukážky latinských textov, Bratislava 1982; and Id., Základné diplomatické kategórie, Bratislava 1988.

8 Archív mesta Bratislavy. Inventár stredovekých listín, listov a iných príbuzných písomností, ed. Darina Lehotská et al. (1956). This volume publishes sources to 1500, the continuation with documents to 1563 prepared Vladimír Horváth: Achív mesta Bratislavy. Inventár listín a listov II, ed. Vladimír Horváth (1966).

9 Slovenské listy a listiny z XV. a XIV. storočia, ed. Branislav Varsik (1956).

10 Urbáre feudálnych panstiev na Slovensku I-II, ed. Richard Marsina/Michal Kušík (1959).

11 Codex diplomaticus et epistolaris Slovaciae I–II, ed. Richard Marsina (1971/1987).

12 Regesta diplomatica nec non epistolaria Slovaciae I–II, ed. Vincent Sedlák (1980/1987).

After the Velvet Revolution (1989)

After the cancellation of the Slovak diplomatary and regestary projects in the early 1990s, the editorial work was revived at two universities: University of Trnava and Comenius University in Bratislava. The employees of the former work on two main series. The Monumenta Vaticana Slovaciae project focuses on publishing sources from the Vatican archives concerning the territory of nowadays Slovakia. In its first volume, V. Sedlák edited the Slovak related parts of the register of the papal taxes collected in Hungary in 1332–1337[13]. The second volume, edited by Vladimír Rábik, publishes supplications registered in Registra supplicationum (Vatican Apostolic Archive) from 1342–1415[14]. At the moment, the third volume consists of two parts, in which Miloš Marek edited charters from the Vatican register issued during the pontificates of popes Clement VI and Innocent VI[15]. The so far last volume was edited by V. Rábik, who this time brought to light documents of the Libri formatarum[16].

The only editor in the other series of the University of Trnava, called *Fontes rerum Slovacarum*, is the mentioned M. Marek. In each of the three volumes, he edited archives of noble families, specifically the Motešický[17], Majtényi[18] and Očkaj[19] families. In context of the University, we must mention other editions as well. V. Rábik also published the mediaeval charters from the archive of the Society of St. Adalbert[20], but mainly editions of municipal books of Trnava (book of incomes of the city parish 1495[21], the oldest municipal book of the city 1394–1530[22], and

13 Rationes collectorum pontificiorum in annis 1332–1337, ed. Vincent Sedlák, Monumenta Vaticana Slovaciae I (2008).

14 Registra supplicationum ex actis pontificum Romanorum res gestas Slovacas illustrantia (1342–1415), ed. Vladimír Rábik, Monumenta Vaticana Slovaciae II (2009).

15 Registra Vaticana ex actis Innocentii papae VI. res gestas Slovaciae illustrantia 2 (1342–1352), 3 (1352–1362), ed. Miloš Marek, Monumenta Vaticana Slovaciae III (2010/2014).

16 Camera apostolica 1 (Libri formatarum 1425–1524), ed. Vladimír Rábik, Monumenta Vaticana Slovaciae IV (2015).

17 Archivum familiæ Motešický. Stredoveké listiny z archívu rodiny Motešickovcov, ed. Miloš Marek (2010).

18 Archivum familiæ Majténi. Stredoveké dejiny rodiny Majténiovcov a listiny z jej archívu, Kraków, ed. Miloš Marek (2013).

19 Archivum familiæ Očkaj. Stredoveké dejiny rodiny Očkajovcov a listiny z jej archívu, ed. Miloš Marek (2015).

20 Diplomatarium Sancto-Adalbertinum. Stredoveké listiny v Literárnom archíve Spolku sv. Vojtecha (1181) 1214–1543, ed. Vladimír Rábik (2008).

21 Mestská kniha príjmov trnavskej farnosti sv. Mikuláša z roku 1495, ed. Vladimír Rábik, Bibliotheca historica Tyrnaviensis 3 (2005).

22 Mestská kniha Trnavy (1392/1393) 1394–1530, ed. Vladimír Rábik, Bibliotheca historica Tyrnaviensis 3 (2006).

other sources[23]). Unfortunately, R. Marsina did not live to see the publication of his last edition, on which he collaborated with Jozef Meliš. The duo edited sources about the history of the Bishopric and Chapter of Nitra and the Zobor Cloister to years 1300[24].

The Comenius University also played and still plays a significant role in the field of source editing. Besides the already introduced editions, Leon Sokolovský published regests of charters from the archive of the town Rimavská Sobota[25]. Following the release of this volume and after a long wait, the editorial work was intensified at the end of 2010s. By the initiative of Juraj Šedivý, the Documenta Posoniensia series was established. Its primarily goal is to publish sources about the history of Bratislava and its region. The first volume was edited by Rastislav Luz, who published the earliest account registers of the Bratislava collegiate Chapter[26]. Balázs Csiba in collaboration with archivist Marián Babirát edited the medieval charters from the archive of the noble family Kondé[27]. The former later became the unofficial coordinator and main editor of the project. In the recent years, he mainly focuses on editing of the so-called authentic protocols of the Bratislava Chapter containing thousands of rough copies of charters, which in most cases did not survive in any other form. So far, he edited the second oldest protocol[28], and the other editions will follow in the near future. The editor plans to publish the whole mediaeval archive of the mentioned chapter, as well as the archive of Bratislava and noble families, which lived in the territory of the historic Bratislava County. Hoping that students will follow in his footsteps, at the Department of archive studies and museology was created a course about source editing.

Digitalisation

In the past decades, Slovakia experiences the 'digital turn' in the academic fields as well. Several institutions started the process of digitalisation and enabling elec-

23 Trnavas/Tyrnaus mittelalterliche Stadtbücher, ed. Vladimír Rábik, Bibliotheca historica Tyrnaviensis 7 (2013).

24 Codex diplomaticus episcopatus Nitriensis I (796) 880–(910), (1100)–1300, ed. Richard Marsina/Jozef Meliš 89 (2021).

25 Regestár stredovekých listín Štátneho okresného archívu v Rimavskej Sobote (1335–1524), ed. Leon Sokolovský (1985).

26 Účtovné registre Bratislavskej kapituly 1417–1529, ed. Rastislav Luz, Documenta Posoniensia I (2018).

27 Diplomatár šľachtického rodu Kondé, ed. Marián Babirát/Balázs Csiba, Documenta Posoniensia II (2019).

28 Autentický protokol Bratislavskej kapituly (1504–1513), ed. Balázs Csiba, Documenta Posoniensia IV (2021).

tronic access to sources. In publishing of the most valuable cimelia of the mediaeval book culture participated mainly the employees of the Slovak National Library (Ľ. Jankovič), Slovak Academy of Sciences (J. Sopko, E. Veselovská), Slovak National Gallery (D. Buran) and Comenius University (J. Šedivý)[29]. In the field of codicology the process began promisingly, however in the recent years the advancement shows signs of stagnations.

The digitalisation of diplomatic diplomatic sources started slightly slower. Back in 2005, digitalised copies – in contrast to standard photocopies – were considered as insufficiently durable and fit only for studying the sources[30]. In the same year, J. Šedivý, supported by the Austrian Science and Research Liaison Office, initiated a project called Virtuelles Haus der Geschichte Mitteleuropas (Virtual House of Central European History). Its goal was to establish an academic network of potential partners (archives from Slovakia and Austria with participation of partners from the Czech Republic) and organisation of two workshops for exchange of experience in the digitisation and publishing of historical sources. In the long-term perspective, the plan was to create a joint central European portal of digitalised mediaeval charters. In the opening workshop in Bratislava (June 2005), the representants of the leading digitalisation projects in the bordering countries (Z. Uhlíř – Manuscriptorium, S. Psohlavec – activities of digitisation-company AiP Beroun, K. J. Damjanov – activities of digitisation-company Bach, T. Aigner and K. Heinz – Monasterium.net, J. Šedivý – possible involvment of the Slovak institutions in a consortia like Monasterium.net) shared their experiences with the Slovak partakers. After the workshop in Bratislava, another two followed (Göttweig, Vienna), and a collective volume was issued too[31]. The spiritus movens of the project tried to integrate the Slovak archives in central European digital databases but could achieve only unsatisfying results due to lack of interest. Therefore, at the conference of Digital Diplomatics in München (February 2007), he had to point out the reluctance of his home country in comparison with other states (Hungary, Czech Republic)[32]. Several years later, after Jozef Hanus, the former director of the Archival Administration, acknowledged the importance of the digitalisation, approximately 35 000 mediaeval charters were digitalised from the Slovak archives. In the

29 Bratislavský antifonár II (Hanov kódex) [CD-ROM], ed. Július Sopko et al., Memoria Slovaciae. Medii Aevi Manuscripta (2000).

30 Jozef Hanus, Vyhotovovanie konzervačných kópií a študijných kópií archívnych dokumentov, in: Slovenská archivistika 40/2 (2005) p. 168–174.

31 More about the project and plans for digitisation see Juraj Šedivý, Digitalisierung der schriftlichen historischen Quellen in der Slowakei, in: Alte Archive – Neue Technologien, hg. von Thomas Aigner/Karin Winter, St.Pölten 2006, p. 257–265.

32 Juraj Šedivý, Archive in Tschechien, Slowakei und Ungarn – Perspektiven im „vernetzten Zeitalter", in: Digitale Diplomatik: neue Technologien in der historischen Arbeit mit Urkunden, hg. von Georg Vogeler (AfD Beiheft 12), Köln u. a. 2009, p. 172–187.

project called OPIS (Operačný program informatizácia spoločnosti – Operational Programme Informatisation of Society)[33] the Digital Archive portal was supposed to be created[34], however the realisation did not go as planned. In the present days, the portal offers only access to PDF inventories and few digitalised copies (mostly of maps).

Even though the state-wide portal does not function according to expectation, it is possible to search mediaeval charters from Slovak archives in other databases. The so-called Diplomatikai Fényképgyűjtemény (Diplomatic Photocopy Collection) database of the National Archives of Hungary, accessible online on the Hungaricana portal[35], contains archival materials from almost every Slovak institute. The disadvantage of this platform is that it offers only digital copies of black and white photos taken in the 1950s and 1960s. The majority of the fonds of the Slovak National Archives[36], and the whole collection of mediaeval charters and letters of the Bratislava City Archives is accessible on Monasterium.net[37]. The CRARC (crossborderarchives SK-AT) project provides digital copies of the official books of Bratislava and modern period documents from the archive of the Bratislava County[38]. None of these portals has full texts yet. In some cases, short regests are at disposal, but mostly only the basic information (mainly date and issuer).

The most complex and progressive Slovak portal is called PamMap.sk, also initiated by J. Šedivý[39]. So far, it includes – among other types of documents from different eras – over 4000 mediaeval charters with short regests, formal description, in some case even transcription, and in the future, translations will be added too. The portal enables to tag localities, persons, themes, dates, archives, languages, and many other features making the search – possible in four (Slovak, English, German, Hungarian) languages – more effective and comfortable[40]. Most of the documents are from the archives of two cities (Bratislava and Košice), but thanks to the arrangement made in 2022 with the Section of Archives and Registry (Odbor archívov a registratúry) of the Ministry of Interior, charters are going to be added from other state archives as well. It is also in plan to find a solution for implementation of commentaries on the transcribed texts.

---

33 https://www.opis.gov.sk/documents-opis/index.html?csrt=1630600441590799972

34 https://portal.minv.sk/wps/wcm/connect/sk/site/main/zivotne-situacie/Elektronicky-archiv-Slovenska/

35 https://archives.hungaricana.hu/en/charters

36 https://www.monasterium.net/mom/SK-SNA/archive

37 https://www.monasterium.net/mom/SK-AMB/archive

38 https://www.crarc.findbuch.net/php/main.php

39 The basic information about the project see Juraj Šedivý, Digitale Erschließung der (kurialen) Quellen in der Slowakei, in: Reti medievali rivista 20/1 (2019) p. 53–66 [online].

40 https://www.pammap.sk/

IV. Charters and Archives

The *Digitale Charterbank Nederland*

A digital portal to more than 200.000 charters in Dutch archives[1]

Jan Burgers, Rik Hoekstra

In medieval and early modern times, hundreds of thousands of charters have been issued on the territory of the current Netherlands. An estimated 220,000 original charters have survived in Dutch archives, with a comparable number only in copies.

Of course, this corpus is an important source for historians. Since the seventeenth century, editions with exclusively charters have been issued. The oldest editions are inadequate by current criteria – they are methodologically outdated and selected by antiquated criteria[2]. In the twentieth century, a number of mostly regional charter books have been issued that were edited conform the established diplomatic method[3]. They all run until circa the year 1300. After that, too many

1 This article is based on the paper 'Digitale Charterbank Nederland (DCN): a digital portal to 200.000 charters in Dutch archives', given by the authors on September 28, 2022, at the Digital Diplomatics Conference in Graz, which paper in its turn was based on: Jan BURGERS/Rik HOEKSTRA, De Digitale Charterbank Nederland. Grootschalige digitale bronontsluiting en het historische onderzoek, in: BMGN – Low Countries Historical Review 136/3 (2021) p. 92–119; https://doi.org/10.51769/bmgn-lchr.6997.

2 Some examples, still useful as they contain unpublished charters from the late Middle Ages and beyond, are Frans VAN MIERIS, Groot charterboek der graaven van Holland ..., 4 vols., Leiden 1754–1756; Georg Frederik THOE SCHWARTZENBERG EN HOHENLANSBERG, Groot placaat en charterboek van Vriesland, 6 vols., Leeuwarden 1768–1793; Pieter BONDAM, Charterboek der hertogen van Gelderland en graaven van Zutphen [...], 4 vols., Utrecht 1783–1809.

3 The most important are Samuel MULLER/Arie Cornelis BOUMAN/Klaas HEERINGA/Frans KETNER, Oorkondenboek van het Sticht Utrecht tot 1301, 5 vols., Utrecht 1920-1959; Anton Carl Frederik KOCH/Jaap Gerardus KRUISHEER/Everardus Cornelis DIJKHOF, Oorkondenboek van Holland en Zeeland tot 1299, 's-Gravenhage etc. 1970-2005; Ed HARENBERG/Menno Sander POLAK/Everardus Cornelis DIJKHOF, Oorkondenboek van Gelre en Zutphen tot 1326, 's-Gravenhage 1980–2003; Hugo P.H. CAMPS/Martien DILLO/Geertrui A.M. VAN SYNGHEL, Oorkondenboek van Noord-Brabant tot 1312, 2 vols. in 4 books, 's-Gravenhage etc. 1979-2000, continued as Geertrui A.M. VAN SYNGHEL, Het Digitaal Oorkondenboek Noord-Brabant: http://www.donb.nl.

charters were issued for the meticulous but time-consuming editing method. Therefore, later documents are only accessible partially and deficiently in the old editions mentioned above; charters after 1500 are almost completely terra incognita.

One of the core tasks of the Huygens Institute in Amsterdam is to edit and publish sources for Dutch history, and therefore many of the twentieth-century charter books were published under its auspices. At the turn of the last century, the institute began to consider publishing Dutch charters from after 1300. From the start, it was obvious that these could only be made accessible with the help of the new computerized methods if only because of their sheer numbers. The intent was to concentrate, at least initially, on charters that survived in their original form, as these are easy to recognize and localize in the archives.

In 2012, a first plan was made to make all original charters in Dutch archives accessible in a central portal, a Digitale Charterbank Nederland (DCN). With the example of Monasterium in mind, the possibility was investigated to scan all documents, provide them with essential metadata and collect these into a central, online accessible database, a charter portal. In spite of initial support from the Dutch archivists, the plan proved too ambitious because of financial reasons and shifting priorities. Therefore, in 2016 a new plan for the realization of DCN was conceived. The idea was not, like before, to take as a point of departure the actual charters as they are held in the archives, but to concentrate on their descriptions in the archival inventories. The origin of many of these texts is in the inventories in print or in typescript, that have been produced in the twentieth century by archivists, according to a fixed system that had been devised around 1900[4]. During digitisation, these inventories were often adapted to the new medium, but their content was hardly ever revised. In this fixed pattern, the materiality of the charters is described with archival or diplomatic terms like 'charter', 'akte', 'transfix', 'vidimus', etcetera. These terms could be used to select the relevant items from the already digitized and online accessible inventories, and collect them in a database, which would be made available for researchers in an internet portal.

A pilot project was initiated together with the National Archives in The Hague, that holds many relevant archival funds. At the Huygens Institute, data were extracted from the relevant archive inventories and made accessible in an application. The first results were encouraging and we demonstrated an initial version in December 2017 at a colloquium in the Tilburg Archive[5]. Still, progress was slow, as harvesting and data alignment proved to need more manual work than the institute could provide. Moreover, the data of many archives were not readily available, and

4 See: Normblad archiefinventaris, published by Nationaal Archief (2019).

5 https://www.regionaalarchieftilburg.nl/home/blog-detail/algemeen/2017/11/21/symposium-'van-scriptorium-naar-charterbank.-trends-in-het-ontsluiten-van-oorkonden'.

reaching an agreement with around a hundred institutions would not only be very time consuming, but would also yield mainly snapshots that are hard to update.

Two fortunate factors made it possible to realize the plan after all. First, the Dutch Organisation of Scientific Research (NWO) provided a modest fund of 15.000 euros. This enabled us to recruit an assistant who for a year carried out many of the organizing and coordinating activities. Even more important was the cooperation with an external partner, the firm of De Ree in Groningen[6]. This company provides as a commercial service the archive inventory management of three quarters of the Dutch archival institutions, large provincial and regional archives as well as tiny municipal ones. De Ree's director, Gerard Mulder, agreed to spend considerable time and money to realize DCN, motivated by the idea that this portal would serve to make the archives of his clients accessible for a larger audience.

The design of the plan remained the same – harvesting relevant data from digital archival inventories – but the coverage of De Ree's databases made it possible to size this up considerably and at a great speed. The company manages the access to the inventories of the participating institutions in its own system, called MAIS-Flexis, in which the archival data conform to a fixed scheme. The collected descriptions are searchable in MAIS-(M)DWS that is used, among other, for the user application Archieven.nl. From this infrastructure, De Ree could adapt a user application for charters [Fig. 1]. The resulting application DCN is made accessible through a portal of the Huygens Institute.

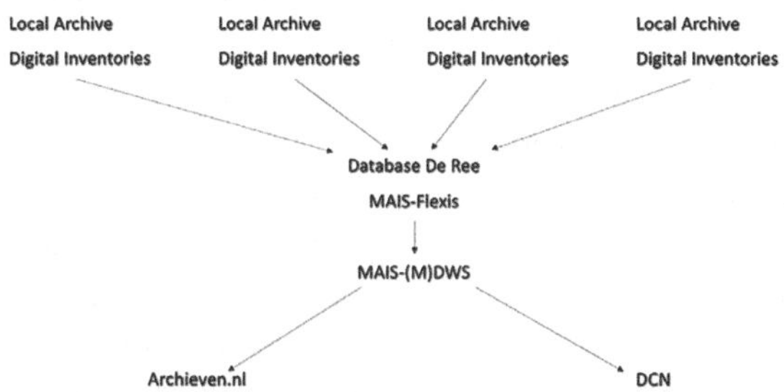

Fig. 1: The structure of the data flow from the archives via De Ree to DCN.

Within a short time, a search portal had been effectuated, containing the data of many thousands of original charters from the holdings of the archives participating with De Ree. They had to be supplemented with the archives with a different inventory management provider. These included some sizable and important archives, such as that of the city of Amsterdam, but with the cooperation of the archivists, our assistant was able to finish much of this work within the year 2018. On 25 Jan-

6 https://www.de-ree.nl.

uary, 2019, DCN was presented at a colloquium in the Utrecht Archives, an event that made the national television news.

DCN's goal is to make all surviving original charters accessible, including archive inventories that are not in MAIS-Flexis[7]. These 'external' charters currently represent about twenty percent of the total number of documents in DCN. In practice, a lot of project work was spent on adding those external inventories, since the information they contained showed quite a bit of variation. For various reasons, some archival institutions are still missing, but the vast majority of Dutch charters can now be found via DCN[8]. In the case of the MAIS-Flexis archives, all additions and improvements made to them are immediately visible in DCN; it is a dynamic collection. Non-MAIS archives have to be re-harvested periodically, either by the institutions themselves or the Huygens Institute[9]. It is encouraging that institutions that are not yet included in DCN often do have the intention to join. In August 2022 this resulted in the insertion of 5,358 charters that were provided by the Delft city archives, and in January 2023 the city archives of 's-Hertogenbosch submitted the data of their 6.997 charters.

The result is the DCN portal, that at the moment of writing contains 211,700 searchable charters from 4,234 archival funds in 95 institutions, but as this is a dynamic database, the numbers are subject to change[10]. Users can search full-text in the data extracted from the inventories. In addition, they have the option of selecting per year or per period, as well as per archival institution or archival fund. Within the inventories, the descriptions of the individual charters are in most cases quite brief, often limited to the date of issue and a short summary of the contents of the document. With a minority of the charters, a somewhat more detailed summary (a 'regest') is also included; in even fewer cases complete transcripts are available. Full-text search gives in many cases basic information about a charter, such as the archival location and signature and data from its content: the date, persons involved, nature of the legal act, place of issue and data about the seals. Especially welcome for the users are the scans that in a significant minority of cases have been linked to the inventories, which pictures are accessible from the search results. Currently, DCN contains 42.822 charters (20 percent) that have one or more images attached, while for other archives, especially the non-MAIS ones, users can click through to images on the websites of those institutions.

7 Obviously DCN does not yet contain currently uninventarised charters; from consults with archivists, it appears this occurs frequently.

8 The most important missing archives are currently Regional archive Midden-Holland (Gouda), the Koninklijk Huisarchief and some library collections that contain charters.

9 The external archive inventories are delivered in EAD, the standard XML archive description format, and imported into the database. These inventories are exclusively visible in the DCN environment. For ead, see: https://www.loc.gov/ead.

10 For this article, data were extracted from DCN in the period January 24-February 3, 2023.

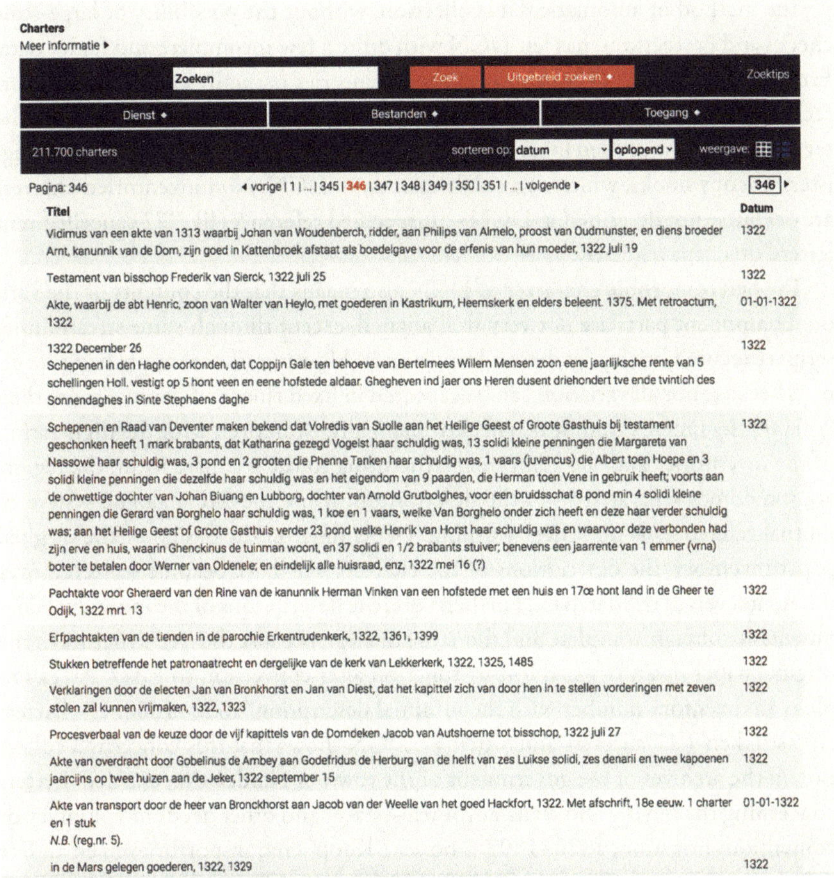

Fig. 2: Screen shot of the DCN public portal. With the button 'Dienst', the user can select an archival institution, with 'Toegang' an archival fund, and with 'Bestanden' whether all records will be found or only those with scans attached. Under 'Uitgebreid zoeken' are more search options, including one for a certain year or period.

All in all, DCN offers a fairly restricted search option. On the other hand, a search always returns data from the underlying tree structure of the inventory, as well as from the data added by the archives, such as date, year or keywords. For example, a search for the term 'hanze' (Hansa) gives 59 results; in 37 cases the word 'hanze' does not appear in the description text, but it was found by the system elsewhere in the data of the inventory[11].

11 One example: a charter from the Streekarchivariaat Noordwest-Veluwe, '5001 Archief Stadsbestuur Harderwijk (1190) 1231-1813, inv.nr. 1154', shows in DCN only the description 'Volmacht van burgers van Lubeck en Thoron, 1307 Augustus 7' ('Authorization by the citizens

The method of automatic data collection, without the possibility of large-scale checks and corrections, has left DCN with quite a few incomplete and faulty data. Errors or incomplete information in the inventories naturally enter DCN uncorrected. There are for instance references to non-charter documents because the term 'oorkonde' was used in an inventory while referring to texts in cartularies, registers or copy books, which as a result turn up in DCN. Non-inventoried charters are of course not described in DCN – unspecified references like '72 cancelled rent letters' do occur regularly.

The heteromorphic character of DCN also means that the contents of the various component parts are not very well aligned, except through some streamlining scripts executed by the database administrator. However, those scripts had side effects because not all variation can be captured in fixed rules and because more than 200,000 documents cannot be checked manually. Moreover, with the digitization of the inventories and the additional structuring to the database form, the regests are sometimes separated from the descriptions, while the old analogue system of mutual references is no longer working. Depending on the design of the original paper inventory, the descriptions of the charters may have become scattered over different levels in the database. Furthermore, the descriptions of the individual documents are often incomplete and therefore unclear, because the tree structure of the original paper inventory had lost its function after conversion to EAD. An example is an inventory number with the minimal description '1320–1608. 17 charters en 5 stukken' ('17 charters and 5 items'). DCN shows that this concerns a collection in the archives of the government of the town of Harderwijk, entitled 'Letters concerning the buying and transfer (of real-estate) and other deeds of voluntary or contentious litigation, 1320–1807. 2 boxes' ('Koop- en transportbrieven en andere voluntaire en contentieuze acten, 1320–1807. 2 doozen'). On the site of this archival institution, one can then click through to the regests of the charters concerned, which can be found in a separate section of the analogue inventory, but which are unfortunately not linked to the inventory number in the digital inventory and are therefore not searchable in DCN[12]. In the non-MAIS-Flexis archives, extra information is sometimes available, including scans of charters, via a link to the website of the institution.

Especially serious obstacles when searching the database are the missing, incomplete and faulty dates. For example, the charter bank lists 3,962 charters between 1000 and 1300, but closer inspection reveals here hundreds of incorrectly dated

---

of Lübeck and Toruń/Thorn'. Only after 'expanding' this hit one sees the structure of the inventory, in which this item is classified under '1.2.19. Hanzezaken' ('Hanseatic matters'), as well as a separate field 'Thema trefwoorden: Hanze' ('Theme keywords: Hanze').

12 For example, this leads to regest no. 1025, the sale of a forty-eighth part of the 'Coeberensteghe' in Voorthuizen, 1562.

charters which are in fact from a later period. Such errors can often be traced back to wrong assumptions when entering the data, either manually by an archivist or automatically by the DCN system. With uncertain or unknown dates, DCN sometimes omits or garbles the reconstructed date from the inventory (often put between square brackets). Undated or incorrectly dated charters are given an automatically generated 'year' by the system, often based on a four-digit number found in the relevant description, such as an amount of money, the size of a land, an inventory or regest number, or a year from the name of the archive inventory[13]. When searching DCN, this dating problem can be partly overcome by avoiding 'round' numbers such as 1200 or 1300, which occur relatively often in functions other than a year. Still, if we select the charters of the thirteenth century (using the period 1201–1299), the first two hundred documents give just 86 'good' results (including some later vidimuses of thirteenth-century charters). It is especially with the older charters, from before 1300, that users should be aware of this dating problem; we have the impression that the dates in DCN are much better in later periods. Random samples in charters from the period 1550–1565 show that about ten percent of the documents do not date from these years. Fortunately, upon inspection of the descriptions of the individual documents in DCN, the correct dating is almost always immediately apparent from the text of the inventory.

All these peculiarities do not easily lead to problems in the presentation of a single archive inventory in serial form, but in DCN's collective presentation all individual defects cumulate and are therefore magnified. Although the biggest flaws in the project have been solved, the many remaining errors must be corrected by the individual archival institutions who have the knowledge – and, as owners of the data, the authority – to change the content of their inventories. Some institutions are currently correcting their data for DCN, but due to a lack of time and manpower, these improvements are not always implemented swiftly. As mentioned, the changes that actually have been made are immediately visible in DCN's dynamic system[14]. Because of this, and as more and more scans of the charters are added, the database will keep improving over time[15].

13 Such as is the case with the 151 undated charters in Het Utrechts Archief, Archief van de Dom te Utrecht, 1220-1811, which were automatically assigned the date '01-01-1220' by the DCN system.

14 This does not apply to the aforementioned archival institutions that do not work in MAIS-Flexis; their changes must be submitted via EADs and then uploaded into DCN.

15 For an example of such a correction recently made by an archival institution, see below, footnote 18.

A first overview of the contents of DCN

The following overview of the content is inevitably exploratory in nature, in which we try to indicate as transparently as possible what we found with our searches. As with all large databases, it is not clear in advance exactly what DCN contains, and with such a large corpus it is not possible to understand it intuitively, just by leafing through or searching it randomly[16]. A system such as DCN also has its specific problems, which the more experienced researcher can sometimes overcome with a smart search strategy.

A quantitative analysis shows that a total of 95 archival institutions are represented in DCN. Het Utrechts Archief provides the most charters with 28,495 documents (15.5 percent of the total number), followed by Gelders Archief (20,758 charters), Groninger Archieven (17,617), Nationaal Archief (15,367) and Brabants Historisch Informatie Centrum (14,834). Table 1 summarizes the distribution of charters across the various institutions.

Table 1: Overview of the distribution of charters over different archival institutions.

Number of charters	Number of institutions	Total number of charters	Percentage
5000–28495	13	155,334	73.4
1000–5000	19	43,002	20.3
500–1000	12	8,126	3.8
100–500	17	4,293	2
0–100	34	951	0.4

The institutions each house many archival funds with varying numbers of charters. There are currently 4,234 funds in total, in which numbers of charters range from one to several thousand (see table 2 for the breakdown). The six largest funds are the Charter collection Erfgoed 's-Hertogenbosch (6,997 charters), the Charter collection Stadsarchief Delft (5,358) (both in fact compositions of various local funds), Order of the German Knights, Balije van Utrecht (4,409), the Chapter of Saint Mary in Utrecht (3,729 charters), the Dom chapter in Utrecht (2,485) and

16 Virtually none of the databases that are composed of various sub-databases – such as umbrella inventories (many institution-wide inventories of large institutions, the image and sound database) or library catalogues (NCC, WorldCat) – make it clear that the metadata is of uneven composition and quality. An exception to this is the media suite (https://mediasuite.clariah.nl) and in particular the 'collection inspector' of the Nederlands Instituut voor Beeld en Geluid. See also about this: Marijn Koolen/Jasmijn van Gorp/Jacco van Ossenbruggen, Toward a model for digital tool criticism. Reflection as integrative practice, in: Digital Scholarship in the Humanities 34/2 (2019) p. 368–385; https://doi.org/10.1093/llc/fqy048.

the city government of Zwolle (2,477)[17]. There are mainly many small funds: about half have five or fewer charters, and of those about a thousand have only one charter.

Table 2: Overview of archival funds.

Number of charters	Number of funds	Total number of charters	Percentage
1000–6997	36	69,755	33
500–1000	45	29,757	14.1
200–500	132	40,444	19.1
100–200	158	22,552	10.7
20–100	748	33,660	15.9
10–20	496	7,486	3.5
5–10	483	3,648	1.7
0–5	2129	4,371	2.1

The identity of the creators of these archival funds concerns in 802 cases a 'gemeente', a term covering both a town or village government and an ecclesiastical congregation – and a parish in another 143 cases. In addition, there are 777 archives with the word 'family' and 249 with the word 'house'. In the list of the most general terms with regard to the funds we also find 'monastery' (120), 'lordship' (173) and 'schepenbank' (alderman's court) (66).

Even a first glance at DCN gives interesting observations about the use of Dutch charters through the ages. In Graph. 1 is an overview of the number of charters per year; Table 3 gives the numbers broken down per century. It is clear that 'Dutch' charters have only been handed down in considerable numbers from the mid-thirteenth century onward[18]. Some unlikely peaks of more than 100 charters per year before 1250 can be attributed to the dating errors just mentioned. After 1300 the number rises steeply, until the highest point is reached in the mid-sixteenth century. From the fifteenth century to the third quarter of the seventeenth century there are often more than 1,000 charters per year. Charters are certainly not an

17 As well as the Archives of the Heilige Geesttafels, Huisarmen, Gast- en Godshuizen (5,755 charters) and the Archive of the Commissie van Openbare Ondrestand (3,174), both of the city archives of Mechelen, which Belgian institution is included in DCN for reasons that are not wholly clear.

18 In DCN there are only a few charters dated before the year 1000; theRegionaal Historisch Centrum Limburg has a few tenth-century charters, the oldest from 950 (01.187A Vrije Rijksheerlijkheid Thorn, 10e eeuw-1550, voorlopig inv.nr. 1). In DCN this document was first dated '1500', after the year in the title of the archival fund, but the institution has since corrected this to '01-10-9500'.

exclusively medieval phenomenon: they remained common throughout the entire Ancien Régime. Institutional changes around 1800 abruptly terminated the use of the charter as an administrative document[19]. Besides, we see a remarkable dip in the third quarter of the sixteenth century, which might be ascribed to the Dutch Revolt, an upheaval that must have reduced administrative activities. However, we cannot give a ready explanation for the clear decrease of charter numbers around the turn of the sixteenth century.

Graph 1: Overview of the number of charters per year, 1000–1850.

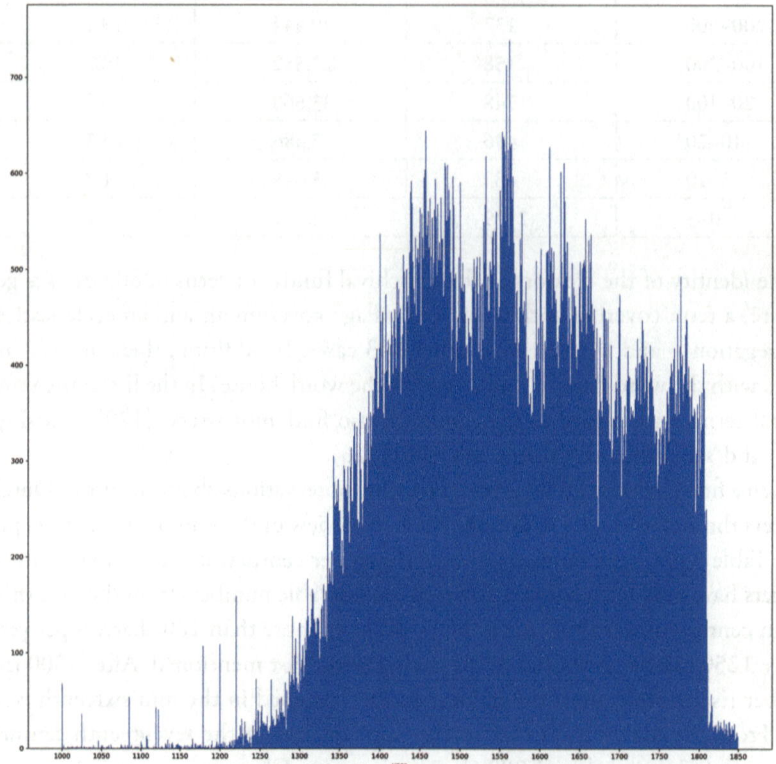

Table 3. Number of charters per century.

PERIOD	NUMBER OF CHARTERS
1001–1100	194
1101–1200	524
1201–1300	3,176

19 The charters after 1800 mostly concern university doctoral degrees.

1301–1400	23,334
1401–1500	49,350
1501–1600	48,625
1601–1700	44,297
1701–1800	36,615

Examples of possibilities for historical research in DCN

DCN offers the researcher many opportunities for historical research, in which old and new questions can be answered. As mentioned, the DCN search possibilities are limited to a full-text search of the charter descriptions and the date, supplemented by an option to select a year or period. However, as mentioned before, search actions also return data from the underlying inventory tree structure, including additional data that were added by the archives, such as date, year or a subject term.

Together with the selection of a time period, specific data can be collected about a person or a place. For example, a search for the high nobleman Jan van Arkel in the fifteenth century (search terms 'Jan', 'Arkel', and the period 1401–1501) produces 218 results. A big advantage is that DCN also finds results in unexpected archives that probably would not have been included in a traditional pre-digital search. In this case, for example, a charter from the French king in the city archives of Kampen, about robberies committed by Jan van Arkel[20].

Another example: the noble Van Brederode family played a prominent role in Holland from the thirteenth to the seventeenth century. Searching on this name yields 504 results, and another 23 hits on the archaic spellings 'Brederoede' and 'Bredero', all from the period 1248–1798. Some of the hits relate not so much to the family as to the toponym of the same name, but most indeed concern various family members, or at least persons with the surname 'van Brederode'. In DCN it is then possible to see at a glance in which archival institutions the found documents are stored. It is immediately clear that members of this Dutch family have left archives all over the country. The charters were found in no fewer than 28 institutions, with most of the documents in the Nationaal Archief (154 stuks), Het Utrechts Archief (154), Noord-Hollands Archief (63), Gelders Archief (46) and Regionaal Archief Zuid-Utrecht (Wijk bij Duurstede, 26). Without DCN, the researcher would probably have started looking there anyway, but he or she might not have come across the unique documents in the archives in Groningen, Leeuwarden, Hoorn, Wassenaar, Woerden, The Hague (Haags Gemeentearchief), Vlaardingen, Middelharnis,

20 Stadsarchief Kampen, 00001 Stadsbestuur van Kampen, 1251-1813, inv.nr. 2075. d.d. 27 August 1404.

Middelburg, Tilburg, Tiel, Harderwijk, Delden and Maastricht[21]. The search can of course also be focused on a specific person, for example on Jan van Brederode (1390–1415), the nobleman to whom Frits van Oostrom recently devoted a book. The combination of 'Jan' and 'Brederode' in the search screen yields 99 results, but the majority of these do not relate to a single person Jan van Brederode (several hits deal with *Jan* van Blois and Reinoud van *Brederode*, for example). However, it is also possible to search directly for "Jan van Brederode" (with double quotation marks), and we find two charters that relate to this person. One of those two pieces is indeed mentioned in Van Oostrom's study, but the other is missing[22].

Similarly, one can of course look at a particular place. To take a random example: Wijchen, formerly a small village southwest of Nijmegen. Searching on that toponym, and of course on historical variants such as 'Wychen', 'Wichen', 'Wijchgen' etcetera, yields 88 hits, from the period 1369–1724. Unsurprisingly, most finds come from Gelders Archief and Regionaal Archief Nijmegen, but incidental cases are found far away, from the Nationaal Archief (the Hague) to Regionaal Historisch Centrum Limburg (Maastricht). We find various persons called 'van Wijchen', as well as mentions of the local church (in 1491; the parish is mentioned in 1369), a house 'de Liliart', and various names of neighborhoods, streets and fields.

Toponymic research in DCN yields a lot, of course especially in a larger town. When we combine the place name Leiden with the words 'straat', 'steeg', 'gracht', 'brug', 'poort' (also with an asterisk for any prefixes: '*straat', '*steeg', et cetera), we arrive at 1541 results. This still needs serious weeding, as there are many duplicats and street names outside Leiden also occur occasionally. Nevertheless, these results give the researcher a head start. A nice addition in this context is research into the distribution of a specific street name. A 'Peperstraat' is found in fifteen cities, towns and villages (141 hits, from the period 1311–1867), while Overschie, Vlaardingen

21 Or across archival institutions with a handful of hits: Deventer (11 hits), Amsterdam (10), Rotterdam (9), Amersfoort (Eemland) (8), Dordrecht (7), Den Bosch BHIC (8), Alkmaar (4), Zwolle (3) and Leiden (2). Even within an archival institution, the documents are not always to be found in the obvious funds. In the National Archives, the Brederode charters are spread over two dozen archival funds, most of them with only one, two or three relevant documents.

22 Frits van Oostrom, Nobel streven. Het onwaarschijnlijke maar waargebeurde verhaal van ridder Jan van Brederode, Amsterdam 2017. The missing charter concerns Regionaal Archief Dordrecht, Gemeente Hardinxveld (648), inv.nr. 96: 'Oktrooi door Johanna van Brabant tot verlening van tolvrijdom binnen Brabant aan Jan van Brederode, heer van Hardinxveld en aan de inwoners van Hardinxveld, 1400' ('Patent by [duchess] Johanna van Brabant granting exemption from tolls within Brabant to Jan van Brederode, lord of Hardinxveld and to the inhabitants of Hardinxveld, 1400'). This document would have fit into Van Oostrom's story, not only because it sheds light on Brederode's interest in the economic well-being of his subjects, but also because he had a serious clash with the duchess at the end of 1400 over his illegal mint in Waalwijk (o.c., 101-103). This charter is also missing in the exhaustive study by Jan H. Verhoog, Onvoltooide roem. De Heeren van Brederode in de Middeleeuwen; geschiedenis van een riddergeslacht, 1203-1473, Bergen 1997.

and Delft have a 'Pepersteeg' (14 hits, mostly from the eighteenth century) and Nijmegen a 'Pepergas' (7 hits, mostly from the sixteenth century)[23].

Especially interesting for professional researchers are the possibilities DCN offers for analyzing developments over a long time period. One can answer all kinds of research questions with the help of a clever choice of one or more keywords. Thus, the digital data make it possible to provide a first global sketch of possible chronological shifts, the nature of legal acts and distributions between the town and the countryside. Some examples have been created by taking a systematic sample that involved the charters of an entire year every ten years from 1005 to 1850. A frequency distribution has been made of the words from the descriptions, and on the basis of this a number of collective terms have been composed with related words. Finally, the frequency development over time was analysed[24].

The result is plotted in eight graphs, showing the cumulative numbers per half century. The scale of the quantities has been kept constant for comparability. As expected, the most common are archival terms assigned by the archivist in the descriptions, such as 'charter(s)' and 'akte' (meaning 'deed')[25]. These do not even fit the standard scale and recur over the entire period. Something similar applies to author names and book titles that refer to existing charter editions.

An analysis of more substantive terms must necessarily remain superficial, but a few examples are outlined below. 'Land' (land, field) and related terms are always common. 'Kerk' (church) and related terms such as 'bisschop' (bishop), 'abt' (abbot), and 'klooster' (monastery) are especially common until the sixteenth century, much less afterwards. Terms related to the feudal system occur regularly throughout the eight centuries. Although 'Leen' (fief, loan) returns only 2,584 results, '*leen' and 'leen*' (which yield, for instance, *erfleen, dienstleen, mansleen, leenbrief, leenman* and *leenhulde* – but also *alleen* ('alone') and the placename *Geleen*) yield another 15,353 and 11,660 hits respectively. The terms 'pacht' ('lease') and 'rente ('rent') (and related ones) are more common in the medieval period, while 'koop' ('sale') is clearly most commonly found in the early modern period. We see terms around the concept of 'benoeming' ('appointment') more and more as time goes on[26].

---

23 With such results it is regularly necessary to click through in DCN to deeper levels of access or to images.

24 An export of search results from DCN is not possible directly, but it can be done by means of so-called 'web scraping'. The method used is documented separately for those interested with programming knowledge (https://github.com/HoekR/charterbank_analysis).

25 Terms are matched with regular expression patterns 'chart.*', '^a[ck]+te.*', '^nummer', '\b(nr)', 'inventarisn(umme)?r'.

26 *Leen* was searched by using the regular expression patterns '*leen' and 'leen*', which resulted in the following list of terms: 'beleend', 'beleening', 'beleent', 'borgleen', 'leen', 'leen-', 'leen-en', 'leenakte', 'leenbrief', 'leendert', 'leengoed', 'leengoederen', 'leenhof', 'leenhulde', 'leenkamer', 'leenmannen', 'leenroerig', 'leenten', 'leenten:1/4', 'leentyen', 'ringie-leen', 'sleen'. From this, 'leendert' was ma-

Graph 2: Frequencies through time of some key terms in DCN.

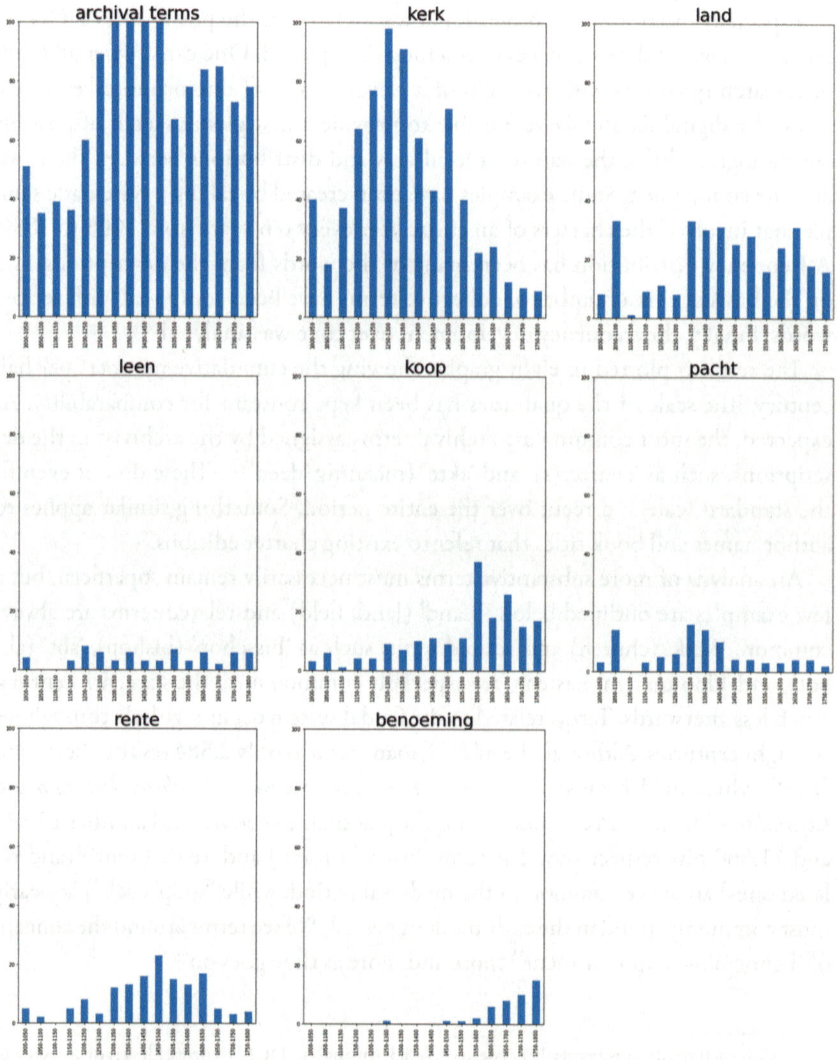

These rough results already give rise to some interesting observations, for example regarding the temporal boundaries of concepts. Thus, it is shown that the feudal

nually removed. *Pacht* was searched by using the regular expression pattern '.*pa[g|ch]+t.*', *rente* by '*rente*', *koop* by 'ko[ch|g]+t' and 'koop', *benoeming* by 'noeming*' and 'aanstelling', *land* by '^land\s+', 'morgen*', '^akker' and '*grond.*'. On regular expressions, see: Jeffrey FRIEDL, Mastering Regular Expressions, Cambridge ³2006. An interactive tester is available at https://regex101.com.

system continued to operate in the early modern period. This comes as no surprise to the experts, but it is nicely confirmed in DCN. We also see that after 1600 real estate transactions continued to be recorded in the form of charters, despite the massive use of the notarial deed, which was often only recorded in notary protocols and can therefore not be found in DCN[27]. The rise in the number of charters with appointments reflects the trend to increasingly record such bureaucratic acts in official deeds, which is related to the general growth of administrative literacy.

By way of a more detailed example of research of the *longue durée*, we explored the historical term 'erfpacht', the leasing of property, usually agricultural land, against a fixed rent, whereby the lease passes from the leaseholder to his or her heir. In this respect, 'erfpacht' differs from leases for a certain period (in Dutch terminology the so-called 'tijdpachten' or 'termijnpachten'), such as 'lijfpacht' (during the life of the tenant) or 'jaarpacht' (an agreement for the period of one year)[28].

A search for *erfpacht* yielded 6,826 results (3.2 percent of all charters in DCN). The locally used variant term 'erfhuur' (or 'erfhure') yielded another 62 hits (the variant 'erfhure' was not found)[29]. Searching for the related terms 'erfcijns', 'erftijns', 'erfthijns' and 'erfthins' (often indicating the same kind of leasehold) gave 3,670 results (per term 3,473, 119, 78 and 0 hits respectively). In Table 4 are the hits, broken down per century, including the corresponding percentage.

Table 4: Search terms 'erfpacht', 'erfhuur' and 'erfcijns', broken down per century.

Period	Number of 'erfpacht'	Percentage 'erfpacht'	Including 'erfhuur', 'erfcijns' etc.	Percentage of all combined
1100–1300[30]	103	2.8	148	4.0
1301–1400	993	4.3	1,844	7.9
1401–1500	2,945	6.0	3,007	6.1
1501–1600	1,359	2.8	2,247	4.6

27 Searching for 'notari*' (for notary, notarial) yields 5,604 hits, mostly notarial copies of deeds. A targeted search for notarial deeds with sale of property (search terms 'notari*' plus 'koop') yields only 50 results, almost all from the end of the sixteenth century onward.

28 For an overview of the nature and origin of the medieval forms of leasehold, see: Hubertus Petrus Henricus Jansen, Landbouwpacht in Brabant in de veertiende en vijftiende eeuw, Assen 1955, p. 2–21.

29 The term 'erfhuur' is rare everywhere, but is found relatively more often in the west of the country: in Nationaal Archief 16 times, in Gemeentearchief Den Haag 10 times, in Noord-Hollands Archief 9 times.

30 In the first period, the twelfth and thirteenth centuries have been combined, because the small number of charters before about 1250 produces unreliable results.

1601–1700	800	1.8	1,132	2.6
1701–1800	545	1.4	558	1.0
TOTAL	6,745	4.3	8,900	5.7

Erfpacht charters were found in 62 archival institutions, in 615 different archival funds, in which the numbers vary from one deed per fund (in 247 cases) to 1,612 deeds in Charterverzameling Erfgoed 's-Hertogenbosch. As mentioned earlier, this charter collection is listed as an unit in DCN, because it concerns externally supplied material, but the charters are drawn from different funds, which can be determined by clicking on the individual items; it seems that most of the documents come from the semi-ecclesiastical archives of the *Tafel van de Heilige Geest* and the *Groot Ziekengasthuis*. This is in agreement with what we find elsewhere: *erfpacht* letters are mainly kept in the archives of ecclesiastical institutions. The next eleven archival funds with more than 100 of these charters are the Teutonic Order in Utrecht (662 pieces), the chapter of Saint Mary there (220), the Nijmegen fraternities (155 pieces), the Utrecht chapter of Saint Peter (132) and the Utrecht Dom chapter (113)[31]. In that top eleven we find only two non-ecclesiastical archives, namely the judicial archives of Tiel and Zandwijk (86 items) and the charters belonging to, or deposited with, the city government of Utrecht, departments I and II I, with respectively 84 and 98 items. In the latter collection, apart from the guild archives, the majority of the pieces also come from religious institutions, such as fraternities, monasteries, almshouses and hospices, and foundations[32]. It should be noted, however, that it is precisely the ecclesiastical archives that have survived relatively well, in contrast to those of some secular institutions, and especially those of private individuals.

By analyzing the numbers per archival institution, we can also say something about the regional distribution of the phenomenon of hereditary leasehold. To this end, the *erfpacht* charters in the various archival institutions have been counted per (current) province; see the map [Fig. 2], which shows the documents as a percentage of the total number of charters in that province. It is clear that the erfpacht system was considerably less widespread in the West and North of the country than in the center and South. The provinces of Utrecht and North Brabant stand out, whereby it should be noted that in the province of Gelderland the area of the great rivers, which is the western part between Utrecht and Brabant, also shows large

31 Furthermore, the Sint Stevensabdij in Oudwijk near Utrecht (98 items), the Commandery of the Teutonic Order in Gemert (94) and the Norbertine priory Sint-Catharinadal (86). Not counted are the 99 items in Stadsarchief Vlaardingen, 1035 Handschriften- en documentatieverzameling Maassluis, because these concern mainly fief loans and deeds of property transfer; there is only one explicit *erfpacht* charter.

32 See the introduction to the inventories, Het Utrechts Archief, archival funds 708 and 709.

numbers of *erfpacht* charters[33]. This conclusion is reinforced when we include *erfcijns* charters; we find this term by far the most in Brabant (no less than 3039 times in the two archives in 's-Hertogenbosch), so that the total percentage of hereditary leasehold in the province even rises to 22 percent[34]. *Erfpachten* apparently had the least distribution in the most outlying regions, Groningen and Friesland in the north and Zeeland in the south west – but they are found in relatively large numbers in Limburg in the south east.

Fig. 3: The modern-day Dutch provinces with the number of erfpacht charters, as a percentage of the total number of charters in the province[35].

When looking at the chronological distribution of the figures it can be deduced that *erfpachten* started early in Utrecht and Brabant: in the former in the thirteenth century, in the latter in the fourteenth. In many areas the fourteenth and fifteenth

33 In Regionaal Archief Nijmegen 8 percent of the total number of charters, in Regionaal Archief Rivierenland (Tiel) 4,6 percent. In the other parts of the province the numbers are much lower: Gelders Archief 1,3 percent, Erfgoedcentrum Achterhoek Liemers 0,4 percent, Regionaal Archief Zutphen 1,8 percent.

34 Numbers of *erfcijns* charters: in Brabants Historisch Informatiecentrum 1339 charters, in Erfgoed 's-Hertogenbosch 1700.

35 The province of Flevoland is a twentieth-century construct, lacking archival documents from the Middle Ages and early modern times.

centuries were the high point of the system, while in the regions with a lower *erfpacht* dissemination that high point was actually later: in the province of South Holland in the sixteenth century, in Drenthe even only in the seventeenth century[36]. Other areas show a clear decline in the numbers of *erfpacht* charters in the seventeenth and eighteenth centuries, although remarkably enough in Utrecht the numbers remain more or less the same in that later period and are hardly inferior to the medieval ones. Furthermore, it could tentatively be assumed that the relatively low density of *erfpacht* charters in Zuid-Holland was caused by the fact that here the ecclesiastical institutions lagged behind in issuing them: only 10 percent of the numbers of in the Nationaal Archief appear to be preserved in church archives. The rest is preserved in the archives of various noble families, in particular in the rich archives of the Nassause Domeinraad, and of secular institutions such as the Court of Holland and the Knighthood of the States of Holland[37].

Subsequently, DCN allows us to zoom in a bit more deeply on the search results, thanks to the information found in the inventories' descriptions and regests. This shows that in the vast majority of cases, even as early as the fourteenth century, the documents do not so much refer to the establishment of an *erfpacht* leasehold on a piece of land, but rather to the transfer of the income from such a leasehold[38]. So this is actually about the *erfcijns* which, as it turns out, is usually called 'erfpacht', or 'rente' as well[39]. This is the case, for example, in a charter from 1338, described as 'Deed of transfer by Willem Koenenzoon and his wife Korstiin to Danyel van den Bossche of the *erfpacht* of a house and homestead in the [Utrechts] Smeesteeg'[40]. From that charter, and hundreds of others, it becomes clear that this type of leasehold not only occurred in agricultural areas, but also frequently in cities and towns, where houses were also issued in *erfpacht*[41]. It is also clear that not only immovable property was transferred as *erfpacht*, but also tithes and certain rights[42], and that the

36 See also Van Bavel, *Goederenverwerving*, 218-220: the abbey of the Mariënweerd (in the rivers area) began in the first half of the fourteenth century with large-scale lease of its land as *erfpacht*, just like other large monasteries in and outside the region.

37 Although the archive of the abbey of Egmond (held in Noord-Hollands Archief) contains twenty *erfpacht* charters, issued between 1228 and 1541.

38 An example of an issue of an *erfpacht*: Het Utrechts Archief, Vrouwenklooster van of Benedictinessen te De Bilt (1005-4), inv.no. 107: 'Akte van uitgifte in erfpacht door priorin en convent van Vrouwenklooster aan Johannes den Clover van 2 morgen land te Linschoten, 1357 mei 6'.

39 In DCN it is usually unclear whether these terms appear like that in the documents or have been introduced by a modern archivist writing the inventory.

40 Het Utrechts Archief, Verzameling losse aanwinsten van de Gemeentelijke Archiefdienst Utrecht (802), inv.nr. 1420: 'Akte van transport door Willem Koenenzoon en zijn vrouw Korstiin aan Danyel van den Bossche van de erfpacht van een huis en hofstede in de Smeesteeg'. See for instance also in the same archive, inv.nr. 1427.

41 For example, in the same archival fund, inv.nr. 1375.

42 See for example Regionaal Archief Zutphen, Kapittel van Sint Walburgis (0325) inv.nr. 167, con-

rent, or part of it, often had to be paid in kind[43]. Payment of the rent in kind was beneficial to the lessor: unlike a fixed sum of money, 'two barrels of rye' per year are not subject to inflation[44].

All this explains why the *erfpacht* figures so frequently and for so long in the charter material. Once a plot or house had been issued on a hereditary lease, the rent, which after all remained in existence forever, could be transferred to other parties again and again, for example as security or to repay a debt[45]. And indeed *erfpacht* deeds from the sixteenth, seventeenth and eighteenth centuries often are about the transfer of rent from – mostly urban – leaseholds, although new issues of land in *erfpacht* still occur[46].

Of course, these results are no more than a first indication of the distribution of this type of leasehold. The findings are too coarse-grained to draw dependable conclusions from them, and they are moreover contaminated by the limitations of DCN's system. The researcher can (and should) check the results manually. But such an initial exploration shows that DCN can be of a great help to the researcher, and that in a short time and with little effort. Of course, with more in-depth research, the trip to the archives will have to be made to study the 'real' charters themselves and to supplement the research corpus with relevant documents that are not in DCN, such as real estate transport registers or cartularies with copies of deeds.

---

cerning the right on a gross tithe ('grove tiende'), and Het Utrechts Archief, Huis Amerongen (1001), inv.nrs. 2077-2079, about the 'right on the wind' ('recht van de wind', that is the right to exploit a windmill).

43 Brabants Historisch Informatiecentrum, Commanderij Duitse Orde in Gemert (272), inv.nr. 1382, *erfpacht* of two barrels of rye.

44 See JANSSEN, Landbouwpacht p. 39–40.

45 This was in fact the difference between *erfpacht*, being the issue of a plot on a hereditary lease, and *erfcijns*, the establishment of a rent, but in the sources, both are often hard to distinguish; see Peter C.M. HOPPENBROUWERS, Een middeleeuwse samenleving. Het land van Heusden (c. 1360-1515) vol. 1 (Afdeling Agrarische Geschiedenis Bijdragen 32), Wageningen 1992, p. 399–400. The author concludes that in the Land of Heusden (at the banks of the Meuse river) *erfcijnsen* are much more common than the issue of *erpachten*, and that the latter were only issued by the large noble and institutional landowners. Indeed, searching for 'erfpacht' in the Heusden archives in DCN gives nine hits, but they all concern the establishment of a rent, notwithstanding the use of the term *erfpacht*.

46 For instance, also the issue on a short lease ('termijnpacht') of land that was already held in an *erfpacht* leasehold; see Het Utrechts Archief, Domkapittel te Utrecht (216), inv.nr. 4359. Sometimes a good reverted to the owner when the *erfpacht* rent was not paid; for instance, Brabants Historisch Informatiecentrum, Kapittel van Heusden (243), inv.nr. 423.

Methodical reflection and the future of DCN

DCN is a product of the 'digital turn', which has radically changed the practice of history in several respects in recent decades. This development has of course not gone unnoticed[47]. Much attention from both IT specialists and users is devoted to the application of digital methods and tools, such as digital maps, databases and visualizations. Equally important is the arrival of large digital resource complexes, which influence almost all aspects of the practice of history. Every historian uses such collections, ranging from bibliographic indexes such as the Netherlands Central Catalogue, Worldcat and Google Books to all kinds of sites with digitized historical sources, such as can be found in the *resources* of the Huygens Institute[48]. With few exceptions, in the traditional print media discussions of such digital collections are lacking, even if there are major differences in their size, quality and degree of accessibility[49].

DCN differs from many other digital collections of historical sources, both in its size and in that it is not set up from a well-defined corpus of sources or with a view to a specific research question. We hope to have shown that DCN opens up new possibilities for the historical researcher, both professional and amateur, but also that in the case of research with DCN there really is no question of a dichotomy between traditional demand-driven historical research and a data-driven method such as which would naturally result from the use of large data complexes[50]. The automatic generation of a numerical analysis of DCN's content, such as the frequency distributions of the most common words per period, is an example of a data-oriented approach. Moreover, the distribution of certain terms over the centuries immediately shows that the combination of both methods not only works excellently, but is also necessary. Starting from a specific question, such as the devel-

47 Recent literature: Ian MILLIGAN, History in the Age of Abundance? How the Web is Transforming Historical Research, Montreal 2019; Shawn GRAHAM/Ian MILLIGAN/Scott WEINGART, Exploring Big Historical Data: The Historian's Macroscope, Londen 2015; https://doi.org/10.1142/p981; Christof SCHÖCH, Big? Smart? Clean? Messy? Data in the Humanities', in: Journal of Digital Humanities 2/3 (2013) p. 2–13.

48 https://resources.huygens.knaw.nl.

49 An exception is the review by Jan BURGERS of 'Diplomata Belgica. Les sources diplomatiques des Pays-Bas méridionaux aux Moyen Âge', in: Tijdschrift voor Geschiedenis 131/2 (2018) p. 343–345; https://doi.org/10.5117/TVGESCH2018.2.BOEK. Even specialized digital media rarely discuss such datasets. For example, two of the three reviews in the June 2020 issue of *Digital Medievalist* concern paper books.

50 See also: Joris VAN EIJNATTEN/Toine PIETERS/Jaap VERHEUL, Big Data for Global History. The Transformative Promise of Digital Humanities, in: BMGN – Low Countries Historical Review 128/4 (2013) p. 55–77; https://doi.org/10.18352/bmgn-lchr.9350; Rens BOD, Het einde van de geesteswetenschappen 1.0, Inaugurele rede 14 december 2012, Amsterdam 2012; Jo GULDI/David ARMITAGE, The History Manifesto, Cambridge 2014.

opment of the feudal loans, big data provides an initial insight within minutes, but with the result the researcher only scratches the surface. Moreover, the data is often still somewhat polluted and it is not clear what exactly they mean. The automatic outcomes are therefore not so much ready-made results, but rather a semi-finished product for analysis and further research. Further elaborated examples such as "Van Brederode" and "erfpacht" make it clear that it is possible in DCN to carry out continued research into a specific subject, both at the micro level to a particular person and to the long-term development of a widespread economic system. Conversely, DCN makes it possible to place specific research in a broader perspective with data-oriented methods, for example with a few charters or a person, family or locality as a starting point.

As data sets become larger and more complex, it becomes more important to be transparent in the methods used and indeed to report on them[51]. From a methodological point of view, this presents the researcher with a number of tasks that are partly related to the digital nature of the material, and that are actually an extension of traditional historical source criticism as well. DCN, as a composite instrument, contains all the gaps and idiosyncrasies that the archival researcher has always had to be aware of; archives have been lost in whole or in part, and people and institutions from the past mainly preserved what they themselves considered valuable. Because DCN brings together all available material, this drawback is sometimes partly overcome because scattered data together form a more complete corpus. Previously scattered deeds thus help to lend context to each other, and sub-collections that have survived from one archive raise questions about the lack of data from other archives[52]. What is so unique about one collection compared to another? Is it a coincidence or is there more to it? These are just some of the questions that could be answered with DCN's panorama.

The 'old' issues of source criticism also have a digital extension. As expressed by the American historian Jo Guldi:

51 See for instance: Arguing with Digital History working group. 2017. Digital History and Argument, (white paper). Roy Rosenzweig Center for History and New Media, November 13, 2017; Andreas Fickers, Towards A New Digital Historicism? Doing History In The Age Of Abundance, in: VIEW. Journal of European Television History and Culture 1/1 (2012) p. 19–26; http://doi.org/10.18146/2213-0969.2012.jethc004; Hieke Huistra/Bram Mellink, Phrasing history. Selecting sources in digital repositories, in. Historical Methods: A Journal of Quantitative and Interdisciplinary History 49/4 (2016) p. 220–229; https://doi.org/10.1080/01615440.2016.1205964; Helle Strandgaard Jensen, Digital Archival Literacy for (All) Historians, in: Media History 27/2 (2020) p. 251–265; https://doi.org/10.1080/13688804.2020.1779047 ; Jack Dougherty/Kristen Nawrotzki (ed.), Writing History in the Digital Age, Ann Arbor 2013, p. 159–170; https://doi.org/10.3998/dh.12230987.0001.001.

52 Compare for instance the composite corpus of letters in EMLO (http://emlo.bodleian.ox.ac.uk/), and on this subject: Howard Hotson/Thomas Wallnig (ed.), Reassembling the Republic of Letters in the Digital Age, Göttingen 2019; https://doi.org/10.17875/gup2019-1146.

> Understanding digital algorithms as having this perspectival ability to open up different dimensions of an archive reminds us that no search is complete until all of its aspects – the choice of keywords, the algorithm, the exceptions, and the particular texts taken as exemplary evidence of the result – have been subjected to iterative examination[53].

Although large data collections such as DCN enable forms of 'data-driven research', they must be used wisely. The historical handicrafts can therefore certainly not be skipped.

We already pointed out that navigation in DCN is adversely affected by the change of context of the inventories, and because sometimes old regests collections have lost their link with the descriptions in the database[54]. However, there are also some structural features that distinguish databases from paper sources[55]. Databases by definition contain structured data, but the structure is a model imposed on the underlying data, and is therefore an abstraction. In the case of DCN, this is even a double abstraction, because the descriptions in the inventories were often made on paper a long time ago and then digitized. In DCN, the searchable structure has been deliberately kept very simple because we wanted to include as many charters as possible while we depended on existing descriptions that cannot simply be expanded. Our research examples indicate that even this very limited structuring of the charters leads to problems. Dates are uncertain and the method of description in the inventory is often derived from the paper form, which, although already standardized, is much more tolerant of variation than the rigid database form. DCN is therefore an umbrella instrument and not a replacement for the underlying inventories and archive descriptions. Clicking on results deliberately leads users to that other context of the archive fund, where they can sometimes find much more relevant information and conduct in-depth research. This forces researchers to be creative: DCN is a starting point for further research.

This is particularly important when the research results are further processed, because the nature and structure of the original data quickly become obscured by the aggregations and data abstractions that result from that processing. Ultimately, the historical methods that have existed for a long time are enriched and supplemented by the new data-oriented methods, which allow the rapid and broader col-

53 Jo GULDI, Critical Search. A Procedure for Guided Reading in Large-Scale Textual Corpora, in: Journal of Cultural Analytics 1/2 (2018) p. 5; https://doi.org/10.22148/16.030.

54 See also: Tim HITCHCOCK, Confronting the Digital. Or How Academic History Writing Lost the Plot, in: Cultural and Social History 10/1 (2013) p. 9–23; https://doi.org/10.2752/147800413X13515292098070.

55 More on this in: Rik HOEKSTRA/Marijn KOOLEN, Data scopes for digital history research, in: Historical Methods: A Journal of Quantitative and Interdisciplinary History 52/2 (2019) p. 79–94; https://doi.org/10.1080/01615440.2018.1484676.

lection of material and at the same time make it possible to test results obtained with other methods against a much larger corpus.

Finally, we reflect on the perspective that DCN offers. In addition to the examples we have given, other types of research are also possible, for example into the charter itself as a material object, especially if more images become available in DCN. One can think of the development of writing culture and writing styles during a certain period or in a certain region, and of a phenomenon such as the transition from Latin to the vernacular in administrative documents. With the help of DCN, specialist disciplines such as diplomatics and palaeography can be practiced on a much larger scale and at the same time much faster and more efficiently. In addition, diplomatic research is greatly accelerated and broadened when advanced tools, such as automatic recognition of writer's hands or automatic dating of handwriting, are enabled. Handwritten text recognition (HTR) can of course also be considered in this context. In the last few years, in this area huge leaps forward have been made and reliable results can now be obtained, also for older types of writing. The best known program is Transkribus, but the number of alternatives is increasing. HTR is easy to implement in DCN, because in fact all that is needed are pictures of charters and a database to link the results to, and both are readily available. Most of the work here is in the training that is needed for the software to perform optimally on charters. HTR would of course greatly expand the possibilities of a full text search. Moreover, based on the recognized text, other operations could then be considered, such as automatic recognition and identification of entities like persons and places; experiments are already underway[56].

Other possibilities for the (near) future are offered by linking DCN to other digital or digitized charter editions. In the first instance, the old paper charter books of the Netherlands can be considered. They contain about 20,000 charters from before 1300, with all kinds of metadata, including personal and place names. Most of the work here is to convert the scans of the charter books, which are already digitized, from book pages to individual charter numbers and to link them to DCN. Also eligible are the many archival regest collections and other charter editions such as the *Registers van de Hollandse grafelijkheid 1299–1345* and the *Digitale Oorkondenboek Noord-Brabant*[57].

---

56 Named Entity Recognition software still causes problems for historical corpora, but see: Marijn Koolen/Rik Hoekstra, Reusing Existing Structures for Accessibility of Large Historical Corpora, paper Digital Humanities Benelux 2019, Luik 11-13 September 2019.

57 The digitized charter books can be found at http://resources.huygens.knaw.nl; for the mentioned digital-born edition, see: http://resources.huygens.knaw.nl/registershollandsegrafelijkheid and www.donb.nl. For an overview of digital charter editions, see: Georg Vogeler, Digitale Urkundenbücher. Eine Bestandsaufnahme, in: AfD 56 (2010) p. 363–392, and, more recent: Jan Burgers, Editing medieval charters in the digital age, in: Peter Boot et al. (ed.), Advances in

Thirdly, internationalization of DCN is possible by establishing a link with digital charter projects outside the Netherlands. Charters are ideally suited for an international approach because of their identical formal features and the common language of Latin, which was often used until the late Middle Ages. This would give the DCN charters a broader context, as they would become part of a much larger corpus, making international comparisons possible. A logical candidate would be the Belgian database *Diplomata Belgica*[58], as well as the gigantic collection of *Monasterium*, in which the images and data of hundreds of thousands of charters mainly from ecclesiastical archives from Central and Southern Europe are searchable[59].

As it is, DCN is already a valuable research tool. In spite of the disadvantages described, the chosen method has the great advantage that the portal could be realized within a short period of time, making tens of thousands of previously hidden documents available to the researcher. Research into the Dutch Middle Ages and the Early modern period has suddenly become a lot easier and faster. In a very short time, the researcher can find a lot of relevant data, even in places that are not obvious beforehand. The latter aspect is inherent to the use of digital editions of extensive source corpora. The researcher is given a broader view than was previously the case, so that old questions can be answered more quickly and more completely and new questions become feasible. DCN facilitates both detailed research, for example into a person or place, and large-scale studies that cover a long period of time or a geographically broad area. The database is excellently suited to get a first impression of certain long-term developments and possible regional differences therein. In short, the possibilities for both professional and amateur historians are endless. DCN is intended to be the starting point rather than the end point in the advance of digital source access and the new forms of historical research based on it.

---

digital scholarly editing. Papers presented at the DiXiT conferences in The Hague, Cologne, and Antwerp, Leiden 2017, p. 383–389.

58 The database of www.diplomata-belgica.be contains data from about 35,000 'Belgian' charters up to about 1250, including nearly 19,000 full text transcripts as well as nearly 6,500 images.

59 https://icar-us.eu/cooperation/online-portals/monasterium-net. There are currently advanced plans to integrate DCN's charters into *Monasterium*.

Die Urkunden der Pfalzgrafen Friedrich und Philipp 1449–1508

Ein Projekt zur digitalen Erschließung und Präsentation eines herausragenden spätmittelalterlichen Urkundenbestandes

Stefan Bröhl

Die Arbeit an den Regesten der Pfalzgrafen bei Rhein kann auf eine lange Tradition zurückblicken. Bereits in der ersten Sitzung der neugegründeten Badischen Historischen Kommission im Jahr 1883 beantragte der Historiker Eduard Winkelmann die Finanzierung eines großangelegten Erschließungsprojekts für den Zeitraum 1214–1508 mit der Begründung:

> Die Rheinpfalz ist von den grösseren Territorien des alten Reichs dasjenige, dessen geschichtliche Behandlung in der neueren Zeit ganz unverhältnismässig vernachlässigt worden ist, hauptsächlich wohl deshalb, weil es in keines der neueren Staatengebilde aufgegangen, sondern vollständig aufgelöst ist. Die Archive sind ebenfalls ganz zerstreut[1].

Das Großprojekt blieb bis heute unvollendet. 1894 erschien der erste Teilband mit bis zum Jahre 1400 reichenden Regesten. Auf welche Schwierigkeiten die Pfalzgrafenregesten bei der Umsetzung stießen, zeigt sich darin, dass der Abschluss des zweiten Bandes – die Regierungszeit König Ruprechts (1400–1410) umfassend – mit allen Nachträgen bis zum Jahr 1939 dauerte. Seitdem ist die Fortsetzung des Regestenwerks für das späte Mittelalter ein immer wieder moniertes Desiderat, dessen wissenschaftliche Bedeutung für die Reichs- und Landesgeschichte grundsätzlich außer Frage, dem aber vor allem die Fülle des Materials im Wege stand. Mit dem 2022 begonnenen, auf drei Jahre angelegten und von der Deutschen Forschungs-

1 Regesten der Pfalzgrafen am Rhein 1214–1508, Bd. 1: 1214–1400, ed. Adolf Koch/Jakob Wille, Innsbruck 1894; Regesten der Pfalzgrafen am Rhein 1214–1508, Bd. 2: Regesten König Ruprechts, ed. Lambert Graf von Oberndorff/Manfred Krebs, Innsbruck 1939.

gemeinschaft (DFG) geförderten Projekt „Urkunden der Pfalzgrafen bei Rhein. Erschließung, Digitalisierung und virtuelle Zusammenführung zwischen 1449 und 1508 entstandener Dokumente aus Baden-Württemberg, Bayern, Hessen und Rheinland-Pfalz als Themenportal im Archivportal-D" soll anhand der Veröffentlichung eines ausgewählten Ensembles von ca. 7.000 Urkunden die Grundlage für zukünftige Forschungen geschaffen werden.

Die Pfalzgrafschaft bei Rhein zählte im späten Mittelalter trotz ihrer territorialen Fragmentierung zu den bedeutendsten weltlichen Fürstentümern des Alten Reiches. Nachdem Ludwig von Wittelsbach im Jahr 1214 mit der rheinischen Pfalzgrafschaft belehnt worden war, gelang seinen Nachfolgern – stets sollten sie den vornehmen Pfalzgrafentitel dem eines Herzogs von Bayern voranstellen – die Etablierung einer hegemonialen Stellung im deutschen Südwesten. Das späte Mittelalter sah den Höhepunkt des pfalzgräflichen Einflusses; ihr Rang spiegelte sich im Ausbau von Heidelberg zu einer königsgleichen Residenz mit dem berühmten Schloss, einer repräsentativen Stiftskirche und der Gründung der Heidelberger Universität wider. Die Ambitionen der rheinischen Wittelsbacher, die spätestens seit der goldenen Bulle 1356 fest als Kurfürsten und Königswähler im Reichsgefüge verankert waren, gipfelten im Aufstieg Ruprechts III. zum römisch-deutschen König im Jahr 1400. Mit ihrer politischen und wirtschaftlichen Potenz entfalteten die Pfalzgrafen bei Rhein eine Strahlkraft, die auch weit über ihre engeren Besitzungen am Ober- und Mittelrhein sowie in der Oberpfalz hinauswirkte.

Als eigenständige politische Entität hat die Kurpfalz ihr Ende in napoleonischer Zeit gefunden, was langfristige Folgen für die Überlieferungssituation und die historische Forschung – bzw. das landeskundliche Interesse und die Finanzierungsmöglichkeiten ebensolcher Vorhaben – nach sich ziehen sollte. Nach wie vor sind die Urkunden der kurfürstlichen Kanzleien über Archive im ganzen Süden Deutschlands zerstreut[2]. Umso erfreulicher mutet an, dass die historische Forschung trotz dieser Widrigkeiten in den letzten Jahrzehnten durchaus rege war. So sind in jüngerer Zeit eine merkliche Zahl an Detailstudien zu den wittelsbachischen Pfalzgrafen und ihrem Fürstentum vorgelegt worden[3]. Große Ausstellungen

2 Hinsichtlich der Archivgeschichte der Kurpfalz sei auf den grundlegenden Aufsatz von Max Josef Neudegger, Geschichte der Pfalz-bayerischen Archive der Wittelsbacher, in: Archivalische Zeitschrift NF 1 (1890) S. 202–240; und NF 2 (1891) S. 289–373 verwiesen.

3 Den neuesten Überblick über die Forschungslage bietet Benjamin Müsegades, Erreichtes und Erstrebenswertes. Forschungen zur Pfalzgrafschaft bei Rhein im Mittelalter, in: Blätter für deutsche Landesgeschichte 157 (2021) S. 455–505. An Monographien seien hier nur exemplarisch genannt: Thorsten Huthwelker, Tod und Grablege der Pfalzgrafen bei Rhein im Spätmittelalter (1327–1508) (Heidelberger Veröffentlichungen zur Landesgeschichte und Landeskunde 14), Heidelberg 2009; Jörg Peltzer, Der Rang der Pfalzgrafen bei Rhein: die Gestaltung der politisch-sozialen Ordnung des Reichs im 13. und 14. Jahrhundert (Rank. Politisch-soziale Ordnungen im mittelalterlichen Europa 2), Ostfildern 2013; Anuschka Holste-Massoth, Ludwig

in den Jahren 2000 und 2013/14 haben dazu beigetragen, die Kurpfalz in das Bewusstsein der Öffentlichkeit (zurück-)zurufen[4].

Dabei darf die Überlieferungslage der Kurlinie der Pfalzgrafschaft für das Spätmittelalter als reichhaltig, ja überreich gelten. Trotz Kriegen und Flüchtungen des kurpfälzischen Archivs in der frühen Neuzeit hat sich eine beachtliche Masse der Urkundenüberlieferung erhalten, wobei die um die Mitte des 14. Jahrhunderts einsetzenden Kopialbücher, die heute hauptsächlich im Generallandesarchiv Karlsruhe liegen, eine zentrale Bedeutung einnehmen. Nicht zuletzt der Komplexität und Masse der Überlieferung ist geschuldet, dass die ursprünglich bis zum Jahre 1508 geplanten Regesten Fragment geblieben sind.

Die nunmehr begonnene Arbeit an den Urkunden der Pfalzgrafen erlaubt, einen merklichen Teil dieser Lücke zu schließen und die verstreuten Archivbestände virtuell zusammenzuführen. Das Projekt fokussiert sich, um von vornherein der Gefahr eines grenzen- und uferlosen Langzeitvorhabens zu entgehen, auf einen Teil der Überlieferung der pfalzgräflichen Kurlinie. Als definiertes Ziel werden knapp 7.000 Urkunden aus der Regierungszeit der Kurfürsten Friedrich („der Siegreiche", † 1476) und Philipp („der Aufrichtige", † 1508) erschlossen. Die Konzentration auf die zweite Hälfte des 15. Jahrhunderts ist der Bedeutung der beiden Kurfürsten im Gefüge der Reichsgeschichte als Protagonisten der „Blütezeit" der spätmittelalterlichen Kurpfalz und der sogenannten Arrogation[5] als Sonderfall der Rechtsgeschichte geschuldet. Der biographisch gewählte Zuschnitt ergibt sich mitunter aus der Überlieferungssituation, da der Tod eines Kurfürsten und der Regierungsantritt seines Erben zum Anfall einer Schriftproduktion führte (z. B. bei den Lehnsmutungen und Huldigungen) und viele Kopialbücher beim Tod eines

---

II. Pfalzgraf bei Rhein und Herzog von Bayern: Felder fürstlichen Handelns im 13. Jahrhundert (Rank. Politisch-soziale Ordnungen im mittelalterlichen Europa 6), Ostfildern 2019. Immer noch grundlegend als Überblicksdarstellung ist: Meinrad SCHAAB, Geschichte der Kurpfalz. Bd. 1: Mittelalter, Stuttgart u. a. 1999.

4 Mittelalter. Der Griff nach der Krone. Die Pfalzgrafschaft bei Rhein im Mittelalter. Begleitpublikation zur Ausstellung der Staatlichen Schlösser und Gärten Baden-Württemberg und des Generallandesarchivs Karlsruhe, bearb. von Volker RÖDEL (Schätze aus unseren Schlössern 4), Regensburg 2000; Die Wittelsbacher am Rhein. Die Kurpfalz und Europa, ed. Alfried WIECZOREK u. a., 2 Bände (Publikationen der Reiss-Engelhorn-Museen 60), Regensburg 2013.

5 Friedrich adoptierte 1452 unter Bekundung des eigenen Eheverzichts und mit Zustimmung maßgeblicher Vertreter der kurpfälzischen Räte und der Ritterschaft seinen minderjährigen Neffen Philipp – den erbberechtigten Sohn des jung verstorbenen Kurfürsten Ludwig IV. – unter Bezugnahme auf das römische Rechtsinstrument der Arrogation. Friedrich ließ sich seine Regentschaft auch nach der Volljährigkeit seines Neffen bestätigen und nahm die kurfürstliche Würde und Regierung der Pfalzgrafschaft bis zu seinem Tod 1476 wahr. Zu seinen Lebzeiten sollte die Arrogation vom Kaiser nicht anerkannt werden, was zu schweren Verwerfungen und Kriegsläufen im deutschen Südwesten führte. Vgl. bspw. Karl-Friedrich KRIEGER, Der Prozeß gegen Pfalzgraf Friedrich den Siegreichen auf dem Augsburger Reichstag vom Jahre 1474, in: Zeitschrift für historische Forschung 12 (1985) S. 257–286.

Kurfürsten und Regierungsantritt seines Erben neu angelegt wurden. Das Sterbedatum eines Regenten stellte somit einen tatsächlichen Einschnitt in die Arbeit der Kanzleien dar. Die Urkunden der seit 1410 bestehenden pfalzgräflichen Nebenlinien sind nicht Teil des Projekts, wobei die Fürsten von Pfalz-Mosbach, Pfalz-Neumarkt und Pfalz-Zweibrücken-Simmern bzw. ihrer jeweiligen Rechtsnachfolger in den Angelegenheiten der Kurlinie häufig vorkommen.

Mit ihren Beständen beteiligt sind das Staatsarchiv Amberg, das Bayerische Hauptstaatsarchiv in München mit den Abteilungen I und III (Geheimes Hausarchiv), das Hessische Staatsarchiv Darmstadt, das Landeshauptarchiv Koblenz, das Landesarchiv Speyer und das Landesarchiv Baden-Württemberg, Abt. Generallandesarchiv Karlsruhe, wobei letzterem die Projektkoordination obliegt. Die jeweiligen Palatina-Bestände der Häuser sind freilich sehr heterogen. Bei der Konzeption des Vorhabens einigte man sich darauf, zuvorderst die Ausfertigungen der beiden Kurfürsten aus gesichteten Beständen in das Projekt aufzunehmen. Für das Generallandesarchiv Karlsruhe heißt das beispielsweise, dass die einschlägigen Ausfertigungen aus einer Reihe besonders relevanter Bestände und dazu 15 Kopialbücher, die in Gänze erschlossen werden, im Projekt aufgenommen sind[6]. Dabei wurde sich vorbehalten, weitere wichtige Dokumente, die aus dieser strengen Systematik der Ausfertigungen herausfallen, z. B. Reverse und Urkunden, in denen die Pfalzgrafen im Kontext der Besiegelung oder Bestätigung erscheinen, ebenfalls aufzunehmen. Die Gesamtauswahl bildet somit einen definierten Urkunden-Selekt, bei dem von zentraler Bedeutung ist, dass gegenüber den Nutzerinnen und Nutzern klar kommuniziert wird, welche Bestände systematisch ausgewertet und für das Projekt herangezogen wurden und welche Urkunden trotz wie auch immer gearteter Beteiligung der Pfalzgrafen (noch) nicht in dem derart veröffentlichten Bestand inkludiert sind. Die Informationen über die ausgewählten Bestände und Urkunden werden auf dem Themenportal zugänglich gemacht werden.

Das Projekt versteht sich als Serviceangebot an die Forschung und alle an der kurpfälzischen Geschichte interessierten Nutzerinnen und Nutzer, die mit Abschluss dieses Vorhabens auf einen umfangreichen Kernbestand an erschlossenen Urkunden mit verknüpften Digitalisaten zugreifen können, selbstverständlich kostenlos und jederzeit von zu Hause aus verfügbar. Dabei ermöglicht die hinter dem Projekt stehende Infrastruktur, den Nukleus an Regesten sukzessive zu erweitern, und zwar sowohl durch Einspeisung seitens der bereits beteiligten Projektpartner, wie auch weiterer Archive und Bibliotheken, die sich mit ihren Urkunden beteiligen möchten. Derzeit finden zudem Vorüberlegungen statt, wie im Anschluss an

6 Alleine die 15 Kopialbücher sind insgesamt ca. 6.300 Blatt stark, wobei in jedem dieser Bände etwa 250 bis 500 Urkunden kopial überliefert sind. Das Generallandesarchiv Karlsruhe steuert aufgrund der Hinzunahme dieses Quellenbestandes ca. 80% der Gesamtmasse der 7.000 Urkunden für das Projekt bei.

das Projekt die Urkunden der Pfalzgrafen Ludwig III. und Ludwig IV. erschlossen und inkludiert werden können. Die Pfalzgrafenregesten sind im 21. Jahrhundert nunmehr ein weitgehend digitales und kooperatives Projekt.

Einen wesentlichen Vorteil dieser digitalen Erschließung stellt die Modellierbarkeit der Datensätze, Metadaten und externen Referenzdaten dar. Denn erst einmal gilt, dass die Arbeit an den Pfalzgrafenregesten durch eine Reihe von Mitarbeiterinnen und Mitarbeitern der beteiligten Archive durchgeführt wird, wobei die einzelnen Häuser ihre eigenen Traditionen und Richtlinien der Urkundenerschließung mitbringen, nicht zuletzt auch ihre eigene Erschließungssoftware verwenden. Grundsätzlich findet die Erschließung dezentral in den jeweiligen Partnerarchiven und anhand der dort jeweils geltenden Erschließungsrichtlinien und Vorgaben statt, wobei sich vorab bei einigen essentiellen Punkten und Parametern (z. B. hinsichtlich der kurfürstlichen Titulatur und Fragen der Erschließungstiefe) auf einen gemeinsamen Nenner geeinigt wurde. Dass das Endergebnis letztlich noch größer als die Summe der jeweiligen – schon für sich wertvollen – Erschließungsarbeit in den Archiven ist, ergibt sich aus einem anschließenden Redaktionsdurchgang, der die eingehenden Datensätze für die Veröffentlichung in einem Themenportal im Archivportal-D vorbereitet. Die Erstellung des Themenportals findet im Zusammenarbeit mit dem FIZ Karlsruhe – Leibniz-Institut für Informationsinfrastruktur statt. Ziel bei diesem Projektschritt ist nicht der Eingriff in die Erschließung auf einer Mikroebene, wie beispielsweise in die Satzstellung im Regest oder die Normierung von formelhaften Rechtsbegriffen, sondern die Datenanreicherung und -modellierung im Hinblick auf die Normdaten. Vorab wurde entschieden, zu diesem Zweck die Gemeinsame Normdatei (GND) zu verwenden. Die Hinzuziehung einer externen Normdatei als Referenzrahmen ermöglicht es, das Auffinden und die Nutzbarkeit der Regesten durch die Verknüpfung mit eindeutigen Identifikatoren erheblich zu verbessern. Zudem ist dadurch die Anschlussmöglichkeit an weitere digitale Vorhaben gesichert. Die Verwendung von Normdaten wird in den am Projekt beteiligten Archiven bislang unterschiedlich gehandhabt, wobei häufig eine Vergabe von archivinternen Deskriptoren üblich ist. Die Verknüpfung der Urkunden aller beteiligten Projektpartner mit einheitlichen Indices und Normdaten erweitert den Blick auf die in den Urkunden vorkommenden Orte, Gemeinschaften und Personen ungemein. Gerade in prosopographischer Perspektive eröffnet sich hier für die Nutzerinnen und Nutzer ein Blick auf Personen und Gruppen, die ansonsten meist „unterhalb des Radars“ bleiben, man denke hier an die Ebene der kurpfälzischen Amtleute, Räte und Spezialisten. Anhand der GND-ID lässt sich ein rascher Überblick über alle mit einem eindeutigen Identifikator verknüpften Urkunden aus den Beständen der am Projekt beteiligten Archive herausgeben, was zuvor lediglich nach aufwendigen Einzelrecherchen vor Ort oder in den jeweiligen Archivportalen möglich gewesen wäre.

Die Regesten und Digitalisate werden im Archivportal-D innerhalb eines eigenen Themenportals präsentiert. Dies hat den Vorteil, dass seitens der Nutzerinnen und Nutzer eine Recherche anhand eines dreifachen Zugriffs erfolgen kann: über die Volltextsuche, über die Indices wie auch über einen thematischen Zugriff im Themenportal, d. h. über die den Archivalien zugeordneten Schlagworte und Kategorien (wie bspw.: „Krieg und Frieden", „Mainzer Stiftsfehde".). Als Vorbild dienen bereits aufgebaute Portale wie etwa jenes zur Weimarer Republik[7].

Unter den erschlossenen Urkunden eröffnet sich mit Belehnungen, politischen Verträgen, Schirm- und Geleitbriefen, Burgfrieden, Erbbestandsbriefen, Hofgerichtsurteilen, Kundschaften, Kredit- und Pfandbriefen usw. die ganze Bandbreite der Produkte der gut funktionierenden spätmittelalterlichen Kanzleibetriebe. Inhaltlich bilden sie das Agieren von zwei der bedeutendsten südwestdeutschen Fürsten an der Wende vom Mittelalter zur Frühneuzeit ab, wobei der Bestand aus mannigfaltigen historiographischen Perspektiven nutzbar gemacht werden kann. So finden sich in den Urkunden Nachrichten über Kriegsereignisse, Rheinfluten und Verhandlungen mit Papst und Kaiser. Es wird auch die große Schar der pfalzgräflichen Satelliten und Vasallen, Räte, Diener und Waffenknechte sichtbar, aber auch von kleinen Müllern, Pächtern und in Ungnade gefallenen Amtleuten sprechen die Quellen. Sie zeugen vom Interesse der Pfalzgrafen an ihren Fachleuten, an gut besoldeten Büchsen- und Baumeistern, gelehrten Juristen und oberpfälzischen Montanunternehmern und Bergbauspezialisten. In den Urkunden erwähnte Bücherverzeichnisse, Seelgeräte, Stiftungen und Präsentationen gewähren Einblicke in die geistigen und geistlichen Interessen der wittelsbachischen Fürsten, wie auch die eifrige Wahrung ihrer Jagd- und Fischereirechte von ihren weltlichen Freuden Kunde bringt – um nur einige Stichworte zu nennen. Aufgrund der weitreichenden kurpfälzischen Interessensphäre und des umfangreichen Lehnshofs der Kurpfalz finden sich in dem Bestand auch zahlreiche Urkunden, die weiter entfernt liegende Herrschaften und Orte, z. B. in den elsässischen und lothringischen Landen, betreffen. Die relativ dichte Masse von 7.000 Urkunden mit weitgehend vereinheitlichten Normdaten mag den Fundus darüber hinaus auch beispielsweise für den Bereich der Digital Humanities interessant machen. Das Urkundenkorpus dürfte somit aus mannigfaltigen Perspektiven ein fruchtbares Feld für die weitere Forschung bilden.

7 Siehe https://www.archivportal-d.de/themenportale/weimarer-republik. Neben der Präsentation im übergreifenden Archivportal werden die Erschließungssätze selbstverständlich auch in den Online-Findmitteln der jeweiligen Landesarchive gemäß den dort geltenden Regularien und Workflows freigeschaltet.

Zusammenfassung

Auf Initiative des Landesarchivs Baden-Württemberg, Abt. Generallandesarchiv Karlsruhe, werden bis Mitte des Jahres 2025 Urkunden (Ausfertigungen und Kopialbucheinträge) der kurpfälzischen Überlieferung im Zusammenwirken mit Partnerarchiven in Amberg, München, Darmstadt, Koblenz und Speyer in dem dreijährigen DFG-geförderten Projekt „Urkunden der Pfalzgrafen bei Rhein. Erschließung, Digitalisierung und virtuelle Zusammenführung zwischen 1449 und 1508 entstandener Dokumente aus Baden-Württemberg, Bayern, Hessen und Rheinland-Pfalz als Themenportal im Archivportal-D" erschlossen. Inhaltlich erstreckt sich das Projekt auf rund 7.000 Urkunden aus den Regierungszeiten der Kurfürsten Friedrich I. und Philipp. Die mit Deskriptoren und Normdaten angereicherten Urkunden werden mit Digitalisaten im übergreifenden Archivportal-D (https://www.archivportal-d.de/) zur Verfügung gestellt und über ein Themenportal der Öffentlichkeit präsentiert.

The digital methods of publishing 15th century papal sources

Adam Zapała

The documentation created as a result of the activity of the Holy See in the late Middle Ages is one of the most important collection of European sources for historical study of this era. Its special value derives from its universal character (it concerns the whole of Western Christendom), the wide range of matters covered (diplomacy, politics, religious issues, individual careers, etc.) and the relatively good preservation of the entire corpus.

The materials created by papal bureaucracy during the 15th century constitute a heterogeneous collection. Only a small fraction of it has survived in the form of original charters. These are mainly documents of a perpetual validity for ecclesiastical institutions, preserved in the archives of the recipients. The vast majority of the material are copies in the papal registers produced in the Curia at various stages of the procedure, mostly stored in the Vatican Apostolic Archives. The most important sources from the 15th century are the registers of the Apostolic Chancery: registers of petitions (*Registra Supplicationum*[1]), registers of bullae (*Regestra Lateranensia*[2], *Registra Vaticana*[3]); records of Apostolic Penitentiary; as well as books produced by the Apostolic Chamber in connection with the financial operations at the Roman Curia: records of incomes and expenses (*Introitus et Exitus*), obligations (*Obligationes et Solutiones, Annatae*), confirmations of payment (*L. quitantiarum, L. taxae*) etc.[4]. In addition to original charters and registers, papal sources also include

1 Fondo described in: Bruno KATTERBACH, Inventario dei Registri delle suppliche, Città del Vaticano 1932.

2 Fondo described in Germano GUALDO, Sussidi per La consultazione dell'Archivio Vaticano, Città del Vaticano 1989, p. 245–315.

3 Fondo described in Ibid. p. 135–245.

4 Fondo described in: Ibid. p. 315–333; and more comprehensively: Marek Daniel KOWALSKI, Proventus Camerae Apostolicae Debiti. Opłaty duchowieństwa polskiego na rzecz papiestwa w latach 1417–1484, Kraków 2012, p. 165–191; ID., Die päpstlichen Rechnungsbücher zu Benefizienabgaben 1417–1484, in: Editionswissenschaftliche Kolloquien 2009. Zahlen und Erin-

documents produced by papal delegates acting outside the Curia (legates, deputies, collectors, judge delegates, executors etc.). The Vatican Apostolic Archives alone hold approximately 3 000 volumes of registers from the 15th century[5], each of them containing hundreds of cases. It is not possible to estimate the approximate number of documents held in the recipients' archives, but it goes into the thousands. Not to mention the unquantifiable material preserved in various registers of local chancelleries, which makes papal sources very broad and scattered resource.

Unlike the sources from the Avignon era[6], most of the papal material from the 15th century has not yet been published. Only small part of it was made available selectively by national projects. Unfortunately, the local nature of these editions means that the immense amount of work dedicated to exploring the Vatican Archives yields a not fully satisfactory result. As a consequence, researchers of the 15th-century papacy have dozens of publications of sources, which, however, cover only a fragment of the corpus. Moreover, some parts of it has been published several times (e.g. the bullae concerning Silesia in the beginning of the 15th century[7]), while others have never been edited (for example those related to France, Spain, most of Italy and Hungary, as well as the most of books of the Apostolic Camera). What is more, there is no comprehensive index to effectively find documents containing the information sought[8], which makes it often impossible to find specific information in the papal source material. This situation severely limits the research potential of the corpus.

The aim of this article is to show how modern digital technologies can help to accelerate research on late medieval papal source material and make it more accessible to a wide range of researchers.

---

nerung von der Vielfalt der Rechnungsbücher und vergleichbarer Quellengattungen, ed. Janusz Tandecki/Helmut von Flachenecker, Toruń 2010, p. 135–168.

5 This number consists of approximately: more than 1120 volumes of Lateran Registers, 580 volumes of Vatican Registers: Gualdo, Sussidi (as n. 2) p. 175–195, 265–285, 1989; more than 1050 books of Registers of Supplications: Katterbach, Inventario dei registri delle suppliche (as n. 1) p. 11–68; as well as several hundred books from the fondo Camera Apostolica.

6 Laurent Vallière, Les lettres pontificales du XIVe siècle: histoire de leur édition et questionnement actuels, in: Lusitania Sacra 22 (2010) p. 25–43

7 Due to changes in the state affiliation of Silesia over the centuries, it was included in German, Czech and Polish publications ('Monumenta Vaticana Res Gestas Bohemicas Illustrantia', 'Repertorium Germanicum' and in part also in 'Bullarium Poloniae').

8 The only source for orientation in the papal material are the indexes in the AAV. For the most part, they describe the contents only at the level of the register (book). Part of the registers of bullae from the second half of the 15th century also have very abbreviated tables of contents (Indices 274–343). On the basis of these, it is possible to find documents relating to individual dioceses (however, this involves a demanding manuscript query). It is not possible to search for persons, institutions, localities or dates.

The most important problem of editions of papal sources is not only quantity but also complexity. Dealing with any issue at the Curia resulted in the production of a whole group of documents. It is the easiest to illustrate this problem through a concrete example. I will use the most common papal grace in the source material, a commission for a non-consistorial ecclesiastical benefice. Curial procedure was already broadly presented in historiography[9], thus, I will just concentrate on the written sources produced by it.

The curial procedure began with the submission of a written supplication containing a request for a grace together with all information necessary to create the final document. Once accepted by the authorised person (the pope, *referendarius domesticus* or vice-chancellor), it was copied to the registers of petitions[10]. Original supplications almost never survived, while the registers of petitions are the most voluminous collection of papal sources from the 15th century. In order to use the grace, the applicant mostly had to apply for a bulla. Before expedition final document was copied into the registers of bullae[11]. However, the copies in the registers were not identical to the original document. First, copies were abbreviated. In case of provisions for benefices, only the typical parts of the salutation or sanction were usually shortened, but in case of more standardised privileges, such as spiritual graces, the copy often contained only information on the recipient, the first words of the *arenga* and date of issue. This means that in such cases the copies in registers are completely different in form from the original document. All copies from registers lack chancery notes as well, which identified those who were involved in the preparation of the document, but instead, they recorded additional information such as the payment of taxes, the date of the expedition of the document (the official date of the document was the day when the supplication was accepted), or names of those responsible for copying the text into the registers. After being copied, the document was sent to the Apostolic Camera, where the supplicant had to make an obligation for *annata* and had to actually pay this fee. These stages of the procedure were followed by entries in the books of the Camera (*Annatae, Introitus et Exitus, Libri Quietantiarum*)[12]. These records contain very valuable information from a historian's perspective, which do not appear neither in the bulla nor in the supplication. Finally, the supplicant had to pay the so-called *taxa quinta*, which allowed him to collect the document and was recorded in the books of taxation (*Taxae*) and in the registers of the bulla. Moreover, the original document was often

9 Thomas FRENZ, I documenti pontifici nel medioevo e nell'età moderna, Città del Vaticano 2008, p. 71–92.

10 FRENZ, I documenti (as n. 9) p. 73–75.

11 Practica Cancellariae Apostolicae saeculi XV. exeuntis, ed. Ludwig SCHMITZ-KALLENBERG, Münster 1904, p. 34–35.

12 On this subject: KOWALSKI, *Proventus* (as n. 4) p. 133–157.

accompanied by bullae for executors, which described the same matter but differed in content from the main document. The executors may also have issued documents (very rarely preserved) in which the original document was summarised or even transcribed[13]. Out of this entire list of documents, historians today usually only have access to copies of supplications and/or bullae and notes from the Camera records. The rest are usually not preserved.

Even this brief description shows the complexity of the problems that editors of 15th century papal material have to face. Can they limit the publication only to a copy of the bulla? How to distinguish between the information contained in the copies of the supplication and bulla? How to link records of different nature concerning the same case? And further, what if the copy of the bulla and the original document do not exist, but a copy of the supplication has survived (which happens very often)? How to indicate in print the differences between the versions and abbreviations of the text? How to include information from the records of the Camera Apostolica in the publication?

Although historians have been working on 15th -century papal sources for more than a century, it has not been established universally accepted method of editing that shows the complexity and comprehensiveness of this corpus[14]. In the age of print, publishers have always had to focus on only a small part of the whole. The work has been usually limited by geographical borders (usually within a single contemporary country), chronological scope (usually within a single pontificate), and also by archival organisation (usually including only selection of fonds). If only one type of the sources (e.g. annates, breve) were published, the editors could edit the text *in extenso*. Publishers dealing with bullae from registers did not have such an opportunity. Their volume and repetitive form led editors to opt for abbreviations in the publication. Most often regesta, or sometimes excerpts (where parts of the documents were cut out – mostly the formulae and the marginal notes) of the original source were published. Unfortunately, each project used a different methodology for abbreviating the documents. The situation became even more complicated, when supplications were included, as they contained the same information, but formulated in the form of a request and a response to it. Although a proper analysis of the products of papal bureaucracy requires knowledge of the entire set

13 For documents issued by the executors see: Marek Daniel Kowalski, Spór kanonika Wernera von Czettritz z klasztorem św. Macieja we Wrocławiu – proces sądowy w Rocie Rzymskiej i jego dokumentacja źródłowa, in: Studia Źródłoznawcze 58 (2020) p. 33–54; These papers will soon be published in the first volume of the series: Monumenta Vaticana res gestas Polonicas illustrantia: Acta Urbani VI pape (1378–1389).

14 On the different concepts of 15th-century papal source publications: Anna Zajchowska, Monumenta Vaticana – koncepcje edycji późnośredniowiecznych źródeł papieskich. Przyczyny sukcesów i porażek, in: Editiones sine fine 1, ed. Janusz Tandecki/Krzysztof Kopiński/Wojciech Mrozowicz, Toruń 2017, p. 143–162.

of documents (e.g. the absence of information in the Camera Apostolica books indicates that the provision copied into the registers was never expedited[15]), the only project so far trying to show the complexity of material was *Repertorium Germanicum*[16]. It described information from all types of papal records (excluding sources preserved in the recipients' archives) in extremely abbreviated regesta, mostly in one sentence. This form requires the use of original sources for analysis but makes it possible to encompass all the material related to Germany (in its 19th – century imperial borders), which is an unprecedented achievement. New, broader concept of publication of papal material including all type of sources and interconnection between them was presented by Prof. M.D. Kowalski[17]. New perspective of publication papal sources offers also digital technology. It allows, on the one hand, the processing of a large full-text corpus and, on the other hand, the publication of information in the form of a database or assertive edition. Moreover, the use of digital tools enables to show the complexity of a resource, link different sources together and increasingly automatize the work. These changes provide an opportunity to think about the processing of the 15th-century papal sources as a whole, something that has previously been impossible. These changes require a reconsideration of the way papal sources are published.

The most common method of making archival material accessible in recent years has been the repository of digital facsimiles published on the internet. This type of project makes it relatively easy and quick to publish material with basic metadata. Unfortunately, due to the restrictive licensing policy of the Vatican Apostolic Archives[18], it is not, and, it seems, will not be possible in the foreseeable future to create an open digital repository of sources from that institution. Thus, publication of 15th-century papal source material must focus on texts and information in

15 Marek Daniel Kowalski, Opłaty annatowe w piętnastowiecznych aktach Kamery Apostolskiej. Uwagi na temat interpretacji źródeł proweniencji papieskiej, in: Roczniki Historyczne 67 (2001) p. 175–178; Adam Zapała, Kontakty Polaków i Litwinów ze Stolicą Apostolską za pontyfikatu papieża Mikołaja V (1447–1455), Warszawa 2021, p. 83–89.

16 A multi-volume publication published since 1916. Currently available also at the website: http://www.romana-repertoria.net/993.html?&L=24#c3033.

17 This concept has been described by: Marek Daniel Kowalski, Monumenta Vaticana res gestas Polonicas illustrantia – The Programme of Editing Medieval Papal Sources Relating to Poland, in: Editionswissenschaftliche Kolloquien 2011. Quellen Kirchlicher Provenienz. Neue Editionsvorhaben und aktuelle EDV-Projekte, ed. Janusz Tandecki/Helmut von Flachenecker/Krzysztof Kopiński, Toruń 2011, p. 30–35; this idea was to be implemented in the project 'Monumenta Vaticana res gestas Polonicas illustrantia' in 2013–2018. A team of editors processed almost 3000 documents but the results have not yet been published in print. The continuation of this project in digital way is currently underway.

18 The Vatican Apostolic Archives only allows private use of images purchased there. A licence to publish a single image on the internet costs 150 euros. The publication of even a small section of the material stored there is far beyond the financial capacity of any research project.

image-free form. In planning the work, it is also necessary to take into account the achievements of historiography – especially editions – as well as the needs of historians, for whom the lack of a usable index is a huge limitation. Therefore, future work on the papal sources should be divided into three levels:

1. Harmonisation and unification of existing editions.
2. Indexing of the resource and publishing of data.
3. Full-text editions.

The topic of digital processing of papal documents has recently entered scholarly discourse through Georg Vogeler[19]. Although his text concerned the 13th-century material (preserved mainly in the form of original charters) and did not focus strictly on digital editions, but rather it discussed more broadly the possibilities of using digital technology to work with papal documents (especially in their cataloguing and analysis), it highlighted two very important needs: to make papal material available within Linked Open Data, and to use permanent identifiers. Both of these propositions must be kept in mind of any researcher proposing a digital method for editing papal sources (or indeed sources in general) in the digital age.

In recent years, the discussion on the processing and publication of source material has moved towards the use of machine learning for text and information processing[20] (Handwritten Text Recognition[21], Named Entity Recognition[22]). New possibilities, not yet well described in literature, offer also the usage of Large Language Models. Despite the vast development of these types of tools in last years, today we still do not have the technology that can cope with the researcher's ability to retrieve the text of the papal registers, or to extract named entities from them. Although the ongoing development of models writing HTR and especially LLM gives hope for such solutions, in this text I would like to focus on tools that are available now. I will not enter into a discussion on the best serialisation of the data, considering this a secondary issue; rather, I would like to point out the most important principles of working with 15th-century papal source material and show examples of their implementation.

---

19 Georg Vogeler, Digitale Methoden bei der Erforschung von Papsturkunden? – Stand der Dinge, in: Innocenz III., Honorius III. und ihre Briefe, ed. Andrea Sommerlechner/Herwig Weigl, Wien 2023, p. 225–242, https://doi.org/10.7767/9783205217718.225.

20 Tobias Hodel, Chapter 6: Supervised and Unsupervised: Approaches to Machine Learning for Textual Entities, in: Archives, Access and Artificial Intelligence: Working with Born-Digital and Digitalized Archival Collections, ed. Lise Jaillant, Bielefeld 2022, p. 157–177, https://doi.org/10.1515/9783839455845-007.

21 Tobias Hodel, Konsequenzen der Handschriftenerkennung und des maschinellen Lernens für die Geschichtswissenschaft. Anwendung, Einordnung und Methodenkritik, in: Historische Zeitschrift 316/1 (2023), p. 151–180; https://doi.org/10.1515/hzhz-2023-0006.

22 Pierre Chastang/Sergio Torre Aquilar/Xavier Tannier, A Named Entity Recognition Model for Medieval Latin Charters, in: Digital Humanities Quartarly 15/4 (2021); https://www.digitalhumanities.org/dhq/vol/15/4/000574/000574.html.

Harmonisation and unification of traditional editions

Harmonisation of international projects, especially those with such a long tradition as editions of papal materials, is a very serious challenge on the organisational, legal and technological levels. In this article, I will only discuss the last aspect.

The discussion of the harmonisation of the various editions should begin with Vogeler's postulate about making the material available as Linked Open Data[23]. Publishing in this environment requires the use of accepted standards, such as domain ontologies, Simple Knowledge Organization System (SKOS), or reference databases. However, in case of the materials in question, the first step must be to bring them to the data level as the vast majority of publications (even digital once) is not released at data level at all[24]. The first step of publishing papal sources in Linked Open Data is to convert the current publications into a structured form, which is not a trivial task. Considering the quantity of the existing material, transforming it into data form is impossible without digital tools using automation.

The technology for extracting entities from text is called Named Entity Recognition (NER)[25]. NER should in theory allow the automatic extraction of personal names, place names and information about offices and institutions from texts[26]. In practice, however, NLP engines still do not work effectively enough on medieval Latin texts, especially in the form of regesta, where the information density is greater than in natural text. Of course, further work on NLP will in time inevitably enable to identify named entities and link them to reference databases (Named Entity Linking) automatically, but at the moment, we still have to cope with other, less advanced solutions.

The features of historical sources editions make it possible to use methods that are not based on linguistic models and artificial intelligence (such as NLP), but that operate on the structure of the text. This is because traditional editions usually are a structured collection of text, data and metadata expressed in print. This structure is of course not expressed in a computer-understandable way (table, tags), but by the

23 Definition of the LOD: https://www.w3.org/egov/wiki/Linked_Open_Data.

24 An example of such digitisation is the 'Repertorium Germanicum'. Although an online database has been created on the basis of this publication (http://www.romana-repertoria.net/993.html), it still operates on text and not on entities modelled with Universal Identifiers.

25 Named Entity Recognition is a subfield of Natural Language Processing. The main purpose of NER is to find and recognise named entities in the text.

26 On the use of NER in Latin texts e.g.: Alexander Erdmann/Christopher Brown7Brian Joseph/Mark Janse/Petra Ajaka/Micha Elsner/Marie-Catharine de Marneffe, Challenges and Solutions for Latin Named Entity Recognition, in: Proceedings of the Workshop on Language Technology Resources and Tools for Digital Humanities (LT4DH), Osaka 2016, p. 85–93; Chastang, A named entity (as n. 22).

layout of the content on the page (format, position on the page, font types, order in which the information is written), and also by indexes.

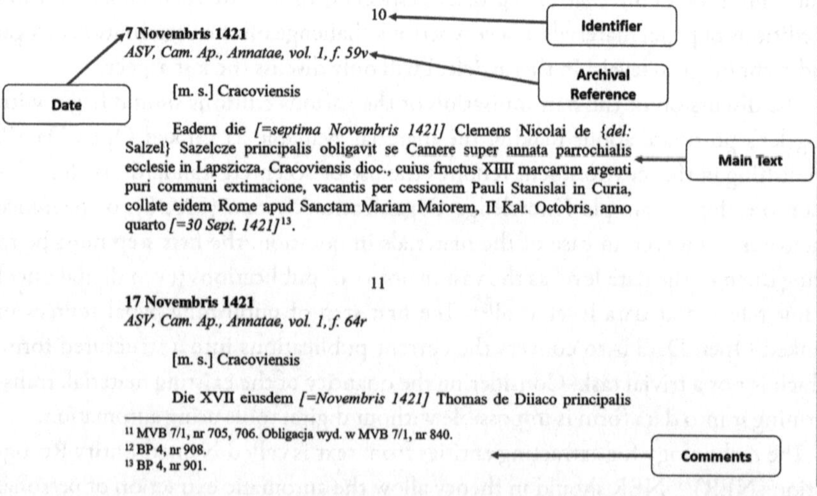
10

7 Novembris 1421
ASV, Cam. Ap., Annatae, vol. 1, f. 59v

[m. s.] Cracoviensis

Eadem die *[=septima Novembris 1421]* Clemens Nicolai de *{del:* Salzel} Sazelcze principalis obligavit se Camere super annata parrochialis ecclesie in Lapszicza, Cracoviensis dioc., cuius fructus XIIII marcarum argenti puri communi extimacione, vacantis per cessionem Pauli Stanislai in Curia, collate eidem Rome apud Sanctam Mariam Maiorem, II Kal. Octobris, anno quarto *[=30 Sept. 1421]*[13].

11

17 Novembris 1421
ASV, Cam. Ap., Annatae, vol. 1, f. 64r

[m. s.] Cracoviensis

Die XVII eiusdem *[=Novembris 1421]* Thomas de Diiaco principalis

[11] MVB 7/1, nr 705, 706. Obligacja wyd. w MVB 7/1, nr 840.
[12] BP 4, nr 908.
[13] BP 4, nr 901.

Fig. 1a: Data structure in main text of Annatae e Regno Poloniae saeculi decimi quinti (MPV 10)[27].

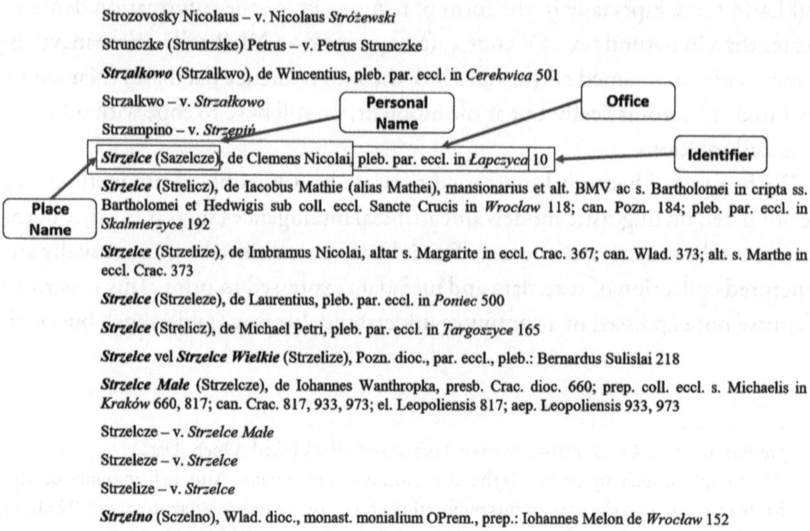
Strozovosky Nicolaus – v. Nicolaus *Stróżewski*

Strunczke (Struntzske) Petrus – v. Petrus Strunczke

Strzałkowo (Strzalkwo), de Wincentius, pleb. par. eccl. in *Cerekwica* 501

Strzalkwo – v. *Strzałkowo*

Strzampino – v. *Strzepiń*

Strzelce (Sazelcze), de Clemens Nicolai, pleb. par. eccl. in *Łapczyca* 10

Strzelce (Strelicz), de Iacobus Mathie (alias Mathei), mansionarius et alt. BMV ac s. Bartholomei in cripta ss. Bartholomei et Hedwigis sub coll. eccl. Sancte Crucis in *Wrocław* 118; can. Pozn. 184; pleb. par. eccl. in *Skalmierzyce* 192

Strzelce (Strzelize), de Imbramus Nicolai, altar s. Margarite in eccl. Crac. 367; can. Wlad. 373; alt. s. Marthe in eccl. Crac. 373

Strzelce (Strzeleze), de Laurentius, pleb. par. eccl. in *Poniec* 500

Strzelce (Strelicz), de Michael Petri, pleb. par. eccl. in *Targoszyce* 165

Strzelce vel ***Strzelce Wielkie*** (Strzelize), Pozn. dioc., par. eccl., pleb.: Bernardus Sulislai 218

Strzelce Małe (Strzelcze), de Iohannes Wanthropka, presb. Crac. dioc. 660; prep. coll. eccl. s. Michaelis in *Kraków* 660, 817; can. Crac. 817, 933, 973; el. Leopoliensis 817; aep. Leopoliensis 933, 973

Strzelcze – v. *Strzelce Małe*

Strzeleze – v. *Strzelce*

Strzelize – v. *Strzelce*

Strzelno (Sczelno), Wlad. dioc., monast. monialium OPrem., prep.: Iohannes Melon de *Wrocław* 152

Fig. 1b: Data structure in the index of MPV 10.

27 Annatae e Regno Poloniae saeculi XV (1421-1503), ed. Marek Daniel KOWALSKI, Monumenta Poloniae Vaticana 10 (2002) Kraków (MPV 10).

Fig. 1 provides an example of the data structure in a traditional source publication[28]. The editor has visually highlighted the following data and metadata: identifier, date, archival reference, main text and comments. The identifier was distinguished by the layout (middle of the page), the date was formatted in bold, the archive reference in italics, and the commentary was specified by its position at the bottom of the page. The editor also detailed the most important data in an index [Fig. 1b]. These have been structured by placing the information in a specific order, with reference to the record identifier. In other editions, the information in the indexes is sometimes even more extensive (e.g. in the *Repertorium Germanicum*[29]) but it is always structured. In this situation, the most important information from the edition can be extracted using simple operations on the structure and layout of the text. The workflow of such extraction is shown in Fig. 2.

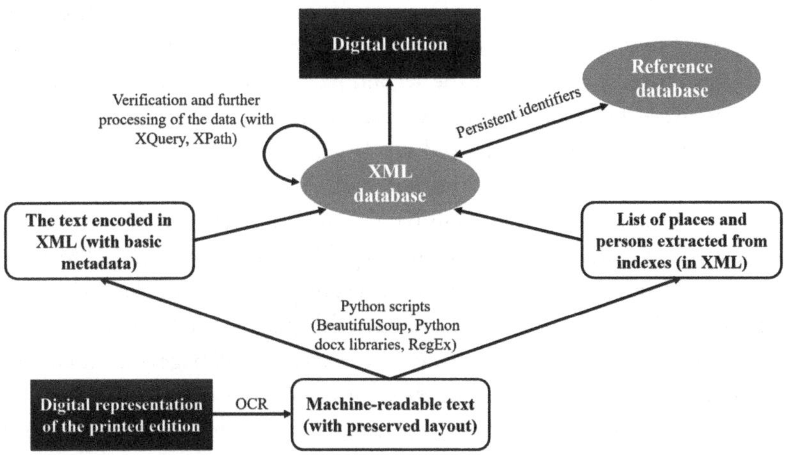

Fig. 2: Workflow of extraction data and metadata from printed editions.

The first step is to convert the digital representation of the edition (e.g. scans) into a machine-readable text form. To do this, OCR must be carried out with layout preservation. Not all commonly available OCR engines handle this type of operation well. FineReader[30], for example, stands out in this aspect, as it can save the results in ALTO format[31], preserving the layout of the text on the page and its formatting (font type, size, bold, italics, underlining, etc.). With the ability to select individual blocks of text, semantics can be easily assigned. Further processing with

28 Ibid.
29 http://rg-online.dhi-roma.it/denqRG/index.htm
30 https://pdf.abbyy.com
31 https://www.loc.gov/standards/alto/description

python scripts, the use of Regex and text processing libraries allow the annotation in XML of individual parts of the text as well as indices. One of the standards such as TEI[32] or CEI[33] can be used for annotation. The produced XML can be stored in a database (e.g. eXistDB[34] or BaseX[35]). However, such annotated text is not yet satisfactory for harmonisation purposes. Further transformations still need to be made in order to disambiguate the information. Firstly, the metadata should be unified, e.g. the ID number should be described together with the resource name (instead of '1', can be 'MVP10_1'). Such unification will make it unambiguous after merging different datasets. Then, information should be converted to the standards (e.g. dates to ISO, archival signatures to recommendations from the Vatican Apostolic Archives) and saved as attributes of the tags. The next, and in my opinion the most important step, is to give the entities unambiguous and permanent identifiers from reference databases.

This method was applied at the Department of Historical Atlas in the Institute of History of the Polish Academy of Sciences. The test sample was editions of papal sources related to Poland in the second half of the 15th century. Specifically, the *Repertorium Germanicum* (downloaded from the website)[36], the *Bullarium Poloniae* (obtained from scans)[37] and the *Monumenta Polonie Vaticana* (from the text file)[38]. Despite the different forms of these three publications, the above-mentioned transformations made it possible to combine them into a single database and then to search and compare the various publications using queries (XQuery[39]). Of course, a database prepared in this way is not perfect. Particularly problematic are, for example, the differences in the way of displaying the same information in joined resources (e.g. the *Bullarium Poloniae* referred to all pages on which the text in the source was located, while the *Repertorium Germanicum* indicated only the first page and then abbreviated the fact that the document still had more pages). Ambiguous data, like two documents appearing on the same page in the source, can also be a problem. Such things need to be verified manually by a historian. Verification could also involve further improvement of the base, like granting identifiers for particular cases, or identifying references between cases.

Material prepared in this way is not yet ready to be fed directly into the Semantic Web. For this, the database would need to be further processed into RDF. How-

32 https://tei-c.org

33 http://www.cei.lmu.de

34 http://exist-db.org/exist/apps/homepage/index.html

35 https://basex.org

36 http://www.romana-repertoria.net/index_rro.html

37 Bullarium Poloniae: litteras apostolicas aliaque monumenta Poloniae Vaticana continens 6, ed. Stanisław Kuraś/Irena Sułkowska-Kuraś, Romae-Lublin 1998.

38 Kowalski, MPV 10.

39 https://www.w3.org/TR/xquery-31/

ever, this does not change the fact that such preparation would be a significant step towards linking the various editions of papal sources, and the existence of such database would be a great help for researchers studying papal letters and could also encourage editors working on the new projects to take a more diligent approach to the question of persistent identification and linking their data with external databases.

Indexing the resource and making the data available

The second level of improving the accessibility of papal material is the publication of data from archival sources. As I have already mentioned, editors realised it already at the beginning of the 20th century that a full-text edition of the papal sources in print was not possible. This is the reason why the form of regesta or excerpts became widespread. The purpose of this form was to provide information from the text, without transcribing and editing of archival documents. In practice, even the regesta form proved to be too demanding to process all the papal material (or even 'only' the part of it which is held in the Vatican Archives). Therefore, there is no modern index to find the required information in the registers (and beyond). A database makes it easier to achieve such a goal by exploiting the benefits of information engineering without the need for time-consuming text processing. Such a solution can be indexing of manuscripts using GIS technology. This solution has been successfully implemented for the mass historical sources at the Department of Historical Atlas of the Institute of History of the Polish Academy of Sciences[40]. An INDXR system has been developed there, to facilitate this process[41].

INDXR uses Geographic Information System (GIS) standards to connect places on the scan with a database (PostgreSQL). In practice, it provides a user-friendly interface with easy entry of data from the manuscript into the database. Drawing a polygon on the scan creates a new record in the database and opens a pop-up window on the page, allowing researcher to enter data. To speed up input, it is possible to define dictionaries and default values as well as to use external resources (e.g. Wi-

40 Marek Słoń/Urszula Zachara-Związek, The Court Records of Wschowa (1495–1526). Digital Edition, in: Studia Geohistorica 6 (2019) p. 206–220, https://atlas.ihpan.edu.pl/gis/agad_wschowa_i2_pub/index.php; Arkadiusz Borek/Tomasz Związek/Michał Słomski/Michał Gochna/Grzegorz Myrda/Marek Słoń, Technical and methodological foundations of digital indexing of medieval and early modern court books, in: Digital Scholarship in the Humanities 35/II (2020) p. 233–253; https://atlas.ihpan.edu.pl/indxr/app/kspk_pub/index.php; https://atlasfontium.pl/ksiegi-miejskie-kalisza/ ; https://atlas.ihpan.edu.pl/indxr/app/kkk_pub/index.php.

41 The functioning of INDXR and an example of its implementation in the editorial project are described in: Borek, Technical (as n. 40).

kidata) do provide identifiers. This solution accelerates the extraction of data from the scans, and binds the information with the exact location in the manuscript. A great advantage of INDXR is the flexibility in creating the data model for many layers of data. Therefore, a separate data model can be developed for the books, a separate one for their parts (chapter, contributions), another for individual documents and another for entities. Importantly, the data stored in INDXR can be accessed not only by this application, but by any SQL database manager, allowing it to be further processed in the user's preferred environment. The application has been used successfully to compile court books[42], tax records[43] and historical maps[44]. It can also be implemented for papal sources.

A database created for papal sources should contain at least three layers of data. Physical object level (e.g. book, charter), document level and entity level. At the physical object level, basic codicological information should be recorded, at the document level the most important metadata about text should be described, while the most extensive indexing should take place at the entity level. Entities such as places, people, dates, offices, institutions and dioceses have to be identified.

The most important issue related to data publication is the use of established standards. The use of standard data formats (at the data level), controlled vocabularies and domain ontologies (at the definition and relations level), as well as persistent identifiers and reference databases (at the entity level) allows data from different projects to be harmonised and used together.

A widely used ontology in the humanities is CIDOC-CRM[45], but it does not always meet the needs of the project. Therefore, it is important to work on lower-level domain ontologies. An important need is the creation of an ontology to describe the institutions and procedures of the Roman Curia. Even more problematic are reference databases for entities. Historians tend to use resources created for other fields of study, e.g. GeoNames for places[46] or VIAF for people[47]. Unfortunately, these resources do not fully meet the requirements of historical research. Geographic databases do not consider changes over time, while databases of per-

42 Marek Słoń/Urszula Zachara-Związek, The Court Records of Wschowa (1495–1526). Digital Edition, in: Studia Geohistorica 6 (2019) p. 206–220, https://atlas.ihpan.edu.pl/gis/agad_wschowa_i2_pub/index.php; Borek, Technical (as n. 40); https://atlas.ihpan.edu.pl/indxr/app/kspk_pub/index.php; https://atlasfontium.pl/ksiegi-miejskie-kalisza/ ; https://atlas.ihpan.edu.pl/indxr/app/kkk_pub/index.php.

43 An edition of 16th-century Polish tax registers was prepared as part of the project „Atlas historyczny Polski XVI wieku – dopełnienie serii", https://atlasfontium.pl/rejestry-poborowe-korony/

44 Bogumił Szady/Tomasz Panecki, Source-driven data model for geohistorical records' editing: a case study of the works of Karol Perthées, in: Miscellanea Geographica 26/I (2022) p. 52–62, https://doi.org/10.2478/mgrsd-2020-0070

45 https://www.cidoc-crm.org

46 https://www.geonames.org

47 https://viaf.org

sons often lack the relevant entities (e.g. lesser-known supplicants to the Roman Curia). For this reason, the creation of domain-specific historical reference databases is extremely important. Such a database on Polish history is WikiHum[48], which is being developed within the Dariah.lab[49] infrastructure. It is an aggregator of Polish historical research data using Wikibase technology[50]. It provides persistent identifiers via Handle.net system[51] for people, places, offices, coat of arms etc. from the past, modelled according to the needs of historians. It allows combining data from different projects in one place and linked to the most important LOD nodes (Wikidata, VIAF).

INDXR was conceived for publication data with scans, however, due to the restrictive licensing policy of the Vatican Apostolic Archives the scans of papal sources will be used only to create a database, without publishing them. Even the dissemination of data would be a great benefit in making the papal source material more available. It would provide researchers with information in an accessible form and would allow them to search more efficiently in the Vatican Archives[52]. Material from other archives could be published according to the licensing rules of the institutions.

Importantly, indexing of papal sources can take place at both the national level (for documents related to a particular region or country) and the universal level (at the level of the entire resource). The use of standards can still allow data to be combined and used together.

Full text edition

The third level of work on papal sources with digital methods is the creation of full-text editions. Until now, the vast majority of projects have shied away from this task for practical reasons. This made research on papal sources very time-consuming and led to inefficient use of the corpus, especially in fields like papal diplomatics. Digital technologies provide opportunities for full-text processing, as they significantly speed up the work. They can be used, firstly, to retrieve machine-readable texts, secondly, to improve the quality of the copied text, thirdly to extract data from the

48 https://wikihum.lab.dariah.pl/wiki/Main_Page

49 Works financed by the project: 'Cyfrowa infrastruktura badawcza dla humanistyki i nauk o sztuce DARIAH-PL', n°: POIR.04.02.00-00-D006/20.

50 https://wikiba.se

51 https://www.handle.net

52 This approach is used to process papal sources on Poland from the second half of the 15th century in the project "Polscy dyplomaci przy Stolicy Apostolskiej w drugiej połowie XV wieku – kwerenda biblioteczna i archiwalna", NCN, Miniatura 5, nr 2021/05/X/HS3/01142.

texts, and lastly, to publish the editions considering the volume and complexity of the papal source material.

The first type of the usage of digital tools is the acquisition of text in machine-readable form. The tool of the future in this regard is Handwritten Text Recognition (HTR). HTR is a technology that uses machine learning to create handwriting models and then automatically read manuscripts. Successful solutions already exist, both commercial (e.g. Transkribus[53]) and open sourced (e.g. eScriptorium[54] with the Kraken engine[55]). In HTR, it is essential to prepare a broad and representative training sample adapted to the handwriting style. Since hundreds of scribes worked in the 15th-century Roman Curia, the preparation of such a sample is time-consuming, although not impossible, hence the creation of a satisfactory model of writing for the 15th-century Roman Curia is only a matter of time. Currently the use of HTR in editing papal sources is still rather an experimental solution and most of the work must be done manually, however, digital tools can speed up even this traditional part of the work.

As I have already mentioned, a large proportion of the surviving papal sources concerning individual privileges are built with repetitive formulas. The documents are not identical; however, recurring parts are easily distinguished. These features enable to speed up the process of manually transcribing a large part of the source material, by using a software that allows the memorisation and copying of repeated text. This option is available, for example, in standard office software like MS Word. For this reason, a considerable part of papal documents does not need to be rewritten at all, but merely constructed from repeated parts of the formulary and proofread. This approach helps to essentially speed up transcription process.

The formulaic form of most papal sources also enables to automatically improve the quality of the copies with the usage of "text re-use detection" tools (e.g. Passim[56], TRACER[57] or CollateX[58]). The identification of repetitive phrases makes it easy for the researcher to find anomalies (which are likely errors). It has also research applications in other fields, especially in diplomatic studies.

A crucial issue for digital editing is the transfer of text to data level (as described for traditional editing). Only this way of publishing will truly bring the edited text to contemporary standards satisfying both for traditional historians and those working with data. The format most commonly used to annotate information in the text is XML, especially in its TEI or CEI standards. XML tags allow to change

53 https://readcoop.eu/transkribus/

54 https://www.escriptorium.uk

55 https://kraken.re/master/index.html

56 Matteo Romanello/Simon Hengchen, Detecting Text Reuse with Passim, in: Programming Historian (2021) https://doi.org/10.46430/phen0092

57 https://www.etrap.eu/research/tracer/

58 https://collatex.net

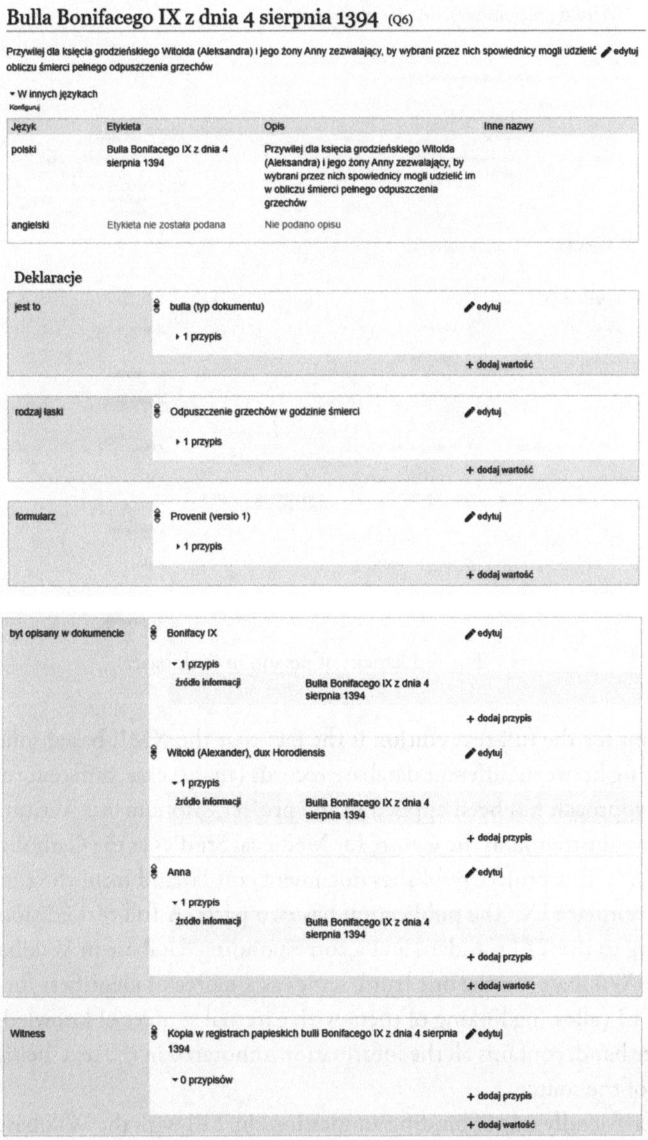

Fig. 3a-b: Element of document in Wikibase.

text into a database. It is important to emphasize that XML tags mark not only the semantics of the different parts of the text, but also create the possibility to describe the data with standards and reference databases – as it was already described. The way data is extracted and described in the full-text edition does not differ from that of the methods mentioned in earlier chapters (on traditional editions and data).

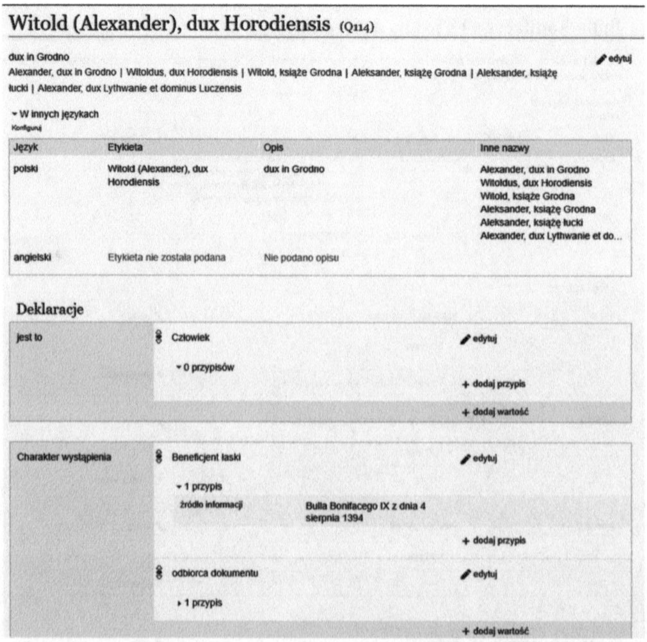

Fig. 4: Element of person in Wikibase.

Important for the full-text edition is the fact that the XML-based solution allows referencing between different database records (in our case, different texts).

This approach has been applied in the project 'Monumenta Vaticana res gestas Polonicas illustrantia' at the Centre for Medieval Studies at the Catholic University of Lublin[59]. This project publishes documents on Poland from the time of Urban VI and Boniface IX. The publication has two parts. A full-text edition annotated according to the TEI standard and a corresponding database in Wikibase technology. The Wikibase, on the one hand, serves as a source of identifiers for annotation in the TEI (allowing linking of them with external sources of knowledge) and, on the other hand, contains all the information annotated in the text, being a database version of the source.

A user-friendly way of binding annotations in TEI with the Wikibase is through the annotation sample interface in TEI Publisher. The annotation contains not only the semantics derived from the tags, but also the unambiguous identification of Wiki entities (via the @ref attribute). In our project we also annotate the character of every entity occurrence in the document, e.g. "issuer of the document" (via the

59 Project funded by the Ministry of Science and Higher Education of the Republic of Poland in the framework of: "Centrum Studiów Mediewistycznych: podstawowe badania edytorskie i inwentaryzacyjne do dziejów średniowiecznej Polski", n. MEIN/2022/DPI/3503.

```xml
<text>
   <body>
      <p>
         <persName ref="va-Q249" ana="wystawca">Bonifacius</persName> etc., dilecto filio
            <persName ref="va-Q114" ana="odbiorca beneficjent_laski tytulatura">
            <roleName ana="pochodzenie_spoleczne" ref="va-Q108">nobili viro</roleName>
               Alexandro,<region ref="va-Q257" ana="diecezja"> </region>
            <affiliation ref="va-Q113" ana="zajmowane_stanowisko">duci Horodiensi</affiliation>
         </persName> et dilecte in Christo filie <persName ref="va-Q115"
            ana="odbiorca beneficjent_laski tytulatura">
            <roleName ana="pochodzenie_spoleczne" ref="va-Q108">nobili mulieri</roleName> Anne,
               <persName ref="va-Q114" ana="wspolmalzonek">eius</persName> uxori, <region
               ref="va-Q257" ana="diecezja">Wilnensis diocesis</region>
         </persName>, salutem etc. Provenit etc. <supplied source="Q352" resp="edytor"
            cert="hipotetyczna">Hinc est, quod nos ...., ut confessor tuus, quem duxeris
            eligendum, omnium peccatorum tuorum .... semel tantum in mortis articulo plenam
            remissionem tibi .... auctoritate apostolica concedere valeat, devocioni tue tenore
            presencium indulgemus; sic tamen, quod ....</supplied> Datum <placeName ref="va-Q67"
            ana="miejsce_wystawienia_dokumentu">Rome apud Sanctum Petrum</placeName>, <date
            type="data_" when="1394-08-04">secundo non. augusti, anno quinto</date>. <handShift/>
         <note type="document_fee" place="in_line">
            <persName ref="va-Q66" ana="urzednik_kurialny">N(icolaus). <measure quantity="16"
                  ana="taksa_dokumentu">XVI</measure>. de Ben(even)to</persName>. </note>
      </p>
   </body>
</text>
```

Fig. 5: Annotation of the document in TEI.

@ana attribute). Such annotation enables to easily extract information from TEI and import them into the Wikibase (in form of triples). Then the identifier of the parent element becomes subject, the value of the @ana attribute becomes predicate while the identifier of the child element becomes object. The document's metadata, including links to other sources, is also expressed in both the TEI (teiHeader) and the Wikibase. This solution, which has so far been applied to a sample of 90 documents, will be further developed, while it is already clear that it will enable a large full-text corpus of papal sources from the 15th century to be satisfactorily processed.

Significantly automating and speeding up work with text using digital tools makes it possible to return to the concepts of publishing that were abandoned at the beginning of the 20th century and bring the full texts of the papal sources into scholarly circulation. This will allow a wider group of researchers to get to know the sources, which they have often only used through regests. This will facilitate and allow a significant development of research related to the Holy See in the 15th century.

Conclusions and outlook

The use of digital technology described above allows us to decisively improve the accessibility of papal sources for researchers. They ensure both easier extraction of relevant data from the source and the creation of easy-to-use indexes, as well as the development of a full-text corpus ready for use in research. Progressive automation and the possibility of harmonising different resources are also very important aspects of these solutions. All the practices described above can be used together and interconnected to optimise the effect and open papal sources to a wider public. In order to do this, the mindset of researchers must change. For traditional historians in particular, publication is associated with print or a closed web application with a user interface. The development of Linked Open Data shifts the centre of gravity from the interface to the data itself. The ability to search through a variety of data resources linked by permanent identifiers makes the display of data more important than the creation of an interface or print.

The greatest challenge the research community faces is harmonising projects and synchronising work. There are long-established publishing projects for papal sources in most European countries. The use of new technologies would have to be combined with a change in the way we think about the papal material. We should recognise it as our common pan-European heritage and work together to make it accessible to the public. From a technological point of view, it is much simpler than from the legal and organisational perspective. However, it is necessary in order to achieve an optimal use of 15th-century papal sources. This can happen either by centralising the work (e.g. the Vatican Archives taking the lead, or organising an international research project) or by creating a decentralised community trying to set and implement standards in the various existing projects. The use of digital infrastructure helps in this, e.g. through the possibility of creating an ontology about the Pontifical Curia and the existence of generally accepted standards for organising information. The removal of geographical barriers is also not insignificant. Researchers from all over the world can work on the development of a single database. To process all 15th – century papal source material would take decades, however, the result would be worth such an effort.

Support of Hungaricana research

A database of diplomatic sources and an experience of 3D scanning of wax seals[1]

Ádám Novák, Sándor Ónadi

Introduction

Our research group started its work in 2014 within the "*Lendület*" [Momentum] programme of the Hungarian Academy of Sciences, and is currently supported by the University of Debrecen. Under the leadership of Professor Attila Bárány, the research group has carried out and is currently running two digital projects based on original medieval sources, which we will be presented in this paper. One of these was a digital online source database, focusing on the history of medieval Hungarian diplomacy, and the other was a pilot project carried out in 2016 in collaboration with the University of Prešov as part of the 2016 exhibition entitled "Gothic in the Monastery of Pilis – King Andrew II's French Relations". Using 3D measurement, we digitised original medieval wax seals and their plastic copies. We gained a considerable amount of experience, on which we reported at the conference and which we will attempt to explain in more detail in this paper.

1 The authors are member of the "Hungary in Medieval Europe" Research Group at the University of Debrecen. The research on which this study is based project no. TKP2021-NKTA-34 has been implemented with the support provided by the Ministry of Culture and Innovation of Hungary from the National Research, Development and Innovation Fund, financed under the TKP2021-NKTA funding scheme.

The Memoria Hungariae Source Database

Charters are the most important sources of information on the Hungarian Middle Ages. This is due to the scarcity of narrative sources that have survived, unlike in Western Europe, and to the fact that the built heritage of Hungary suffered considerable losses due to Ottoman destruction. Only a fraction of the documents has been preserved, as a large part of them were destroyed during the Ottoman rule and the storms of history (World War II, the 1956 revolution, communist secularisation and nationalisation). Their importance was recognised already at the end of the 19th century, at the dawn of the professionalisation of Hungarian historiography, then the concept of "*Hungarica*" was created[2]. This has changed considerably over the years, but today, according to the 1971/205 directive of the Hungarian Academy of Sciences we call Hungarica all documents which relate to

A. the territory, population, inhabitants, political, administrative, judicial, socio-economic, scientific, etc., relations of the Kindome of Hungary and also the modern Hungary at any given time;
B. the relations of Hungary and its residents with foreign lands and foreigners;
C. the views of foreign states, organisations and residents regarding the views and activities of residents (bodies) living (working) in Hungary or its territory;
D. significant persons of Hungarian origin who have lived or are living abroad, and their activities;
E. memories that contain data of historical value on Hungarian ethnic groups living or having lived abroad.

The exploration of "Hungarica" documents began in the 19th century, and around the turn of the 19th to 20th centuries, it was organized within a coordinated framework. Milestones in this process included the initiation of thematic source publication series and the establishment of the *Collegium Hungaricum* institution in the 1920s. The institutions established in major European cities were primarily intended to support and assist Hungarian-origin researchers' professional journeys abroad. They provided accommodation and professional support for numerous researchers conducting archival studies abroad. Additionally, they played an important role in cultivating Hungarian international relations. After the signing of the Treaty of Trianon, foreign source exploration became even more critical, as many important collections ended up beyond the borders, making the accessibility and study of archival materials challenging. Documents related to "Hungarica" became, for instance, the former records of Upper Hungarian cities, which were now situated in the territory and under the control of the Czechoslovak state. With the de-

2 István Kollega Tarsoly, Levéltári hungarika kutatás [Archival Hungarica Research], in: Levéltári Szemle 42/2 (1992) p. 40–52. This concept gave rise to the name of the Hungarian digital public collection portal, Hungaricana.

velopment of technology, a new method has been used to study them: microfilming. In a short time, it was possible to record large archival material and processing could be done at home. Antal Fekete Nagy and Bálint Ila were the first to research the archive of the authentication place of the Spiš Chapter using this method in 1935[3]. From this point on, the Hungarica research was carried out by microfilming the documents selected during the longer or shorter research trips. The detailed process can be traced back through the writings of Iván Borsa and István Kollega Tarsoly in the columns of the *Levéltári Szemle* [Archival Review][4]. And the result can be seen in the database of the Diplomatic Archives–Diplomatic Photo Collection of the Hungarian National Archives, which was conceived by Borsa and implemented by György Rácz[5]. Research availability has been greatly enhanced by the fact that, as of 2009, the Archive has made it accessible online with metadata and photographs. The resulting *Collectio Diplomatica Hungarica* has greatly facilitated research on medieval Hungarian history[6]. Our research team is exploring the positionof the Kingdom of Hungary in Europe, its image, its dynastic-diplomatic relations and expanding its base of sources. The project fits in with the burgeoning international contact studies that are rethinking the relationship between the "West" and the "periphery". We seek to better grasp the role and image of Hungary in the European political scene, and in Latin Christianity. Our main question is how the country was able to "join" Europe, remain a powerful monarchy and stand its ground in the bloodstream of large-scale politics. The results show that in many respects that Hungary was closer to the European centre in certain periods of the Middle Ages than in later times[7]. Since 2014, in the framework of this research, we

3 The Chapter of Spiš was one of the most important "locus credibilis", which fulfilled the role of notary in medieval Hungary, as it is a specificum of Hungarian Diplomatics.

4 Iván Borsa, A magyar medievisztika forráskérdései. (Medievisztika és levéltári anyag) [Source Issues of Hungarian Medieval Studies (Medieval Studies and Archival Material)], in: Levéltári Közlemények 44–45. (1974) p. 114; Id., A hungarikakutatás aktuális kérdései [Current Issues of Hungarica Research], in: Levéltári Szemle 36/2 (1986) p. 8–13; Id., A Magyar Országos Levéltár középkori gyűjteményei [The Medieval Collections of the Hungarian National Archives], in: Erdélyi Múzeum 58 (1996) p. 314–321.

5 In Hungarian: Magyar Nemzeti Levéltár Országos Levéltára Diplomatikai Levéltár–Diplomatikai Fényképgyűjtemény [Diplomatic Archive–Diplomatic Photo Collection of the National Archives of Hungary], abbreviation: MNL OL DL–DF.

6 A középkori Magyarország levéltári forrásainak adatbázisa [Database of archival sources of medieval Hungary] (DL–DF 4.2.) CD–ROM, ed. György Rácz, Budapest 2003. Online as of 2009: Collectio Diplomatica Hungarica, ed. György Rácz. More recently: https://adatbazisokonline.mnl.gov.hu/adatbazis/dldf. More details on the current developments of the database were presented by Krisztina Aranyi at the conference.

7 More about the research objectives: Attila Bárány, Magyarország helye és képe a középkori Európában [The Place and Image of Hungary in Medieval Europe], in: Debreceni Szemle 3 (2014) p. 268–274.

have been actively collecting and processing sources in both Western and Central Europe.

In this spirit, new documentary material has been discovered, or the original texts of documents already known from the printed source publications have been uncovered. An important cornerstone of our research is that we have also managed to record the seals of the diplomas of the MNL OL DF[8], which are only available in microfilm (black and white) copies both in the National Archives of Hungary and online. We also drew from a wider range of sources, such as diplomatic correspondence, reports of envoys, commissions, tombstones and notes from chambers.

In addition to presenting these sources in studies and monographs, we have also created a freely accessible, online searchable database of sources. Although the tradition of Hungarian historiography requires the publication of edited, printed, limited-edition source publications, this database represents a new step in the process of source publication. Its main purpose is to enable the sources cited to be retrieved and exploited in different ways. The "Memoria Hungariae" database is a JAVA based application, where the records are always based on an image (source), which is associated with 20 metadata[9]. 17 of these are searchable for more precise browsing options. Each record has a unique identifier (ID) to facilitate future reference. Records can be entered manually, one by one; neither import nor export is possible. However, the content of the records can be downloaded as a PDF file. The database allows the creation of internal links for connected records (e.g. in the case of multiple pages of a manuscript, or polysigillic charters). In the input fields, users can embed an external link that directs to related or external content (e.g. to a previous edition of a charter, or a microfilm copy of an original diploma in the DF.)

A successful search requires at least three characters in the search field or selecting an item from the drop-down menus. The images in the database were taken or have been taken by the research team and its members for the purpose of scientific processing. The database can be accessed free of charge, and the images are watermarked to prevent them from being used commercially. The images cannot be saved directly, thus safeguarding the rights of the holding institutions. The aim of our research group is to make the digitised sources available to foreign colleagues as well who are studying the history of medieval Hungary, therefore the search interface of the website offers both English and French language options. Currently, version 2.6.1.11 of the database is available on the server of the University of Debrecen[10]. Since the birth of the portal, we have uploaded more than 1000 records, to which

8 See footnote 4.

9 Registry number (ID), set, date, contemporary dating, survival form, place, character, origin, author, language, folio/page range, image data, publication data, bibliography, personal names, short summary, geographical names, other 1–2–3, and uploader name.

10 Memoria Hungariae database: http://lendulet.memhung.unideb.hu – Abbreviation: MH

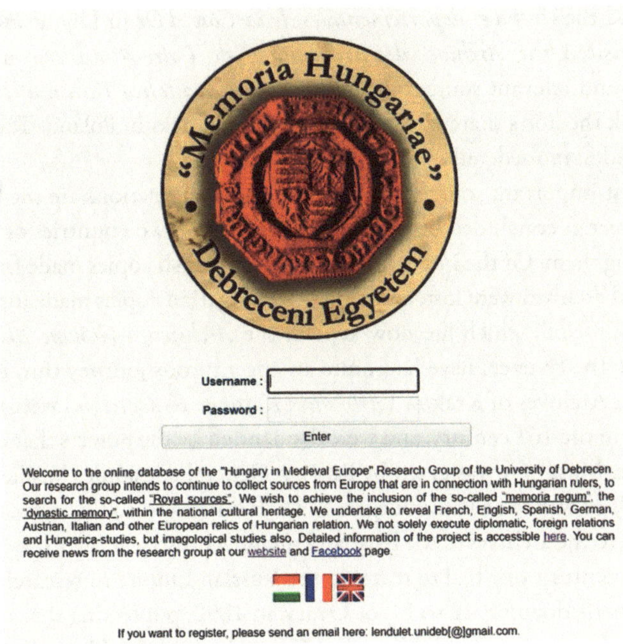

Fig. 1: Welcome screen of the database.

we have also added short entries. In 2016, we signed a cooperation agreement with the Hungarian National Archives to synchronise our database with the collection of the Diplomatikai Levéltár – Diplomatikai Fényképgyűjtemény (DL-DF) after the end of the project. The collection is still under construction, and not all sources have been published yet. In the following, we will describe the nature and content of the sources available through a few examples.

Our colleagues have carried out research and digitisation in archives in several countries. Attila Bárány and Attila Györkös conducted research in England[11]. In France, Gergely Kiss collected materials from the *Archives nationales de France*

11 The original letter of King Louis II of Hungary from the British Library, asking Henry VIII for military and financial aid against the Ottomans in 1526: MH 10011–12.; Cf.: Attila Bárány, A szulejmáni ajánlat. Magyarország, a Török Birodalom és a Nyugat (1521–1524) [The Offer of Suleiman. Hungary, the Ottoman Empire and the West (1521–1524),], Máriabesnyő 2014; Pierre Choque, breton herold leírása Foix-i Anna francia grófnő, leendő magyar királyné utazásáról, esküvőjéről és megkoronázásáról Magyarországon [Description by Pierre Choque, Breton herald, on the journey, wedding and Hungarian coronation of Anne of Foix, French Countess and future Queen of Hungary]: MH 23125. Cf.: Attila Györkös, Reneszánsz utazás. Anna királyné 1502-es fogadtatásának ünnepségei Észak-Itáliában és Magyarországon [A Renaissance Journey. The Celebrations of the Reception of Queen Anne in Northern Italy and Hungary in 1502] (Scriptores Rerum Hungaricarum 9), Máriabesnyő 2016.

in Paris and the *Archives départementales de la Côte d'Or* in Dijon[12], while Attila Györkös visited the *Archives départementales de Loire-Atlantique* in Nantes[13]. We also found relevant sources in the *Biblioteca Apostolica Vaticana*[14], and Adam Novák took the lion's share in the search for Hungaricas in Poland. The latter will be explained in more detail.

The most important sources of Polish–Hungarian relations are the bilateral or trilateral treaties concluded between the rulers of the two countries or the envoys representing them. Of the important treaties, the Polish copies made for the Hungarian royal archives were lost, and only the Hungarian copies made for the Polish side have survived, which are now kept in the *Archiwum Główne Akt Dawnych* in Warsaw. The charters have had quite an adventurous journey through history. The Crown Archives of Krakow (*Arhiwum Koronne Krakowskie*) were transferred to Warsaw in the 16th century, and were dismantled by the powers that divided the Polish state. Most of it was taken by Russian General Alexander Vasilievich Suvorov as spoils of war to St Petersburg in 1794 after he captured Warsaw, then it was transferred to the archives of the Russian Foreign Ministry in Moscow. Thus, at the turn of the century, one had to travel to the Russian Empire to research the medieval diplomatic documents, so Lipót Óváry, in 1890, publishing the copies of the diplomatic documents of the Historical Committee of the Hungarian Academy of Sciences, also cited the Moscow archives as the place where these documents were kept[15]. The Polish-Soviet war that broke out after the First World War ended with the Peace of Riga, signed on 18 March 1921, under which the parties agreed that the contents of Polish archives that had been taken to Moscow would be re-

12 The seal of Bishop-Cardinal István Báncsa of Preneste from Paris: MH 24021. Cf. Gergely Kiss, Dél-Magyarországtól Itáliáig. Báncsa nembeli István (1205 k. – 1270) váci püspök, esztergomi érsek, az első magyarországi bíboros életpályája [From Southern Hungary to Italy. The Career of István of the House of Báncsa (1205 c. – 1270), Bishop of Vác, Archbishop of Esztergom, the First Cardinal of Hungary], Pécs 2015; Original charter of King Béla IV of Hungary from Dijon: MH 24041.

13 Letter of commission from King Vladislaus II of Hungary to Miklós Bacskai, Bishop of Nitra, and István Telegdi, Royal Councillor, on the occasion of their visit to France: MH 23104. Cf. Györkös, Reneszánsz utazás. (as n. 11).

14 The original will and testament of Bishop-Cardinal István Báncsa, Bishop of Praeneste: MH 24002. Cf.: Gergely Kiss, Dél-Magyarországtól Itáliáig (as n. 12); Manuscript depicting Ladislaus the Posthumous, King of Hungary, Bohemia and Prince of Austria: MH 29001. Cf.: Ádám Novák, Hungarikák V. László gyámságának időszakából [Hungaricas from the period of Ladislaus the Posthumous' guardianship], in: Száműzetés, fogság, szabadulás a középkori és koraújkori Európában, ed. Attila Bárány/László Pósán, Debrecen 2021, p. 159–184.

15 Lipót Óváry, A Magyar Tudományos Akadémia történelmi bizottságának oklevélmásolatai 1. A Mohácsi vész előtti okiratok kivonatai [Charter Copies of the Historical Committee of the Hungarian Academy of Sciences 1. Extracts from Documents Prior to the Battle of Mohács], Budapest 1890.

turned[16]. The documents kept in Warsaw were first included in the MNL OL DF in 1987, following the research of Péter Tóth–who was the chief archivist of the Somogy County Archives in Kaposvár at the time–designated the Hungarian-related documents for microfilming[17].

In 2014, during our personal archival research, we were able to look through the documentary material on the basis of the archival aid and add a few more documents to the corpus. Furthermore, we also ordered photocopies of the large number of polysigillic charters. Subsequently, in 2022, at the end of a six-year-long research programme, the records of the Hungarian-related charters kept in Warsaw were uploaded to the online database created by the research group, allowing the browsing of 98 charters and their 785 records. When creating the database, we considered it very important to provide the seals with a unique, referenceable mark as well. An interesting example can be seen in the case of the charter dated 18 January 1440 signed in Buda by the 18 Hungarian nobles who sent envoys to King Władysław III of Poland. Some of their seals found here are the only known intact specimen[18]. We have also produced a modern edition of the charter texts in a four-volume series[19], in which we have modernised and supplemented the hundreds of years old editions, or published hitherto unpublished charters. Each edition is accompanied

16 Adorján DIVÉKY, A lengyelországi könyv- és levéltárak magyar vonatkozású kézirati anyaga [Hungarian-Related Manuscripts in Polish Libraries and Archives], in: Levéltári Közlemények 5 (1927) p. 27–58. Cf.: Dr. József SEIMIENSKI, A lengyel állami levéltárak [The Polish National Archives], in: Levéltári Közlemények 8 (1930) p. 1–29. See also: Istvánné FÁBIÁN, Lengyel levéltárakban [In Polish Archives], in: Levéltári Szemle 20/1 (1970) p. 233–240.; Hanna KRAJEWSKA, A Varsói Régi Iratok Levéltárának története és iratállománya [The History and Holdings of the Archive of Old Documents in Warsaw], in: Levéltári Szemle 42 (1992) p. 81–86, p. 81.

17 The 75 charters in the DF database were assigned the reference numbers 288959-289022, 289127 and 292993-293002. From the research report of Péter TÓTH. File No: MNL OL Y section 12134/87. For a more detailed discussion on this topic, see Ádám NOVÁK, Bevezetés a Fontes Memoriae Hungariae sorozat Varsóban őrzött magyar vonatkozású oklevelek című kötet első füzetéhez (1350–1386) [Introduction to the First Booklet of the Series Fontes Memoriae Hungariae – Hungarian-Related Documents Kept in Warsaw (1350–1386)], in: Péter TÓTH/Ádám NOVÁK, Varsóban őrzött magyar vonatkozású oklevelek (1350–1386), Debrecen 2017, p. 8–14.

18 MH 11336–11350. Ádám NOVÁK, The Seals of the Monarch Electing Lords From the Beginning of 1440, in: Történeti Tanulmányok 28/1 (2020) p. 67–89.

19 Fontes Memoriae Hungariae I. (as n. 17); Fontes Memoriae Hungariae II. Varsóban őrzött magyar vonatkozású oklevelek, 1388–1427 [Fontes Memoriae Hungariae II. Hungarian-Related Documents Kept in Warsaw, 1388–1427], ed. Ádám NOVÁK, pub. Ádám NOVÁK/Péter TÓTH, Debrecen 2018; Fontes Memoriae Hungariae III. Varsóban őrzött magyar vonatkozású oklevelek, 1439–1489 [Fontes Memoriae Hungariae III. Hungarian-Related Documents Kept in Warsaw, 1439–1489], ed. Ádám NOVÁK, pub. Ádám NOVÁK/Orsolya TÓTH/Péter TÓTH, Debrecen 2019; Fontes Memoriae Hungariae IV. Varsóban őrzött magyar vonatkozású oklevelek, 1490–1521 [Fontes Memoriae Hungariae IV. Hungarian-Related Documents Kept in Warsaw, 1490–1521], ed. Ádám NOVÁK, Debrecen 2022.

Fig. 2: Polysigillic charter issued by the Hungarian nobels 18 January 1440.

with a relevant introductory study on Polish–Hungarian relations. An important goal was to publish them online in digital format, and to make our materials available not only on the website of our Research Group, but also on the Hungarian public collections database, the *Hungaricana*[20]. The records in the database contain links to these online access points[21].

We did not only search for polysigillic charters in Polish archives, but also visited other institutions such as the *Österreichisches Staatsarchiv, Abteilung Haus-, Hof- und Staatsarchiv*, the *Stadtarchiv Freiburg im Breisgau*, or the *Arhiv Republike Slovenije*. The corpus of medieval Hungarian seals is very fragmentary, as is the case with the charters, but while most of the relevant charters can be found in the DL-DF, we are far from having a similar database of seals. Polysigillic charters provide an excellent opportunity to explore the medieval Hungarian seal corpus. The Memoria Hungariae database–mainly thanks to the Hungarian-related material from Warsaw–now provides a representative selection of the 15th century Hungarian baronial and archpriestly seal material[22].

20 https://library.hungaricana.hu/hu/collection/kozepkori_magyar_okmanytarak_egyebek/

21 Although the full texts of the charters have not been uploaded to the database for each record (the technical background for this was not established during development), feedback from the conference in September 2022 suggests that this may be desirable.

22 Some of our relevant publications on the subject, in addition to those mentioned earlier: Ádám Novák/Balázs Antal Bacsa, Polish and Hungarian lords in the entourage of Władysław. King of Poland and Hungary 1440–1442, in: Studia Z Dziejów Skredniowiecza 23 (2019) p. 183–

3D digitisation of medieval seals

The research on medieval seals in Europe and Hungary has a long history dating back to the 18th century[23]. We can speak of scholarly sphragistic examinations and seal publications from the 19th century onwards. In Hungary, the first monograph on sphragistics was compiled by György Pray, and printed posthumously in 1805[24]. He has already published the drawings of the seals he studied with particular care on several panels. In other words, the fact that the publication of seals and the making of drawing copies was a particularly important task of sigillography was already recognised at the dawn of the 19th century. Later, photography became a means of publishing the seals, which allowed the remaining imprints to be published without any distortion[25]. Admittedly, unlike drawings, this technique is not suitable for reconstructing the damaged seals; but neither does it record conclusions that cannot be supported by evidence. The phenomenon was well illustrated by John Alexander McEwan, in his 2018 paper in the History Compass[26]. In the same paper, he pointed out the advantages of the Reflectance Transformation Imaging (RTI) technique, whereby digitised seals can be examined from multiple illuminated angles without the need to move the original.

I was introduced to the potential of 3D technology in cultural heritage during my professional internship at the University of Prešov in 2014–15. With the support of our research group, we carried out a pilot project on medieval seals kept in the *Štátny archív v Prešove*. With the help of Mensor 3D Ltd. (now part of the 4iG group), we conducted photogeometric measurements and recorded 12 seals of different types, condition and size. We briefly describe below the theoretical and technical background of the procedure used[27].

198; Ádám Novák, Diplomats and Supporters of Matthias Corvinus. Seals of the Treaty of Ófalu/ Spišská Stará Ves 1474, in: Zapiski Historyczne 2 (2022) p. 5–21, p. 17; Ádám Novák, Sokpecsétes oklevelek a Cillei család levéltárából [Polysigillic Charters from the Archive of the Cillei Family], in: AETAS: Történettudományi folyóirat 37/2 (2022) p. 87–94.

23 Lajos Bernát Kumorovitz, A magyar szfragisztika multja [The Past of Hungarian Sphragistics], in: Emlékkönyv Szentpétery Imre születése 60-ik évfordulója ünnepére, Pécs 1938, p. 251–311.

24 György Pray, Syntagma historicum de sigillis regum et reginarum Hungariae pluribusque aliis, Buda 1805.

25 One of the first works to appear in print with a thematic selection of photographs of Hungarian seals: A magyar királyi Országos Levéltár diplomatikai osztályában őrzött pecsétek mutatója [Index of Seals kept in the Diplomatic Department of the Hungarian Royal National Archives], ed. Dezső Csánki, Budapest 1889. The appendix of the index contains 52 images of seals taken by György Klösz, one of the most renowned photographers of the period in Budapest.

26 John Alexander McEwan, Reflectance Transformation Imaging and the Future of Medieval Sigillography, in: History Compass 16/9 (2018) https://doi.org/10.1111/hic3.12477.

27 For the summary, thanks are due to András Fehér, Director of Business Development at 4iG Mensor3D. https://www.mensor3d.com/hu/.

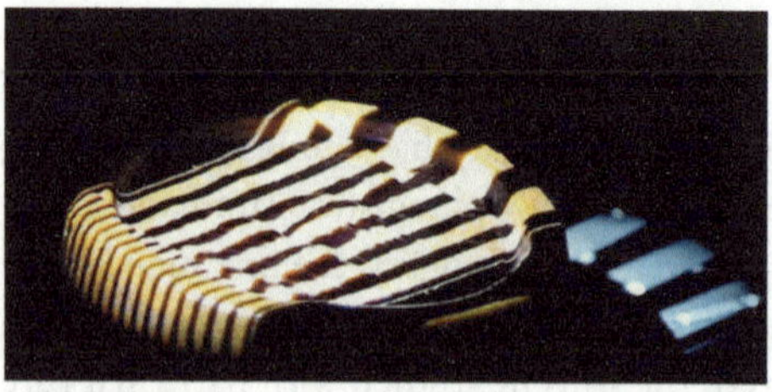

Fig. 3: The projector casts a "light and dark" image of increasingly thinning bands onto the object.

The basic tools for spatial imaging are the so-called three-dimensional scanners and measuring machines, which use various techniques. The fundamental difference between scanners and measuring machines is that scanners do not make physical contact with the object under examination. Non-contact data collection is particularly important in the field of cultural heritage, as physical contact with a high-value artefact could cause damage. Object scanners can be divided into two main groups (1) optical object scanners (that use structured light), and (2) laser-based object scanners. According to the design and application of the object scanners, they can be distinguished as hand-held, arm-held and fixed systems.

Optical scanners, which work with white (or other coloured) light, use the reflection of light to create images, i.e. they generate a point cloud in space that can be positioned in any coordinate system. The devices work in the range of visible light. The measurement is based on the intensity of reflected light and the differences in contrast. The basis of the method is the classic principle of triangulation. The process used by these instruments is also known as active stereo vision. The main difference compared to a conventional dual-camera close-up photogrammetry system is that one camera is replaced by an active light source that illuminates the object to be scanned with a series of known patterns and then records an image containing both the pattern and the object being scanned.

The two main units of the scanner are the projector, which projects the pattern onto the surface, and the video camera, which "captures" the projected image and converts it into a signal stream that can be interpreted by the processing software. The projector casts a "light and dark" image of increasingly thinning bands onto the object. The difference between the angle of incidence and the angle of reflection gives the shape and extent of the object at a given point. The result of averaging based on the differences is an undistorted data, which means that, unlike with two-dimensional cameras, perfect measurements are obtained without any distortion.

Coded structured light technology is based on the unique allocation of individual light signals (similar to the encoding of a barcode) projected onto the object to be measured. When a light signal is identified in the image, the matching can be done directly by decoding, but this requires a complex projection system. The most commonly used solution is time multiplexing, also known as transitional zoning,

Fig. 4: Optical object scanner (front).

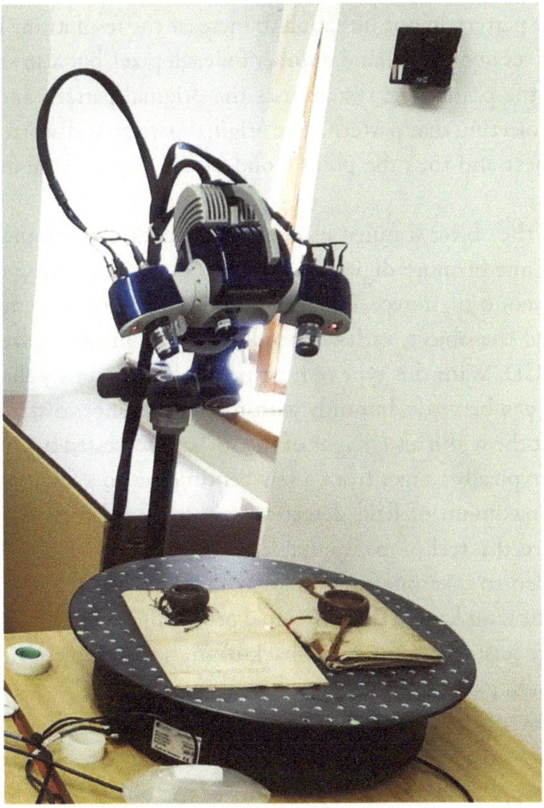

Fig. 5: Optical object scanner (in work).

with Gray coding and phase stepping[28]. For systems that use coded structured light, the use of Gray coding is more efficient, as it better eliminates inconsistencies at

28 A Gray code is a binary number system in which two consecutive numbers differ by only one value, e.g. 000, 001, 010, 011 in the traditional binary system corresponds to 000, 001, 011, 010 in the Gray binary system.

the edges of successive patterns. The projection unit casts a Gray-coded binary sequence of patterns onto the object to be measured.

This divides the object into 2^n parts ("sections"), where 'n' is the number of sample sequences, so in the case of n=7, the object is divided into 128 parts. Thus, a code can be assigned to each pixel, which is a sequence of zeros and ones that can be derived from the order of the sections. This creates a link between the image pixels and the projected bars. Pixels that belong to the same band in the sample with the highest frequency (where n is the highest) are given the same code, so the maximum resolution is half that of the sample with the finest resolution.

In addition, the system projects a periodic pattern onto the object several times, by stepping the pattern in one direction to increase the resolution. Thanks to phase shifting, this gives not only a band number for each pixel, but also an in-band value. To determine the points, the system uses the original pattern and a photograph taken while projecting that pattern. The original pattern is distorted by the geometry of the object and thus the point cloud of the object being measured can be generated.

The data of the object scanned using the light-dark pattern, the reflected light, is captured by one or more digital cameras in colour, depending on whether the equipment is mono or stereo. The resolution of the resulting image, the digital reproduction of the object, varies depending on the imaging plate of the digital camera, the CCD. With this type of instrument, high accuracy three-dimensional measurements can be made, but only within relatively short distances. In practice, this means that the width and height of the surface processed by the system during the recording typically ranges from a few centimetres to a few times 10 centimetres, and the maximum of field detection (maximum depth) is also within this range. Therefore, this technique is suitable for recording small objects, such as seals. The time needed to take one single shot is short, a few seconds at most for the projecting of the samples and the individual processing of images. Finding the right setting, and processing the front and back of the seal completely can take 20–30 minutes, depending on the size.

The digital model may not only be a monochrome point cloud or one intensity values, but may also contain chromatic information. The resulting colour data are RGB colour mappings of the visible colours of the object. To achieve the perfect reproduction of the colours, it is necessary to illuminate the subject with neutral, global light, and to avoid shadows.

The scanned images of the object, taken from a number of points, are matched using software optimised for the scanner, based on the common points of the surfaces. The scanners and their associated software reconstruct the examined object from the points of the coordinate system. The points with X, Y, Z coordinates mapped into 3 dimensions are processed by the program and a surface mesh is fitted to the measured points (TIN model). The resulting 3-dimensional model, consisting of small triangles, already provides a good representation of the shape and surface of the original scanned object – depending, of course, on the resolution and mapping accuracy of the device. The accuracy of scanners allows the creation of models with a resolution of a few microns, but the resolution and accuracy are usually below 1 millimetre. Another advantage of these scanners is that they do not determine the coordinates of a single point during each measurement (image capturing), but of all points in the field of view, with a resolution that depends on the specific solution. The main drawbacks are the small angle of view/recording range, limited maximum depth of field, and sensitivity to external light conditions. Therefore, it is particularly important to assess the condition of the seals in advance and to set up a suitable measuring environment.

The steps of the 3D object digitization process: (A) preparation of the scanning - (B) execution of the scanning - (C) merging of the datasets - (D) point cloud cutting and cleaning - (E) polygon model creation - (F) formation and correction of the surface model - (G) texturing - (H) model exporting - (I) production and publication of the results[29].

The main conclusion of the project is that, although the process requires considerable technical background and expertise, the results can be widely used. Of course, the primary use is the digital (now online) presentation of the seals. There is no doubt that even the less stable wax seals can be more thoroughly inspected with this technique, as the light conditions can be freely calibrated and the points are fixed with extreme precision[30]. Medieval sigillography can only gain from this procedure.

The second fundamental insight is that 3D technology is saving medieval wax seals from inevitable destruction. Indeed, wax seals are very fragile and can be easily damaged during packing, storage or even research, especially the closing seals and the underpressed seals. With 3D measurement, we are practically performing heritage

29 For the technical background, procedure, and tools of 3D digitisation, see: 3D Imaging, Analysis and Applications, ed. Yonghuai LIU/Nick PEARS/Paul L. ROSIN/Patrik HUBER, London/Heidelberg/New York/Dordrecht 2020.

30 Seals selected and recorded for 3D digitisation: (1) The authentication seal of the Chapter of Spiš, 1350; (2) The middle seal of Louis I (the Great), 1359; (3) The secret seal of Queen Mary, 1387; (4) Second Hungarian royal seal of King Sigismund of Luxembourg, 1411; (5) The seal of Jan Jiškra, Czech mercenary captain and Prince of Šariš, 1445; (6) The seal of János Perényi, master of the treasury, 1447; (7) The Hungarian royal secret seal of King Ladislaus the Posthumous, 1455; (8) Seal of the Polish Prince John I Albert, elected King of Hungary, 1490; (9) The seal of László Losonci, master of the treasury, 1497; (10) The seal of the city of Prešov, 1506; (11) The seals of the vicecomes of the county of Šariš and of the noble judges (Iudex nobelium, a. k. a. szolgabíró), 1508; (12) Royal secret seal of King Vladislaus II of Hungary, 1512. Some of the models created during the project were uploaded to our Sketchfab site: https://sketchfab.com/memhung. Supplemented with historical data, they are also included in the Memoria Hungariae database under the reference numbers MH 31001– 31011.

Fig. 6: 3D model of the Hungarian royal secret seal of King Ladislaus the Posthumous, 1455.

conservation. The need to copy the seals was recognised long ago. The history of seal copying in Hungary dates to the beginning of the 20th century, which will be briefly summarised to see to what extent the RTI processing of seals represents a step forward. The making of plaster copies was already a common practice at the beginning of the 20th century, and Lajos Bernát Kumorovitz made several copies this way for his monograph on seal usage, which is still the definitive work today. The plaster cast collection of the Budapest History Museum is one of the most valuable plaster collections regarding the medieval Hungarian seal material. It was created between 1959 and 1967 as a result of the work of Kumorovitz. Although it is a very fine material, plasticine comes into direct contact with the seal, and the process must be carried out with extreme caution to avoid damaging the original object. The copies bear the fronts and backs in separate pieces. This method is of little use for the thin closing and underpressed seals, because they will crumble under the slightest pressure. Although the copies made by this method are particularly easy to study, the copies themselves are extremely fragile as well[31]. In the early 1960s, on the initiative of art historian Katalin Dávid, restorers at the National Archives developed a new procedure for making copies of old wax seals. The method involved the replacement of plasticine with liquid silicone rubber and the pouring of a hot PVC mass into the resulting negative. The PVC copy was then hand-coloured, which requires a skilled professional. The advantage is that an exact replica of the original can be made and the front and back can be studied at the same time. The downside is that the silicone negative, despite all its flexibility, is still more rigid than plasticine. It is risky to use when copying damaged, saponified seals. When making a copy, the cord of the seal and the parchment of the charter must be carefully sealed, as silicone leaves an irremovable mark[32].

31 On the methods used to make plaster copies of medieval seals, see: László Magyari, Pecsétmásolatok készítése [The Making of Seal Copies], in: Levéltári Közlemények 24 (1946) p. 290–292. For the collection of the Budapest History Museum, see: https://varmuzeum.hu/a-diplomatikai-oklevel-oklevelfenykep-es-pecsetmasolati-gyujtemeny/

32 For more information on the making of plastic copies, see: Imre Bodor /Erik Fügedi /Imre Takács, A középkori Magyarország főpapi pecsétjei a Magyar Tudományos Akadémia Művészettörténeti Kutató Csoportjának pecsétmásolat-gyűjteménye alapján [Archpriestly Seals of Medieval Hungary Based on the Collection of Seal Copies of the Art History Research Group of the Hungarian Academy of Sciences], Budapest 1984, p. 7.

Fig. 7: Seal of Bertalan bishop of Veszprém, 1231. A: original (MNL OL DL 165). B: plaster copy (BTM 64.16.). C: PVC copy (MNL OL V8.157.). D: 3D printed.

In comparison, 3D measurement means non-contact copying and recording, something that neither plaster nor plastic copying can offer. In this way, copying can be extended to seals that are fragmentary, in very poor condition or are found in very fragile, thin layers on the closing of paper or parchment charters. Furthermore, the camera can also capture – although only an RGB – colour-coded image of the seals, so the post-processed model contains and carries shades that are close to the original colours. The measurement can also be used to create a digital collection[33].

However, it is not necessary for the collection to remain digital, since with 3D printing, tangible copies can be made. There are many ways to do this, but for one-to-one ratio copies, precision is essential due to the small size. The simplest method is to use a layer-by-layer FDM (Fused Deposit Modeling) printer. This is widely used, but the accuracy of the copy depends on the quality of the printer. Another very common method of additive manufacturing is powder 3D printing. Unlike FDM printing, which prints using filaments, powder 3D printing – as suggested by its name – uses powder as the primary printing material. There are two main powder printing processes: powder bed fusion and binder jetting. With powder bed fusion, powder 3D printers sinter or laser fuse powder particles layer by layer into the desired object, while a reflow blade adds more powder to each new layer. Instead of a laser, binder jetting uses a print head that delivers a liquid binder to the powder bed. The liquid binds the powder particles together to form the individual layers of the desired object. Then another layer of powder is added and the process is repeated layer by layer. Powder-based 3D printing can work with a wide range of materials, including metals, which can be relevant when making copies of bulls. 3D printers using powder bed fusion typically print with greater accuracy and can produce more complex prints. Some printers can also print the colours that are captured in the 3D model, saving the slow and skill-intensive restorative painting process.

During our pilot project, we were able to use the 3D printer at the Centres of Excellence department at Prešovskej univerzity v Prešove. The ZPRINTER 650 printer with its five printheads was able to work on a 254 x 381 x 203 mm tray, allowing multiple seal copies to be produced in a single print run. The printer is capable of producing a layer thickness between 0.089–0.102 mm, so it was able to reproduce the digital files in near-perfect quality. The five printheads ensured colour printing as well, and an epoxy coating was applied to improve the vividness of the prints. The printer itself is an expensive investment, but its rental and operation

33 Cultural heritage protection has turned to digitisation in the wake of the coronavirus epidemic. Gabriele Guidi/Bernard D. Frischer, 3D Digitization of Cultural Heritage. 3D Imaging, Analysis and Applications (as n. 29) p. 631–699. See also: Emma Cieslik, 3D Digitization in Cultural Heritage Institutions Guidebook, Baltimore 2020/21.

is sustainable and can be envisaged for the processing of small projects or even the material of small archives[34].

Building on the experience of 2015, our research team started to work on some parts of our exhibition planned for 2016. For the exhibition in the Ferenczy Museum in Szentendre entitled "Gothic in the Monastery of Pilis – King Andrew II's French Relations", we digitised the royal seals of Andrew II, his golden bull of 1221, the seals of several contemporary archpriests, and the convent seal of the Cistercian Abbey of Pilisszentkereszt[35]. At that time, we were mainly interested in exploring the educational potential of technology. We created an animation of the major historical chronology of the period using the 3D models, and demonstrated the process of digitisation and printing[36]. With a museum pedagogical purpose, for the opening of the exhibition we created the seal matrix of the pontifical or larger seal of the French-born bishop of Veszprém, Bertalan (1226–1244). We digitally augmented the negative of the digitised seal impression, added an artificial handle, which we also printed from plastic. With the help of the resulting seal matrix, we were able to recreate the seal from wax, thus familiarising visitors with the medieval authentication process. We did the same with the seal of the monastery of Pilis, which this time was turned from metal. The devices have since been used as demonstration tools at the University of Debrecen.

Finally, we would like to point out the academic usefulness of the technique. We put the known copies of the second double royal seal of King Andrew II of Hungary under hypothetical examination. The seal has not survived in its entirety, we know of 14 fragments in total. In our opinion, as part of a comprehensive project – the specimens are kept in five different institutions and their transportation is difficult – the remaining fragments could be digitised using the RTI technique, and the individual fragments could be pieced together through post-processing, thus obtaining a much more complete impression. In addition to recreating a historical source that is thought to have disappeared, other sphragistic observations could also be made. For example, to prevent the forgery of the seal used between 1213 and 1235, authentication marks may have been made on it, which is not unprecedented in royal seal usage[37].

---

34 Here we would like to express our gratitude once again to the esteemed Rector of the Prešovskej univerzity v Prešove, Peter Kónya, who allowed us to use the Centres of Excellence laboratory. Thanks are also due to Martin Javor, David Palaščák and Tibor Dohnanec for all the assistance they provided.

35 Pilisi gótika II. András francia kapcsolatai [Gothic in the Monastery of Pilis – King Andrew II's French Relations], ed. Attila Bárány/Elek Benkő/Zoltán Kárpáti (Memoria Hungariae 3), Szentendre 2016.

36 Presentation film on the Three-Dimensional Digitisation of Medieval Seals. https://www.youtube.com/watch?v=4XodITMVZIQ&ab_channel=MemoriaHungariae.

37 Ádám Novák, Use of seals in the Árpád era, in: Kings and Saints The Age of the Árpáds, ed.

We have chosen this seal of King Andrew II because of the above-mentioned exhibition, but other examples could also be given for the sake of the investigation. Hungarian sphragistics, however, lacks a comprehensive guide to seals, which would greatly facilitate the scholarly preparation of such a pilot project[38].

In the above, we attempted to summarise the observations and experiences of the digital projects of our medieval historical workshop. The main purpose of our participation in the conference in September 2022 was to present the results of our workshop and receive feedback on the projects. We are therefore very grateful for the opportunity to have been able to gain useful experiences in the field of digital humanities and to meet many fellow researchers from all over Europe. In the hope that digital humanities will become more and more popular in Hungary as well, a report on the conference has been published by our colleagues[39].

Final thoughts

We plan to further expand the Memoria Hungariae source database, as during the period of our research group's operation, we have managed to identify a number of sources that we have not yet been able to publish. As of 2023, the portal has been moved to a new server, ensuring secure access and stable operation.

Another objective of this paper is to encourage the institutions that keep original medieval sources to try to preserve the very easily decaying seal material in the above-mentioned way, thus making our cultural heritage available to future generations.

Ciprián Horváth/Gábor Horváth-Lugossy/Attila Kovács/Miklós Makoldi/Dóra Nagy/Éva Teiszler/László Tamás Vizi (Publications of the Institute of Hungarian Research 6), Budapest/Székesfehérvár 2022, p. 277–294.

38 We have a clear, reliable catalogue only of the Árpád period's royal seal material: Imre Takács, Az Árpád-házi királyok pecsétjei [The Seals of the Kings of the House of Árpád] (Corpus sigillorum hungariae mediaevalis 1), Budapest 2012.

39 Gábor Berecz/Gergő Németh, Informatika és történettudomány – A Digital Diplomatics 2022 konferencián jártunk [Informatics and Historiography - We were at the Digital Diplomatics 2022 conference.]. Újkor.hu https://ujkor.hu/content/informatika-es-tortenettudomany-a-digital-diplomatics-2022-konferencian-jartunk.

The Post-Mohács Era of the Hungarian Kingdom

Database of the Records from 1526–1570 in the Holdings of the National Archives of Hungary

Krisztina Arany, György Laczlavik

1. Introduction

It was a defining event in Hungarian history when, almost 500 years ago, on 29 August 1526, the troops of the Ottoman Empire inflicted a crushing defeat on the plain of Mohács on the army of King Louis II of Hungary. It is this event that we associate with the fall of the medieval Kingdom of Hungary, and indeed with the end of the Hungarian Middle Ages. From 1875 onwards our archivist predecessors in the National Archives of Hungary (NAH), in order to promote medieval research in Hungary, collected the documents dating from the period prior to 1526 from the archival material that had survived the turbulent centuries of Hungarian history and had been scattered in many different places. This collection is the Diplomatic Archives, which today contains more than 108,000,000 documents and has been searchable online for nearly 20 years[1] and online for nearly 10 years[2]. However, the Battle of Mohács marked not only the end of an era but also the beginning of a new one. The records issued during the decades after the battle are no different from those before 1526, but we do not have a tool like the one mentioned above to help us research them.

The Hungarian National Archives had a long-cherished plan to continue this work with the documents created after 1526. In spring 2016 we started to identify

1 A középkori Magyarország levéltári forrásainak adatbázisa (Database of archival sources of medieval Hungary), ed. György Rácz (CD-ROM) Arcanum, Budapest 2003.

2 https://archives.hungaricana.hu/hu/charters/ György Rácz, Collectio Diplomatica Hungarica. The online portal of the National Archives of Hungary on medieval charters, in: AfD 56 (2010) p. 423–444.

the records issued in the time from 29 August 1526 to 1570 in the collections of the National Archives, initially with the financial help of the Reformation Memorial Committee (until 30 June 2018), and then with the support of the National Research, Development and Innovation Office (NRDI) grant application K 128695 "Processing and online publication of the MNL OL 1526–1570 documents"[3] (between 1 September 2018 and 30 August 2020) – of course under new conditions[4]. Unfortunately, extending the period of processing to 1608, as we had originally planned, would not have been feasible, given the huge increase in the number of surviving central government documents after 1570, so the decision on the end date of the investigated period was primarily influenced by practical reasons.

In the National Archives, there are about 500 archival units (archival collections) that can be assumed to contain documents within the proposed time limits. The objective set at the time of planning was to 'find' all the documents from 1526 to 1570 in originals or copies, an estimated corpus of around 100,000 documents. We also intended to make the digital images of the documents accessible online, through a searchable database, to both professional and amateur researchers and to the general public. The construction of the database was planned with the use of the NAH namespace, for the first time in the history of the archives, in order to achieve a higher professional output. The huge undertaking of the archives can be divided into three (or four) major work phases: 1) identification and preparation of the records for digitisation, 2) digitisation, 3) processing of the records, 4) online publication.

The investigation was carried out using our existing finding aids, no new research was conducted. The documents recovered are therefore incomplete both in the cases of the originals and copies. The preparation of the documents for digitisation was carried out according to the principles developed by the archivists of the National Archives. However, the experience accumulated in the past was not always sufficient, and many new problems had to be solved in the course of the work. Moving nearly 90,000 documents was no easy task either: We had to keep track of the documents, during transferring them to digitisation and reprocessing, to ensure that the documents that had passed through several hands were returned to their place and not lost during a process that could take several months[5].

3 György Laczlavik, Az MNL OL 1526–1570 közötti iratainak feldolgozása és online publikálása című projekt kutatási terve. (Research plan of the project entitled Processing and online publication of the MNL OL 1526–1570), in: Turul 92 (2019) p. 130–135.

4 One of the most striking differences is that, unlike the Diplomatic Archives, the selected documents remain in their original location, only forming a virtual collection.

5 See more in György Laczlavik, Egy merész vállalkozás és tapasztalatai (2016–2018). A Magyar Nemzeti Levéltár Országos Levéltára 1526–1570 közötti iratainak feltárása, digitalizálása és feldolgozása. (A bold undertaking and its experiences (2016–2018): the identification, digitisation and processing of the records of the National Archives of the Hungarian National Archi-

2. *The database*

After the enormous work invested in identification and digitisation, we would have been left with not researchable digital copies of archival records from a number of collections (nearly 500,000 records) if the grant had not been used to process the documents and publish them online. The archives did not have and will probably never have their own resources to do this. The documents were processed in the online database developed for this purpose and in the NAH namespace database.

Due to the expected large amount of available archival sources, we developed a method of processing that has not been used in the archives before: we combined the method of description (inventory) and indexing (index of places, names and objects). To ensure consistency, a thesaurus is used for frequently recurring elements (e.g. document type, subject, etc.). In all cases, the document name/title must be given during processing, in accordance with international descriptive standards. This should aim to describe the essential content of the document, but should not be done in the form of an abstract, for example, not all names of persons and places should be listed. As a general rule, each document is systematically processed, and even transcribed documents are kept in a separate record, of course linked to the document in which they are incorporated. The indication of the transcribed documents is distinguished from the indication of the transcribing documents by the elements /1, /2, etc. in the physical order of occurrence. The same is true for the documents preserved in copy books. In summary, we have used the terms "incorporated" and "incorporating" documents for these. If the documents and deeds that are incorporated in the records predate 1526, they are also recorded in the database with basic data.

A very important achievement is the processing of personal, corporate and place names using a namespace database. We record the names of all the persons who are in the text of the document and who signed it[6]. For technical reasons, corporate bodies have been given a separate field, so convents, the Hungarian Chamber, counties, etc. are listed there. We also indicate, by means of an expandable list, the capacity (role) in which the person appears in the document[7]. The name is entered

---

ves from 1526–1570.), in: Levéltári Szemle 68 (2018) p. 41–49; György Laczlavik, Magyar Nemzeti Levéltár Országos Levéltára 1526–1570 közötti iratainak adatbázisa és felhasználásának lehetőségei (The database of the records from 1526–1570 preserved in the holdings of the National Archives of Hungary and its research possibilities), in: Certamen VII. Előadások a Magyar Tudomány Napján az Erdélyi Múzeum-Egyesület I. szakosztályában, ed. Emese Egyed/László Pakó/Emese Sófalvi, Kolozsvár 2020, p. 349–360.

6 However, it is not compulsory to include those listed in the census, those listed in the dignity list, those mentioned in the proclamation clause. They must, however, be referred to in the "Comment" data field at the end of the form.

7 The most common roles are: 'Name of originator', 'Recipient', 'Beneficiary', 'Other person', 'Other

in the database in the normalised form recorded in the namespace, linked to it, if it can be determined with certainty[8]. If, in the absence of identification, the name cannot be recorded in normalised form, it is recorded in transliterated form. It is important to further enhance the effectiveness of query by recording also the name spelling variants in the namespace.

Places are also processed according to roles[9]. The field "Place of creation" must be filled in, even if it is missing for some reason[10]. The place names are listed in the normalised form taken from the namespace, with the spelling versions not yet known being indicated in the namespace. Place names which could not be identified during processing are included in transliterated form.

It is important to note that the date (the date on which the document was created is mandatory) is also given in normalised form even if the date format in the record is not such. If the "Sealed" option is selected, an answer is given as to whether the document was sealed when it was issued. For the time being, we cannot provide more detailed information on the seal, as this would considerably slow down the processing.

One of the very important features of the database interface used for processing is that it is in the online space, which is important because processing can be done from outside the walls of the archives, even from another continent, by creating a "virtual workstation"[11].

But what would the database be worth without online publication? The first official launch of the public version of the database took place on 30 October 2018 at NAH's Reformation project closing event[12]. The database records and their digital images have been available at https://adatbazisokonline.hu/adatbazis/reformacio-kora-mnl-ol-1526–1570, with a renewed interface from 22 January 2020. The online publication of the records is only possible at fixed intervals, as automatic synchronisation is unfortunately not possible. The archives' IT staff initiates the process whereby the metadata of the processing interface will be transferred to the public interface and the records here will be linked to the watermarked image files. The images are published in their original size for better readability. Currently only 20,395 records are published which currently have 66,921 digital images of the documents linked to them. The table below clearly shows that there are more

person involved in the execution of the document'.

8 The principles of normalisation are of course detailed in the work instructions.

9 Possible roles: 'Place of creation', 'Place of issue of copy', 'Place of authentication', 'Property', 'Other place described in text'.

10 In this case "No data" will be entered in the field.

11 For more on work organisation, see Laczlavik, Egy merész vállalkozás (as n. 5) p. 41–47.

12 See more at http://mnl.gov.hu/mnl/ol/hirek/beszamolo_a_reformacio_mnl_projekt_zarounnepsegerol

than twice as many processed records as published. The next online publication is scheduled for 2024.

Table 1: Processed and published records in result figures.

Year	Processed records	Published records	Published images
2016	3473		
2017	9345		
2018	6231	13725	56773
2019	7662		
2020	5542	6670	10148
2021	6815		
2022–2024	6358	20469	42741
Total	45426	40864	109662

3. Research possibilities

A total of 288 archival collections of documents were explored to identify records created between 1526 and 1570, the most significant collections involved in the processing being the Benignae resolutiones (HU-MNL-OL-E 21), the Neoregestrata Acta collection (HU-MNL-OL-E 148), both are part of the Hungarian Chamber Archives. These collections mainly preserve official documents of a legal nature (e.g. letters of grant, privileges, warrants, last wills, litigation documents, etc.). The majority of the types of documents listed either secure rights to land or relate to the possession of houses and other immovable property, animals, tools, movables, money, etc., in addition to land. The most common causes of litigation were donations, pledges, sales, exchanges, loans, confiscations and inheritance issues.

The other significant source base of the database is the group of family archives preserved by NAH, among which the *Missiles* collection of the Batthyány family (HU-MNL-OL-P 1314) stands out. In addition to the correspondence of the Batthyány family, the research was also carried out in the archives of the Balassa, Bánffy, Baranyay, Barkóczi, Bethlen, Dessewffy, Károlyi and Eszterházy families, among others.

Table 2: The 30 archival collections with the most identified and digitised records.

Archival Signature		Title	number of digitised documents	number of digital files	number of processed records
P	184	Archives of the Princely branch of the Esterházy family – Oláh family	248	645	258
P	423	Kende (kölcsei) family	250	650	296
F	3	Central Archives of the Convent of Gyulafehérvár (Alba Julia), Centuriae	290	2049	–
P	285	The Festetics Family Archives in Keszthely – Sallér family – Documents arranged by the family	295	1547	–
P	108	Archives of the Princely branch of the Esterházy family – Princely branch of the Esterházy family – Repository[13]	315	2570	–
P	646	Szulyovszky – Sirmiensis family	318	747	–
P	11	Balassa family archives – Documents registered by the family	385	1792	588
P	644	Sztáray family	407	1341	613
P	419	Károlyi Family Archives – Bosnyák family	478	1791	657
P	430	Kisfaludy family	502	1284	642
R	314	Municipal archival collections	525	1851	–
E	172	Archivum familiae Dobó	553	1959	–
F	4	Central Archives of the Convent of Gyulafehérvár (Alba Julia), Cista Comitatuum	569	4498	535
P	608	Soós (sóvári) family	587	1853	820
P	45	Békássy family	625	1637	899
I	4	Staatsarchiv, Abschriften ungarischer Urkunden	643	7303	–

13 Not all of the material has been researched.

Archival Signature		Title	number of digitised documents	number of digital files	number of processed records
P	1313	Batthyány Family Archives – Batthyány Family Main Archives[14]	653	2458	–
F	17	Central Archives of the Convent of Kolozsmonostor (Cluj-Mănăștur), Deeds of possessions by County and Department	731	4240	–
E	204	Missiles	836	1944	–
E	136	Instructiones	864	17751	–
E	249	Benigna mandata	961	4030	–
P	707	Archives of the Zichy family – Archives of the Zichy family in Zély[15]	1036	2387	894
E	254	Repraesentationes, informationes et instantiae	1062	3009	–
E	159	Regesta decimarum	1079	29625	–
E	41	Hungarian Chamber registry, Litterae ad cameram exaratae	2601	7117	2169
P	1314	Batthyány Family Archives – Missiles	5706	23183	4593
E	148	Neo-regestrata acta	5900	34579	14153
E	21	Hungarian Chamber registry, Benignae resolutions	7291	23546	8779
E	15	Hungarian Chamber registry, Expeditiones camerales	7294	20778	–
E	185	Archivum familiae Nádasdy	19661	58036	–

It is also worth taking a look at the characteristics of the digital copies available in the database. The types of sources that can be searched in the database reflect the characteristics of the collections covered by the research: mandates/orders are the largest group of documents, with a total 15237/8832[16] records (34/43% of

14 Not all of the material has been researched.

15 Not all of the material has been researched.

16 The first number represents the total number of records processed, the second the number of records published.

the documents in the database). In addition, the typical document type of family archives, the *missilis*, totals 8633/5058 (19/25%), and the *relationes* 4121/1138 (9/5%) are also represented, whereas also other interesting document types, such as last wills, accounts, etc. are available in lesser number in the database.

Most of the documents available in the database are in Latin (40515/17414). In addition, there are 2914/1683 documents in Hungarian, a slightly smaller number of documents in German (1707/1271) and a lesser number of documents in Slovak, Croatian, Italian and Slavic can also be accessed.

The distribution of the geographical regions covered by the documents in any form (place of origin, name of creator, other place, etc.) also reflects the characteristics of the archival collections explored during the project. The distribution is primarily influenced by the place of residence of the rulers and, in the case of the family archives, by the main geographical interests of the families (centres of possession, official functions linked to certain geographical regions) and, finally, by the location of the administrative offices' seats.

Table 3: Some examples of the cities most frequently mentioned as places of expenditure.

Geographical places	total number of records
Vienna	8324
Bratislava	6383
Prague	994
Nagyszombat	1124
Varaždin	629
Güssing	563
Wiener Neustadt	369
Kosice	344
Linz	310
Zagreb	240
Graz	185
Innsbruck	123
Ptuj	70
Brno	37
Constantinople/Istanbul	8

Among the issuers of the documents, the Hungarian king Ferdinand I (1526–1564), who reigned the longest in the researched period, has the most records (6718 records), followed by his son, Maximilian II (1563–1576) (4196 records). However, in the case of the Hungarian kings, we must take into account that the documents issued by the chief justice, that is the personal legal representative of the King of Hungary (*personalis praesentiae regiae in judiciis locumtenens*) were also issued on behalf of the ruler in his name, with his judicial seal, but without their participation. Of the Habsburgs' opponents, John I (John Szapolyai, 1526–1540)[17] 591 records are accessible in the database, and his son John II (John Sigismund Szapolyai, 1540–1551, 1556–1570) 548 records have been processed. The Habsburg rulers spent little time in Hungary, so they appointed a governor in their absence. The database also contains a number of documents issued by Royal Lieutenants of Hungary (Elek Thurzó, Pál Várday, Ferenc Újlaki, Tamás Nádasdy, Miklós Oláh)[18]. In addition to the Lieutenant, Habsburg Archdukes were also involved in the administration of the Kingdom of Hungary[19]. Finally, a significant number of documents issued by places of authentication and by the country's central magistrates can be found among these records. The database also contains 186 royal publications, issued by Queens, Queen Isabella Jagiellon, Queen Mary of Hungary and Queen Anne of Bohemia and Hungary. The number of records issued by municipalities is much smaller: 286 documents in total.

Table 4: Records issued by municipalities.

Varaždin	37
Trnava	18
Bratislava	16
Kremnica	14
Skalica	13
Kosice	10
Prešov	9
Levoča	9
Brezno	9
Bardejov	8

17 András Péter Szabó is publishing the itinerary of John Szapolyai in a separate volume in 2023, for the publication he has also used the database.

18 György Laczlavik, The Royal Lieutenants (Locum tenentes) of Hungary in the 16th Century (1526–1608), in: Les alter ego des souverains Vice-rois et lieutenants généraux en Europe et dans les Amériques XVe–XVIIe siècle Pau France, ed. Philippe Chareyre/Álvaro Adot Lerga/Dénes Harai, Pau 2021, p. 281–299.

19 For more on the activities of the archdukes in Hungary, see. György Laczlavik. Adalékok a Habsburg főhercegek (elsősorban Miksa főherceg) magyarországi tevékenységéhez a 16. század második felében [Contribution to the activity of Habsburg archdukes in Hungary (especially archduke Maximilian) in the second half of the 16th century], in: "Az ifjak tanítása oly nagy jó" (The teaching of youth is so great good), Tanulmányok Ágnes Kovács tiszteletére, ed. Zoltán Fogarassy/Kálmán Mészáros/Péter Török, Debrecen 2021, p. 271–280.

Trenèín	7
Banská Štiavnica	6
Sopron	6
Cluj Napoca	5
Radkersburg	5
Miskolc	5
Lipova	4
Ptuj	4
Kežmarok	4
Szombathely	4
Mád	4
Krupina	4
Sibiu	3
Baia Mare	3
Turda	3
Krakow	3
Berehovo	2
Graz	2
Zagreb	2
Buda	2
Rožňava	2
Mezőkövesd	2
Kőszeg	2
Šamorín	2
Jelšava	2
Prievidza	2
Ľubietová	2
Uzhhorod	1
Modra	1
Fiľakovo	1
Pukanec	1
Dobrá Niva	1
Fürstenfeld	1
Huszt	1

Brno	1
Sighisoara	1
Jászberény	1
Olaszliszka	1
Mosonmagyaróvár	1
Telkibánya	1
Újhely	1
Hegyeshalom	1
Győr	1

In parallel with the processing of records, we are continuously developing NAH's namespace database. This is a background database specialised in persons, corporate bodies and geographical names, without which it is no longer worth creating this type of database in the 21st century. It is a knowledge aggregator that will greatly facilitate not only our work, but also that of future database builders, as it can serve as the basis for any other database. The namespace will not only record the results of ongoing research[20] but will also try to incorporate archontological and prosopographical results published in the literature so far – the database will of course include precise bibliographical references. Based on the experience accumulated so far, it will provide a suitable basis for identifying actors in the central justice system and county administration, for establishing hitherto unknown genealogical relationships, and for promoting research on family, estate and local history, not only in present-day Hungary but also in the whole Carpathian Basin.

One of the priority areas in which we expect to make great progress with the help of the database is the history of county administration. There are very few sources on the history of county administration and the judiciary in the 16th century. There are hardly any coherent archival records for the period. This is also true for the records of the county councils, as there is little written evidence of the 16th century. Only a few counties have records from the 16th century, such as Borsod (1569–1581), Gömör (1571–1579), Győr (1580–1637), Nógrád (1597–1603), Sopron (1579–1589, 1595–1608), Szabolcs (1550–1848), Szatmár (1593–1616), Vas (1595–1602), Zala (1555–1609, 1611–1655) and Zemplén (1558–1563)[21].

20 So much so that the person's position is only recorded in the database as " Name of Creator ", but in the namespace in all cases.

21 16–18. századi vármegyei jegyzőkönyvek regesztái. (Abstracts of 16th–18th century county records), ed. László Varga/István Kenyeres/Péter Tóth. DVD Arcanum, Budapest 2009. The DVD-ROM includes Borsod county 1569–1581, Esztergom county 1638–1702, 1710–1723, Fejér county 1692–1711, Gömör county 1571–1579, Győr county 1580–1637, Nógrád county 1597–1603, 1652–1656, Pest-Pilis-Solt county 1632, 1638–1644, 1664, 1656–1712, 1715–

On the basis of the processed documents, we have now recorded 2204 documents issued by 58 counties, as well as records of the county officers in the namespace, not only on the basis of documents issued by the counties. Based on the current state of processing, these and the following data are of course still only indicative and not yet suitable for drawing conclusions. Most of the data relate to elected judges and administrative officers of the county (*iudex nobelium*), deputy county administrators (*vicecomes*) and lord lieutenants of counties. The latter have the lowest percentage of new data. The majority of the remaining actors in county management are tax collectors, notaries or jury assessors.

Table 5: The 30 counties with the largest number of recorded documents, with the total number of officials recorded in the register.

County	number of publications	number of officers
Sáros (Slovakia)	385	76
Vas (small part of Austria)	192	84
Abaúj (greater part of Slovakia)	144	69
Nyitra (Slovakia)	132	56
Szepes (Slovakia)	131	43
Zemplén (greater part of Slovakia)	125	51
Ung (Ukraine)	107	61
Bars (Slovakia)	104	43
Zala (small part of Austria)	80	62
Trencsén (Slovakia)	79	57
Pozsony (Slovakia)	79	48
Szabolcs	63	61
Sopron (small part of Austria)	56	41
Satu Mare (Partly Romania)	54	59
Gömör (Slovakia)	51	42
Kraszna (Romania)	47	39
Zólyom (Slovakia)	47	18
Borsod	45	39
Ugocsa (Ukraine)	33	40

1740, Somogy county 1710–1715, Sopron county 1579–1589, 1595–1608, Szatmár county 1593–1616, 1629–1640, Tolna county 1696–1703, 1714–1717, Vas county 1595–1600, 1601–1620, 1631–1641, Zala county 1555–1609, 1611–1655 and Zemplén county 1558–1563. material from the following periods. Online at https://archives.hungaricana.hu/hu/lear/Jegyzokonyvek/ Last download: 27.02.2023.

County	number of publications	number of officers
Bereg (greater part of Ukraine)	27	31
Liptó (Slovakia)	26	34
Hont (partly Slovakia)	24	42
Turóc (Slovakia)	24	23
Küküllő (Romania)	18	21
Nógrád	15	20
Máramaros (Romania)	14	68
Bihar (partly Romania)	12	29
Veszprém	8	14
Kőrös (Croatia)	8	11
Doboka (Romania)	7	37

A report of Komárom County, written between 22 May 1569 and 16 December 1570, gives an insight into the process of county justice, in which the trial of the nuns of Nyulak Island (Budapest, Margit sziget) concerning the village of Ekecs is transferred to the royal court. In addition to the deputy county administrator and the elected judge (*iudex nobilium*), the county jury members were also involved in the investigation. The 10 jurors are listed by name in the document[22]. In 2018, we added another role of person to the database to enhance the research on the county administration. We now include in the "county person" role column those persons who are involved in any capacity and in any way in the administrative or judicial functions of the county, without their function being clearly defined[23].

To find documents relating to litigation, one can search for specific types of documents in the document type field, such as trial 'transmitting (*transmissionalis*), suspending, introducing (*introductoria cause*), *prorogatoria*, terminating, resuming, other relating to litigation' types. The number of letters of sentence is 1289. A further way of examining the activity of lawyers in the 16th century is to record in over 600 documents the names of persons acting as lawyers[24].

Another very important area is the archontology of the central courts of the Kingdom of Hungary. A systematic research of the organisation of the central courts in the 16th century has not yet been carried out, and unlike the period before 1526, the organisation of the central courts after Mohács can only be researched through

22 MNL OL E 148 - a. - Fasc. 336. - No. 7. Ákos Csábi, Albert Csóka, Ferenc Czudar, Mihály Gadóczy, Péter Gadóczy, György Markházy, András Ollé, Ambrus Sipos, Gergely Tőke, István Vértesy.

23 This is a fairly new category, but we have already recorded 93 such roles.

24 For example, MNL OL P 536 - 1. - 1564 - No. 3. Before Mihály Mérey, Gáspár Pécsi and his wife Margit Dóczy testified as lawyers of twenty persons in Pécsújfalu on 12 May 1564. Including the as yet unpublished records, we know of a total of 105 records.

the texts of statutes. Relatively few people have dealt with this topic: in the 20th century, the work of Árpád Gellért, Ákos Timon, János Vinkler and Alajos Degré can be highlighted. Although the names of the grand magistrates (the royal lieutenant, the count palatine, the count palatine's lieutenant, the judge royal etc.) are known, very little details are known about their activities. As was the practice in the Middle Ages, the most of judicial tasks were certainly not carried out by the grand magistrates but of their deputies and magistrates, many of whose names have not yet been known. We can learn more about the activity of pre-Mohács legal intellectuals from the work of György Bónis[25]. However, no such summary has been compiled for the period after 1526, so we know very little about the magistrates, their archontology has not even been completed, not to mention other members of the court staff. So far, a total of 47 magistrates have been recorded in the register, not all of whom were unknown, but few of whose terms of office were known[26]. In addition to building up the archontology, we are also examining the operation of the smaller chancellery, where most of the documents related to central legislation were drawn up. Far exceeding our expectations, we have already identified 63 members of the staff of the smaller chancellery, the vast majority of whom (45) are notaries.

We have also tried to contribute to the history of public administration by recording the names of 50 chamber officials (secretaries, councillors, clerks, auditors,

25 György Bónis: A jogtudó értelmiség a Mohács előtti Magyarországon (The legal intellectuals in pre-Mohács Hungary), Budapest 1971.

26 Exceptions are Frederik Federmayer, who collected the archontology of the deputies of the governors of the provinces in the 16th century, see Frederik Federmayer, Klement Literát Beczenczy (a archontologie zástupcov palatínskych miestodržiteľov), in: Historický časopis 59 (2011) p. 493–514, and the period of the royal governorship of Pál Várday. See György Laczlavik, Várday Pál helytartói működése 1542–1549. (Várday Pál's function as Lord Lieutenant 1542–1549), in: Levéltári Közlemények 83 (2012) p. 3–67. and Id., A központi bíráskodás szervezetének vázlata a Magyar Királyságban a 16. század első felében. (The central jurisdictional system in the Hungarian Kingdom in the first half of the 16th century), in: Jogtörténeti Szemle s.n. (2015) p. 16–19. The situation is much better in the case of the Principality of Transylvania, as several studies have recently dealt with the topic, see Zsolt Bogdándi, A fejedelemség kori törvénykezési szakaszokról (1556–1600), in: Erdélyi Múzeum 77 (2015) p. 64–83; Zsolt Bogdándi, Az Erdélyi Fejedelemség személyes jelenléti bírósága és a táblai elnökök a 16. század második felében. (Transylvanian Principality's *praesentiae personalis* court and the presidents of the magistrate in the second half of the 16th century), in: Erdélyi Múzeum 78 (2016) p. 47–55; Zsolt Bogdándi, Az erdélyi és a partiumi jogügyigazgatók a 16. század második felében = Hivatalnok értelmiség a kora újkori Erdélyben. (The Transylvanian and Partium Law Administrators in the Second Half of the 16th Century – Official Intellectuals in Early Modern Transylvania) Erdélyi Tudományos Füzetek 287, ed. Zsolt Bogdándi/Tamás Fejér, in: Erdélyi Múzeum Egyesület s.n. (2017) p. 9–24; Tamás Fejér, Kancelláriai jegyzetek az erdélyi fejedelmi kancellária okleveles gyakorlatában a Báthoriak korában (1571–1602) (Chancellery notes in the documentary practice of the Transylvanian princely chancellery in the Báthorian era 1571–1602), in: Turul 88 (2015) p. 81–96.

assistant auditors, couriers, etc.), 31 clerks and 25 paymasters, many of whom are not yet known in the literature. The data on the captains and castellans discovered are important not only for military history research, but also for the history of estates, together with the data on economic officials, provisors, etc. To better understand regional history, it is very important that the names of all the places in the documents are recorded, in a normalised form.

The database is also an extremely rich source of data for genealogical research. We record all the names in the documents and, until 2018, we even included family relationships in the namespace, which means that complete family trees can be drawn from them. As an experiment, we have also conducted such type of research on the Bejczy family[27]. We did not however decode the names of witnesses, mainly serfs during processing. Nevertheless, on several occasions these names are included in the comment field[28].

A wider use of the database is the research of land tenure and social relations in the county. The vast majority of the documents discovered are in fact inextricably linked to estates, such as donation of property, registration of property, lawsuit, sale, exchange, class, etc. The advantage of these types of documents over the various censuses and tax registers is that they do not reflect one single moment in time, instead, they make processes visible. Through the various types of witnesses, on-site estate border visits, etc., we can learn about the network of relationships of the holders of a given territory, and through persistent work we can discover hitherto unknown kinships links.

In its present state, the database is primarily useful for Hungarian-speaking researchers, because on the one hand the data fields and the query are only available in Hungarian for the time being, and on the other hand proper names, especially geographical names, are usually given with their Hungarian names. We hope that in the future we will be able to provide German and English versions of the database, at least for data fields, in order to make the metadata content of the database accessible for a wider international public.

27 Csaba Farkas, A Bejcyek. Egy Vas megyei köznemesi család a 15–16. században (The Bejcyek. A noble family of Vas County in the 15th–16th centuries), in: Turul 92 (2019) p. 107–117.

28 For example, MNL OL P 45 - 1. - No. 16. - No. 19., ibid. 1528 - No. 1.; MNL OL P 1960 - 24. - No. 18.; MNL OL P 14 - I. - 1. - 1543 - No. 3.

Appendices

Abstracts

I. Diplomatics and Computational Methods: Internal Features

Michael Gervers, Gelila Tilahun

Patterns of Change. The DEEDS Database, Topic Modeling and Network Analysis in English Medieval Charters, and the Future of Digital Diplomatics

This paper describes the challenges of working in digital diplomatics over the past half century. In the 1970s, prior to the introduction of the laptop, digital research was performed on mainframe computers and the relational database was unknown. Microfiche replaced microfilm as a standard means of reproducing large numbers of images in a still physical medium. Data transfer was by dial-up telephone connections. The 1980s saw the foundation of the journals *History and Comp*uting, and *Le médiéviste et l'ordinateur*, both of which appeared regularly into the early twentieth century when the field broadened to make way for the *Journal of Digital Humanities.* 2011 saw the on-line launch of the DEEDS Project in Toronto featuring a database of the rare English charters from the period 1066–1307 that were issued with dates. Using statistical applications, the DEEDS 'Dater' was subsequently developed to attribute dates to the 97% of documents from the period which are undated. Topic modeling, using Latent Dirichlet Allocation applied to nearly seventeen thousand internally dated charters, has provided clear indications of diplomatic variance which in turn reflect major societal change across the kingdom. Further examination of individual topics explains why the occasional charter was dated, while heat mapping of common diplomatic terms points to disruptions caused by political confrontations. Future directions in Humanities computing see the abandonment of stand-alone databases in favour of their integration.

Marlene Ernst, Alina Ostrowski, Malte Rehbein

Delegated Jurisdiction in the Iberian Peninsula of the 12th Century. Considerations on a Computational Approach to Personal Networks and Formulaic Language

The paper offers first insights into researching papal charters dealing with delegated jurisdiction on the Iberian Peninsula during the 12th century. Perhaps the greatest challenge to a wide-ranging investigation into the delegated judicial practice is the mass of (papal) documents generated in the proceedings. An obvious way to meet this challenge is to use digital humanities methods that enable big data analysis.

First concepts for the digital processing range from network analysis to formulaic language and text reuse detection. The presented methods from digital humanities will help to gain a macroscopical view over the temporal, geographical, and qualitative evolution of delegated jurisdiction as well as the subsequent consolidation of papal jurisdictional primacy on the Iberian Peninsula.

Timo Korkiakangas

Linguistic research on medieval Latin charters. What to expect of digital diplomatics?

This paper reviews how medieval Latin charters have been used as a source of linguistic research and discusses what kind of prospects digital diplomatic advances open up for such research. Current Latin linguistics tends towards increasingly complex research settings based on large text corpora. Since charters provide crucial evidence for the history and evolution of Latin, there is an urgent need to find ways to put diplomatic information meaningfully into the service of historical Latin corpus linguistics. Diplomatically informed corpus-linguistic approaches are likely to help in ruling out extra-linguistic artefacts and epiphenomenal features from language data and, thus, lead to an increased precision and reliability in linguistic argumentation. Three fields of application will be discussed in particular: digitization of previously inaccessible charters into electronic text, automated detection of metadata, and automated detection of diplomatic parts of charters.

Eveline Leclercq

Reflections on charter redaction. An assessment of a stylometric approach in studying the Cambrai bishop's diplomatic landscape (12th c.)

The episcopal chancery of Cambrai has proven a fruitful subject for testing the use of stylometry in the research of medieval charters. Since then, this case-study has led to further stylometric analyses. This article entails a review of the method, the current results, the possibilities and the problems presenting themselves during such research, in particular problems of corpus size and bias, of 'reading' the result and of technicality. The use of stylometric methods permits on the other hand the study of larger corpora in a short period of time, the unveiling of results lost to the diplomatists' naked eye in a mass of data, and opening up to new research questions. As such, ongoing testing is envisioned, especially the research avenue of 'mixed media' - analysing charters alongside other types of text produced by chancery members – to determine the usefulness of stylometry for the diplomatist.

II. Diplomatics and Computational Methods: External Features

Zahra Ziran, Francesco Leotta, Massimo Mecella, Antonella Ghignoli

Image processing and semantic technologies in digital humanities. The NOTAE experience

The ERC project NOTAE has the potential to make a significant contribution to the field of digital humanities, mainly in some potential issues that could be generated by investigating typologies of documentary records: legal contracts, petitions, official letters, private letters, lists, authentic from relics, etc. By developing a digital library metadata of documents from Late Antiquity to early medieval Europe and incorporating image processing techniques, the project aims to enhance our understanding of graphic symbols traced by individuals within these records. The use of a knowledge graph to integrate data with other authoritative sources and the development of an interactive symbol identification system could provide valuable insights into the origin, meanings, and functions of these symbols. Additionally, image processing techniques applied in the project, such as document pre-processing, image enhancement, graphic symbol identification and classification, have the potential to improve the quality and accessibility of these ancient documents for scholars and researchers. This work has the potential to greatly enhance our understanding of medieval graphic symbols and could lead to new discoveries and advancements in the digital and computational humanities field.

Serena Ammirati, Lorenzo Lastilla, Paolo Merialdo, Marco Maiorino

Roman medieval documents meet machine learning. An experience of research and teaching.

In this contribution, we present the results and future developments of two research projects (*In codice ratio* and *Matrices*) dedicated to develop innovative methodologies and tools for the analysis and study of manuscript sources, in particular of the Roman medieval documentation (pontifical registers and private charters). Techniques, approaches and new research paths (in particular, one dedicated to explainability) are described, with the aim of consolidating an effective synergy between computer engineers and historians of manuscript sources.

Nicole Bergk-Pinto, Jacqueline Schindler, Niklas Tscherne

BeCoRe – Between Composition and Reception. The Authority of Medieval Charters

The project "BeCoRe – Between Composition and Reception: The Authority of Medieval Charters" uses machine learning techniques to investigate the graphical signs found on medieval charters on the examples of French and Austrian Monasteries (Cluny, Fontenay, Göttweig, Lilienfeld, Lambach), and thereby seeks to learn more about their use as expressions of power and authority in the creation and reception of charters. It takes up the "diplomatic landscapes" concept by Heinrich Fichtenau and it explores the usefulness of modern digital approaches to longstanding challenges in diplomatics, while simultaneously enhancing the Monasterium.net platform's data and metadata structure, and providing it with new tools for automatized analysis of the visual aspects of historical charters.

John A. McEwan

From archives to archaeology via machine learning. An automated approach to dating medieval seal matrices from Britain

Seal catalogue entries typically include information about the size, shape, content and date of seals. The date is a critical element in a seal catalogue entry, because it situates a seal in its historical context. How cataloguers date seals depends on whether they are working with seal matrices (stamps that people used to make seal impressions), or the seal impressions themselves. Cataloguers can generally date seal impressions, which are usually attached to documents, based on information in the documents. By contrast, cataloguers often date medieval seal matrices by comparing them to other seals. This method, if done manually, is time-consuming. This paper explores the feasibility of using archival seal catalogues to create an automated system for dating medieval seal matrices, using machine learning. The computer may never rival a skilled human cataloguer in accuracy, but a computer can date vast numbers of seal matrices quickly, at minimal cost, and in a consistent manner. Thus, a computational approach to dating seal matrices offers a potential method for improving catalogues of seal matrices, especially in situations where there are insufficient human resources available to date seals manually.

Mark Bell, Eirini Goudarouli, John Stell, Jane Winters

Qualitative Space in Digital Diplomatics

This paper is driven by the idea that existing modes of access, such as keyword searching, are unable to deliver the views of digital archives that contemporary scale, complexity, and heterogeneity demand. It argues that enabling the exploration and identification of evidence based on their qualitative spatial and temporal relationships, offers exciting new research avenues.

The paper introduces Qualitative Spatial Representation (QSR) as a method to explore the spatial and temporal dimensions of digital document collections, focusing on the structure of the documents themselves and how they may have developed over time. It suggests that QSR can enable exploration of heritage collections as traces of dynamic processes, approaching documents as processual narratives, emphasising their spatial structure and interconnections. The concepts of QSR are presented by applying existing spatial relation algebras to historical documents, demonstrating how spatial and temporal relationships in documents can contribute significantly to their meaning and interpretation.

Tobias Hodel, Jonas Widmer

Combining Automatic Text Recognition with Digital Paleography. New Trajectories for Digital Diplomatics

Text recognition based on machine learning can not only be used to recognize text properly. Some engines also offer the opportunity to output similar readings, e.g., in the form of a confidence matrix. For this article, we use confidence matrices not (as intended) to construct highly reliable text from images but to determine if the output can be leveraged to identify scribes. For the article, we rely on 87 charters from the monastery of Einsiedeln that have been automatically recognized. Based on confidence matrices outputted by HTR+, we demonstrate that visual and semantical similarities are identifiable in the patterns. Using PCA-based dimension reduction, we identify clusters that indicate similarity in the language and, to a certain degree, also in the handwriting. In short, a more in-depth and elaborate analysis would be required to use the approach for scribal identification but already some behavior of text recognition engines are explainable based on the limited data set.

III. Charters and their Digital Edition

Martin Glessgen, Marguerite Dallas

The *Documents et analyses linguistiques de la Galloromania médiévale* (*GallRom*). A new potential for interpretive research

The principal aims of the project GallRom are at least twofold. A first concerns the integration into a new database of an enlarged version of the *Documents linguistiques galloromans* (DocLing), a collection of philologically impeccable editions of over 6000 original vernacular documentary texts in electronic format, which will eventually cover the medieval Gallo-Romance territory in its entirety. A second concerns the restructuring of the lexical material contained in the various electronic reference dictionaries available for medieval Gallo-Romance in order to form the *Lexique étymologique de la Galloromania médiévale* (LEGaMe), which includes all the essential accompanying bibliographical and philological information gathered over the previous decades. A bibliographical reference tool for Old Occitan and Old Gascon inspired by that of Frankwalt Möhren for Old French is also envisaged. The project thus constitutes a network linking the textual production and the independent resources available for medieval Gallo-Romance, rendering them accessible for linguistic and philological research.

The paper will focus primarily on the textual database, its powerful interrogation tool and encoding principles. Examples of the potential afforded by the project for a rich contribution to historical linguistics will also be provided, currently consisting in lexicological and scriptological analysis carried out on the basis of the electronic editions of the documentary texts in conjunction with the data stemming from the linked reference works within the lexical network LEGaMe.

Miguel Calleja-Puerta

El etiquetado de los documentos notariales para el análisis diplomático. Experiencias del proyecto NotFor

The study of public notariate, based on the many thousands of charters preserved, has been one of the most developed branches of iberian Diplomatics in recent decades.

The NotFor research project (*Notariado y construcción social de la realidad. Hacia una codificación del documento notarial, siglos XII–XVII*) focuses on public notaries in the kingdoms of Castille and Portugal, their development, their social implantation and their documentary production. Analyzing the diplomatic structure of notarial charters has been one of the fundamental objectives of the project. Markup languages provide a useful tool to accomplish this task, but the standards in use such as TEI or CEI still offer a tagset that is limited to the basic metadata or the main elements of the diplomatic discourse. The objective of this paper is to show how a specific set of tags has been developed to describe and analyze the diplomatic structure of notarial documents.

Žarko Vujošević

Diplomatarium Serbicum Digitale. A project resuming in between of database and digital edition

The EU-funded project "Diplomatarium Serbicum Digitale" (DSD) started in 2015 with the aim of editorial and critical processing the entire corpus of charters and letters issued by Serbian medieval actors (late 12th – late 15th century), as well as presenting them in digital form. In 2018, a database was put online, where a majority of 600 identified documents were presented through new editions, metadata and images. After the EU support programme had been finished, the project was discontinuited, until being taken over by the Audiovisual Archive and Digitization Center of the Serbian Academy of Sciences and Arts (AVA Center). The activities were resumed in 2022 with the task to transfer all existing files to the newly created online application of the AVA Center and to carry out the editorial processing of the remaining documents.
Revived in a new format, the database keeps its basic structure corresponding to a traditional printed edition. Although electronically accessible and searchable, it still does not represent a digital edition as it remains a local SQL database. It is nevertheless considered an important contribution to the regional research community, which otherwise lacks a complete collection of editions or regesta, even in printed form.
However, the resuming of the DSD project also opens the new perspective of transferring the database content to XML format. The work on establishing a "real" digital edition started by using the TEI standard, whose elements and attributes were adapted with certain modifications to the terminology of the Vocabulaire international de la Diplomatique. The created schema allows detailed description of metadata as well as the direct markup of the charter texts, which enables enhancing the potential for computer-assisted charter processing and integration with other corpora provided in the similar way.
In addition to the brief history of the project and an overview of the corpus processed so far in both formats (local database, XML), the paper also includes some

experiences in gaining new diplomatic insights through the use of the existing database.

Christian Domenig

Quellen zur Geschichte des Alpen-Adria-Raumes. Digitale Urkundenedition auf Basis von MediaWiki

In the recent years digitalization made big steps forward. Even the edition of historical sources is now affected by digital techniques. Since 1987 the Text Encoding Initiative exists. It soon became a standard in Humanities. But until now a software is missing to edit historical sources. The paper deals with the use of Semantic MediaWiki to edit medieval charters. This way all modern demands are fulfilled. Historical sources can be edited for all digital purposes and even for print.

Balázs Csiba

Editing Mediaeval Diplomatic Sources in Slovakia

The first Slovak editions of mediaeval diplomatic sources were published in the second half of the 19th century without a profound method of editing. The first critical editions were brought to light after 1921, however those were results of uncoordinated efforts of individuals. The first systematic editions were introduced in the 1970s and 1980s by R. Marsina and V. Sedlák. In the present days, the employees of the Comenius University and the University of Trnava do editorial work. In the recent years, after overcoming the initial difficulties, the process of digitalisation began as well, nevertheless the majority of the Slovak archival materials are still not available in electronic databases.

IV. Charters and Archives

Jan Burgers, Rik Hoekstra

The *Digitale Charterbank Nederland*. A digital portal to more than 200.000 charters in Dutch archives

The Dutch archives hold tens of thousands of charters from the Middle Ages and early modern period, providing an invaluable source of information on various societal aspects. Yet, this material is scarcely used in historical research mainly due to its complicated heuristics: the documents are spread across dozens of archives and hundreds of archival funds. The *Digitale Charterbank Nederland* (DCN) now makes most of this corpus accessible through an integrated database that holds the data of the vast majority of the original charters kept in Dutch archives. It is based on the database of the commercial firm of De Ree, which provides the inventory management of three quarters of the Dutch archival institutions. The article gives an overview of the contents of DCN and discusses its set-up and its practical consequences for the user. The database has specific possibilities but also certain limitations, and examples are shown how DCN can help with both detailed research into persons or places, and with more broadly oriented research covering a long period of time. The article further includes a methodical reflection on the impact of new large scale digital source retrieval systems and the associated tools and techniques on historical research, as well as some thoughts about future development of DCN.

Stefan Bröhl

Die Urkunden der Pfalzgrafen Friedrich und Philipp 1449–1508. Ein Projekt zur digitalen Erschließung und Präsentation eines herausragenden spätmittelalterlichen Urkundenbestandes

The continuation of the *Regesten der Pfalzgrafen* – abstracts of the charters of the counts palatine of the Rhine – for the later Middle Ages has long been a historiographical desideratum. As prince-electors and powerful lords, the counts palatine of the Rhine stood among the highest-ranking secular princes of the Empire in the 15th century. In a project coordinated by the Landesarchiv Baden-Württemberg, Dep. Generallandesarchiv Karlsruhe, the state archives in Amberg, Munich, Darmstadt, Koblenz and Speyer contribute their Palatine charters from the years 1449 until 1508, during the reign of the electors Frederick I "the Victorious" and Philipp "the Upright", for cooperative description and presentation. In mid-2025, about 7.000 abstracts will be published along with their digital images via Archivportal-D (https://www.archivportal-d.de/). The abstracts will be enriched with normative data and further keywords that allow a digital thematic presentation as well as several types of access and research from a user's perspective. The framework can be used to further expand the core of 7.000 charters in the future.

Adam Zapała

The digital methods of publishing 15th century papal sources

The material produced by the papal bureaucracy in the 15th century, mostly stored in the Vatican Archives, offers crucial insights into European history. However, due to its vastness and complexity, much of it remains unpublished or unprocessed. The existing source editions shed light only on a small fraction of the whole. Furthermore, the lack of a comprehensive index of the papal registers, combined with the restrictive copyright policy of archives hampers querying. The present paper describes the possibilities that digital methods offer to process this resource more efficiently. It outlines procedures for harmonizing existing editions, indexing scans using INDXR software, as well as transcribing and preparing text for full-text publications. Additionally, it draws the attention to the importance of an international collaboration to comprehensively process 15th-century papal sources.

Ádám Novák, Sándor Ónadi

Support of Hungaricana research. A database of diplomatic sources and an experience of 3D scanning of wax seals

In this paper, we present two digital projects based on original medieval sources carried out by the "Hungary in Medieval Europe" Research Group at the University of Debrecen. Our main activity is the exploration of the so-called *Hungaricana*. To publish them, we created a digital online database called *Memoria Hungariae*. Its significance lies in the fact that the records include not only medieval charters, but also manuscripts, seals, letters and other material sources. In the framework of a pilot project on 3D seal digitisation, twelve medieval seals kept in the *Štátny archív v Prešove* were digitised. Later, the process was also used for installation purposes in an exhibition on medieval history. During the project, it became apparent that 3D technology not only makes medieval wax seals more presentable, but also saves this type of source from inevitable destruction. In addition, the technique also has academic, educational and museum-educational potential. In this paper, we endeavour to share with the readers our experiences on these projects.

Krisztina Arany, György Laczlavik

The Post-Mohács Era of the Hungarian Kingdom. Database of the Records from 1526–1570 in the Holdings of the National Archives of Hungary

On 29 August 2026, it will be 500 years since the troops of the Ottoman Empire inflicted a crushing defeat on the Hungarian army of King Louis II of Hungary on the plain of Mohács. This tragic event was decisive in many ways. Many of us associate it with the end of the Hungarian Middle Ages. The sources available for the decades following the battle are no different from those before 1526, but researching them has so far required a considerable effort on the part of researchers, since, unlike the online database available for the former, the necessary documents had to be collected from hundreds of archival collections. In the spring of 2016, the National Archives of Hungary (NAH) started the identification, digitisation and processing of the documents issued from 29 August 1526 to 1570 in the holdings of the National Archives. The first publication of the results (nearly 20,000 records) took place in the autumn of 2018, followed by the second in the spring of 2020, as the work is ongoing. In parallel with the processing of the records, the development of NAH's namespace is taking place. The two databases will provide a wealth of resources on the history of the of the Kingdom of Hungary (and Transylvania), the history of county legislation and administration, the possibility to establish hitherto unknown genealogical data, and to enhance the research of family, estate, social and regional history in the region of the Carpathian Basin.

The Authors

Serena AMMIRATI
Università degli Studi Roma Tre
serena.ammirati@uniroma3.it

Krisztina ARANY
Ungarische Archivdelegation beim Haus-, Hof- und Staatsarchiv, ÖStA
ung.archdel@gmail.com

Mark BELL
The National Archives (United Kingdom)
Mark.Bell@nationalarchives.gov.uk

Nicole BERGK-PINTO
Aubervilliers, Institut de Recherche et d'histoire des textes
nicole.bergk.pinto@chartes.psl.eu

Stefan BRÖHL
Landesarchiv Baden-Württemberg, Generallandesarchiv Karlsruhe
Projektmitarbeiter „Urkunden der Pfalzgrafen bei Rhein" 1449–1508
stefan.broehl@la-bw.de

Jan BURGERS
Royal Netherlands Academy of Arts & Sciences
Huygens Institute
J.W.J.Burgers@uva.nl

Miguel CALLEJA-PUERTA
Universidad de Oviedo
Laboratorio de documentación histórica
mcalleja@uniovi.es

Balázs CSIBA
Faculty of Arts of Comenius University Bratislava
Department of Archive Studies and Museology
balazs.csiba@uniba.sk

Marguerite DALLAS
Universität Zürich

Romanisches Seminar
marguerite.dallas@uzh.ch

Christian DOMENIG
Universität Klagenfurt
Institut für Geschichte
christian.domenig@aau.at

Marlene ERNST
Stadtarchiv Salzburg
marlene.ernst@stadt-salzburg.at

Michael GERVERS
University of Toronto
Department of Historical and Cultural Studies
m.gervers@utoronto.ca

Antonella GHIGNOLI
Sapienza Università di Roma
antonella.ghignoli@uniroma1.it

Martin GLESSGEN
Universität Zürich
Romanisches Seminar
Paris, ÉPHÉ -PSL
glessgen@rom.uzh

Eirini GOUDAROULI
The National Archives (United Kingdom)
eirini.goudarouli@nationalarchives.gov.uk

Tobias HODEL
Universität Bern
tobias.hodel@unibe.ch

Rik HOEKSTRA
Royal Netherlands Academy of Arts & Sciences
DHLab
rik.hoekstra@di.huc.knaw.nl

Timo Korkiakangas
University of Helsinki
Department of Languages
timo.korkiakangas@helsinki.fi

György Laczlavik
Magyar Nemzeti Levéltár
laczlavik.gyorgy@mnl.gov.hu

Lorenzo Lastilla
Università degli Studi Roma Tre
lorenzo.lastilla@uniroma3.it

Eveline Leclercq
Gemeentelijke Bibliotheek Kraainem
eveline.leclercq@gmail.com

Francesco Leotta
Sapienza Università di Roma
leotta@diag.uniroma1.it

Daniel Luger
Universität Wien
Institut für Österreichische Geschichtsforschung
daniel.luger@univie.ac.at

Marco Maiorino
Archivio Apostolico Vaticano
marco.maiorino2109@gmail.com

John A. McEwan
University of Kansas
john.mcewan@ku.edu

Massimo Mecella
Sapienza Università di Roma
mecella@dis.uniroma1.it

Paolo Merialdo
Università degli Studi *Roma Tre*
paolo.merialdo@uniroma3.it

Ádám Novák
University of Debrecen
"Hungary in Medieval Europe" Research Group
adamanovak@unideb.hu

Sándor Ónadi
University of Debrecen
"Hungary in Medieval Europe" Research Group
onadi.sandor@arts.unideb.hu

Alina Ostrowski
University of Passau
Chair of Computational Humanities
Alina.Ostrowski@uni-passau.de

Malte Rehbein
University of Passau
Chair of Computational Humanities
Malte.Rehbein@uni-passau.de

Jacqueline Schindler
St. Pölten, NÖ Landesarchiv – NÖ Institut für Landeskunde
jacqueline.schindler@noel.gv.at

John Stell
University of Leeds
School of Computing
J.G.Stell@leeds.ac.uk

Gelila Tilahun
University of Toronto
DEEDS Project
gelila.tilahun@utoronto.ca

Niklas Tscherne
Universität Graz
Institut für Digitale Geisteswissenschaften
niklas.tscherne@uni-graz.at

Georg Vogeler
Universität Graz
Institut für Digitale Geisteswissenschaften
georg.vogeler@uni-graz.at

Žarko Vujošević
Univerzitet Beograd, Filozofski fakultet/
Universität Graz, Institut für Digitale Geisteswissenschaften
zarko.vujosevic@f.bg.ac.rs

Jonas Widmer
Universität Bern
jonas.widmer@unibe.ch

Jane Winters
University of London
School of Advanced Study
jane.winters@sas.ac.uk

Adam Zapała
Tadeusz Manteuffel Institute of History Polish Academy of Sciences
Department of Historical Atlas
adam.j.zapala@gmail.com

Zahra Ziran
Sapienza Università di Roma
zahra.ziran@uniroma1.it